THE MONSTER THEORY READER

CONTENTS

Part II. Monsterizing Difference

Part III. Monsters and Culture

Part IV. The Promises of Monsters

ACKNOWLEDGMENTS

This one is dedicated to JJC, whose monstrous support has been unwavering for more years than I'd care to admit. Thanks go as well to the frightfully competent team at the University of Minnesota Press, especially Douglas Armato and Gabriel Levin, for overseeing the transformation of this project from idea to reality.

INTRODUCTION

A Genealogy of Monster Theory

Jeffrey Andrew Weinstock

JEFFREY JEROME COHEN'S 1996 essay "Monster Culture (Seven Theses),"
from his edited collection *Monster Theory: Reading Culture,* holds a prominent
position in this reader as the introduction to a volume that named a field—and
the naming of a field or subdiscipline can exert a powerful gravitational effect,
allowing dispersed scholarship to coalesce around its banner and start to form
into something coherent. In this sense, to name a field is a type of performative
speech act, bringing something into being that did not previously exist: "I dub
thee monster theory." *Presto!* And then, having been named, the larger a field
grows, the stronger its gravity becomes as scholarship begets scholarship and
scholars acknowledge affiliations with one another. Once there is monster theory,
there can be monster theory scholars, monster theory journals, monster theory
organizations, monster theory conferences, and so on.

One difficulty confronting monster theory researchers, however, has been
the dispersed nature of the scholarship—a difficulty exacerbated by the transnational and transdisciplinary nature of the investigation. Like the monsters it
theorizes, monster theory transgresses categorical boundaries, spreading out
into different disciplines. What monsters are, where they come from, what they
mean, and the cultural work they do are questions that have preoccupied philosophers, theologians, psychologists, physicians, and cultural critics. Because all
cultures have their own monsters, monster theory is by necessity an international
endeavor—and one that, bearing in mind shifting cultural norms and expectations,

1

must tread carefully when it comes to broad generalizations (the same monster resonates differently in different times and places). And because monsters and monstrosity appear in contexts ranging from art to medicine and religion to sociology and beyond, the theorization of monsters and their meanings has followed suit, with historians and anthropologists, queer theorists, and even computer scientists all attempting to think through what monstrosity is and how it functions.

Focusing on contemporary theorizations of monstrosity with an emphasis on the humanities, this collection, then, is itself inevitably a kind of monster—a Frankenstein's creature assembled out of diverse approaches and perspectives. It first supplies a set of "tools" for researchers and students—common approaches to and vocabulary for theorizing monstrosity—and then provides an interdisciplinary selection of important readings theorizing monsters and monstrosity from disciplines ranging from medieval studies to ecocriticism to terrorism studies.

This assemblage of different methods offers a convenient overview of the field for those with interests in monster theory. However, because the study of monsters, including theorization about what they are, where they come from, and what they mean, goes back many thousands of years—as does the understanding of how anxieties concerning monsters, as well as the tabooed desires they reflect, can be strategically deployed to prohibit or enable particular behaviors—it may be useful before turning to the contemporary perspectives that compose this volume to take a step back and consider a kind of monster theory genealogy, thereby acknowledging that, although newly named, monster theory is in fact a very old endeavor.

Definitions

The place to begin, even before turning our attention to genealogy, is with the question of definition: just what constitutes a "monster" in the first place? Etymology is suggestive here, although it is of limited overall utility. Timothy Beal tells us in *Religion and Its Monsters* (one of many places where this derivation is rehearsed) that "'monster' derives from the Latin *monstrum,* which is related to the verbs *monstrare* ('show' or 'reveal') and *monere* ('warn' or 'portend')."[1] The *monstrum,* then, at least for the ancients, had a portentous quality, as it was "a message that breaks into this world from the realm of the divine."[2] Stephen Asma, too, notes the Latin connotation of *monstrum* as a kind of omen, a sign from the gods indicating their displeasure, before elaborating that the monster is "a kind of *cultural category*" employed in various domains ranging from religion to biology.[3] Such discussions do help us understand where the term *monster* came from and begin to help us think about their functions; however, they are not particularly useful in delimiting what does or does not qualify as a monster. Are monsters purely imaginary, like Minotaurs and manticores and zombies? Does monstrosity inhere in substantial deviation from established physical or behavioral norms for a species—like begetting *un*like? Are serial killers and other human beings who engage in depraved acts monsters? Must a monster be physically threatening?

Synthesizing the work of Beal, Noël Carroll, Massimo Leone, and others, Asa Mittman seeks to answer these questions by proposing that the monster is that which unsettles or challenges established cognitive categories and interpretive strategies: "Above all, the monstrous is that which creates [a] sense of vertigo, that which calls into question our (their, anyone's) epistemological worldview, highlights its fragmentary and inadequate nature, and thereby asks us . . . to acknowledge the failures of our systems of categorization."[4] Mittman thus highlights here the relativity of monstrosity: the monster is the thing that, from a particular perspective in a given context, shouldn't be, but is. The monster is that which threatens understandings of the world, the self, and the relations between the two—and these are understandings that vary depending upon time and place. Mittman also shifts the emphasis from object to subject, from the intrinsic qualities of the thing considered monstrous to the subject doing the considering. The monster, suggests Mittman, comes into being at the moment affective vertigo is translated into the catch-all conceptual category for things that don't fit; that is (like a disciplinary field), the monster comes into being the moment it is called a monster.

Mittman's formulation is broad—given human idiosyncrasies and phobias, on the level of the individual, it could encompass almost anything. And it does raise some questions. For one thing, is something still a monster if one believes in its existence and has a category to define it? Is a troll, for example, still a monster to someone who has grown up believing trolls are part of their world—in which case, they might be scary but presumably would not provoke a sense of epistemological crisis or vertigo? For another, when does something transition from being unsettling or uncanny to vertigo inducing? How profound must epistemological vertigo be for something to be construed as monstrous (assuming there are degrees of vertigo)? Despite these questions, however, Mittman's emphasis on monstrosity being "rooted in the vertigo of redefining one's understanding of the world" is useful for thinking about why the same thing can be regarded differently by different individuals and groups and at different times. It also helps to explain the anxiety that monsters provoke above and beyond any physical threat they present and the hyperbolic response that that which is considered monstrous provokes. The "intolerable ambiguity" of the monster, to reference the title of Elizabeth Grosz's inclusion in this volume, compels two types of responses: to understand it and find a category to contain it—that is, to assimilate it into an existing or altered epistemological framework—or to stamp it out of existence.

To understand monsters or to eradicate them is a succinct formulation of the difference between what we may refer to as the scholarly and political approaches to monstrosity, with philosophers, theologians, and academics seeking to explain monsters—what they are, where they come from, what they mean—and those in or aspiring to positions of power deploying the rhetoric of monstrosity as a tool to manipulate opinion and promote specific political agendas.

Focusing first on the scholarly approach to monstrosity, theorization of monstrosity from antiquity to today has tended to divide along three tracks: *teratology*, the study of "monstrous" births; *mythology*, the consideration of fantastical creatures; and *psychology*, the exploration of how human beings come to act in monstrous or inhuman ways. Teratology and psychology are more immediately connected to what we may think of as the "real world" than mythology, which often has to do with fantasy or dream; however, all three divisions find their grounding in the human experience of overlaying meaning upon existence. Whether the monstrous comes to us or we conjure it up, monstrosity is a loose and flexible epistemological category that allows us a space to define that which complicates or seems to resist definition.

Teratology

Ambroise Paré (circa 1510–90) thought seriously about monsters. This French surgeon and scholar—who tended to Kings Henry II, Francis II, Charles IX, and Henry III; invented surgical instruments; and is considered one of the fathers of modern forensic pathology—wrote about monstrous births in his 1573 *On Monsters and Marvels* (*Des Monstres Tant Terrestres que Marines avec Leurs Portraits*, part of his *Deux Livres de Chirurgie*). As Bates observes, *On Monsters and Marvels* is the best-known attempt from the early modern period to theorize monstrous births, and, in its opening chapter, Paré offers a list of "several things that cause Monsters":[5]

> The first is the glory of God.
> The second, His wrath.
> The third, too great a quantity of semen.
> The fourth, too small a quantity.
> The fifth, imagination.
> The sixth, the narrowness or smallness of the womb.
> The seventh, the unbecoming sitting position of the mother, who, while
>   pregnant, remains seated too long with her thighs crossed or pressed
>   against her stomach.
> The eighth, by a fall or blows struck against the stomach of the mother during
>   pregnancy.
> The ninth, by hereditary or accidental illnesses.
> The tenth, by the rotting or corruption of the semen.
> The eleventh, by the mingling or mixture of seed.

The twelfth, by the artifice of wandering beggars.
The thirteenth, by Demons or Devils.[6]

Paré's list, which collects causes for monstrous births generally accepted in his time, is fascinating for the way it intermingles superstition with science, as it covers what we could consider the five most important teratological theories: supernatural intervention, hybridization, maternal impression, accident, and what we today would call genetics. We will begin our survey with the supernatural explanations (causes 1, 2, and 13), which themselves can be divided into three subcategories—portents, punishments, and intercourse with diabolic forces— before giving some consideration to the natural causes.

Supernatural Theories

Although the term *teratology,* referring to the study of abnormal gestational development, wasn't introduced until the nineteenth century,[7] human beings have always been interested in understanding the causes and potential meanings of "monstrous births"—animals and human beings demonstrating physiological and/ or mental abnormalities. In keeping with the etymology of the word *monster,* there is a long history of monstrous births being regarded as divine portents of things to come. Babylonian priests kept careful records of congenital malformations on clay tablets for purposes of divination—the "appearance of malformations of the ears, nose, mouth, sex organs, and digits," Warkany writes, "had meaning for the future of the king, the land, and the parents."[8] The Babylonians' "extensive system of monster interpretation based on emblematic symbolism,"[9] in which particular deformations were interpreted as mapping onto future events or reflecting divine will, was then inherited by the Greeks and Romans.[10]

Among the Romans, Livy (59 B.C.E. to 17 C.E.), Tacitus (circa 56–120 C.E.), and the mysterious fourth-century C.E. Julius Obsequens discuss monstrous births as supernatural expressions of divine displeasure and as signs of calamitous things to come. Smith explains that "of a hundred or so portentous events in Livy's history, at least fifteen are frightening monsters, such as 'a pig born with a human face' (IIVII.iv.14–5) and a boy with the head of an elephant (XXVII. xi.4–6)."[11] Tacitus's *Histories,* continues Smith, "is a dark and bloody chronicle of the coups and usurpations of first-century Rome, and among the divine portents of these disasters are animals that 'give birth to strange young' (I.lxxvi)."[12] And Julius's fourth-century C.E. *Liber Prodigiorum* (Book of prodigies)—not published until 1508—found its basis in Livy and presents an account of Roman wonders and portents from 249 to 12 B.C.E. For the Greeks and Romans, as for the Babylonians, monstrous births—both animal and human—were not chance events but meaningful, and they required interpretation to ferret out their occult significance.

Early Christian thinkers as well were inclined to consider monstrous births as messages from God. While Smith notes that both Tertullian (160–220 C.E.) and Eusebius (263–339 C.E.) discuss the portentous quality of monstrous births, it is St. Augustine (354–430 C.E.) who established in the fifth century "a definitive Christian doctrine of the monstrous."[13] For Augustine, all natural processes are directed by God—nothing in the world happens without God's permission, and God is able to act without constraint. Thus Augustine writes in book X of *City of God* that "monstrous births" are "arranged and appointed by Divine Providence."[14] When a human woman or animal gives birth to something "monstrous"—something physiologically abnormal—it is God sending us a message, although what exactly it portends is always the matter of debate and conjecture.

The view of monstrous births as supernatural omens persisted through the Middle Ages and Renaissance; however, as Surekha Davies explains, a shift began in the late fifteenth century such that monstrous births were regarded less as "portents of general misfortune" and more as "signs of particular crimes and impending divine retribution for a range of failings indicating wrongful political and religious allegiances."[15] Martin Luther's influential pamphlet from 1523, for example, composed together with Philipp Melanchthon, explained the manifestations of the "Papal Ass"—a creature allegedly appearing on the banks of the Tiber in 1495 with the head of an ass, a woman's breasts and belly, an elephant's truck in place of one arm, one cloven foot, and one birdlike foot, and with scales covering its neck, arms, and legs—and the "Monk Calf," a malformed calf born in Saxony in 1522 with a fold of skin over its head shaped like a cowl, as emblems of the corruption of the Roman Catholic Church and signs of God's displeasure. Thirty-five years later, Conradus Lycosthenes wrote in his *Prodigiorum ac Ostentorum Chronicon,* a year-by-year chronicle starting with what Lycosthenes proposed as the year of creation (3959 B.C.E.), of "God's marvelous warnings and portents—monsters, comets, earthquakes, rains of blood or frogs or stones, heavenly visions, and so on."[16]

While monstrous births could be interpreted as portents of catastrophes to come that would afflict an entire community or region, in some cases, they were construed as signs of divine disapproval for more personal actions already taken—that is, as punishments for moral lapses, often specifically sexual ones, including sodomy, bestiality, adultery, incest, and "impure thoughts" and "unnatural desire" writ large. Overlapping with hybridity theory, to be discussed shortly, the bull-headed Minotaur of Greek mythology, for example, was divine punishment for Queen Pasiphaë of Crete after her coupling with a bull (through the machinations of Poseidon, who inflamed her desire for it). And Peggy McCracken observes in *The Curse of Eve* that some medieval romances took their cue from the biblical passage 2 Esdras 5, interpreted as saying that intercourse with a woman during menstruation will beget monsters, to suggest monstrous births were divine punishment

Der Bapstesel zu Rom

Figure I.1. The Papal Ass.

for "impure" copulation.[17] Monstrous births could also be interpreted as signs of God's displeasure outside of specifically sexual immortality. Some seventeenth-century North American Puritans, for example, construed the abnormal offspring of Mary Dyer and Anne Hutchinson as signs of divine disapprobation.[18]

In addition to divine portents and punishments, monstrous births could also reflect the other side of the theological divide: not God's will but diabolical intervention. At the end of Paré's list, he includes "by Demons or Devils," and a final supernatural explanation for monstrous births was found in direct copulation—wittingly or not—with demons, succubi, incubi, witches, the devil himself, and other assorted magical creatures that many used to believe (and some still do) roamed the world, or through the influence of such creatures in the form of a spell, curse, or possession. Narratives of sexual congress with demonic entities can be traced back to ancient Sumeria—the demons Ardat lili and Irdu lili would beget children from sleeping men and women, respectively. St. Augustine believed in the existence of succubi and incubi,[19] as did Thomas Aquinas, although the latter doubted whether such creatures could themselves sire children, proposing instead that they stole semen from sleeping men and transported it to sleeping women.[20] In literature, the sorcerer Merlin is revealed by Geoffrey of Monmouth to be the son of an incubus and a king's daughter.

Interestingly, while the idea of demonic entities copulating with humans and siring monstrous children is generally given little credence today, the idea still finds considerable purchase in contemporary popular culture—consider, for example, *Rosemary's Baby* (Polanski, 1968), the *Omen* films, and the ending of *The Witches of Eastwick* (Miller, 1987), in which the devil has sired children with three human witches. Half-human, half-monstrous hybrids like the *dhampir*—a half-human, half-vampire synthesis—also stalk through the pages of contemporary fantasy and gaming narratives.

Hybridization

Theorization of part-human, part-animal offspring as the consequence of bestiality or copulation with a supernatural creature points us toward a second prominent teratological explanation: hybridization or the "mingling or mixing of seed" of different species, which can function as an explanation for monstrous birth even outside of the frameworks of divine punishment and moral disapprobation. Warkany, Barrow, and others note that belief in the possibility of monstrous hybrids was widespread and deeply entrenched up until the nineteenth century—when it then migrated from presumed scientific fact into literary fantasy.

The idea of human–animal hybridization flourished in the ancient world, where Egyptian gods and Greco-Roman monsters often combined human and animal aspects, and monstrous races of people with dogs' heads or covered in hair or with horns were reported to live at the ends of the earth. Warkany proposes as well that belief in reincarnation and the transmigration of souls from human to animal in India and Egypt fostered an attitude of, if not reverence, at least acceptance of the idea of human–animal hybridity in those regions.[21] Mosaic and Christian law, however, didn't mince words when it came to the idea of human–animal sexual congress: "And if a man lie with a beast, he shall surely be put to death: and ye shall slay the beast. And if a woman approach unto any beast, and lie down thereto, thou shalt kill the woman, and the beast: they shall surely be put to death; their blood [shall be] upon them."[22] Bestiality was an abomination punishable by death, and any offspring of such congress would be accursed as well.

The idea that bestiality could produce offspring was not universally accepted—Aristotle, for example, rejected the prospect of interspecies copulation yielding hybrid progeny; however, this skeptical position was the exception rather than the rule, as its possibility was taken as an article of faith by most until at least the nineteenth century. Paré, for example, writes, "There are monsters that are born with a form that is half-animal and the other [half] human, or retaining everything [about them] from animals, which are produced by sodomists and atheists who 'join together' and break out of their bounds—unnaturally—with animals, and from this are born several hideous monsters that bring great shame on those who look at them or speak to them."[23] Paré then goes on to give a list of examples of such monstrous births.[24]

Monstrosity in general, it should be noted, is frequently correlated with hybridity perceived to be unnatural. Cohen's third thesis from "Monster Culture" is that the monster "is the harbinger of category crisis": "This refusal to participate in the classificatory 'order of things' is true to monsters generally," writes Cohen. "[T]hey are disturbing hybrids whose externally incoherent bodies resist attempts to include them in any systematic structuration."[25] Because of their "ontological liminality,"[26] disturbing hybrids possess the potential to evoke the kind of epistemological vertigo proposed by Mittman and are frequently met with a violent response out of all proportion to the actual physical threat they present as a result. The widespread acceptance of hybridity theory up until at least the nineteenth century, along with the deep-seated Western antipathy toward the idea of bestiality and the rigid policing of the border between human and animal, meant that a child born resembling in some way an animal and the mother who bore it were objects of suspicion, as were animals born with humanlike characteristics—or characteristics of another species—and their mothers. Malformed children perceived in some way to resemble an animal and malformed animals in some way perceived to resemble a human being were often put to death—as, in many cases, were the mothers who birthed them.

In the nineteenth and the first part of the twentieth centuries, individuals presented as human–animal hybrids were stock features of freak shows. Bogdan notes that from approximately 1840 to 1940, "the formally organized exhibition for amusement and profit of people with physical, mental, or behavioral anomalies, both alleged and real, was an accepted part of American life."[27] Such exhibitions would include a variety of nonnormative body types, ranging from the excessively hairy (bearded women and "dog-faced boys") to the extremely tall or short to those with physical deformations. As Fielder discusses, such displays would often routinely include "wild men"—often non-Western people pitched as "savages" and "cannibals"—and "feral children."[28] Stories were woven around these figures by carnival barkers for their audiences, often explaining the appearance of the performer on display as the consequence of miscegenation, bestiality, or, as

Figure I.2. Charles Eisenmann's photograph of Jojo the Dog-Faced Boy (circa 1870).

will be discussed later, maternal impression. With the waning of the freak show in the mid-twentieth century, fantasies about monstrous hybrid births migrated to science fiction, where hybrids either were the project of "unnatural" human tampering, as in H. G. Wells's *The Island of Dr. Moreau* (1896) or Michael Crichton's *Jurassic Park* (1990), or populated other planets (consider, for example, the famous Cantina scene from George Lucas's first Star Wars film, *Episode IV: A New Hope* [1977]).

Maternal Impression

Hybridity theory bears a close connection to another prominent teratological theory—what is sometimes called maternal impression—premised on the idea that what a woman thinks about or sees during conception and the gestation of the embryo can influence its development and appearance. Succinctly presented by Paré as "imagination" in his list of causes of monstrous births, Huet traces this theory back to antiquity, noting the theory, attributed to Empedocles, that "progeny can be modified by the statues and paintings that the mother gazes upon during her pregnancy"[29] and that Pliny wrote that both maternal and paternal thoughts during conception can shape the child.[30] The belief that the mother's imagination played a crucial role in shaping development of progeny, however, gained traction in the seventeenth and eighteenth centuries. Montaigne, for example, expressed this belief in his essay "On the Power of Imagination" (1850), writing, "We know by experience that women transmit marks of their fancies to the bodies of the children they carry in their wombs."[31] Huet observes that "several stories of monstrosities caused by a mother's troubled contemplation of images became extremely popular in the Renaissance" and were included in the various treatises on monsters of the period, including Paré's.[32]

While, in one sense, maternal impression theory is an extension of hybridity theory, in which one need not physically copulate for hybridization to occur, if followed to its logical conclusion, the consequences of maternal impression theory are significant for patriarchal culture, as paternity is rendered inherently uncertain. Paré mentions, for example, a princess accused of adultery because of having birthed a black child but who was saved by Hippocrates, who pointed out the influence of a portrait of a Moor near her bed.[33] A child could thus differ in appearance from its parents as a consequence of the mother's imagination or images that impressed themselves on her. Huet, however, points out that this logic can work in both directions: an adulterous woman could conceal her crime by thinking about her husband during intercourse with another man. Paternity is thus always speculative.

Maternal impression theory could extend to include the effect not just of imaginative fantasy or the images viewed but also of emotional stimuli experienced by the pregnant woman. The family of Joseph Merrick, the famous "Elephant

Man," explained, for example, that his symptoms resulted from his mother being frightened and knocked over by a fairground elephant while she was pregnant. Merrick apparently subscribed to this belief throughout his life.[34] Stevenson, writing in 1992, notes that maternal impression theory remains widely accepted in parts of the world.[35]

Accident

Another common theory for monstrous births from antiquity to today—and one on much safer scientific ground—foregrounds circumstances that affect the development of the fetus, such as intrauterine trauma; ingestion of substances; or conditions, such as illness, that influence the pregnant woman and developing fetus. This theory was at the core of Aristotle's consideration of teratology (although no doubt an understanding that intrauterine trauma, maternal deprivation, or ingestion of particular substances could cause birth defects or induce abortion goes back much further). For Aristotle, gestation is directed by an essence or essential form or character, which ensures that like generates like—a kind of early DNA theory.[36] Aristotle thus proposed that what we call monsters are in fact the consequence of developmental errors introduced during procreation or gestation, resulting in the failure of something to realize its essence fully. Significantly, for Aristotle, monstrous births were not omens or signs. Their monstrosity inhered in their being "contrary to Nature," but this was indicative only of a natural process thwarted, not of the gods' displeasure.[37] Monstrous births were not augurs of things to come but only indications of a process thwarted or incomplete. Aristotle also dismisses the idea that human copulation with an animal could produce a hybrid, noting, "That . . . it is impossible for such a monstrosity to come into existence—I mean one animal in another—is shown by the great difference in the period of gestation between man, sheep, dog, and ox, it being impossible for each to be developed except in its proper time."[38]

According to Barrow, the accident theory became more prominent after Paré's inclusion among his causes for monstrous births "a fall or blows struck against the stomach of the mother during pregnancy" and "accidental illness," as well as poor posture or a narrow uterus.[39] Beginning in the eighteenth century, researchers began to explore the effects of changing environmental conditions on the hatching of eggs. René Antoine Ferchault de Réaumer (1683–1757) investigated artificial incubation of chicken eggs, noting the effect of different temperatures on development. The French naturalist Étienne Geoffroy Saint-Hilaire (1772–1844) explored the effects of manipulating eggs in various ways, including shaking them.[40] Charles Féré (1852–1907) found that various drugs, including alcohol and nicotine, could induce birth defects in developing eggs, and this then led the way for twentieth-century scientists, including Charles Stockard (1879–1939), who offered increasingly precise explanations for how and why changing environmental conditions could influence the development of embryos in both animals and humans.

The effect that drugs in particular could have on the developing fetus was rendered in stark relief by use of the drug thalidomide in the late 1950s. First marketed in 1957 to alleviate the symptoms of morning sickness, the drug's use resulted in infants being born with malformed limbs and other deformities. Hofland notes that of the more than ten thousand babies born with deformities as a consequence of thalidomide use, over 40 percent died before their first birthdays.[41] In the twenty-first century, various contemporary public health campaigns have sought to highlight the effects of smoking, alcohol, and use of other drugs on developing fetuses. In the literary world, Katherine Dunn's celebrated novel *Geek Love* (1989) concerns a married couple who induce birth defects in their children using various drugs and radioactive material to create a freak show for their traveling carnival.

Genetics

The genetic theory of teratology complements the accident theory by suggesting that malformations may be accounted for by intrinsic genetic causes rather than environmental factors. While the founding of genetics as a science has been credited to Gregor Mendel, who worked in the nineteenth century, the understanding that something like a code directs fetal development and that diseases and anomalies may be inherited goes back much further. As noted, Aristotle believed that species have a kind of essence that directs fetal development such that like generates like. Along these lines, Paré writes that "crookt-back begets crookt-back" and notes among his causes of monstrous births inherited diseases and "corrupt" sperm.[42] The modern understanding of the role of genetics in directing fetal development, however, is primarily a twentieth-century innovation.

Mythology

In medicine and biology, teratology is the scientific study of congenital abnormalities and abnormal formations. Although many reports of monstrous births were apocryphal (like the Papal Ass) or exaggerated, "monstrous births"—deviations from the normal form for a species—are of course real, and the more striking occurrences, such as conjoined twins or dramatic deformations, have always excited wonder. In contrast to these real-world occurrences are tales of mythical creatures that some claim to have encountered but the existence of which has been discredited or at the very least disputed. We can divide up this discussion into three categories: monstrous races of human beings, monstrous creatures of myth and fantasy, and cryptids—creatures proposed by some to exist but the existence of which is generally disputed by science.

The Monstrous Races

Those who write about monsters are fond of lists—and John Block Friedman's study *The Monstrous Races in Medieval Art and Thought* includes a fascinating one. In his first chapter, Friedman notes that tales of marvelous races of unusual men suffused the ancient world and that such races were speculated about extensively in the works of several authors, including most notably the fifth-century B.C.E. Ctesias, the fourth-century B.C.E. Megasthenes, and the first-century C.E. Pliny the Elder, as well as in works commissioned by and attributed to Alexander the Great in the fourth century B.C.E. Far more extensive than Paré's list of causes of monstrous births, Friedman's list consists of forty different races presented as objects of wonder in Ctesias, Megasthenes, Pliny, and the Alexander cycle and is particularly intriguing for the way it includes actual races, such as Pygmies and dark-skinned Ethiopians; individual difference generalized as a characteristic of race, such as the Androgini, who have both male and female sex organs, and Speechless Men, who communicate by gesture; and more fanciful races, such as the Astomi, who lack mouths and live by smell,[43] the Blemmyae, who lack heads and necks and whose faces are on their chests,[44] the Cynocephali, who have the heads of dogs,[45] the Panotii, whose ears reach to their feet and can serve as blankets,[46] and the Sciopods, who have one leg and a giant foot that they use to shade themselves against the sun.[47]

Friedman notes that there may be explanations for even the more improbable-sounding races, including perceptual errors—ornamented shields, for example, could have given rise to the belief in men with faces on their chests, and baboons or apes may have been mistaken for dog-headed men—mistranslations, and cultural differences construed as monstrous.[48] In an observation concerning Greco-Roman accounts of monstrous races, but generalizable far beyond that, Friedman explains that such tales "exhibit a marked ethnocentrism which made the observer's culture, language, and physical appearance the norm by which to evaluate all other people."[49] Even a practice such as yoga could have suggested monstrosity to Greek observers: "Probably the Sciapod who shields his head from the sun with his foot while lying on his back derives from observation of people in yoga positions."[50] Friedman also notes, however, that while sources for many of the monstrous races can be traced, their elaboration—often "willful, poetic, and imaginative"—filled a psychological need.[51] Their appeal is rooted in "fantasy, escapism, delight in the exercise of the imagination, and—very important—fear of the unknown." Friedman continues, "If the monstrous races had not existed, it is likely that people would have created them."[52] As will be developed more fully later in this chapter, "monsterizing" an existing group, as Asma observes, can also promote imperialist political agendas.[53]

As Friedman details, interest in monstrous races persisted through the Middle Ages, with various natural philosophers and theologians grappling with questions

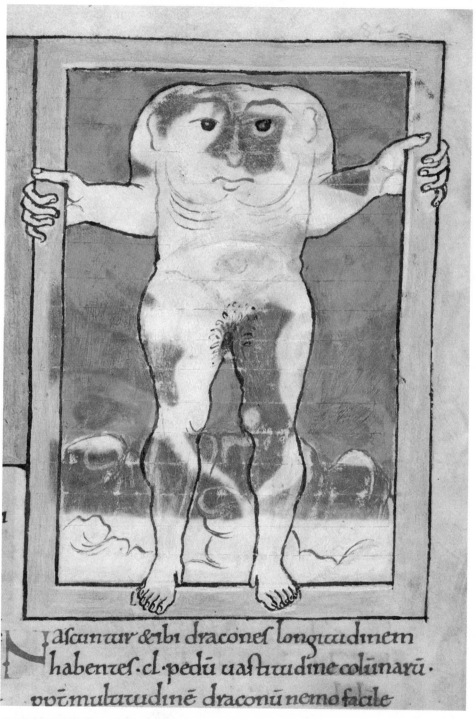

ascuntur &ibi dracones longitudinem
habentes . cl . pedū uastitudine colūnarū .
uti multitudinē draconū nemo facile

Figure I.3. The Blemmyae from *The Marvels of the East* (circa fifth century C.E.).

of their origins and significance. The questions for St. Augustine in his fifth-century *City of God* were whether monstrous races possessed reason, which would elevate them above animals, and if they are descended from Adam (by way of Noah). Augustine hedges his bets a little, writing, "Wherefore, to conclude this question cautiously and guardedly, either these things which have been told of some races have no existence at all; or if they do exist, they are not human races; or if they are human, they are descended from Adam."[54] As characterized by Friedman, Augustine "combined missionary zeal with the Roman cosmopolitan tolerance of ethnic diversity" in his consideration of monstrous races as "potential Christians."[55] In his seventh-century *Etymologiae,* a wide-ranging encyclopedia, Isidore of Seville draws heavily on Pliny's *Natural History* to discuss monstrous races as those that deviate from a given mean. This allows him to share Augustine's conclusion that monstrous appearance is not necessarily antithetical to Christian salvation.[56]

Other works from the Middle Ages were less invested in philosophical theorization than simply in provoking wonder. The eleventh-century Old English *Marvels of the East,* for example, mixes together fantastic tales of dragons and phoenixes with accounts of huge-eared Panotti; half-human, half-donkey Homodubii; and cannibalistic Donestre. The fourteenth-century *Travels of Sir John Mandeville* includes among Mandeville's famous adventures encounters with one-legged Sciapods and dog-headed Cynocephales—both of which, it is worth noting, come off better than his representation of Jews.

As Davies observes, tales of monstrous peoples continued to circulate in the Renaissance and early modern period: "During the first two centuries of printed books beings such as apple-smellers, troglodytes, anthropophagi, and sciapods, who had sniffed, huddled, chomped, or hopped their way across medieval manuscripts of *The Marvels of the East* and Pliny the Elder's *Historia naturalis,* continued to pass through the hands and minds of European writers, readers, and viewers."[57] What changed, however, was their proximity. During the Middle Ages, monstrous races were always imagined "at the very edges of the world."[58] During the long sixteenth century, in contrast, those edges began to contract as Christopher Columbus and other navigators moved outward—taking their predispositions and expectations with them. Columbus recorded an encounter with cannibals as well as anecdotal accounts of other kinds of monstrous races, including the Cyclops and cynocephali.[59] Of course, as Davies notes, characterizing indigenous populations as monstrous had significant implications for European colonial enterprises.[60]

Davies argues that beginning in the sixteenth century, the "category of monster expanded enormously, while its subdivisions became less pronounced."[61] Cabinets of curiosity collected various kinds of unusual artifacts, while exhibitions at fairs and shows mixed deformed human beings and non-European humans (especially Native Americans, notes Davies[62]) with exotic and deformed animals. Davies writes that "from the mid-sixteenth century, such fairs exhibited inhabitants of America, Africa, and even Asia with increasing frequency."[63] Such exhibitions, working in concert with fanciful travel narratives like Mandeville's, arguably influenced and inflected public opinion in ways that facilitated imperialist programs and colonialist endeavors. Indeed, the question of whether the African species of man was fundamentally related to the European variety or of different extraction was central to the debate over African slavery.

Toward the end of the nineteenth century, as it became clear that variation in human morphology was relatively circumscribed—groups of people could have fair skin or dark, be tall or short, but none had dog heads or heads that "do grow beneath their shoulders," as Shakespeare puts it in *Othello*[64]—the appeal of the idea of monstrous races discussed by Friedman migrated into literature and, later, film. Science fiction, fantasy, and horror in particular permit authors, artists, and filmmakers unchecked expression of the imagination. That depictions of monstrous races in speculative media has often mapped unsubtly onto real-world terrestrial groups suggests the entrenched perniciousness of stereotype.[65]

Mythical Creatures

Despite beginning this survey with a consideration of monstrous births and races, it seems likely that when people think of monsters, what first comes to mind is not conjoined twins or people with exceptionally big ears but the panoply of fantastic creatures that testifies to the fecundity of the human imagination—Godzilla and golems, basilisks and blobs, vampires, ghouls, zombies, werewolves, wendigos, dragons, krakens, and so on: an immense litany of wondrous, fearsome beasties inhabiting the earth, the air, the seas, and worlds beyond. Theorizing the origins of such beasts is a complicated endeavor. In some cases, the possibility of strange or gigantic beasts was certainly suggested by fossils—what is a dragon, after all, if not a kind of dinosaur, the existence of which was made plain by uncovered gigantic bones? In other cases, gigantic specimens of living creatures could suggest even larger ones lurking in inaccessible places—giant squid washed up on the shore could lead one to conjure the kraken, for example. Superstition and incomplete knowledge of the world, of physical processes, and of the self obviously participated in populating the world with monsters—medieval bestiaries mixed together bears, beavers, and bats with unicorns, dragons, phoenixes, and griffins. Tales told by travelers, such as Marco Polo's reports of unicorns and serpents (likely Asian rhinos and crocodiles), must have excited the imagination of audiences, and outright chicanery has played an important role—P. T. Barnum sewed the torso and head of a monkey onto the back half of a fish and marketed it in the nineteenth century as the "Feejee Mermaid," while Bigfoot and Slenderman now have lives of their own despite identifiable origin points.

Figure I.4. P. T. Barnum and the Feejee Mermaid.

Many monsters, too, have been cut wholesale from the cloth of fancy for various purposes, ranging from prohibition (go here and get eaten, do this and become a monster) to entertainment (often with a profit motive). And then, of course, there are dreams, which have always been a powerful force in suggesting to humans the existence of other worlds and marvelous creatures.

While the origin of each type of monster must be investigated individually (and one must bear in mind that the same monster functions differently in different contexts), theorization of monsters has offered some general insight into the nature and functions of monstrous creatures. As concerns what monsters are, Noël Carroll in "Nightmare and the Horror Film: The Symbolic Biology of Fantastic Beings," as well as in his later *The Philosophy of Horror,* offers a straightforward answer. Restricting his consideration to what he refers to as "art-horror," representations of monsters in art and narrative, Carroll asserts that monsters are entities that represent a threat on some level and evoke disgust as a consequence of "impurity" connected to categorical ambiguity.[66] In some cases, this impurity is the result of what Carroll calls "fusion," which occurs when something is an "unnatural" or confusing composite, such as the "living dead" or a Minotaur or a Frankenstein's monster literally pieced together from parts of different corpses.[67] The opposite of fusion, but equally monstrous, is fission, which takes something unified and breaks it into pieces—doppelgangers, alter egos, werewolves, and so on.[68] Another key strategy for creating a monster is impurity through magnification—take a spider or crab or ape and make it huge, and you have a monster.[69] Congruent with Cohen's third thesis, Carroll concludes that monsters are essentially defined by what Cohen calls "ontological liminality."[70] Neither this nor that—or both this and that—monsters, as Mittman suggests, frustrate our epistemological strategies for making sense of the world.

This raises a question however: if monsters are repulsive and epistemological vertigo is unpleasant, what explains the human fascination with monsters? Carroll's answer in *The Philosophy of Horror* is that we don't so much love monsters as seeing human protagonists contend with them. That is, narrative elicits curiosity—how will the monster be dealt with? Will the heroes win? If our curiosity is stronger than our repulsion, we keep turning the pages, or our eyes stay glued to the screen.

Cohen, however, suggests that there is more to it than this with his sixth thesis, "Fear of the Monster Is Really a Kind of Desire."[71] The monster, as Cohen observes, does not just repulse; it simultaneously attracts. The monster is powerful and linked to forbidden desires and practices: "Through the body of the monster fantasies of aggression, domination, and inversion are allowed safe expression in a clearly delimited and permanently liminal space." Monsters are seldom good citizens, decorous and respectful. They instead are bringers of chaos, violators of boundaries: "We distrust and loathe the monster," writes Cohen, "at the same time we envy its freedom, and perhaps its sublime despair."[72] Monsters in this sense may be considered a kind of language, a way to give symbolic shape to and communicate affect and experience. The body of the monster is a text expressing human fear and desire—one language we speak through is monsters.

And perhaps we can go even further: we love our monsters because through them we indulge our desire for other worlds (after death, beneath our feet, out in space, all around us). Few thoughts can be more terrifying (if for some liberating) than the consideration that *this* is all there is: this life, circumscribed by birth and death; this body, subject to disease and decay; this world, the concrete, intersubjective one we perceive through our senses; this universe, and we are the only ones in it. The epistemological vertigo evoked by the monster on the local level from a remove becomes euphoria. Ghosts and the undead are impure and threatening, but they also testify to the persistence of spirit after death. Demons, witches, and aliens tell us there are other worlds—eschatological, magical, or extraterrestrial. The one thing that the world's great wealth of monsters shares is that all of them insist that there is more to our world than what we can see and touch. The monster threatens, but also promises liberation—a liberation that itself can seem threatening.

Cryptids

Somewhere between mythical beasts and real animals are cryptids, creatures supposed by some to exist but whose existence has not been confirmed by science. As Bernadette Bosky summarizes, the term *cryptid* is derived from *cryptozoology*, the "study of hidden or mysterious animals," and was invented in 1983 by John E. Wall in the newsletter of the International Society of Cryptozoology.[73] The category of cryptids, as Bosky explains, can cover creatures amenable to ordinary zoology, including variants that redefine a species and creatures thought to be extinct. "[G]orillas, the Congo peacock, giant pandas, and the okapi, a stripped relative of the giraffe, were all cryptids before proof of their existence was established."[74] The more famous cryptids, however, are those whose existence is unlikely or impossible—creatures such as the Loch Ness Monster and other surviving dinosaurs, giant hominids such as the Sasquatch or Australian Yowie, the goat-eating Chupacabra alleged to stalk the southwestern deserts of the United States, and the kraken.

In 2005, cryptozoologist George Eberhart proposed (in yet another monster-related list) "10 categories of mystery animal":

1. "distribution anomalies": well-known animal species found in unexpected areas
2. undescribed, unusual, or outsized variations of known species
3. survivals of recently extinct species
4. survivals into the present of species known only from the fossil record

5. survivals of creatures known only from the fossil record into periods much later than previously thought
6. animals not known from the fossil record but related to known species
7. animals not known from the fossil record and not related to any known species
8. mythical animals with a zoological basis
9. seemingly paranormal or supernatural entities with some animal-like characteristics
10. known hoaxes or probably misidentifications.

Eberhart also proposes that cryptozoology should exclude aliens, angels and demons, "bizarre humans," animals relocated by human agency, animals about which there is no controversy, and, curiously, "insignificant" animals whose mysterious features are not "big, weird, dangerous, or significant to humans in some way."[75]

What is perhaps most notable about cryptids is their staying power—once purchase is attained in the imagination, cryptids persist even when their origins can be traced to a hoax, mistake, or misperception. This is because—perhaps to a degree even greater than mythical creatures—cryptids "weird" our world, suggesting that it is stranger than we think: more dangerous, but more interesting. No matter how many investigations into the Loch Ness Monster come up empty or prove that footage of Bigfoot is faked, we still—to borrow from monster theorist Fox Mulder of the program *The X-Files*—want to believe.

Psychology

Our final category of monstrosity shifts our attention from weirdness without to the weird within; to develop this thread, we can focus briefly on another television series—this one about a serial killer. In the television series *Dexter*, which ran for eight seasons from 2006 to 2013, the main character, Dexter Morgan (Michael C. Hall), is a serial killer—but an unusual one. Recognizing homicidal psychopathic tendencies in his adopted son—tendencies we as viewers learn stem from Dexter having observed the brutal murder of his mother as a young child—Dexter's dad, a police officer, taught him to channel his irresistible urges into killing only those guilty of heinous crimes who have somehow escaped justice. Dexter still experiences great pleasure and satisfaction in killing but limits his serial murdering to pedophiles, other serial killers, rapists, and so on. Most considerations of monstrous humans would list serial killers at or near the top. But is Dexter a monster? And if not, is it because we have a sympathetic origin story for his psychosis? Or because we do not feel sympathy for his victims? Or some combination of this and other factors, such as the relationships we see him establish with others on the program?

As the audacious case of Dexter suggests (and I say "audacious" because the premise of asking viewers to sympathize with a serial killer is certainly a bold one), theorizing monstrosity in relation to human psychology is a tricky business and returns us to the vexed issue of definition and the drawing of boundaries. At what point does a human being violate culturally specific expectations to such an extent that he elicits the kind of epistemological vertigo marking monstrosity proposed by Mittman? At what point does deviance make someone a monster? Context is of course key here, because there are few universal human taboos—although prohibitions against cannibalism, murder of group members, and certain sexual practices (necrophilia and incest chief among them) prevail in the majority of societies, nowhere is the idea of monstrosity being in the eye of the beholder more apropos than in considering human monsters.

I would like to suggest that, from a contemporary perspective, human monstrosity is defined most immediately by a lack of sympathy on the part of someone committing or contemplating what are perceived to be physically and/or psychologically harmful acts by an observer who considers those affected as deserving of compassion—particularly if an individual is driven to commit harmful acts by either allegiance to ideology antithetical to that of an observer or sadistic desire. This definition covers the genocidal dictator, on one hand, and the sadistic serial killer who derives enjoyment from his acts, on the other. Also included here are individuals rendered monstrous through their conformity with what Asma calls "monstrous institutional systems"[76]—that is, those who, acting like machines, participate in what one construes as the immoral abuse of others.

The general issue of human psychological deviation from cultural norms of course has received considerable attention for millennia. For the ancient Greeks, such as Socrates and Plato, human monstrosity resulted when human reason failed to govern emotion and appetite.[77] Also originating in antiquity and extending across cultures into the eighteenth century was the idea that temperament was connected to bodily fluids—called *humors*. The four humors proposed by Hippocrites were black bile, yellow bile, phlegm, and blood—and an excess or deficiency of any of them could alter a person's health or psychological condition. Medical practices like bleeding a sick person were intended to restore the balance. An updated version of humorism was eighteenth-century mesmerism. Developed by German doctor Franz Mesmer, mesmerism was premised on the belief in a kind of magnetic fluid that flowed through the body. Physiological and psychological ailments were proposed to be due to the blockage of this fluid, the flow of which could be restored by a trained mesmerist.

In the late nineteenth and early twentieth centuries, Sigmund Freud developed an influential theory concerning human psychology, called *psychoanalysis,* that in interesting ways resonated both with classical Greek philosophy and with theories of internal energy. Freud proposed a divided self—an internal contest between desires (the Id) and internalized social expectations (the Superego) mediated by the Ego. Freud asserted that human beings are divided in another way as well: between the conscious mind and the unconscious, the latter a repository for tabooed desires. For Freud, whose practice focused on those deemed psychologically ill, human behavior (both acceptable and deviant) found its roots in psychosexual development during childhood. Neuroses and psychoses could therefore be traced back to repressed childhood experiences and desires. As Asma explains it, "after Freud, monstrous murderers and abusive people could be theoretically dissected and understood through an examination of their own childhood. Metaphorically speaking, one's childhood is the parent of one's adulthood."[78] In trying to understand the forces that channeled childhood development toward normative adult behavior, Freud also speculated broadly on religion and culture, with a focus on the incest taboo.

Contemporary theories of psychological illness typically break with Freud's emphasis on childhood psychosexual development but generally accept the notions of repression, unconscious desires, and that childhood experiences (whether real or imagined) can have profound effects on later behavior. The roots of psychological dysfunction in adults still are often traced back to childhood. However, modern treatment of psychological illness also to varying degrees considers physiological causes or triggers for behavior considered deviant, as mental illness can be caused by chemical imbalances, diseases, and physical conditions like tumors.

Comprehending psychological illness as the product of childhood trauma and/or physiological factors may help us feel sympathy for those affected and thus undercut their monstrosity in our eyes. We understand in such instances that individuals do not choose to act in ways considered irrational or deviant but rather are compelled by powerful forces outside their control. Tolerance has its limits, of course—it would be much harder to regard Dexter kindly if his victims were children, even recognizing his traumatic backstory and uncontrollable impulses—and the contemporary media still has a tendency to demonize those with mental illness (most dramatically dissociative identity disorder). Nevertheless, twenty-first-century narratives explaining the causes of mental illness undercut the knee-jerk reaction to categorize those affected as monsters.

The situation, however, is vastly different where action perceived as harmful and motivated by political or religious ideology or mercenary self-interest is concerned. As relates to politics and religion, monstrosity inheres in the perception that one's opponents choose to act immorally. No one, of course, consciously chooses to embrace a belief system she feels to be wrong; nevertheless, the rhetoric of monstrosity that circulates in contemporary culture often assumes that if only one's opponents would think rationally—or sometimes in conformity with the perceiver's understanding of religious or political doctrine—they would reach different decisions. These are monsters due to lack of reflection or understanding.

Figure I.5. Nazi propaganda monsterizing Jews during World War II.

Monster Politics

The foregoing overview of teratology, mythology, and psychology attempts to trace various threads in the theorization of what monsters are, where they come from, and what they mean. Although far from complete, this consideration suggests the deep psychic investment human beings have had in contemplating monsters for millennia. There is another thread to this discussion of monster theory, however, that has to be briefly introduced—and that is what we could refer to as the strategic deployment of monsters for sociopolitical ends. This perspective on monsters thinks in terms not of "what is this thing?" but rather of "how can I use this thing to achieve my goals?"

Cohen foregrounds the political utility of monsters in his fourth and fifth theses: "The Monster Dwells at the Gates of Difference" and "The Monster Polices the Borders of the Possible."[79] Where difference is concerned, Cohen observes that representing another culture as monstrous "justifies its displacement or extermination by rendering the act heroic"[80]—and this is something that demagogues have understood all too well across human history. Whether one is discussing Roman attitudes toward "barbarians" in antiquity, French demonization of Muslims in the Middle Ages, the displacement and destruction of indigenous populations in many parts of the world beginning in the sixteenth century, the Nazi "Final Solution," genocidal campaigns in Bosnia or Rwanda or Armenia, the twenty-first-century immigrant crisis, and so many other instances across time, the exaggeration of cultural difference into monstrosity has always served as an essential preliminary step toward domination. From this perspective, a complete genealogy of monster theory would need to be expanded to include a range of works that explore how manipulation of human fear through the exaggeration of physical and/or cultural difference can and has been used to achieve social or political ends. Such a genealogy would be broad indeed (certainly beyond the scope of this introduction), including primary texts ranging from political screeds against particular groups to propaganda posters, programs, and films.

Contemporary Monster Theory

What differentiates contemporary monster theory from the theorization of monsters in earlier periods is primarily the position that monstrosity is a socially constructed category reflecting culturally specific anxieties and desires, and often deployed—wittingly or not—to achieve particular sociopolitical objectives. Contemporary monster theory thus disavows (or at least sidesteps the question of) the monstrosity of human subjects based on morphology and instead focuses on the means through which such subjects are "monsterized" and the implications of this process. Adopting a skeptical (or at least agnostic) position in relation to the existence of actual monsters, contemporary monster theory also prefers to focus on images of and narratives involving monsters (human and nonhuman) to tease out what such images and narratives say about their creators and their cultures. Monsters from this perspective remain, as they have been for millennia, texts in need of interpretation; however, they are messages originating from human beings rather than the gods. Put concisely, contemporary monster theory tends to explore "monsters" rather than monsters.

Where contemporary monster theory is concerned, a special position in this monster theory genealogy must be afforded to the work of French philosopher Michel Foucault. Throughout his work, Foucault consistently emphasized the social construction of ideas of normalcy and deviancy, exploring how understandings of what is "natural" and "unnatural" shift across time and from place to place, but invariably participate in the constitution of power hierarchies and the regulation of social behaviors. In *Madness and Civilization* (1961), Foucault explored changing understandings of madness from the Middle Ages to the end of the eighteenth century and the ways in which the label of "mad" created a divide between socially acceptable and unacceptable behavior. Foucault's *The History of Sexuality*—most especially the first volume, *The Will to Knowledge* (1976)—focuses on the way ideas of normalcy and deviancy in relation to sexuality are produced and policed. In *Discipline and Punish: The Birth of the Prison* (1975), Foucault considers in more general terms the coercive regimes that seek to regulate human behavior. In these works and others, Foucault emphasized that, rather than being universal and immutable, understandings of normalcy and deviancy are context dependent and mutable; the result is that what one culture construes as monstrous aberration could be considered normal by another.

Foucault turned his attention explicitly to monsters in his lectures at the Collège de France in 1974–75, which clustered around the theme of the "emergence of the abnormal individual in the nineteenth century"[81] and focused in particular on the "human monster," the "individual to be corrected," and the onanist.[82] In these lectures, Foucault shows how monstrosity is not only a relational term—monstrosity is always defined against that which is not monstrous—but also part of a regulatory regime that disciplines human beings into acting and thinking in particular ways. In relation to the human monster, Foucault in his lecture of January 22, 1975, asserts that the "frame of reference" for the human monster is always the law.[83] The human monster, according to Foucault, violates both the laws of society and the laws of nature.[84] Beyond this, though, the human monster exceeds the capacity of the law to respond to it: "the monster's power and its capacity to create anxiety are due to the fact that it violates the law while leaving it with nothing to say. . . . [It] is a breach of the law that automatically stands outside the law."[85] As a consequence, the response evoked by the human monster is either violence or pity.

Indeed, Foucault's interests often extended explicitly to subjects conventionally regarded as monstrous. Representative here as well is Foucault's brief introduction to the English-language publication of *Herculine Barbin (Being the Recently Discovered Memoirs of a Nineteenth-Century French Hermaphrodite)* (1980), in which he considers the history of hermaphroditism and shifting attitudes regarding it—a topic he had touched on in his lectures of 1974–75.[86] Foucault notes that in the Middle Ages, European hermaphrodites were typically assigned a sex at baptism but were later free to decide for themselves whether they preferred to continue with the sex assigned to them.[87] As time passed, however, sexuality was increasingly regarded as singular and less fluid: "Biological theories of sexuality, juridical conceptions of individuals, forms of administrative control in modern nations, led little by little to rejecting the idea of a mixture of the two sexes in a single body, and consequently to limiting the free choice of indeterminate individuals. Henceforth, everyone was to have one and only one sex."[88]

Foucault's concise consideration of the history of and attitudes regarding hermaphroditism in his introduction to *Herculine Barbin* constitutes a pithy and accessible encapsulation not only of Foucault's general method but of the approach of much contemporary monster theory. Through his repeated considerations of the social construction of the ideas of normalcy and deviancy, and the ways in which these ideas vary and shift, as well as coerce certain behaviors while retarding others, Foucault—often referred to as the great theoretician of power—can also be considered as the great theoretician of monstrosity. His work makes clear that monsters are always "monsters"—not "naturally," universally, or eternally monsters but rather constructed as monstrous through the influence of social conventions, expectations, and attitudes.

Foucault's work was part of a larger twentieth-century social milieu in which marginalized populations—women, people of color, gays and lesbians, and so on—were agitating actively for social justice and equal rights, and his research was influenced by and in turn exerted influence on those seeking to explore how entrenched power dynamics rendered particular populations vulnerable to exploitation and exclusion. Foucault's method and research arguably have been central to the development of numerous disciplines within the humanities and social sciences that have been invested in exploring, highlighting, and resisting the forces that have historically marginalized—or monsterized—particular groups, including postcolonial studies, Jewish studies, feminist studies, disability studies, and gender and sexuality studies. Although the rhetoric of monstrosity may not always be explicit, texts that would need to be highlighted in a genealogy of Foucaultian-influenced monster theory would need to include Edward Said's *Orientalism* (1978), which considers how the West's representations of the East as backward and degraded facilitated imperialist agendas; Stephen Greenblatt's *Marvelous Possessions: The Wonders of the New World* (1992), which explores how Europeans in the late Middle Ages and early modern period represented non-Europeans in ways also facilitating an imperialist agenda; Sander Gilman's

The Jew's Body (1991), which focuses on anti-Semitic representations of Jewish morphology; Rosemarie Garland-Thomson's *Extraordinary Bodies: Figuring Physical Disability in American Culture and Literature* (1997), a foundational text within disability studies; and Gayle Rubin's 1984 essay "Thinking Sex," which explores how value systems are overlaid on sexual behavior.

These titles—and many others—would then supplement a listing of earlier studies that similarly explore the mechanisms through which particular populations are constructed as monstrous others. Such a catalog would need to include, for example, Simone de Beauvoir's *The Second Sex* (1949), which frames women's oppression as rooted in being constructed as other to man; Frantz Fanon's *Black Skins, White Masks* (1952), which addresses the association of Blackness with inadequacy; philosopher René Girard's exploration of scapegoating in *The Scapegoat* (1982); Hannah Arendt's *The Origins of Totalitarianism* (1951), which scrutinizes anti-Semitism but extends beyond that focus; Erving Goffman's research on social stigmas in *Stigma: Notes on the Management of Spoiled Identity* (1963); and Eric Hoffer's *True Believer: Thoughts on the Nature of Mass Movements* (1951), which analyzes how and why mass movements start and the ways in which they position themselves in opposition to other groups perceived as monstrous.

Foucault's work in the second half of the twentieth century arguably constitutes a "tipping point" as concerns monster theory, as it insists that we consider the label of monster as a mechanism of social control and form of oppression—and it is this understanding of monsters as disenfranchised victims of an oppressive dominant culture that informs the twentieth century's most significant development in monstrous representation: giving voice to the monster. As I've pointed out in a different context, beginning arguably in 1971 with John Gardner's retelling of Beowulf from the monster Grendel's perspective, a central contemporary trend in monstrous narrative has been to let monsters tell their own stories, rendering them comprehensible and often sympathetic (see my "Invisible Monsters" in this volume). Particularly in films ostensibly targeted at children, such as the *Shrek* and *Monsters, Inc.* franchises, the "true monster" is shown not to be the fairy tale creature or exotic beast but rather the human society that demonizes somatic difference. Such narratives—products of twentieth- and twenty-first-century civil rights movements—clearly convey a message of tolerance and the valuing of diversity. Monstrosity inheres not in looking different but rather in acting in harmful ways.

The Monster Theory Reader

This, then, brings us back to our beginning, with Jeffrey Jerome Cohen's "Monster Theory (Seven Theses)" essay, the coalescing of the monster theory discipline, and this volume. Following this introduction is Cohen's 1996 essay, which presents a foundational—and, as he himself acknowledges on the first page, thoroughly Foucaultian—analysis of monsters as reflections of culturally specific anxieties and desires, as mechanisms of social control, and also as potential sites of resistance to oppressive paradigms. Cohen's formulations implicitly or explicitly guide much of the analysis in the latter sections of this reader. As my foregoing monster theory genealogy makes clear, Cohen didn't invent monster theory; however, he did name it, and his essay provides a clear set of parameters for what monsters are and how they function that has directed or informed subsequent investigation into monsters.

Following Cohen's essay is what I'm calling "The Monster Theory Toolbox"—a set of readings that introduce important concepts and terminology and that model approaches often utilized in contemporary discussions of monsters and monstrosity. Much of this section is psychoanalytic in orientation, as that is where monstrosity and the affect it elicits have been theorized most fully. This section starts with Sigmund Freud and his concept of the uncanny—the affect elicited under certain conditions when the familiar becomes strange or something strange seems oddly familiar. That this concept has proven to be a very productive tool in analyzing monsters and their functions is then demonstrated by the piece that follows: Masahiro Mori's "The Uncanny Valley," which addresses the way human beings respond to representations of the human form that are almost, but not quite, human. Although often cited in discussions of dolls and automata, this essay has never been reprinted. As important to discussions of monsters as Freud's idea of the uncanny is Julia Kristeva's concept of abjection, which refers to the process through which the self separates itself from the nonself, and the repulsion elicited by that which was once a part of the self but no longer is. Accordingly, Kristeva's discussion of abjection from her *The Powers of Horror* is included here. Robin Wood and Noël Carroll follow, presenting more general psychoanalytic approaches to monsters. Wood, in "An Introduction to the American Horror Film," focuses in particular on repression, arguing that monsters in horror films reflect the "return of the repressed"; that is, they give shape to what a particular culture fears and desires. Carroll, in the selection taken from his study *The Philosophy of Horror,* offers us a recipe for the making of monsters. Reaffirming Cohen's thesis that the monster is the "harbinger of category crisis," Carroll considers the different kinds of categorical transgressions that precipitate monstrosity. The toolbox section then rounds out with a selection from Jack Halberstam's (writing as Judith) *Skin Shows: Gothic Horror and the Technology of Monsters,* in which he theorizes monsters as "meaning machines." Making use of some of the psychoanalytic concepts introduced earlier in this section, Halberstam argues that monsters, refusing any simple one-to-one correspondence with an underlying fear or desire, instead give shape to multiple meanings simultaneously.

The three parts that follow part I, "The Monster Theory Toolbox," overlap in various ways but also break along obvious fault lines. Part II, "Monsterizing Difference," clusters together essays considering the "monsterizing" of different populations and the consequences of monstrous rhetoric. These essays explore how difference—somatic, religious, sexual, and so on—becomes elaborated into monstrosity as a tool of domination. Alexa Wright begins part II by exploring the "monstrous races" and their placement on medieval maps. Her essay is followed by Bettina Bildhauer's examination of monsterization of Jews in medieval culture. With a focus on film, Barbara Creed, making use of Kristeva's concept of abjection, considers the monsterization of the feminine, Harry Benshoff looks at the monsterizing of homosexuals, and Annalee Newitz explores the monsterizing of race. Rounding out this section—and returning us to its initial focus on monsterous races and somatic difference—is Elizabeth Grosz's consideration of somatic "freaks."

Broader in its focus than "Monsterizing Difference," part III, "Monsters and Culture," includes scholarship that explores how monsters intersect with social beliefs, attitudes, and trends ranging from religious belief and ideas about the "proper" body to technology, terrorism, and displaced peoples. Stephen T. Asma starts off part III with a consideration of the appeal of monsters and the roles they play in the "moral imagination." Timothy Beal follows, connecting the experience of horror and the fear of the monster to religion and the transcendental. Margrit Shildrick, taking us back to Kristeva, emphasizes the self–other dichotomy inherent in monstrosity and how the abjection of the monster helps to shore up the boundaries of the self. In his chapter, Michael Dylan Foster shifts our focus to Japan and shows how monsters are very much products of their moment as he considers the relationship between tales of the shape-shifting *tanuki* and the development of the locomotive in the nineteenth and early twentieth centuries. In my own contribution, I consider the decoupling of ideas of monstrosity from physical difference in the twenty-first century and the consequent generalization of threat: what do we do when we can't identify the monster? Jasbir K. Puar and Amit S. Rai take this consideration of modern monstrosity to the next step by focusing on the figure of the monstrous terrorist constructed as a foil to twenty-first-century white, heterosexual patriotism. Concluding part III is Jon Stratton's exploration of the monsterization of displaced people. Although first published in 2011, this essay's argument has become ever more significant as issues of migration and displaced people have become increasingly visible.

Then, taking its cue from Cohen's final thesis, "The Monster Stands at the Threshold . . . of Becoming," this reader's final section, part IV, "The Promises of Monsters," collects four essays that show us how monsters can be figures not just of fear but of hope. Erin Suzuki's essay looks at monsters of the Pacific as enacting a kind of cultural critique. Drawing language from filmmaker Guillermo del Toro's *Pacific Rim* (2013), she proposes a kind of "openness to alien otherness." Anthony Lioi's ecocritical approach to monstrosity focuses on the swamp dragon, asking us not just to "give dirt its due" but also to form "serpentine alliances" in our defense of natural spaces. Donna Haraway's essay, from which the name of this section is drawn, offers a daring deconstruction of deeply entrenched binaries, with a focus on the power dynamics at play in self–other oppositions and an ethical imperative to rethink the monstrous. The collection ends with Patricia MacCormack's assertion that our monsters are "seductive present promises of extending thoughts of human potentiality." They can show us the way to becoming something other than we are, and more just.

Further Reading

This suggested reading is far from a complete list of sources that address monsters—indeed, as soon as one starts to focus on a particular monster, such as the vampire or the zombie or Frankenstein, the list swells to monstrous proportions. Instead, the following list primarily includes monographs and edited collections those researching monsters and monster theory are likely to find useful and that themselves can lead researchers on to other sources.

Bilhauer, Bettina, and Robert Mills, eds. *The Monstrous Middle Ages.* Toronto: University of Toronto Press, 2003.

Blanco, María del Pilar, and Esther Peeren, eds. *The Spectralities Reader: Ghosts and Haunting in Contemporary Cultural Theory.* New York: Bloomsbury, 2013.

Braidotti, Rosi. "Mothers, Monsters, and Machines." In *Writing on the Body: Female Embodiment and Feminist Theory,* ed. Katie Conboy, Nadia Medina, and Sarah Stanbury, 59–79. New York: Columbia University Press, 1997.

Braidotti, Rosi. "Signs of Wonder and Traces of Doubt: On Teratology and Embodied Differences." In *Between Monsters, Goddesses and Cyborgs: Feminist Confrontations with Science, Medicine and Cyberspace,* ed. Nina Lykke and Rosi Braidotti, 135–52. London: Zed Books, 1996.

Brenner, Alletta. "'The Good and Bad of That Sexe': Monstrosity and Womanhood in Early Modern England." *Intersections* 10, no. 2 (2009): 161–75.

Cohen, Jeffrey Jerome, ed. *Monster Theory: Reading Culture.* Minneapolis: University of Minnesota Press, 1996.

Crawford, Julie. *Marvelous Protestantism: Monstrous Births in Post-Reformation England.* Baltimore: Johns Hopkins University Press, 2005.

Cutler-Broyles, Teresa, and Marko Teodorski, eds. *Monstrosity from the Inside Out.* Oxford, U.K.: Inter-Disciplinary Press, 2014.

Gelder, Ken. *New Vampire Cinema.* New York: Palgrave Macmillan, 2012.

Gilmore, David D. *Monsters: Evil Beings, Mythical Beasts, and All Manner of Imaginary Terrors.* Philadelphia: University of Pennsylvania Press, 2003.

Hubner, Laura, Marcus Leaning, and Paul Manning, eds. *The Zombie Renaissance in Popular Culture*. New York: Palgrave Macmillan, 2015.

Hudson, Dale. "'Of Course There Are Werewolves and Vampires': *True Blood* and the Right to Rights for Other Species." *American Quarterly* 65, no. 3 (2012): 661–87.

Hutchison, Sharla, and Rebecca A. Brown, eds. *Monsters and Monstrosity from the Fin de Siècle to the Millennium*. New York: McFarland, 2015.

Ingebretsen, Edward J. *At Stake: Monsters and the Rhetoric of Fear in Public Culture*. Chicago: University of Chicago Press, 2001.

Kaplan, Matt. *Medusa's Gaze and Vampire's Bite: The Science of Monsters*. New York: Scribner, 2012.

Keetley, Dawn, and Angela Tenga, eds. *Plant Horror: Approaches to the Monstrous Vegetal in Fiction and Film*. New York: Palgrave, 2016.

Kukla, Rebecca. *Mass Hysteria: Medicine, Culture, and Mothers' Bodies*. New York: Rowman and Littlefield, 2005.

Lauro, Sarah Juliet, ed. *Zombie Theory: A Reader*. Minneapolis: University of Minnesota Press, 2017.

Lawrence, Elizabeth A. "Werewolves in Psyche and Cinema: Man-Beast Transformation and Paradox." *Journal of American Culture* 19, no. 3 (1996): 103–12.

Leeder, Murray, ed. *Cinematic Ghosts: Haunting and Spectrality from Silent Cinema to the Digital Era*. New York: Bloomsbury, 2015.

Levina, Marina, and Diem-My T. Bui, eds. *Monster Culture in the 21st Century: A Reader*. New York: Bloomsbury, 2013.

McIntosh, Shawn, and Marc Leverette, eds. *Zombie Culture: Autopsies of the Living Dead*. New York: Scarecrow Press, 2008.

McNally, David. *Monsters of the Market: Zombies, Vampires and Global Capitalism*. Chicago: Haymarket Books, 2011.

Mieville, China. "Theses on Monsters." *Conjunctions* 59 (2012). http://www.conjunctions.com/print/article/china-mieville-c59.

Mittman, Asa Simon. "Are the 'Monstrous Races' Races?" *Postmedieval: A Journal of Medieval Cultural Studies* 6, no. 1 (2015): 36–51.

Mittman, Asa Simon, and Susan M. Kim. "Monsters and the Exotic in Early Modern England." *Literature Compass* 6, no. 2 (2009): 332–48.

Paradiso-Michau, Michael R., ed. "Listening to Our Monsters" (special issue). *Listening: Journal of Communication Ethics, Religion, and Culture* 52, no. 3 (2017).

Picart, Caroline Joan S., and John Edgar Browning, eds. *Speaking of Monsters: A Teratological Anthology*. New York: Palgrave Macmillan, 2012.

Poole, W. Scott. *Monsters in America: Our Historical Obsession with the Hideous and the Haunting*. Houston, TX: Baylor University Press, 2011.

Pulliam, June. *Monstrous Bodies: Feminine Power in Young Adult Horror Fiction*. New York: McFarland, 2014.

Richardson, Niall, and Adam Locks. "Monstrosity, Enfreakment and Disability." In *Body Studies: The Basics*, 50–71. New York: Routledge, 2014.

Smith, Preserved. "The Mooncalf." *Modern Philology* 11, no. 3 (1914): 355–61.

Spinks, Jennifer. *Monstrous Births and Visual Culture in Sixteenth-Century Germany.* London: Pickerings and Chatto, 2009.

Weinstock, Jeffrey Andrew. "The American Ghost Story." In *A Company to the Ghost Story,* ed. Scott Brewster and Luke Thurston, 206–14. New York: Routledge, 2018.

Weinstock, Jeffrey Andrew. "American Monsters." In *A Companion to the American Gothic,* ed. Charles L. Crow, 41–55. New York: Wiley-Blackwell, 2014.

Weinstock, Jeffrey Andrew. "American Vampires." In *Edinburgh Companion to the American Gothic,* ed. Jason Haslam and Joel Faflak, 203–21. Edinburgh: Edinburgh University Press, 2015.

Weinstock, Jeffrey Andrew, ed. *The Ashgate Encyclopedia of Literary and Cinematic Monsters.* Burlington, Vt.: Ashgate, 2014.

Weinstock, Jeffrey Andrew. *The Vampire Film: Undead Cinema.* New York: Columbia University Press, 2012.

Wilson, Natalie. "Civilized Vampires versus Savage Werewolves: Race and Ethnicity in the Twilight Series." In *Bitten by Twilight: Youth Culture, Media, and the Vampire Franchise,* 55–70. Berlin: Peter Lang, 2010.

Notes

1. Timothy Beal, *Religion and Its Monsters* (New York: Routledge, 2002), 6–7.

2. Beal, 7.

3. Stephen Asma, *On Monsters: An Unnatural History of Our Worst Fears* (New York: Oxford University Press, 2009), 13.

4. Asa Simon Mittman, "Introduction: The Impact of Monsters and Monster Studies," in *The Ashgate Research Companion to Monsters and the Monstrous,* ed. Asa Simon Mittman (Surrey, U.K.: Ashgate, 2013), 8.

5. Alan W. Bates, *Emblematic Monsters: Unnatural Conceptions and Deformed Births in Early Modern Europe* (Amsterdam: Rodopi, 2004), 74.

6. Ambrose Paré, *On Monsters and Marvels,* trans. Janis L. Pallister (Chicago: University of Chicago Press, 1995), 3–4.

7. On this point, see Eduard Ulházy et al., "Teratology—Past, Present and Future," *Interdisciplinary Toxicology* 5, no. 4 (2012): 163–68.

8. Josef Warkany, "History of Teratology," in *The Handbook of Teratology: General Principles and Etiology,* ed. James G. Wilson and F. Clarke Fraser (New York: Springer, 1977), 24.

9. Norman R. Smith, "Portent Lore and Medieval Popular Culture," *Journal of Popular Culture* 14, no. 1 (1980): 47.

10. Mark V. Barrow, "A Brief History of Teratology to the Early 20th Century," *Teratology* 4, no. 119 (1971): 18.

11. Smith, "Portent Lore," 48.

12. Smith, 48.

13. Smith, 50.

14. Saint Augustine of Hippo, *The City of God,* trans. Marcus Dods (New York: The Modern Library, 1950), X.16: 321

15. Surekha Davies, "The Unlucky, the Bad and the Ugly: Categories of Monstrosity from the Renaissance to the Enlightenment," in *The Ashgate Research Companion to Monsters and the Monstrous,* ed. Asa Simon Mittman (Surrey, U.K.: Ashgate, 2013), 52.

16. Smith, "Portent Lore," 57.

17. See chapter 4 of Peggy McCracken's *The Curse of Eve, the Wound of the Hero: Blood, Gender, and Medieval Literature* (Philadelphia: University of Pennsylvania Press, 2003). See also Alexandra Walsham, *Providence in Early Modern England* (Oxford: Oxford University Press, 1999), 202–3.

18. See Anne Jacobson Schutte, "'Such Monstrous Births': A Neglected Aspect of the Antinomian Controversy," *Renaissance Quarterly* 38, no. 1 (1985): 85–106.

19. Saint Augustine, *City of God,* 15:23.

20. Saint Thomas Aquinas, *The "Summa Theologica" of St. Thomas Aquinas* (London: Burns, Oates, and Washburne, 1920–42), I, q. 51, art. 3, rep. 6.

21. Warkany, "History of Teratology," 27.

22. Leviticus 20:15, 16.

23. Paré, *On Monsters and Marvels,* 67. Brackets in original.

24. See chapter 20 of Paré; see also Warkany, "History of Teratology," 27–29.

25. Jeffrey Jerome Cohen, "Monster Culture (Seven Theses)," in *Monster Theory: Reading Culture,* ed. Jeffrey Jerome Cohen (Minneapolis: University of Minnesota Press, 1996), 6.

26. Cohen, 6.

27. Robert Bogdan, *Freak Show: Presenting Human Oddities for Amusement and Profit* (Chicago: University of Chicago Press, 1988), 2.

28. See chapter 6, "Wild Men and Feral Children," in Leslie Fiedler, *Freaks: Myths and Images of the Secret Self* (New York: Anchor Books, 1978).

29. Marie-Hélène Huet, *Monstrous Imagination* (Cambridge, Mass.: Harvard University Press, 1993), 3–4.

30. Warkany, "History of Teratology," 30.

31. Montaigne, quoted in Wes Williams, "Montaigne on Imagination," in *The Oxford Handbook of Montaigne,* ed. Phillipe Desan (Oxford: Oxford University Press, 2016), 696.

32. Huet, *Monstrous Imagination,* 19.

33. Paré, *On Monsters and Marvels,* 39.

34. Michael Howell and Peter Ford, *The True History of the Elephant Man* (New York: Penguin Books, 1981), 128.

35. Ian Stevenson, "A New Look at Maternal Impressions: An Analysis of 50 Published Cases and Reports of Two Recent Examples," *Journal of Scientific Exploration* 6, no. 4 (1992): 353.

36. See book 1, part 1 of Aristotle, *On the Parts of Animals,* trans. William Ogle, http://classics.mit.edu/Aristotle/parts_animals.html.

37. Aristotle, 770b: 10.

38. Aristotle, 769b: 25.

39. Barrow, "A Brief History of Teratology," 21.

40. Warkany, "History of Teratology," 33.

41. Peter Hofland, "Reversal of Fortune: How a Vilified Drug Became a Life-Saving Agent in the 'War' against Cancer," *Onco'Zine: The International Oncology Nework,* November 30, 2013, https://oncozine.com/reversal-of-fortune-how-a-vilified-drug-became-a-life -saving-agent-in-the-war-against-cancer/.

42. Paré, quoted in Barrow, "A Brief History of Teratology," 23.

43. John Block Friedman, *The Monstrous Races in Medieval Art and Thought* (Syracuse, N.Y.: Syracuse University Press, 2003), 11.

44. Friedman, 13.

45. Friedman, 15.

46. Friedman, 18.

47. Friedman, 18.

48. Friedman, 24.

49. Friedman, 26.

50. Friedman, 25.

51. Friedman, 25.

52. Friedman, 24.

53. Asma, *On Monsters,* 37–38.

54. Saint Augustine, *City of God,* 16.8, 532.

55. Friedman, *Monstrous Races,* 90.

56. See Friedman, 112–16.

57. Davies, "The Unlucky, the Bad and the Ugly," 63.

58. Friedman, *Monstrous Races,* 46.

59. Davies, "The Unlucky, the Bad and the Ugly," 65.

60. Davies, 69.

61. Davies, 73.

62. Davies, 73.

63. Davies, 74.

64. Shakespeare, *Othello,* 1.3.167–69.

65. See, e.g., my "Freaks in Space: 'Extraterrestrialism' and 'Deep-Space Multiculturalism,'" in *Freakery: Cultural Spectacles of the Extraordinary Body,* ed. Rosemarie Garland Thomson, 327–37 (New York: New York University Press, 1996). See also Helen Young's *Race and Popular Fantasy Literatures: Habits of Whiteness* (New York: Routledge, 2015).

66. Noël Carroll, *The Philosophy of Horror or Paradoxes of the Heart* (New York: Routledge, 1990), 43.

67. Carroll, 43.

68. Carroll, 46.

69. Carroll, 49.

70. Cohen, "Monster Culture," 6.

71. Cohen, 16.

72. Cohen, 17.

73. Bernadette Bosky, "Cryptids," in *The Ashgate Encyclopedia of Literary and Cinematic Monsters,* ed. Jeffrey Andrew Weinstock (Burlington, Vt.: Ashgate, 2013), 105.

74. Bosky, 105.

75. George M. Eberhart, "Mysterious Creatures: Creating a Cryptozoological Encyclopedia," *Journal of Scientific Exploration* 19, no. 1 (2005): 109.

76. Asma, *On Monsters,* 244.

77. Asma, 53.

78. Asma, 210.

79. Cohen, "Monster Culture," 7–16.

80. Cohen, 7–8.

81. Arnold I. Davidson, introduction to *Abnormal: Lectures at the Collège de France 1974–1975,* by Michel Foucault, ed. Valerio Marchetti and Antonella Salomoni, trans. Graham Burchell (New York: Picador, 1999), xvii.

82. Michel Foucault, *Abnormal: Lectures at the Collège de France 1974–1975*, ed. Valerio Marchetti and Antonella Salomoni, trans. Graham Burchell (New York: Picador, 1999), 55.

83. Foucault, 55.

84. Foucault, 55–56.

85. Foucault, 56.

86. Foucault, 70–74.

87. Michel Foucault, introduction to *Herculine Barbin (Being the Recently Discovered Memoirs of a Nineteenth-Century French Hermaphrodite)* (New York: Pantheon, 1980), viii.

88. Foucault, viii.

MONSTER CULTURE (SEVEN THESES)

Jeffrey Jerome Cohen

W HAT I WILL PROPOSE HERE by way of a first foray, as entrance into this book of monstrous content, is a sketch of a new *modus legendi*: a method of reading cultures from the monsters they engender. In doing so, I will partially violate two of the sacred dicta of recent cultural studies: the compulsion to historical specificity and the insistence that all knowledge (and hence all cartographies of that knowledge) is local. Of the first I will say only that in cultural studies today history (disguised perhaps as "culture") tends to be fetishized as a *telos*, as a final determinant of meaning; post de Man, post Foucault, post Hayden White, one must bear in mind that history is just another text in a procession of texts, and not a guarantor of any singular signification. A movement away from the *longue durée* and toward microeconomics (of capital or of gender) is associated most often with Foucauldian criticism; yet recent critics have found that where Foucault went wrong was mainly in his details, in his minute specifics. Nonetheless, his methodology—his archaeology of ideas, his histories of unthought—remains with good reason the chosen route of inquiry for most cultural critics today, whether they work in postmodern cyberculture or in the Middle Ages.

And so I would like to make some grand gestures. We live in an age that has rightly given up on Unified Theory, an age when we realize that history (like "individuality," "subjectivity," "gender," and "culture") is composed of a multitude of fragments, rather than of smooth epistemological wholes. Some fragments will be collected here and bound temporarily together to form a loosely integrated net—or, better, an unassimilated hybrid, a monstrous body. Rather than argue a "theory of teratology," I offer by way of introduction to the essays that follow a set of breakable postulates in search of specific cultural moments. I offer seven theses toward understanding cultures through the monsters they bear.

Thesis I: The Monster's Body Is a Cultural Body

Vampires, burial, death: inter the corpse where the road forks, so that when it springs from the grave, it will not know which path to follow. Drive a stake through its heart: it will be stuck to the ground at the fork, it will haunt that place that leads to many other places, that point of indecision. Behead the corpse, so that, acephalic, it will not know itself as subject, only as pure body.

The monster is born only at this metaphoric crossroads, as an embodiment of a certain cultural moment—of a time, a feeling, and a place.[1] The monster's body quite literally incorporates fear, desire, anxiety, and fantasy (ataractic or incendiary), giving them life and an uncanny independence. The monstrous body is pure culture. A construct and a projection, the monster exists only to be read: the *monstrum* is etymologically "that which reveals," "that which warns," a glyph that seeks a hierophant. Like a letter on the page, the monster signifies something other than itself: it is always a displacement, always inhabits the gap between the time of upheaval that created it and the moment into which it is received, to be born again. These epistemological spaces between the monster's bones are Derrida's familiar chasm of *différance*: a genetic uncertainty principle, the essence of the monster's vitality, the reason it always rises from the dissection table as its secrets are about to be revealed and vanishes into the night.

Thesis II: The Monster Always Escapes

We see the damage that the monster wreaks, the material remains (the footprints of the yeti across Tibetan snow, the bones of the giant stranded on a rocky cliff), but the monster itself turns immaterial and vanishes, to reappear someplace else (for who is the yeti if not the medieval wild man? Who is the wild man if not the biblical and classical giant?). No matter how many times King Arthur killed the ogre of Mount Saint Michael, the monster reappeared in another heroic chronicle, bequeathing the Middle Ages an abundance of *morte d'Arthurs*. Regardless of how many times Sigourney Weaver's beleaguered Ripley utterly destroys the ambiguous Alien that stalks her, its monstrous progeny return, ready to stalk again in another bigger-than-ever sequel. No monster tastes of death but once. The anxiety that condenses like green vapor into the form of the vampire can be dispersed temporarily, but the revenant by definition returns. And so the monster's body is both corporal and incorporeal; its threat is its propensity to shift.

Each time the grave opens and the unquiet slumberer strides forth ("come from the dead, / Come back to tell you all"), the message proclaimed is transformed by the air that gives its speaker new life. Monsters must be examined within the intricate matrix of relations (social, cultural, and literary-historical) that generate them. In speaking of the new kind of vampire invented by Bram Stoker, we might explore the foreign count's transgressive but compelling sexuality, as subtly alluring to Jonathan Harker as Henry Irving, Stoker's mentor, was to Stoker.[2] Or we might analyze Murnau's self-loathing appropriation of the same demon in *Nosferatu,* where in the face of nascent fascism the undercurrent of desire surfaces in plague and bodily corruption. Anne Rice has given the myth a modern rewriting in which homosexuality and vampirism have been conjoined, apotheosized; that she has created a pop culture phenomenon in the process is not insignificant, especially at a time when gender as a construct has been scrutinized at almost every social register. In Francis Coppola's recent blockbuster, *Bram Stoker's Dracula,* the homosexual subtext present at least since the appearance of Sheridan Le Fanu's lesbian lamia (*Carmilla,* 1872) has, like the red corpuscles that serve as the film's leitmotif, risen to the surface, primarily as an AIDS awareness that transforms the disease of vampirism into a sadistic (and very medieval) form of redemption through the torments of the body in pain. No coincidence, then, that Coppola was putting together a documentary on AIDS at the same time he was working on *Dracula.*

In each of these vampire stories, the undead returns in slightly different clothing, each time to be read against contemporary social movements or a specific, determining event: *la décadence* and its new possibilities, homophobia and its hateful imperatives, the acceptance of new subjectivities unfixed by binary gender, a fin de siècle social activism paternalistic in its embrace. Discourse extracting a transcultural, trans-temporal phenomenon labeled "the vampire" is of rather limited utility; even if vampiric figures are found almost worldwide, from ancient Egypt to modern Hollywood, each reappearance and its analysis is still bound in a double act of construction and reconstruction.[3] "Monster theory" must therefore concern itself with strings of cultural moments, connected by a logic that always threatens to shift; invigorated by change and escape, by the impossibility of achieving what Susan Stewart calls the desired "fall or death, the stopping" of its gigantic subject,[4] monstrous interpretation is as much process as epiphany, a work that must content itself with fragments (footprints, bones, talismans, teeth, shadows, obscured glimpses—signifiers of monstrous passing that stand in for the monstrous body itself).

Thesis III: The Monster Is the Harbinger of Category Crisis

The monster always escapes because it refuses easy categorization. Of the night-marish creature that Ridley Scott brought to life in *Alien,* Harvey Greenberg writes:

> It is a Linnean nightmare, defying every natural law of evolution; by turns
> bivalve, crustacean, reptilian, and humanoid. It seems capable of lying
> dormant within its egg indefinitely. It sheds its skin like a snake, its carapace
> like an arthropod. It deposits its young into other species like a wasp. . . . It
> responds according to Lamarckian and Darwinian principles.[5]

This refusal to participate in the classificatory "order of things" is true of monsters generally: they are disturbing hybrids whose externally incoherent bodies resist attempts to include them in any systematic structuration. And so the monster is dangerous, a form suspended between forms that threatens to smash distinctions.

Because of its ontological liminality, the monster notoriously appears at times of crisis as a kind of third term that problematizes the clash of extremes—as "that which questions binary thinking and introduces a crisis."[6] This power to evade and to undermine has coursed through the monster's blood from classical times, when despite all the attempts of Aristotle (and later Pliny, Augustine, and Isidore) to incorporate the monstrous races[7] into a coherent epistemological system, the monster always escaped to return to its habitations at the margins of the world (a purely conceptual locus rather than a geographic one).[8] Classical "wonder books" radically undermine the Aristotelian taxonomic system, for by refusing an easy compartmentalization of their monstrous contents, they demand a radical rethinking of boundary and normality. The too-precise laws of nature as set forth by science are gleefully violated in the freakish compilation of the monster's body. A mixed category, the monster resists any classification built on hierarchy or a merely binary opposition, demanding instead a "system" allowing polyphony, mixed response (difference in sameness, repulsion in attraction), and resistance to integration—allowing what Hogle has called with a wonderful pun "a deeper play of differences, a nonbinary polymorphism at the 'base' of human nature."[9]

The horizon where the monsters dwell might well be imagined as the visible edge of the hermeneutic circle itself: the monstrous offers an escape from its hermetic path, an invitation to explore new spirals, new and interconnected methods of perceiving the world.[10] In the face of the monster, scientific inquiry and its ordered rationality crumble. The monstrous is a genus too large to be encapsulated in any conceptual system; the monster's very existence is a rebuke to boundary and enclosure; like the giants of *Mandeville's Travels,* it threatens to devour "all raw & quyk" any thinker who insists otherwise. The monster is in this way the living embodiment of the phenomenon Derrida has famously labeled the "supplement" *(cedangereux supplément)*:[11] it breaks apart bifurcating, "either/ or" syllogistic logic with a kind of reasoning closer to "and/or," introducing what Barbara Johnson has called "a revolution in the very logic of meaning."[12]

Full of rebuke to traditional methods of organizing knowledge and human experience, the geography of the monster is an imperiling expanse, and therefore always a contested cultural space.

Thesis IV: The Monster Dwells at the Gates of Difference

The monster is difference made flesh, come to dwell among us. In its function as dialectical Other or third-term supplement, the monster is an incorporation of the Outside, the Beyond—of all those loci that are rhetorically placed as distant and distinct but originate Within. Any kind of alterity can be inscribed across (constructed through) the monstrous body, but for the most part monstrous difference tends to be cultural, political, racial, economic, sexual.

The exaggeration of cultural difference into monstrous aberration is familiar enough. The most famous distortion occurs in the Bible, where the aboriginal inhabitants of Canaan are envisioned as menacing giants to justify the Hebrew colonization of the Promised Land (Numbers 13). Representing an anterior culture as monstrous justifies its displacement or extermination by rendering the act heroic. In medieval France the *chansons de geste* celebrated the Crusades by transforming Muslims into demonic caricatures whose menacing lack of humanity was readable from their bestial attributes; by culturally glossing "Saracens" as "monstra," propagandists rendered rhetorically admissible the annexation of the East by the West. This representational project was part of a whole dictionary of strategic glosses in which "monstra" slipped into significations of the feminine and the hypermasculine.

A recent newspaper article on Yugoslavia reminds us how persistent these divisive mythologies can be, and how they can endure divorced from any grounding in historical reality:

> A Bosnian Serb militiaman, hitchhiking to Sarajevo, tells a reporter in all earnestness that the Muslims are feeding Serbian children to the animals in the zoo. The story is nonsense. There aren't any animals left alive in the Sarajevo zoo. But the militiaman is convinced and can recall all the wrongs that Muslims may or may not have perpetrated during their 500 years of rule.[13]

In the United States, Native Americans were presented as unredeemable savages *so* that the powerful political machine of Manifest Destiny could push westward with disregard. Scattered throughout Europe by the Diaspora and steadfastly refusing assimilation into Christian society, Jews have been perennial favorites for xenophobic misrepresentation, for here was an alien culture living, working, and even at times prospering within vast communities dedicated to becoming homogeneous and monolithic. The Middle Ages accused the Jews of crimes ranging from the bringing of the plague to bleeding Christian children to make their Passover meal, Nazi Germany simply brought these ancient traditions of hate to their conclusion, inventing a Final Solution that differed from earlier persecutions only in its technological efficiency.

Political or ideological difference is as much a catalyst to monstrous representation on a micro level as cultural alterity in the macrocosm. A political figure suddenly out of favor is transformed like an unwilling participant in a science experiment by the appointed historians of the replacement regime: "monstrous history" is rife with sudden, Ovidian metamorphoses, from Vlad Tepes to Ronald Reagan. The most illustrious of these propaganda-bred demons is the English king Richard III, whom Thomas More famously described as "little of stature, ill fetured of limmes, croke backed, his left shoulder much higher then his right, hard fauoured of visage. . . . hee came into the worlde with feete forward, . . . also not vntothed."[14] From birth, More declares, Richard was a monster, "his deformed body a readable text"[15] on which was inscribed his deviant morality (indistinguishable from an incorrect political orientation).

The almost obsessive descanting on Richard from Polydor Vergil in the Renaissance to the Friends of Richard III Incorporated in our own era demonstrates the process of "monster theory" at its most active: culture gives birth to a monster before our eyes, painting over the normally proportioned Richard who once lived, raising his shoulder to deform simultaneously person, cultural response, and the possibility of objectivity.[16] History itself becomes a monster: defeaturing, self-deconstructive, always in danger of exposing the sutures that bind its disparate elements into a single, unnatural body. At the same time Richard moves between Monster and Man, the disturbing suggestion arises that this incoherent body, denaturalized and always in peril of disaggregation, may well be our own.

The difficult project of constructing and maintaining gender identities elicits an array of anxious responses throughout culture, producing another impetus to teratogenesis. The woman who oversteps the boundaries of her gender role risks becoming a Scylla, Weird Sister, Lilith ("die erste Eva," "la mère obscuré"),[17] Bertha Mason, or Gorgon.[18] "Deviant" sexual identity is similarly susceptible to monsterization. The great medieval encyclopedist Vincent of Beauvais describes the visit of a hermaphroditic cynocephalus to the French court in his *Speculum naturale* (31.126).[19] Its male reproductive organ is said to be disproportionately large, but the monster could use either sex at its own discretion. Bruno Roy writes of this fantastic hybrid: "What warning did he come to deliver to the king? He came to bear witness to sexual norms, . . . He embodied the punishment earned by those who violate sexual taboos."[20] This strange creature, a composite of the supposedly discrete categories "male" and "female," arrives before King Louis to validate heterosexuality over homosexuality, with its supposed inversions and transformations ("Equa fit equus," one Latin writer declared; "The horse becomes a mare").[21] The strange dog-headed monster is a living excoriation of gender ambiguity and sexual abnormality, as Vincent's cultural moment defines them: heteronormalization incarnate.

From the classical period into the twentieth century, race has been almost as powerful a catalyst to the creation of monsters as culture, gender, and sexuality. Africa early became the West's significant other, the sign of its ontological difference simply being skin color. According to the Greek myth of Phaeton, the denizens of mysterious and uncertain Ethiopia were black because they had been scorched by the too-close passing of the sun. The Roman naturalist Pliny assumed nonwhite skin to be symptomatic of a complete difference in temperament and attributed Africa's darkness to climate; the intense heat, he said, had burned the Africans' skin and malformed their bodies (*Natural History*, 2.80). These differences were quickly moralized through a pervasive rhetoric of deviance. Paulinus of Nola, a wealthy landowner turned early church homilist, explained that the Ethiopians had been scorched by sin and vice rather than by the sun, and the anonymous commentator to Theodulus's influential *Ecloga* (tenth century) succinctly glossed the meaning of the word *Ethyopium*: "Ethiopians, that is, sinners. Indeed, sinners can rightly be compared to Ethiopians, who are black men presenting a terrifying appearance to those beholding them."[22] Dark skin was associated with the fires of hell, and so signified in Christian mythology demonic provenance. The perverse and exaggerated sexual appetite of monsters generally was quickly affixed to the Ethiopian; this linking was only strengthened by a xenophobic backlash as dark-skinned people were forcibly imported into Europe early in the Renaissance. Narratives of miscegenation arose and circulated to sanction official policies of exclusion; Queen Elizabeth is famous for her anxiety over "blackamoores" and their supposed threat to the "increase of people of our own nation."[23]

Through all of these monsters the boundaries between personal and national bodies blur. To complicate this category confusion further, one kind of alterity is often written as another, so that national difference (for example) is transformed into sexual difference. Giraldus Cambrensis demonstrates just this slippage of the foreign in his *Topography of Ireland*; when he writes of the Irish (ostensibly simply to provide information about them to a curious English court, but actually as a first step toward invading and colonizing the island), he observes:

> It is indeed a most filthy race, a race sunk in vice, a race more ignorant than
> all other nations of the first principles of faith. . . . These people who have
> customs so different from others, and so opposite to them, on making signs

either with the hands or the head, beckon when they mean that you should go away, and nod backwards as often as they wish to be rid of you. Likewise, in this nation, the men pass their water sitting, the women standing. . . . The women, also, as well as the men, ride astride, with their legs stuck out on each side of the horse.[24]

One kind of inversion becomes another as Giraldus deciphers the alphabet of Irish culture—and reads it backward, against the norm of English masculinity. Giraldus creates a vision of monstrous gender (aberrant, demonstrative): the violation of the cultural codes that valence gendered behaviors creates a rupture that must be cemented with (in this case) the binding, corrective mortar of English normalcy. A bloody war of subjugation followed immediately after the promulgation of this text, remained potent throughout the High Middle Ages, and in a way continues to this day.

Through a similar discursive process the East becomes feminized (Said) and the soul of Africa grows dark (Gates).[25] One kind of difference becomes another as the normative categories of gender, sexuality, national identity, and ethnicity slide together like the imbricated circles of a Venn diagram, abjecting from the center that which becomes the monster. This violent foreclosure erects a self-validating, Hegelian master/slave dialectic that naturalizes the subjugation of one cultural body by another by writing the body excluded from personhood and agency as in every way different, monstrous. A polysemy is granted so that a greater threat can be encoded; multiplicity of meanings, paradoxically, iterates the same restricting, agitprop representations that narrowed signification performs. Yet a danger resides in this multiplication: as difference, like a Hydra, sprouts two heads where one has been lopped away, the possibilities of escape, resistance, disruption arise with more force.

René Girard has written at great length about the real violence these debasing representations enact, connecting monsterizing depiction with the phenomenon of the scapegoat. Monsters are never created *ex nihilo,* put through a process of fragmentation and recombination in which dements are extracted "from various forms" (including—indeed, especially—marginalized social groups) and then assembled as the monster, "which can then claim an independent identity."[26] The political-cultural monster, the embodiment of radical difference, paradoxically threatens to *erase* difference in the world of its creators, to demonstrate

> the potential for the system to differ from its own difference, in other words not to be different at all, to cease to exist as a system. . . . Difference that exists outside the system is terrifying because it reveals the truth of the system, its relativity, its fragility, and its mortality. . . . Despite what is said around us persecutors are never obsessed with difference but rather by its unutterable contrary, the lack of difference.[27]

By revealing that difference is arbitrary and potentially free-floating, mutable rather than essential, the monster threatens to destroy not just individual members of a society, but the very cultural apparatus through which individuality is constituted and allowed. Because it is a body across which difference has been repeatedly written, the monster (like Frankenstein's creature, that combination of odd somatic pieces stitched together from a community of cadavers) seeks out its author to demand its raison d'être—and to bear witness to the fact that it could have been constructed Otherwise. Godzilla trampled Tokyo; Girard frees him here to fragment the delicate matrix of relational systems that unite every private body to the public world.

Thesis V: The Monster Polices the Borders of the Possible

The monster resists capture in the epistemological nets of the erudite, but it is something more than a Bakhtinian ally of the popular. From its position at the limits of knowing, the monster stands as a warning against exploration of its uncertain demesnes. The giants of Patagonia, the dragons of the Orient, and the dinosaurs of Jurassic Park together declare that curiosity is more often punished than rewarded, that one is better off safely contained within one's own domestic sphere than abroad, away from the watchful eyes of the state. The monster prevents mobility (intellectual, geographic, or sexual), delimiting the social spaces through which private bodies may move. To step outside this official geography is to risk attack by some monstrous border patrol or (worse) to become monstrous oneself.

Lycaon, the first werewolf in Western literature, undergoes his lupine metamorphosis as the culmination of a fable of hospitality.[28] Ovid relates how the primeval giants attempted to plunge the world into anarchy by wrenching Olympus from the gods, only to be shattered by divine thunderbolts. From their scattered blood arose a race of men who continued their fathers' malignant ways.[29] Among this wicked progeny was Lycaon, king of Arcadia. When Jupiter arrived as a guest at his house, Lycaon tried to kill the ruler of the gods as he slept, and the next day served him pieces of a servant's body as a meal. The enraged Jupiter punished this violation of the host–guest relationship by transforming Lycaon into a monstrous semblance of that lawless, godless state to which his actions would drag humanity back:

> The king himself flies in terror and, gaining the fields, howls aloud, attempting in vain to speak. His mouth of itself gathers foam, and with his accustomed greed for blood he turns against the sheep, delighting still in slaughter. His garments change to shaggy hair, his arms to legs. He turns into a wolf, and yet retains some traces of his former shape.[30]

The horribly fascinating loss of Lycaon's humanity merely reifies his previous moral state; the king's body is rendered all transparence, instantly and insistently readable. The power of the narrative prohibition peaks in the lingering description of the monstrously composite Lycaon, at that median where he is both man and beast, dual natures in a helpless tumult of assertion. The fable concludes when Lycaon can no longer speak, only signify.

Whereas monsters born of political expedience and self-justifying nationalism function as living invitations to action, usually military (invasions, usurpations, colonizations), the monster of prohibition polices the borders of the possible, interdicting through its grotesque body some behaviors and actions, envaluing others. It is possible, for example, that medieval merchants intentionally disseminated maps depicting sea serpents like Leviathan at the edges of their trade routes in order to discourage further exploration and to establish monopolies.[31] Every monster is in this way a double narrative, two living stories: one that describes how the monster came to be and another, its testimony, detailing what cultural use the monster serves. The monster of prohibition exists to demarcate the bonds that hold together that system of relations we call culture, to call horrid attention to the borders that cannot—must not—be crossed.

Primarily these borders are in place to control the traffic in women, or more generally to establish strictly homosocial bonds, the ties between men that keep a patriarchal society functional. A kind of herdsman, this monster delimits the social space through which cultural bodies may move, and in classical times (for example) validated a tight, hierarchical system of naturalized leadership and control where every man had a functional place.[32] The prototype in Western culture for this kind of "geographic" monster is Homer's Polyphemos. The quintessential xenophobic rendition of the foreign (the barbaric—that which is unintelligible within a given cultural-linguistic system),[33] the Cyclopes are represented as savages who have not "a law to bless them" and who lack the *techne* to produce (Greek-style) civilization. Their archaism is conveyed through their lack of hierarchy and of a politics of precedent. This dissociation from community leads to a rugged individualism that in Homeric terms can only be horrifying. Because they live without a system of tradition and custom, the Cyclopes are a danger to the arriving Greeks, men whose identities are contingent upon a compartmentalized function within a deindividualizing system of subordination and control. Polyphemos's victims are devoured, engulfed, made to vanish from the public gaze: cannibalism as incorporation into the wrong cultural body.

The monster is a powerful ally of what Foucault calls "the society of the panopticon," in which "polymorphous conducts [are] actually extracted from people's bodies and from their pleasures . . . [to be] drawn out, revealed, isolated, intensified, incorporated, by multifarious power devices."[34] Susan Stewart has observed that "the monster's sexuality takes on a separate life";[35] Foucault helps us to see why. The monster embodies those sexual practices that must not be committed, or that may be committed only through the body of the monster. *She* and *Them!*: the monster enforces the cultural codes that regulate sexual desire.

Anyone familiar with the low-budget science fiction movie craze of the 1950s will recognize in the preceding sentence two superb films of the genre, one about a radioactive virago from outer space who kills every man she touches, the other a social parable in which giant ants (really, Communists) burrow beneath Los Angeles (that is, Hollywood) and threaten world peace (that is, American con-servatism). I connect these two seemingly unrelated titles here to call attention to the anxieties that monsterized their subjects in the first place, and to enact syntactically an even deeper fear: that the two will join in some unholy miscege-nation. We have seen that the monster arises at the gap where difference is per-ceived as dividing a recording voice from its captured subject; the criterion of this division is arbitrary, and can range from anatomy or skin color to religious belief, custom, and political ideology. The monster's destructiveness is really a deconstructiveness: it threatens to reveal that difference originates in process, rather than in fact (and that "fact" is subject to constant reconstruction and change). Given that the recorders of the history of the West have been mainly European and male, women (*She*) and nonwhites (*Them!*) have found themselves repeatedly transformed into monsters, whether to validate specific alignments of masculinity and whiteness, or simply to be pushed from its realm of thought.[36] Feminine and cultural others are monstrous enough by themselves in patriarchal society, but when they threaten to mingle, the entire economy of desire comes under attack.

As a vehicle of prohibition, the monster most often arises to enforce the laws of exogamy, both the incest taboo (which establishes a traffic in women by mandating that they marry outside their families) and the decrees against inter-racial sexual mingling (which limit the parameters of that traffic by policing the boundaries of culture, usually in the service of some notion of group "purity").[37] Incest narratives are common to every tradition and have been extensively docu-mented, mainly owing to Lévi-Strauss's elevation of the taboo to the founding base of patriarchal society. Miscegenation, that intersection of misogyny (gender anxiety) and racism (no matter how naive), has received considerably less criti-cal attention. I will say a few words about it here.

The Bible has long been the primary source for divine decrees against inter-racial mixing. One of these pronouncements is a straightforward command from God that comes through the mouth of the prophet Joshua (Joshua 23:12ff.); another is a cryptic episode in Genesis much elaborated during the medieval period, alluding to "sons of God" who impregnate the "daughters of men" with a race of wicked giants (Genesis 6:4). The monsters are here, as elsewhere, expedient rep-resentations of other cultures, generalized and demonized to enforce a strict notion of group sameness. The fears of contamination, impurity, and loss of identity that produce stories like the Genesis episode are strong, and they reappear incessantly. Shakespeare's Caliban, for example, is the product of such an illicit mingling, the "freckled whelp" of the Algerian witch Sycorax and the devil. Charlotte Brontë reversed the usual paradigm in *Jane Eyre* (white Rochester and lunatic Jamaican Bertha Mason), but horror movies as seemingly innocent as *King Kong* demonstrate miscegenation anxiety in its brutal essence. Even a film as recent as 1979's immensely successful *Alien* may have a cognizance of the fear in its under-workings; the grotesque creature that stalks the heroine (dressed in the final scene only in her underwear) drips a glistening slime of K-Y Jelly from its teeth; the jaw tendons are constructed of shredded condoms; and the man inside the rubber suit is Bolaji Badejo, a Masai tribesman standing seven feet tall who happened to be studying in England at the time the film was cast.[38]

The narratives of the West perform the strangest dance around that fire in which miscegenation and its practitioners have been condemned to burn. Among the flames we see the old women of Salem hanging, accused of sexual relations with the black devil; we suspect they died because they crossed a different border, one that prohibits women from managing property and living solitary, unmanaged lives. The flames devour the Jews of thirteenth-century England, who stole children from proper families and baked seder matzo with their blood; as a menace to the survival of English race and culture, they were expelled from the country and their property confiscated. A competing narrative again implicates monstrous economics—the Jews were the money lenders, the state and its commerce were heavily indebted to them—but this second story is submerged in a horrifying fable of cultural purity and threat to Christian continuance. As the American frontier expanded beneath the banner of Manifest Destiny in the nineteenth century, tales circulated about how "Indians" routinely kidnapped white women to furnish wives for themselves; the West was a place of danger waiting to be tamed into farms, its menacing native inhabitants fit only to be dispossessed. It matters little that the protagonist of Richard Wright's *Native Son* did not rape and butcher his employer's daughter; that narrative is supplied by the police, by an angry white society, indeed by Western history itself. In the novel, as in life, the threat occurs when a nonwhite leaves the reserve abandoned to him; Wright envisions what happens when the horizon of narrative expectation is firmly set, and his conclusion (born out in seventeenth-century Salem, medieval England, and nineteenth-century America) is that the actual circumstances of history tend to vanish when a narrative of miscegenation can be supplied.

The monster is transgressive, too sexual, perversely erotic, a lawbreaker; and so the monster and all that it embodies must be exiled or destroyed. The repressed, however, like Freud himself, always seems to return.

Thesis VI: Fear of the Monster Is Really a Kind of Desire

The monster is continually linked to forbidden practices, in order to normalize and to enforce. The monster also attracts. The same creatures who terrify and interdict can evoke potent escapist fantasies; the linking of monstrosity with the forbidden makes the monster all the more appealing as a temporary egress from constraint. This simultaneous repulsion and attraction at the core of the monster's composition accounts greatly for its continued cultural popularity, for the fact that the monster seldom can be contained in a simple, binary dialectic (thesis, antithesis . . . no synthesis). We distrust and loathe the monster at the same time we envy its freedom, and perhaps its sublime despair.

Through the body of the monster fantasies of aggression, domination, and inversion are allowed safe expression in a clearly delimited and permanently liminal space. Escapist delight gives way to horror only when the monster threatens to overstep these boundaries, to destroy or deconstruct the thin walls of category and culture. When contained by geographic, generic, or epistemic marginalization, the monster can function as an alter ego, as an alluring projection of (an Other) self. The monster awakens one to the pleasures of the body, to the simple and fleeting joys of being frightened, or frightening—to the experience of mortality and corporality. We watch the monstrous spectacle of the horror film because we know that the cinema is a temporary place, that the jolting sensuousness of the celluloid images will be followed by reentry into the world of comfort and light.[39] Likewise, the story on the page before us may horrify (whether it appears in the *New York Times* news section or Stephen King's latest novel matters little), so long as we are safe in the knowledge of its nearing end (the number of pages in our right hand is dwindling) and our liberation from it. Aurally received narratives work no differently; no matter how unsettling the description of the giant, no matter how many unbaptized children and hapless knights he devours, King Arthur will ultimately destroy him. The audience knows how the genre works.

Times of carnival temporally marginalize the monstrous, but at the same time allow it a safe realm of expression and play: on Halloween everyone is a demon for a night. The same impulse to ataractic fantasy is behind much lavishly bizarre manuscript marginalia, from abstract scribblings at the edges of an ordered page to preposterous animals and vaguely humanoid creatures of strange anatomy that crowd a biblical text. Gargoyles and ornately sculpted grotesques, lurking at the crossbeams or upon the roof of the cathedral, likewise record the liberating fantasies of a bored or repressed hand suddenly freed to populate the margins. Maps and travel accounts inherited from antiquity invented whole geographies of the mind and peopled them with exotic and fantastic creatures; Ultima Thule, Ethiopia, and the Antipodes were the medieval equivalents of outer space and virtual reality, imaginary (wholly verbal) geographies accessible from anywhere, never meant to be discovered but always waiting to be explored. Jacques Le Goff has written that the Indian Ocean (a "mental horizon" imagined, in the Middle Ages, to be completely enclosed by land) was a cultural space

> where taboos were eliminated or exchanged for others. The weirdness of this world produced an impression of liberation and freedom. The strict morality imposed by the Church was contrasted with the discomfiting attractiveness of a world of bizarre tastes, which practiced coprophagy and cannibalism; of bodily innocence, where man, freed of the modesty of clothing, rediscovered nudism and sexual freedom; and where, once rid of restrictive monogamy and family barriers, he could give himself over to polygamy, incest, and eroticism.[40]

The habitations of the monsters (Africa, Scandinavia, America, Venus, the Delta Quadrant—whatever land is sufficiently distant to be exoticized) are more than dark regions of uncertain danger: they are also realms of happy fantasy, horizons of liberation. Their monsters serve as secondary bodies through which the possibilities of other genders, other sexual practices, and other social customs can be explored. Hermaphrodites, Amazons, and lascivious cannibals beckon from the edges of the world, the most distant planets of the galaxy.

The co-optation of the monster into a symbol of the desirable is often accomplished through the neutralization of potentially threatening aspects with a liberal dose of comedy: the thundering giant becomes the bumbling giant.[41] Monsters may still function, however, as the vehicles of causative fantasies even without their valences reversed. What Bakhtin calls "official culture" can transfer all that is viewed as undesirable in itself into the body of the monster, performing a wish-fulfillment drama of its own; the scapegoated monster is perhaps ritually destroyed in the course of some official narrative, purging the community by eliminating its sins. The monster's eradication functions as an exorcism and, when retold and promulgated, as a catechism. The monastically manufactured *Queste del Suint Graal* serves as an ecclesiastically sanctioned antidote to the looser morality of the secular romances; when Sir Bors comes across a castle where "ladies of high descent and rank" tempt him to sexual indulgence, these ladies are, of course, demons in lascivious disguise. When Bors refuses to sleep with one of these transcorporal devils (described as "*so* lovely and so fair that it seemed all earthly beauty was embodied in her"), his steadfast assertion of control banishes them all shrieking back to hell.[42] The episode valorizes the celibacy so central to the authors' belief system (and so difficult to enforce) while inculcating a lesson in morality for the work's intended secular audience, the knights and courtly women fond of romances.

Seldom, however, are monsters as uncomplicated in their use and manufacture as the demons that haunt Sir Bors. Allegory may flatten a monster rather thin, as when the vivacious demon of the Anglo-Saxon hagiographic poem *Juliana* becomes the one-sided complainer of Cynewulf's *Elene*. More often, however, the monster retains a haunting complexity. The dense symbolism that makes a thick description of the monsters in Spenser, Milton, and even *Beowulf* so challenging reminds us how permeable the monstrous body can be, how difficult to dissect.

This corporal fluidity, this simultaneity of anxiety and desire, ensures that the monster will always dangerously entice. A certain intrigue is allowed even Vincent of Beauvais's well-endowed cynocephalus, for he occupies a textual space of allure before his necessary dismissal, during which he is granted an undeniable charm. The monstrous lurks somewhere in that ambiguous, primal space between fear and attraction, close to the heart of what Kristeva calls "abjection":

> There looms, within abjection, one of those violent, dark revolts of being, directed against a threat that seems to emanate from an exorbitant outside or inside, ejected beyond the scope of the possible, the tolerable, the thinkable. It lies there, quite close, but it cannot be assimilated. It beseeches, worries, fascinates desire, which, nonetheless, does not let itself be seduced. Apprehensive, desire turns aside; sickened, it rejects. . . . But simultaneously, just the same, that impetus, that spasm, that leap is drawn toward an elsewhere as tempting as it is condemned. Unflaggingly, like an inescapable boomerang, a vortex of summons and repulsion places the one haunted by it literally beside himself.[43]

And the self that one stands so suddenly and so nervously beside is the monster.

The monster is the abjected fragment that enables the formation of all kinds of identities—personal, national, cultural, economic, sexual, psychological, universal, particular (even if that "particular" identity is an embrace of the power/status/knowledge of abjection itself); as such it reveals their partiality, their contiguity. A product of a multitude of morphogeneses (ranging from somatic to ethnic) that align themselves to imbue meaning to the Us and Them behind every cultural mode of seeing, the monster of abjection resides in that marginal geography of the Exterior, beyond the limits of the Thinkable, a place that is doubly dangerous: simultaneously "exorbitant" and "quite close." Judith Butler calls this conceptual locus "a domain of unlivability and unintelligibility that bounds the domain of intelligible effects," but points out that even when discursively closed off, it offers a base for critique, a margin from which to reread dominant paradigms.[44] Like Grendel thundering from the mere or Dracula creeping from the grave, like Kristeva's "boomerang, a vortex of summons" or the uncanny Freudian–Lacanian return of the repressed, the monster is always coming back, always at the verge of irruption.

Perhaps it is time to ask the question that always arises when the monster is discussed seriously (the inevitability of the question a symptom of the deep anxiety about what is and what should be thinkable, an anxiety that the process of monster theory is destined to raise): Do monsters really exist?

Surely they must, for if they did not, how could we?

Thesis VII: The Monster Stands at the Threshold . . . of Becoming

"This thing of darkness I acknowledge mine."

Monsters are our children. They can be pushed to the farthest margins of geography and discourse, hidden away at the edges of the world and in the forbidden recesses of our mind, but they always return. And when they come back, they bring not just a fuller knowledge of our place in history and the history of knowing our place, but they bear self-knowledge, *human* knowledge—and a discourse all the more sacred as it arises from the Outside. These monsters ask us how we perceive the world, and how we have misrepresented what we have attempted to place. They ask us to reevaluate our cultural assumptions about race, gender, sexuality, our perception of difference, our tolerance toward its expression. They ask us why we have created them.

Notes

1. Literally, here, *Zeitgeist*: Time Ghost, the bodiless spirit that uncannily incorporates a "place" that is a series of places, the crossroads that is a point in a *movement* toward an uncertain elsewhere. Bury the Zeitgeist by the crossroads: it is confused as it awakens, it is not going anywhere, it intersects everyplace; all roads lead back to the monster.

2. I realize that this is an interpretive biographical maneuver Barthes would surely have called "the living death of the author."

3. Thus the superiority of Joan Copjec's "Vampires, Breast-Feeding, and Anxiety," *October* 58 (Fall 1991): 25–43, to Paul Barber's *Vampires, Burial, and Death: Folklore and Reality* (New Haven, Conn.: Yale University Press, 1988).

4. "The giant is represented through movement, through being in time. Even in the ascription of the still landscape to the giant, it is the activities of the giant, his or her legendary actions, that have resulted in the observable trace. In contrast to the still and perfect universe of the miniature, the gigantic represents the order and disorder of historical forces." Susan Stewart, *On Longing: Narratives of the Miniature, the Gigantic, the Souvenir, the Collection* (Baltimore: Johns Hopkins University Press, 1984), 86.

5. Harvey R. Greenberg, "Reimaging the Gargoyle: Psychoanalytic Notes on *Alien*," in *Close Encounters: Film, Feminism, and Science Fiction,* ed. Constance Penley, Elisabeth Lyon, Lynn Spigel, and Janet Bergstrom (Minneapolis: University of Minnesota Press, 1991), 90–91.

6. Marjorie Garber, *Vested Interests: Cross-Dressing and Cultural Anxiety* (New York Routledge, 1992), 11. Garber writes at some length about "category crisis," which she defines as "a failure of definitional distinction, a borderline that becomes permeable, that permits

of border crossings from one (apparently distinct) category to another: black/white, Jew/Christian, noble/bourgeois, master/servant, master/slave. . . . [That which crosses the border, like the transvestite] will always function as a mechanism of overdetermination—a mechanism of displacement from one blurred boundary to another. An analogy here might be the so-called 'tagged' gene that shows up in a genetic chain, indicating the presence of some otherwise hidden condition. It is not the gene itself, but its presence, that marks the trouble spot, indicating the likelihood of a crisis somewhere, elsewhere" (16–17). Note, however, that whereas Garber insists that the transvestite must be read *with* rather than *through,* the monster can be read only *through—for* the monster, pure culture, is nothing of itself.

7. These are the ancient monsters recorded first by the Greek writers Ctesias and Megasthenes, and include such wild imaginings as the Pygmies, the Sciapods (men with one large foot with which they can hop about at tremendous speed or that they can lift over their reclining bodies as a sort of beach umbrella), Blemmyae ("men whose heads/Do grow beneath their shoulders," in Othello's words), and Cynocephali, ferocious dog-headed men who are anthropophagous to boot. John Block Friedman has called these creatures the Plinian races, after the classical encyclopedist who bestowed them to the Middle Ages and early modern period. Friedman, *The Monstrous Races in Medieval Art and Thought* (Cambridge, Mass.: Harvard University Press, 1981).

8. The discussion of the implication of the monstrous in the manufacture of heuristics is partially based upon my essay "The Limits of Knowing: Monsters and the Regulation of Medieval Popular Culture," *Medieval Folklore* 3 (Fall 1994): 1–37.

9. Jerrold E. Hogle, "The Struggle for a Dichotomy: Abjection in Jekyll and His Interpreters," in *Dr. Jekyll and Mr. Hyde after One Hundred Years,* ed. William Veeder and Gordon Hirsch (Chicago: University of Chicago Press, 1988), 161.

10. "The hermeneutic circle does not permit access or escape to an uninterrupted reality; but we do not [have to] keep going around in the same path." Barbara Herrnstein Smith, "Belief and Resistance: A Symmetrical Account," *Critical Inquiry* 18 (Autumn 1991): 137–38.

11. Jacques Derrida, *Of Grammatology,* trans. Gayatri Chakravorty Spivak (Baltimore: Johns Hopkins University Press, 1974).

12. Barbara Johnson, introduction to Jacques Derrida, *Dissemination,* trans. Barbara Johnson (Chicago: University of Chicago Press, 1981), xiii.

13. H. D. S. Greenway, "Adversaries Create Devils of Each Other," *Boston Globe,* December 15, 1992, 1.

14. Thomas More, *The Yale Edition of the Complete Works of Thomas More,* vol. 2, *The History of King Richard III,* ed. Richard S. Sylvester (New Haven, Conn.: Yale University Press, 1963), 7.

15. Marjorie Garber, *Shakespeare's Ghost Writers: Literature as Uncanny Causality* (New York: Routledge, Chapman and Hall, 1988), 30. My discussion of Richard is indebted to Marjorie Garber's provocative work.

16. "A portrait now in the Society of Antiquaries of London, painted about 1505, shows a Richard with straight shoulders. But a second portrait, possibly of earlier date, in the Royal Collection, seems to emblematize the whole controversy [over Richard's supposed

monstrosity], for in it, X-ray examination reveals an original straight shoulder line, which was subsequently painted over to present the raised right shoulder silhouette *so* often copied by later portraitists." Garber, 35.

17. I am hinting here at the possibility of a feminist recuperation of the gendered monster by citing the titles of two famous books about Lilith (a favorite figure in feminist writing): Jacques Bril's *Lilith, ou, La Mere obscure* (Paris: Payot, 1981), and Siegmund Hurwitz's *Lilith, die erste Eva: Eine Studie uber dunkle Aspekte des Weiblichen* (Zurich: Daimon, 1980).

18. "The monster-woman, threatening to replace her angelic sister, embodies intransigent female autonomy and thus represents both the author's power to allay 'his' anxieties by calling their source bad names (witch, bitch, fiend, monster) and simultaneously, the mysterious power of the character who refuses to stay in her textually ordained 'place' and thus generates a story that 'gets away' from its author." Sandra M. Gilbert and Susan Gubar, *The Madwoman in the Attic: The Woman Writer and the Nineteenth Century Literary Imagination* (New Haven, Conn.: Yale University Press, 1984), 28. The "dangerous" role of feminine will in the engendering of monsters is also explored by Marie-Hélène Huet in *Monstrous Imagination* (Cambridge, Mass.: Harvard University Press, 1993).

19. A cynocephalus is a dog-headed man, like the recently decanonized Saint Christopher. Bad enough to be a cynocephalus without being hermaphroditic to boot: the monster accrues one kind of difference on top of another, like a magnet that draws differences into an aggregate, multivalent identity around an unstable core.

20. Bruno Roy, "En marge du monde connu: Les races de monstres," in *Aspects de la marginalité au Moyen Age,* ed. Guy-H Allard (Quebec: Les Editions de l'Aurore, 1975), 77. This translation is mine.

21. See, e.g., Monica E. McAlpine, "The Pardoner's Homosexuality and How It Matters," *PMLA* 95 (1980): 8–22.

22. Cited by Friedman, *Monstrous Races,* 64.

23. Elizabeth deported "blackamoores" in 1596 and again in 1601. See Karen Newman, "'And Wash the Ethiop White': Femininity and the Monstrous in Othello," in *Shakespeare Reproduced: The Text in History and Ideology,* ed. Jean E. Howard and Marion F. O'Connor (New York: Methuen, 1987), 148.

24. See Giraldus Cambrensis, *Topographia Hibernae* [The history and topography of Ireland], trans. John J. O'Meara (Atlantic Highlands, N.J.: Humanities Press, 1982), 24.

25. See Edward Said, *Orientalism* (New York: Pantheon, 1978); Henry Louis Gates Jr., *The Signifying Monkey: A Theory of Afro-American Literature* (New York: Oxford University Press, 1988).

26. René Girard, *The Scapegoat,* trans. Yvonne Freccero (Baltimore: Johns Hopkins University Press, 1986), 33.

27. Girard, 21–22.

28. Extended travel was dependent in both the ancient and medieval world on the promulgation of an ideal of hospitality that sanctified the responsibility of host to guest. A violation of that code is responsible for the destruction of the biblical Sodom and Gomorrah, for the devolution from man to giant in *Sir Gawain and the Carl of Carlisle,* and for the first punitive transformation in Ovid's *Metamorphoses.* This popular type of

narrative may be conveniently labeled the fable of hospitality; such stories envalue the practice whose breach they illustrate through a drama repudiating the dangerous behavior. The valorization is accomplished in one of two ways: the host is a monster already and learns a lesson at the hands of his guest, or the host becomes a monster in the course of the narrative and audience members realize how they should conduct themselves. In either case, the cloak of monstrousness calls attention to those behaviors and attitudes the text is concerned with interdicting.

29. Ovid, *Metamorphoses* (Loeb Classical Library no. 42), ed. G. P. Goold (1916; repr., Cambridge, Mass.: Harvard University Press, 1984), I.156–62.

30. Ovid, I.231–39.

31. I am indebted to Keeryung Hong of Harvard University for sharing her research on medieval map production for this hypothesis.

32. A useful (albeit politically charged) term for such a collective is *Männerbunde*, "all-male groups with aggression as one major function." See Joseph Harris, "Love and Death in the *Männerbund*: An Essay with Special Reference to the *Bjarkamál* and *The Battle of Maldon*," in *Heroic Poetry in the Anglo-Saxon Period*, ed. Helen Damico and John Leyerle (Kalamazoo: Medieval Institute/Western Michigan State University, 1993), 78. See also the *Interscripta* discussion of "Medieval Masculinities," moderated and edited by Jeffrey Jerome Cohen, http://www.george-town.edu/labyrinth/e-center/interscripta/mm.html (the piece is also forthcoming in a nonhypertext version in *Arthuriana*, as "The Armour of an Alienating Identity").

33. The Greek word *barbaros*, from which we derive the modern English word *barbaric*, means "making the sound *bar bar*"—that is, not speaking Greek, and therefore speaking nonsense.

34. Michel Foucault, *The History of Sexuality*, vol. 1, *An Introduction*, trans. Robert Hurley (New York: Vintage, 1990), 47–48.

35. Stewart, *On Longing*. See especially "The Imaginary Body," 104–31.

36. The situation was obviously far more complex than these statements can begin to show; "European," for example, usually includes only males of the Western Latin tradition. Sexual orientation further complicates the picture, as we shall see.

Donna Haraway, following Trinh Minh-ha, calls the humans beneath the monstrous skin "inappropriate/d others": "To be 'inappropriate/d' does not mean 'not to be in relation with'—i.e., to be in a special reservation, with the status of the authentic, the untouched, in the allochronic and allotropic condition of innocence. Rather to be an 'inappropriate/d other' means to be in critical deconstructive relationality, in a diffracting rather than reflecting (ratio)nality—as the means of making potent connection that exceeds domination." "The Promises of Monsters," in *Simians, Cyborgs, and Women: The Reinvention of Nature* (New York: Routledge, 1991), 299.

37. This discussion owes an obvious debt to Mary Douglas, *Purity and Danger: An Analysis of the Concepts of Pollution and Taboo* (New York: Routledge and Kegan Paul, 1966).

38. John Eastman, *Retakes: Behind the Scenes of 500 Classic Movies* (New York: Ballantine Books, 1989), 9–10.

39. Paul Coates interestingly observes that "the horror film becomes the essential form of cinema, monstrous content manifesting itself in the monstrous form of the gigantic

screen." Coates, *The Gorgon's Gaze* (Cambridge: Cambridge University Press, 1991), 77. Carol Clover locates some of the pleasure of the monster film in its cross-gender game of identification; see Clover, *Men, Women, and Chain Saws: Gender in the Modern Horror Film* (Princeton, N.J.: Princeton University Press, 1992). Why not *go* further, and call the pleasure cross-somatic?

40. Jacques Le Goff, "The Medieval West and the Indian Ocean," in *Time, Work and Culture in the Middle Ages,* trans. Arthur Goldhammer (Chicago: University of Chicago Press, 1980), 197. The postmodern equivalent of such spaces is Gibsonian cyberspace, with its MOOs and MUSHes and other arenas of unlimited possibility.

41. For Mikhail Bakhtin, famously, this is the transformative power of laughter: "Laughter liberates not only from external censorship but first of all from the great internal censor; it liberates from the fear that developed in man during thousands of years: fear of the sacred, fear of the prohibitions, of the past, of power." Bakhtin, *Rabelais and His World,* trans. Hélène Iswolsky (Indianapolis: Indiana University Press, 1984), 94. Bakhtin traces the moment of escape to the point at which laughter became a part of the "higher levels of literature," when Rabelais wrote *Gargantua et Pantagruel.*

42. *The Quest for the Holy Grail,* trans. Pauline Matarasso (London: Penguin Books, 1969), 194.

43. Julia Kristeva, *The Powers of Horror: An Essay on Abjection,* trans. Leon S. Roudiez (New York: Columbia University Press, 1982), 1.

44. Judith Butler, *Bodies That Matter: On the Discursive Limits of "Sex"* (New York: Routledge, 1993), 22. Both Butler and I have in mind here Foucault's notion of an emancipation of thought "from what it silently thinks" that will allow "it to think differently." Michel Foucault, *The Use of Pleasure,* trans. Robert Hurley (New York: Vintage, 1985), 9. Michael Uebel amplifies and applies this practice to the monster in his essay in this volume.

I
The Monster Theory Toolbox

THE UNCANNY

Sigmund Freud

I

It is only rarely that a psychoanalyst feels impelled to investigate the subject of aesthetics, even when aesthetics is understood to mean not merely the theory of beauty but the theory of the qualities of feeling. He works in other strata of mental life and has little to do with the subdued emotional impulses which, inhibited in their aims and dependent on a host of concurrent factors, usually furnish the material for the study of aesthetics. But it does occasionally happen that he has to interest himself in some particular province of that subject; and this province usually proves to be a rather remote one, and one which has been neglected in the specialist literature of aesthetics.

The subject of the "uncanny"[1] is a province of this kind. It is undoubtedly related to what is frightening—to what arouses dread and horror; equally certainly, too, the word is not always used in a clearly definable sense, so that it tends to coincide with what excites fear in general. Yet we may expect that a special core of feeling is present which justifies the use of a special conceptual term. One is curious to know what this common core is which allows us to distinguish as "uncanny" certain things within the field of what is frightening.

As good as nothing is to be found upon this subject in comprehensive treatises on aesthetics, which in general prefer to concern themselves with what is beautiful, attractive and sublime—that is, with feelings of a positive nature—and with the circumstances and the objects that call them forth, rather than with the opposite feelings of repulsion and distress. I know of only one attempt in medico-psychological literature, a fertile but not exhaustive paper by Jentsch (1906). But I must confess that I have not made a very thorough examination of the litera-ture, especially the foreign literature, relating to this present modest contribution of mine, for reasons which, as may easily be guessed, lie in the times in which we live;[2] so that my essay is presented to the reader without any claim to priority.

In his study of the "uncanny" Jentsch quite rightly lays stress on the obstacle presented by the fact that people vary so very greatly in their sensitivity to this quality of feeling. The writer of the present contribution, indeed, must himself plead guilty to a special obtuseness in the matter, where extreme delicacy of perception would be more in place. It is long since he has experienced or heard of anything which has given him an uncanny impression, and he must start by translating himself into that state of feeling, by awakening in himself the possibil-ity of experiencing it. Still, such difficulties make themselves powerfully felt in many other branches of aesthetics; we need not on that account despair of find-ing instances in which the quality in question will be unhesitatingly recognized by most people.

Two courses are open to us at the outset. Either we can find out what mean-ing has come to be attached to the word "uncanny" in the course of its history; or we can collect all those properties of persons, things, sense-impressions, experi-ences and situations which arouse in us the feeling of uncanniness, then infer the unknown nature of the uncanny from what all these examples have in common. I will say at once that both courses lead to the same result: the uncanny is that class of the frightening which leads back to what is known of old and long familiar. How this is possible, in what circumstances the familiar can become uncanny and frightening, I shall show in what follows. Let me also add that my investigation was actually begun by collecting a number of individual cases, and was only later confirmed by an examination of linguistic usage. In this discussion, however, I shall follow the reverse course.

The German word "unheimlich" is obviously the opposite of "heimlich" ["homely"], "heimisch" ["native"]—the opposite of what is familiar; and we are tempted to conclude that what is "uncanny" is frightening precisely because it is *not* known and familiar. Naturally not everything that is new and unfamiliar is frightening, however; the relation is not capable of inversion. We can only say that what is novel can easily become frightening and uncanny; some new things are frightening but not by any means all. Something has to be added to what is novel and unfamiliar in order to make it uncanny.

On the whole, Jentsch did not get beyond this relation of the uncanny to the novel and unfamiliar. He ascribes the essential factor in the production of the feeling of uncanniness to intellectual uncertainty; so that the uncanny would always, as it were, be something one does not know one's way about in. The better orientated in his environment a person is, the less readily will he get the impression of something uncanny in regard to the objects and events in it.

It is not difficult to see that this definition is incomplete, and we will therefore try to proceed beyond the equation "uncanny" = "unfamiliar." We will first turn to other languages. But the dictionaries that we consult tell us nothing new, perhaps only because we ourselves speak a language that is foreign. Indeed, we get an impression that many languages are without a word for this particular shade of what is frightening.

I should like to express my indebtedness to Dr. Theodor Reik for the following excerpts:—

LATIN: (K. E. Georges, *Deutschlateinisches Wörterbuch,* 1898). An uncanny place: *locus suspectus;* at an uncanny time of night: *intempesta nocte.*

GREEK: (Rost's and Schenkl's Lexikons). ξένος (i.e. strange, foreign).

ENGLISH: (from the dictionaries of Lucas, Bellows, Flügel and Muret-Sanders). Uncomfortable, uneasy, gloomy, dismal, uncanny, ghastly; (of a house) haunted; (of a man) a repulsive fellow.

FRENCH: (Sachs-Villatte). *Inquiétant, sinistre, lugubre, mal à son aise.*

SPANISH: (Tollhausen, 1889). *Sospechoso, de mal agüero, lúgubre, siniestro.*

The Italian and Portuguese languages seem to content themselves with words which we should describe as circumlocutions. In Arabic and Hebrew "uncanny" means the same as "daemonic," "gruesome."

Let us therefore return to the German language. In Daniel Sanders's *Wörterbuch der Deutschen Sprache* (1860, 1, 729), the following entry, which I here reproduce in full, is to be found under the word *"heimlich."* I have laid stress on one or two passages by italicizing them.[3]

Heimlich, adj., subst. *Heimlichkeit* (pi. *Heimlichkeiten*): I. Also *heimelich, heimelig,* belonging to the house, not strange, familiar, tame, intimate, friendly, etc.

(*a*) (Obsolete) belonging to the house or the family, or regarded as so belonging (cf. Latin *familiaris,* familiar): *Die Heimlichen,* the members of the household; *Der heimliche Rat* (Gen. xli, 45; 2 Sam. xxiii. 23; 1 Chron. xii. 25; Wisd. viii. 4), now more usually *Geheimer Rat* [Privy Councillor].

(*b*) Of animals: tame, companionable to man. As opposed to wild, e.g. "Animals which are neither wild nor *heimlich,*" etc. "Wild animals . . . that are trained to be *heimlich* and accustomed to men." "If these young creatures are brought up from early days among men they become quite *heimlich,* friendly" etc.—So also: "It (the lamb) is so *heimlich* and eats out of my hand." "Nevertheless, the stork is a beautiful, *heimelich* bird."

(c) Intimate, friendlily comfortable; the enjoyment of quiet content, etc., arousing a sense of agreeable restfulness and security as in one within the four walls of his house.[4] "Is it still *heimlich* to you in your country where strangers are felling your woods?" "She did not feel too *heimlich* with him." "Along a high, *heimlich*, shady path . . . , beside a purling, gushing and babbling woodland brook." "To destroy the *Heimlichkeit* of the home." "I could not readily find another spot so intimate and *heimlich* as this." "We pictured it so comfortable, so nice, so cosy and *heimlich*." "In quiet *Heimlichkeit*, surrounded by close walls." "A careful housewife, who knows how to make a pleasing *Heimlichkeit* (*Häuslichkeit* [domesticity]) out of the smallest means." "The man who till recently had been so strange to him now seemed to him all the more *heimlich*." "The protestant land-owners do not feel . . . *heimlich* among their catholic inferiors." "When it grows *heimlich* and still, and the evening quiet alone watches over your cell." "Quiet, lovely and *heimlich*, no place more fitted for their rest." "He did not feel at all *heimlich* about it."—Also, [in compounds] "The place was so peaceful, so lonely, so shadily-*heimlich*." "The in- and outflowing waves of the current, dreamy and lullaby-*heimlich*." Cf. in especial *Unheimlich* [see below]. Among Swabian Swiss authors in especial, often as a trisyllable: "How *heimelich* it seemed to Ivo again of an evening, when he was at home." "It was so *heimelig* in the house." "The warm room and the *heimelig* afternoon." "When a man feels in his heart that he is so small and the Lord so great—that is what is truly *heimelig*." "Little by little they grew at ease and *heimelig* among themselves." "Friendly *Heimeligkeit*." "I shall be nowhere more *heimelich* than I am here." "That which comes from afar . . . assuredly does not live quite *heimelig* (*heimatlich* [at home], *freundnachbarlich* [in a neighbourly way]) among the people." "The cottage where he had once sat so often among his own people, so *heimelig*, so happy." "The sentinel's horn sounds so *heimelig* from the tower, and his voice invites so hospitably." "You go to sleep there so soft and warm, so wonderfully *heim'lig*."—*This form of the word deserves to become general in order to protect this perfectly good sense of the word from becoming obsolete through an easy confusion with* II [see below]. Cf: *"The Zecks* [a family name] *are all 'heimlich.'"* (in sense II) *"'Heimlich'? . . . What do you understand by 'heimlich'?"* "Well, . . . *they are like a buried spring or a dried-up pond. One cannot walk over it without always having the feeling that water might come up there again."* "Oh, *we call it 'unheimlich'; you call it 'heimlich.' Well, what makes you think that there is something secret and untrustworthy about this family?"* (Gutzkow).

(d) Especially in Silesia: gay, cheerful; also of the weather.

II. Concealed, kept from sight, so that others do not get to know of or about it, withheld from others. To do something *heimlich*, i.e. behind someone's back; to steal away *heimlich*; *heimlich* meetings and appointments; to look on with *heimlich* pleasure at someone's discomfiture; to sigh or weep *heimlich*; to behave *heimlich*, as though there was something to conceal; *heimlich* love-affair, love, sin; *heimlich* places (which good manners oblige us to conceal) (1 Sam. v. 6). "The *heimlich* chamber" (privy) (2 Kings x. 27.). Also, "the *heimlich* chair." "To throw into pits or *Heimlichkeiten*."—"Led the steeds *heimlich* before Laomedon."—"As secretive, *heimlich,* deceitful and malicious towards cruel masters . . . as frank, open, sympathetic and helpful towards a friend in misfortune." "You have still to learn what is *heimlich* holiest to me." "The *heimlich* art" (magic). "Where public ventilation has to stop, there *heimlich* machinations begin." "Freedom is the whispered watchword of *heimlich* conspirators and the loud battle-cry of professed revolutionaries." "A holy, *heimlich* effect." "I have roots that are most *heimlich*. I am grown in the deep earth." "My *heimlich* pranks." "If he is not given it openly and scrupulously he may seize it *heimlich* and unscrupulously." "He had achromatic telescopes constructed *heimlich* and secretly." "Henceforth I desire that there should be nothing *heimlich* any longer between us."—To discover, disclose, betray someone's *Heimlichkeiten*; "to concoct *Heimlichkeiten* behind my back." "In my time we studied *Heimlichkeit*." "The hand of understanding can alone undo the powerless spell of the *Heimlichkeit* (of hidden gold)." "Say, where is the place of concealment . . . in what place of hidden *Heimlichkeit*?" "Bees, who make the lock of *Heimlichkeiten*" (i.e. sealing-wax). "Learned in strange *Heimlichkeiten*" (magic arts).

For compounds see above, Ic. Note especially the negative '*un-*': eerie, weird, arousing gruesome fear: "Seeming quite *unheimlich* and ghostly to him." "The *unheimlich,* fearful hours of night." "I had already long since felt an *unheimlich,* even gruesome feeling." "Now I am beginning to have an *unheimlich* feeling." . . . "Feels an *unheimlich* horror." "*Unheimlich* and motionless like a stone image." "The *unheimlich* mist called hill-fog." "These pale youths are *unheimlich* and are brewing heaven knows what mischief." "'*Unheimlich*' *is the name for everything that ought to have remained . . . secret and hidden but has come to light*" (Schelling).— "To veil the divine, to surround it with a certain *Unheimlichkeit*."—*Unheimlich* is not often used as opposite to meaning II (above).

What interests us most in this long extract is to find that among its different shades of meaning the word "*heimlich*" exhibits one which is identical with its opposite, "*unheimlich*." What is *heimlich* thus comes to be *unheimlich*. (Cf. the quotation from Gutzkow: "We call it '*unheimlich*'; you call it '*heimlich*.'") In general we are reminded that the word "*heimlich*" is not unambiguous, but belongs to two sets of ideas, which, without being contradictory, are yet very different: on the one hand it means what is familiar and agreeable, and on the other, what is concealed and kept out of sight.[5] "*Unheimlich*" is customarily used, we are told, as the contrary only of the first signification of "*heimlich*," and not of the second.

Sanders tells us nothing concerning a possible genetic connection between these two meanings of *heimlich*. On the other hand, we notice that Schelling says something which throws quite a new fight on the concept of the *Unheimlich,* for which we were certainly not prepared. According to him, everything is *unheimlich* that ought to have remained secret and hidden but has come to light.

Some of the doubts that have thus arisen are removed if we consult Grimm's dictionary. (1877, 4, Part 2, 873 ff.)

We read:

Heimlich; adj. and adv. *vernaculus, occultus*; MHG. heimelich, heimlich.

(P. 874.) In a slightly different sense: "I feel *heimlich,* well, free from fear." . . .

[3] *(b) Heimlich* is also used of a place free from ghostly influences . . . familiar, friendly, intimate.

(P. 875: *β*) Familiar, amicable, unreserved.

4. *From the idea of "homelike," "belonging to the house," the further idea is developed of something withdrawn from the eyes of strangers, something concealed, secret; and this idea is expanded in many ways . . .*

(P. 876.) "On the left bank of the lake there lies a meadow *heimlich* in the wood." (Schiller, *Wilhelm Tell,* I. 4.) . . . Poetic licence, rarely so used in modern speech . . . *Heimlich* is used in conjunction with a verb expressing the act of concealing: "In the secret of his tabernacle he shall hide me *heimlich.*" (Ps. xxvii. 5.) . . . *Heimlich* parts of the human body, *pudenda* . . . "the men that died not were smitten on their *heimlich* parts." (1 Samuel v. 12.) . . .

(c) Officials who give important advice which has to be kept secret in matters of state are called *heimlich* councillors; the adjective, according to modern usage, has been replaced by *geheim* [secret] . . . "Pharaoh called Joseph's name 'him to whom secrets are revealed'" (*heimlich* councillor). (Gen. xli. 45.)

(P. 878.) 6. *Heimlich,* as used of knowledge—mystic, allegorical: a *heimlich* meaning, *mysticus, divinus, occultus, figuratus.*

(P. 878.) *Heimlich* in a different sense, as withdrawn from knowledge, unconscious . . . *Heimlich* also has the meaning of that which is obscure, inaccessible to knowledge . . . "Do you not see? They do not trust us; they fear the *heimlich* face of the Duke of Friedland." (Schiller, *Wallensteins Lager,* Scene 2.)

9. *The notion of something hidden and dangerous, which is expressed in the last paragraph, is still further developed, so that "heimlich" comes to have the meaning usually ascribed to "unheimlich."* Thus: "At times I feel like a man who walks in the night and believes in ghosts; every corner is *heimlich* and full of terrors for him." (Klinger, *Theater,* 3. 298.)

Thus *heimlich* is a word the meaning of which develops in the direction of ambivalence, until it finally coincides with its opposite, *unheimlich. Unheimlich* is in some way or other a sub-species of *heimlich.* Let us bear this discovery in mind, though we cannot yet rightly understand it, alongside of Schelling's[6] definition of the *Unheimlich*. If we go on to examine individual instances of uncanniness, these hints will become intelligible to us.

II

When we proceed to review the things, persons, impressions, events and situations which are able to arouse in us a feeling of the uncanny in a particularly forcible and definite form, the first requirement is obviously to select a suitable example to start on. Jentsch has taken as a very good instance "doubts whether an apparently animate being is really alive; or conversely, whether a lifeless object might not be in fact animate"; and he refers in this connection to the impression made by wax-work figures, ingeniously constructed dolls and automata. To these he adds the uncanny effect of epileptic fits, and of manifestations of insanity, because these excite in the spectator the impression of automatic, mechanical processes at work behind the ordinary appearance of mental activity. Without entirely accepting his author's view, we will take it as a starting-point for our own investigation because in what follows he reminds us of a writer who has succeeded in producing uncanny effects better than anyone else.

Jentsch writes: "In telling a story, one of the most successful devices for easily creating uncanny effect is to leave the reader in uncertainty whether a particular figure in the story is a human being or an automation, and to do it in such a way that his attention is not focused directly upon his uncertainty, so that he may not be led to go into the matter and clear it up immediately. That, as we have said, would quickly dissipate the peculiar emotional effect of the thing. E. T. A. Hoffmann has repeatedly employed this psychological artifice with success in his fantastic narratives."

This observation, undoubtedly a correct one, refers primarily to the story of "The Sand-Man" in Hoffmann's *Nachtstücken*,[7] which contains the original of Olympia, the doll that appears in the first act of Offenbach's opera, *Tales of Hoffmann*. But I cannot think—and I hope most readers of the story will agree with me—that the theme of the doll Olympia, who is to all appearances a living being, is by any means the only, or indeed the most important, element that must be held responsible for the quite unparalleled atmosphere of uncanniness evoked by the story. Nor is this atmosphere heightened by the fact that the author himself treats the episode of Olympia with a faint touch of satire and uses it to poke fun at the young man's idealization of his mistress. The main theme of the story is, on the contrary, something different, something which gives it its name, and which is always re-introduced at critical moments: it is the theme of the "Sand-Man" who tears out children's eyes. This fantastic tale opens with the childhood recollections of the student Nathaniel. In spite of his present happiness, he cannot banish the memories associated with the mysterious and terrifying death of his beloved father. On certain evenings his mother used to send the children to bed early, warning them that "the Sand-Man was coming"; and, sure enough, Nathaniel would not fail to hear the heavy tread of a visitor, with whom his father would then be occupied for the evening. When questioned about the Sand-Man, his mother, it is true, denied that such a person existed except as a figure of speech; but his nurse could give him more definite information: "He's a wicked man who comes when children won't go to bed, and throws handfuls of sand in their eyes so that they jump out of their heads all bleeding. Then he puts the eyes in a sack and carries them off to the half-moon to feed his children. They sit up there in their nest, and their beaks are hooked like owls' beaks, and they use them to peck up naughty boys' and girls' eyes with."

Although little Nathaniel was sensible and old enough not to credit the figure of the Sand-Man with such gruesome attributes, yet the dread of him became fixed in his heart. He determined to find out what the Sand-Man looked like; and one evening, when the Sand-Man was expected again, he hid in his father's study. He recognized the visitor as the lawyer Coppelius, a repulsive person whom the children were frightened of when he occasionally came to a meal; and he now identified this Coppelius with the dreaded Sand-Man. As regards the rest of the scene, Hoffmann already leaves us in doubt whether what we are witnessing is the first delirium of the panic-stricken boy, or a succession of events which are to be regarded in the story as being real. His father and the guest are at work at a brazier with glowing flames. The little eavesdropper hears Coppelius call out: "Eyes here! Eyes here!" and betrays himself by screaming aloud. Coppelius seizes him and is on the point of dropping bits of red-hot coal from the fire into his eyes, and then of throwing them into the brazier, but his father begs him off and saves his eyes. After this the boy falls into a deep swoon; and a long illness brings his experience to an end. Those who decide in favour of the rationalistic interpretation of the Sand-Man will not fail to recognize in the child's phantasy the persisting influence of his nurse's story. The bits of sand that are to be thrown into the child's eyes turn into bits of red-hot coal from the flames; and in both cases they are intended to make his eyes jump out. In the course of another visit of the Sand-Man's, a year later, his father is killed in his study by an explosion. The lawyer Coppelius disappears from the place without leaving a trace behind.

Nathaniel, now a student, believes that he has recognized this phantom of horror from his childhood in an itinerant optician, an Italian called Giuseppe Coppola, who at his university town, offers him weather glassed for sale. When Nathaniel refuses, the man goes on: "Not weather-glasses? not weather-glasses? also got fine eyes, fine eyes!" The student's terror is allayed when he finds that the proffered eyes are only harmless spectacles, and he buys a pocket spy-glass from Coppola. With its aid he looks across into Professor Spalanzani's house opposite and there spies Spalanzani's beautiful, but strangely silent and motionless daughter, Olympia. He soon falls in love with her so violently that, because of her, he quite forgets the clever and sensible girl to whom he is betrothed. But Olympia is an automaton whose clock-work has been made by Spalanzani, and whose eyes have been put in by Coppola, the Sand-Man. The student surprises the two Masters quarrelling over their handiwork. The optician carries off the wooden eyeless doll; and the mechanician, Spalanzani, picks up Olympia's bleeding eyes from the ground and throws them at Nathaniel's breast, saying that Coppola had stolen them from the student. Nathaniel succumbs to a fresh attack of madness, and in his delirium his recollection of his father's death is mingled with this new experience. "Hurry up! hurry up! ring of fire!" he cries. "Spin about, ring of fire—Hurrah! Hurry up, wooden doll! lovely wooden doll, spin about—." He then falls upon the professor, Olympia's "father," and tries to strangle him.

Rallying from a long and serious illness, Nathaniel seems at last to have recovered. He intends to marry his betrothed, with whom he has become reconciled. One day he and she are walking through the city market-place, over which the high tower of the Town Hall throws its huge shadow. On the girl's suggestion, they climb the tower, leaving her brother, who is walking with them, down below. From the top, Clara's attention is drawn to a curious object moving along the street. Nathaniel looks at this thing through Coppola's spy-glass, which he finds in his pocket, and falls into a new attack of madness. Shouting "Spin about, wooden doll!" he tries to throw the girl into the gulf below. Her brother, brought to her side by her cries, rescues her and hastens down with her to safety. On the tower above, the madman rushes round, shrieking "Ring of fire, spin about!"— and we know the origin of the words. Among the people who begin to gather below there comes forward the figure of the lawyer Coppelius, who has suddenly returned. We may suppose that it was his approach, seen through the spy-glass, which threw Nathaniel into his fit of madness. As the onlookers prepare to go up and overpower the madman, Coppelius laughs and says: "Wait a bit; he'll come down of himself." Nathaniel suddenly stands still, catches sight of Coppelius, and with a wild shriek "Yes! 'Fine eyes—fine eyes'!" flings himself over the parapet. While he lies on the paving-stones with a shattered skull the Sand-Man vanishes in the throng.

This short summary leaves no doubt, I think, that the feeling of something uncanny is directly attached to the figure of the Sand-Man, that is, to the idea of being robbed of one's eyes, and that Jentsch's point of an intellectual uncertainty has nothing to do with the effect. Uncertainty whether an object is living or inanimate, which admittedly applied to the doll Olympia, is quite irrelevant in connection with this other, more striking instance of uncanniness. It is true that the writer creates a kind of uncertainty in us in the beginning by not letting us know, no doubt purposely, whether he is taking us into the real world or into a purely fantastic one of his own creation. He has, of course, a right to do either;

and if he chooses to stage his action in a world peopled with spirits, demons and ghosts, as Shakespeare does in *Hamlet*, in *Macbeth* and, in a different sense, in *The Tempest* and *A Midsummer-Night's Dream*, we must bow to his decision and treat his setting as though it were real for as long as we put ourselves into his hands. But this uncertainty disappears in the course of Hoffmann's story, and we perceive that he intends to make us, too, look through the demon optician's spectacles or spy-glass—perhaps, indeed, that the author in his very own person once peered through such an instrument. For the conclusion of the story makes it quite clear that Coppola the optician really *is* the lawyer Coppelius[8] and also, therefore, the Sand-Man.

There is no question therefore, of any intellectual uncertainty here: we know now that we are not supposed to be looking on at the products of a madman's imagination, behind which we, with the superiority of rational minds, are able to detect the sober truth; and yet this knowledge does not lessen the impression of uncanniness in the least degree. The theory of intellectual uncertainty is thus incapable of explaining that impression.

We know from psychoanalytic experience, however, that the fear of damaging or losing one's eyes is a terrible one in children. Many adults retain their apprehensiveness in this respect, and no physical injury is so much dreaded by them as an injury to the eye. We are accustomed to say, too, that we will treasure a thing as the apple of our eye. A study of dreams, phantasies and myths has taught us that anxiety about one's eyes, the fear of going blind, is often enough a substitute for the dread of being castrated. The self-blinding of the mythical criminal, Oedipus, was simply a mitigated form of the punishment of castration— the only punishment that was adequate for him by the *lex talionis*. We may try on rationalistic grounds to deny that fears about the eye are derived from the fear of castration, and may argue that it is very natural that so precious an organ as the eye should be guarded by a proportionate dread. Indeed, we might go further and say that the fear of castration itself contains no other significance and no deeper secret than a justifiable dread of this rational kind. But this view does not account adequately for the substitutive relation between the eye and the male organ which is seen to exist in dreams and myths and phantasies; nor can it dispel the impression that the threat of being castrated in especial excites a peculiarly violent and obscure emotion, and that this emotion is what first gives the idea of losing other organs its intense colouring. All further doubts are removed when we learn the details of their "castration complex" from the analysis of neurotic patients, and realize its immense importance in their mental life.

Moreover, I would not recommend any opponent of the psychoanalytic view to select this particular story of the Sand-Man with which to support his argument that anxiety about the eyes has nothing to do with the castration complex. For why does Hoffmann bring the anxiety about eyes into such intimate connection

with the father's death? And why does the Sand-Man always appear as a dis-
turber of love? He separates the unfortunate Nathaniel from his betrothed and
from her brother, his best friend; he destroys the second object of his love, Olympia, the lovely doll; and he drives him into suicide at the moment when he has
won back his Clara and is about to be happily united to her. Elements in the story
like these, and many others, seem arbitrary and meaningless so long as we deny
all connection between fears about the eye and castration; but they become intelligible as soon as we replace the Sand-Man by the dreaded father at whose hands
castration is expected.[9]

We shall venture, therefore, to refer the uncanny effect of the Sand-Man to
the anxiety belonging to the castration complex of childhood. But having reached
the idea that we can make an infantile factor such as this responsible for feelings of uncanniness, we are encouraged to see whether we can apply it to other
instances of the uncanny. We find in the story of the Sand-Man the other theme
on which Jentsch lays stress, of a doll which appears to be alive. Jentsch believes
that a particularly favourable condition for awakening uncanny feelings is created when there is intellectual uncertainty whether an object is alive or not, and
when an inanimate object becomes too much like an animate one. Now, dolls are
of course rather closely connected with childhood life. We remember that in
their early games children do not distinguish at all sharply between living and
inanimate objects, and that they are especially fond of treating their dolls like live
people. In fact, I have occasionally heard a woman patient declare that even at
the age of eight she had still been convinced that her dolls would be certain to
come to fife if she were to look at them in a particular, extremely concentrated,
way. So that here, too, it is not difficult to discover a factor from childhood. But,
curiously enough, while the Sand-Man story deals with the arousing of an early
childhood fear, the idea of a "living doll" excites no fear at all; children have no
fear of their dolls coming to life, they may even desire it. The source of uncanny
feelings would not, therefore, be an infantile fear in this case, but rather an infantile wish or even merely an infantile belief. There seems to be a contradiction
here; but perhaps it is only a complication, which may be helpful to us later on.

Hoffmann is the unrivalled master of the uncanny in literature. His novel, *Die
Elixire des Teufels* [*The Devil's Elixir*], contains a whole mass of themes to which
one is tempted to ascribe the uncanny effect of the narrative;[10] but it is too obscure
and intricate a story for us to venture upon a summary of it. Towards the end of
the book the reader is told the facts; hitherto concealed from him, from which
the action springs; with the result, not that he is at last enlightened, but that he
falls into a state of complete bewilderment. The author has piled up too much
material of the same kind. In consequence one's grasp of the story as a whole

suffers, though not the impression it makes. We must content ourselves with selecting those themes of uncanniness which are most prominent, and with seeing whether they too can fairly be traced back to infantile sources. These themes are all concerned with the phenomenon of the "double," which appears in every shape and in every degree of development. Thus we have characters who are to be considered identical because they look alike. This relation is accentuated by mental processes leaping from one of these characters to another—by what we should call telepathy—so that the one possesses knowledge, feelings and experience in common with the other. Or it is marked by the fact that the subject identifies himself with someone else, so that he is in doubt as to which his self is, or substitutes the extraneous self for his own. In other words, there is doubling, dividing and interchanging of the self. And finally there is the constant recurrence of the same thing[11]—the repetition of the same features or character-traits or vicissitudes, of the same crimes, or even the same names through several consecutive generations.

The theme of the "double" has been very thoroughly treated by Otto Rank (1914). He has gone into the connections which the "double" has with reflections in mirrors, with shadows, with guardian spirits, with the belief in the soul and with the fear of death; but he also lets in a flood of light on the surprising evolution of the idea. For the "double" was originally an insurance against the destruction of the ego, an "energetic denial of the power of death," as Rank says; and probably the "immortal" soul was the first "double" of the body. This invention of doubling as a preservation against extinction has its counterpart in the language of dreams, which is fond of representing castration by a doubling or multiplication of a genital symbol.[12] The same desire led the Ancient Egyptians to develop the art of making images of the dead in lasting materials. Such ideas, however, have sprung from the soil of unbounded self-love, from the primary narcissism which dominates the mind of the child and of primitive man. But when this stage has been surmounted, the "double" reverses its aspect. From having been an assurance of immortality, it becomes the uncanny harbinger of death.

The idea of the "double" does not necessarily disappear with the passing of primary narcissism, for it can receive fresh meaning from the later stages of the ego's development. A special agency is slowly formed there, which is able to stand over against the rest of the ego, which has the function of observing and criticizing the self and of exercising a censorship within the mind, and which we become aware of as our "conscience." In the pathological case of delusions of being watched, this mental agency becomes isolated, dissociated from the ego, and discernible to the physician's eye. The fact that an agency of this kind exists, which is able to treat the rest of the ego like an object—the fact, that is, that man is capable of self-observation—renders it possible to invest the old idea of a "double" with a new meaning and to ascribe a number of things to it—above all, those things which seem to self-criticism to belong to the old surmounted narcissism of earliest times.[13]

But it is not only this latter material, offensive as it is to the criticism of the ego, which may be incorporated in the idea of a double. There are also all the unfulfilled but possible futures to which we still like to cling in phantasy, all the strivings of the ego which adverse external circumstances have crushed, and all our suppressed acts of volition which nourish in us the illusion of Free Will.[14] [Cf. Freud, 1901b, Chapter XII (B).]

But after having thus considered the *manifest* motivation of the figure of a "double," we have to admit that none of this helps us to understand the extraordinarily strong feeling of something uncanny that pervades the conception; and our knowledge of pathological mental processes enables us to add that nothing in this more superficial material could account for the urge towards defence which has caused the ego to project that material outward as something foreign to itself. When all is said and done, the quality of uncanniness can only come from the fact of the "double" being a creation dating back to a very early mental stage, long since surmounted—a stage, incidentally, at which it wore a more friendly aspect. The "double" has become a thing of terror, just as, after the collapse of their religion, the gods turned into demons.[15]

The other forms of ego-disturbance exploited by Hoffmann can easily be estimated along the same fines as the theme of the "double." They are a harking-back to particular phases in the evolution of the self-regarding feeling, a regression to a time when the ego had not yet marked itself off sharply from the external world and from other people. I believe that these factors are partly responsible for the impression of uncanniness, although it is not easy to isolate and determine exactly their share of it.

The actor of the repetition of the same thing will perhaps not appeal to everyone as a source of uncanny feeling. From what I have observed, this phenomenon, does undoubtedly, subject to certain conditions and combined with certain circumstances, arouse an uncanny feeling, which, furthermore, recalls the sense of helplessness experienced in some dream-states. As I was walking, one hot summer afternoon, through the deserted streets of a provincial town in Italy which was unknown to me, I found myself in a quarter of whose character I could not long remain in doubt. Nothing but painted women were to be seen at the windows of the small houses, and I hastened to leave the narrow street at the next turning. But after having wandered about for a time without enquiring my way, I suddenly found myself back in the same street, where my presence was now beginning to excite attention. I hurried away once more, only to arrive by another *détour* at the same place yet a third time. Now, however, a feeling overcame me which I can only describe as uncanny, and I was glad enough to find myself back at the piazza I had left a short while before, without any further voyages of discovery. Other situations which have in common with my adventure an unintended recurrence of the same situation, but which differ radically from it in other respects, also result in the same feeling of helplessness and of uncanniness. So, for instance, when, caught in a mist perhaps, one has lost one's way in a mountain forest, every attempt to find the marked or familiar path may bring one back again and again to one and the same spot, which one can identify by some particular landmark. Or one may wander about in a dark, strange room, looking for the door or the electric switch, and collide time after time with the same piece of furniture—though it is true that Mark Twain succeeded by wild exaggeration in turning this latter situation into something irresistibly comic.[16]

If we take another class of things, it is easy to see that there, too, it is only this factor of involuntary repetition which surrounds what would otherwise be innocent enough with an uncanny atmosphere, and forces upon us the idea of something fateful and inescapable when otherwise we should have spoken only of chance. For instance, we naturally attach no importance to the event when we hand in an overcoat and get a cloakroom ticket with the number, let us say, 62; or when we find that our cabin on a ship bears that number. But the impression is altered if two such events, each in itself indifferent, happen close together—if we come across the number 62 several times in a single day, or if we begin to notice that everything which has a number—addresses, hotel rooms, compartments in railway trains—invariably has the same one, or at all events one which contains the same figures. We do feel this to be uncanny. And unless a man is utterly hardened and proof against the lure of superstition, he will be tempted to ascribe a secret meaning to this obstinate recurrence of a number; he will take it, perhaps, as an indication of the span of life allotted to him.[17] Or suppose one is engaged in reading the works of the famous physiologist, Hering, and within the space of a few days receives two letters from two different countries, each from a person called Hering, though one has never before had any dealings with anyone of that name. Not long ago an ingenious scientist (Kammerer, 1919) attempted to reduce coincidences of this kind to certain laws, and so deprive them of their uncanny effect. I will not venture to decide whether he has succeeded or not.

How exactly we can trace back to infantile psychology the uncanny effect of such similar recurrences is a question I can only lightly touch on in these pages; and I must refer the reader instead to another work,[18] already completed, in which this has been gone into in detail, but in a different connection. For it is possible to recognize the dominance in the unconscious mind of a "compulsion to repeat" proceeding from the instinctual impulses and probably inherent in the very nature of the instincts—a compulsion powerful enough to overrule the pleasure principle, lending to certain aspects of the mind their daemonic character, and still very clearly expressed in the impulses of small children; a compulsion, too, which is responsible for a part of the course taken by the analyses of neurotic patients. All these considerations prepare us for the discovery that whatever reminds us of this inner "compulsion to repeat" is perceived as uncanny.

Now, however, it is time to turn from these aspects of the matter, which are in any case difficult to judge, and look for some undeniable instances of the uncanny, in the hope that an analysis of them will decide whether our hypothesis is a valid one.

In the story of "The Ring of Polycrates,"[19] the King of Egypt turns away in horror from his host, Polycrates, because he sees that his friend's every wish is at once fulfilled, his every care promptly removed by kindly fate. His host has become "uncanny" to him. His own explanation, that the too fortunate man has to fear the envy of the gods, seems obscure to us; its meaning is veiled in mythological language. We will therefore turn to another example in a less grandiose setting. In the case history of an obsessional neurotic,[20] I have described how the patient once stayed in a hydropathic establishment and benefited greatly by it. He had the good sense, however, to attribute his improvement not to the therapeutic properties of the water, but to the situation of his room, which immediately adjoined that of a very accommodating nurse. So on his second visit to the establishment he asked for the same room, but was told that it was already occupied by an old gentleman, whereupon he gave vent to his annoyance in the words: "I wish he may be struck dead for it." A fortnight later the old gentleman really did have a stroke. My patient thought this an "uncanny" experience. The impression of uncanniness would have been stronger still if less time had elapsed between his words and the untoward event, or if he had been able to report innumerable similar coincidences. As a matter of fact, he had no difficulty in producing coincidences of this sort; but then not only he but every obsessional neurotic I have observed has been able to relate analogous experiences. They are never surprised at their invariably running up against someone they have just been thinking of, perhaps for the first time for a long while. If they say one day "I haven't had any news of so-and-so for a long time," they will be sure to get a letter from him the next morning, and an accident or a death will rarely take place without having passed through their mind a little while before. They are in the habit of referring to this state of affairs in the most modest manner, saying that they have "presentiments" which "usually" come true.

One of the most uncanny and wide-spread forms of superstition is the dread of the evil eye, which has been exhaustively studied by the Hamburg oculist Seligmann (1910–11). There never seems to have been any doubt about the source of this dread. Whoever possesses something that is at once valuable and fragile is afraid of other people's envy, in so far as he projects on to them the envy he would have felt in their place. A feeling like this betrays itself by a look[21] even though it is not put into words; and when a man is prominent owing to noticeable, and particularly owing to unattractive, attributes, other people are ready to believe that his envy is rising to a more than usual degree of intensity and that this intensity will convert it into effective action. What is feared is thus a secret intention of doing harm, and certain signs are taken to mean that that intention has the necessary power at its command.

These last examples of the uncanny are to be referred to the principle which I have called "omnipotence of thoughts," taking the name from an expression used by one of my patients.[22] And now we find ourselves on familiar ground. Our analysis of instances of the uncanny has led us back to the old, animistic conception of the universe. This was characterized by the idea that the world was peopled with the spirits of human beings; by the subject's narcissistic overvaluation of his own mental processes; by the belief in the omnipotence of thoughts and the technique of magic based on that belief; by the attribution to various outside persons and things of carefully graded magical powers, or "*mana*"; as well as by all the other creations with the help of which man, in the unrestricted narcissism of that stage of development, strove to fend off the manifest prohibitions of reality. It seems as if each one of us has been through a phase of individual development corresponding to this animistic stage in primitive men, that none of us has passed through it without preserving certain residues and traces of it which are still capable of manifesting themselves, and that everything which now strikes us as "uncanny" fulfils the condition of touching those residues of animistic mental activity within us and bringing them to expression.[23]

At this point I will put forward two considerations which, I think, contain the gist of this short study. In the first place, if psychoanalytic theory is correct in maintaining that every affect belonging to an emotional impulse, whatever its kind, is transformed, if it is repressed, into anxiety, then among instances of frightening things there must be one class in which the frightening element can be shown to be something repressed which *recurs*. This class of frightening things would then constitute the uncanny; and it must be a matter of indifference whether what is uncanny was itself originally frightening or whether carried some *other* affect. In the second place, if this is indeed the secret nature of the uncanny, we can understand why linguistic usage has extended *das Heimliche* ["homely"] into its opposite, *das Unheimliche*; for this uncanny is in reality nothing new or alien, but something which is familiar and old-established in the mind and which has become alienated from it only through the process of repression. This reference to the factor of repression enables us, furthermore, to understand Schelling's definition of the uncanny as something which ought to have remained hidden but has come to light.

It only remains for us to test our new hypothesis on one or two more examples of the uncanny.

Many people experience the feeling in the highest degree in relation to death and dead bodies, to the return of the dead, and to spirits and ghosts. As we have seen some languages in use to-day can only render the German expression 'an *unheimlich* house' by 'a *haunted* house'. We might indeed have begun our investigation with this example, perhaps the most striking of all, of something uncanny, but we refrained from doing so because the uncanny in it is too much intermixed with what is purely gruesome and is in part overlaid by it. There is scarcely any other matter, however, upon which our thoughts and feelings have changed so little since the very earliest times, and in which discarded forms have been so completely preserved under a thin disguise, as our relation to death. Two things account for our conservatism: the strength of our original emotional re-action to death and the insufficiency of our scientific knowledge about it. Biology has not yet been able to decide whether death is the inevitable fate of every living being or whether it is only a regular but yet perhaps avoidable event in life.[24] It is true that the statement "All men are mortal" is paraded in text-books of logic as an example of a general proposition; but no human being really grasps it, and our unconscious has as little use now as it ever had for the idea of its own mortality.[25] Religions continue to dispute the importance or the undeniable fact of individual death and to postulate a life after death; civil governments still believe that they cannot maintain moral order among the living if they do not uphold the prospect of a better life hereafter as a recompense for mundane existence. In our great cities, placards announce lectures that undertake to tell us how to get into touch with the souls of the departed; and it cannot be denied that not a few of the most able and penetrating minds among our men of science have come to the conclusion, especially towards the close of their own lives, that a contact of this kind is not impossible. Since almost all of us still think as savages do on this topic, it is no matter for surprise that the primitive fear of the dead is still so strong within us and always ready to come to the surface on any provocation. Most likely our fear still implies the old belief that the dead man becomes the enemy of his survivor and seeks to carry him off to share his new life with him. Considering our unchanged attitude towards death, we might rather enquire what has become of the repression, which is the necessary condition of a primitive feeling recurring in the shape of something uncanny. But repression is there, too. All supposedly educated people have ceased to believe officially that the dead can become visible as spirits, and have made any such appearances dependent on improbable and remote conditions; their emotional attitude towards their dead, moreover, once a highly ambiguous and ambivalent one, has been toned down in the higher strata of the mind into an unambiguous feeling of piety.[26]

We have now only a few remarks to add—for animism, magic and sorcery, the omnipotence of thoughts, man's attitude to death, involuntary repetition and the castration complex comprise practically all the factors which turn something frightening into something uncanny.

We can also speak of a living person as uncanny, and we do so when we ascribe evil intentions to him. But that is not all; in addition to this we must feel that his intentions to harm us are going to be carried out with the help of special powers. A good instance of this is the *"Gettatore,"*[27] that uncanny figure of Romanic superstition which Schaeffer, with intuitive poetic feeling and profound psycho-analytic understanding, has transformed into a sympathetic character in his *Josef Montfort*. But the question of these secret powers brings us back again to the realm of animism. It was the pious Gretchen's intuition that Mephistopheles possessed secret powers of this kind that made him so uncanny to her.

> Sie fühlt dass ich ganz sicher ein Genie,
> Vielleicht sogar der Teufel bin.[28]

The uncanny effect of epilepsy and of madness has the same origin. The layman sees in them the working of forces hitherto unsuspected in his fellow-men, but at the same time he is dimly aware of them in remote corners of his own being. The Middle Ages quite consistently ascribed all such maladies to the influence of demons, and in this their psychology was almost correct. Indeed, I should not be surprised to hear that psychoanalysis, which is concerned with laying bare these hidden forces, has itself become uncanny to many people for that very reason. In one case, after I had succeeded—though none too rapidly—in effecting a cure in a girl who had been an invalid for many years, I myself heard this view expressed by the patient's mother long after her recovery.

Dismembered limbs, a severed head, a hand cut off at the wrist, as in a fairy tale of Hauff's,[29] feet which dance by themselves, as in the book by Schaeffer which I mentioned above—all these have something peculiarly uncanny about them, especially when, as in the last instance, they prove capable of independent activity in addition. As we already know, this kind of uncanniness springs from its proximity to the castration complex. To some people the idea of being buried alive by mistake is the most uncanny thing of all. And yet psychoanalysis has taught us that this terrifying phantasy is only a transformation of another phantasy which had originally nothing terrifying about it at all, but was qualified by a certain lasciviousness—the phantasy, I mean, of intra-uterine existence.[30]

There is one more point of general application which I should like to add, though, strictly speaking, it has been included in what has already been said about animism and modes of working of the mental apparatus that have been surmounted;

for I think it deserves special emphasis. This is that an uncanny effect is often and easily produced when the distinction between imagination and reality is effaced, as when something that we have hitherto regarded as imaginary appears before us in reality, or when a symbol takes over the full functions of the thing it symbolizes, and so on. It is this factor which contributes not a little to the uncanny effect attaching to magical practices. The infantile element in this, which also dominates the minds of neurotics, is the over-accentuation of psychical reality in comparison with material reality—a feature closely allied to the belief in the omnipotence of thoughts. In the middle of the isolation of war-time a number of the English *Strand Magazine* fell into my hands; and, among other somewhat redundant matter, I read a story about a young married couple who move into a furnished house in which there is a curiously shaped table with carvings of crocodiles on it. Towards evening an intolerable and very specific smell begins to pervade the house; they stumble over something in the dark; they seem to see a vague form gliding over the stairs—in short, we are given to understand that the presence of the table causes ghostly crocodiles to haunt the place, or that the wooden monsters come to life in the dark, or something of the sort. It was a naïve enough story, but the uncanny feeling it produced was quite remarkable.

To conclude this collection of examples, which is certainly not complete, I will relate an instance taken from psychoanalytic experience; if it does not rest upon mere coincidence, it furnishes a beautiful confirmation of our theory of the uncanny. It often happens that neurotic men declare that they feel there is something uncanny about the female genital organs. This *unheimlich* place, however, is the entrance to the former *Heim* [home] of all human beings, to the place where each one of us lived once upon a time and in the beginning. There is a joking saying that "Love is home-sickness"; and whenever a man dreams of a place or a country and says to himself, while he is still dreaming: "this place is familiar to me, I've been here before," we may interpret the place as being his mother's genitals or her body.[31] In this case too, then, the *unheimlich* is what was once *heimisch*, familiar; the prefix "*un*" ["un-"] is the token of repression.[32]

III

In the course of this discussion the reader will have felt certain doubts arising in his mind; and he must now have an opportunity of collecting them and bringing them forward.

It may be true that the uncanny [*unheimlich*] is something which is secretly familiar [*heimlich-heimisch*], which has undergone repression and then returned from it, and that everything that is uncanny fulfils this condition. But the selection of material on this basis does not enable us to solve the problem of the uncanny. For our proposition is clearly not convertible. Not everything that fulfils this condition—not everything that recalls repressed desires and surmounted modes of thinking belonging to the prehistory of the individual and of the race—is on that account uncanny.

Nor shall we conceal the fact that for almost every example adduced in support of our hypothesis one may be found which rebuts it. The story of the severed hand in Hauff's fairy tale certainly has an uncanny effect, and we have traced that effect back to the castration complex; but most readers will probably agree with me in judging that no trace of uncanniness is provoked by Herodotus's story of the treasure of Rhampsinitus, in which the master-thief, whom the princess tries to hold fast by the hand, leaves his brother's severed hand behind with her instead. Again, the prompt fulfilment of the wishes of Polycrates undoubtedly affects us in the same uncanny way as it did the king of Egypt; yet our own fairy stories are crammed with instantaneous wish-fulfilments which produce no uncanny effect whatever. In the story of "The Three Wishes," the woman is tempted by the savoury smell of a sausage to wish that she might have one too, and in an instant it lies on a plate before her. In his annoyance at her hastiness her husband wishes it may hang on her nose. And there it is, dangling from her nose. All this is very striking but not in the least uncanny. Fairy tales quite frankly adopt the animistic standpoint of the omnipotence of thoughts and wishes, and yet I cannot think of any genuine fairy story which has anything uncanny about it. We have heard that it is in the highest degree uncanny when an inanimate object—a picture or a doll—comes to life; nevertheless in Hans Andersen's stories the household utensils, furniture and tin soldiers are alive, yet nothing could well be more remote from the uncanny. And we should hardly call it uncanny when Pygmalion's beautiful statue comes to life.

Apparent death and the re-animation of the dead have been represented as most uncanny themes. But things of this sort too are very common in fairy stories. Who would be so bold as to call it uncanny, for instance, when Snow-White opens her eyes once more? And the resuscitation of the dead in accounts of miracles, as in the New Testament, elicits feelings quite unrelated to the uncanny. Then, too, the theme that achieves such an indubitably uncanny effect, the unintended recurrence of the same thing, serves other and quite different purposes in another class of cases. We have already come across one example in which it is employed to call up a feeling of the comic; and we could multiply instances of this kind. Or again, it works as a means of emphasis, and so on. And once more: what is the origin of the uncanny effect of silence, darkness and solitude? Do not these factors point to the part played by danger in the genesis of what is uncanny, notwithstanding that in children these same factors are the most frequent determinants of the expression of fear [rather than of the uncanny]? And are we after all justified in entirely ignoring intellectual uncertainty as a factor, seeing that we have admitted its importance in relation to death?

It is evident therefore, that we must be prepared to admit that there are other elements besides those which we have so far laid down as determining the production of uncanny feelings. We might say that these preliminary results have satisfied *psychoanalytic* interest in the problem of the uncanny, and that what remains probably calls for an *aesthetic* enquiry. But that would be to open the door to doubts about what exactly is the value of our general contention that the uncanny proceeds from something familiar which has been repressed.

We have noticed one point which may help us to resolve these uncertainties: nearly all the instances that contradict our hypothesis are taken from the realm of fiction, of imaginative writing. This suggests that we should differentiate between the uncanny that we actually experience and the uncanny that we merely picture or read about.

What is *experienced* as uncanny is much more simply conditioned but comprises far fewer instances. We shall find, I think, that it fits in perfectly with our attempt at a solution, and can be traced back without exception to something familiar that has been repressed. But here, too, we must make a certain important and psychologically significant differentiation in our material, which is best illustrated by turning to suitable examples.

Let us take the uncanny associated with the omnipotence of thoughts, with the prompt fulfilment of wishes, with secret injurious powers and with the return of the dead. The condition under which the feeling of uncanniness arises here is unmistakable. We—or our primitive forefathers—once believed that these possibilities were realities, and were convinced that they actually happened. Nowadays we no longer believe in them, we have *surmounted* these modes of thought; but we do not feel quite sure of our new beliefs, and the old ones still exist within us ready to seize upon any confirmation. As soon as something *actually happens* in our lives which seems to confirm the old, discarded beliefs we get a feeling of the uncanny: it is as though we were making a judgment something like this: "So, after all, it is *true* that one can kill a person by the mere wish!" or, "So the dead *do* live on and appear on the scene of their former activities!" and so on. Conversely, anyone who has completely and finally rid himself of animistic beliefs will be insensible to this type of the uncanny. The most remarkable coincidences of wish and fulfilment, the most mysterious repetition of similar experiences in a particular place or on a particular date, the most deceptive sights and suspicious noises—none of these things will disconcert him or raise the kind of fear which can be described as "a fear of something uncanny." The whole thing is purely an affair of "reality-testing," a question of the material reality of the phenomena.[33]

The state of affairs is different when the uncanny proceeds from repressed infantile complexes, from the castration complex, womb-phantasies, etc.; but experiences which arouse this kind of uncanny feeling are not of very frequent occurrence in real life. The uncanny which proceeds from actual experience belongs for the most part to the first group [the group dealt with in the previous paragraph]. Nevertheless the distinction between the two is theoretically very important. Where the uncanny comes from infantile complexes the question of material reality does not arise; its place is taken by psychical reality. What is involved is an actual repression of some content of thought and a return of this repressed content, not a cessation of *belief in the reality* of such a content. We might say that in the one case what had been repressed is a particular ideational content, and in the other the belief in its (material) reality. But this last phrase no doubt extends the term "repression" beyond its legitimate meaning. It would be more correct to take into account a psychological distinction which can be detected here, and to say that the animistic beliefs of civilized people are in a state of having been (to a greater or lesser extent) *surmounted* [rather than repressed]. Our conclusion could then be stated thus: an uncanny experience occurs either when infantile complexes which have been repressed are once more revived by some impression, or when primitive beliefs which have been surmounted seem once more to be confirmed. Finally, we must not let our predilection for smooth solutions and lucid exposition blind us to the fact that these two classes of uncanny experience are not always sharply distinguishable. When we consider that primitive beliefs are most intimately connected with infantile complexes, and are, in fact, based on them, we shall not be greatly astonished to find that the distinction is often a hazy one.

The uncanny as it is depicted in *literature,* in stories and imaginative productions, merits in truth a separate discussion. Above all, it is a much more fertile province than the uncanny in real life, for it contains the whole of the latter and something more besides, something that cannot be found in real life. The contrast between what has been repressed and what has been surmounted cannot be transposed on to the uncanny in fiction without profound modification; for the realm of phantasy depends for its effect on the fact that its content is not submitted to reality-testing. The somewhat paradoxical result is that *in the first place a great deal that is not uncanny in fiction would be so if it happened in real life; and in the second place that there are many more means of creating uncanny effects in fiction than there are in real life.*

The imaginative writer has this licence among many others, that he can select his world of representation so that it either coincides with the realities we are familiar with or departs from them in what particulars he pleases. We accept his ruling in every case. In fairy tales, for instance, the world of reality is left behind from the very start, and the animistic system of beliefs is frankly adopted. Wish-fulfilments, secret powers, omnipotence of thoughts, animation of inanimate objects, all the elements so common in fairy stories, can exert no uncanny influence here; for, as we have learnt, that feeling cannot arise unless there is a conflict of judgement as to whether things which have been "surmounted" and are regarded as incredible may not, after all, be possible; and this problem eliminated from the outset by the postulates of the world of fairy tales. Thus we see that fairy stories, which have furnished us with most of the contradictions to our hypothesis of the uncanny, confirm the first part of our proposition—that in the realm of fiction many things are not uncanny which would be so if they happened in real life. In the case of these stories there are other contributory factors, which we shall briefly touch upon later.

The creative writer can also choose a setting which though less imaginary than the world of fairy tales, does yet differ from the real world by admitting superior spiritual beings such as daemonic spirits or ghosts of the dead. So long as they remain within their setting of poetic reality, such figures lose any uncanniness which they might possess. The souls in Dante's *Inferno,* or the supernatural apparitions in Shakespeare's *Hamlet, Macbeth,* or *Julius Caesar,* may be gloomy and terrible enough, but they are no more really uncanny than Homer's jovial world of gods. We adapt our judgement to the imaginary reality imposed on us by the writer, and regard souls, spirits and ghosts as though their existence had the same validity as our own has in material reality. In this case too we avoid all trace of the uncanny.

The situation is altered as soon as the writer pretends to move in the world of common reality. In this case he accepts as well all the conditions operating to produce uncanny feelings in real life; and everything that would have an uncanny effect in reality has it in his story. But in this case he can even increase his effect and multiply it far beyond what could happen in reality, by bringing about events which never or very rarely happen in fact. In doing this he is in a sense betraying us to the superstitiousness which we have ostensibly surmounted; he deceives by promising to give us the sober truth, and then after all overstepping it. We react to his inventions as we would have reacted to real experience; by the time we have seen through his trick it already too late and the author has achieved his object. But it must be added that his success is not unalloyed. We retain a feeling of dissatisfaction, a kind of grudge against the attempted deceit. I have noticed this particularly after reading Schnitzler's *Die Weissagung* [*The Prophecy*] and similar stories which flirt with the supernatural. However, the writer has one more means which he can use in order to avoid our recalcitrance and at the same time to improve his chances of success. He can keep us in the dark for a long time about the precise nature of the presuppositions on which the world he writes about is based, or he can cunningly and ingeniously avoid any definite information on the point to the last. Speaking generally, however, we find a confirmation of the second part of our proposition—that fiction presents more opportunities for creating uncanny feelings than are possible in real life.

Strictly speaking, all these complications relate only to that class of the uncanny which proceeds from forms of thought that have been surmounted. The class which proceeds from repressed complexes is more resistant and remains as powerful in fiction as in real experience, subject to one exception [see p. 252]. The uncanny belonging to the first class—that proceeding from forms of thought that have been surmounted—retains its character not only in experience but in fiction as well, so long as the setting is one of material reality; but where it is given an arbitrary and artificial setting in fiction, it is apt to lose that character.

We have clearly not exhausted the possibilities of poetic license and the privileges enjoyed by story-writers in evoking or in excluding an uncanny feeling. In the main we adopt an unvarying passive attitude towards real experience and are subject to the influence of our physical environment. But the storyteller has a *peculiarly* directive power over us; by means of the moods he can put us into, he is able to guide the current of our emotions, to dam it up in one direction and make it flow in another, and he often obtains a great variety of effects from the same material. All this is nothing new, and has doubtless long since been fully taken into account by students of aesthetics. We have drifted into this field of research half involuntarily, through the temptation to explain certain instances which contradicted our theory of the causes of the uncanny. Accordingly we will now return to the examination of a few of those instances.

We have already asked why it is that the severed hand in the story of the treasure of Rhampsinitus has no uncanny effect in the way that the severed hand has in Hauff's story. The question seems to have gained in importance now that we have recognized that the class of the uncanny which proceeds from repressed complexes is the more resistant of the two. The answer is easy. In the Herodotus story our thoughts are concentrated much more on the superior cunning of the master-thief than on the feelings of the princess. The princess may very well have had an uncanny feeling, indeed she very probably fell into a swoon; but *we* have no such sensations, for we put ourselves in the thief's place, not in hers. In Nestroy's farce, *Der Zerrissene* [*The Torn Man*], another means is used to avoid any impression of the uncanny in the scene in which the fleeing man, convinced that he is a murderer, lifts up one trapdoor after another and each time sees what he takes to be the ghost of his victim rising up out of it. He calls out in despair, "But I've only killed *one* man. Why this ghastly multiplication?" We know what went before this scene and do not share his error, so what must be uncanny to him has an irresistibly comic effect on us. Even a "real" ghost, as in Oscar Wilde's *Canterville Ghost,* loses all power of at least arousing *gruesome* feelings in us as soon as the author begins to amuse himself by being ironical about it and allows liberties to be taken with it. Thus we see how independent emotional effects can be of the actual subject-matter in the world of fiction. In fairy stories feelings of fear—including therefore uncanny feelings—are ruled out altogether. We understand this, and that is why we ignore any opportunities we find in them for developing such feelings.

Concerning the factors of silence, solitude and darkness, we can only say that they are actually elements in the production of the infantile anxiety from which the majority of human beings have never become quite free. This problem has been discussed from a psychoanalytic point of view elsewhere.[34]

Appendix

Extract from Daniel Sanders's Worterbuch der Deutschen Sprache[35]

Heimlich, a. (-keit, f. -en): 1. auch Heimelich, heimelig, zum Hause gehörig, nicht fremd, vertraut, zahm, traut und traulich, anheimelnd etc. (*a*) (veralt.) zum Haus, zur Familie gehörig oder: wie dazu gehörig betrachtet, vgl. lat. familiaris, vertraut: Die Heimlichen, die Hausgenossen; Der heimliche Rath. 1. Mos. 41, 45; 2. Sam. 23, 23. 1 Chr. 12, 25. Weish. 8, 4., wofür jetzt: Geheimer (s. *d* 1.) Rath üblich ist, s. Heimlicher—(*b*) von Thieren zahm, sich den Menschen traulich anschließend. Ggstz. wild, z. B.: Thier, die weder wild noch heimlich sind, etc. Eppendorf. 88; Wilde Thier . . . so man sie h. und gewohnsam um die Leute aufzeucht. 92. So diese Thierle von Jugend bei den Menschen erzogen, werden sie ganz h., freundlich etc., Stumpf 608a etc.—So noch: So h. ist's (das Lamm) und frißt aus meiner Hand. Hölty; Ein schöner, heimelicher (s. *c*) Vogel bleibt der Storch immerhin. Linck, Schl. 146. s. Häuslich 1 etc.—(*c*) traut, traulich anheimelnd; das Wohlgefühl stiller Befriedigung etc., behaglicher Ruhe u. sichern Schutzes, wie das umschlossne, wohnliche Haus erregend (vgl. Geheuer): 1st dir's h. noch im Lande, wo die Fremden deine Wälder roden? Alexis H. 1, 1, 289; Es war ihr nicht allzu h. bei ihm. Brentano Wehm. 92; Auf einem hohen h—en Schattenpfade . . . , längs dem rieselnden rauschenden und plätschernden Waldbach. Forster B. 1, 417. Die H—keit der Heimath zerstören. Gervinus Lit. 5, 375. So vertraulich und h. habe ich nicht leicht ein Plätzchen gefunden. G[oethe], 14, 14; Wir dachten es uns so bequem, so artig, so gemüthlich und h. 15, 9; In stiller H—keit, umzielt von engen Schranken. Haller; Einer sorglichen Hausfrau, die mit dem Wenigsten eine vergnügliche H—keit (Häuslichkeit) zu schaffen versteht. Hartmann Unst. 1, 188; Desto h—er kam ihm jetzt der ihm erst kurz noch so fremde Mann vor. Kerner 540; Die protestantischen Besitzer fühlen sich . . . nicht h. unter ihren katholischen Unterthanen. Kohl. Irl. 1, 172; Wenns h. wird und leise/die Abendstille nur an deiner Zelle lauscht. Tiedge 2, 39; Still und lieb und h., als sie sich/zum Ruhen einen Platz nur wünschen möchten. W[ieland], 11, 144; Es war ihm garnicht h. dabei 27. 170, etc.—Auch: Der Platz war so still, so einsam, so schatten-h. Scherr Pilg. 1, 170; Die ab- und zuströmenden Fluthwellen, träumend und wiegenlied-h. Körner, Sch. 3, 320, etc.—Vgl. namentl. Un-h.—Namentl. bei schwäb., schwzr. Schriftst. oft dreisilbig: Wie 'heimelich' war es dann Ivo Abends wieder, als er zu Hause lag. Auerbach, D. 1, 249; In dem Haus ist mir's so heimelig gewesen. 4. 307; Die warme Stube, der heimelige Nachmittag. Gotthelf, Sch. 127, 148; Das ist das wahre Heimelig, wenn der Mensch so von Herzen fühlt, wie wenig er ist, wie groß der Herr ist. 147; Wurde man nach und nach recht gemüthlich und heimelig mit einander. U. 1, 297; Die trauliche Heimeligkeit. 380, 2, 86; Heimelicher wird es mir wohl nirgends werden als hier. 327; Pestalozzi 4, 240; Was von ferne herkommt... lebt gw. nicht ganz heimelig (heimatlich, freundnachbarlich) mit den Leuten. 325; Die Hütte, wo/er sonst so heimelig, so froh/... im Kreis der Seinen oft gesessen. Reithard 20; Da klingt das Horn des Wächters so heimelig vom Thurm/da ladet seine Stimme so gastlich. 49; Es schläft sich da so lind und warm/so wunderheim'lig ein. 23, etc.—Diese Weise verdiente allgemein zu werden, um das gute Wort vor dem Veralten wegen nahe liegender Verwechslung mit 2 zu bewahren. vgl.: 'Die Zecks sind alle h. (2)' H.? .. Was verstehen sie unter h.? ..—'Nun ... es kommt mir mit ihnen vor, wie mit einem zugegrabenen Brunnen oder einem ausgetrockneten Teich. Man kann nicht darüber gehen, ohne daß es Einem immer ist, als könnte da wieder einmal Wasser zum Vorschein kommen.' Wir nennen das un-h.; Sie nennen's h. Worin finden Sie denn, daß diese Familie etwas Verstecktes und Unzuverlässiges hat? etc. Gutzkow R. 2, 61.[36]—(d) (s. c) namentl. schles.: fröhlich, heiter, auch vom Wetter, s. Adelung und Weinhold.

2. versteckt, verborgen gehalten, so daß man Andre nicht davon oder darum wissen lassen, es ihnen verbergen will, vgl. Geheim (2), von welchem erst nhd. Ew. es doch zumal in der älteren Sprache, z. B. in der Bibel, wie Hiob 11, 6; 15, 8; Weish. 2, 22; 1. Kor. 2, 7 etc., und so auch H—keit statt Geheimnis. Math. 13, 35 etc., nicht immer genau geschieden wird: H. (hinter Jemandes Rücken) Etwas thun, treiben; Sich h. davon schleichen; H—e Zusammenkünfte, Verabredungen; Mit h—er Schadenfreude zusehen; H. seufzen, weinen; H. thun, als ob man etwas zu verbergen hätte; H—e Liebschaft, Liebe, Sünde; H—e Orte (die der Wohlstand zu verhüllen gebietet). 1. Sam. 5, 6; Das h—e Gemach (Abtritt). 2. Kön. 10, 27; W[ieland], 5, 256 etc., auch: Der h—e Stuhl. Zinkgräf 1, 249; In Graben, in H—keiten werfen. 3, 75; Rollenhagen Fr. 83 etc.—Führte h. vor Laomedon/die Stuten vor. B[ürger], 161 b etc.—Ebenso versteckt, h., hinterlistig und boshaft gegen grausame Herren ... wie offen, frei, theilnehmend und dienstwillig gegen den leidenden Freund. Burmeister gB 2, 157; Du sollst mein h. Heiligstes noch wissen. Chamisso 4, 56; Die h—e Kunst (der Zauberei). 3, 224; Wo die öffentliche Ventilation aufhören muß, fängt die h—e Machination an. Forster, Br. 2, 135; Freiheit ist die leise Parole h. Verschworener, das laute Feldgeschrei der öffentlich Umwälzenden. G[oethe], 4, 222; Ein heilig, h. Wirken. 15; Ich habe Wurzeln/die sind gar h., /im tiefen Boden/bin ich gegründet. 2, 109; Meine h—e Tücke (vgl. Heimtücke). 30, 344; Empfängt er es nicht offenbar und gewissenhaft, so mag er es h. und gewissenlos ergreifen. 39, 33; Ließ h. und geheimnisvoll achromatische Fernröhre zusammensetzen. 375; Von nun an, will ich, sei nichts H—es/ mehr unter uns. Sch[iller], 369 b.—Jemandes H—keiten entdecken, offenbaren,

verrathen; H—keiten hinter meinem Rücken zu brauen. Alexis. H. 2, 3, 168; Zu meiner Zeit/befliß man sich der H—keit. Hagedorn 3, 92; Die H—keit und das Gepuschele unter der Hand. Immermann, M. 3, 289; Der H—keit (des verborgnen Golds) unmächtigen Bann/kann nur die Hand der Einsicht lösen. Novalis. 1, 69; / Sag'an, wo du sie . . . verbirgst, in welches Ortes verschwiegener H. Sch[iller], 495 b; Ihr Bienen, die ihr knetet/der H—keiten Schloß (Wachs zum Siegeln). Tieck, Cymb. 3, 2; Erfahren in seltnen H—keiten (Zauberkünsten). Schlegel Sh. 6, 102 etc., vgl. Geheimnis L[essing], 10: 291 ff.

Zsstzg. s. 1 c, so auch nam. der Ggstz.: Un-: unbehagliches, banges Grauen erregend: Der schier ihm un-h., gespenstisch erschien. Chamisso 3, 238; Der Nacht un-h., bange Stunden. 4, 148; Mir war schon lang' un-h., ja graulich zu Muthe. 242; Nun fängts mir an, un-h. zu werden. G[oethe], 6, 330; . . . Empfindet ein u—es Grauen. Heine, Verm. 1, 51; Un-h. und starr wie ein Steinbild. Reis, 1, 10; Den u—en Nebel, Haarrauch geheißen. Immermann M., 3, 299; Diese blassen Jungen sind un-h. und brauen Gott weiß was Schlimmes. Laube, Band. 1, 119; Un-h. nennt man Alles, was im Geheimnis, im Verborgnen . . . bleiben sollte und hervorgetreten ist. Schelling, 2, 2, 649 etc.—Das Göttliche zu verhüllen, mit einer gewissen U—keit zu umgeben 658, etc.—Unüblich als Ggstz. von (2), wie es Campe ohne Beleg anführt.

Notes

Notes in brackets have been provided by the translator, David McLintock. Unbracketed notes are those provided by Freud.

1. [The German word translated throughout this essay by the English "uncanny," is "*unheimlich*," literally "unhomely." The English term is not, of course, an exact equivalent of the German one.]

2. [An allusion to the First World War only just concluded.]

3. [In the translation which follows in the text above, a few details, mainly giving the sources of the quotations, have been omitted. For purposes of reference, we reprint in an appendix the entire extract from Sanders's Dictionary exactly as it is given in German in Freud's original paper except that a few minor misprints have been put right. (Cf. p. 253.)]

4. [It may be remarked that the English 'canny', in addition to its more usual meaning of "shrewd," can mean "pleasant," "cosy."]

5. [According to the *Oxford English Dictionary*, a similar ambiguity attaches to the English 'canny', which may mean not only 'cosy' but also 'endowed with occult or magical powers'.]

6. [In the original version of the essay (1919) only, the name "Schleiermacher" was printed here, evidently in error.]

7. Hoffmann's *Sämtliche Werke*, Grisebach Edition, 3. [A translation of "The Sand-Man" is included in *Eight Tales of Hoffmann*, trans. J. M. Cohen (London: Pan Books, 1952).]

8. Frau Dr. Rank has pointed out the association of the name with *"coppella"* = crucible, connecting it with the chemical operations that caused the father's death; and also with *"coppo"* = eye-socket. [Except in the first (1919) edition, this footnote was attached, it seems erroneously, to the first occurrence of the name Coppelius on this page.]

9. In fact, Hoffmann's imaginative treatment of his material has not made such wild confusion of its elements that we cannot reconstruct their original arrangement. In the story of Nathaniel's childhood, the figures of his father and Coppelius represent the two opposites into which the father-imago is split by his ambivalence; whereas the one threatens to blind him—that is, to castrate him— the other, the "good" father, intercedes for his sight. The part of the complex which is most strongly repressed, the death-wish against the "bad" father, finds expression in the death of the "good" father, and Coppelius is made answerable for it. This pair of fathers is represented later, in his student days, by Professor Spalanzani and Coppola the optician. The Professor is in himself a member of the father-series, and Coppola is recognized as identical with Coppelius the lawyer. Just as they used before to work together over the secret brazier, so now they have jointly created the doll Olympia; the Professor is even called the father of Olympia. This double occurrence of activity in common betrays them as divisions of the father-imago: both the mechanician and the optician were the father of Nathaniel (and of Olympia as well). In the frightening scene in childhood, Coppelius, after sparing Nathaniel's eyes, had screwed off his arms and legs as an experiment; that is, he had worked on him as a mechanician would on a doll. This singular feature, which seems quite outside the picture of the Sand-Man, introduces a new castration equivalent; but it also points to the inner identity of Coppelius with his later counterpart, Spalanzani the mechanician, and prepares us for the interpretation of Olympia. This automatic doll can be nothing else than a materialization of Nathaniel's feminine attitude towards his father in his infancy. Her fathers, Spalanzani and Coppola, are, after all, nothing but new editions, reincarnations of Nathaniel's pair of fathers. Spalanzani's otherwise incomprehensible statement that the optician has stolen Nathaniel's eyes (see above) so as to set them in the doll, now becomes significant as supplying evidence of the identity of Olympia and Nathaniel. Olympia is, as it were, a dissociated complex of Nathaniel's which confronts him as a person, and Nathaniel's enslavement to this complex is expressed in his senseless obsessive love for Olympia. We may with justice call love of this kind narcissistic, and we can understand why someone who has fallen victim to it should relinquish the real, external object of his love. The psychological truth of the situation in which the young man, fixated upon his father by his castration complex, becomes incapable of loving a woman, is amply proved by numerous analyses of patients whose story, though less fantastic, is hardly less tragic than that of the student Nathaniel.

Hoffmann was the child of an unhappy marriage. When he was three years old, his father left his small family, and was never united to them again. According to Grisebach, in his biographical introduction to Hoffmann's works, the writer's relation to his father was always a most sensitive subject with him.

10. [Under the rubric "Varia" in one of the issues of the *Internationale Zeitschrift für Psychoanalyse* for 1919 (5, 308), the year in which the present essay was first published, there appears over the initials "S.F." a short note which it is not unreasonable to attribute

to Freud. Its insertion here, though strictly speaking irrelevant, may perhaps be excused. The note is headed: "E. T. A. Hoffmann on the Function of Consciousness" and it proceeds: "In *Die Elixire des Teufels* (Part II, p. 210, in Hesse's edition)—a novel rich in masterly descriptions of pathological mental states—Schönfeld comforts the hero, whose consciousness is temporarily disturbed, with the following words: 'And what do you get out of it? I mean out of the particular mental function which we call consciousness, and which is nothing but the confounded activity of a damned toll-collector—excise-man—deputy-chief customs officer, who has set up his infamous bureau in our top storey and who exclaims, whenever any goods try to get out: "Hi! hi! exports are prohibited . . . they must stay here . . . here, in this country . . ."'"]

11. [This phrase seems to be an echo from Nietzsche (e.g. from the last part of *Also Sprach Zarathustra*). In Chapter III of *Beyond the Pleasure Principle* (1920g), *Standard Ed.*, 18, 22, Freud puts a similar phrase "the perpetual recurrence of the same thing" in quotation marks.]

12. [Cf. *The Interpretation of Dreams, Standard Ed.*, 5, 357.]

13. I believe that when poets complain that two souls dwell in the human breast, and when popular psychologists talk of the splitting of people's egos, what they are thinking of is this division (in the sphere of ego-psychology) between the critical agency and the rest of the ego, and not the antithesis discovered by psychoanalysis between the ego and what is unconscious and repressed. It is true that the distinction between these two antitheses is to some extent effaced by the circumstance that foremost among the things that are rejected by the criticism of the ego are derivatives of the repressed.—[Freud had already discussed this critical agency at length in Section III of his paper on narcissism (1914c), and is was soon to be further expanded into the "ego-ideal" and "super-ego" in chapter XI of his *Group Psychology* (1921c) and Chapter III of *The Ego and the Id* (1923b) respectively.]

14. In Ewers's *Der Student von Prag,* which serves as the starting-point of Rank's study on the "double," the hero has promised his beloved not to kill his antagonist in a duel. But on his way to the duelling-ground he meets his "double," who has already killed his rival.

15. Heine, *Die Götter im Exil.*

16. [Mark Twain, *A Tramp Abroad* (London, 1880), 1, 107.]

17. [Freud had himself reached the age of sixty-two a year earlier, in 1918.]

18. [This was published a year later as *Beyond the Pleasure Principle* (1920g). The various manifestations of the "compulsion to repeat" enumerated here are enlarged upon in chapters II and III of that work. The "compulsion to repeat" had already been described by Freud as a clinical phenomenon, in a technical paper published five years earlier (1914g).]

19. [Schiller's poem based on Herodotus.]

20. "Notes upon a Case of Obsessional Neurosis" (1909d) [*Standard Ed.*, 10, 234].

21. ["The evil eye" in German is '*der böse Blick*', literally 'the evil look'.]

22. [The obsessional patient referred to just above—the "Rat Man" (1909d), *Standard Ed.*, 10, 233f.]

23. Cf. my book *Totem and Taboo* (1912–13), Essay III, "Animism, Magic and the Omnipotence of Thoughts," where the following footnote will be found: "We appear to attribute an 'uncanny' quality to impressions that seek to confirm the omnipotence of thoughts

and the animistic mode of thinking in general, after we have reached a stage at which, in our *judgement,* we have abandoned such beliefs." [*Standard Ed.,* 13, 86.]

24. [This problem figures prominently in *Beyond the Pleasure Principle* (1920*g*), on which Freud was engaged while writing the present essay. See *Standard Ed.,* 18, 44 ff.]

25. [Freud had discussed the individual's attitude to death at greater length in the second part of his paper "Thoughts for the Times on War and Death" (1915*b*).]

26. Cf. *Totem and Taboo* [*Standard Ed.,* 13, 66].

27. [Literally "thrower" (of bad luck), or "one who casts" (the evil eye). Schaeffer's novel was published in 1918.]

28. ["She feels that surely I'm a genius now,—Perhaps the very Devil indeed!" Goethe, *Faust,* Part I (Scene 16), (Bayard Taylor's translation).]

29. [*Die Geschichte von der abgehauenen Hand* ("The Story of the Severed Hand").]

30. [See Section VIII of Freud's analysis of the "Wolf Man" (1918*b*), above p. 101 ff.]

31. [Cf. *The Interpretation of Dreams* (1900*a*), *Standard Ed.,* 5, 399.]

32. [See Freud's paper on "Negation" (1925*h*).]

33. Since the uncanny effect of a "double" also belongs to this same group it is interesting to observe what the effect is of meeting one's own image unbidden and unexpected. Ernst Mach has related two such observations in his *Analyse der Empfindungen* (1900, 3). On the first occasion he was not a little startled when he realized that the face before him was his own. The second time he formed a very unfavourable opinion about the supposed stranger who entered the omnibus, and thought "What a shabby-looking school-master that man is who is getting in!"—I can report a similar adventure. I was sitting alone in my *wagon-lit* compartment when a more than usually violent jolt of the train swung back the door of the adjoining washing-cabinet, and an elderly gentleman in a dressing-gown and a travelling cap came in. I assumed that in leaving the washing-cabinet, which lay between the two compartments, he had taken the wrong direction and come into my compartment by mistake. Jumping up with the intention of putting him right, I at once realized to my dismay that the intruder was nothing but my own reflection in the looking-glass on the open door. I can still recollect that I thoroughly disliked his appearance. Instead, therefore, of being *frightened* by our "doubles," both Mach and I simply failed to recognize them as such. Is it not possible, though, that our dislike of them was a vestigial trace of the archaic reaction which feels the "double" to be something uncanny?

34. [See the discussion of children's fear of the dark in Section V of the third of Freud's *Three Essays* (1905*d*), *Standard Ed.,* 7, 224 n.]

35. [Cf. p. 222.]

36. [Spaced type, here and below, is introduced by Freud.]

THE UNCANNY VALLEY

Masahiro Mori

A Valley in One's Sense of Affinity

The mathematical term *monotonically increasing function* describes a relation in which the function $y = f(x)$ increases continuously with the variable x. For example, as effort x grows, income y increases, or as a car's accelerator is pressed, the car moves faster. This kind of relation is ubiquitous and easily understood. In fact, because such monotonically increasing functions cover most phenomena of everyday life, people may fall under the illusion that they represent all relations. Also attesting to this false impression is the fact that many people struggle through life by persistently pushing without understanding the effectiveness of pulling back. That is why people usually are puzzled when faced with some phenomenon that this function cannot represent.

An example of a function that does not increase continuously is climbing a mountain—the relation between the distance (x) traveled by a hiker toward the summit and the hiker's altitude (y)—owing to the intervening hills and valleys. I have noticed that, in climbing toward the goal of making robots appear like a human, our affinity for them increases until we come to a valley (Figure 3.1), which I call the *uncanny valley*.

Nowadays, industrial robots are increasingly recognized as the driving force behind reductions in factory personnel. However, as is well known, these robots just extend, contract, and rotate their arms; without faces or legs, they do not look human. Their design policy is clearly based on functionality. From this standpoint, the robots must perform functions similar to those of human factory workers, but whether they look similar does not matter. Thus, given their lack of resemblance to human beings, in general, people hardly feel any affinity for them.[1] If we plot the industrial robot on a graph of affinity versus human likeness, it lies near the origin in Figure 3.1.

In contrast, a toy robot's designer may focus more on the robot's appearance than its functions. Consequently, despite its being a sturdy mechanical figure, the robot will start to have a roughly human-looking external form with a face, two arms, two legs, and a torso. Children seem to feel deeply attached to these toy robots. Hence, the toy robot is shown more than halfway up the first hill in Figure 3.1.

Since creating an artificial human is itself one of the objectives of robotics, various efforts are underway to build humanlike robots.[2] For example, a robot's arm may be composed of a metal cylinder with many bolts, but by covering it with skin and adding a bit of fleshy plumpness, we can achieve a more humanlike appearance. As a result, we naturally respond to it with a heightened sense of affinity.

Many of our readers have experience interacting with persons with physical disabilities, and all must have felt sympathy for those missing a hand or leg and wearing a prosthetic limb. Recently, owing to great advances in fabrication technology, we cannot distinguish at a glance a prosthetic hand from a real one. Some models simulate wrinkles, veins, fingernails, and even fingerprints. Though similar to a real hand, the prosthetic hand's color is pinker as if it had just come out of the bath.

One might say that the prosthetic hand has achieved a degree of resemblance to the human form, perhaps on par with false teeth. However, once we realize that the hand that looked real at first sight is actually artificial, we experience an eerie sensation. For example, we could be startled during a handshake by its limp boneless grip together with its texture and coldness. When this happens, we lose our sense of affinity, and the hand becomes uncanny. In mathematical terms, this can be represented by a negative value. Therefore, in this case, the appearance of the prosthetic hand is quite human-like, but the level of affinity is negative, thus placing the hand near the bottom of the valley in Figure 3.1.

I don't think that, on close inspection, a *bunraku* puppet appears similar to a human being. Its realism in terms of size, skin texture, and so on, does not even reach that of a realistic prosthetic hand. But when we enjoy a puppet show in the theater, we are seated at a certain distance from the stage. The puppet's absolute size is ignored, and its total appearance, including hand and eye movements, is close to that of a human being. So, given our tendency as an audience to become absorbed in this form of art, we might feel a high level of affinity for the puppet.

From the preceding discussion, the readers should be able to understand the concept of the uncanny valley. Now let us consider in detail the relation between the uncanny valley and movement.

The Effect of Movement

Movement is fundamental to animals—including human beings—and thus to robots as well. Its presence changes the shape of the uncanny valley graph by amplifying the peaks and valleys (Figure 3.2). For illustration, when an industrial robot is switched off, it is just a greasy machine. But once the robot is programmed to move its gripper like a human hand, we start to feel a certain level of affinity for it. (In this case, the velocity, acceleration, and deceleration must approximate human movement.) Conversely, when a prosthetic hand that is near the bottom of the uncanny valley starts to move, our sensation of eeriness intensifies.

Some readers may know that recent technology has enabled prosthetic hands to extend and contract their fingers automatically. The best commercially available model was developed by a manufacturer in Vienna. To explain how it works, even if a person's forearm is missing, the intention to move the fingers produces a faint current in the arm muscles, which can be detected by an electromyogram. When the prosthetic hand detects the current by means of electrodes on the skin's surface, it amplifies the signal to activate a small motor that moves its fingers. As this myoelectric hand makes movements, it could make healthy people feel uneasy. If someone wearing the hand in a dark place shook a woman's hand with it, the woman would assuredly shriek.

I predict that it is possible to create a safe level of affinity by deliberately pursuing a nonhuman design.

Since the negative effects of movement are apparent even with a prosthetic hand, to build a whole robot would magnify the creepiness. This is just one robot. Imagine a craftsman being awakened suddenly in the dead of the night. He searches downstairs for something among a crowd of mannequins in his workshop. If the mannequins started to move, it would be like a horror story.

Movement-related effects could be observed at the 1970 World Exposition in Osaka, Japan. Plans for the event had prompted the construction of robots with some highly sophisticated designs. For example, one robot had twenty-nine pairs of artificial muscles in the face (the same number as a human being) to make it smile in a humanlike fashion. According to the designer, a smile is a dynamic sequence of facial deformations, and the speed of the deformations is crucial.

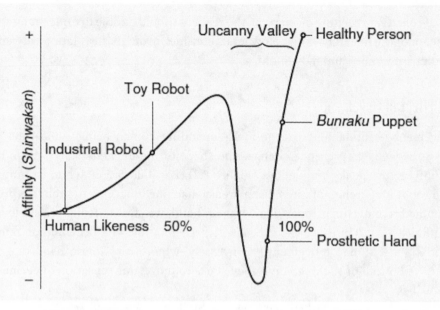

Figure 3.1. The graph depicts the uncanny valley, the proposed relation between the human likeness of an entity, and the perceiver's affinity for it.[3]

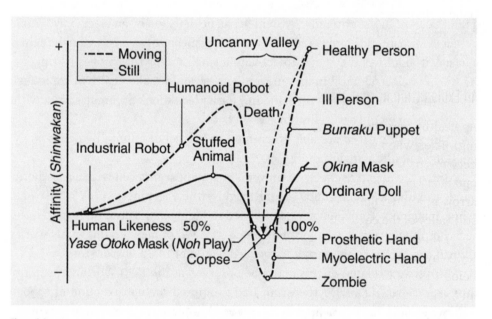

Figure 3.2. The presence of movement steepens the slopes of the uncanny valley. The arrow's path represents the sudden death of a healthy person.[4]

When the speed is cut in half in an attempt to make the robot bring up a smile more slowly, instead of looking happy, its expression turns creepy. This shows how, because of a variation in movement, something that has come to appear close to human—like a robot, puppet, or prosthetic hand—could easily tumble down into the uncanny valley.

Escape by Design

We hope to design and build robots and prosthetic hands that will not fall into the uncanny valley. Thus, because of the risk inherent in trying to increase their degree of human likeness to scale the second peak, I recommend that designers instead take the first peak as their goal, which results in a moderate degree of human likeness and a considerable sense of affinity. In fact, I predict that it is possible to create a safe level of affinity by deliberately pursuing a nonhuman design. I ask designers to ponder this. To illustrate the principle, consider eyeglasses. Eyeglasses do not resemble real eyeballs, but one could say that their design has created a charming pair of new eyes. So we should follow the same principle in designing prosthetic hands. In doing so, instead of pitiful-looking realistic hands, stylish ones would likely become fashionable.

As another example, consider the model of a human hand created by a wood-carver who sculpts statues of Buddhas. The fingers bend freely at the joints. The hand lacks fingerprints, and it retains the natural color of the wood, but its roundness and beautiful curves do not elicit any eerie sensation. Perhaps this wooden hand could also serve as a reference for design.

An Explanation of the Uncanny

As healthy persons, we are represented at the second peak in Figure 3.2 (moving). Then when we die, we are unable to move; the body goes cold, and the face becomes pale. Therefore, our death can be regarded as a movement from the second peak (moving) to the bottom of the uncanny valley (still), as indicated by the arrow's path in Figure 3.2. We might be glad that this arrow leads down into the still valley of the corpse and not the valley animated by the living dead.

I think this descent explains the secret lying deep beneath the uncanny valley. Why were we equipped with this eerie sensation? Is it essential for human beings? I have not yet considered these questions deeply, but I have no doubt it is an integral part of our instinct for self-preservation.[5]

We should begin to build an accurate map of the uncanny valley so that through robotics research we can begin to understand what makes us human. This map is also necessary to create—using nonhuman designs—devices to which people can relate comfortably.

Notes

1. However, industrial robots are considerably closer in appearance to humans than general machinery, especially in their arms.

2. Others believe that the true appeal of robots is their potential to exceed and augment humans.

3. [*Bunraku* is a traditional Japanese form of musical puppet theater dating to the seventeenth century. The puppets range in size but are typically a meter in height, dressed in elaborate costumes, and controlled by three puppeteers obscured only by their black robes.—Trans.]

4. [*Noh* is a traditional Japanese form of musical theater dating to the fourteenth century in which actors commonly wear masks. The *yase otoko* mask bears the face of an emaciated man and represents a ghost from hell. The *okina* mask represents an old man.—Trans.]

5. The sense of eeriness is probably a form of instinct that protects us from proximal, rather than distal, sources of danger. Proximal sources of danger include corpses, members of different species, and other entities we can closely approach. Distal sources of danger include windstorms and floods.

APPROACHING ABJECTION

Julia Kristeva

No Beast is there without glimmer of infinity,
No eye so vile nor abject that brushes not
Against lightning from on high, now tender, now fierce.
　　　　　—Victor Hugo, *La Légende des siècles*

Neither Subject nor Object

There looms, within abjection, one of those violent, dark revolts of being, directed against a threat that seems to emanate from an exorbitant outside or inside, ejected beyond the scope of the possible, the tolerable, the thinkable. It lies there, quite close, but it cannot be assimilated. It beseeches, worries, and fascinates desire, which, nevertheless, does not let itself be seduced. Apprehensive, desire turns aside; sickened, it rejects. A certainty protects it from the shameful—a certainty of which it is proud holds on to it. But simultaneously, just the same, that impetus, that spasm, that leap is drawn toward an elsewhere as tempting as it is condemned. Unflaggingly, like an inescapable boomerang, a vortex of summons and repulsion places the one haunted by it literally beside himself.

When I am beset by abjection, the twisted braid of affects and thoughts I call by such a name does not have, properly speaking, a definable *object*. The abject is not an ob-ject facing me, which I name or imagine. Nor is it an ob-jest, an otherness ceaselessly fleeing in a systematic quest of desire. What is abject is not my correlative, which, providing me with someone or something else as support, would allow me to be more or less detached and autonomous. The abject has only one quality of the object—that of being opposed to *I*. If the object, however, through its opposition, settles me within the fragile texture of a desire for meaning, which, as a matter of fact, makes me ceaselessly and infinitely homologous to it, what is *abject,* on the contrary, the jettisoned object, is radically excluded and draws me toward the place where meaning collapses. A certain "ego" that merged with its master, a superego, has flatly driven it away. It lies outside, beyond the set, and does not seem to agree to the latter's rules of the game. And yet, from its place of banishment, the abject does not cease challenging its master. Without a sign (for him), it beseeches a discharge, a convulsion, a crying out. To each ego its object, to each superego its abject. It is not the white expanse or slack boredom of repression, not the translations and transformations of desire that wrench bodies, nights, and discourse; rather it is a brutish suffering that "I" puts up with, sublime and devastated, for "I" deposits it to the father's account [*verse au père—père-version*]: I endure it, for I imagine that such is the desire of the other. A massive and sudden emergence of uncanniness, which, familiar as it might have been in an opaque and forgotten life, now harries me as radically separate, loathsome. Not me. Not that. But not nothing, either. A "something" that I do not recognize as a thing. A weight of meaninglessness, about which there is nothing insignificant, and which crushes me. On the edge of nonexistence and hallucination, of a reality that, if I acknowledge it, annihilates me. There, abject and abjection are my safeguards. The primers of my culture.

The Improper/Unclean

Loathing an item of food, a piece of filth, waste, or dung. The spasms and vomiting that protect me. The repugnance, the retching that thrusts me to the side and turns me away from defilement, sewage, and muck. The shame of compromise, of being in the middle of treachery. The fascinated start that leads me toward and separates me from them.

Food loathing is perhaps the most elementary and most archaic form of abjection. When the eyes see or the lips touch that skin on the surface of milk—harmless, thin as a sheet of cigarette paper, pitiful as a nail paring—I experience a gagging sensation and, still farther down, spasms in the stomach, the belly; and all the organs shrivel up the body, provoke tears and bile, increase heartbeat, cause forehead and hands to perspire. Along with sight-clouding dizziness, *nausea* makes me balk at that milk cream, separates me from the mother and father who proffer it. "I" want none of that element, sign of their desire; "I" do not want to listen, "I" do not assimilate it, "I" expel it. But since the food is not an "other" for "me," who am only in their desire, I expel *myself,* I spit *myself* out, I abject *myself* within the same motion through which "I" claim to establish *myself.* That detail, perhaps an insignificant one, but one that they ferret out, emphasize, evaluate, that trifle turns me inside out, guts sprawling; it is thus that *they* see that "I" am in the process of becoming an other at the expense of my own death. During that course in which "I" become, I give birth to myself amid the violence of sobs, of vomit. Mute protest of the symptom, shattering violence of a convulsion that, to be sure, is inscribed in a symbolic system, but in which, without either wanting or being able to become integrated in order to answer to it, it reacts, it abreacts. It abjects.

The corpse (or cadaver: *cadere,* to fall), that which has irremediably come a cropper, is cesspool, and death; it upsets even more violently the one who confronts it as fragile and fallacious chance. A wound with blood and pus, or the sickly, acrid smell of sweat, of decay, does not *signify* death. In the presence of signified death—a flat encephalograph, for instance—I would understand, react, or accept. No, as in true theater, without makeup or masks, refuse and corpses *show me* what I permanently thrust aside in order to live. These body fluids, this defilement, this shit are what life withstands, hardly and with difficulty, on the part of death. There, I am at the border of my condition as a living being. My body extricates itself, as being alive, from that border. Such wastes drop so that I might live, until, from loss to loss, nothing remains in me and my entire body falls beyond the limit— *cadere,* cadaver. If dung signifies the other side of the border, the place where I am not and which permits me to be, the corpse, the most sickening of wastes, is a border that has encroached upon everything. It is no longer I who expel, "I" is expelled. The border has become an object. How can I be without border? That elsewhere that I imagine beyond the present, or that I hallucinate so that I might, in a present time, speak to you, conceive of you—it is now here, jetted, abjected, into "my" world. Deprived of world, therefore, I *fall in a faint.* In that compelling, raw, insolent thing in the morgue's full sunlight, in that thing that no longer matches and therefore no longer signifies anything, I behold the breaking down of a world that has erased its borders: fainting away. The corpse, seen without God and outside of science, is the utmost of abjection. It is death infecting life. Abject. It is something rejected from which one does not part, from which one does not protect oneself as from an object. Imaginary uncanniness and real threat, it beckons to us and ends up engulfing us.

It is thus not lack of cleanliness or health that causes abjection but what disturbs identity, system, order. What does not respect borders, positions, rules. The in-between, the ambiguous, the composite. The traitor, the liar, the criminal with a good conscience, the shameless rapist, the killer who claims he is a savior. . . . Any crime, because it draws attention to the fragility of the law, is abject, but premeditated crime, cunning murder, hypocritical revenge are even more so because they heighten the display of such fragility. He who denies morality is not abject; there can be grandeur in amorality and even in crime that flaunts its disrespect for the law—rebellious, liberating, and suicidal crime. Abjection, on the other hand, is immoral, sinister, scheming, and shady: a terror that dissembles, a hatred that smiles, a passion that uses the body for barter instead of inflaming it, a debtor who sells you up, a friend who stabs you. . . .

In the dark halls of the museum that is now what remains of Auschwitz, I see a heap of children's shoes, or something like that, something I have already seen elsewhere, under a Christmas tree, for instance, dolls I believe. The abjection of Nazi crime reaches its apex when death, which, in any case, kills me, interferes with what, in my living universe, is supposed to save me from death: childhood, science, among other things.

The Abjection Self

If it be true that the abject simultaneously beseeches and pulverizes the subject, one can understand that it is experienced at the peak of its strength when that subject, weary of fruitless attempts to identify with something on the outside, finds the impossible within; when it finds that the impossible constitutes its very *being*, that it *is* none other than abject. The abjection of self would be the culminating form of that experience of the subject to which it is revealed that all its objects are based merely on the inaugural *loss* that laid the foundations of its own being. There is nothing like the abjection of self to show that all abjection is in fact recognition of the *want* on which any being, meaning, language, or desire is founded. One always passes too quickly over this word "want," and today psychoanalysts are finally taking into account only its more or less fetishized product, the "object of want." But if one imagines (and imagine one must, for it is the working of imagination whose foundations are being laid here) the experience of *want* itself as logically preliminary to being and object—to the being of the object—then one understands that abjection, and even more so abjection of self, is its only signified. Its signifier, then, is none but literature. Mystical Christendom turned this abjection of self into the ultimate proof of humility before God, witness Elizabeth of Hungary who "though a great princess, delighted in nothing so much as in abasing herself."[1]

The question remains as to the ordeal, a secular one this time, that abjection can constitute for someone who, in what is termed knowledge of castration, turning away from perverse dodges, presents himself with his own body and ego as the most precious non-objects; they are no longer seen in their own right but forfeited, abject. The termination of analysis can lead us there, as we shall see. Such are the pangs and delights of masochism.

Essentially different from "uncanniness," more violent, too, abjection is elaborated through a failure to recognize its kin; nothing is familiar, not even the shadow of a memory. I imagine a child who has swallowed up his parents too soon, who frightens himself on that account, "all by himself," and, to save himself, rejects and throws up everything that is given to him—all gifts, all objects. He has, he could have, a sense of the abject. Even before things for him *are*—hence before they are signifiable—he drives them out, dominated by drive as he is, and constitutes his own territory, edged by the abject. A sacred configuration. Fear cements his compound, conjoined to another world, thrown up, driven out, forfeited. What he has swallowed up instead of maternal love is an emptiness, or rather a maternal hatred without a word for the words of the father; that is what he tries to cleanse himself of, tirelessly. What solace does he come upon within such loathing? Perhaps a father, existing but unsettled, loving but unsteady, merely an apparition but an apparition that remains. Without him the holy brat would probably have no sense of the sacred; a blank subject, he would remain, discomfited, at the dump for non-objects that are always forfeited, from which, on the contrary, fortified by abjection, he tries to extricate himself. For he is not mad, he through whom the abject exists. Out of the daze that has petrified him before the untouchable, impossible, absent body of the mother, a daze that has cut off his impulses from their objects, that is, from their representations, out of such daze he causes, along with loathing, one word to crop up—fear. The phobic has no other object than the abject. But that word, "fear"—a fluid haze, an elusive clamminess— no sooner has it cropped up than it shades off like a mirage and permeates all words of the language with nonexistence, with a hallucinatory, ghostly glimmer. Thus, fear having been bracketed, discourse will seem tenable only if it ceaselessly confront that otherness, a burden both repellent and repelled, a deep well of memory that is unapproachable and intimate: the abject.

Beyond the Unconscious

Put another way, it means that there are lives not sustained by *desire,* as desire is always for objects. Such lives are based on *exclusion.* They are clearly distinguishable from those understood as neurotic or psychotic, articulated by *negation* and its modalities, *transgression, denial,* and *repudiation.* Their dynamics challenges the theory of the unconscious, seeing that the latter is dependent upon a dialectic of negativity.

The theory of the unconscious, as is well known, presupposes a repression of contents (affects and presentations) that, thereby, do not have access to consciousness but effect within the subject modifications, either of speech (parapraxes, etc.), or of the body (symptoms), or both (hallucinations, etc.). As correlative to the notion of *repression,* Freud put forward that of *denial* as a means of figuring out neurosis, that of *rejection (repudiation)* as a means of situating psychosis. The asymmetry of the two repressions becomes more marked owing to denial's bearing on the object whereas repudiation affects desire itself (Lacan, in perfect keeping with Freud's thought, interprets that as "repudiation of the Name of the Father").

Yet, facing the ab-ject and more specifically phobia and the splitting of the ego (a point I shall return to), one might ask if those articulations of negativity germane to the unconscious (inherited by Freud from philosophy and psychology) have not become inoperative. The "unconscious" contents remain here *excluded* but in strange fashion: not radically enough to allow for a secure differentiation between subject and object, and yet clearly enough for a defensive *position* to be established—one that implies a refusal but also a sublimating elaboration. As if the fundamental opposition were between I and Other or, in more archaic fashion, between Inside and Outside. As if such an opposition subsumed the one between Conscious and Unconscious, elaborated on the basis of neuroses.

Owing to the ambiguous opposition I/Other, Inside/Outside—an opposition that is vigorous but pervious, violent but uncertain—there are contents, "normally" unconscious in neurotics, that become explicit if not conscious in "borderline" patients' speeches and behavior. Such contents are often openly manifested through symbolic practices, without by the same token being integrated into the judging consciousness of those particular subjects. Since they make the conscious/unconscious distinction irrelevant, borderline subjects and their speech constitute propitious ground for a sublimating discourse ("aesthetic" or "mystical," etc.), rather than a scientific or rationalist one.

An Exile Who Asks, "Where?"

The one by whom the abject exists is thus a *deject* who places (himself), *separates* (himself), situates (himself), and therefore *strays* instead of getting his bearings, desiring, belonging, or refusing. Situationist in a sense, and not without laughter—since laughing is a way of placing or displacing abjection. Necessarily dichotomous, somewhat Manichaean, he divides, excludes, and without, properly speaking, wishing to know his abjections is not at all unaware of them. Often, moreover, he includes himself among them, thus casting within himself the scalpel that carries out his separations.

Instead of sounding himself as to his "being," he does so concerning his place: "*Where* am I?" instead of "*Who* am I?" For the space that engrosses the deject, the excluded, is never *one*, nor *homogeneous*, nor *totalizable*, but essentially divisible, foldable, and catastrophic. A deviser of territories, languages, works, the *deject* never stops demarcating his universe whose fluid confines—for they are constituted of a non-object, the abject—constantly question his solidity and impel him to start afresh. A tireless builder, the deject is in short a *stray*. He is on a journey, during the night, the end of which keeps receding. He has a sense of the danger, of the loss that the pseudo-object attracting him represents for him, but he cannot help taking the risk at the very moment he sets himself apart. And the more he strays, the more he is saved.

Time: Forgetfulness and Thunder

For it is out of such straying on excluded ground that he draws his jouissance. The abject from which he does not cease separating is for him, in short, a *land of oblivion* that is constantly remembered. Once upon blotted-out time, the abject must have been a magnetized pole of covetousness. But the ashes of oblivion now serve as a screen and reflect aversion, repugnance. The clean and proper (in the sense of incorporated and incorporable) becomes filthy, the sought-after turns into the banished, fascination into shame. Then, forgotten time crops up suddenly and condenses into a flash of lightning an operation that, if it were thought out, would involve bringing together the two opposite terms but, on account of that flash, is discharged like thunder. The time of abjection is double: a time of oblivion and thunder, of veiled infinity and the moment when revelation bursts forth.

Jouissance and Affect

Jouissance, in short. For the stray considers himself as equivalent to a Third Party. He secures the latter's judgment, he acts on the strength of its power in order to condemn, he grounds himself on its law to tear the veil of oblivion but also to set up its object as inoperative. As jettisoned. Parachuted by the Other. A ternary structure, if you wish, held in keystone position by the Other, but a "structure" that is skewed, a topology of catastrophe. For, having provided itself with an *alter ego,* the Other no longer has a grip on the three apices of the triangle where subjective homogeneity resides; and so, it jettisons the object into an abominable real, inaccessible except through jouissance. It follows that jouissance alone causes the abject to exist as such. One does not know it, one does not desire it, one joys in it [*on en jouit*]. Violently and painfully. A passion. And, as in jouissance where the object of desire, known as object *a* [in Lacan's terminology], bursts with the shattered mirror where the ego gives up its image in order to contemplate itself in the Other, there is nothing either objective or objectal to the abject. It is simply a frontier, a repulsive gift that the Other, having become *alter ego,* drops so that "I" does not disappear in it but finds, in that sublime alienation, a forfeited existence. Hence a jouissance in which the subject is swallowed up but in which the Other, in return, keeps the subject from foundering by making it repugnant. One thus understands why so many victims of the abject are its fascinated victims—if not its submissive and willing ones.

We may call it a border; abjection is above all ambiguity. Because, while releasing a hold, it does not radically cut off the subject from what threatens it—on the contrary, abjection acknowledges it to be in perpetual danger. But also because abjection itself is a composite of judgment and affect, of condemnation and yearning, of signs and drives. Abjection preserves what existed in the archaism of pre-objectal relationship, in the immemorial violence with which a body becomes separated from another body in order to be—maintaining that night in which the outline of the signified thing vanishes and where only the imponderable affect is carried out. To be sure, if I am affected by what does not yet appear to me as a thing, it is because laws, connections, and even structures of meaning govern and condition me. That order, that glance, that voice, that gesture, which enact the law for my frightened body, constitute and bring about an effect and not yet a sign. I speak to it in vain in order to exclude it from what will no longer be, for myself, a world that can be assimilated. Obviously, *I am* only *like* someone else: mimetic logic of the advent of the ego, objects, and signs. But when I *seek* (myself), *lose* (myself), or experience *jouissance*—then "I" is *heterogeneous*. Discomfort, unease, dizziness stemming from an ambiguity that, through the violence of a revolt *against,* demarcates a space out of which signs and objects arise. Thus braided, woven, ambivalent, a heterogeneous flux marks out a territory that I can call my own Because the Other, having dwelt in me as *alter* ego, points it out to me through loathing.

This means once more that the heterogeneous flow, which portions the abject and sends back abjection, already dwells in a human animal that has been highly altered. I experience abjection only if an Other has settled in place and stead of what will be "me." Not at all an other with whom I identify and incorporate, but an Other who precedes and possesses me, and through such possession causes me to be. A possession previous to my advent: a being-there of the symbolic that a father might or might not embody. Significance is indeed inherent in the human body.

At the Limit of Primal Repression

If, on account of that Other, a space becomes demarcated, separating the abject from what will be a subject and its objects, it is because a repression that one might call "primal" has been effected prior to the springing forth of the ego, of its objects and representations. The latter, in turn, as they depend on another repression, the "secondary" one, arrive only *a posteriori* on an enigmatic foundation that has already been marked off; its return, in a phobic, obsessional, psychotic guise, or more generally and in more imaginary fashion in the shape of *abjection*, notifies us of the limits of the human universe.

On such limits and at the limit one could say that there is no unconscious, which is elaborated when representations and affects (whether or not tied to representations) shape a logic. Here, on the contrary, consciousness has not assumed its rights and transformed into signifiers those fluid demarcations of yet unstable territories where an "I" that is taking shape is ceaselessly straying. We are no longer within the sphere of the unconscious but at the limit of primal repression that, nevertheless, has discovered an intrinsically corporeal and already signify-ing brand, symptom, and sign: repugnance, disgust, abjection. There is an effer-vescence of object and sign—not of desire but of intolerable significance; they tumble over into non-sense or the impossible real, but they appear even so in spite of "myself" (which is not) as abjection.

Premises of the Sign, Linings of the Sublime

Let us pause a while at this juncture. If the abject is already a wellspring of sign for a non-object, on the edges of primal repression, one can understand its skirt-ing the somatic symptom on the one hand and sublimation on the other. The *symptom*: a language that gives up, a structure within the body, a non-assimilable alien, a monster, a tumor, a cancer that the listening devices of the unconscious do not hear, for its strayed subject is huddled outside the paths of desire. *Subli-mation,* on the contrary, is nothing else than the possibility of naming the pre-nominal, the pre-objectal, which are in fact only a trans-nominal, a trans-objectal. In the symptom, the abject permeates me, I become abject. Through sublimation, I keep it under control. The abject is edged with the sublime. It is not the same moment on the journey, but the same subject and speech bring them into being.

For the sublime has no object either. When the starry sky, a vista of open seas or a stained glass window shedding purple beams fascinate me, there is a cluster of meaning, of colors, of words, of caresses, there are light touches, scents, sighs, cadences that arise, shroud me, carry me away, and sweep me beyond the things that I see, hear, or think. The "sublime" object dissolves in the raptures of a bottomless memory. It is such a memory, which, from stopping point to stop-ping point, remembrance to remembrance, love to love, transfers that object to the refulgent point of the dazzlement in which I stray in order to be. As soon as I perceive it, as soon as I name it, the sublime triggers—it has always already trig-gered—a spree of perceptions and words that expands memory boundlessly. I then forget the point of departure and find myself removed to a secondary universe, set off from the one where "I" am—delight and loss. Not at all short of but always with and through perception and words, the sublime is a *something added* that expands us, overstrains us, and causes us to be both *here,* as dejects, and *there,* as others and sparkling. A divergence, an impossible bounding. Everything missed, joy—fascination.

Before the Beginning: Separation

The abject might then appear as the most *fragile* (from a synchronic point of view), the most *archaic* (from a diachronic one) sublimation of an "object" still inseparable from drives. The abject is that pseudo-object that is made up *before* but appears only *within* the gaps of secondary repression. *The abject would thus be the "object" of primal repression.*

But what is primal repression? Let us call it the ability of the speaking being, always already haunted by the Other, to divide, reject, repeat. Without *one* division, *one* separation, *one* subject/object having been constituted (not yet, or no longer yet). Why? Perhaps because of maternal anguish, unable to be satiated within the encompassing symbolic.

The abject confronts us, on the one hand, with those fragile states where man strays on the territories of *animal*. Thus, by way of abjection, primitive societies have marked out a precise area of their culture in order to remove it from the threatening world of animals or animalism, which were imagined as representatives of sex and murder.

The abject confronts us, on the other hand, and this time within our personal archeology, with our earliest attempts to release the hold of *maternal* entity even before ex-isting outside of her, thanks to the autonomy of language. It is a violent, clumsy breaking away, with the constant risk of falling back under the sway of a power as securing as it is stifling. The difficulty a mother has in acknowledging (or being acknowledged by) the symbolic realm—in other words, the problem she has with the phallus that her father or her husband stands for— is not such as to help the future subject leave the natural mansion. The child can serve its mother as token of her own authentication; there is, however, hardly any reason for her to serve as go-between for it to become autonomous and authentic in its turn. In such close combat, the symbolic light that a third party, eventually the father, can contribute helps the future subject, the more so if it happens to be endowed with a robust supply of drive energy, in pursuing a reluctant struggle against what, having been the mother, will turn into an abject. Repelling, rejecting; repelling itself, rejecting itself. Ab-jecting.

In this struggle, which fashions the human being, the *mimesis,* by means of which he becomes homologous to another in order to become himself, is in short logically and chronologically secondary. Even before being *like,* "I" am not but do *separate, reject, ab-ject.* Abjection, with a meaning broadened to take in subjective diachrony, *is a precondition of narcissism.* It is coexistent with it and causes it to be permanently brittle. The more or less beautiful image in which I behold or recognize myself rests upon an abjection that sunders it as soon as repression, the constant watchman, is relaxed.

The "Chora," Receptacle of Narcissism

Let us enter, for a moment, into that Freudian aporia called primal repression. Curious primacy, where what is repressed cannot really be held down, and where what represses always already borrows its strength and authority from what is apparently very secondary: language. Let us therefore not speak of primacy but of the instability of the symbolic function in its most significant aspect—the prohibition placed on the maternal body (as a defense against autoeroticism and incest taboo). Here, drives hold sway and constitute a strange space that I shall name, after Plato (*Timeus,* 48–53), a *chora,* a receptacle.

For the benefit of the ego or its detriment, drives, whether life drives or death drives, serve to correlate that "not yet" ego with an "object" in order to establish both of them. Such a process, while dichotomous (inside/outside, ego/not ego) and repetitive, has nevertheless something centripetal about it: it aims to settle the ego as center of a solar system of objects. If, by dint of coming back towards the center, the drive's motion should eventually become centrifugal, hence fasten on the Other and come into being as sign so as to produce meaning—that is, literally speaking, exorbitant.

But from that moment on, while I recognize my image as sign and change in order to signify, another economy is instituted. The sign represses the *chora* and its eternal return. Desire alone will henceforth be witness to that "primal" pulsation. But desire ex-patriates the *ego* toward an *other* subject and accepts the exactness of the ego only as narcissistic. Narcissism then appears as a regression to a position set back from the other, a return to a self-contemplative, conservative, self-sufficient haven. Actually, such narcissism never is the wrinkleless image of the Greek youth in a quiet fountain. The conflicts of drives muddle its bed, cloud its water, and bring forth everything that, by not becoming integrated with a given system of signs, is abjection for it.

Abjection is therefore a kind of *narcissistic crisis*: it is witness to the ephemeral aspect of the state called "narcissism" with reproachful jealousy, heaven knows why; what is more, abjection gives narcissism (the thing and the concept) its classification as "seeming."

Nevertheless, it is enough that a prohibition, which can be a superego, block the desire craving an other—or that this other, as its role demands, not fulfill it—for desire and its signifiers to turn back toward the "same," thus clouding the waters of Narcissus. It is precisely at the moment of narcissistic perturbation (all things considered, the permanent state of the speaking being, if he would only hear himself speak) that secondary repression, with its reserve of symbolic means, attempts to transfer to its own account, which has thus been overdrawn, the resources of primal repression. The archaic economy is brought into full light of day, signified, verbalized. Its strategies (rejecting, separating, repeating/abjecting) hence find a symbolic existence, and the very logic of the symbolic—arguments, demonstrations, proofs, etc.—must conform to it. It is then that the object ceases to be circumscribed, reasoned with, thrust aside: it appears as abject.

Two seemingly contradictory causes bring about the narcissistic crisis that provides, along with its truth, a view of the abject. *Too much strictness on the part of the Other,* confused with the One and the Law. The *lapse of the Other,* which shows through the breakdown of objects of desire. In both instances, the abject appears in order to uphold "I" within the Other. The abject is the violence of mourning for an "object" that has always already been lost. The abject shatters the wall of repression and its judgments. It takes the ego back to its source on the abominable limits from which, in order to be, the ego has broken away—it assigns it a source in the non-ego, drive, and death. Abjection is a resurrection that has gone through death (of the ego). It is an alchemy that transforms death drive into a start of life, of new significance.

Perverse or Artistic

The abject is related to perversion. The sense of abjection that I experience is anchored in the superego. The abject is perverse because it neither gives up nor assumes a prohibition, a rule, or a law; but turns them aside, misleads, corrupts; uses them, takes advantage of them, the better to deny them. It kills in the name of life—a progressive despot; it lives at the behest of death—an operator in genetic experimentations; it curbs the other's suffering for its own profit—a cynic (and a psychoanalyst); it establishes narcissistic power while pretending to reveal the abyss—an artist who practices his art as a "business." Corruption is its most common, most obvious appearance. That is the socialized appearance of the abject.

An unshakable adherence to Prohibition and Law is necessary if that perverse interspace of abjection is to be hemmed in and thrust aside. Religion, Morality, Law. Obviously always arbitrary, more or less; unfailingly oppressive, rather more than less; laboriously prevailing, more and more so.

Contemporary literature does not take their place. Rather, it seems to be written out of the untenable aspects of perverse or superego positions. It acknowledges the impossibility of Religion, Morality, and Law—their power play, their necessary and absurd seeming. Like perversion, it takes advantage of them, gets round them, and makes sport of them. Nevertheless, it maintains a distance where the abject is concerned. The writer, fascinated by the abject, imagines its logic, projects himself into it, introjects it, and as a consequence perverts language—style and content. But on the other hand, as the sense of abjection is both the abject's judge and accomplice, this is also true of the literature that confronts it. One might thus say that with such a literature there takes place a crossing over of the dichotomous categories of Pure and Impure, Prohibition and Sin, Morality and Immorality.

For the subject firmly settled in its superego, a writing of this sort is necessarily implicated in the interspace that characterizes perversion; and for that reason, it gives rises in turn to abjection. And yet, such texts call for a softening of the superego. Writing them implies an ability to imagine the abject, that is, to

see oneself in its place and to thrust it aside only by means of the displacements of verbal play. It is only after his death, eventually, that the writer of abjection will escape his condition of waste, reject, abject. Then, he will either sink
into oblivion or attain the rank of incommensurate ideal. Death would thus be
the chief curator of our imaginary museum; it would protect us in the last resort
from the abjection that contemporary literature claims to expend while uttering
it. Such a protection, which gives its quietus to abjection, but also perhaps to the
bothersome, incandescent stake of the literary phenomenon itself, which, raised
to the status of the sacred, is severed from its specificity. Death thus keeps house
in our contemporary universe. By purifying (us from) literature, it establishes our
secular religion.

As Abjection—So the Sacred

Abjection accompanies all religious structurings and reappears, to be worked out
in a new guise, at the time of their collapse. Several structurations of abjection
should be distinguished, each one determining a specific form of the sacred.

Abjection appears as a rite of defilement and pollution in the paganism that
accompanies societies with a dominant or surviving matrilinear character. It takes
on the form of the *exclusion* of a substance (nutritive or linked to sexuality), the
execution of which coincides with the sacred since it sets it up.

Abjection persists as *exclusion* or taboo (dietary or other) in monotheistic
religions, Judaism in particular, but drifts over to more "secondary" forms such
as *transgression* (of the Law) within the same monotheistic economy. It finally
encounters, with Christian sin, a dialectic elaboration, as it becomes integrated
in the Christian Word as a threatening otherness—but always nameable, always
totalizeable.

The various means of *purifying* the abject—the various catharses—make up
the history of religions, and end up with that catharsis par excellence called art,
both on the far and near side of religion. Seen from that standpoint, the artistic
experience, which is rooted in the abject it utters and by the same token purifies,
appears as the essential component of religiosity. That is perhaps why it is destined
to survive the collapse of the historical forms of religions.

Note

1. Francis de Sales, *Introduction to a Devout Life,* trans. Thomas S. Kepler (New York:
World, 1952), 125. [Modified to conform to the French text, which reads "l'abjection de
soy-mesme." –Trans.]

AN INTRODUCTION TO
THE AMERICAN HORROR FILM

Robin Wood

I. Repression, the Other, the Monster

The most significant development—in film criticism, and in progressive ideas generally—of the past few decades has clearly been the increasing confluence of Marx and Freud, or more precisely of the traditions of thought arising from them: the recognition that social revolution and sexual revolution are inseparably linked and necessary to each other. From Marx we derive our awareness of the dominant ideology—the ideology of bourgeois capitalism—as an insidious all-pervasive force capable of concealment behind the most protean disguises, and the necessity of exposing its operation whenever and wherever possible. It is psychoanalytic theory that has provided (without Freud's awareness of the full revolutionary potential of what he was unleashing) the most effective means of examining the ways in which that ideology is transmitted and perpetuated, centrally through the institutionalization of the patriarchal nuclear family. The battle for liberation, the battle against oppression (whether economic, legal or ideological), gains enormous extra significance through the addition of that term *patriarchal*, since patriarchy long *pre*cedes and far *ex*ceeds what we call capitalism. It is here, through the medium of psychoanalytic theory, that Feminism and Gay Liberation join forces with Marxism in their progress toward a common aim: the overthrow of patriarchal capitalist ideology and the structures and institutions that sustain it and are sustained by it.

Psychoanalytic theory, like Marxism, now provides various models, inflecting basic premises in significantly different ways. It is not certain that the Lacanian model promoted by (among others) *Screen* magazine is the most satisfactory.[1] On the evidence so far it seems certainly not the most potentially *effective,* leading either to paralysis or to a new academicism perhaps more sterile than the old, and driving its students into monastic cells rather than the streets. I want to indicate briefly a possible alternative model, developed out of Freud by Marcuse and given definitive formulation in a recent book by Gad Horowitz, *Repression:*[2] a model that enables us to connect theory closely with the ways we actually think and feel and conduct our lives—those daily practicalities from which the theorizing of *Screen* seems often so remote. The book's subtitle is *Basic and Surplus Repression in Psychoanalytic Theory: Freud, Reich, Marcuse.* It is the crucial distinction between basic and surplus repression that is so useful in relation to direct political militancy and so suggestive in relation to the reading of our cultural artifacts (among them our horror films), and through them, our culture itself. Horowitz has devoted a dense, often difficult and closely argued book to the subject; in the space at my disposal I can offer only a bald and simplified account.

Basic repression is universal, necessary, and inescapable. It is what makes possible our development from an uncoordinated animal capable of little beyond screaming and convulsions into a human being; it is bound up with the ability to accept the postponement of gratification, with the development of our thought and memory processes, of our capacity for self-control, of our recognition of and consideration for other people. Surplus repression, on the other hand, is specific to a particular culture and is the process whereby people are conditioned from earliest infancy to take on predetermined roles within that culture. In terms of our own culture, then, *basic* repression makes us distinctively human, capable of directing our own lives and coexisting with others; *surplus* repression makes us (if it works) into monogamous heterosexual bourgeois patriarchal capitalists ("bourgeois" even if we are born into the proletariat, for we are talking here of ideological norms rather than material status). *If* it works: if it doesn't, the result is either a neurotic or a revolutionary (or both), and if revolutionaries account for a very small proportion of the population, neurotics account for a very large one. Hardly surprising. All known existing societies are to some degree surplus-repressive, but the degree varies enormously, from the trivial to the overwhelming. Freud saw long ago that our own civilization had reached a point where the burden of repression was becoming all-but-insupportable, an insight Horowitz (following Marcuse) brilliantly relates to Marx's theory of alienated labor: the most immediately obvious characteristics of life in our culture are frustration, dissatisfaction, anxiety, greed, possessiveness, jealousy, neuroticism: no more than what psychoanalytic theory shows to be the logical product of patriarchal capitalism. What needs to be stressed is that the kinds of challenges now being made to the system—and the kinds of perceptions and recognitions that structure those challenges and give them impetus—become possible (become in the literal sense *thinkable*) only in the circumstances of the system's imminent disintegration. While the system retained sufficient conviction, credibility, and show of coherence to suppress them, it did so. The struggle for liberation is not utopian but a practical necessity.

Given that our culture offers an extreme example of surplus repressiveness, one can ask what, exactly, in the interests of alienated labor and the patriarchal family, is repressed. One needs here both to distinguish between the concepts of *re*pression and *op*pression and to suggest the continuity between them. In psychoanalytic terms, what is *re*pressed is not accessible to the conscious mind (except through analysis or, if one can penetrate their disguises, in dreams). We may also not be conscious of ways in which we are *op*pressed, but it is much easier to become so: we are oppressed by something "out there." One might perhaps define repression as fully internalized Oppression (while reminding ourselves that all the groundwork of repression is laid in infancy), thereby suggesting both the difference and the connection. A specific example may make this clearer: our social structure demands the *re*pression of the bisexuality that psychoanalysis shows to be the natural heritage of every human individual, and the *op*pression of homosexuals: obviously, the two phenomena are not identical, but equally obviously they are closely connected. What escapes *re*pression has to be dealt with by *op*pression.

What, then, is repressed in our culture? First, sexual energy itself, together with its possible successful sublimation into nonsexual creativity—sexuality being the source of creative energy in general. The "ideal" inhabitant of our culture will be the individual whose sexuality is sufficiently fulfilled by the monogamous heterosexual union necessary for the reproduction of future ideal inhabitants, and whose sublimated sexuality (creativity) is sufficiently fulfilled in the totally noncreative and nonfulfilling labor (whether in factory or office) to which our society dooms the overwhelming majority of its members. The "ideal," in other words, is as close as possible to an automaton in whom both sexual and intellectual energy has been reduced to a minimum. Otherwise, the "ideal" is a contradiction in terms and a logical impossibility, hence the *necessary* frustration, anxiety, and neuroticism of our culture.

Secondly, bisexuality—which should be understood both literally (in terms of possible sexual orientation and practice) and in a more general sense. Bisexuality represents the most obvious and direct affront to the principle of monogamy and its supportive romantic myth of "the one right person"; the homosexual impulse in both men and women represents the most obvious threat to the "norm" of sexuality as reproductive and restricted by the "ideal" of family. But more generally we confront here the whole edifice of clear-cut sexual differentiation that bourgeois-capitalist ideology erects on the flimsy and dubious foundations of biological difference: the social norms of masculinity and femininity, the social definitions of manliness and womanliness, the whole vast apparatus of oppressive male/female myths, the systematic repression from infancy ("blue for a boy . . .") of the man's "femininity" and the woman's "masculinity," in the interests of forming human beings for specific predetermined social roles.

Thirdly, the particularly severe repression of female sexuality/creativity; the attribution to the female of passivity, her preparation for her subordinate and dependent role in our culture. Clearly, a crucial aspect of the repression of bisexuality is the denial to women of drives culturally associated with masculinity: activeness, aggression, self-assertion, organizational power, creativity itself.

Fourthly—and fundamentally—the repression of the sexuality of children, taking different forms from infancy, through "latency" and puberty, and into adolescence—the process moving, indeed, from *re*pression to *op*pression, from the denial of the infant's nature as sexual being to the veto on the expression of sexuality before marriage.

None of these forms of repression is necessary for the existence of civilization in some form (i.e., none is "basic")—for the development of our humanness. Indeed, they impose limitations and restrictions on that development, stunting human potential. All are the outcome of the requirements of the particular, surplus-repressive civilization in which we live.

Closely linked to the concept of repression—indeed, truly inseparable from it—is another concept necessary to an understanding of ideology on which psychoanalysis throws much light, the concept of "the Other": that which bourgeois ideology cannot recognize or accept but must deal with (as Barthes suggests in *Mythologies*) in one of two ways: either by rejecting and if possible annihilating it, or by rendering it safe and assimilating it, converting it as far as possible into a replica of itself. The concept of Otherness can be theorized in many ways and on many levels. Its psychoanalytic significance resides in the fact that it functions not simply as something external to the culture or to the self, but also as what is repressed (but never destroyed) in the self and projected outwards in order to be hated and disowned. A particularly vivid example—and one that throws light on a great many classical Westerns—is the relationship of the Puritan settlers to the Indians in the early days of America. The Puritans rejected any perception that the Indians had a culture, a civilization, of their own; they perceived them not merely as savage but, literally, as devils or the spawn of the Devil; and, since the Devil and sexuality are inextricably linked in the Puritan consciousness, they perceived them as sexually promiscuous, creatures of unbridled libido. The connection between this view of the Indian and Puritan repression is obvious: a classic and extreme case of the projection on to the Other of what is repressed within the Self, in order that it can be discredited, disowned, and if possible annihilated. It is repression, in other words, that makes impossible the healthy alternative: the full recognition and acceptance of the Other's autonomy and right to exist.

Some versions then, of the figure of the Other as it operates within our culture, of its relation to repression and oppression, and of how it is characteristically dealt with:

1. *Quite simply, other people.* It is logical and probable that under capitalism all human relations will be characterized by power, dominance, possessiveness, manipulation: the extension into relationships of the property-principle. Given the subordinate and dependent position of women, this is especially true of the culture's central relationship, the male/female, and explains why marriage as we have it is characteristically a kind of mutual imperialism/colonization, an exchange of different forms of possession and dependence, both economic and emotional. In theory, relations between people of the same sex stand more chance of evading this contamination, but in practice most gay and lesbian relationships tend to rely on heterosexual models. The "otherness," the autonomy, of the partner, her/his right to freedom and independence of being, is perceived as a threat to the possession/dependence principle and denied.

2. *Woman.* In a male-dominated culture, where power, money, law, social institutions are controlled by past, present, and future patriarchs, woman as the Other assumes particular significance. The dominant images of women in our culture are entirely male-created and male-controlled. Woman's autonomy and independence are denied; on to women men project their own innate, repressed femininity in order to disown it as inferior (to be called "unmanly"—i.e., like a woman—is the supreme insult).

3. *The proletariat*—insofar as it still has any autonomous existence, escaping its colonization by bourgeois ideology. It remains, at least, a conveniently available object for projection: the bourgeois obsession with cleanliness, which psychoanalysis shows to be closely associated, as outward symptom, with sexual repression, and bourgeois sexual repression itself, find their inverse reflections in the myths of working-class squalor and sexuality.

5. *Other cultures.* If they are sufficiently remote, no problem: they can be simultaneously deprived of their true character and exoticized (e.g., Polynesian cultures as embodied by Dorothy Lamour). If they are inconveniently close, we already have the example of the American Indian: the procedure is very precisely represented in Ford's *Drums along the Mohawk,* with its double vision of the Indians as "sons of Belial" fit only for extermination, or the Christianized, domesticated, servile, and (hopefully) comic Blueback.

5. *Ethnic groups within the culture.* Again, an easily available projection-object (myths of black sexuality, "animality," etc.). Acceptable in either of two ways:

either they keep to their ghettoes and don't trouble us with their "otherness," or they behave as we do and become replicas of the good bourgeois, their otherness reduced to the one unfortunate difference of color. We are more likely to invite a Pakistani to dinner if he dresses in a business suit.

6. *Alternative ideologies or political systems.* The exemplary case is of course Marxism, the strategy that of parody. Still almost totally repressed within our preuniversity education system (despite the key importance of Marx—whatever way you look at it—in the development of twentieth-century thought), Marxism exists generally in our culture only in the form of bourgeois myth that renders it indistinguishable from Stalinism (rather like confusing the teachings of Christ with the Spanish Inquisition).

7. *Deviations from ideological sexual norms*—notably bisexuality and homosexuality. One of the clearest instances of the operation of the repression/projection mechanism: homophobia (the irrational hatred and fear of homosexuals) is only explicable as the outcome of the unsuccessful repression of bisexual tendencies: what is hated in others is what is rejected (but nonetheless continues to exist) within the self.

8. *Children.* When we have worked our way through all the other liberation movements, we may discover that children are the most oppressed section of the population (unfortunately, we cannot expect to liberate our children until we have successfully liberated ourselves). Most clearly of all, the "otherness" of children (see Freudian theories of infantile sexuality) is that which is repressed within ourselves, its expression therefore hated in others: what the previous generation repressed in us, and what we, in turn, repress in our children, seeking to mold them into replicas of ourselves, perpetuators of a discredited tradition.

All this may seem to have taken us rather far from our immediate subject. In fact, I have been laying the foundations, stone by stone, for a theory of the American horror film which (without being exhaustive) should provide us with a means of approaching the films seriously and responsibly. One could, I think, approach any of the genres from the same starting point; it is the horror film that responds in the most clear-cut and direct way, because central to it is the actual dramatization of the dual concept the repressed/the other, in the figure of the Monster. One might say that the true subject of the horror genre is the struggle for recognition of all that our civilization *re*presses or *op*presses: its reemergence dramatized, as in our nightmares, as an object of horror, a matter for terror, the "happy ending" (when it exists) typically signifying the restoration of repression. I think my analysis of what is repressed, combined with my account of the Other as it functions within our culture, will be found to offer a comprehensive survey of horror film monsters from German Expressionism on. It is possible to produce "monstrous" embodiments of virtually every item in the list. Let me preface this by saying that the general sexual content of the horror film has long been recognized, and the list of monsters representing a generalized sexual threat would be interminable; also, the generalized concept of "otherness" offered by the first item on my list cannot be represented by specific films.

Female sexuality. Earlier examples are the panther-woman of *Island of Lost Souls* and the heroine of *Cat People* (the association of women with cats runs right through and beyond the Hollywood cinema, cutting across periods and genres from *Bringing Up Baby* to *Alien*); but the definitive Feminist horror film is clearly De Palma's *Sisters* (co-scripted by the director and Louisa Rose) among the most complete and rigorous analyses of the oppression of women under patriarchal culture in the whole popular cinema.

The proletariat. I would claim here Whale's *Frankenstein,* partly on the strength of its pervasive class references, more on the strength of Karloff's costume: Frankenstein *could* have dressed his creature in top hat, white tie, and tails, but in fact chose laborer's clothes. Less disputable, in recent years we have *The Texas Chainsaw Massacre,* with its monstrous family of retired, but still practicing, slaughterhouse workers; the underprivileged devil worshippers of *Race with the Devil*; and the revolutionary army of *Assault on Precinct 13.*

Other cultures. In the 1930s the monster was almost invariably foreign; the rebellious animal-humans of *Island of Lost Souls* (though created by the white man's science) on one level clearly signify a "savage," unsuccessfully colonized culture. Recently, one horror film, *The Manitou,* identified the monster with the American Indian (*Prophecy* plays tantalizingly with this possibility—also linking it to urban blacks—before opting for the altogether safer and less interesting explanation of industrial pollution).

Ethnic groups. The Possession of Joel Delaney links diabolic possession with Puerto Ricans; blacks (and a leader clad as an Indian) are prominent, again, in *Assault on Precinct 13*'s monstrous army.

Alternative ideologies. The 1950s science fiction cycle of invasion movies is generally regarded as being concerned with the Communist threat.

Homosexuality and bisexuality. Both Murnau's *Nosferatu* and Whale's *Frankenstein* can be claimed as implicitly (on certain levels) identifying their monsters with repressed homosexuality. Recent, less arguable, instances are Dr. Frank 'n' Furter of *The Rocky Horror Picture Show* (he, not his creation, is clearly the film's real monster) and, more impressively, the bisexual god of Larry Cohen's *Demon.*

Children. Since *Rosemary's Baby,* children have figured prominently in horror films as the monster or its medium: *The Exorcist, The Omen,* etc. Cohen's two It's Alive films again offer perhaps the most interesting and impressive example. There is also the Michael of *Halloween*'s remarkable opening.

This offers us no more than a beginning, from which one might proceed to interpret specific horror films in detail as well as further exploring the genre's social significance, the insights it offers into our culture. I shall add here simply that these notions of repression and the Other afford us not merely a means of access but a rudimentary categorization of horror films in social-political terms, distinguishing the progressive from the reactionary, the criterion being the way in which the monster is presented and defined.

II. Return of the Repressed

I want first to offer a series of general propositions about the American horror film, then attempt to define the particular nature of its evolution in the 1960s and 1970s.

1. Popularity and Disreputability

The horror film has consistently been one of the most popular and, at the same time, the most disreputable of Hollywood genres. The popularity itself has a peculiar characteristic that sets the horror film apart from other genres: it is restricted to aficionados and complemented by total rejection, people tending to go to horror films either obsessively or not at all. They are dismissed with contempt by the majority of reviewer-critics, or simply ignored. (The situation has changed somewhat since *Psycho,* which conferred on the horror film something of the dignity that *Stagecoach* conferred on the Western, but the disdain still largely continues. I have read no serious or illuminating accounts of, for example, *Raw Meat, It's Alive,* or *The Hills Have Eyes.*) The popularity, however, also continues. Most horror films make money; the ones that don't are those with overt intellectual pretensions, obviously "difficult" works like *God Told Me To (Demon)* and *Exorcist II.* Another psychologically interesting aspect of this popularity is that many people who go regularly to horror films profess to ridicule them and go in order to laugh—which is not true, generally speaking, of the Western or the gangster movie.

2. Dreams and Nightmares

The analogy frequently invoked between films and dreams is usually concerned with the experience of the audience. The spectator sits in darkness, and the sort of involvement the entertainment film necessitates a certain switching-off of consciousness, a losing of oneself in a fantasy-experience. But the analogy is also useful from the point of view of the filmmakers. Dreams—the embodiment of repressed desires, tensions, fears that our conscious mind rejects—become possible when the "censor" that guards our subconscious relaxes in sleep, though even then the desires can only emerge in disguise, as fantasies that are "innocent" or apparently meaningless.

One of the functions of the concept of "entertainment"—by definition, that which we don't take seriously, or think about much ("It's only entertainment")—

is to act as a kind of partial sleep of consciousness. For the filmmakers as well as for the audience, full awareness stops at the level of plot, action, and character, in which the most dangerous and subversive implications can disguise themselves and escape detection. This is why seemingly innocuous genre movies can be far more radical and fundamentally undermining than works of conscious social criticism, which must always concern themselves with the possibility of reforming aspects of a social system whose basic rightness must not be challenged. The old tendency to dismiss the Hollywood cinema as escapist always defined escape merely negatively as escape *from,* but escape logically must also be escape *to.* Dreams are also escapes, from the unresolved tensions of our lives into fantasies. Yet the fantasies are not meaningless; they can represent attempts to resolve those tensions in more radical ways than our consciousness can countenance.

Popular films, then, respond to interpretation as at once the personal dreams of their makers and the collective dreams of their audiences—the fusion made possible by the shared structures of a common ideology. It becomes easy, if this is granted, to offer a simple definition of horror films: they are our collective nightmares. The conditions under which a dream becomes a nightmare are (1) that the repressed wish is, from the point of view of consciousness, so terrible that it must be repudiated as loathsome, and (2) that it is so strong and powerful as to constitute a serious threat. The disreputability noted above—the general agreement that horror films are not to be taken seriously—works clearly *for* the genre viewed from this position. The censor (in both the common *and* the Freudian sense) is lulled into sleep and relaxes vigilance.

3. The Surrealists

It is worth noting here that one group of intellectuals *did* take American horror movies very seriously indeed: the writers, painters, and filmmakers of the Surrealist movement. Luis Buñuel numbers *The Beast with Five Fingers* among his favorite films and paid homage to it in *The Exterminating Angel*; and Georges Franju, an heir of the Surrealists, numbers *The Fly* among his. The association is highly significant, given the commitment of the Surrealists to Freud, the unconscious, dreams, and the overthrow of repression.

4. Basic Formula

At this stage it is necessary to offer a simple and obvious basic formula for the horror film: normality is threatened by the Monster. I use *normality* here in a strictly nonevaluative sense, to mean simply "conformity to the dominant social norms"; one must firmly resist the common tendency to treat the word as if it were more or less synonymous with "health."

The very simplicity of this formula has a number of advantages:

a. It covers the entire range of horror films, being applicable whether the Monster is a vampire, a giant gorilla, an extraterrestrial invader, an amorphous gooey mass, or a child possessed by the Devil, and this makes it possible to connect the most seemingly heterogeneous movies.

b. It suggests the possibility of extension to other genres: substitute for *Monster* the term *Indians,* for example, and one has a formula for a large number of classical Westerns.

c. Although so simple, the formula provides three variables: normality, the Monster, and, crucially, the relationship between the two. The definition of normality in horror films is in general boringly constant: the heterosexual monogamous couple, the family, and the social institutions (police, church, armed forces) that support and defend them. The Monster is, of course, much more protean, changing from period to period as society's basic fears clothe themselves in fashionable or immediately accessible garments— rather as dreams use material from recent memory to express conflicts or desires that may go back to early childhood.

It is the third variable, the relationship between normality and the Monster, that constitutes the essential subject of the horror film. It, too, changes and develops, the development taking the form of a long process of clarification or revelation. The relationship has one privileged form: the figure of the doppelgänger, alter ego, or double, a figure that has recurred constantly in Western culture, especially during the past hundred years. The *locus classicus* is Stevenson's Dr. Jekyll and Mr. Hyde, where normality and Monster are two aspects of the same person. The figure recurs throughout two major sources of the American horror film, German Expressionist cinema (the two Marias of *Metropolis,* the presentation of protagonist and vampire as mirror reflections in *Nosferatu,* the very title of F. W. Murnau's lost Jekyll and Hyde film *Der Januskopf*), and the tales of Poe. Variants can be traced in such oppositions as Ahab/the white whale in *Moby Dick* and Ethan/Scar in *The Searchers.* The Westerns of Anthony Mann are rich in doubles, often contained within families or family patterns; *Man of the West,* a film that relates very suggestively to the horror genre, represents the fullest elaboration.

I shall limit myself for the moment to one example from the horror film, choosing it partly because it is so central, partly because the motif is there less obvious, partially disguised, partly because it points forward to Larry Cohen and *It's Alive*: the relationship of Monster to creator in the Frankenstein films. Their identity is made explicit in *Son of Frankenstein,* the most intelligent of the Universal series, near the start of which the title figure (Basil Rathbone) complains bitterly that everyone believes "Frankenstein" to be the name of the monster. (We discover subsequently that the town has also come to be called Frankenstein, the symbiosis of Monster and creator spreading over the entire environment.) But we should be alerted to the relationship's true significance from the moment in the James Whale original when Frankenstein's decision to create his monster is juxtaposed very precisely with his decision to become engaged. The doppelgänger motif reveals the Monster as normality's shadow.

5. Ambivalence

The principle of ambivalence is most eloquently elaborated in A. P. Rossiter's *Angel with Horns,* among the most brilliant of all books on Shakespeare. Rossiter first expounds it with reference to Richard III. Richard, the "angel with horns," both horrifies us with his evil and delights us with his intellect, his art, his audacity; while our moral sense is appalled by his outrages, another part of us gleefully identifies with him. The application of this to the horror film is clear. Few horror films have totally unsympathetic Monsters (*The Thing* is a significant exception); in many (notably the Frankenstein films) the Monster is clearly the emotional center, and much more human than the cardboard representatives of normality. The Frankenstein monster suffers, weeps, responds to music, longs to relate to people; Henry and Elizabeth merely declaim histrionically. Even in *Son of Frankenstein*—the film in which the restructured monster is explicitly designated evil and superhuman—the monster's emotional commitment to Ygor and grief over his death carries far greater weight than any of the other relationships in the film.

But the principle goes far beyond the Monster's being sympathetic. Ambivalence extends to our attitude to normality. Central to the effect and fascination of horror films is their fulfillment of our nightmare wish to smash the norms that oppress us and which our moral conditioning teaches us to revere. The overwhelming commercial success of *The Omen* cannot possibly be explained in terms of a simple, unequivocal *horror* at the Devil's progress.

6. Freudian Theses

Finally, one can simply state the two elementary (and closely interconnected) Freudian theses that structure this article: that in a society built on monogamy and family, there will be an enormous surplus of sexual energy that will have to be repressed, and that what is repressed must always strive to return.

Before considering how the horror film has developed in the past decade, I want to test the validity of the above ideas by applying them to a classical horror film. I have chosen Robert Florey's *Murders in the Rue Morgue* (1932)—because it is a highly distinguished example, and generally neglected; because its images suggest Surrealism as much as Expressionism; and because it occupies a particularly interesting place in the genre's evolution, linking two of the most famous, though most disparate, horror films ever made. On the one hand it looks back very clearly to *The Cabinet of Dr. Caligari*: the Expressionist sets and lighting, with Karl

Freund as cinematographer; the fairground that provides the starting point for the action; the figure of the diabolical doctor, who shows off his exhibit and later sends it to kidnap the heroine; the flight over the rooftops. On the other hand it looks forward, equally clearly, to *King Kong*: instead of *Caligari*'s sleepwalker, a gorilla, which falls in love with the heroine, abducts her at night and is shot down from a roof. It is as important to notice the basic motifs that recur obstinately throughout the evolution of the horror film in Western culture as it is to be aware of the detailed particularities of individual films. *Murders in the Rue Morgue* responds well to the application of my formula.

    a. *Normality*. The film is quite obsessive about its heterosexual couples. At the opening, we have two couples responding to the various spectacles of the fairground; there is a scene in the middle where numerous carefree couples disport themselves picturesquely amid nature. Crucial to the film, however, is Pierre's love-speech to Camille on her balcony, with its exaggerated emphasis on purity: she is both a "flower" and a "star"; she is told not to be curious about what goes on in the houses of the city around them ("Better not to know"); she is also prevented from obtaining knowledge of the nature of Pierre's activities in the morgue (a "horrid old place"). Even the usual gay stereotype, Pierre's plump and effeminate friend, fits very well into the pattern. He is provided with a girl friend, to recuperate him into the heterosexual coupling of normality. His relationship with Pierre (they share an apartment, he wears an apron, cooks the dinner, and fusses) is a parody of bourgeois marriage, the incongruity underlining the relationship's repressive sexlessness. And he underlines the attempts at separating "pure" normality from the pervasive contamination of outside forces by complaining that Pierre "beings the morgue into their home."

    b. *The Monster*. *Murders in the Rue Morgue* has a divided Monster, a phenomenon not uncommon in the horror film. (In *The Cabinet of Dr. Caligari* the Monster is both Caligari and Cesar; in *Island of Lost Souls* both Dr. Moreau and his creatures.) Here the division is tripartite: Dr. Mirakle (Bela Lugosi), his servant-assistant, and Erik, "the beast with a human soul." The servant's role is small, but important because of his appearance: half-human, half-animal, he bridges the gap between Mirakle and Erik. Scientist and ape are linked, however, in another way: Mirakle himself lusts after Camille, and Erik (the animal extension of himself) represents the instrument for the satisfaction of that lust. Together, they combine the two great, apparently contradictory, dreads of American culture as expressed in its cinema: intellectuality and eroticism.

    c. *Relationship*. The film's superficial project is to insist that purity-normality can be separated from contaminating eroticism-degradation; its deeper project is to demonstrate the impossibility of such a separation. In the opening sequence, the couples view a series of fairground acts as spectacles (the separation of stage from audience seeming to guarantee safety): an erotic dance by "Arabian" girls, a Wild Red Indian show, and finally Erik the ape. The association of the three is suggestive of the link between the horror film and the Western—the link of Horror, Indians, and released libido. In each case the separation of show and audience is shown to be precarious: Pierre's sidekick asks his girl if she "could learn to do that dance" for him; two spectators adopt the name "apache" to apply to the savages of Paris; the audience enters the third booth between the legs of an enormous painted ape, where its phallus would be. Dr. Mirakle's introduction uses evolutionary theory to deny separation: Erik is "the darkness at the dawn of Man." His subsequent experiments are carried out to prove that Erik's blood can be "mixed with the blood of man"—and as the experiments all involve women, the sexual connotations are plain.

Though not obvious, the "double" motif subtly structures the film. It comes nearest to explicitness in the effeminate friend's remark that Pierre is becoming fanatical, "like that Dr. Mirakle." But Pierre and Mirakle are paralleled repeatedly, both in the construction of the scenario and through the mise-en-scène. At the end of the balcony love scene Florey cuts from the lovers' kiss to Mirakle and Erik watching from their carriage. Later, the juxtaposition is reversed, the camera panning from Mirakle-Erik lurking in the shadows to Pierre-Camille embracing on the balcony; it is as if the Monster were waiting to be released by the kiss. Mirakle sends Camille a bonnet; she assumes it is from Pierre. After Pierre leaves her at night, there is a knock at her door. She assumes it is Pierre come back and opens; it is Mirakle. Bearing in mind that Mirakle and Erik are not really distinct from one another, one must see Pierre and this composite Monster paralleled throughout as rival mates for Camille, like Jonathan and Nosferatu, or like David Ladd and the underworld man of *Raw Meat*. (The motif's recurrence across different periods and different continents testifies to its importance.) At the climax, Pierre and Erik confront each other like mirror images on the rooftop, and Erik is shot down by Pierre: the hero's drive is to destroy the doppelgänger who embodies his repressed self.

Murders in the Rue Morgue is fascinating for its unresolved self-contradiction. In the fairground, Mirakle is denounced as a heretic, in the name of the biblical/ Christian tradition of God's creation of man; the whole notion of purity/normality clearly associates with this—explicitly, in the very prominent, carefully lit crucifix above Camille's bed. Yet Mirakle's Darwinian theories are also obviously meant to be correct. Erik and humanity are *not* separable; the ape exists in all of us; the "morgue" cannot be excluded from the "home."

The horror film since the 1960s has been dominated by five recurrent motifs. The list of examples offered in each case begins with what I take to be the decisive source-film of each trend—not necessarily the first, but the film that, because of its distinction or popularity, can be thought of as responsible for the ensuing cycle. I have included a few British films that seem to me American-derived (*Raw Meat,* arguably the finest British horror film, was directed by an American, Gary Sherman); they lie outside the main British tradition represented by Hammer Productions, a tradition very intelligently treated in David Pirie's book *A Heritage of Horror.* The lists are not, of course, meant to be exhaustive.

    a. The Monster as human psychotic or schizophrenic: *Psycho, Homicidal, Repulsion, Sisters, Schizo.*
    b. The revenge of Nature: *The Birds, Frogs, Night of the Lepus, Day of the Animals, Squirm.*
    c. Satanism, diabolic possession, the Antichrist: *Rosemary's Baby, The Exorcist, The Omen, The Possession of Joel Delaney, The Car, God Told Me To (Demon),* and *Race with the Devil,* which, along with *High Plains Drifter,* interestingly connects this motif with the Western.
    d. The Terrible Child (often closely connected to the above). To the first three films in (c) add: *Night of the Living Dead, Hands of the Ripper, It's Alive, Cathy's Curse;* also, although here the "children" are older, *Carrie* and *The Fury.*
    e. Cannibalism: *Night of the Living Dead, Raw Meat, Frightmare, The Texas Chainsaw Massacre, The Hills Have Eyes.*

These apparently heterogeneous motifs are drawn deeper together by a single unifying master-figure: the Family. The connection is most tenuous and intermittent in what has proved, on the whole, the least interesting and productive of these concurrent cycles, the "revenge of Nature" films; but even there, in the more distinguished examples (outstandingly, of course, *The Birds,* but also in *Squirm*), the attacks are linked to, or seem triggered by, familial or sexual tensions. Elsewhere, the connection of the Family to Horror has become overwhelmingly consistent: the psychotic/schizophrenic, the Antichrist and the child-monster are all shown as products of the family, whether the family itself is regarded as guilty (the "psychotic" films) or innocent (*The Omen*).

The "cannibalism" motif functions in two ways. Occasionally members of a family devour each other (*Night of the Living Dead,* and *Psycho*'s Mrs. Bates is a metaphorical cannibal who swallows up her son). More frequently, cannibalism is the family's means of sustaining or nourishing itself (*The Texas Chainsaw Massacre, The Hills Have Eyes*). Pete Walker's revoltingly gruesome and ugly British horror film *Frightmare* deserves a note here, its central figure being a sweet and gentle old mother who has the one unfortunate flaw that she can't survive without eating human flesh, a craving guiltily indulged by her devoted husband.

If we see the evolution of the horror film in terms of an inexorable "return of the repressed," we will not be surprised by this final emergence of the genre's real significance—together with a sense that it is currently the most important of all American genres and perhaps the most progressive, even in its overt nihilism—in a period of extreme cultural crisis and disintegration, which alone offers the possibility of radical change and rebuilding. To do justice to the lengthy process of that emergence would involve a dual investigation too complex for the framework of this chapter: into the evolution of the horror film, and into the changing treatment of the family in the Hollywood cinema. I shall content myself here with a few further propositions.

1. The family (or marital) comedy in which the 1930s and 1940s are so rich, turns sour (*Father of the Bride, The Long Long Trailer*) in the 1950s and peters out; the family horror film starts (not, of course, without precedents) with *Psycho* in 1960, and gains impetus with *Rosemary's Baby* and *Night of the Living Dead* toward the end of the decade.

2. As the horror film enters into its apocalyptic phase, so does the Western. *The Wild Bunch* appeared in 1969, the year after *Rosemary's Baby.* And *High Plains Drifter* (1973) fused their basic elements in a Western in which the Hero from the Wilderness turns out to be the Devil (or his emissary) and burns the town (American civilization) to the ground after revealing it as fundamentally corrupt and renaming it Hell.

3. The family comedies that seemed so innocent and celebratory in the 1930s and 1940s appear much less so in retrospect from the 1970s. In my book *Personal Views* I pointed to the remarkable anticipation in *Meet Me in St. Louis* of the Terrible Child of the 1970s horror film, especially in the two scenes (*Halloween,* and the destruction of the snow people) in which Margaret O'Brien symbolically kills parent figures. What is symbolic in 1944 becomes literal in *Night of the Living Dead,* where a little girl kills and devours her parents—just as the implications of another anticipatory family film of the early 1940s, *Shadow of a Doubt,* becomes literally enacted in *It's Alive* (the monster as product of the family).

4. The process whereby horror becomes associated with its true milieu, the family, is reflected in its steady *geographical* progress toward America.

a. In the 1930s, horror is always foreign. The films are set in Paris (*Murders in the Rue Morgue*), Middle Europe (*Frankenstein, Dracula*), or on uncharted islands (*Island of Lost Souls, King Kong*); it is always external to Americans, who may be attacked by it physically but remain (superficially, that is) uncontaminated by it morally. The designation of horror as foreign stands even when the "normal" characters are Europeans. In *Murders in the Rue Morgue,* for example, the young couples, though nominally French, are to all intents and purposes nice clean-living Americans (with American accents); the foreignness of the horror characters is strongly underlined, both by Lugosi's accent and by the fact that nobody knows where he comes from. The foreignness of horror in the Thirties can be interpreted in two ways: simply, as a means of disavowal (horror exists, but is un-American), and, more interestingly and unconsciously, as a means of locating horror as a "country of the mind," as a psychological state: the films set on uncharted (and usually nameless) islands lend themselves particularly to interpretation of this kind.

b. The Val Lewton films of the 1940s are in some ways outside the mainstream development of the horror film. They seem to have had little direct influence on its evolution (certain occasional haunted-house movies like *The Uninvited* and *The Haunting* may owe something to them), though they strikingly anticipate, by at least two decades, some of the features of the modern horror film. *Cat People* is centered on the repression of female sexuality, in a period where the Monster is almost invariably male and phallic. (Other rare exceptions are the panther-woman of *Island of Lost Souls* and, presumably, *Dracula's Daughter,* which I have not seen.) *The Seventh Victim* has strong undertones of sibling envy and sexual jealousy (the structure and editing of the last scene suggesting that Jacqueline's suicide is willed by her "nice" husband and sister rather than by the "evil" devil worshippers), as well as containing striking anticipations of *Psycho* and *Rosemary's Baby*; it is also set firmly in America, with no attempt to disown evil as foreign.

Above all, *I Walked with a Zombie* explicitly locates horror at the heart of the family, identifying it with sexual repressiveness in the cause of preserving family unity. *The Seventh Victim* apart, horror is still associated with foreignness; Irena in *Cat People* is from Serbia, *Zombie* is set in the West Indies, *The Leopard Man* in Mexico, etc. Yet the best of the series are concerned with the undermining of such distinctions—with the idea that no one escapes contamination. Accordingly, the concept of the Monster becomes diffused through the film (closely linked to the celebrated Lewton emphasis on atmosphere, rather than overt shock), no longer identified with a single figure.

Zombie, one of the finest of all American horror films, carries this furthest. It is built on an elaborate set of apparently clear-cut structural oppositions—Canada–West Indies, white–black, light–darkness, life–death, science–black magic, Christianity–Voodoo, conscious–unconscious, etc.—and it proceeds systematically to blur all of them. Jessica is both living and dead; Mrs. Rand mixes medicine, Christianity, and voodoo; the figurehead is both St. Sebastian and a black slave; the black-white opposition is poetically undercut in a complex patterning of dresses and voodoo patches; the motivation of *all* the characters is called into question; the messenger-zombie Carrefour can't be kept out of the white domain.

c. The 1950s science fiction cycles project horror onto either extraterrestrial invaders or mutations from the insect world, but they are usually set in America; even when they are not (*The Thing*), the human characters are American. The films, apparently simple, prove on inspection often very difficult to "read." The basic narrative patterns of the horror film repeat themselves obstinately and continue to carry their traditional meanings, but they are encrusted with layers of more transient, topical material. *Them!* for example, seems to offer three layers of meaning. Explicitly, it sets out to cope with the fear of nuclear energy and atomic experiment: the giant ants are mutants produced by the radioactive aftermath of a bomb explosion; they are eventually destroyed under the guidance of a humane and benevolent science embodied in the comfortingly paternal figure of Edmund Gwenn. The fear of Communist infiltration also seems present, in the emphasis on the ants as a subversive subterranean army and on their elaborate communications system. Yet the film continues to respond convincingly to the application of my basic formula and its Freudian implications. The ants rise up from underground (the unconscious); they kill by holding their victims and injecting into them huge (excessive) quantities of formic acid (the release of repressed phallic energy); and both the opening and final climax of the film are centered on the destruction (respectively actual and potential) of family groups.

Since *Psycho,* the Hollywood cinema has implicitly recognized Horror as both American and familial. I want to conclude this section by briefly examining two key works that offer particularly illuminating and suggestive contrasts and comparisons: *The Omen* and *The Texas Chainsaw Massacre.*

One can partly define the nature of each by means of a chart of oppositions:

The Omen	*The Texas Chainsaw Massacre*
big budget	low budget
glossy production values	raw, unpolished
stars	unknown actors
bourgeois entertainment	nonbourgeois "exploitation"
Good Taste	Bad Taste
"good" family	"bad" family
the Monster	the Monster
imported from Europe	indigenously American
child destroys parents	parent figures destroy "children"
traditional values reaffirmed	traditional values negated

I don't wish to make any claims for *The Omen* as a work of art: the most one could say is that it achieves a sufficient level of impersonal professional efficiency to ensure that the "kicks" inherent in its scenario are not dulled. (I would add here that my description above of *Massacre* as "raw, unpolished" refers to the overall effect of the film, as it seems to be generally experienced.) Its mise-en-scène is,

without question, everywhere more intelligent, more inventive, more cinemati-
cally educated and sophisticated, than that of *The Omen*. Hooper's cinematic intelligence, indeed, becomes more apparent on every viewing, as one gets over the
initial traumatizing impact and learns to respect the pervasive felicities of camera
placement and movement.

In obvious ways *The Omen* is old-fashioned, traditional, reactionary: the
"goodness" of the family unit isn't questioned, "horror" is disowned by having the
devil-child a product of the Old World, unwittingly *adopted* into the American
family, the devil-child and his independent-female guardian (loosely interpretable
in "mythic" terms as representing child liberation and women's liberation) are
regarded as purely evil (oh for a cinematic Blake to reverse all the terms).

Yet the film remains of great interest. It is about the end of the world, but
the "world" the film envisages ending is very particularly defined within it: the
bourgeois-capitalist patriarchal Establishment. Here "normality" is not merely
threatened by the monster, but totally annihilated: the state, the church, the family.
The principle of ambivalence must once again be invoked: with a film so shrewdly
calculated for box-office response, it is legitimate to ask what general satisfaction
it offers its audience.

Superficially, the satisfaction of finding traditional values reaffirmed (even if
"our" world is ending, it was still the good, right, true one); more deeply, and far
more powerfully, under cover of this, the satisfaction of the ruthless logic with
which the premise is carried through—the supreme satisfaction (masquerading
as the final horror) being the revelation, as the camera cranes down in the last
shot, that the Devil has been adopted by the president and first lady of the United
States. The translation of the film into Blakean terms is not in fact that difficult:
the devil-child is its implicit hero, whose systematic destruction of the bourgeois
Establishment the audience follows with a secret relish. *The Omen* would make
no sense in a society that was not prepared to enjoy and surreptitiously condone
the working out of its own destruction.

As Andrew Britton pointed out to me, *The Omen* and *The Texas Chainsaw
Massacre* (together with numerous other horror films) have one premise disturbingly in common: the annihilation is inevitable, humanity is now completely
powerless, there is nothing anyone can do to arrest the process. (Ideology, that
is, can encompass despair, but not the imagining of constructive radical alternatives.) *The Omen* invokes ancient prophecy and shows it inexorably fulfilling itself
despite all efforts at intervention; we infer near the opening of *Massacre* that the
Age of Aquarius whose advent was so recently celebrated in *Hair* has already
passed, giving way to the Age of Saturn and universal malevolence. Uncontrol is
emphasized throughout the film: not only have the five young victims no control
over their destiny, their slaughterers (variously psychotic and degenerate) keep
losing control of themselves and each other.

This is partly (in conjunction with the film's relentless and unremitting intensity) what gives *Massacre* to such a degree (beyond any other film in my experience) the authentic quality of nightmare. I have had since childhood a recurring nightmare whose pattern seems to be shared by a very large number of people within our culture: I am running away from some vaguely terrible oppressors who are going to do dreadful things to me; I run to a house or a car, etc., for help; I discover its occupants to be precisely the people I am fleeing. This pattern is repeated twice in *Massacre,* where Sally "escapes" from Leatherface first to his own home, then to the service station run by his father.

The application of my formula to *Massacre* produces interesting results: the pattern is still there, as is the significant relationship between the terms, but the definitions of *normality* and *monster* have become partly reversed. Here "normality" is clearly represented by the quasi-liberated, permissive young (though still forming two couples and a brother/sister family unit, hence reproducing the patterns of the past); the monster is the family, one of the great composite monsters of the American cinema, incorporating four characters and three generations, and imagined with an intensity and audacity that far transcend the connotations of the term "exploitation movie." It has a number of important aspects:

1. The image of the "Terrible House" stems from a long tradition in American (and Western capitalist) culture.[3] Traditionally, it represents an extension or "objectification" of the personalities of the inhabitants. *Massacre* offers two complementary "terrible houses": the once imposing, now totally decayed house of Franklyn's and Sally's parents (where we keep *expecting* something appalling to happen), and the more modest, outwardly spruce, inwardly macabre villa of the monstrous family wherein every item of decor is an expression of the characters' degeneracy. The borderline between home and slaughterhouse (between work and leisure) has disappeared—the slaughterhouse has invaded the home, humanity has begun literally to "prey upon itself, like monsters of the deep." Finally, what the "terrible house" (whether in Poe's "Fall of the House of Usher," in *Psycho,* in *Mandingo,* or here) signifies is the dead weight of the past crushing the life of the younger generation, the future—an idea beautifully realized in the shot that starts on the ominous gray, decayed Franklyn house and tilts down to show Kirk and Pam, dwarfed in long-shot, playing and laughing as they run to the swimming-hole, and to their doom.

2. The contrast between the two houses underlines the distinction the film makes between the affluent young and the psychotic family, representatives of an exploited and degraded proletariat. Sally's father used to send his cattle to the slaughterhouse of which the family are products.

3. The all-male family (the grandmother exists only as a decomposing corpse) also derives from a long American tradition, with notable antecedents in Ford's Westerns (the Clantons of *My Darling Clementine,* the Cleggses of

Wagonmaster) and in *Man of the West*. The absence of Woman (conceived of as a civilizing, humanizing influence) deprives the family of its social sense and social meaning while leaving its strength of primitive loyalties largely untouched. In *Massacre*, Woman becomes the ultimate object of the characters' animus (and, I think, the film's, since the sadistic torments visited on Sally go far beyond what is necessary to the narrative).

4. The release of sexuality in the horror film is always presented as perverted, monstrous, and excessive (whether it takes the form of vampires, giant ants, or Mrs. Bates), both the perversion and the excess being the logical outcome of repression. Nowhere is this carried further than in *Massacre*. Here sexuality is totally perverted from its functions, into sadism, violence, and cannibalism. It is striking that there is no suggestion anywhere that Sally is the object of an overtly sexual threat: she is to be tormented, killed, dismembered, eaten, but not raped. Ultimately, the most terrifying thing about the film is its total negativity; the repressed energies—represented most unforgettably by Leatherface and his continuously whirring phallic chainsaw—are presented as irredeemably debased and distorted. It is no accident that the four most intense horror films of the Seventies at "exploitation" level (*Night of the Living Dead, Raw Meat,* and *The Hills Have Eyes* are the other three) are all centered on cannibalism, and on the specific notion of present and future (the younger generation) being devoured by the past. Cannibalism represents the ultimate in possessiveness, hence the logical end of human relations under capitalism. The implication is that "liberation" and "permissiveness," as defined within our culture, are at once inadequate and too late—too feeble, too unaware, too undirected to withstand the legacy of long repression.

5. This connects closely with the recurrence of the "double" motif in *Massacre*. The young people are, on the whole, uncharacterized and undifferentiated (the film's energies are mainly with its monsters—as usual in the horror film, the characteristic here surviving the reversal of definitions), but in their midst is Franklyn, who is as grotesque, and almost as psychotic, as his nemesis Leatherface. (The film's refusal to sentimentalize the fact that he is crippled may remind one of the blind beggars of Bunuel.) Franklyn associates himself with the slaughterers by imitating the actions of Leatherface's brother the hitchhiker: wondering whether he, too, could slice open his own hand, and toying with the idea of actually doing so. (Kirk remarks, "You're as crazy as he is.") Insofar as the other young people are characterized, it is in terms of a pervasive petty malice. Just before Kirk enters the house to meet his death, he teases Pam by dropping into her hand a human tooth he has found on the doorstep; later, Jerry torments Franklyn to the verge of hysteria by playing on his fears that the hitchhiker will pursue and kill him. Franklyn resents being neglected by the others, Sally resents being burdened with him on her vacation. The monstrous cruelties of the slaughterhouse family have their more pallid reflection within

"normality." (The reflection pattern here is more fully worked out in *The Hills Have Eyes,* with its stranded "normal" family besieged by its dark mirror-image, the terrible shadow-family from the hills, who want to kill the men, rape the women, and eat the baby.)

6. Despite the family's monstrousness, a degree of ambivalence is still present in the response they evoke. Partly, this is rooted in our sense of them as a *family.* They are held together—and torn apart—by bonds and tensions with which we are all familiar—with which, indeed, we are likely to have grown up. We cannot cleanly dissociate ourselves from them. Then there is the sense that *they* are victims, too—of the slaughterhouse environment, of capitalism—*our* victims, in fact. Finally, they manifest a degraded but impressive creativity. The news reporter at the start describes the tableau of decomposing corpses in the graveyard (presumably the work of the hitchhiker, and perhaps a homage to his grandparents: a female corpse is posed in the lap of a male corpse in a hideous parody of domesticity) as "a grisly work of art." The phrase, apt for the film itself, also describes the art-works among which the family live, some of which achieve a kind of hideous aesthetic beauty: the light-bulb held up by a human hand, the sofa constructed out of human and animal bones, surmounted by ornamental skulls, the hanging lamp over the dining table that appears to be a shrunken human head. The film's monsters do not lack that characteristically human quality, an aesthetic sense, however perverted its form; also, they waste nothing, a lesson we are all taught as children.

7. Central to the film—and centered on its monstrous family—is the sense of grotesque comedy, which in no way diminishes (rather intensifies) its nightmare horror: Leatherface chasing Sally with the chainsaw, unable to stop and turn, skidding, wheeling, like an animated character in a cartoon; the father's response to Leatherface's devastations, which by that time include four murders and the prolonged terrorization of the heroine ("Look what your brother did to that door"); Leatherface dressed up in jacket and tie and fresh black wig for formal dinner with Grandpa; the macabre farce of Grandpa's repeated failures to kill Sally with the hammer. The film's sense of fundamental horror is closely allied to a sense of the fundamentally absurd. The family, after all, only carry to its logical conclusion the basic (though unstated) tenet of capitalism, that people have the right to live off other people. In twentieth century art, the sense of the absurd is always closely linked to total despair (Beckett, Ionesco . . .). The fusion of nightmare and absurdity is carried even further in *Death Trap,* a film that confirms that the creative impulse in Hooper's work is centered in his monsters (here, the grotesque and pathetic Neville Brand) and is essentially nihilistic.

The Texas Chainsaw Massacre, unlike *The Omen,* achieves the force of authentic art, profoundly disturbing, intensely personal, yet at the same time far more than personal, as the general response it has evoked demonstrates. As a "collective nightmare," it brings to a focus a spirit of negativity, an undifferentiated lust for destruction, that seems to lie not far below the surface of the modern collective consciousness. Watching it recently with a large, half-stoned youth audience who cheered and applauded every one of Leatherface's outrages against their representatives on the screen was a terrifying experience. It must not be seen as an isolated phenomenon: it expresses, with unique force and intensity, at least one important aspect of what the horror film has come to signify: the sense of a civilization condemning itself, through its popular culture, to ultimate disintegration, and ambivalently (with the simultaneous horror/wish-fulfillment of nightmare) celebrating the fact. We must not, of course, see that as the last word.

III. The Reactionary Wing

I suggested earlier that the theory of repression offers us a means toward a political categorization of horror movies. Such a categorization, however, can never be rigid or clear-cut. While I have stressed the genre's progressive or radical elements, its potential for the subversion of bourgeois patriarchal norms, it is obvious enough that this potential is never free from ambiguity. The genre carries within itself the capability of reactionary inflection, and perhaps no horror film is entirely immune from its operations. It need not surprise us that there is a powerful reactionary tradition to be acknowledged—so powerful it may at times appear the dominant one. Its characteristics are, in extreme cases, very strongly marked.

Before noting them, however, it is important to make one major distinction between the reactionary horror film and the "apocalyptic" horror film. The latter expresses, obviously, despair and negativity, yet its very negation can be claimed as progressive: the "apocalypse," even when presented in metaphysical terms (the end of the world), is generally reinterpretable in social/political ones (the end of the highly specific world of patriarchal capitalism). The majority of the most distinguished American horror films (especially in the 1970s) are concerned with this particular apocalypse; they are progressive insofar as their negativity is not recuperable into the dominant ideology, but constitutes (on the contrary) the recognition of that ideology's disintegration, its untenability, as all it has repressed explodes and blows it apart. *The Texas Chainsaw Massacre, Sisters, Demon* are all apocalyptic in this sense; so are Romero's two Living Dead movies. (Having said that, it must be added that important distinctions remain to be made between these works.)

Some of the characteristics, then, that have contributed to the genre's reactionary wing:

1. The designation of the monster as *simply* evil. Insofar as horror films are typical manifestations of our culture, the *dominant* designation of the monster must necessarily be "evil": what is repressed (in the individual,

in the culture) must always return as a threat, perceived by the consciousness as ugly, terrible, obscene. Horror films, it might be said, are progressive precisely to the degree that they refuse to be satisfied with this simple designation—to the degree that, whether explicitly or implicitly, consciously or unconsciously, they modify, question, challenge, seek to invert it. All monsters are by definition destructive, but their destructiveness is capable of being variously explained, excused, and justified. To identify what is repressed with "evil incarnate" (a metaphysical, rather than a social, definition) is automatically to suggest that there is nothing to be done but strive to *keep* it repressed. Films in which the "monster" is identified as the Devil clearly occupy a privileged place in this group; though even the Devil can be presented with varying degrees of (deliberate or inadvertent) sympathy and fascination—*The Omen* should not simply be bracketed with *The Sentinel* for consignment to merited oblivion.

2. The presence of Christianity (insofar as it is given weight or presented as a positive force) is in general a portent of reaction. (This is a comment less on Christianity itself than on what it signifies within the Hollywood cinema and the dominant ideology.) *The Exorcist* is an instructive instance—its validity is in direct proportion to its failure convincingly to impose its theology.

3. The presentation of the monster as totally nonhuman. The "progressiveness" of the horror film depends partly on the monster's capacity to arouse sympathy; one can feel little for a mass of viscous black slime. The political (McCarthyite) level of 1950s science fiction films—the myth of Communism as total dehumanization—accounts for the prevalence of this kind of monster in that period.

4. The confusion (in terms of what the film wishes to regard as "monstrous") of *repressed* sexuality with sexuality itself. The distinction is not always clear-cut; perhaps it never can be, in a culture whose attitudes to sexuality remain largely negative and where a fear of sex is implanted from infancy. One can, however, isolate a few extreme examples where the sense of horror is motivated by sexual disgust.

A very common generic pattern plays on the ambiguity of the monster as the "return of the repressed" and the monster as punishment for sexual promiscuity (or, in the more extreme puritanical cases, for *any* sexual expression whatever: two teenagers kiss; enter, immediately, the Blob). Both the Jaws films (their sources in both 1950s McCarthyite science fiction and all those beach party/monster movies that disappeared with the B feature) are obvious recent examples, Spielberg's film being somewhat more complex, less blatant, than Szwarc's, though the difference is chiefly one of ideological sophistication.

I want to examine briefly here some examples of the "reactionary" horror film in the 1970s, of widely differing distinction but considerable interest in clarifying these tendencies.

David Cronenberg's *Shivers* (formerly *The Parasite Murders*) is, indeed, of very special interest here, as it is a film single-mindedly about sexual liberation, a prospect it views with unmitigated horror. The entire film is premised on and motivated by sexual disgust. The release of sexuality is linked inseparably with the spreading of venereal disease, the scientist responsible for the experiments having seen fit (for reasons never made clear) to include a VD component in his aphrodisiac parasite. The parasites themselves are modeled very obviously on phalluses, but with strong excremental overtones (their color) and continual associations with blood; the point is underlined when one enters the Barbara Steele character through her vagina. If the film presents sexuality in general as the object of loathing, it has a very special animus reserved for female sexuality (a theme repeated, if scarcely developed, in Cronenberg's subsequent *Rabid*). The parasites are spread initially by a young girl (the original subject of the scientist's experiments), the film's Pandora whose released eroticism precipitates general cataclysm; throughout, sexually aroused preying women are presented with a particular intensity of horror and disgust. *Shivers* systematically chronicles the breaking of every sexual-social taboo—promiscuity, lesbianism, homosexuality, age difference, finally incest—but each step is presented as merely one more addition to the accumulation of horrors. At the same time, the film shows absolutely no feeling for traditional relationships (or for human beings, for that matter): with its unremitting ugliness and crudity, it is very rare in its achievement of *total* negation.

The Brood, again, is thematically central to the concept of the horror film proposed here (its subject being the transmission of neurosis through the family structure) and the precise antithesis of the genre's progressive potential. It carries over all the major structural components of its two predecessors (as an *auteur*, Cronenberg is nothing if not consistent): the figure of the Scientist (here psychotherapist) who, attempting to promote social progress, precipitates disaster; the expression of unqualified horror at the idea of releasing what has been repressed; the projection of horror and evil on to women and their sexuality, the ultimate dread being of women usurping the active, aggressive role that patriarchal ideology assigns to the male. The film is remarkable for its literal enactment, at its climax, of the Freudian perception that, under patriarchy, the child becomes the woman's penis-substitute—Samantha Eggar's latest offspring representing, unmistakeably, a monstrous phallus. The film is laboriously explicit about its meaning: the terrible children are the physical embodiments of the woman's rage. But that rage is never seen as the logical product of woman's situation within patriarchal culture; it is blamed entirely on the woman's mother (the father being culpable only in his weakness and ineffectuality). The film is useful for offering an extremely instructive comparison with *Sisters* on the one hand and *It's Alive* on the other.

In turning from Cronenberg's films to *Halloween,* I do not want to suggest that I am bracketing them together. John Carpenter's films reveal in many ways an engaging artistic personality: they communicate, at the very least, a delight in skill and craftsmanship, a pleasure in play with the medium, that is one of the essential expressions of true creativity. Yet the film-buff innocence that accounts for much of the charm of *Dark Star* can go on to combine (in *Assault on Precinct 13*) *Rio Bravo* and *Night of the Living Dead* without any apparent awareness of the ideological consequences of converting Hawks' fascists (or Romero's ghouls, for that matter) into an army of revolutionaries. The film buff is very much to the fore again in *Halloween,* covering the film's confusions, its lack of real *thinking,* with a formal/stylistic inventiveness that is initially irresistible. If nothing in the film is new, everything testifies to Carpenter's powers of assimilation (as opposed to mere imitation): as a resourceful amalgam of *Psycho, The Texas Chainsaw Massacre, The Exorcist,* and *Black Christmas, Halloween* is cunning in the extreme.

The confusions, however, are present at its very foundation, in the conception of the monster. The opening is quite stunning both in its virtuosity and its resonances. The long killer's-point-of-view tracking-shot with which the film begins, establishes the basis for the first murder as sexual repression: the girl is killed because she arouses in the voyeur-murderer feelings he has simultaneously to deny and enact in the form of violent assault. The second shot reveals the murderer as the victim's bewildered six-year-old brother. Crammed into those first two shots (in which *Psycho* unites with the Hallowe'en sequence of *Meet Me in St. Louis*) are the implications for the definitive family horror film: the child-monster, product of the nuclear family and the small-town environment; the sexual repression of children; the incest taboo that denies sexual feeling precisely where the proximities of family life most encourage it. Not only are those implications not realized in the succeeding film, their trace is obscured and all but obliterated. The film identifies the killer with "the Bogeyman," as the embodiment of an eternal and unchanging evil which, by definition, can't be understood; and with the Devil ("those eyes . . . the Devil's eyes"), by none other than his own psychoanalyst (Donald Pleasence)—surely the most extreme instance of Hollywood's perversion of psychoanalysis into an instrument of repression.

The film proceeds to lay itself wide open to the reading Jonathan Rosenbaum offered in Take One: the killer's victims are all sexually promiscuous, the one survivor a virgin; the monster becomes (in the tradition of all those beach party monster movies of the late 1950s to early 1960s) simply the instrument of Puritan vengeance and repression rather than the embodiment of what Puritanism repressed.

Halloween is more interesting than that—if only because more confused. The basic premise of the action is that Laurie is the killer's real quarry throughout (the other girls merely distractions en route), because she is for him the reincarnation of the sister he murdered as a child (he first sees her in relation to a little boy who resembles him as he was then, and becomes fixated on her from that moment). This compulsion to reenact the childhood crime keeps Michael tied at least to the *possibility* of psychoanalytical explanation, thereby suggesting that Donald Pleasence may be wrong. If we accept that, then one tantalizing unresolved detail becomes crucial: the question of how Michael learned to drive a car. There are only two possible explanations: either he *is* the Devil, possessed of supernatural powers; or he has *not* spent the last nine years (as Pleasence would have us believe) sitting staring blackly at a wall meditating further horrors. (It is to Carpenter's credit that the issue is raised in the dialogue, not glossed over as an unfortunate plot necessity we aren't supposed to notice; but he appears to use it merely as another tease, a bit of meaningless mystification.) The possibility this opens up is that of reading the whole film against the Pleasence character: Michael's "evil" is what his analyst has been projecting on to him for the past nine years. Unfortunately, this remains merely a possibility in the material that Carpenter chose not to take up: it does not constitute a legitimate (let alone a coherent) reading of the actual film. Carpenter's interviews suggest that he strongly resists examining the connotative level of his own work; it remains to be seen how long this very talented filmmaker can preserve this false innocence.

At first glance, *Alien* seems little more than *Halloween*-in-outer-space: more expensive, less personal, but made with similar professional skill and flair for manipulating its audiences. Yet it has several distinctive features that give it a limited interest in its own right: it clearly wants to be taken, on a fairly simple level, as a "progressive" movie, notably in its depiction of women. What it offers on this level amounts in fact to no more than a "pop" feminism that reduces the whole involved question of sexual difference and thousands of years of patriarchal oppression to the bright suggestion that a woman can do anything a man can do (almost). This masks (not very effectively) its fundamentally reactionary nature.

Besides its resemblance to *Halloween* in general narrative pattern and suspense strategies (Where is the monster hiding? Who will be killed next? When? How? etc.), *Alien* has more precise parallels with *The Thing*. There is the enclosed space, cut off from outside help; the definition of the monster as both non- and superhuman; the fact that it feeds on human beings; its apparent indestructibility. Most clearly of all, the relationship of Ash, the robot science officer, to the alien is very close to that of Professor Carrington to the Thing; in both films, science regards the alien as a superior form of life to which human life must therefore be subordinate; in both films, science is initially responsible for bringing the monster into the community and thereby endangering the latter's existence.

What strikingly distinguishes *Alien* from both *Halloween* and *The Thing* (and virtually every other horror movie) is the apparently total absence of sexuality. Although there are two women among the space-ship's crew of seven, there is no "love interest," not even any sexual banter—in fact, with the characters restricted exclusively to the use of surnames, no recognition anywhere of sexual difference (unless we see Parker's ironic resentment of Ripley's domineeringness as motivated partly by the fact that she is a woman; but he reacts like that to all displays of authority in the film, and his actual phrase for her is "son of a bitch"). Only at the end of the film, after all the men have been killed, is female sexuality allowed to become a presence (as Ripley undresses, not knowing that the alien is still alive and in the compartment). The film constructs a new "normality" in which sexual differentiation ceases to have effective existence—on condition that sexuality be obliterated altogether.

The term *son of a bitch* is applied (by Ripley herself) to one other character in the film: the alien. The cinematic confrontation of its two "sons of bitches" is the film's logical culmination. Its resolution of ideological contradictions is clear in the presentation of Ripley herself: she is a "safe threat," set against the real threat of the alien. On the one hand, she is the film's myth of the "emancipated woman": "masculine," aggressive, self-assertive, she takes over the ship after the deaths of Kane and Dallas, rebelling against and dethroning both "Mother" (the computer) and father (Ash, the robot). On the other hand, the film is careful to supply her with "feminine," quasi-maternal characteristics (her care for Jones, the cat) and gives her, vis-à-vis the alien, the most reactionary position of the entire crew (it is she who is opposed to letting it on board, even to save Kane's life). She is, of course, in the film's terms, quite right; but that merely confirms the ideologically reactionary nature of the film, in its attitude to the Other.

If male and female are superficially and trendily united in Ripley, they are completely fused in the alien (whose most striking characteristic is its ability to transform itself). The sexuality so rigorously repressed in the film returns grotesquely and terrifyingly in its monster (the more extreme the repression, the more excessive the monster). At first associated with femaleness (it begins as an egg in a vast womb), it attaches itself to the most "feminine" of the crew's males (John Hurt, most famous for his portrayal of Quentin Crisp) and enters him through the mouth as a preliminary to being "born" out of his stomach. The alien's phallic identity is strongly marked (the long reptilian neck); but so is its large, expandable mouth, armed with tiers of sharp metallic teeth. As a composite image of archetypal sexual dreads it could scarcely be bettered: the monstrous phallus combined with *vagina dentata*. Throughout the film, the alien and the cat are repeatedly paralleled or juxtaposed, an association that may remind us of the panther/domestic cat opposition in *Cat People* (the cats even have the same surname, the John Paul Jones of Tourneur's movie reduced here to a mere "Jones" or "Jonesey"). The film creates its image of the emancipated woman only to subject her to massive terrorization (the use of flashing lights throughout *Alien*'s climactic scenes strikingly recalls the finale of *Looking for Mr. Goodbar*) and enlist her in the battle for patriarchal repression. Having destroyed the alien, Ripley can become completely "feminine"—soft and passive, her domesticated pussy safely asleep.

It is not surprising, though disturbing and sad, that at present it is the reactionary horror film that dominates the genre. This is entirely in keeping with the overall movement of Hollywood in the past five years. Vietnam, Nixon, and Watergate produced a crisis in ideological confidence which the Carter administration has temporarily resolved; *Rocky, Star Wars, Heaven Can Wait* (all overwhelming popular successes) are but the echoes of a national sigh of relief. *Sisters, Demon, Night of the Living Dead, The Texas Chainsaw Massacre,* in their various ways reflect ideological disintegration and lay bare the possibility of social revolution; *Halloween* and *Alien,* while deliberately evoking maximum terror and panic, variously seal it over again.

Notes

1. Andrew Britton, "The Ideology of *Screen,*" *Movie* 26 (Winter 1978–79): 26.

2. Gad Horowitz, *Repression—Basic and Surplus Repression in Psychoanalytic Theory: Freud, Reich, Marcuse* (Toronto: University of Toronto Press, 1977).

3. For a fuller treatment of this, see Andrew Britton's magisterial account of *Mandingo* in "Mandingo," *Movie* 22 (Spring 1976): 1–22.

FANTASTIC BIOLOGIES AND THE STRUCTURES OF HORRIFIC IMAGERY

Noël Carroll

THE OBJECTS OF ART-HORROR are essentially threatening and impure. The creator of horror presents creatures that are salient in respect to these attributes. In this, certain recurring strategies for designing monsters appear with striking regularity across the arts and media. The purpose of this chapter is to take note of some of the most characteristic ways in which monsters are produced for the reading and viewing public. This chapter could be subtitled "How to make a monster."

Horrific monsters are threatening. This aspect of the design of horrific monsters is, I think, incontestable. They must be dangerous. This can be satisfied simply by making the monster lethal. That it kills and maims is enough. The monster may also be threatening psychologically, morally, or socially. It may destroy one's identity (William Blatty's *The Exorcist* or Guy de Maupassant's "The Horla"), seek to destroy the moral order (Ira Levin's *Rosemary's Baby* et al.), or advance an alternative society (Richard Matheson's *I Am Legend*). Monsters may also trigger certain enduring infantile fears, such as those of being eaten or dismembered, or sexual fears, concerning rape and incest. However, in order to be threatening, it is sufficient that the monster be physically dangerous. If it produces further anxieties that is so much icing on the cake. So the creators of art-horror must be sure that the creatures in their fictions are threatening and this can be done by assuring that they are at least physically dangerous. Of course, if a monster is psychologically threatening but not physically threatening—i.e., if it's after your mind, not your body—it will still count as a horrific creature if it inspires revulsion.

Horrific creatures are also impure. Here, the means for presenting this aspect of horrific creatures are less obvious. So I will spend some time looking at the characteristic structures through which horrific impurity is portrayed.

Many cases of impurity are generated by what, adapting Mary Douglas, I call *interstitiality* and *categorical contradictoriness*. Impurity involves a conflict between two or more standing cultural categories. Thus, it should come as no surprise that many of the most basic structures for representing horrific creatures are combinatory in nature.

One structure for the composition of horrific beings is *fusion*. On the simplest physical level, this often entails the construction of creatures that transgress categorical distinctions such as inside–outside, living–dead, insect–human, and flesh–machine. Mummies, vampires, ghosts, zombies, and Freddy, *Elm Street*'s premier nightmare, are fusion figures in this respect. Each, in different ways, blurs the distinction between living and dead. Each, in some sense, is both living *and* dead. A fusion figure is a composite that unites attributes held to be categorically distinct and/or at odds in the cultural scheme of things in *unambiguously* one, spatiotemporally discrete entity.

The caterpillars in E. F. Benson's story of the same name are fusion figures insofar as they defy biology not only due to their extraordinary length but also because their legs are outfitted with crab pincers. Similarly, the blighted victim in John Metcalfe's "Mr. Meldrum's Mania" falls into this category since he is a combination of a man with the Egyptian god Thoth, already a fusion creature compounding an ibis head with a human body, not to mention his moon-disk and crescent accoutrements. Lovecraft's amalgams of octopi and crustaceans with humanoid forms are paradigmatic fusion figures, as are the pig-men in William Hope Hodgson's *The House on the Borderland*. Fusion examples from film would include figures such as the babies in the It's Alive series and the grotesqueries in *Alligator People* and *The Reptile*.

The central mark of a fusion figure is the compounding of ordinarily disjoint or conflicting categories in an integral, spatiotemporally unified individual. On this view, many of the characters in possession stories are fusion figures. They may be inhabited by many demons—"I am legion"—or one. But as long as they are composite beings, locatable in an unbroken spatiotemporal continuum with a single identity, we shall count them as fusion figures.

Also, I tend to see the Frankenstein monster, especially as he is represented in the Universal Pictures movie cycle, as a fusion figure. For not only is it emphasized that he is made from distinct bodies, along with electrical attachments, but the series presents him as if he had different brains imposed upon him—first a criminal's and later Igor's. In this, the films appear to uphold the unlikely hypothesis that somehow the monster has a kind of continuing identity—one that is perhaps innocent and benign—in spite of the brain it has. Obviously, this is, to say the least, paradoxical, but if we allow the fiction of brain transplants, why quibble about whether the monster is in some sense still the same monster it would have been had it not had a criminal's or Igor's brain foisted upon it?

The fusion aspect of the Frankenstein monster becomes quite hysterical in Hammer Films's *And Frankenstein Created Woman*. Dr. Frankenstein transfers the soul of his dead assistant Hans into the body of Hans's dead, beloved Christina, and Hans, in Christina's body, seduces and dispatches the hooligans who had driven Christina (i.e., Christina unified in mind and body) to her death.

The fusion figure may find its prototype in the sort of symbolic structure that Freud called the *collective figure* or *condensation* with respect to dreams. Freud writes that one way

> in which a "collective figure" can be produced for the purposes of dream-condensation [is] by uniting the actual features of two or more people into a single dream-image. It was in this way that Dr. M. of my dream was constructed. He bore the name of Dr. M., he spoke and acted like him; but his physical characteristics and his malady belonged to someone else, namely to my eldest brother. One single feature, his pale appearance, was doubly determined, since it was common to both of them in real life.
>
> Dr. R. in my dream about my uncle with the yellow beard was a similar composite figure. But in his case the dream-image was constructed in yet another way. I did not combine the features of one person with those of another and in the process omit from the memory-picture certain features of each of them. What I did was to adopt the procedure by means of which Galton produced family portraits: namely by projecting two images onto a single plate, so that certain features common to both are emphasized, while those which fail to fit in with one another cancel one another out and are indistinct in the picture. In my dream about my uncle the fair beard emerged prominently from a face which belonged to two people and which was consequently blurred.[1]

For Freud, the condensatory or collective figure superimposes, in the manner of a photograph, two or more entities in one individual. Similarly, the fusion figure of art-horror is a composite figure, conflating distinct *types* of beings. In his discussion of condensation, Freud stresses that the fused elements have something in common. However, in art-horror what the combined elements have in common need not be salient—in T. E. D. Klein's "Nadelman's God," the horrific entity has literally been constructed from a hodgepodge of garbage. As in the associationist writings of the British Empiricists, the fantastic fusion beings of horror are colligations of ontologically or biologically separate orders.[2] They are single figures in whom distinct and often clashing types of elements are superimposed or condensed, resulting in entities that are impure and repulsive.

Freud notes that the collective structures we find in the dream-work are not unlike "the composite animals invented by the folk imagination of the Orient."[3] Presumably, Freud has in mind here figures like the winged lions of ancient Assyria. Other examples of this type of condensation-figure would include the gargoyles on medieval cathedrals, the demon-priest (part rodent, part man) in the central panel of Hieronymus Bosch's *Temptation of St. Anthony* triptych, the chickens with the heads of human babies in Goya's "Ya van desplumados" in *Los Caprichos,* and characters like The Thing (aka Ben Grimm)—literally a man of stone—in the Marvel comic book series The Fantastic Four.

Of course, in these examples, the elements that go into the condensation or fusion are visually perceptible. However, this is not necessary. One might condense different ontological orders such as the animate and inanimate—e.g., a haunted house—and here nothing that meets the naked eye signals the fusion. And, furthermore, whether any of the preceding examples shall count as *horrific* fusion depends upon whether or not, in the representational context in which they appear, the beings so concocted match the criteria of art-horror.

As a means of composing horrific beings, fusion hinges upon conflating, combining, or condensing distinct and/or opposed categorical elements in a spatiotemporally continuous monster. In contrast, another popular means for creating interstitial beings is *fission.* In fusion, categorically contradictory elements are fused or condensed or superimposed in one unified spatiotemporal being whose identity is homogeneous. But with fission, the contradictory elements are, so to speak, distributed over *different,* though metaphysically related, identities. The type of creatures that I have in mind here include doppelgängers, alter egos, and werewolves.

Werewolves, for example, violate the categorical distinction between humans and wolves. In this case, the animal and the human inhabit the same body (understood as spatially locatable protoplasm); however, they do so at *different times.* The animal and the wolf identities are not temporally continuous, though presumably their protoplasm is numerically the same; at a given point in time (the rise of the full moon), the body, inhabited by the human, is turned over to the wolf. The human identity and the wolf identity are not fused, but, so to speak, they are sequenced. The human and the wolf are spatially continuous, occupying the same body, but the identity changes or alternates over time; the two identities—and the opposed categories they represent—do not overlap temporally in the same body. That protoplasm is heterogeneous in terms of accommodating different, mutually exclusive identities at different times.

The werewolf figure embodies a categorical contradiction between man and animal which it distributes over time. Of course, what is being said of werewolves here applies to shape-shifters of every variety. In Kipling's *Mark of the Beast,* the victim is on his way to becoming a leopard, while in Machen's *The Novel of the Black Seal,* the boy-idiot seems to be transmutating into a sea lion. One form of fission, then, *divides* the fantastic being into two or more (categorically distinct) identities that alternatively possess the body in question. Call this temporal fission.[4] Temporal fission can be distinguished from fusion in that the categories combined in the figure of the fantastic being are not temporally simultaneous; rather, they are split or broken or distributed over time.

A second mode of fission distributes the categorical conflict over space through the creation of doubles. Examples here include the portrait in Oscar Wilde's *Picture of Dorian Gray*, the dwarf in the cavalier's body in Mary Shelley's "Transformation," and the doppelgängers in movies like *The Student of Prague* and *Warning Shadows*. Structurally, what is involved in spatial fission is a process of *multiplication*, i.e., a character or set of characters is multiplied into one or more new facets, each standing for another aspect of the self, generally one that is either hidden, ignored, repressed, or denied by the character who has been cloned. These new facets generally contradict cultural ideals (usually morally charged ones) of normality. The alter ego represents a normatively alien aspect of the self. Most of my examples so far employ some mechanism of reflection—a portrait, a mirror, shadows—as the pretext for doubling. But this sort of fission figure can appear without such devices.

In the movie *I Married a Monster from Outer Space*, a young bride begins to suspect that her new husband is not quite himself. Somehow he's different from the man she used to date. And, she's quite right. Her boyfriend was kidnapped by invaders from another planet on his way back from a bachelor party and replaced by an alien. This double,[5] however, initially lacks feelings—the essential characteristic of being human in 1950s sci-fi films of this sort—and his bride intuits this. Thus, the categorical distinction between humanity and inhumanity—marked in terms of the possession versus the lack of feelings—is projected symbolically by splitting the boyfriend in two, with each corresponding entity standing for a categorically distinct order of being.

The basic story of *I Married a Monster from Outer Space*—its sci-fi elements aside—resembles a very specific paranoid delusion called the Capgras delusion. The delusion involves the patient's belief that his or her parents, lovers, etc. have become minatory doppelgängers. This enables the patient to deny his fear or hatred of a loved one by splitting the loved one in half, creating a bad version (the invader) and a good one (the victim). The new relation of marriage in *I Married a Monster from Outer Space* appears to engender a conflict, perhaps over sexuality, in the wife that is expressed through the fission figure.[6] Just as condensation suggests a model for fusion figuration, splitting as a psychic trope of denial may be the root prototype for spatial fission in art-horror, organizing conflicts, categorical and thematic, through the multiplication of characters.

Fission, then, in horror occurs in two major forms—spatial fission and temporal fission. Temporal fission, which the split between Dr. Jekyll and Mr. Hyde exemplifies, *divides characters in time,* while spatial fission—for instance, the case of doppelgängers—*multiplies characters in space.* Here characters become symbols for categorically distinct or opposed elements. In the case of fusion, on the other hand, categorically distinct or opposed elements are conflated or colligated or condensed into a single, spatiotemporally continuous entity whose identity is stable. Both fission and fusion are symbolic structures that facilitate—in different ways—the linkage of distinct and/or opposed categories, thereby providing vehicles for projecting the themes of interstitiality, categorical contradictoriness, and impurity. The fantastic biologies of horrific monsters are, to a surprising extent, reducible to the symbolic structures of fusion and fission.

In order to make a horrific monster—in terms of the impurity requirement—it is enough to link distinct and/or opposed categories by fission or fusion. In terms of fusion, one can put claws on Rosemary's baby, the devil in Regan, or a fly's head on Vincent Price's body. By fission, discrete and/or contradictory categories can be connected by having different biological or ontological orders take turns inhabiting one body, or by populating the fiction with numerically different but otherwise identical bodies, each representing one of the opposed categories. In the most fundamental sense of fusion and fission, these structures are meant to apply to the organization of opposed cultural categories, generally of a deep biological or ontological sort: human–reptile, living–dead, etc. But it is also true that in much horror, especially that which is considered to be classic, the opposition of such cultural categories in the biology of the horrific creatures portend further oppositions, oppositions that might be thought of in terms of thematic conflicts or antinomies which, in turn, are generally deep-seated in the culture in which the fiction has been produced.

For example, the horrific creatures in Blackwood's celebrated *Ancient Sorceries* are were-cats. An entire French town goes feline, at night indulging all manner of unmentionable (and unmentioned) debaucheries in the presence of Satan. In terms of my model, these creatures are the product of temporal fission. But this division—between cat and human—heralds other oppositions in the context of the story. An Englishman (perhaps the reincarnation of a cat-man from bygone days) visits the town and is gradually tempted to join the coven. The opposition of cat versus human plays into further oppositions—sensual versus staid, nondirective activity versus conscientious, female versus male, and maybe even French versus British. That is, the salient opposition of different elements at the categorical level of biology might be thought of as prefiguring a series of further thematic oppositions.

Another example along the same lines would be Val Lewton's film *Cat People.* Irena is a shape-changer whose divided self is not only categorically fissured but also represents the opposition of chaste love versus violent sexuality. In terms of fusion, the vampire in Sheridan Le Fanu's *Camilla* may be a case in point; for the opposition between living and dead in the monster's makeup portends a further thematic conflict concerning lesbianism.[7]

The notions of fission and fusion are meant to apply strictly to the biological and ontological categorical ingredients that go into making monsters. So it is sufficient for a being to be part man and part snake for it to qualify as a horrific fusion figure, or for a woman to be a lady by day and a troll or gorgon by night in order for her to qualify as a horrific fission figure. However, it is frequently the case that the oppositional biologies of fantastic beings correlate to an oppositional thematics. This is generally the case with what are thought to be the better specimens of horror. As a result, much of the work of the critic of horror, as opposed to the theoretician of horror, will be to trace the thematic conflicts that appear in her objects of study. That the creatures are fission or fusion figures may be less interesting than what this dimension of categorical interstitiality prefigures at the thematic level.[8] However, for purposes of theoretically identifying the symbolic structures through which myriad monsters are made, the notions of fission and fusion are crucial.

Along with fission and fusion, another recurring symbolic structure for generating horrific monsters is the *magnification* of entities or beings already typically adjudged impure or disgusting within the culture. In the concluding paragraphs of M. R. James's *The Ash-Tree,* the gardener looks into the hollow of a tree trunk, his face contorts "with an incredulous terror and loathing," and he cries out with a "dreadful voice" before fainting. What he has seen is a poisonous spider—spawned from a witch's body for the purposes of revenge—that is as big as a man's head.[9] The spider, already a phobic object in our culture, exceeds in horribleness not only because of its supernatural provenance and unearthly abilities but especially because of its increase in size beyond the normal.

Things that creep and crawl—and that tend to make our flesh creep and crawl—are prime candidates for the objects of art-horror; such creatures already disgust, and augmenting their scale increases their physical dangerousness. In Stephen King's "Jerusalem's Lot," a hellish creature is summoned by means of an unholy book:

> Calvin pushed me and I tottered, the church whirling before me, and fell to the floor. My head crashed against the edge of an upturned pew, and red fire filled my head—yet seemed to clear it.
>
> I groped for the sulphur matches I had brought.
>
> Subterranean thunder filled the place. Plaster fell. The rusted bell in the steeple pealed a choked devil's clarion in sympathetic vibration.
>
> My match flared. I touched it to the book just as the pulpit exploded upward in a rending explosion of wood. A huge black maw was discovered beneath; Cal tottered on the edge, his hands held out, his face distended in a wordless scream that I shall hear forever.

> And then there was a huge surge of gray, vibrating flesh. The smell
> became a nightmare tide. It was a huge outpouring of a viscid, pustulant jelly,
> a huge and awful form that seemed to skyrocket from the very bowels of the
> ground. And yet, with a sudden horrible comprehension which no man can
> have known, I perceived *that it was but one ring, one segment, of a monster
> worm that had-existed eyeless for years in the chambered darkness beneath that
> abominated church*!
>
> The book flared alight in my hands, and the Thing seemed to scream
> soundlessly above me. Calvin was struck glancingly and flung the length of the
> church like a doll with a broken neck.

Monsters of the magnified phobia variety were quite popular in 1950s movies (undoubtedly, they were suggested by the first radiation experiments on seeds). Some examples include *Them!, Tarantula, Attack of the Crab Monsters, The Deadly Mantis, Giant Gila Monster, Monster from Green Hell, Attack of the Giant Leeches, The Spider, Black Scorpion, The Fly, The Monster That Challenged the World, The Giant Spider Invasion, Mothra, The Return of the Fly,* the humongous octopus in *It Came from Beneath the Sea,* the big crawlers in *Rodan,* the giant grasshoppers in *The Beginning of the End,* and the proportionately towering black widow in *The Incredible Shrinking Man,* among others. Insofar as detached body parts can elicit revulsion, we encounter the *Crawling Eye* attempting to conquer the world. More recently, giant ants have eaten Joan Collins in *Empire of the Ants* and outsized rats have surrounded Marjoe Gortner in *Food of the Gods.* Of course, one cannot magnify just anything and hope for a horrific creature; few seem to have been convinced by the monster rabbits in *Night of the Lepus.* What needs to be magnified are things that are already potentially disturbing and disgusting.[10]

For the purposes of art-horror, one may exploit the repelling aspect of existing creatures not only by magnifying them, but also by *massing* them. In Richard Lewis's novel *Devil's Coach Horse,* armies of bloodthirsty beetles are on the rampage, while the identity of the monstrous masses in Guy Smith's *Killer Crabs* and Peter Tremayne's *Ants* requires no further comment. These swarms of crawling things, grouped for an ultimate showdown with humanity, are, of course, really fantastical beings, invested with strategic abilities, virtual invulnerability, a hankering for human flesh, and often mutated powers unknown to present-day biological science. Carl Stephenson's "Leiningen versus the Ants"—surely the *Moby Dick* of the insect genre—is based on the scientifically correct observation that certain types of ants forage in large, coordinated collectives, but he imbues these ants with qualities and powers that experts of the day would have found unprecedented.[11] They are hunting people and horses—rather than other insects like spiders, cockroaches, and grasshoppers—and the story strongly suggests that they knock out Leiningen's weir *in order to* cross the channel. Saul Bass's movie *Phase IV* presents the army of ants as a superior intelligence, while in *Kingdom of the Spiders* the invading tarantulas enwrap an entire town in their web for purposes of food storage; in *Kiss of the Tarantulas,* the spiders become hit men. As with the case of magnification, with massification it is not the case that any kind of entity can be grouped into horrific hordes. It must be the sort of thing we are already prone to find repellent—a point made comically by *The Attack of the Killer Tomatoes* (and its sequel, *The Return of . . .*). Massing mountains of already disgusting creatures, unified and guided by unfriendly purposes, generates art-horror by augmenting the threat posed by these antecedently phobic objects.

Fantastic biologies, linking different and opposed cultural categories, can be constructed by means of fission and fusion, while the horrific potential of already disgusting and phobic entities can be accentuated by means of magnification and massification. These are primary structures for the construction of horrific creatures. These structures pertain primarily to what might be thought of as the biologies of horrific monsters. However, another structure, not essentially connected to the biology of these creatures, warrants discussion in a review of the presentation of horrific beings, for though not a matter of biology, it is an important recurring strategy in the staging of monsters. This strategy might be called *horrific metonymy.*

Often the horror of horrific creatures is not something that can be perceived by the naked eye or that comes through a description of the look of the monster. Frequently, in such cases, the horrific being is *surrounded* by objects that we antecedently take to be objects of disgust and/or phobia. In "The Spectre Bride," the Wandering Jew, a fusion figure, does not initially appear disgusting; however, the wedding is associated by contiguity with disgust:

> [The Wandering Jew] "Poor girl, I am leading thee indeed to our nuptials; but the priest will be death, thy parents the mouldering skeletons that rot in heaps around; and the witnesses [of] our union, the lazy worms that revel on the carious bones of the dead. Come, my young bride, the priest is impatient for his victim." As they proceeded, a dim blue light moved swiftly before them, and displayed at the extremity of the churchyard the portals of a vault. It was open, and they entered it in silence. The hollow wind came rushing through the gloomy abode of the dead; and on every side were the mouldering remnants of coffins, which dropped piece by piece upon the damp earth. Every step they took was on a dead body; and the bleached bones rattled horribly beneath their feet. In the centre of the vault rose a heap of unburied skeletons, whereon was seated a figure too awful even for the darkest imagination to conceive. As they approached it, the hollow vault rung with a hellish peal of laughter; and every mouldering corpse seemed endued with unearthly life.

Here, though the horrific bridegroom himself doesn't elicit disgust perceptually, everything that surrounds him and his hellish ministrations is impure by the lights of the culture. In a similar vein, Dracula, both in literature and on stage and screen, is associated with vermin; in the novel, he commands armies of rats. And undoubtedly, the association of horrific beings with disease and contamination is related to the tendency to surround horrific beings with further impurities.

In Clive Barker's *The Damnation Game*—a sort of update of *Melmoth the Wanderer*—the Mephistophelian character Mamoulian is ostensibly normal-looking but his associated minion, the Razor-Eater is a hulking zombie undergoing graphically described putrefaction throughout the novel, a feature made more unsettling by his always messy indulging of his sweet tooth. Likewise, the child possessed by the spirit of Beth in John Saul's *Suffer the Children*, though not outwardly disgusting herself, is surrounded by stomach-turning ceremonies such as a make-believe tea party attended by blood-splattered children, the skeleton of Beth, and a decapitated cat in a doll's outfit whose head keeps rolling off its shoulders. With Mamoulian and Beth, the fantastic being is not perceptually repulsive but is linked by metonymy to perceptually disgusting things. Of course, even those creatures like Dracula though they may not, in the main, be portrayed as *perceptually* loathsome, are nevertheless still disgusting and impure; one doesn't require perceptually detectable grotesquerie in order to be reviling. Dracula strikes Harker as sickening though his appearance is not literally monstrous. In such cases, the association of such impure creatures with perceptually pronounced gore or other disgusting trappings is a means of underscoring the repulsive nature of the being.

In James Herbert's novel *The Magic Cottage*, the villainous magus Mycroft is a stately, altogether human figure who has at his disposal agencies marked by incredible noxiousness. In the final confrontation with the narrator, he summons them: the "carpet was ripping explosively all around me, and sluglike monsters oozed over the edges in shiny slimes. Hands that were scabbed and dripping pus clawed at the frayed carpet in an effort to drag the rest of their life forms out into the open. Those membranes, full of wriggling life, quivered their snouts in the air before curling over the edge. Wispy black smoke tendrils drifted up in lazy spirals, and these were full of diseased microorganisms, the corrupting evil that roamed the depths, subversives that searched for ways to surface, intent on finding exposure, definition—*actuality*. These were the infiltrating substances of evil."

Horrific metonymy need not be restricted to cases where the monsters do not look gruesome; an already misshapen creature can be associated with entities already antecedently thought of in terms of impurity and filth. Think of Murnau's *Nosferatu* and the remake by Werner Herzog, where the vampire is linked to unclean, crawling things. Similarly, zombies with great gobs of phlegm dangling from their lips exemplify horrific metonymy.

Fusion, fission, magnification, massification, and horrific metonymy are the major tropes for presenting the monsters of art-horror.[12] Fusion and fission are means for constructing horrific biologies; magnification and massification are means for augmenting the powers of already disgusting and phobic creatures. Horrific metonymy is a means of emphasizing the impure and disgusting nature of the creature—from the outside, so to speak—by associating said being with objects and entities that are already reviled: body parts, vermin, skeletons, and all manner of filth. The horrific creature is essentially a compound of danger and disgust and each of these structures provides a means of developing these attributes in tandem.

Notes

1. Sigmund Freud, *The Interpretation of Dreams,* trans. James Strachey (New York: Avon Books, 1965), 327–28.

2. Recall Hume's notion that the fantastic beasts of mythology are recombinations of elements previously experienced in perception. David Hume, *Treatise on Human Nature,* I, 1, 3.

3. Sigmund Freud, *On Dreams,* trans. James Strachey (New York: Norton Library, 1952), 46.

4. The distinction between temporal and spatial fission is an elaboration of Robert Rogers, *A Psychoanalytic Study of the Double in Literature* (Detroit, Mich.: Wayne State University Press, 1970).

5. The real boyfriend is hanging on some kind of ray-gun meat hook in an alien spaceship whose interior resembles that of a large icebox.

6. *I Married a Monster from Outer Space* belongs to a subgenre of space-possession films including *Invasion of the Body Snatchers* (both versions), *Creation of the Humanoids, Man from Planet X, Invaders from Mars* (both versions), *Phantom from Space, It Came from Outer Space, Killers from Space,* etc. Depending on the specific context of the film, the possessed earthlings in these films can be examples of either spatial or temporal fission. For an interpretation of *Invasion of the Body Snatchers,* see my "You're Next" in *Soho Weekly News,* December 21, 1978.

7. Carmilla may not represent an absolutely pure case of fusion since at times she is described as a dark figure that may be an animal. Thus, she may be a shape-changer, but I think the text is somewhat ambiguous.

8. At the same time, the distinction between fission and fusion can be useful to the critic as a means of penetrating the symbolic organization of the fantastic being in question in such a way that the thematic oppositions that the creature's biology prefigures are clarified.

9. James has prepared for this denouement by emphasizing the "*poysonous Rage*" and "*venomous*" aspect of the witch in the opening of the story.

10. One also suspects that one could also generate a horrific being by miniaturization. There is a story in the movie *Stephen King's Cat's Eye* where the troll monster is all the more horrifying for being tiny, insofar as this allows him to endanger the child heroine by being effectively invisible to adults (but luckily not to cats).

11. See William Morton Wheeler, *Ants: Their Structure, Development and Behavior* (New York: Columbia University Press, 1910), 246–56. "Leiningen versus the Ants" was made into a movie called *The Naked Jungle* by Byron Haskin.

12. These tropes may not be mutually preclusive and the list may not be exhaustive; however, I think that it does supply a useful characterization of a number of the most recurrent structures of horrific imagery.

PARASITES AND PERVERTS

An Introduction to Gothic Monstrosity

Jack Halberstam

So many monsters; so little time.
—promotional slogan for *Hellraiser*

Skin Shows

In *The Silence of the Lambs* (1991) by Jonathan Demme, one of many modern adaptations of *Frankenstein*, a serial killer known as Buffalo Bill collects women in order to flay them and use their skins to construct a "woman suit." Sitting in his basement sewing hides, Buffalo Bill makes his monster a sutured beast, a patchwork of gender, sex, and sexuality. Skin, in this morbid scene, represents the monstrosity of surfaces and as Buffalo Bill dresses up in his suit and prances in front of the mirror, he becomes a layered body, a body of many surfaces laid one upon the other. Depth and essence dissolve in this mirror dance, and identity and humanity become skin deep.

My subject is monsters, and I begin in Buffalo Bill's basement, his "filthy workshop of creation," because it dramatizes precisely the distance traveled between current representations of monstrosity and their genesis in nineteenth-century Gothic fiction. Where the monsters of the nineteenth century metaphorized modern subjectivity as a balancing act between inside–outside, female–male, body–mind, native–foreign, proletarian–aristocrat, monstrosity in postmodern horror

148

films finds its place in what Baudrillard has called the obscenity of "immediate visibility"[1] and what Linda Williams has dubbed "the frenzy of the visible."[2] The immediate visibility of a Buffalo Bill, the way in which he makes the surface itself monstrous, transforms the cavernous monstrosity of Jekyll/Hyde, Dorian Gray, or Dracula into a beast who is all body and no soul.

Victorian monsters produced and were produced by an emergent conception of the self as a body which enveloped a soul, as a body, indeed, enthralled to its soul. Michel Foucault writes in *Discipline and Punish* that "the soul is the prison of the body," and he proposes a genealogy of the soul that will show it to be born out of "methods of punishment, supervision and constraint."[3] Foucault also claims that, as modern forms of discipline shifted their gaze from the body to the soul, crime literature moved from confession or gallows speeches or the cataloging of famous criminals to the detective fiction obsessed with identifying criminality and investigating crime. The hero of such literature was now the middle- or upper-class schemer whose crime became a virtuoso performance of skill and enterprise.

There are many congruities between Gothic fiction and detective fiction, but in the Gothic, crime is embodied within a specifically deviant form—the monster—that announces itself (de-monstrates) as the place of corruption. Furthermore, just as the detective character appears across genres in many different kinds of fiction (in the sensation novel, in Dickens), so Gothic infiltrates the Victorian novel as a symptomatic moment in which boundaries between good and evil, health and perversity, crime and punishment, truth and deception, inside and outside, dissolve and threaten the integrity of the narrative itself. While many literary histories, therefore, have relegated Gothic to a subordinate status in relation to realism, I will be arguing that nineteenth-century literary tradition *is* a Gothic tradition and that this has everything to do with the changing technologies of subjectivity that Foucault describes.

Gothic fiction is a technology of subjectivity, one which produces the deviant subjectivities opposite which the normal, the healthy, and the pure can be known. Gothic, within my analysis, may be loosely defined as the rhetorical style and narrative structure designed to produce fear and desire within the reader. The production of fear in a literary text (as opposed to a cinematic text) emanates from a vertiginous excess of meaning. Gothic, in a way, refers to an ornamental excess (think of Gothic architecture—gargoyles and crazy loops and spirals), a rhetorical extravagance that produces, quite simply, too much. Within Gothic novels, I argue, multiple interpretations are embedded in the text, and part of the experience of horror comes from the realization that meaning itself runs riot. Gothic novels produce a symbol for this interpretive mayhem in the body of the monster. The monster always becomes a primary focus of interpretation, and its monstrosity seems available for any number of meanings. While I will examine closely the implications of embodied horror (monstrosity) in nineteenth-century Gothic, I will also be paying careful attention to the rhetorical system which produces it (Gothic).

Many histories of the Gothic novel begin with the Gothic Romances of the later eighteenth century by Mrs. Radcliffe, Horace Walpole, and Matthew Lewis.[4] While, obviously, there are connections to be made between these stories of mad monks, haunted castles, and wicked foreigners and the nineteenth-century Gothic tales of monsters and vampires, we should not take the connections too far. I argue that the emergence of the monster within Gothic fiction marks a peculiarly modern emphasis upon the horror of particular kinds of bodies. Furthermore, the ability of the Gothic story to take the imprint of any number of interpretations makes it a hideous offspring of capitalism itself. The Gothic novel of the nineteenth century and the Gothic horror film of the late twentieth century are both obsessed with multiple modes of consumption and production, with dangerous consumptions and excessive productivity, and with economies of meaning. The monster itself is an economic form in that it condenses various racial and sexual threats to nation, capitalism, and the bourgeoisie in one body. If the Gothic novel produces an easy answer to the question of what threatens national security and prosperity (the monster), the Gothic monster represents many answers to the question of who must be removed from the community at large. I will be considering, therefore, nineteenth- and twentieth-century Gothic as separate from eighteenth-century Gothic, but I will also be tracing Gothic textuality across many modes of discourse.

Within the nineteenth-century Gothic, authors mixed and matched a wide variety of signifiers of difference to fabricate the deviant body—Dracula, Jekyll/Hyde, and even Frankenstein's monster before them are lumpen bodies, bodies pieced together out of the fabric of race, class, gender, and sexuality. In the modern period, and with the advent of cinematic body horror, the shift from the literary Gothic to the visual Gothic was accompanied by a narrowing rather than a broadening of the scope of horror. One might expect to find that cinema multiplies the possibilities for monstrosity, but in fact, the visual register quickly reaches a limit of visibility. In *Frankenstein* the reader can only imagine the dreadful spectacle of the monster, and so its monstrosity is limited only by the reader's imagination; in the horror film, the monster must always fail to be monstrous enough, and horror therefore depends upon the explicit violation of female bodies as opposed to simply the sight of the monster.

Furthermore, as I noted, while nineteenth-century Gothic monstrosity was a combination of the features of deviant race, class, and gender, within contemporary horror, the monster, for various reasons, tends to show clearly the markings of deviant sexualities and gendering but less clearly the signs of class or race. Buffalo Bill in *The Silence of the Lambs,* for example, leads one to suppose that the monstrous body is a sexed or gendered body only, but this particular body, a borrowed skin, is also clearly inscribed with a narrative of class conflict. To give just one example of deviant class in this film, the heroine, Clarice Starling, is identified by Hannibal Lecter as a woman trying to hide her working-class roots behind "bad perfume" and cheap leather shoes. Given the emphases in this film upon skins and hides, it is all too significant that cheap leather gives Starling away. Poor skin, in this film, literally signifies poverty, or the trace of it. As we will see, however, the narrative of monstrous class identity has been almost completely subsumed within *The Silence of the Lambs* by monstrous sexuality and gender.

The discourse of racialized monstrosity within the modern horror film proves to be a discursive minefield. Perhaps because race has been so successfully Goth-icized within our recent history, filmmakers and screenplay writers tend not to want to make a monster who is defined by a deviant racial identity. Euro-pean anti-Semitism and American racism toward black Americans are precisely Gothic discourses given over to the making monstrous of particular kinds of bod-ies. This study will delineate carefully the multiple strands of anti-Semitism within nineteenth-century Gothic, and I will attempt to suggest why anti-Semitism in particular used Gothic methods to make Jews monstrous. But when it comes to tracing the threads of Gothic race into modern horror, we often draw a blank.

The Gothicization of certain "races" over the last century, one might say, has been all too successful. This does not mean that Gothic race is not readable in the contemporary horror text, but it is clear that, within Gothic, the difference between representing racism and representing race is extremely tricky to negoti-ate. I will be arguing, in relation to *The Silence of the Lambs,* that the film clearly represents homophobia and sexism and punishes actions motivated by them; it would be very difficult in a horror film to show and punish racism simultaneously. To give an example of what I am arguing here, one can look at a contemporary horror film, *Candyman* (1990), and the way it merges monstrosity and race.

In *Candyman,* two female graduate students in anthropology at the Univer-sity of Illinois at Chicago are researching urban legends when they run across the story of Candyman, the ghost of a murdered black man who haunts the Cabrini Green projects. Candyman was the son of a former slave who made good by in-venting a procedure for the mass production of shoes. Despite his wealth, Candy-man still ran into trouble with the white community by falling in love with a white woman. He was chased by white men to Cabrini Green, where they caught him, cut his right hand off, and drove a hook into the bloody stump. Next Candy-man was covered in honey and taken to an apiary, where the bees killed him. Now, the urban myth goes, Candyman responds to all who call him. The two researchers, a white woman and a black woman, go to Cabrini Green to hunt for information on Candyman. Naturally, the black woman, Bernadette, is killed by Candyman, and the white woman, Helen, is seduced by him. While the film on some level attempts to direct all kinds of social criticisms at urban planners, historians, and racist white homeowners, ultimately the horror stabilizes in the ghastly body of the black man whose monstrosity turns upon his desire for the white woman and his murderous intentions toward black women.

No amount of elaborate framing within this film can prevent it from confirming racist assumptions about black male aggression toward white female bodies. Monstrosity, in this tired narrative, never becomes mobile; rather, it remains anchored by the weight of racist narratives. The film contains some clever visual moves, like a shot of Helen going through the back of a mirror into a derelict apartment. She next passes through a hole in the wall, and the camera reverses to show her stepping through a graffiti painting of a black man's face. She stops for a moment in the mouth of the black man, and this startling image hints at the various forms of oral transmission that the film circulates. Is Helen contained by the oral history of the Candyman, or is she the articulate voice of the academy that disrupts its transmission and brings violence to the surface? Inevitably, Helen's character stabilizes under the sign of the white woman victim, and Candyman's horror becomes a static signifier of black male violence. If race in nineteenth-century Gothic was one of many clashing surfaces of monstrosity, in the context of twentieth-century Gothic, race becomes a master signifier of monstrosity, and when invoked, it blocks out all other possibilities of monstrous identity.

Moving from nineteenth-century Gothic monsters to the monsters of contemporary horror films, my study will show that within the history of embodied deviance, monsters always combine the markings of a plurality of differences even if certain forms of difference are eclipsed momentarily by others. The fact that monstrosity within contemporary horror seems to have stabilized into an amalgam of sex and gender demonstrates the need to read a history of otherness into and out of the history of Gothic fiction. Gothic fiction of the nineteenth century specifically used the body of the monster to produce race, class, gender, and sexuality within narratives about the relation between subjectivities and certain bodies.

Monstrosity (and the fear it gives rise to) is historically conditioned rather than a psychological universal. Tracing the emergence of monstrosity from *Frankenstein* through to the contemporary horror film (in both its high- and low-budget forms), I will attempt to show that monsters not only reveal certain material conditions of the production of horror, but they also make strange the categories of beauty, humanity, and identity that we still cling to. While the horror within *Frankenstein* seemed to depend upon the monster's actual hideous physical aspect, his status as anomaly, and his essential foreignness, the threat of Buffalo Bill depends upon the violence of his identity crisis, a crisis that will exact a price in female flesh. Buffalo Bill's identity crisis is precisely that: a crisis of knowledge, a "category crisis";[5] but it no longer takes the form of the anomaly—now a category crisis indicates a crisis of sexual identity.

It is in the realm of sexuality, however, that Buffalo Bill and Frankenstein's monster seem to share traits, and it is here that we may be inclined to read Buffalo Bill as a reincarnation of many of the features of nineteenth-century monstrosity. As a sexual being, Frankenstein's monster is foreign, and as an outsider to the community, his foreign sexuality is monstrous and threatens miscegenation. Frankenstein's lonely monster is driven out of town by the mob when he threatens to reproduce. Similarly, Buffalo Bill threatens the community with his indeterminate gender and sexuality. Indeed, sexuality and its uneasy relation to gender identity creates Buffalo Bill's monstrosity. But much ground has been traveled between the stitched monstrosity of Frankenstein and the sutured gender horror of Buffalo Bill; while both monsters have been sewn into skin bodysuits, and while both want to jump out of their skins, the nineteenth-century monster is marked by racial or species violation, while Buffalo Bill seems to be all gender. If we measure one skin job against the other, we can read transitions between various signifying systems of identity.

Skin, I will argue with reference to certain nineteenth-century monsters, becomes a kind of metonym for the human; and its color, its pallor, its shape, mean everything within a semiotic of monstrosity. Skin might be too tight (Frankenstein's creature), too dark (Hyde), too pale (Dracula), too superficial (Dorian Gray's canvas), too loose (Leatherface), or too sexed (Buffalo Bill). Skin houses the body, and it is figured in Gothic as the ultimate boundary, the material that divides the inside from the outside. The vampire will puncture and mark the skin with his fangs, Mr. Hyde will covet white skin, Dorian Gray will desire his own canvas, Buffalo Bill will covet female skin, Leatherface will wear his victim's skin as a trophy and recycle his flesh as food. Slowly but surely the outside becomes the inside, and the hide no longer conceals or contains; it offers itself up as text, as body, as monster. The Gothic text, whether novel or film, plays out an elaborate skin show.

How sexuality became the dominant mark of otherness is a question that we may begin to answer by deconstructing Victorian Gothic monsters and examining the constitutive features of the horror they represent. If, for example, many nineteenth-century monsters seem to produce fears more clearly related to racial identity than gender identity, how is it that we as modern readers have been unable to discern these more intricate contours of difference? Obviously, the answer to such a question, and many others like it, lies in a history of sexuality, a history introduced by Michel Foucault and continued by recent studies that link Foucault's work to a history of the novel.[6]

In this study I am not simply attempting to add racial, national, or class difference to the already well-defined otherness of sexual perversion, nor am I attempting merely another reading of the Gothic tradition; I am suggesting that, where the foreign and the sexual merge within monstrosity in Gothic, a particular history of sexuality unfolds. It is indeed necessary to map out a relation between the monstrous sexuality of the foreigner and the foreign sexuality of the monster, because sexuality, I will argue, is itself a beast created in nineteenth-century literature. Where sexuality becomes an identity, other "others" become invisible, and the multiple features of monstrosity seem to degenerate back into a primeval sexual slime. Class, race, and nation are subsumed, in other words, within the monstrous sexual body; accordingly, Dracula's bite drains pleasure rather than capital, Mr. Hyde symbolizes repression rather than the production of self, and both figure foreign aspect as a threat to domestic security. While I will attempt here to delineate the mechanism by which multiple otherness is subsumed by the unitary otherness of sexuality, it is actually beyond the scope of this study to account for the very particular and individual histories of race, nation, and class within the nineteenth century. I am concerned specifically with representational strategies and with the particularities of deviant race, class, national, and gender markings.

Past studies of the Gothic have tended toward the psychological, or more precisely, the psychoanalytic, because the unconscious is assumed to be the proper seat of fear. So, for example, there are studies of the Gothic that associate Gothic with masochism,[7] with the abject maternal,[8] with women's "fear of self,"[9] with the very construction of female identity.[10] And yet, as critics like Michel Foucault and Gilles Deleuze and Félix Guattari have shown, the unconscious itself and all of its mechanisms are precisely the effects of historical and cultural production. Therefore, to historicize monstrosity in literature, and especially in the Gothic novel, reveals a specificity within the way that, since the age of Frankenstein and Dracula, monsters mark difference within and upon bodies. A historical study of Gothic and of Gothic monstrosity must actually avoid psychoanalytic readings just long enough to expose the way that Gothic actually participates in the production of something like a psychology of self. However, as will be clear, certain psychoanalytic positions on fear and desire are useful ways of negotiating between the psychic and the social and of showing how some social mechanisms are internalized to the point that they are experienced as internal mechanisms. In order to examine such a process, a detour through Freud's case histories of paranoia will be necessary.

The body that scares and appalls changes over time, as do the individual characteristics that add up to monstrosity, as do the preferred interpretations of that monstrosity. Within the traits that make a body monstrous—that is, frightening or ugly, abnormal or disgusting—we may read the difference between an other and a self, a pervert and a normal person, a foreigner and a native. Furthermore, in order to read monsters as the embodiments of psychic horror, one must first of all subscribe to psychoanalysis's own tale of human subjectivity—a fiction intent upon rewriting the Gothic elements of human subjectivity. As I have said, my study refuses the universality of what Deleuze and Guattari call the "daddy-mommy-me triangle,"[11] but it cannot always escape the triangle. With characteristic grim humor, Deleuze and Guattari describe the psychoanalytic encounter between analyst and patient: "The psychoanalyst no longer says to the patient: 'Tell me a little bit about your desiring machines, won't you?' Instead he screams: 'Answer daddy-and-mommy when I speak to you!' Even Melanie Klein. So the entire process of desiring-production is trampled underfoot and reduced to parental images, laid out step by step in accordance with supposed pre-oedipal stages, totalized in Oedipus."[12] Within modern Western culture, we are disciplined through a variety of social and political mechanisms into psychoanalytic relations, and then psychoanalytic explanations are deployed to totalize our submission. Resistance in such a circular system, as many theorists have noted, merely becomes part of the oppressive mechanism. However, psychoanalysis, with its emphases on and investments in the normal, quickly reveals itself to be inadequate to the task of unraveling the power of horror.

In relation to Gothic monstrosity, it is all too easy to understand how the relation between fear and desire may be oedipalized, psychologized, humanized. Psychoanalysis itself has a clinical term for the transformation of desire into fear and of the desired/feared object into monster: *paranoia*. Freud believed that his theory of paranoia as a repressed homosexual desire could be applied to any and all cases of paranoia regardless of race or social class. This, of course, is where the psychoanalytic crisis begins and ends—in its attempt to reduce everything to the sexual and then in its equation of sexuality and identity. The process by which political material becomes sexual material is one in which the novel plays a major role. And the Gothic novel, particularly the late-Victorian Gothic novel, provides a metaphor for this process in the form of the monster. The monster is the product of and the symbol for the transformation of identity into sexual identity through the mechanism of failed repression.

One Lacanian account of monstrosity demonstrates simultaneously the appeal and the danger of psychoanalytic explanations. In Slavoj Žižek's essay "Grimaces of the Real; or, When the Phallus Appears," he reads the phantom from *The Phantom of the Opera* alongside such enigmatic images as the vampire, Edvard Munch's *The Scream* (1893), and David Lynch's *Elephant Man* (1980).[13] Žižek attempts to position images of the living-dead as both mediators between high art and mass culture and as "the void of the pure self" (67). Žižek is at his most persuasive when he discusses the multiplicity of meaning generated by the monster. The fecundity of the monster as a symbol leads him to state, "The crucial question is not 'What does the phantom signify?' but 'How is the very space constituted where entities like the phantom can emerge?'" (63). The monster/phantom, in other words, never stands for a simple or unitary prejudice; it always acts as a "fantasy screen" upon which viewers and readers inscribe and sexualize meaning.

Žižek also seems to be very aware of the dangers of what he calls "the so-called psychoanalytic interpretation of art," which operates within a kind of spiral of interpretation so that everything *means* psychoanalysis. Accordingly, rather than explain the mother's voice in *Psycho* as the maternal superego, he suggests "turn(ing) it around, to explain the very logic of the maternal superego by means of this vocal stain" (51). But Žižek does not always sustain his challenge to the hegemonic structure of psychoanalysis. Indeed, he often stays firmly within the interpretive confines of the psychoanalytic model and merely uses cultural texts as examples of psychoanalytic functions (particularly Lacanian functions). Within this model, the phantom of the opera, for example, is a "fetish"; it literally stands in for various kinds of antagonisms: class based, racial, economic, national, etc. But the fetish remains always a sexual mechanism, and this is where Žižek's analysis is doomed to reproduce the process it attempts to explain; the fetish is a sexualized object that stands in for and indeed covers up other kinds of antagonism. Žižek gives, as an example of the fetishistic role of the phantom, the Jew of anti-Semitic discourse. It is crucial to an interpretation of Gothic to understand that the Jew/phantom/monster is sexualized within fictional narratives (and this includes pseudoscientific and social-scientific narratives that are usually classified as nonfiction) as a part of the narrative process that transforms class/race/gender threat into sexual threat.

Žižek's claim, then, that "the Jew is the anal object par excellence, that is to say, the partial object stain that disturbs the harmony of the class relationship" (57) precisely leaves intact the sexualization of Jewishness; his assertion that the phantom of the living-dead is the emergence of "the anal father" or "primal father" and the opposite of paternal law reinscribes parental (symbolic or otherwise) relations into a scene that precisely seems to escape the familial; his claim, finally, that vampires do not appear in mirrors because "they have read their Lacan" and know, therefore, that "they materialize object *a* which, by definition, *cannot be mirrored*" (55), begs to be read as a parody of what it invokes but instead actually continues to posit subjects that simply do not exist independent of their production in Lacanian psychoanalysis.

The vampire of the nineteenth-century narrative has most certainly not read his or her Lacan (avant la lettre) and does not know that he or she cannot be mirrored. This vampire crawls face down along the wall dividing self from other, class from race from gender and drains metaphoricity from one place only to infuse it in another. While Žižek claims often in his work to be using psychoanalysis and specifically Lacan to explain popular culture paradigms, too often he merely uses popular culture to explain Lacan. And, of course, this particular relationship between host and parasite is the only one that psychoanalytic discourse can endorse. Žižek warns, "The analysis that focuses on the 'ideological meaning' of monsters overlooks the fact that, before signifying something, before serving as a vessel of meaning, monsters embody enjoyment qua the limit of interpretation, that is to say, *nonmeaning as such*" (64). The idea that a realm of "nonmeaning" exists prior to interpretation is only possible in a structural universe in which form and content can easily be separated. Gothic literature in particular is a rhetorical form which resists the disintegration of form and content.[14] Monstrosity always unites monstrous form with monstrous meaning.

In its typical form, the Gothic topos is the monstrous body à la Frankenstein, Dracula, Dorian Gray, Jekyll/Hyde; in its generic form, Gothic is the disruption of realism and of all generic purity. It is the hideous eruption of the monstrous in the heart of domestic England, but it is also the narrative that calls genre itself into question. Mary Shelley's *Frankenstein*, which I think functions as an allegory of Gothic production, contains a domestic tableau of family life (the De Laceys) right in the heart of the narrative. This structure inverts and threatens to maintain a reversal whereby, rather than the Gothic residing in the dark corners of realism, the realistic is buried alive in the gloomy recesses of Gothic. It may well be that the novel is always Gothic.

Gothic Gnomes

In her 1832 introduction to *Frankenstein*, Shelley writes, "I bid my hideous progeny go forth and prosper."[15] Shelley's "hideous progeny" was not merely her novel but the nineteenth-century Gothic novel itself. The Gothic, of course, did indeed prosper and thrive through the century. It grew in popularity until, by the turn of the century, its readership was massive enough that a writer could actually make a living from the sale of his Gothic works. In 1891, for example, Robert Louis Stevenson loosed his "shilling shocker" *Dr. Jekyll and Mr. Hyde* upon the reading public hoping for commercial returns. Stevenson described his novella as a "Gothic gnome" and worried that he had produced a gross distortion of literature.[16] Such an anxiety marked Gothic itself as a monstrous form in relation to its popularity and its improper subject matter. The appellation "Gothic gnome" labeled the genre as a mutation or hybrid form of true art and genteel literature.

But monsters do indeed sell books, and books sell monsters, and the very popularity of the Gothic suggests that readers and writers collaborate in the production of the features of monstrosity. Gothic novels, in fact, thematize the monstrous aspects of both production and consumption—*Frankenstein* is, after all, an allegory about a production that refuses to submit to its author, and *Dracula* is a novel about an arch-consumer, the vampire, who feeds upon middle-class women and then turns them into vampires by forcing them to feed upon him. The Gothic, in fact, like the vampire itself, creates a public who consumes monstrosity, who revels in it, and who then surveys its individual members for signs of deviance or monstrosity, excess or violence.

Anxiety about the effects of consuming popular literature revealed itself in England in the 1890s in the form of essays and books that denounced certain works as "degenerate" (a label defined by Max Nordau's book *Degeneration*).[17] Although Gothic fiction obviously fell into this category, the censors missed the mark in denouncing such works. Rather than condoning the perversity they recorded, Gothic authors, in fact, seemed quite scrupulous about taking a moral stand against the unnatural acts that produce monstrosity. Long sentimental sermons on truth and purity punctuate many a gruesome tale and leave few doubts as to its morality by the narrative's end. Bram Stoker, for example, sermonizes both in his novels and in an essay printed in the journal *The Nineteenth Century* called "The Censorship of Fiction." In this essay, Stoker calls for stricter surveillance of popular fiction and drama. Stoker thinks censorship would combat human weakness on two levels, namely, "the weakness of the great mass of people who form audiences, and of those who are content to do base things in the way of catering for these base appetites."[18] Obviously, Stoker did not expect his own writing to be received as a work that "catered to base appetites" because, presumably, it used perverse sexuality to identify what or who threatened the dominant class.

Similarly, Oscar Wilde was shocked by the critics who called *The Picture of Dorian Gray* "poisonous" and "heavy with the mephitic odours of moral and spiritual putrefaction." Wilde's novel, after all, tells the story of a young man seduced by a poisonous book and punished soundly for his corruptions. Wilde defends his work by saying, "It was necessary, sir, for the dramatic development of this story to surround Dorian Gray with an atmosphere of moral corruption." He continues, "Each man sees his own sin in Dorian Gray."[19]

Producing and consuming monsters and monstrous fictions, we might say, adds up to what Eve Kosofsky Sedgwick has called, in her study of Gothic conventions, "an aesthetic of pleasurable fear."[20] The Gothic, in other words, inspires fear and desire at the same time—fear of and desire for the other, fear of and desire for the possibly latent perversity lurking within the reader herself. But fear and desire within the same body produce a disciplinary effect. In other words, a Victorian public could consume Gothic novels in vast quantities without regarding such a material as debased because Gothic gave readers the thrill of reading about so-called perverse activities while identifying aberrant sexuality as a condition of otherness and as an essential trait of foreign bodies. The monster, of course, marks the distance between the perverse and the supposedly disciplined sexuality of a reader. Also, the signifiers of "normal" sexuality maintain a kind of hegemonic power by remaining invisible.

So, the aesthetic of pleasurable fear that Sedgwick refers to makes pleasure possible only by fixing horror elsewhere, in an obviously and literally foreign body, and by then articulating the need to expel the foreign body. Thus, both Dracula and Hyde are characters with markedly foreign physiognomies; they are dark and venal, foreign in both aspect and behavior. Dracula, for example, is described by Harker as an angular figure with a strong face notable for "peculiarly arched nostrils . . . a lofty domed forehead," bushy hair and eyebrows, "sharp white teeth," and ears pointed at the tops.[21] Hyde is described as small and deformed, "pale and dwarfish . . . troglodytic."[22] By making monstrosity so obviously a physical condition and by linking it to sexual corruption, such fictions bind foreign aspects to perverse activities.

The most telling example I can find of a monstrous foreigner in Gothic is Bram Stoker's Count Dracula, who obviously comes to England from a distant "elsewhere" in search of English blood. Critics have discussed at length the perverse and dangerous sexuality exhibited by the vampire, but, with a few exceptions, criticism has not connected Dracula's sexual attacks with the threat of the foreign. Dracula condenses the xenophobia of Gothic fiction into a very specific horror—the vampire embodies and exhibits all the stereotyping of nineteenth-century anti-Semitism. The anatomy of the vampire, for example, compares remarkably to anti-Semitic studies of Jewish physiognomy—peculiar nose, pointed ears, sharp teeth, clawlike hands—and furthermore, in Stoker's novel, blood and money (central facets in anti-Semitism) mark the corruption of the vampire. The vampire merges Jewishness and monstrosity and represents this hybrid monster as a threat to Englishness and English womanhood in particular. In the Jew, then, Gothic fiction finds a monster versatile enough to represent fears about race, nation, and sexuality, a monster who combines in one body fears of the foreign and the perverse.

Perversion and Parasitism

Within nineteenth-century anti-Semitism, the Jew was marked as a threat to capital, to masculinity, and to nationhood. Jews in England at the turn of the century were the objects of an internal colonization. While the black African became the threatening other abroad, it was closer to home that people focused their real fears about the collapse of nation through a desire for racial homogeneity.[23] Jews were referred to as "degenerate," the bearers of syphilis, hysterical, neurotic, as bloodsuckers, and, on a more practical level, Jews were viewed as middlemen in business.[24] Not all Gothic novels are as explicit as *Dracula* about their identification of monster and Jew. In some works we can read a more generalized code of fear that links horror to the Oriental,[25] and in others we must interpret a bodily semiotic that marks monsters as symbols of a diseased culture. But to understand better how the history of the Gothic novel charts the entanglement of race, nation, and sexuality in productions of otherness, we might consider the Gothic monster as the antithesis of "Englishness."

Benedict Anderson has written about the cultural roots of the nation in terms of "imagined communities" that are "conceived in language, not in blood."[26] By linking the development of a print industry, particularly the popularization of novels and newspapers, to the spread of nationalism, Anderson pays close attention to the ways in which a shared conception of what constitutes "nationness" is written and read across certain communities. If the nation, therefore, is a textual production that creates national community in terms of an inside and an outside and then makes those categories indispensable, Gothic becomes one place to look for a fiction of the foreign, a narrative of who and what is not-English and not-native. The racism that becomes a mark of nineteenth-century Gothic arises out of the attempt within horror fiction to give form to what terrifies the national community. Gothic monsters are defined both as other than the imagined community and as the being that cannot be imagined as community.

"Racism and anti-Semitism," Anderson writes, "manifest themselves, not across national boundaries, but within them. In other words, they justify not so much foreign wars as domestic oppression and domination" (136). The racism and anti-Semitism that I have identified as a hallmark of nineteenth-century Gothic literature certainly direct themselves toward a domestic rather than a foreign scene. Gothic in the 1890s, as represented by the works of Robert Louis Stevenson, Bram Stoker, and Oscar Wilde, takes place in the backstreets of London in laboratories and asylums, in old abandoned houses and decaying city streets, in hospitals and bedrooms, in homes and gardens. The monster, such a narrative suggests, will find you in the intimacy of your own home; indeed, it will make your home its home (or you its home) and alter forever the comfort of domestic privacy. The monster peeps through the window, enters through the back door, and sits beside you in the parlor; the monster is always invited in but never asked to stay. The racism that seems to inhere to the nineteenth-century Gothic monster, then, may be drawn from imperialistic or colonialist fantasies of other lands and peoples, but it concentrates its imaginative force upon the other peoples in "our" lands, the monsters at home. The figure of the parasite becomes paramount within Gothic precisely because it is an internal, not an external, danger that Gothic identifies and attempts to dispel.

In *The Origins of Totalitarianism,* Hannah Arendt has argued convincingly that the modern category of anti-Semitism emerges from both nineteenth-century attempts to make race the "key to history" and the particular history of the Jews as "a people without a government, without a country, and without a language."[27] As such, the Jew, with regard to nation and, for our purposes, to English nationality, might be said to represent the not-English, the not-middle-class, the parasitical tribe that drains but never restores or produces. Arendt shows how the decline of the aristocracy and of nationalism by the mid-nineteenth century made people seek new ground for both commonality and superiority. She writes, "For if race doctrines finally served more sinister and immediately political purposes, it is still true that much of their plausibility and persuasiveness lay in the fact that they helped anybody feel himself an aristocrat who had been selected by birth on the strength of 'racial' qualification." Arendt's point is of central importance to an understanding of the history of Gothic. We might note in passing that, from the late eighteenth century to the nineteenth century, the terrain of Gothic horror shifted from the fear of corrupted aristocracy or clergy, represented by the haunted castle or abbey, to the fear embodied by monstrous bodies. Reading Gothic with nineteenth-century ideologies of race suggests why this shift occurs. If, then, with the rise of bourgeois culture, aristocratic heritage became less and less of an index of essential national identity, the construction of national unity increasingly depended upon the category of race and class. Therefore, the blood of nobility now became the blood of the native, and both were identified in contradistinction to so-called impure races such as Jews and Gypsies. The nobility, furthermore, gave way to a middle class identified by both their relation to capital as producers and consumers and a normal sexuality that leads to reproduction.[28]

The Gothic novel, I have been arguing, establishes the terms of monstrosity that were to be, and indeed were in the process of being, projected onto all who threatened the interests of a dwindling English nationalism. As the English empire stretched over oceans and continents, the need to define an essential English character became more and more pressing. Nonnationals, like Jews, for example, but also like the Irish or Gypsies, came to be increasingly identified by their alien natures, and the concept of "foreign" became ever more closely associated with a kind of parasitical monstrosity, a nonreproductive sexuality, and an anti-English character. Gothic monsters in the 1880s and 1890s made parasitism—vampirism— the defining characteristic of horror. The parasitical nature of the beast might be quite literal, as in Stoker's vampire, or it might be a more indirect trait, as suggested by the creeping and homeless Hyde; it might be defined by a homoerotic influence, as exerted by Dorian Gray. Parasitism, especially with regard to the vampire, represents a bad or pathological sexuality, nonreproductive sexuality, a sexuality that exhausts and wastes and exists prior to and outside of the marriage contract.

The ability of race ideology and sexology to create a new elite to replace the aristocracy also allows for the staging of historical battles within the body. This suggests how Gothic monstrosity may intersect with, participate in, and resist the production of a theory of racial superiority. The Gothic monster—Frankenstein's creature, Hyde, Dorian Gray, and Dracula—represents the dramatization of the race question and of sexology in their many different incarnations. If Frankenstein's monster articulates the injustice of demonizing one's own productions, Hyde suggests that the most respectable bodies may be contaminated by bad blood; and if Dorian Gray's portrait makes an essential connection between the homosexual and the uncanny, Dracula embodies once and for all the danger of the hybrid race and the perverse sexuality within the form of the vampire.

The Power of Horror

In Gothic, as in many areas of Victorian culture, sexual material was not repressed but produced on a massive scale, as Michel Foucault has argued.[29] The narrative, then, that professed outrage at acts of sexual perversion (the nightly wanderings of Hyde, for example, or Dracula's midnight feasts) in fact produced a catalog of perverse sexuality by first showcasing the temptations of the flesh in glorious technicolor and then by depicting so-called normal sex as a sickly enterprise devoid of all passion. One has only to think of the contrast between Mina Harker's encounter with Count Dracula—she is found lapping at blood from his breast—and her sexually neutral, maternal relations with her husband.

The production of sexuality as identity and as the inversion of identity (perversion—a turning away from identity) in Gothic novels consolidates normal sexuality by defining it in contrast to its monstrous manifestations. Horror, I have suggested, exercises power even as it incites pleasure and/or disgust. Horror, indeed, has a power closely related to its pleasure-producing function and the twin mechanism of pleasure-power perhaps explains how it is that Gothic may empower some readers even as it disables others. An example of how Gothic appeals differently to different readers may be found in contemporary slasher movies like *The Texas Chainsaw Massacre* (1974) and *Halloween* (1978). Critics generally argue that these films inspire potency in a male viewer and incredible vulnerability in a female viewer. However, the mechanisms of Gothic narrative never turn so neatly around gender identifications. A male viewer of the slasher film, like a male reader of the nineteenth-century Gothic, may find himself on the receiving end of countless acts of degradation in relation to monstrosity and its powers, while the female reader and spectator may be able to access a surprising source of power through monstrous forms and monstrous genres.

In her psychoanalytic study of fear, *Powers of Horror,* Julia Kristeva defines horror in terms of "abjection." The abject, she writes, is "something rejected from which one does not part, from which one does not protect oneself as from an object. Imaginary uncanniness and real threat, it beckons to us and ends up engulfing us."[30] In a chapter on the writings of Celine, Kristeva goes on to identify abjection with the Jew of anti-Semitic discourse. Anti-Semitic fantasy, she suggests, elevates Jewishness to both mastery and weakness, to "sex tinged with femininity and death" (185).

The Jew, for Kristeva, anchors abjection within a body, a foreign body that retains a certain familiarity and that therefore confuses the boundary between self and other. The connection that Kristeva makes between psychological categories and sociopolitical processes leads her to claim that anti-Semitism functions as a receptacle for all kinds of fears—sexual, political, national, cultural, economic. This insight is important to the kinds of arguments that I am making about the economic function of the Gothic monster. The Jew in general within anti-Semitism is Gothicized or transformed into a figure of almost universal loathing who haunts the community and represents its worst fears. By making the Jew supernatural, Gothic anti-Semitism actually makes Jews into spooks and Jew-hating into a psychological inevitability. The power of literary horror, indeed, lies in its ability to transform political struggles into psychological conditions and then to blur the distinction between the two. Literary horror, or Gothic, I suggest, uses the language of race hatred (most obviously anti-Semitism) to characterize monstrosity as a representation of psychological disorder. To understand the way monster may be equated with Jew or foreigner or non-English national, we need to historicize Gothic metaphors like vampire and parasite. We also have to read the effacement of the connection between monster and foreigner alongside the articulation of monster as a sexual category.

The Return of the Repressed

In an introduction to *Studies on Hysteria* written in 1893, Freud identifies the repressed itself as a foreign body. Noting that hysterical symptoms replay some original trauma in response to an accident, Freud explains that the memory of trauma "acts like a foreign body which, long after its entry, must continue to be regarded as an agent that is still at work."[31] In other words, until an original site of trauma reveals itself in therapy, it remains foreign to body and mind but active in both. The repressed, then, figures as a sexual secret that the body keeps from itself, and it figures as foreign because what disturbs the body goes unrecognized by the mind.

The fiction that Freud tells about the foreign body as the repressed connects remarkably with the fiction Gothic tells about monsters as foreigners. Texts, like bodies, store up memories of past fears, of distant traumas. "Hysterics," writes Freud, "suffer mainly from reminiscences" (7). History, personal and social, haunts hysterics, and the repressed always takes on an uncanny life of its own. Freud here has described the landscape of his own science—foreignness is repressed into the depths of an unconscious, a kind of cesspool of forgotten memories, and it rises to the surface as a sexual disturbance. Psychoanalysis Gothicizes sexuality; that is to say, it creates a body haunted by a monstrous sexuality and forced into repressing its Gothic secrets. Psychoanalysis, in the Freudian scenario, is a sexual science able to account for and perhaps cure Gothic sexualities. Gothicization in this formula, then, is the identification of bodies in terms of what they are not. A Gothic other stabilizes sameness; a Gothicized body is one that disrupts the surface–depth relationship between the body and the mind. It is the body that must be spoken, identified, or eliminated.

Sedgwick has advanced a reading of Gothic as the return of the repressed. She reads fear in the Gothic in terms of the trope of "live burial" and finds in Gothic "a carceral sublime of representation, of the body, and potentially of politics and history as well."[32] Live burial as a trope is, of course, standard fare in the Gothic, particularly in eighteenth-century Gothic like Matthew Lewis's *The Monk* and Ann Radcliffe's *The Mysteries of Udolpho*. Live burial also works nicely as a metaphor for a repressed thing that threatens to return. Sedgwick's example of the repressed in Gothic is homosexuality. She characterizes the "paranoid Gothic novel" in terms of its thematization of homophobia and thus, she describes *Frankenstein*'s plot in terms of "a tableau of two men chasing each other across the landscape."[33]

But Sedgwick's reading tells only half the story. The sexual outsider in Gothic, I am suggesting, is always also a racial pariah, a national outcast, a class outlaw. The "carceral sublime of representation" that, for Sedgwick, marks the role of textuality or language in the production of fear does not only symbolize that Gothic language buries fear alive. Live burial is certainly a major and standard trope of Gothic, but I want to read it alongside the trope of parasitism. Parasitism, I think, adds an economic dimension to live burial that reveals the entanglement of capital, nation, and the body in the fictions of otherness sanctified and popularized by any given culture. If live burial, for Sedgwick, reveals a "queerness of meaning," an essential doubleness within language that plays itself out through homoerotic doubles within the text, the carceral in my reading hinges upon a more clearly metonymic structure. Live burial as parasitism, then, becomes a tooth buried in an exposed neck for the explicit purpose of blood sucking or a monstrous Hyde hidden within the very flesh of a respectable Jekyll. Live burial is the entanglement of self and other within monstrosity and the parasitical relationship between the two. The one is always buried in the other.

The form of the Gothic novel, again as Sedgwick remarks, reflects further upon the parasitical monstrosity it creates. The story buried within a story buried within a story that Shelley's *Frankenstein* popularizes evolves into the narrative with one story but many different tellers. This form is really established by Wilkie Collins's *The Woman in White* (1860). In this novel, Collins uses a series of narrators so that almost every character in the novel tells his or her side of the story. Such a narrative device gives the effect of completion and operates according to a kind of judicial model of narration where all witnesses step forward to give an account. Within this narrative system, the author professes to be no more than a collector of documents, a compiler of the facts of the case. The reader, of course, is the judge and jury, the courtroom audience, and often a kind of prosecuting presence expected to know truth, recognize guilt, and penalize monstrosity.

In *Dracula,* Bram Stoker directly copies Collins's style. Stevenson also uses Collins's narrative technique in *Dr. Jekyll and Mr. Hyde,* but he frames his story in a more overtly legal setting so that our main narrator is a lawyer, the central document is the last will and testament of Dr. Jekyll, and all other accounts contribute to the "strange case." All Gothic novels employing this narrative device share an almost obsessive concern with documentation, and they all exhibit a sinister mistrust of the not-said, the unspoken, the hidden, and the silent. Furthermore, most Gothic novels lack the point of view of the monster. Collins does include in his novel a chapter by the notorious Count Fosco, but Fosco's account is written as a forced confession that confirms his guilt and reveals his machinations. Neither Dracula nor Dorian Gray ever directly gives his versions of events, and Jekyll stands in at all times for his monstrous double, Hyde.

Collins's novel is extremely important to the Victorian Gothic tradition in that it establishes a layered narrative structure in which a story must be peeled back to reveal the secret or repressed center. The secret buried in the heart of Gothic, I suggested much earlier, is usually identified as a sexual secret. In an essay on the function of sensationalism in *The Woman in White,* Ann Cvetkovich argues that the sexual secret in this novel ultimately has little to do with a random sexual desire and everything to do with the class structure that brings Walter Hartright into contact with his future bride, Laura Fairlie. Cvetkovich suggests that the novel, in fact, sensationalizes class relations by making the relationship between Laura and her lowly art teacher seem fateful—preordained rather than a product of one man's social ambition.[34]

Novels in a Gothic mode transform class and race, sexual and national relations, into supernatural or monstrous features. The threat posed by the Gothic monster is a combination of money, science, perversion, and imperialism, but by reducing it to solely sexual aberrance, we fail to historicize Gothic embodiments.

The Technology of Monsters

Gothic novels are technologies that produce the monster as a remarkably mobile, permeable, and infinitely interpretable body. The monster's body, indeed, is a machine that, in its Gothic mode, produces meaning and can represent any horrible trait that the reader feeds into the narrative. The monster functions as monster, in other words, when it is able to condense as many fear-producing traits as possible into one body. Hence the sense that Frankenstein's monster is bursting out of his skin—he is indeed filled to bursting point with flesh and meaning both. Dracula, at the other end of the nineteenth century, is a body that consumes to excess—the vampiric body in its ideal state is a bloated body, sated with the blood of its victims.

Monsters are meaning machines. They can represent gender, race, nationality, class, and sexuality in one body. And even within these divisions of identity, the monster can still be broken down. Dracula, for example, can be read as an aristocrat, a symbol of the masses; he is predator and yet feminine, he is consumer and producer, he is parasite and host, he is homosexual and heterosexual, he is even a lesbian. Monsters and the Gothic fiction that creates them are therefore technologies, narrative technologies that produce the perfect figure for negative identity. Monsters have to be everything the human is not, and in producing the negative of human, these novels make way for the invention of human as white, male, middle class, and heterosexual.

But Gothic is also a narrative technique, a generic spin that transforms the lovely and the beautiful into the abhorrent and then frames this transformation within a humanist moral fable. A brilliant postmodern example of what happens when a narrative is Gothicized is Tim Burton's surrealistic *Nightmare before Christmas* (1993). *Nightmare* is an animated fantasy about what happens when Halloween takes over Christmas. Halloween and Christmas, in this film, are conceived as places rather than times or occasions, and each is embodied by its festive representatives, Jack Skellington and Santa Claus. Indeed religious or superstitious meanings of these holidays are almost entirely absent from the plot. Jack Skellington is a kind of melancholic Romantic hero who languishes under the strain of representing fear and maintaining the machinery of horror every year. He stumbles upon the place called Christmas one day after a stroll through the woods beyond his graveyard, and he decides that he wants to do Christmas this year instead of Halloween.

The transformation of Christmas into Halloween is the Gothicization of the sentimental; presents and toys, food and decorations, are all transformed from cheery icons of goodwill into fanged monsters, death masks, and all manner of skullduggery. Kids are frightened, parents are shocked, Santa Claus is kidnapped, and mayhem ensues. Of course, a pathetic sentimental heroine called Sally uses her rag doll body to restore law and order and to woo Jack back to his proper place, but nonetheless, the damage has been done. Christmas, the myth of a transcendent generosity, goodwill, and community love, has been unmasked as just another consumer ritual, and its icons have been exposed as simply toys without teeth or masks that smile instead of grimace. The naturalness and goodness of Christmas has unraveled and shown itself to be the easy target of any and all attempts to make it Gothic.

While *Nightmare* suggests that, at least in a postmodern setting, Gothicization seems to have progressive and even radicalizing effects, it is not always so simple to tell whether the presence of Gothic registers a conservative or a progressive move. Of course, Gothic is, as I have been arguing, mobile, and therefore, we should not expect it to succumb so easily to attempts to make a claim for its political investments. But it does seem as if there has been a transformation in the uses of Gothic from the early nineteenth century to the present. I argue that horror now disrupts dominant culture's representations of family, heterosexuality, ethnicity, and class politics. It disrupts, furthermore, the logic of genre that essentializes generic categories and stabilizes the production of meaning within them. Gothic film horror, I propose, produces models of reading (many in any one location) that allow for multiple interpretations and a plurality of locations of cultural resistance.

I am using terms like *Gothic* and *technology* very specifically. Gothic has typically been used to refer to two sets of novels: first, to refer to Gothic revival novels of the late eighteenth century, and then second, to refer to a cluster of fin-de-siècle novels in England. Gothic is the breakdown of genre and the crisis occasioned by the inability to "tell," meaning both the inability to narrate and the inability to categorize. Gothic, I argue, marks a peculiarly modern preoccupation with boundaries and their collapse. Gothic monsters, furthermore, differ from the monsters that come before the nineteenth century in that the monsters of modernity are characterized by their proximity to humans.

Notes

1. Jean Baudrillard, "The Ecstasy of Communication," in *The Anti-Aesthetic: Essays on Postmodern Culture,* ed. Hal Foster (Port Townsend, Wash.: Bay Press, 1983), 130. Baudrillard writes, "Obscenity begins precisely when there is no more spectacle, no more scene, when all becomes transparence and immediate visibility, when everything is exposed to the harsh and inexorable light of information and communication."

2. Linda Williams, *Hard Core: Power, Pleasure and the "Frenzy of the Visible"* (Berkeley: University of California Press, 1989).

3. Michel Foucault, *Discipline and Punish: The Birth of the Prison,* trans. Alan Sheridan (New York: Vintage, 1979), 30, 29.

4. See, e.g., Edith Birkhead, *The Tale of Terror: A Study of the Gothic Romance* (New York: Russell and Russell, 1963); Montague Summers, *The Gothic Quest: A History of Gothic* (New York: Russell and Russell, 1938); David Punter, *The Literature of Terror: A History of Gothic Fictions from 1765 to the Present Day* (London: Longman, 1980).

5. This term is coined by Marjorie Garber in *Vested Interests: Cross-Dressing and Cultural Anxiety* (New York: Routledge, 1992), 16. In this study of transvestism, Garber suggests that the cross-dresser and the transsexual provoke category crises that are displaced onto the place of gender ambiguity. This argument is useful to the claim I make that all difference in modernity has been subsumed under the aegis of sexual difference.

6. Most notable for my purposes, among such studies are Nancy Armstrong's *Desire and Domestic Fiction: A Political History of the Novel* (New York: Oxford University Press, 1987) and David A. Miller's *The Novel and the Police* (Berkeley: University of California Press, 1988).

7. See Michelle A. Masse, *In The Name of Love: Women, Masochism and the Gothic* (Ithaca, N.Y.: Cornell University Press, 1992). Masse's study looks at the intersections of the Gothic novel, masochism, and feminism. Masse writes, "The novels' central concern

with masochism does not mean that characters (or women) are masochistic, although many are. Instead, my premise is that what characters in these novels represent, whether through repudiation, doubt, or celebration, is the cultural, psychoanalytic, and fictional expectation that they should be masochistic if they are 'normal' women" (2).

8. See Susan Wolstenholme, *Gothic (Re)Visions: Writing Women as Readers* (Albany: State University of New York Press, 1993). Wolstenholme has a chapter titled "Exorcising the Mother" and another called "Why Would a Textual Mother Haunt a House Like This?" She writes, "As linguistic structures novels are always inscribed in paternal law; in one sense (a strictly psychoanalytic one), no text can really have a 'mother' because inscription in language implies differentiation from the maternal. But as I have suggested, Gothic-marked narratives always point to the space where the absent mother might be" (151).

Another study of Gothic similarly invests in exclusively familial metaphors for the relations between authors, Gothic novels, and fear or dread. In *Ghosts of the Gothic: Austen, Eliot, and Lawrence* (Princeton, N.J.: Princeton University Press, 1980), Judith Wilt writes, "Dread is the father and mother of the Gothic. Dread begets rage and fright and cruel horror, or awe and worship and shining steadfastness—all of these have human features, but Dread has no face" (5).

9. Ellen Moers, *Literary Women* (London: Women's Press, 1978).

10. Claire Kahane, "Gothic Mirrors and Feminine Identity," *Centennial Review* 24 (1980): 43–64.

11. Gilles Deleuze and Félix Guattari, *Anti-Oedipus: Capitalism and Schizophrenia,* trans. Robert Hurley, Mark Seem, and Helen R. Lane, preface by Michel Foucault (Minneapolis: University of Minnesota Press, 1983), 51.

12. Deleuze and Guattari, "The Whole and Its Parts," in *Anti-Oedipus,* 45.

13. Slavoj Žižek, "Grimaces of the Real, or When the Phallus Appears," *October* 58 (Fall 1991): 44–68.

14. For more on this, see George E. Haggerty, *Gothic Fiction/Gothic Form* (University Park: The Pennsylvania State University Press, 1989).

15. Mary Shelley, *Frankenstein; or, The Modern Prometheus,* ed. M. K. Joseph (1831; repr., New York: Oxford University Press, 1980), 10.

16. See Patrick Bratlinger and Richard Boyle, "The Education of Edward Hyde: Stevenson's 'Gothic Gnome' and the Mass Readership of Late Victorian England," in *100 Years of Dr. Jekyll and Mr. Hyde,* ed. Gordon Hirsch and William Veeder (Chicago: University of Chicago Press, 1988).

17. Max Simon Nordau, *Degeneration* (New York: D. Appleton, 1895).

18. Bram Stoker, "The Censorship of Fiction," *The Nineteenth Century,* September 1908, 481.

19. See the introduction to Oscar Wilde, *The Picture of Dorian Gray,* ed. and with an introduction by Isobel Murray (1891; repr., Oxford: Oxford University Press, 1981).

20. Eve Kosofsky Sedgwick, *The Coherence of Gothic Conventions* (New York: Methuen, 1986), vi.

21. Bram Stoker, *Dracula* (1897; repr., New York: Bantam, 1981), 18.

22. Robert Louis Stevenson, *The Strange Case of Dr. Jekyll and Mr. Hyde* (1886; repr., New York: Bantam, 1981), 18.

23. In an article on the influence of Spanish models of nationhood upon English debates of "the Jewish question," Michael Ragussis looks at nineteenth-century novels like *Ivanhoe* and their positioning of questions of nationhood alongside calls for Jewish assimilation: "By depicting the persecution of the Jews at a critical moment in history—the founding of the English nation-state—*Ivanhoe* located 'the Jewish question' at the heart of English national identity" (478). See "The Birth of a Nation in Victorian Culture: The Spanish Inquisition, the Converted Daughter, and the 'Secret Race,'" *Critical Inquiry* 20 (Spring 1994): 477–508.

24. See, e.g., Henry Arthur Jones, "Middlemen and Parasites," *New Review* 8 (June 1893): 645–54, and "The Dread of the Jew," *The Spectator* 83 (September 9, 1899): 338–39, where the author discusses references made in popular periodicals of the time to Jews as "a parasitical race with no ideals beyond precious metals." "Parasite" and "degenerate" became coded synonyms for Jews in such literature.

25. See, e.g., Richard Marsh, *The Beetle* (1897), in *Victorian Villainies,* ed. Graham Greene and Sir Hugh Greene (New York: Penguin, 1984). For an excellent article on this little-known Gothic text, see Kelly Hurley, "'The Inner Chambers of All Nameless Sin': *The Beetle,* Gothic Female Sexuality and Oriental Barbarism," in *Virginal Sexuality and Textuality in Victorian Literature,* ed. Lloyd Davis (Albany: State University of New York Press, 1993), 193–213.

26. Benedict Anderson, *Imagined Communities: Reflections on the Origin and Spread of Nationalism* (London: Verso, 1983), 133.

27. Hannah Arendt, *The Origins of Totalitarianism* (New York: Harcourt Brace Jovanovich, 1979), 8.

28. For a fascinating and clever account of the production of heterosexuality within capitalism, see Henry Abelove, "Some Speculations on the History of Sexual Intercourse during the Long Eighteenth Century in England," *Genders* 6 (1989): 125–30.

29. Michel Foucault, *The History of Sexuality,* vol. 1, *An Introduction,* trans. Robert Hurley (New York: Vintage, 1980).

30. Julia Kristeva, *Powers of Horror: An Essay on Abjection,* trans. Leon S. Roudiez (New York: Columbia University Press, 1982), 4.

31. Sigmund Freud and Josef Brauer, *Studies on Hysteria,* ed. and trans. James Strachey (1893; repr., New York: Basic Books, 1987), 6.

32. Sedgwick, *Coherence,* vi.

33. Sedgwick, ix.

34. See Ann Cvetkovich, *Mixed Feelings: Feminism, Mass Culture and Victorian Sensationalism* (New Brunswick, N.J.: Rutgers University Press, 1992).

II
Monsterizing Difference

MONSTROUS STRANGERS AT THE EDGE OF THE WORLD

The Monstrous Races

Alexa Wright

T HE ARNSTEIN BIBLE is a large, heavy book in two volumes.[1] It was hand-written in ink by a German monk, Lunandus of Arnstein, in the late twelfth century. Parts of the text are skillfully illuminated in color, which suggests that the Bible was originally created for public display.[2] But the most interesting and intriguing feature of this ancient book is the collection of sketches on the flyleaves at the back of the second volume. There are several full-page drawings showing cosmographic charts; simple, geometrical world maps; a diagram of related types of human endeavor with philosophy at its head; and, lastly, a pen-and-ink sketch of the Monstrous Races (see Figure 8.3). In these later additions, the images and texts are rendered simply and directly, with none of the certainty of the main manuscript. They appear to be private sketchbook drawings or annotations made by someone trying to work out the order of the world during a time of unsettling social and cultural change. Collectively, the charts and drawings configured here give a fascinating insight into the late medieval worldview as understood by one anonymous individual. But the most remarkable feature of the Bible is the final page of drawings, which is filled with some of the fantastical figures that make up the Monstrous Races. This particular set of drawings may represent one individual's meditation on the order of things, but they also reflect a widespread historical understanding of the body of the human monster as a site for cultural interrogation of the boundaries between nature and culture, human and animal, human and not-human.

The idea of the Monstrous Races is far from unique to this one set of draw-ings. For a long period, lasting from some time before the fifth century B.C.E. until the sixteenth century C.E., they were popularly characterized throughout Europe as real creatures that could not be considered fully human because of their remote existence, far from "civilized" human society. Incorporating human–animal hybrids, exaggerated, misplaced, or missing body parts, and performing curiously inhuman practices, their mixed-up bodies manifest confusion about what might constitute the boundaries of human society and the limits of accept-able human being.

The Monstrous Races are especially interesting because they show that, in Western cultures, there is an established history of articulating narratives of self and other visually, in the form of strange bodies and unconventional behaviors. When searching for an interpretation of these oddly configured bodies, it is impor-tant to bear in mind that, until relatively recently, physical deformity was gen-erally understood to hold negative significance, either for the affected individual or for society as a whole. And yet, like all human monsters, the Races are para-doxical in that they can be read as simultaneously positive and negative, expan-sive and cautionary, playful and discriminatory—depending on the point of view of the observer.

The apparently whimsical drawings in the back of the Arnstein Bible seem to be infused with a curiosity about the unknown. While each figure is accompa-nied by a brief annotation in Latin noting its name and geographical origin, they have no visual context. These strange creatures are arranged on the page in what appear to be a series of theatrical vignettes in which they are either performing individually or interacting with one another. Collectively, they seem to point to a sense of wonder at the potential diversity of nature in regions of the world that would have been unfamiliar to most medieval Europeans. While the majority of the figures have human faces, their social status is ambiguous. None of them is clothed, and yet several are holding or using tools, weapons, or musical instru-ments, all of which represent human culture. The top row of figures are all eating or holding smaller animals, which suggests that they have been attributed a prim-itive nature. The confusion between human and nonhuman is further emphasized by the fact that many of these quasi-human figures have hooves, and yet some of them are playing music or fighting with weapons. In the center of the page is a centaur (half-human, half-horse). The character on the top left has a dog's head and tail. Creatures such as the centaur and the dog-headed cynocephalus, which was believed to communicate by barking rather than speaking, represent a clear transgression of the division between humans and animals, which, as we shall see, is one of the most important boundaries defended by human monsters.

In the particular case of the cynocephalus, the animal head on a human body symbolizes a loss of human rationality, suggesting the domination of bestial nature over human culture.[3] Representing a fundamental breach of the boundary between human and animal, this zoomorphic monstrosity is particularly threatening because it indicates a resistance to human culture. The animal head also indicates a lack of ability to use human language. The use of articulate speech is commonly understood to be the feature that most securely distinguishes civilized humans from beasts, or nonhumans.[4] While the cynocephali were reported to bark like dogs, others of the Monstrous Races—such as the Astomi or apple smellers, the straw-drinkers, the snake-eating troglodytes, and a race of speechless, gesturing people—were said to lack any kind of speech at all. This in itself would render these particular Races less than human and exclude them from human society in the eyes of medieval scholars, for whom language was a crucial attribute of all socialized peoples.[5]

History of the Monstrous Races

The long and fascinating history of the Monstrous Races is well documented by the art historian Rudolf Wittkower in chapter 3 of his book *Allegory and the Migration of Symbols*.[6] Wittkower describes the "literary transmission" of the Races, from ancient Greek texts, to the Roman naturalist and philosopher Pliny, and then to the encyclopedists of the Middle Ages, charting their gradual decline through the sixteenth and seventeenth centuries. He explains that the confused bodies and strange customs of the Monstrous Races provided a form for anxieties about the limits of human being for a period of perhaps two thousand years, during which time they were discussed and depicted as real, if inaccessible, beings.

Wittkower links the written and verbal history of the Races to a pictorial tradition, claiming that "we know that pictures of the fabulous races existed in antiquity," although none of these has survived. The earliest remaining images are from the Middle Ages.[7] The strength of public confidence in visual representations of the Monstrous Races during the Middle Ages in particular demonstrates how spoken or written narratives can be "realized" visually, both in formal religious and academic contexts and, like the Arnstein Bible drawings, within a more popular or personal framework. Although, as Wittkower has shown, the Monstrous Races do have a literary tradition, the available pictures show most clearly how the body of the monster manifests uncertainty. These literal embodiments of difference demonstrate that, by portraying what is understood to be "other," visual images of human monsters can help to establish and disseminate ideas about what it is to be human within a particular social and cultural context.[8]

The Monstrous Races in Medieval Art and Thought by John Block Friedman provides another detailed account of the Races, again tracing their transmission from antiquity to the Middle Ages and beyond.[9] In addition to a catalog of all the major types, Friedman offers convincing anthropological explanations for their provenance, which, he writes, were often based on "errors of perception" on the part of early travelers.[10] He shows how firsthand written or verbal reports brought back by military leaders such as Alexander the Great (fourth century B.C.E.) influenced subsequent literary or visual records compiled by people who had never traveled to the regions supposedly inhabited by the creatures they were portraying.

One of the earliest known accounts of the Monstrous Races comes from a treatise on India, published by the royal physician Ctesias of Knidos at around the beginning of the fourth century B.C.E. Ctesias describes a number of marvelous creatures, including Sciopods, who have one giant foot that enables them to hop very fast and is also used to provide shelter from the sun; the Blemmaye, who have no heads but have faces in their chests; and the Panotii, people with enormous ears that they use to cover themselves with when they sleep and which can also be used to fly away from unwanted visitors.[11] These descriptions and the visual images derived from them, such as the one shown in Figure 8.1, seem at first glance to be simply naive, charming, and playful. However, further research reveals these monsters to be complex, provocative creatures, open to a variety of conflicting interpretations.

According to the nineteenth-century historian J. W. McCrindle, the Races depicted by Ctesias are often misrepresentations of indigenous tribes, particularly those who resisted invasion by Western colonizers.[12] The contemporary art historian Debra Higgs Strickland pursues this idea further, arguing that, in the Middle Ages, representations of the Monstrous Races were crucial to the Christian portrayal of "godless" non-Christian minorities.[13] But McCrindle also maintains that some of the most influential descriptions of the Races were directly derived from monsters portrayed in two great Indian epic tales and other Brahmanical writings that formed an important part of Indian verbal and literary tradition. For example, the *Mahabharata* describes the Karnapravarana, a people who cover themselves with their ears, which clearly served as a model for the Panotii (Figure 8.1).[14] If this is the case, Western travelers must have taken mainstream Indian culture seriously enough to adopt some of its mythology. Wittkower points to the appearance in Arabic illuminated manuscripts of creatures identical to the dog-headed cynocephali.[15] This again suggests that there was some exchange between cultures, ancient Greece being the source of inspiration for both Western and Arabic imagery. So it seems that not everyone whose appearance or culture differed from that of mainstream Western society was labeled a monster. However, the "East," and especially India, was conceived as a site of potential for wonder and ambiguity for medieval Europeans on account of its distance from their known territories.

The work of the renowned Greek scholars Ctesias and Megasthenes, who was an ambassador to India during the fourth century B.C.E., provided the main source for Western understanding of the culture, history, and religion of the East for many years. Their descriptions of the Monstrous Races formed the basis of

Figure 8.1. Panotii, lintel of Basilique Ste-Madeleine, Vézelay, France, circa 1125–30.

numerous secondary texts during the course of the next fifteen hundred years, reappearing in influential works by Pliny the Elder, Solinus, Saint Augustine, and Isidore of Seville. One of the most significant of these secondary texts is Pliny's encyclopedic *Natural History* (77 C.E.), which includes an extensive list of the most popular of the Races. Like the earlier Greek accounts, Pliny's descriptions reveal a fascination for the strangeness of "outsiders" and a sense of awe at what he understands to be the diversity of nature:

Megasthenes records that on Mount Nulus there are men with their feet
reversed and with eight toes on each foot. On many mountains there are men
with dogs' heads who are covered with wild beasts' skins; they bark instead
of speaking and live by hunting and fowling, for which they use their nails. . . .
Ctesias . . . writes of a tribe of men called the Sciapods who have only one
leg and hop with amazing speed. These people are also called the Umbrella-
footed, because when the weather is hot they lie on their backs stretched out
on the ground and protect themselves by the shade of their feet. . . . Further to
the east of these are some people without necks and with eyes in their shoulders. . . . Among the Nomads of India Megasthenes records a race called Sciri-
tai that has only holes in place of nostrils—like snakes—and has bandy legs. At
the extreme boundaries of India, to the East, near the source of the Ganges,
he locates the Astomi who have no mouth and whose body is covered in hair.
They dress in cotton wool and live only on the air they breathe and the odour
they draw in through their nostrils. . . . Beyond the Astomi, in the depth of the
mountains, so the story goes, live the Trispithami and Pygmies. In height they
do not exceed three spans—that is about two and a half feet.[16]

Pliny does not question the truth of the classical texts on which he bases
his descriptions, but seems to accept these previous accounts as factual descriptions of actual people. Following the earlier writers, he makes no distinction
between clearly mythical characters like the Astomi and real people, such as the
Pygmies.

On the one hand the inclusion of Pygmies among the Monstrous Races could
be taken to indicate that the configuration of many of the Races is based on genuine misperceptions on the part of early travelers, as McCrindle has suggested.
This idea is reinforced by Pliny's account of a race he calls the Gymnosophists,
who "remain standing from sunrise to sunset in the burning sun, all the while
looking at the sun with a fixed gaze, resting first on one foot and then on the
other," which could be a description of Brahmin practicing yoga.[17] However, the
bodies and customs of the Races could also be read as the emblems of discriminatory and racist beliefs of a xenophobic society, rehearsed without question until
travel became more commonplace and people could see the far-off lands they
were supposed to inhabit for themselves. We can only speculate on the spirit
in which these creatures were originally conceived, but as the examples given so
far demonstrate, the Races described by Ctesias clearly do embody many of the
perceptual and emotional confusions experienced by early Western travelers.
The inhabitants of the "East" are mythologized in a way that may be considered
either charming because of its literal naivety or disturbing because of its imperialist nature.

Friedman points out that the Greeks, like many closely integrated communities, "tended to view outsiders as likely to be inferior and untrustworthy."[18] While

the works of classical scholars such as Ctesias and Megasthenes and the writers that followed them demonstrate a fascination with the strangeness of other peoples and places, they do also reveal an intolerance of difference. Friedman maintains that the early accounts of the Monstrous Races are decidedly ethnocentric because the culture, language, and physical appearance of the observer are used as the "norm" by which all other peoples are evaluated.[19] But this is the standard by which all monsters are constructed. Our contemporary understanding of what is monstrous would clearly not include those members of minority cultures who may have provided a source for some of the classical Monstrous Races. And yet the processes by which what is monstrous is identified as "other," embodied and set apart from self and society, have changed little since the Races held currency.

The Monstrous Races have, understandably, been characterized as precursors to modern racism.[20] From a contemporary perspective this is certainly how they appear when mythical races such as the Blemmaye and cynocephali are grouped together with actual forest-dwelling peoples such as Pygmies. Pliny and other writers seeking subjects for scholarly debate on the limits of human being make no distinction between real and mythical "others." These ideas were derived from the ancient Greeks, who imagined themselves to be at the center of the civilized world, judging all outsiders according to their own culture and customs. Homer, writing some time between the twelfth and seventh centuries B.C.E. is one of the earliest known sources. He describes Pygmies as animals because they were considered too small and too different from Europeans to be men. Although in the contemporary context this seems laughable on the one hand and offensive on the other, it graphically highlights the insecurity and lack of knowledge that engendered the Monstrous Races. For those who first imagined them, much of the terrestrial world must have been an unknown and incomprehensible wilderness. Those distant parts of the globe, where extremes of climate and geography were believed to produce extreme bodies and behaviors, were clearly both intriguing and terrifying to early Europeans.

While the Monstrous Races may be problematic because of the racist connotations that are attached to them, they are nevertheless interesting because, like all monsters, they reflect the cultural values invested in "otherness." Because the transgressions they represent are literally displayed on their bodies, the Races provide a clear and straightforward example of the historical function of the human monster as an embodiment of social, moral, or ontological disorder. Their hybrid bodies, which combine human and animal, male and female, cultural and natural elements, operate as signifiers of the known and the unknown. They interrogate the boundaries of what constitutes an acceptable human subject on a direct, somatic level. The Monstrous Races demonstrate that, even when it is physically located elsewhere, human monstrosity is a construct that is intimately related to the social and moral values of the observer. By default, then, they also clarify what it means to be a valid member of a particular society. Human monsters are confusing figures lurking on the margins of society. They are strangers, outsiders, law-breakers, and, above all, inherently transgressive characters that say more about those who create them than about those that are branded monstrous. In the words of Peter Stallybrass and Allon White, "what is socially peripheral is so frequently symbolically central."[21] Individual, social, and cultural identities are inseparable from their limits and from the peripheral figures that help to define accepted norms.

The Monster as Deviant "Other"

Embodying many of the confusing or troubling qualities that must be set apart from self and removed from society, the body of the human monster has historically provided a tangible site for the inscription of transgression. This notion of transgression is interesting because it brings with it the concept of a "limit" that differentiates one thing or way of being from another. Etymologically, *transgression* is defined as a violation of the law. It also means "crossing over" or "going beyond."[22] In the Judeo-Christian tradition, *transgression* is a negative moral term linked, for example, to the biblical account of Adam's "original sin" in the Garden of Eden. In this context it represents a failure, a fall from grace. For Michel Foucault, however, transgression performs a more interesting and complex role. He proposes that "a limit could not exist if it were absolutely uncrossable and, reciprocally, transgression would be pointless if it merely crossed a limit composed of illusions and shadows."[23] In this interpretation, transgression is a creative force that challenges established laws, limits, and social structures and compels them to respond to modifications in human understanding, values, and belief systems. Transgression is also a political force, in that it disrupts the existing order of bodies and cultures.

As an expression of difference that helps to define the self and the social "norm" by manifesting what is currently unacceptable, human monstrosity is also closely bound up with ideas of the "other" and "otherness." *Otherness* literally means "the state of being different."[24] But it has come to be integrally related to notions of representation, in which representation of the other is always linked to representation of self. While the self–other relation is accorded different significance in disciplines such as philosophy, psychology, anthropology, and cultural politics, the "other" is never simply a given in any of these contexts. It is never just found or encountered but is always constructed.[25] Like monstrosity, the "other" represents what is external to the "norms" of self and society, but it is also essential to the constitution of the self. The philosopher Richard Kearney points out the paradoxical relation between self and monstrous other: "in a sense we may say that monsters are our *others* par excellence. Without them we know not what we are. With them we are not what we know."[26] In other words, the subjective position of the observer is always implicated in the construction of the "other," whether monstrous or not.

The *other* and *otherness* are difficult terms to define because, as the anthropologist Malcolm Crick has written,

> a change in the value of the "self" invariably alters the image of the "other" and vice versa; and either change alters the nature of the difference which they constitute and by which they are constituted . . . there can be no final definition of the relation between "ourselves" and "others."[27]

Emmanuel Levinas's philosophical notion of the "other" as an absolute form of difference that cannot be known or articulated is very close to the concept of the monstrous. Levinas writes that "the alien being is as it were naturalized as soon as it commits itself within knowledge," and "the other, in manifesting itself as a being, loses its alterity."[28] This "alien being" is equivalent to the monstrous, which is articulated through the body or behavior of the monster. When what is monstrous has a visually identifiable, tangible form, it can be classified as separate from self and from "normal" society. Once it has been made known in this way, its terrible power is diffused. What is truly monstrous, therefore, is that which refuses representation and cannot be situated. This form of "otherness" is profoundly threatening both because it cannot be seen to stand outside, and apart from, the normal subject and because it undermines existing structures.

On a more practical level, human "otherness" is traditionally constructed in terms of race, sexuality, gender, or physical disability. Culturally and socially, the relationship between self and other is a hierarchical one, based on a need to justify and sustain existing power relations.[29] Racial, sexual, or physically deformed "others" have so often been subordinated to the image of the straight, white, "rational," and able-bodied European male, which in Western culture has traditionally been the standard by which all "others" are judged. From this perspective, all that is familiar and similar to the self is considered good, while what is other is thought to be strange and evil and must be avoided. In the context of anthropology, for example, Susan Sontag identifies the racial "other" as a figure of exclusion: "Europe seeks itself in the exotic . . . among preliterate peoples . . . the 'other' is experienced as a harsh purification of 'self.'"[30]

Within a European tradition that has its roots in ancient Greece, the categorical separation of the European subject from the ethnic "other" is evidenced in early depictions of the Monstrous Races, whose deformed bodies function as literal, visual representations of cultural otherness. In this case, otherness is aligned with monstrosity, which is the tangible manifestation of what is considered monstrous in any particular context.

Monsters and the Law

However, alterity is not always monstrous. Foucault asserts that "there is monstrosity only when the confusion comes up against, overturns or disturbs civil, canon or religious law."[31] In suggesting that the natural and cultural laws infringed by the monster also determine its existence, he highlights the peculiar nature of the relationship between monsters and the law. The monstrous is powerful because it resists containment by social and natural laws and, in itself, defies language. As an articulation of this terrifying but transformative force, human monstrosity has an impact—which is different at different times—on definitions of what is natural and on the limits of acceptable human identity. It is most interesting when this process occurs in the "real" world, rather than in the fictional worlds of literature or film. In both being and at the same time representing what is understood to be neither an accepted part of nature nor an accepted part of culture at any given time, the "real" human monster can act as a powerful and concrete mirror for social and cultural values, while at the same time eliciting human empathy.

One example Foucault uses to illustrate his point about monstrosity that overturns the law is that of a pair of conjoined twins, one of which has committed a crime. This act, he says, confounds the law because it is unclear whether one or both of the twins should be executed for the crime.[32] If we understand this to be a "true" case (as opposed to a fictional one), the potential legal and moral dilemma it raises is simultaneously chilling and fascinating. It is truly monstrous.

In medieval Europe, an indication of both human and animal presence in one being represented a direct violation of social and divine laws. In Foucault's words, "it is because there was a sexual relationship between a man and an animal that a monster appears in which the two kingdoms are mixed. In that respect we are referred to a breach of civil or religious law."[33] This literal image of the monster as the result of a transgression of the laws prohibiting bestiality, which seem to be more or less ubiquitous in the Judeo-Christian tradition, is highly significant. The monstrous human–animal hybrid both acts as a warning of the consequences of behavior that contravenes social codes and reinforces the importance of the codes, or laws, that bind a society together. When a clear boundary is established between humans and animals, the "natural," savage, uncivilized characteristics of animals can be set apart from what is human, which is traditionally defined by the possession of culture and of a coherent language, and by the capacity for self-reflection and self-control.[34]

The very existence of laws calling for a clear division between animals and humans indicates a profound anxiety about the potential contamination of human identity by primitive, animal characteristics.[35] The long-standing popularity of the Monstrous Races, which include many human–animal hybrids, suggests that this anxiety has deeply troubled Western cultures for some time. In the sixteenth century the French surgeon Ambroise Paré forcefully described monsters that transgressed the boundary between human and animal as unnatural expressions of evil:

> There are monsters that are born with a form that is half-animal and half-human . . . which are produced by sodomists and atheists who join together . . . with animals, and from this are born several monsters that are hideous and very scandalous to look at or speak about.[36]

In his seminal essay "Monstrosity and the Monstrous," Georges Canguilhem explains that, until the late eighteenth century, corporeal monstrosity was generally understood to be the result of a monstrous act such as those described by Paré. It did not happen by chance but was brought about by "the license of living beings." According to Canguilhem, monstrous deformity was read as a sign of a conscious act of defiance, representing a contravention of the laws that segregate particular species, races, or types:

> Zoomorphic monstrosity, if one admitted its existence, had to be considered the result of a deliberate attempt at infraction of the order of things, which is one with their perfection; it had to be considered the result of abandoning oneself to the dizzy fascination of the undefined, of chaos.[37]

In Canguilhem's view, therefore, someone is culpable—guilty of deliberately bringing about the state of chaos out of which a monster is born by his or her actions. For him, monstrosity is a direct consequence of deviance. But monsters are always paradoxical, simultaneously signifying that something is not right and providing a vehicle for exploring and "working out" changes to established belief systems. Returning once more to Foucault, we learn that in transgressing the laws of both nature and culture, the monster "combines the impossible and the forbidden." It is "a breach of the law that automatically stands outside the law."[38] He explains this further: "It could be said that the monster's power and its capacity to create anxiety are due to the fact that it violates the law while leaving it with nothing to say."[39] Monsters absorb the horror of what is unknown and unregulated by giving form to the unspeakable, and perhaps even unthinkable, monstrousness that cannot be contained within existing categories.

In most societies, a sexual act involving humans and animals clearly represents a serious and long-standing violation of the laws of both nature and culture. But in medieval images such as the drawings in the Arnstein Bible, even those Monstrous Races whose mixed-up bodies imply that transgressive sexual relations have taken place seem to be depicted as more marvelous than threatening. This is perhaps because, in their geographical location at the very edges of the known world, the Races stood outside the social and symbolic order of

Western cultures. Living in a territory beyond the direct experience of most Europeans, they posed little threat to society. Their bodies could be spectacularly reordered without apparent negative consequence because, in the words of the medieval English monk Ranulph Higden, "at the furthest reaches of the world often occur new marvels and wonders, as though Nature plays with greater freedom secretly at the edges of the world than she does openly and nearer to us in the middle of it."[40] Confined to this remote and uncharted area, the Monstrous Races locate the transgressions they represent at a safe distance, far from "civilized" human society.

Monsters and Maps

Medieval maps such as the Hereford Mappa Mundi (Figure 8.2) show a range of monsters in their "proper" geographical location, at the very edges of the globe. This map, which was drawn on a single sheet of vellum (calf skin) measuring 1.58 × 1.33 meters, dates from the early fourteenth century. While it may be more narrative than utilitarian, the Mappa Mundi functions as an important visual and textual account of medieval cultural values, illustrating the cosmology and theology of the late Middle Ages.[41] Mixing classical agendas with new information provided by more recent commercial travelers, pilgrims, and Crusaders, the Hereford map acted as an important and authoritative source for medieval scholars.

According to this map, Jerusalem is located at center of the (Christian) world, and monstrous "others" are arranged around the edges, beyond the Nile.[42] The monsters depicted include real and imaginary exotic beasts, such as an elephant (with a castle on its back), a manticore (a legendary creature similar to the Egyptian sphinx), a parrot, a camel, a unicorn, and a dragon, as well as many of the Monstrous Races. This grouping of human and animal, fantastical and "real" creatures seems to suggest an openness to the range of possibilities that may exist in the undefined territory beyond the concrete world of immediate experience. However, Friedman paints a rather less benign picture of the presence of the Races at the edges of the map:

> In the antipodal space defined by the edge of what separated us from them, and ringed by the river of Ocean believed to circle the very edges of the earth, is a cultural other, a sciopode or shadow-footed man, whose single great foot protects him from the heat of the sun. . . . His physical form defines the oddness beyond the border, for he is half like us and half like them. This map encloses the cultural other and renders him a harmless anecdotal representation.[43]

From a contemporary perspective, we can only speculate about the true spirit in which the Races were conceived. Perhaps the symbolic other that is being exiled is not so explicitly racial; maybe it is simply difference per se that is anthropomorphized in the bodies of the Monstrous Races.

What is clear is that, even though very few people could claim to have seen any of them "in the flesh," the Monstrous Races played an important role in the order of the world for classical and medieval scholars and laypeople alike. Living at the extremities of the known world, the Races could inhabit the realms of the imaginary and the mythical and yet still be considered entirely "real." This is perhaps because, in medieval culture, figures of the imagination and of myth were

Figure 8.2. Richard of Haldingham, Mappa Mundi, circa 1300.

Figure 8.3. The Monstrous Races, Arnstein Bible, circa 1172. Copyright The British Library Board.

not differentiated from everyday reality in the way that they are today.[44] The historians of science Katherine Park and Lorraine Daston offer an explanation for this: "medieval readers and writers shared an approach to truth more complicated and multivalent than the post-seventeenth-century obsession with the literal fact. . . . For them, truth could exist on various levels, both literal and figurative."[45] In the twenty-first century, we are led to believe that modern science enables us to separate "myth" from "reality," which makes it difficult to understand how people could ever have "believed in" the Monstrous Races. However, these ancient creatures are not so different to the more modern human monsters. They are all, to some degree, mythical figures, constructed to help sort out what is acceptably human from what is unacceptably "other."

Myth

The term *myth* is often used to indicate what is imaginary or fictitious. It is associated with something that is not "real." In the sense it is used here, a myth is a narrative that assigns meaning to a particular body or action. Roland Barthes has explained that myth is "a system of communication, a message . . . a type of speech, everything can be myth provided it is conveyed by a discourse."[46] So mythical human monsters are not necessarily "unreal." They are figures around which narratives have been constructed in order to help explain a newly experienced aspect of, or idea about, human being. As mythical figures, the Monstrous Races are imaginative (as opposed to imaginary) creatures that combine elements of observed material reality with signifying features to explain something. Barthes goes on to argue that "myth does not deny things. . . . Its function is to talk about them. . . . It purifies them, makes them innocent, gives them a natural and eternal justification . . . a clarity which is not that of an explanation, but that of a statement of fact."[47] In this interpretation, a mythical creature is the embodiment of an idea. In giving physical and visual form to a particular belief, the mythical monster can fix it in place and render it "real." While Barthes has claimed that "there is no fixity in mythical concepts—they can come into being, alter, disintegrate, disappear completely," mythical concepts can have lasting effects.[48] This is evidenced by the longevity of the Monstrous Races, whose existence was debated and often defended by scholars throughout the Middle Ages and beyond.[49]

Barthes makes another remark about myth that is particularly interesting. He writes, "Myth is not defined by the object of its message, but by the way in which it utters this message."[50] Here he draws attention to the constructed nature of myth and to how that narrative can change the way in which an existing object is perceived. In relation to creatures such as those that make up the Monstrous Races, myth can assign meaning to that which is otherwise unintelligible or, in the case of modern monsters, it can assign particular significance to an ordinary-looking face or body. Barthes characterizes myth as a form of representation that is informed by history.[51] For him, the signifier of myth "presents itself in an ambiguous way: it is at the same time meaning and form"—this is precisely the place of the human monster.[52]

By the beginning of the sixteenth century, the idea of monsters as symbolic "moral prodigies" was becoming popular in Western culture. Creatures like the Monster of Ravenna appeared, signifying the presence of moral or social unrest within Western society. And yet the strange and distant figures of the Monstrous Races described by early Greek travelers also continued to function as emblems of human difference up until at least the end of the sixteenth century. Wittkower attributes this longevity to the fact that well-educated travelers who knew the classics and understood natural science would have seen the Races marked on their maps and would have heard about them from childhood.[53] Even when geographical knowledge became widespread, therefore, travelers found these monsters in the East simply because they believed they would.[54]

The representational function of the Monstrous Races as corporeal signifiers of difference can perhaps be seen in the context of a classical worldview in which the "normal" human body acted as a model for the universe and social values were directly embodied in the human image. The importance of the "proper" body as an expression of acceptable human identity is illustrated in a comment made by the medieval teacher, papal adviser, and authority on Roman law Baldo degli Ubaldi, who wrote, "That which does not have the body of a man is presumed not to have the soul of a man . . . since form gives essence to a thing, that which does not have the form of a man is not a man."[55] The idea that human monstrosity represents that which is disproportionate or out of place can be examined in the light of a historically widespread belief that a person's character and moral status are mirrored in his or her physical characteristics. This belief, which offers a background to understanding the configuration of the Monstrous Races, is perhaps another factor that contributed to the longevity of belief in their existence.

No matter where the Monstrous Races appeared, they were always geographically distant from their observers. As remote social outsiders, they could pose little threat to established social laws or to the identity of individuals living within society. Because of their historical and geographical distance, the Monstrous Races provide a relatively uncomplicated visual introduction to the study of monsters.

Notes

1. The Arnstein Bible is now kept in the British Library.

2. From a conversation with Alixe Bovey, former curator of manuscripts at the British Library, November 17, 2008.

3. See David Williams, *Deformed Discourse: The Function of the Monster in Medieval Thought and Literature* (Exeter, U.K.: Exeter University Press, 1996), 137. Conversely, creatures such as the centaur, in which a human head is combined with an animal body, symbolize a distortion of form that preserves reason.

4. In *Politics* book I, chapter II, 1253a 9–10, Aristotle states, "Man is the only animal who has the gift of speech." See: Aristotle, *Politics,* trans. B. Jowett, in *The Complete Works of Aristotle,* ed. Jonathan Barnes (Princeton, N.J.: Princeton University Press, 1984), 1988. Also, Kate Soper discusses the legacy of Descartes's seventeenth-century argument that the use of language is exclusively human and offers a clear-cut standard for dividing animals from humans. Soper, *What Is Nature? Culture, Politics and the Non-human* (Oxford: Blackwell, 1995), 52–70. Stephen Horigan identifies Descartes's understanding of language as "the most important criterion used to distinguish between humans and animals" in Horigan, *Nature and Culture in Western Discourses* (London: Routledge, 1988), 75.

5. See Erica Fudge, *Animal* (London: Reaktion Books, 2002), 117–18.

6. Rudolf Wittkower, "Marvels of the East," in *Allegory and the Migration of Symbols* (London: Thames and Hudson, 1977).

7. Wittkower, 50.

8. See Dudley Wilson, *Signs and Portents: Monstrous Births from the Middle Ages to the Enlightenment* (London: Routledge, 1993), 4.

9. John Block Friedman, *The Monstrous Races in Medieval Art and Thought* (Cambridge, Mass.: Harvard University Press, 1981).

10. Friedman, 24–25.

11. The origins of the Monstrous Races are unknown, but Ctesias's treatise is understood to be one of the earliest surviving accounts. See Wittkower, "Marvels of the East," 46, and J. W. McCrindle, *Ancient India as Described by Ctesias the Knidian* (Calcutta: Thacker, Spink, 1882).

12. See, e.g., Wittkower, "Marvels of the East," 47, and McCrindle, *Ancient India,* 5.

13. Debra Higgs Strickland, *Saracens, Demons, and Jews: Making Monsters in Medieval Art* (Princeton, N.J.: Princeton University Press, 2003), 11–12.

14. McCrindle, *Ancient India,* 5. See also Wittkower, "Marvels of the East," 48.

15. Wittkower, "Marvels of the East," 54.

16. Pliny the Elder, *Natural History,* trans. H. Rackham (London: Loeb Classical Library, Harvard University Press, 1999), book VII, 23–25.

17. Pliny, book VII, 22.

18. Friedman, *Monstrous Races,* 26.

19. Friedman, 26–27.

20. See, e.g., Margrit Shildrick, *Embodying the Monster* (London: Sage, 2002), 16, and Gregory Velazco y Trianosky, "Savages, Wild Men, and Monstrous Races: The Social Construction of Race in the Early Modern Era," in *Beauty Revisited,* ed. Peggy Zeglin Brand (Bloomington: Indiana University Press, 2012), 45–71.

21. Peter Stallybrass and Allon White, *The Politics and Poetics of Transgression* (London: Methuen, 1986), 5.

22. Robert Barnhart, ed., *Chambers Dictionary of Etymology* (Edinburgh: Harrap, 2000), 1160.

23. Michel Foucault, "A Preface to Transgression," in *Language, Counter-memory, Practice,* ed. Donald F. Bouchard, trans. Donald F. Bouchard and Sherry Simon (Ithaca, N.Y.: Cornell University Press, 1977), 34.

24. This is the *Oxford English Dictionary* definition.

25. Johannes Fabian, *Time and the Work of Anthropology, Critical Essays, 1971–1991* (London: Routledge, 1991), 208.

26. Richard Kearney, *Strangers, Gods and Monsters: Interpreting Otherness* (London: Routledge, 2003), 117.

27. Malcolm Crick, *Explorations in Language and Meaning: Towards a Semantic Anthropology* (London: Malaby Press, 1976), 165.

28. Emmanuel Levinas, "The Trace of the Other," in *Continental Philosophy: An Anthology,* ed. William McNeill and Karen Feldman (Oxford: Blackwell, 1998), 177.

29. Edward Said, *Orientalism* (London: Routledge and Kegan Paul, 1978).

30. Susan Sontag, "The Anthropologist as Hero," in *Claude Lévi-Strauss: The Anthropologist as Hero,* ed. Eugene Hayes (Cambridge, Mass.: MIT Press, 1970), 185.

31. Michel Foucault, *Les Anormaux: Cours au Collége de France 1974–5,* trans. as *Abnormal* by Graham Burchill (New York: Picador, 2003), 63.

32. Foucault, 65.

33. Foucault, 64.

34. See, e.g., Horigan, *Nature and Culture,* 4, and Hayden White, "The Forms of Wildness," in *The Wild Man Within,* ed. E. Dudley and M. Novak (Pittsburgh: Pittsburgh University Press, 1972), 15.

35. On a conceptual level the boundary between humans and animals is less clearly defined in the contemporary context. See Fudge, *Animal.* However, in the field of genetic science the taboos surrounding the mixture of human and animal material remain strong. See Andrew Sharpe, "Structured Like a Monster: Understanding Human Difference through a Legal Category," *Law and Critique* 18, no. 2 (2007): 221–26.

36. Ambroise Paré, *Monstres et Prodiges; On Monsters and Marvels,* trans. Janis Pallister (Chicago: University of Chicago Press, 1982), 67.

37. Canguilhem, "Monstrosity and the Monstrous," 30–31.

38. Foucault, *Abnormal,* 56.

39. Foucault.

40. Ranulph Higden, *Polycronicon,* trans. John Trevisa (London: William Caxton, 1482). Quoted with reference to the Monstrous Races in Katherine Park and Lorraine Daston, *Wonders and the Order of Nature* (New York: Zone Books, 1998), 25. The Englishman Higden was in this case referring to Ireland as the edge of the world.

41. Park and Daston, *Wonders.* See also N. J. W. Thrower, *Maps and Civilization: Cartography in Culture and Society* (Chicago: University of Chicago Press, 2007), 42–46.

42. Thrower, 43.

43. John Block Friedman, "Cultural Conflicts in Medieval World Maps," in *Implicit Understandings: Observing, Reporting and Reflecting on the Encounters between Europeans and Other People in the Early Modern Era,* ed. Stuart B. Schwartz (Cambridge: Cambridge University Press, 1995), 69.

44. Wittkower, in "Marvels of the East," and Park and Daston, in *Wonders*, indicate that myth still figured strongly in both Eastern and Western interpretations of the world during the Middle Ages.

45. Park and Daston, *Wonders*, 60.

46. Roland Barthes, "Myth Today," in *Selected Writings* (London: Fontana, 1982), 93.

47. Barthes, 132.

48. Barthes, 106.

49. Wittkower, "Marvels of the East," 61–69.

50. Barthes, "Myth Today," 93–94.

51. Barthes.

52. Barthes, 102–3.

53. Wittkower, "Marvels of the East," 72.

54. Wittkower.

55. Baldo Ubaldi, quoted in Friedman, *Monstrous Races*, 180.

BLOOD, JEWS, AND MONSTERS IN MEDIEVAL CULTURE

Bettina Bildhauer

WHETHER THEY ARE THREE-HEADED DRAGONS, one-eyed giants, dog-headed men, or long-haired locusts, monsters have fascinatingly deformed and hybrid bodies. This physical visibility is so obviously a characteristic of the monstrous that it is implied rather than examined by modern critics. "The Monster's Body is a Cultural Body" is the first of Jeffrey Jerome Cohen's slick "seven theses" on monsters, which acknowledges their embodiedness only to sweep it away as a purely cultural construct.[1] While recent "freak" and "disability" studies, such as Rosemarie Garland Thomson's work, recognize that the "extraordinary bodies" under investigation were often labeled "monstrous" in the Middle Ages, the implication for the study of monsters is not accentuated.[2] Research into medieval monsters has also tacitly favored those with visibly deformed bodies. David Williams, for instance, discusses almost exclusively physical deformities (apart from a detour into monstrous alphabets and numbers), while maintaining that monstrosity is primarily an abstract linguistic and theoretical concept.[3] John Block Friedman suggests that those monstrous races who are not "physically anomalous" are in fact "not monstrous at all."[4] More recently, however, Judith Halberstam, in her book on the manufacture of monstrosity in Gothic horror, and Caroline Walker Bynum, in *Metamorphosis and Identity,* explicitly problematize the relation of monstrosity and bodies.[5]

But I shall argue here that it is often not its own misshapen or hybrid body that makes the monster but its relation to other bodies, social or individual. Mary

Douglas observes that social bodies are often imagined in analogy to individual bodies and that both are vulnerable at their margins.[6] What violates social categories and boundaries is vilified and excluded; so are bodily excretions. As one such transgressive phenomenon, she mentions "monstrous births," perceived by the Nuer people as violating the boundary between humans and animals, thus swiftly labeled "hippopotamuses" and physically excluded from human society.[7] The idea that the subject constructs itself by banishing the other, that which it does not want to be, beyond the boundaries of its physical and imagined identity is a commonplace in contemporary thought influenced by psychoanalytic and poststructural theory. But the disruptive interaction of monsters with other bodies has been explored surprisingly rarely in monster studies. I shall here investigate how their challenge to specifically physical and spatial contrasts, to the categories of "inside" and "outside" that mark out the normative social or individual body, makes many monsters what they are.[8] The monstrous races described by Pliny, for instance, do not always have deformed bodies, but always live on the fringes of the known world, outside human society and yet part of it, alien and yet somehow familiar. Likewise, many medieval demons were also commonly located on the peripheries of human settlements. Some of the demons studied by Dyan Elliott disrupt the physical integrity of individual clerics by instigating nocturnal emissions.[9]

Defining monstrosity as physically "borderline" provides an explanation for the pervasiveness of the concept of the monstrous and its juxtapositions with seemingly unrelated concepts in medieval culture. In what follows, I shall explore some examples of such linkages, in this case the connections of monsters in German thirteenth-century texts with ideas about Jews and blood. It was only on rare occasions that Jews were unambiguously described as monsters in medieval anti-Semitic discourse, and monsters were rarely perceived explicitly as Jews. But I will show that their positioning as an other, on the fringes of the metaphorical body of Christendom, opened up multiple parallels between Jews and monsters that were occasionally exploited by anti-Semites in graphic ways. Blood, frequently represented in the same marginal position as Jews and monsters, was used to "stigmatize" both. In looking at the multiple links between these three outwardly very different concepts—monstrosity, Jewishness, and blood—I hope to elucidate medieval attitudes to all three of them, with my focus remaining on the monstrous. I shall do so with close reference to two sermons of the Franciscan Berthold of Regensburg (d. 1272), but first, to the Ebstorf *mappa mundi*.

Locating Anti-Semitism: Gog and Magog on the Ebstorf *Mappa Mundi*

Medieval conceptions of the world are preserved in uniquely eloquent form on *mappae mundi*. The Ebstorf map of the world is by far the largest and arguably the most complex extant example, measuring 3.56 × 3.58 meters, and pieced together from thirty sheets of parchment (Figure 8.1). It is named after the nunnery of Ebstorf in Lower Saxony, where it was rediscovered in 1843, and where it may have been produced in the thirteenth century. The map shows the entire earth as a circle, densely filled with rivers, seas, landmasses, islands, towns, buildings, mountains, historical sites, animals, plants, humans, and plenty of monsters, as well as with Latin names and descriptions, and framed by Latin texts. The orb is organized in a variation of the widespread "T–O-scheme," so called because water bodies forming a "T" divide the orb ("O") into three main landmasses: Asia in the top (eastern) half, and Europe and Africa in the two bottom quarters. Africa, however, extends eastward along the right side of the circle, together

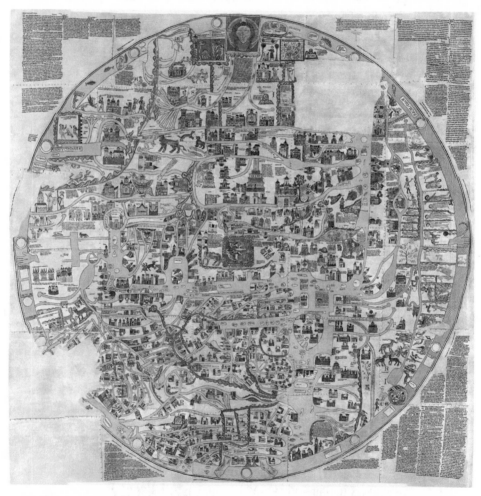

Figure 9.1. Ebstorf world map (circa thirteenth century). Reproduction from Ernst Sommerbrodt, *Die Ebstorfer Weltkarte* (Hanover: Hahn'sche Buchhandlung, 1891). Reprinted by permission of the Syndics of Cambridge University Library.

with an Antipodean zone full of monsters, so that a more "quadripartite" scheme emerges.[10] Research efforts are still to a large extent tied up in determining the circumstances of the Ebstorf map's production, its sources and representational method. Most scholars now assume that the map was conceived in the thirteenth century by a cleric with personal connections to the Guelph court as well as to the Ebstorf nunnery; the name Gervais of Tilbury is still mentioned.

Older scholarship dismissed the *mappa mundi* itself as a "monstrosity" for its failure to conform to modern conceptions of topographical maps.[11] But the Ebstorf map has in the past two decades been shown to provide not only some topographical orientation but also a compendium of information about the world and its inhabitants, as well as about history, theology, and natural philosophy. It creates multilayered meaning through text and images as well as through their spatial arrangement, which has been read as establishing conceptual links through geometrical axes and as moving chronologically from top to bottom, or clockwise, mapping time onto space. The map was destroyed by fire in the Second World War, so our interpretations are now based on modified reproductions of an already damaged map. These readings can thus never be definite, which is oddly appropriate for my argument about the indeterminacy, the irreducible polyvalence, of monsters.[12]

In the northeast corner of the earth as represented on the Ebstorf world map sit two naked men with receding hairlines, each biting into a severed and bleeding human foot (Figure 9.2). Between them, there lies another naked person, bleeding copiously from the severed stumps of his or her hands and feet. Another bloody foot or hand floats in the background; a bleeding hand is held by the man to the left of the viewer. "Here, Alexander has enclosed the two unclean people, Gog and Magog, who will accompany the Antichrist. They eat human flesh and drink blood," explains the caption.

Based on Ezekiel and the Apocalypse, Christian exegesis sees "Gog and Magog" as destroyers who would participate in the Antichrist's terrible reign at the end of time (Ezekiel 38–39; Revelation 20:7–10). Andrew Gow painstakingly traces the emergence of this tradition and its convergence with other stories of the "unclean people," whom Alexander the Great had enclosed behind mountains in the far northeast, as well as with the ten "lost" tribes of Israel (2 Kings 17), "long believed by many Jews (and later by Christians) to be a huge army somewhere in the East in reserve against the day when God would send them out to wreak havoc on a sinful world."[13] By the thirteenth century, Gog and Magog were thought of as Jewish and referred to as the Red Jews in a range of German texts. The men on the Ebstorf map indeed are drawn with stereotypical "Jewish" features, as identified in medieval anti-Semitic visual art by Ruth Mellinkoff: elongated eyes and deformed noses shown in profile.[14] Cannibalism and the use of human blood were also accusations often leveled against Jews; the first recorded

Figure 9.2. Gog and Magog. Detail from northeast corner of the Ebstorf world map (circa thirteenth century). Reproduction from Ernst Sommerbrodt, *Die Ebstorfer Weltkarte* (Hanover: Hahn'sche Buchhandlung, 1891). Reprinted by permission of the Syndics of Cambridge University Library.

allegation of Jews requiring Christian blood as a cure was raised in the German town of Fulda in 1235, resulting in the mass murder of the local Jews.[15] Gow suggests that images of Gog and Magog such as the one on the map could have fueled the belief in "real," contemporary German Jews eating Christian children and consuming their blood.[16]

But such an identification of Gog and Magog with Jews is only one of several possible readings. As Judith Halberstam has demonstrated, a monster's power lies in the fact that it has more than one signified, that it represents surplus alterity;

that, "within the history of embodied deviance, monsters always combine the markings of a plurality of differences even if certain forms of difference are eclipsed momentarily by others."[17] This insight might also be relevant to medieval monstrosity. For example, it can be argued that the distorted features of Gog and Magog have associations not only with Jews but also with executioners, prostitutes, and demons; there are several other figures on the Ebstorf map itself with faces similar to the Gog and Magog pair.[18] Moreover, the caption mentions neither facial features nor Jewishness. Instead, the factors highlighted by text and image are cannibalism and blood drinking, accusations leveled not just against Jews in the Middle Ages but against many monsters and social groups. Williams observes, "Not only does the act of cannibalism in and of itself establish monstrosity, it is also a common characteristic among many kinds of monsters," such as dog heads and giants.[19] *Strigae* or *lamiae,* fantastic night-flying women, were also believed to drink blood and eat humans, as was, according to Norman Cohn, a range of heretics.[20]

As these examples graphically depict, cannibalism constitutes an extreme "deformation" of the victim's body, a mutilation. The cannibals' own bodies are also deformed, as they ingest and digest foreign body parts and visibly form a monstrous conglomerate with them. But Gog and Magog also disrupt another body: the body of Christ. In the north, east, west, and south of the orb, Christ's head, hands, and feet are shown floating above the land (in the case of the head, in a separate square). This cannot be read as Christ standing behind or embracing the world, as in other *mappae mundi,* but rather seems to suggest that Christ's body has merged with the earth.[21] This fits in with the theological interpretation from the mid-twelfth century onward of Christ's body, *corpus mysticum,* as not only the eucharist but also the Church, comprising every Christian as a member.[22] Jeremy Cohen maintains that this new self-image of the Church as a streamlined body politic led to a more fervent exclusion of Jews.[23] But it also excluded other "others," like monsters. Gog and Magog are depicted at the very fringes of this body of Christ, as geographically ex-centric and marginal. The square in which they are placed is situated so far in the northeast corner of the orb that it reaches out into the ocean surrounding the landmass and is only cut off by the lines around the whole picture (which might signify the course of the planets or the elements). Thus, they create a disruption in the otherwise almost perfectly round circumference of Christ's body. Indeed, it is questionable whether they are still part of Christ's body. Text and image stress Gog and Magog's enclosure, their separation from the rest of the world. Their square is surrounded by mountains and walls (the latter built by Alexander the Great), and encircled by the larger country Scythia, which is home to other monsters and is depicted as being cut off by another mountain range, the Caucasus. Gog and Magog's double enclosure is not absolute, however. As the text reminds the viewer, Gog and Magog will enter

Christendom during the reign of the Antichrist. The visual enclosure is not complete either: one cannibal's foot reaches onto the right wall of the square; further to the right, the mountains that form the border of Scythia are interrupted by the Caspian Gates ("porte Caspie"). So Gog and Magog can be seen both as part of Christ's body and as separate from it. This precarious position, on the borderline between inside and out, is typical of monsters. As Jeffrey Jerome Cohen puts it, though without reference to bodies: "the monster's very existence is a rebuke to boundary and closure."[24]

Such a presence of monsters in or near Christ's body disrupts its integrity. Since the monsters are both part of and not part of that body, it is unclear where the *corpus mysticum* ends and the monsters begin. Any body, if it were to incorporate a monstrous part, would become a monstrous composite in itself. More specifically, Christ here embodies the dilemma of all medieval mapmakers and historiographers: what to do with the monsters, how to justify their existence in God's creation, and more generally what to include and what not. If the world image ignores monsters, despite popular and ancient knowledge of their existence, it fails to be all-encompassing, all-explaining. If imperfect creatures are included, as by the authors of the Ebstorf map, this requires justification. But the map offers no concrete explanation of their place in the Christian plan of the world (for example, as signs of God's infinite power or as interpretable portents). Despite scholars' efforts to detect a coherent, integrative pictorial program, the map is so multilayered that it leaves room for a whole host of interpretations. In the case of Gog and Magog, the monstrous seems to disrupt Christendom as much as it forms a part of it. As we shall see, it can even be read as resulting from the construction of the normative body of Christendom.

There is a striking visual parallel between the severed and bloody hands and feet eaten by Gog and Magog, and the separate hands and feet of Christ at the "corners" of the map, Christ's right hand showing its bloody stigma. As with all doubled motifs, a play of correspondence and contrast begins. We could interpret the severed limbs of Christ either as a positive contrast to the monstrous limbs of Gog and Magog, or as uncannily similar to them, highlighting the fragility and vulnerability of Christ's body that is Christendom. Perhaps what appears here is the tension in Christ's body, which represents both a human, individual body and the *corpus mysticum* of the Church. The head, hands, and feet make visual sense if read as part of the symbolic body of Christendom, but they become potentially disturbing if read as parts of a human body. This difficult double role is also evident in the doubling of Christ's body on the map. In a strongly defined and visually striking square, similar to the ones surrounding Christ's head at the top and Gog and Magog on the top left, there appears a second representation of Christ, here seen stepping out from his grave in Jerusalem at the center of the map. So on the one hand he is shown encompassing the world, and on the other

hand he is represented residing in his own navel, at the moment of his resurrection. This tension between two functions of Christ's body is an internal dynamic
of Christian thought.[25] It can be projected on to monsters, or just as easily on to
Jews, because both simply serve as a receptacle of anything "other," anything that
Christians do not want to be.

Blood is also a feature associated with both the monsters and Christ here. Gog
and Magog are visually and textually described as blood-drinkers. Like monsters,
blood is in itself marginal and problematic. We see it here, at the moment when it
exudes from the severed limbs, where it flows around the cannibals' mouths and
where it clings to Christ's wound, as being neither completely interior nor completely exterior to the body. In the context of Christ's body, an added parallel can
perhaps be discerned between, on the one hand, the drinking of blood and the eating of human flesh by Gog and Magog, and, on the other, partaking in the eucharist.
The visual resemblance between the roundness of the host and of the orb highlights this connection, even if the Ebstorf map makes no explicit reference to the
eucharist in text or image. Again, we may read the relationship between the eucharist and the cannibalism of Gog and Magog as a contrast or an analogy, or both. And
again, the tensions inherent in the idea of eating the divine body were, as we have
seen, just as often projected onto Jews in accusations of ritual cannibalism.[26]

The Gog and Magog scene can be compared not just to representations of
Christ but also to representations of Ebstorf. Ebstorf is represented, in the bottom
left corner next to the elaborate towns of Brunswick and Lüneburg, as a small
church labeled "Ebbekestorp" along with a drawing consisting of three small
squares, with the inscription "here rest the blessed martyrs," indicating the martyrs' graves that the cloister was beginning to promote as the site of a cult in the
thirteenth century.[27] Hartmut Kugler sees a geometrical relation between Gog
and Magog and Ebstorf: just as Ebstorf is located at the bottom left corner of the
earth, so Gog and Magog are situated at the top left corner ("corners" denoting
the intersections of the diagonals of the square map with the circumference
of the earth). Ebstorf is surrounded by the Christian northwest, while Gog and
Magog are likewise surrounded by the barbarian Scythia in the northeast.[28] Again,
this juxtaposition could be read as a contrast between the "anti-Christian" Gog and
Magog who drink blood and the martyrs who exude healing oil, between Christian respect for the dead and the monsters' devouring of them. Since the martyrs
died in the ninth century while fighting heathens, Gog and Magog could be seen
as their heathen (not just Jewish) anti-images. But it might also draw attention
to the uncanny parallels between drinking blood and consuming oil, eating bodies and profiting from centuries-old corpses, between heathens in the East and
Slavic heathens at home.

Gog and Magog are here strangely multiplied, as if to amplify their monstrosity and to stress that they cannot be fixed to one place or meaning. The caption of

the northern ocean island Taracontum also informs us that it is inhabited by the cannibalistic Gog and Magog. Several other cannibals are present on the map; one image depicts the cannibalistic Massagetes in Scythia as similarly slaughtering and eating the right foot of a bleeding victim. While this multiplication can be understood as a projection of Christ's problematic multiple roles, it also points us to the fact that the map itself is a hybrid, heterogeneous in origin and appearance; it combines material from various sources, which the authors did not want to, or could not, merge into an entirely unified picture.[29] Like many other Christian texts, the Ebstorf map incorporates material of non-Christian origin: for instance, the ancient Alexander lore, blended with the Old and New Testament stories of Gog and Magog. Moreover, it combines text and image in a highly unusual way: not in manuscript form, but in what can be seen as an image of the world with written explanations or as a text broken down into a picture. While the text is entirely in Latin, the image might also have spoken to the unlearned public. With so much hybridity in sources and media, then, the hybridity of contents is no coincidence.

Gog and Magog are thus not so much Jews as polyvalent monsters situated at the margins of Christendom. Their monstrosity is linked to both Jewishness and blood, but not identical with either. In what follows, I shall extend this analysis by exploring stereotypes that appear on the surface to be more self-consciously and insidiously anti-Semitic. In addition, I will suggest that it is not so much Jewishness in itself that causes fear in these contexts, but the awareness that Jews and Christians are not entirely distinct categories, and that there is hybridity in both.

Locusts and Weed: Judaeo-Christians in the Sermons of Berthold of Regensburg

Among the thirteenth-century German texts that discuss Jews most intensively are the sermons of the Franciscan friar and preacher Berthold of Regensburg. Berthold was a preacher of legendary fame, reportedly attracting crowds in their thousands during his extensive tours of Europe from the 1240s to his death in 1272. His performances are of course irretrievable, but written versions of many of his sermons survive, composed from his Latin homiletic manuals as well as probably from the memory of Augsburg friars—hybrid texts combining Latin and German, orality and literacy, single and collective authorship.[30] These penitential sermons present Christendom and each Christian in an ever-changing world, constantly under threat from the inside—through sin—as well as from the outside—from Jews, heathens and heretics. In his influential *The Friars and the Jews,* Jeremy Cohen argues that thirteenth-century mendicant friars played a key role in spreading anti-Semitism and describes Berthold as a prime example of this.[31] Cohen chooses quotations from Berthold that seem unambiguously to condemn "the Jews." Upon closer examination, however, Berthold's anti-Semitism emerges as more complex, anxious and insidious, insofar as he often sees Jews as much more ambivalent figures, not clearly distinguishable from Christians, and thus even more dangerous.

In his sermon "Of the four traps," for example, Berthold links Jewish–Christian interaction with one of the famous apocalyptic monsters: the locust with lions' teeth, woman's hair, iron armor, a scorpion's tail and a human face (2:137–44).[32] This beast represents the greedy, who are, to Berthold, the most contemptible of all sinners. Like a locust and a lion with his big teeth, the greedy never get enough. Like fickle-minded women, the greedy do not trust God to provide them with all they need. Like solid armor, they are so hardened that they cannot even be moved by Christ's blood and passion. Their ill-gotten gains sting all humanity like a scorpion's tail. And the human face means "daz er kristen namen hât und mit den werken ein jude ist" ("that he [the greedy person?] is a Christian by name and a Jew in his deeds"; 2:144). This last explanation is the most opaque. The relation between signifier (human face or the whole monster) and signified (a Christian doing Jewish deeds or the greedy) is all but clear. The face itself might somehow represent either greed or a combination of Christian name and Jewish deed. Or, it might here be for once the whole combination of a monstrous body and a human face that is the signifier, perhaps expressing the idea that a greedy sinner seems Christian (human face) but turns out to be Jewish (composite body). What is evident is that the monster is not identified specifically as a Jew here, nor are Jews identified as monstrous. Rather it is the Jewish–Christian hybrid—the Christian who behaves like a Jew—who is somehow monstrous here. The monster is not a Jew or a Christian: it is a locust-lion-scorpion-woman-knight-glutton-sinner-greedy-fraudster-Jew-Christian, and simultaneously none of these. Jeremy Cohen sees this passage as revealing how firmly the category "Jewish" had been defined and connected to sinful behavior.[33] I would stress instead that "Jewish" does not describe a stable social, ethnic, or religious group in this context but a kind of behavior that Christians themselves can display.[34] Of course this does not make Berthold less anti-Semitic: "Jewish" behavior (at least that perceived in a Christian) clearly denotes something negative here and elsewhere in his sermons. But it does give an insight into where his anti-Semitism is coming from: his anxious awareness that these categories are fluid provokes even more aggressive attempts at distinction.

The same ambiguous position as both part of and not part of Christians and Christendom characterizes Jews throughout Berthold's work. In the sermon "Of the Three Walls," for instance, this position is linked not so much to monstrosity as to blood (1:357–72).[35] This sermon interprets the biblical example of a field with a treasure, for which a man gladly exchanges all his possessions (Matthew 13:44). This treasure is here read as the Christian's soul, the field as Christendom, which Jesus bought with his body and fertilized with his blood. The equation of Christendom with Christ's body is not made explicit in this particular sermon, although the fact that Christ bought the field with his body suggests that field and body are equivalent in some ways. Jeremy Cohen claims that Jews are entirely excluded from the Christian field: "The Jew, states the friar emphatically, has no rightful access to this field and its treasure; at best he represents a weed planted by the devil in the field, one which will, it is hoped, be removed."[36] As we shall see, Jews are, rather, ambiguously positioned both inside and outside the field.

The field, after all, is surrounded by the three walls of the title. The first wall is made of silk and signifies the stole of the priest, clerical power. Pope and clergy teach Christians how to keep their faith in case Jews, heathens, or heretics try to dissuade them and how to act according to their faith. The second, iron wall, representing the iron sword of worldly legal authority, is the most problematic one: it protects against the same enemies of the faith as well, so that, in case someone breaks the silk wall, "this iron wall is still in front of it and shields the field from Jews and from heathens and from heretics" (1:362). But at the same time, in a paradox that is not resolved in the sermon, Jews are themselves sheltered by it: the worldly authorities "shall also protect the Jews' life [lîbe] and belongings like they protect the Christians', since they are included in the peace" (1:363).[37] So Jews do both belong to the "field" of Christendom that is protected by the second wall and do not belong to it. Again, this seems to result from problems in the construction of Christendom itself, claiming universal status as well as exclusivity.[38]

The third wall is a heavenly wall that protects each side, each patch, each ear of corn of the field, or each kingdom, duchy, diocese, town, village, cloister, farm, dwelling, castle, house, and human being. This again includes Jews as well as heathens, heretics, Slavs, and Tartars. So Jews are separated from Christians, and vice versa, by their individual walls, but included by the ones around each village, town, and so forth. Since the field represents Christendom (as a whole) and the (single) treasure the individual soul, the relation between the individual Christian and Christendom is problematic anyway, but here Christendom definitely no longer appears as a unified field but as fragmented. The image is here shifting from an external threat to Christendom as a whole to a threat to each individual. Everybody has his or her own devil, Berthold explains, which constantly tempts them and which each person's angel is only just able to keep in check. Even on an individual level, Jewishness and Christianity are combined in hybrid entities, as becomes clear in the ensuing image of weeds growing among the wheat of the field. Berthold identifies these weeds as sinners and gives a long list of examples, several of which are figures that are often seen as prototypical Jews: Cain, Esau, Judas.[39] But, due to the common heritage of Christians and Jews, these figures can also be read simply as archetypal sinners. Since they (and their pious counterparts) are both addressed as "you," the (Christian) audience is encouraged to identify with them and repent their own sins. So once again Jewishness, if anything, is mostly feared as a kind of behavior displayed by Christians. The weeds are indistinguishably both Jewish and Christian, and thus form a potentially monstrous hybrid.

Blood is again associated with these weeds/Jews/sinners. Berthold addresses them as blood-drinkers (*bluottrinker*), an epithet he uses throughout his sermons for murderers, especially Cain. Jezebel's blood is lapped up by dogs in hell (1:367).[40] Again here blood is shown as moving from one body to the next, not simply being spilled, but being drunk. Abel's and Jezebel's blood leaves their bodies and enters Cain's and the dogs', being part of both and neither of them. Just as the Jews are situated both inside and outside the field, blood is situated in between bodies here.

There is another instance of an exchange of blood in this sermon: Christ fertilizes the field with his blood, which means that it leaves his body and enters the field. We could again see this image as pointing to the tensions within the Christian ideology contained in the sermon, which result in the production of monstrous Jews/sinners: Christ willingly sheds his own blood here, when bloodshed is normally a violent crime. This creates awkward parallels between Christ and Cain, for example.[41] But I would also like to emphasize that, despite its predominantly negative associations with sin, blood appears here with a positive significance: as Christ's salvific and nourishing blood. This is paralleled by the partly positive and integral function of any "other": it enables the construction of identity. The weeds/Jews/sinners thus also paradoxically have a positive function in this sermon: on a metatextual level, they furnish Berthold with material for his skillful rhetoric to identify what a good Christian is by contrast with what is not, and to make sinners repent, that is, become good Christians themselves. This positive effect is made explicit in the sermon: as Berthold acknowledges, Jews are tolerated inside Christendom for two reasons: not only will they become Christians if they survive the time of the Antichrist, but they are also signs or witnesses (*geziuge*) reminding Christians of the passion Christ suffered at their hands and admonishing them (*ermanen*) lest they forget (1:363).

Blood, Anti-Semitism, and Monstrosity: A Pervasive Juxtaposition

I hope to have shown that by virtue of embodying anything differing from the norm, monsters cannot be pinned down to a single meaning: neither Berthold's locust and weeds nor Gog and Magog exclusively represent Jews. Instead, blood, Jews, and monsters all occupy a position as an "other" on the margins of the normative Christian body: the bloody Gog and Magog on the borders of Christ's enormous body on the Ebstorf map and the bloody weeds simultaneously inside and outside the field of Christendom in Berthold's sermon.

Such implicit juxtaposition of Jews, monsters, and blood was widespread in medieval Europe. It can be argued that most of the accusations leveled against Jews in anti-Semitic writings involve blood, and, to some extent, monstrous behavior. Narratives of host desecration and ritual murder, rumors about the crucifixion of Christian boys, and accounts describing images of Christ being attacked with knives—all partook of the anti-Semitic processes by which Jews were associated with blood, and became, metaphorically speaking, monsters.[42] Blood is usually a central element in these narratives, streaming out of hosts, images, and corpses. Blood in these stories marks, disturbs, and enforces the body of Christ, in the shape of the eucharist, the Church, the little boy, the crucified Christ, and the devotional image. While there is certainly room for much more research in this area, I hope this chapter has demonstrated ways in which Jews could take on more explicitly monstrous associations, too. In the following, I shall briefly contextualize my findings by pointing out analogies to further examples.

If Berthold sees Jews as signs and reminders, so do many other authors. For instance, in his treatise on Christ's blood, *Tractatus de sacratissimo sanguine domini* (1280), the Dominican Gerhard of Cologne gives exactly the same reason as Berthold for tolerating the despised Jews: that they remind Christians of Christ's passion (*conmoneare*).[43] A similar function is of course often ascribed to monsters: many medieval scholars explained the meaning of "monster" etymologically, as derived from some form of either *monstrare* (to show) or *monere* (to remind, admonish, warn), in both senses to indicate that monsters exist in order to show God's power.[44] Interestingly, Christ's blood also has exactly the same role as the Jews in Gerhard's treatise: the eucharist is mentioned in the same breath as Jews as a further reminder (as well as the Bible and the instruments of the passion); and the whole treatise is aimed at defending the value of the reliquary of Christ's blood established in Weingarten as an even more powerful reminder than the previous four.[45] Christ's blood thus becomes dangerously similar to the "monstrous" Jews. Underlying Gerhard's anti-Judaism are again intense concerns about the integrity of Christ's body and in particular about its potential disruption by the blood relic: the text deals at length with questions about the resurrection of his blood together with Christ, about the blood's freshness after his death, and about his bodily fluids remaining on the earth.[46]

Most of the monstrous races represented in the Ebstorf *mappa mundi* and other medieval texts are derived from Pliny's *Natural History*. "But nothing," Pliny concludes, "nothing could easily be found that is more remarkable (*monstrificum*) than the monthly flux of women."[47] Medieval sources continue and augment this view of menstruation as monstrous by stressing its disastrous effects. For example, an excess of menstrual blood (*uberflussigkait der matery*), which constitutes the mother's contribution to the fetus, is one of the common explanations for "monstrous births," given here in a fifteenth-century German translation of the gynecological treatise *Secreta mulierum*.[48] *Menstrum,* menstrual blood, is often written by scribes as *monstrum,* "monster." Several manuscripts of the *Secreta mulierum* include a Latin heading to the section on the question "through which place [the vagina or the anus] menstrual fluids flow": "per quem locum fluant menstrua" or similar. Manuscript J, however, after a convoluted excursus on how much human females resemble animals, has the corrupted "per quem locum fluant monstruum."[49] Williams explains the monstrosity of menstrual blood by its hybrid status as matter without form, according to Aristotelian ideas about conception and the universe.[50] On the basis of my observations in this chapter, I can specify that menstrual blood represents a violation of the boundaries of the body: it is both part of the body and at the same time leaves its confines. This ambiguous position is what makes it "monstrous," and also comparable to anti-Semitic constructions of the Jews. It should thus not be surprising that a number of late medieval texts claimed that Jewish men themselves menstruate: "for this and the following reasons, all Jews are used to having the [menstrual] flow every month," states another German translation of the *Secreta mulierum*.[51] The reasons cited are a mixture of physiology, theology, and prejudice—a need to expel residues due to their diet, constitution, lack of hard work, melancholia, and uncleanness, plus inheritance and astrological influence; but first and foremost that they "called Christ's blood upon them" when Pilate washed his hands of it (Matthew 27:25).[52]

The decrees of the Fourth Lateran Council in 1215 shall be my last example of how a concern with his blood as well as with Jews and monsters accompanies attempts to delineate Christ's body. This Council is trying to impose a strict hierarchy on the body of the Church, not least through the dogma of the transubstantiated eucharist mediated exclusively by priests.[53] The fear expressed is that the Church would turn monstrous if it were to deviate from this structure: if a town or diocese had two bishops, two "heads," it would become monstrous: "as if it were a body with several heads like a monster *(quasi monstrum)*."[54]

It is probably no coincidence that the same Council feels compelled to clarify the position of blood, Jews, and monstrous demons to the Christian world, to eliminate these problematic ambiguities threatening to upset the streamlined Church. Clerics are forbidden to shed blood, for example, to have anything to do with sentences and punishments that involve the shedding of blood, to command "men of blood" like mercenaries or to practice surgery.[55] It is made clear that "the devil and other demons were created by God naturally good, but they became evil by their own doing."[56] Jewish–Christian relations are also regulated, with the most obvious attempt at demarcation probably being the infamous order for Jews to wear distinctive clothes to avoid any further confusion with Christians.[57] It can be argued again that neither of these attempts at differentiation is very successful, since they implicitly confirm that monsters sit uncomfortably with the concept of a perfect creation and that Jews can easily be confused with gentiles. For, as I have tried to show, however desperately one tries to exclude the monstrous other, it remains lurking at the borders.

Notes

Many thanks to Bob Mills, Greg Moore, and Miri Rubin for their very helpful comments on this chapter.

1. Jeffrey Jerome Cohen, "Monster Culture (Seven Theses)," in *Monster Theory: Reading Culture,* ed. Jeffrey Cohen (Minneapolis: University of Minnesota Press, 1996), 4.

2. Rosemarie Garland Thomson, "Introduction: From Wonder to Error—A Genealogy of Freak Discourse in Modernity," in *Freakery: Cultural Spectacles of the Extraordinary Body,* ed. Rosemarie Garland Thomson (New York: New York University Press, 1996), 1–4.

3. David Williams, *Deformed Discourse: The Function of the Monster in Mediaeval Thought and Literature* (Exeter, U.K.: University of Exeter Press, 1996).

4. John Block Friedman, *The Monstrous Races in Medieval Art and Thought* (Cambridge, Mass.: Harvard University Press, 1981), 1.

5. Judith Halberstam, *Skin Shows: Gothic Horror and the Technology of Monsters* (Durham, N.C.: Duke University Press, 1995); Caroline Walker Bynum, *Metamorphosis and Identity* (New York: Zone, 2001).

6. Mary Douglas, *Purity and Danger: An Analysis of the Concepts of Pollution and Taboo* (London: Routledge, 1966), esp. 122–23.

7. Douglas, 40.

8. Michael Uebel, "Unthinking the Monster: Twelfth-Century Responses to Saracen Alterity," in Cohen, *Monster Theory,* 274–80, makes a similar point with reference to Saracens.

9. Dyan Elliott, *Fallen Bodies: Pollution, Sexuality, and Demonology in the Middle Ages* (Philadelphia: University of Pennsylvania Press, 1999), 14–34.

10. This term is introduced by David Woodward, "Medieval *mappaemundi,*" in *The History of Cartography,* vol. 1, *Cartography in Prehistoric, Ancient, and Medieval Europe and the Mediterranean,* ed. John Brian Harley and David Woodward (Chicago: University of Chicago Press, 1987), 296.

11. C. Raymond Beazley, *The Dawn of Modern Geography* (Oxford: Clarendon, 1897–1906), 3:528.

12. Hartmut Kugler, ed., *Ein Weltbild vor Columbus: Die Ebstorfer Weltkarte: Interdisziplinäres Kolloquium 1988,* Acta humaniora (Weinheim: VCH, 1991); Hartmut Kugler, "Hochmittelalterliche Weltkarten als Geschichtsbilder," in *Hochmittelalterliches Geschichtsbewusstsein im Spiegel nichthistorischer Quellen,* ed. Hans-Werner Goetz (Berlin: Akademie, 1998), 179–98; Birgit Hahn-Woernle, *Die Ebstorfer Weltkarte* (Ebstorf: Kloster Ebstorf, 1987); Uwe Ruberg, "Mappae mundi des Mittelalters im Zusammenwirken von Text und Bild," in *Text und Bild: Aspekte des Zusammenwirkens zweier Künste in Mittelalter und früher Neuzeit,* ed. Christel Meier und Uwe Ruberg (Wiesbaden: Reichert, 1980), 550–92.

For editions, see Ernst Sommerbrodt, *Die Ebstorfer Weltkarte* (Hannover: Hahn'sche Buchhandlung, 1891), black and white facsimile with redrawings and accompanying commentary; Konrad Miller, ed., *Monialium Ebstorfensium Mappamundi/Die Ebstorfkarte,* Mappaemundi: Die ältesten Weltkarten 5 (Stuttgart: Roth, 1896), colour redrawing/accompanying commentary.

13. Andrew Colin Gow, *The Red Jews: Antisemitism in an Apocalyptic Age 1200–1600,* Studies in Medieval and Reformation Thought 55 (Leiden: Brill, 1995), 3–4.

14. Ruth Mellinkoff, *Outcasts: Signs of Otherness in Northern European Art of the Late Middle Ages* (Berkeley: University of California Press, 1993), 1:229–30, e.g., ii, Figure 3.4; Ruth Mellinkoff, *Antisemitic Hate Signs in Hebrew Illuminated Manuscripts from Medieval Germany* (Jerusalem: Center for Jewish Art, Hebrew University of Jerusalem, 1999), 23–27. Mellinkoff also mentions other elements frequently found in anti-Semitic images, such as Hebrew letters, or mouths drawn as a long horizontal line or with heavy lips, that are not present here.

15. Gavin I. Langmuir, *Toward a Definition of Antisemitism* (Berkeley: University of California Press, 1990), 262–81. In 1247, Innocent IV had received complaints from German Jews that they were accused of cannibalism, of eating Christian children's hearts at Passover: Julius Aronius, *Regesten zur Geschichte der Juden im fränkischen und deutschen Reiche bis zum Jahre 1273* (Berlin: Nathansen & Lamm, 1902), 242. On later variations of the blood libel legend and ritual murder accusations, see, e.g., Ronnie Po-chia Hsia, *The Myth of Ritual Murder: Jews and Magic in Reformation Germany* (New Haven, Conn.: Yale University Press, 1988).

16. Gow, *Red Jews,* 49–53.

17. Halberstam, *Skin Shows,* 5–6.

18. See Mellinkoff, *Outcasts* (e.g., ii, Figures 1.31 and 3.25); Debra Hassig, "The iconography of rejection: Jews and other monstrous races," in *Image and Belief: Studies in Celebration of the Eightieth Anniversary of the Index of Christian Art,* ed. Colum Hourihane, 25–46 (Princeton, N.J.: Princeton University Press, 1999). Scott Westrem, "Against Gog and Magog," in *Text and Territory: Geographical Imagination in the European Middle Ages,* ed. Sylvia Tomasch and Sealy Gilles (Philadelphia: University of Pennsylvania Press, 1998), 54–78, also forcefully warns against ascribing one particular significance to Gog and Magog in their varied medieval representations.

19. Williams, *Deformed Discourse,* 145–48.

20. Norman Cohn, *Europe's Inner Demons: The Demonization of Christians in Medieval Christendom,* 2nd ed. (London: Pimlico, 1993), esp. 35–41 and 162–66. Historical records of cannibalism by Christian crusaders are discussed, for example, in Geraldine Heng, "Cannibalism, the First Crusade and the Genesis of Medieval Romance," *differences* 10 (1998) 98–173. Mongols were also accused of cannibalism by various writers: see Uebel, "Unthinking the Monster," 282 and 290–91. On blood-sucking women and monsters, see Bettina Bildhauer, "Bloodsuckers: The Construction of Female Sexuality in Medieval Science and Fiction," in *Consuming Narratives: Gender and Monstrous Appetites in the Middle Ages and the Renaissance,* ed. Liz Herbert McAvoy and Teresa Walters (Cardiff: University of Wales Press, 2002), 104–15.

21. Armin Wolf, "Ebstorfer Weltkarte," in *Lexikon des Mittelalters* (Munich: Artemis, 1986), 3:1534–35.

22. Ernst H. Kantorowicz, *The King's Two Bodies: A Study in Mediaeval Political Theology* (Princeton, N.J.: Princeton University Press, 1957), 194–206; Sarah Beckwith, *Christ's Body: Identity, Culture and Society in Late Medieval Writings* (London: Routledge, 1993), esp. 30–33.

23. Jeremy Cohen, *The Friars and the Jews: The Evolution of Medieval Anti-Judaism* (Ithaca, N.Y.: Cornell University Press, 1982), 248–64. The increasing emphasis on Christ's body in another, the eucharistic, sense from the eleventh century onward also went hand in hand with the tightening of the *societas christiana*: see Miri Rubin, *Corpus Christi: The Eucharist in Late Medieval Culture* (Cambridge: Cambridge University Press, 1991), 12–14.

24. Cohen, "Monster Culture," 7.

25. It is repeated in formulations of the Church as Christ's body, of which Christ is simultaneously the head, so that there are two "Christs," one in the head of the other—a two-headed monster: Kantorowicz, *King's Two Bodies*, esp. 194.

26. For cannibalism as featured in discussions of the eucharist, see Rubin, *Corpus Christi*, 359–60.

27. Klaus Jaitner, "Kloster Ebstorf und die Weltkarte," in Kugler, *Weltbild*, 41–53; Jerzy Strzelczyk, "Die Legende von den Ebstorfer Märtyrern als Zeugnis über die politischen und ethnischen Verhältnisse in Nordostdeutschland im Mittelalter," *Lětopis* B18 (1971): 54–79.

28. Hartmut Kugler, "Die Ebstorfer Weltkarte: Ein europäisches Weltbild im deutschen Mittelalter," *Zeitschrift für deutsches Altertum und deutsche Literatur* 116 (1987): 20–22; Kugler, "Hochmittelalterliche Weltkarten," 187–94.

29. See Hartmut Kugler, "Abschreibfehler: Zur Quellenproblematik der Ebstorfer Weltkarte," in Kugler, *Weltbild*, 347–66.

30. *Berthold von Regensburg: Vollständige Ausgabe seiner Predigten*, ed. Franz Pfeiffer, 2 vols. (Vienna: Braumüller, 1862–80). Further references to this edition will be made in parentheses in the text.

31. Cohen, *Friars and Jews*, 229–38.

32. See Revelation 9:7–10.

33. Cohen, *Friars and Jews*, 234.

34. Sara Lipton has observed a similar fluidity of Judaism and Christianity in illustrations to the *Bible moralisée: Images of Intolerance: The Representation of Jews in the Bible moralisée* (Berkeley: University of California Press, 1999), esp. 15–19.

35. A largely unmodified edition of this sermon with commentary and modern German translation appears in *Berthold von Regensburg: Vier Predigten Mittelhochdeutsch/Neuhochdeutsch*, ed. Werner Röcke (Stuttgart: Reclam, 1983), 142–83 and 222–34.

36. Cohen, *Friars and Jews*, 235.

37. If they became too numerous, however, one would have to defend oneself against them as against heathens (1:363).

38. The relationship of the three walls to each other is also unclear. If someone who broke the first wall (presumably from the outside) still faced the second one, and if the third wall is the narrow individual one, it seems likely that the walls are concentric and

treated from the outside to the inside; this in turn implies that the papal Christian community is regarded as more inclusive than worldly society. In another, shorter version of this sermon, worldly and papal walls have changed place (2:238–41).

39. Jezebel is described as wearing yellow, which Berthold condemns throughout his sermons and elsewhere sees fit for demarcating Jewesses (1:415).

40. Judas is also associated with blood since he famously sold Christ's blood for "blood money" with which a "field of blood" was bought (see, e.g., 1:160). Berthold calls blood in general a sign of sin in the Bible: Frank G. Banta, *Predigten und Stücke aus dem Kreise Bertholds von Regensburg (Teilsammlung. YIII)*, Göppinger Arbeiten zur Germanistik 621 (Göppingen: Kümmerle, 1995), 92.

41. In the same way that Christ fertilizes the earth with his blood, the earth is described as "drinking" Abel's blood in the Bible (Genesis 4:11) and by Berthold (Banta, *Predigten*, 89). Christ here assumes Cain's role of a field farmer, his crucifix being likened to a plow and his blood to fertilizer, as opposed to the shepherd Abel. In the shorter version of this sermon, Christ problematically both buys and at the same time fertilizes the field with his blood, perhaps indicating the double role of his blood as having bought salvation for us and still being required as a reminder of his passion, to ensure piety and thus salvation (2:239). Another field of blood that can be uncomfortably linked to this one is the field that was bought with Judas's thirty coins of "blood money" (Matthew 27:6–9; Acts 1:18–19).

42. See, e.g., Miri Rubin, *Gentile Tales: The Narrative Assault on Late Medieval Jews* (New Haven, Conn.: Yale University Press, 1999); Langmuir, *Toward a Definition*; Denise L. Despres, "Cultic Anti-Judaism and Chaucer's Little Clergeon," *Modern Philology* 91 (1994): 413–27.

43. Klaus Berg, "Der Traktat des Gerhard von Köln über das kostbare Blut Christi aus dem Jahre 1280," in *900 Jahre Heilig-Blut-Verehrung in Weingarten, 1094–1994*, ed. Norbert Kruse and Hans-Ulrich Rudolf (Sigmaringen: Thorbecke, 1994), 1:459–60, ll. 28–56.

44. Friedman, *Monstrous Races*, 108–30.

45. Berg, *Traktat*, 459–65.

46. Berg, 465–68.

47. Pliny, *Natural History*, ed. Harris Rackham, Loeb Classical Library (London: Heinemann, 1961), 2:548, ll. 64–65 (7. 15); Friedman, *Monstrous Races*, 5–25.

48. Margaret Rose Schleissner, "Pseudo-Albertus Magnus, 'Secreta Mulierum Cum Commento, Deutsch': Critical Text and Commentary" (PhD diss., Princeton University, 1987), 265–69, ll. 1735–83; 278–79, ll. 1894–1903 (l. 1895). The thirteenth-century Latin original has not been published, but a rough, excerpted English translation is available: Helen Rodnite Lemay, *Women's Secrets: A Translation of Pseudo-Albertus Magnus' "De Secretis Mulierum with Commentaries"* (Albany: State University of New York Press, 1992).

49. Schleissner, "Pseudo-Albertus Magnus," 152, l. 182; Erlangen, *Universitätsbibliothek*, B 33 (Irm. 1492).

50. Williams, *Deformed Discourse*, 174–75.

51. *"Secreta mulierum" mit Glosse in der deutschen Bearbeitung von Johann Hartlieb*, ed. Kristian Bosselmann-Cyran, Würzburger medizinhistorische Forschungen 36 (Pattensen: Wellm, 1985), 134–37. Willis Johnson's important study overlooks this early reference when he claims that the myth was first mentioned in 1503: "The Myth of Jewish

Male Menses," *Journal of Medieval History* 24 (1998): 273–95. Peter Biller also mentions two earlier sources for Jewish male menstruation in "Views of Jews from Paris around 1300: Christian or 'Scientific'?," in *Christianity and Judaism: Papers Read at the 1991 Summer Meeting and the 1992 Winter Meeting of the Ecclesiastical History Society,* Studies in Church History 29, ed. Diana Wood (Oxford: Blackwell, 1992), 199.

52. The latter is a common anti-Semitic accusation and is often used to draw parallels between the Jews and Cain, since Abel's blood calls out to God and accuses Cain in the same way that Christ's blood accuses the Jews. Cain is seen as the forefather not only of Jews but also of monsters: Friedman, *Monstrous Races,* 103; Ruth Mellinkoff, "Cain and the Jews," *Journal of Jewish Art* 6 (1979): 16–38. Many more parallels occur in medieval representations of menstrual blood, Jews, and monsters: menstrual blood, the devil, and Jews, for example, were all believed to have a distinctive smell, thus sneakily invading the Christian male through his nostrils. The motif of Jewish eye affliction, especially blindness, was paralleled by the assumption that menstrual blood is emitted out of the eyes of women and causes infections, and by the glowing eyes of many monsters. Lasciviousness was also ascribed to Jews, certain monsters, and women alike; in women, it was caused by menstrual blood.

53. Norman P. Tanner, ed., *Decrees of the Ecumenical Councils* (London: Sheed and Ward, 1990), 1:230, ll. 33–41 (canon 1).

54. Tanner, 1:239, ll. 14–16 (canon 9).

55. Tanner, 1:244, ll. 1–14 (canon 18).

56. Tanner, 1:230, ll. 13–15 (canon 1).

57. Tanner, 1:266, ll. 5–10 (canon 68).

HORROR AND THE MONSTROUS-FEMININE

An Imaginary Abjection

Barbara Creed

Mother's not herself today.
—Norman Bates, *Psycho*

I

All human societies have a conception of the monstrous-feminine, of what it is about woman that is shocking, terrifying, horrific, abject. "Probably no male human being is spared the terrifying shock of threatened castration at the sight of the female genitals," Freud wrote in his paper "Fetishism" in 1927.[1] Joseph Campbell, in his book *Primitive Mythology,* noted that

> there is a motif occurring in certain primitive mythologies, as well as in modern surrealist painting and neurotic dream, which is known to folklore as "the toothed vagina"—the vagina that castrates. And a counterpart, the other way, is the so-called "phallic mother," a motif perfectly illustrated in the long fingers and nose of the witch.[2]

Classical mythology also was populated with gendered monsters, many of which were female. The Medusa, with her "evil eye," head of writhing serpents, and lolling tongue, was queen of the pantheon of female monsters; men unfortunate enough to look at her were turned immediately to stone.

It is not by accident that Freud linked the sight of the Medusa to the equally horrifying sight of the mother's genitals, for the concept of the monstrous-feminine, as constructed within/by a patriarchal and phallocentric ideology, is related intimately to the problem of sexual difference and castration. In 1922 he argued that the "Medusa's head takes the place of a representation of the female genitals";[3] if we accept Freud's interpretation, we can see that the Perseus myth is mediated by a narrative about the *difference* of female sexuality as a difference that is grounded in monstrousness and that invokes castration anxiety in the male spectator. "The sight of the Medusa's head makes the spectator stiff with terror, turns him to stone."[4] The irony of this was not lost on Freud, who pointed out that becoming stiff also means having an erection. "Thus in the original situation it offers consolation to the spectator: he is still in possession of a penis, and the stiffening reassures him of the fact."[5] One wonders if the experience of horror—of viewing the horror film—causes similar alterations in the body of the male spectator. And what of other phrases that apply to both male and female viewers—phrases such as "It scared the shit out of me"; "It made me feel sick"; "It gave me the creeps"? What is the relationship between physical states, bodily wastes (even if metaphoric ones), and the horrific—in particular, the monstrous-feminine?

II

Julia Kristeva's *Powers of Horror*[6] provides us with a preliminary hypothesis for an analysis of these questions. Although this study is concerned with literature, it nevertheless suggests a way of situating the monstrous-feminine in the horror film in relation to the maternal figure and what Kristeva terms "abjection," that which does not "respect borders, positions, rules"—that which "disturbs identity, system, order" (4). In general terms, Kristeva is attempting to explore the different ways in which abjection, as a source of horror, works within patriarchal societies, as a means of separating the human from the nonhuman and the fully constituted subject from the partially formed subject. Ritual becomes a means by which societies both renew their initial contact with the abject element and then exclude that element.

Through ritual, the demarcation lines between human and nonhuman are drawn up anew and presumably made all the stronger for that process. One of the key figures of abjection is the mother who becomes an abject at that moment when the child rejects her for the father who represents the symbolic order. The problem with Kristeva's theory, particularly for feminists, is that she never makes clear her position on the oppression of women. Her theory moves uneasily between explanation of, and justification for, the formation of human societies based on the subordination of women.

Kristeva grounds her theory of the maternal in the abject, tracing its changing definitions from the period of the pagan or mother-goddess religions through to the time of Judaic monotheism and to its culmination in Christianity. She deals with abjection in the following forms: as a rite of defilement in paganism; as a biblical abomination, a taboo, in Judaism; and as self-defilement, an interiorization, in Christianity. Kristeva, however, does not situate abjection solely within a ritual or religious context. She argues that it is "rooted historically (in the history of religions) and subjectively (in the structuration of the subject's identity), in the cathexis of maternal function—mother, woman, reproduction" (91). Kristeva's central interest, however, lies with the structuring of subjectivity within and by the processes of abjectivity in which the subject is spoken by the abject through both religious and cultural discourses, that is, through the subject's position within the practices of the rite as well as within language:

> But the question for the analyst-semiologist is to know how far one can analyze ritual impurity. The historian of religion stops soon: the critically impure is that which is based on a natural "loathing." The anthropologist goes further: there is nothing "loathsome" in itself; the loathsome is that which disobeys classification rules peculiar to the given symbolic system. But as far as I am concerned, I keep asking questions.... Are there no subjective structurations that, within the organization of each speaking being, correspond to this or that symbolic-social system and represent, if not stages, at least types of subjectivity and society? Types that would be defined, in the last analysis, according to the subject's position in language? (92)

A full examination of this theory is outside the scope of this chapter; I propose to draw mainly on Kristeva's discussion of abjection in its construction in the human subject in relation to her notions of (1) the "border" and (2) the mother–child relationship. At crucial points, I shall also refer to her writing on the abject in relation to religious discourses. This area cannot be ignored, for what becomes apparent in reading her work is that definitions of the monstrous as constructed in the modern horror text are grounded in ancient religious and historical notions of abjection—particularly in relation to the following religious "abominations": sexual immorality and perversion; corporeal alteration, decay and death; human sacrifice; murder; the corpse; bodily wastes; the feminine body; and incest.

The place of the abject is "the place where meaning collapses" (2), the place where "I" am not. The abject threatens life; it must be "radically excluded" (2) from the place of the living subject, propelled away from the body and deposited on the other side of an imaginary border which separates the self from that which threatens the self. Kristeva quotes Bataille:

> Abjection ... is merely the inability to assume with sufficient strength the imperative act of excluding abject things (and that act establishes the foundations of collective existence). (56)

Although the subject must exclude the abject, it must, nevertheless, be tolerated, for that which threatens to destroy life also helps to define life. Further, the activity of exclusion is necessary to guarantee that the subject take up his/her proper place in relation to the symbolic:

> To each ego its object, to each superego its abject. It is not the white expanse or slack boredom of repression, not the translations and transformations of desire that wrench bodies, nights and discourse; rather it is a brutish suffering that "I" puts up with, sublime and devastated, for "I" deposits it to the father's account (verse au pere—pere-version): I endure it, for I imagine such is the desire of the other. . . . On the edge of non-existence and hallucination, of a reality that, if I acknowledge it, annihilates me. There, abject and abjection are my safeguards. The primers of my culture. (2)

The abject can be experienced in various ways—one of which relates to biological bodily functions, the other of which has been inscribed in a symbolic (religious) economy. For instance, Kristeva claims that food loathing is "perhaps the most elementary and archaic form of abjection" (2). Food, however, only becomes abject if it signifies a border "between two distinct entities or territories" (75). Kristeva describes how, for her, the skin on the top of milk, which is offered to her by her father and mother, is a "sign of their desire," a sign separating her world from their world, a sign which she does not want. "But since the food is not an 'other' for 'me,' who am only in their desire, I expel *myself,* I spit *myself* out, I abject *myself* within the same motion through which 'I' claim to establish *myself*" (3). Dietary prohibitions are, of course, central to Judaism. Kristeva argues that these are directly related to the prohibition of incest; she argues this not just because this position is supported by psychoanalytic discourse and structural anthropology but also because "the biblical text, as it proceeds, comes back, at the intensive moments of its demonstration and expansion, to that mytheme of the archaic relation to the mother" (106).

The ultimate in abjection is the corpse. The body protects itself from bodily wastes such as shit, blood, urine, and pus by ejecting these substances just as it expels food that, for whatever reason, the subject finds loathsome. The body extricates itself from them and from the place where they fall, so that it might continue to live:

> Such wastes drop so that I might live, until, from loss to loss, nothing remains in me and my entire body falls beyond the limit—cadere, cadaver. If dung signifies the other side of the border, the place where I am not and which permits me to be, the corpse, the most sickening of wastes, is a border that has encroached upon everything. It is no longer I who expel. "I" is expelled. (3–4)

Within the biblical context, the corpse is also utterly abject. It signifies one of the most basic forms of pollution—the body without a soul. As a form of waste it represents the opposite of the spiritual, the religious symbolic:

> Corpse fanciers, unconscious worshippers of a soulless body, are thus preeminent representatives of inimical religions, identified by their murderous cults. The priceless debt to great mother nature, from which the prohibitions of Yahwistic speech separates us, is concealed in such pagan cults. (109)

In relation to the horror film, it is relevant to note that several of the most popular horrific figures are "bodies without souls" (the vampire), the "living corpse" (the zombie), and corpse-eater (the ghoul). Here, the horror film constructs and confronts us with the fascinating, seductive aspect of abjection. What is also interesting is that such ancient figures of abjection as the vampire, the ghoul, the zombie, and the witch (one of whose many crimes was that she used corpses for her rites of magic) continue to provide some of the most compelling images of horror in the modern cinema. The werewolf, whose body signifies a collapse of the boundaries between human and animal, also belongs to this category.

Abjection also occurs where the individual fails to respect the law and where the individual is a hypocrite, a liar, a traitor:

> Any crime, because it draws attention to the fragility of the law, is abject, but premeditated crime, cunning murder, hypocritical revenge are even more so because they heighten the display of such fragility. He who denies morality is not abject; there can be grandeur in amorality. . . . Abjection, on the other hand, is immoral, sinister, scheming, and shady. (4)

Thus, abject things are those that highlight the "fragility of the law" and that exist on the other side of the border which separates out the living subject from that which threatens its extinction. But abjection is not something of which the subject can ever feel free—it is always there, beckoning the self to take up its place, the place where meaning collapses. The subject, constructed in/through language, through a desire for meaning, is also spoken by the abject, the place of meaninglessness—thus, the subject is constantly beset by abjection which fascinates desire but which must be repelled for fear of self-annihilation. The crucial point is that abjection is always ambiguous. Like Bataille, Kristeva emphasizes the attraction, as well as the horror, of the undifferentiated:

> We may call it a border; abjection is above all ambiguity. Because, while releasing a hold, it does not radically cut off the subject from what threatens it—on the contrary, abjection acknowledges it to be in perpetual danger. But also because abjection itself is a composite of judgement and affect, of

condemnation and yearning, of signs and drives. Abjection preserves what
existed in the archaism of pre-objectal relationship. (9–10)

To the extent that abjection works on the sociocultural arena, the horror
film would appear to be, in at least three ways, an illustration of the work of abjection. Firstly, the horror film abounds in images of abjection, foremost of which
is the corpse, whole and mutilated, followed by an array of bodily wastes such
as blood, vomit, saliva, sweat, tears, and putrifying flesh. In terms of Kristeva's
notion of the border, when we say such-and-such a horror film "made me sick" or
"scared the shit out of me,"[7] we are actually foregrounding that specific horror
film as a "work of abjection" or "abjection at work"—in both a literal and metaphoric sense. Viewing the horror film signifies a desire not only for perverse pleasure (confronting sickening, horrific images, being filled with terror/desire for the
undifferentiated) but also a desire, having taken pleasure in perversity, to throw
up, throw out, eject the abject (from the safety of the spectator's seat).

Secondly, there is, of course, a sense in which the concept of a border is central to the construction of the monstrous in the horror film; that which crosses or
threatens to cross the "border" is abject. Although the specific nature of the border changes from film to film, the function of the monstrous remains the same—
to bring about an encounter between the symbolic order and that which threatens its stability. In some horror films the monstrous is produced at the border
between human and inhuman, man and beast (*Dr. Jekyll and Mr. Hyde, Creature
from the Black Lagoon, King Kong*); in others the border is between the normal
and the supernatural, good and evil (*Carrie, The Exorcist, The Omen, Rosemary's
Baby*); or the monstrous is produced at the border that separates those who take up
their proper gender roles from those who do not (*Psycho, Dressed to Kill, Reflection
of Fear*); or the border is between normal and abnormal sexual desire (*Cruising,
The Hunger, Cat People*).

In relation to the construction of the abject within religious discourses, it is
interesting to note that various subgenres of the horror film seem to correspond
to religious categories of abjection. For instance, blood as a religious abomination
becomes a form of abjection in the "splatter" movie (*Texas Chainsaw Massacre*);
cannibalism, another religious abomination, is central to the "meat" movie (*Night
of the Living Dead, The Hills Have Eyes*); the corpse as abomination becomes the
abject of ghoul and zombie movies (*The Evil Dead, Zombie Flesheaters*); blood as
a taboo object within religion is central to the vampire film (*The Hunger*) as well
as the horror film in general (*Bloodsucking Freaks*); human sacrifice as a religious
abomination is constructed as the abject of virtually all horror films; and bodily
disfigurement as a religious abomination is also central to the slash movie, particularly those in which woman is slashed, the mark a sign of her "difference," her
impurity (*Dressed to Kill, Psycho*).

III

The third way in which the horror film illustrates the work of abjection refers to the construction of the maternal figure as abject. Kristeva argues that all individuals experience abjection at the time of their earliest attempts to break away from the mother. She sees the mother–child relation as one marked by conflict: the child struggles to break free, but the mother is reluctant to release it. Because of the "instability of the symbolic function" in relation to this most crucial area— "the prohibition placed on the maternal body (as a defense against autoeroticism and incest taboo)" (14)—Kristeva argues that the maternal body becomes a site of conflicting desires. "Here, drives hold sway and constitute a strange space that I shall name, after Plato (*Timeus*, 48–53), a *chora*, a receptacle" (14). The position of the child is rendered even more unstable because, while the mother retains a close hold over the child, it can serve to authenticate her existence—an existence which needs validation because of her problematic relation to the symbolic realm:

> It is a violent, clumsy breaking away, with the constant risk of falling back
> under the sway of a power as securing as it is stifling. The difficulty the
> mother has in acknowledging (or being acknowledged by) the symbolic realm—
> in other words, the problem she has with the phallus that her father or hus-
> band stands for—is not such as to help the future subject leave the natural
> mansion. (13)

In the child's attempts to break away, the mother becomes an abject; thus, in this context, where the child struggles to become a separate subject, abjection becomes "a *precondition of narcissism*" (13). Once again we can see abjection at work in the horror text where the child struggles to break away from the mother, representative of the archaic maternal figure, in a context in which the father is invariably absent (*Psycho, Carrie, The Birds*). In these films, the maternal figure is constructed as the monstrous-feminine. By refusing to relinquish her hold on her child, she prevents it from taking up its proper place in relation to the Symbolic. Partly consumed by the desire to remain locked in a blissful relationship with the mother and partly terrified of separation, the child finds it easy to succumb to the comforting pleasure of the dyadic relationship. Kristeva argues that a whole area of religion has assumed the function of tackling this danger:

> This is precisely where we encounter the rituals of defilement and their
> derivatives, which, based on the feeling of abjection and all converging on
> the maternal, attempt to symbolize the other threat to the subject: that of
> being swamped by the dual relationship, thereby risking the loss not of apart
> (castration) but of the totality of his living being. The function of these reli-
> gious rituals is to ward off the subject's fear of his very own identity sinking
> irretrievably into the mother. (64)

How, then, are prohibitions against contact with the mother enacted and enforced? In answering this question, Kristeva links the universal practices of rituals of defilement to the mother. She argues that within the practices of all rituals of defilement, polluting objects fall into two categories: excremental, which threatens identity from the outside, and menstrual, which threatens from within:

> Excrement and its equivalents (decay, infection, disease, corpse, etc.) stand for the danger to identity that comes from without: the ego threatened by the non-ego, society threatened by its outside, life by death. Menstrual blood, on the contrary, stands for the danger issuing from within identity (social or sexual); it threatens the relationship between the sexes within a social aggregate and, through internalization, the identity of each sex in the face of sexual difference. (71)

Both categories of polluting objects relate to the mother; the relation of menstrual blood is self-evident, the association of excremental objects with the maternal figure is brought about because of the mother's role in sphincteral training. Here, Kristeva argues that the subject's first contact with "authority" is with the maternal authority when the child learns, through interaction with the mother, about its body: the shape of the body, the clean and unclean, the proper and improper areas of the body. Kristeva refers to this process as a "primal mapping of the body," which she calls "semiotic." She distinguishes between maternal "authority" and "paternal laws":

> Maternal authority is the trustee of that mapping of the self's clean and proper body; it is distinguished from paternal laws within which, with the phallic phase and acquisition of language, the destiny of man will take shape. (72)

In her discussion of rituals of defilement in relation to the Indian caste system, Kristeva draws a distinction between the maternal authority and paternal law. She argues that the period of the "mapping of the self's clean and proper body" is characterized by the exercise of "authority without guilt," a time when there is a "fusion between mother and nature." However, the symbolic ushers in a "totally different universe of socially signifying performances where embarrassment, shame, guilt, desire etc. come into play—the order of the phallus." In the Indian context, these two worlds exist harmoniously side by side because of the working of defilement rites. Here, Kristeva is referring to the practice of public defecation in India. She quotes V. S. Naipaul, who says that no one ever mentions "in speech or in books, those squatting figures, because, quite simply, no one sees them." Kristeva argues that this split between the world of the mother (a universe without shame) and the world of the father (a universe of shame) would in other social contexts produce psychosis; in India it finds a "perfect socialization":

> This may be because the setting up of the rite of defilement takes on the function of the hyphen, the virgule, allowing the two universes of filth and prohibition to brush lightly against each other without necessarily being identified as such, as object and as law. (74)

Images of blood, vomit, pus, shit, etc., are central to our culturally/socially constructed notions of the horrific. They signify a split between two orders: the maternal authority and the law of the father. On the one hand, these images of bodily wastes threaten a subject that is already constituted, in relation to the symbolic, as "whole and proper." Consequently, they fill the subject—both the protagonist in the text and the spectator in the cinema—with disgust and loathing. On the other hand, they also point back to a time when a "fusion between mother and nature" existed—when bodily wastes, while set apart from the body, were not seen as objects of embarrassment and shame. Their presence in the horror film may invoke a response of disgust from the audience situated as it is within the symbolic but at a more archaic level the representation of bodily wastes may invoke pleasure in breaking the taboo on filth—sometimes described as a pleasure in perversity—and a pleasure in returning to that time when the mother–child relationship was marked by an untrammeled pleasure in "playing" with the body and its wastes.

The modern horror film often "plays" with its audience, saturating it with scenes of blood and gore, deliberately pointing to the fragility of the symbolic order in the domain of the body which never ceases to signal the repressed world of the mother. This is particularly evident in *The Exorcist,* where the world of the symbolic, represented by the priest-as-father, and the world of the presymbolic, represented by woman aligned with the devil, clashes head-on in scenes where the foulness of woman is signified by her putrid, filthy body covered in blood, urine, excrement, and bile. Significantly, a pubescent girl about to menstruate played the woman who is possessed—in one scene blood from her wounded genitals mingles with menstrual blood to provide one of the film's key images of horror. In *Carrie,* the film's most monstrous act occurs when the couple are drenched in pig's blood that symbolizes menstrual blood—women are referred to in the film as "pigs," women "bleed like pigs," and the pig's blood runs down Carrie's body at a moment of intense pleasure, just as her own menstrual blood runs down her legs during a similar pleasurable moment when she enjoys her body in the shower. Here, women's blood and pig's blood flow together, signifying horror, shame, and humiliation. In this film, however, the mother speaks for the symbolic, identifying with an order which has defined women's sexuality as the source of all evil and menstruation as the sign of sin. The horror film's obsession with blood, particularly the bleeding body of woman, where her body is transformed into the "gaping wound," suggests that castration anxiety is a central concern of the horror film—particularly the slasher subgenre. Woman's body is slashed and mutilated, to signify not only her own castrated state but also the possibility of castration for the male. In the guise of a "madman" he enacts on her body the one act he most fears for himself, transforming her entire body into a bleeding wound.

Kristeva's semiotic posits a preverbal dimension of language that relates to sounds and tone and to direct expression of the drives and physical contact with the maternal figure; "it is dependent upon meaning, but in a way that is not that of *linguistic* signs nor of the *symbolic* order they found" (72). With the subject's entry into the symbolic, which separates the child from the mother, the maternal figure and the authority she signifies are repressed. Kristeva argues that it is the function of defilement rites, particularly those relating to menstrual and excremental objects, to point to the "boundary" between the maternal semiotic authority and the paternal symbolic law:

> Through language and within highly hierarchical religious institutions, man hallucinates partial "objects"—witnesses to an archaic differentiation of the body on its way toward ego identity, which is also sexual identity. The defilement from which ritual protects us is neither sign nor matter. Within the rite that extracts it from repression and depraved desire, defilement is the translinguistic spoor of the most archaic boundaries of the self's clean and proper body. In that sense, if it is a jettisoned object, it is so from the mother. . . . By means of the symbolic institution of ritual, that is to say, by means of a system of ritual exclusions, the partial-object consequently becomes scription—an inscription of limits, an emphasis placed not on the (paternal) Law but on (maternal) Authority through the very signifying order. (73)

Kristeva argues that, historically, it has been the function of religion to purify the abject, but with the disintegration of these "historical forms" of religion, the work of purification now rests solely with "that catharsis par excellence called art" (17):

> In a world in which the Other has collapsed, the aesthetic task—a descent into the foundations of the symbolic construct—amounts to retracing the fragile limits of the speaking being, closest to its dawn, to the bottomless "primacy" constituted by primal repression. Through that experience, which is nevertheless managed by the Other, "subject" and "object" push each other away, confront each other, collapse, and start again—inseparable, contaminated, condemned, at the boundary of what is assimilable, thinkable: abject. (18)

This, I would argue, is also the central ideological project of the popular horror film—purification of the abject through a "descent into the foundations of the symbolic construct." In this way, the horror film brings about a confrontation with the abject (the corpse, bodily wastes, the monstrous-feminine) in order, finally, to eject the abject and redraw the boundaries between the human and nonhuman. As a form of modern defilement rite, the horror film works to separate out the symbolic order from all that threatens its stability, particularly the mother and all that her universe signifies. In Kristeva's terms, this means separating out the maternal authority from paternal law.

As mentioned earlier, the central problem with Kristeva's theory is that it can be read in a prescriptive rather than a descriptive sense. This problem is rendered more acute by the fact that, although Kristeva distinguishes between the maternal and paternal figures, when she speaks of the subject who is being constituted, she never distinguishes between the child as male or female. Obviously, the female child's experience of the semiotic chora must be different from that of the male's experience in relation to the way it is spoken to, handled, etc. For the mother is already constituted as a gendered subject living within a patriarchal order and thus aware of the differences between the "masculine" and the "feminine" in relation to questions of desire. Thus, the mother might relate to a male child with a more acute sense of pride and pleasure. It is also possible that the child, depending on its gender, might find it more or less difficult to reject the mother for the father. Kristeva does not consider any of these issues. Nor does she distinguish between the relation of the adult male and female subject to rituals of defilement—for instance, menstruation taboos, where one imagines notions of the gendered subject, would be of crucial importance. How, for instance, do women relate to rites of defilement, such as menstruation rites, that reflect so negatively on them? How do women within a specific cultural group see themselves in relation to taboos that construct their procreative functions as abject? Is it possible to intervene in the social construction of woman as abject? Or is the subject's relationship to the processes of abjectivity, as they are constructed within subjectivity and language, completely unchangeable? Is the abjection of women a precondition for the continuation of sociality? Kristeva never asks questions of this order. Consequently, her theory of abjection could be interpreted as an apology for the establishment of sociality at the cost of women's equality. If, however, we read it as descriptive, as one that is attempting to explain the origins of patriarchal culture, then it provides us with an extremely useful hypothesis for an investigation of the representation of women in the horror film.[8]

IV

The science fiction horror film *Alien* is a complex representation of the monstrous-feminine in terms of the maternal figure as perceived within a patriarchal ideology. She is there in the text's scenarios of the primal scene, of birth and death; she is there in her many guises as the treacherous mother, the oral sadistic mother, the mother as primordial abyss; and she is there in the film's images of blood, of the all-devouring vagina, the toothed vagina, the vagina as Pandora's box; and finally she is there in the chameleon figure of the alien, the monster as fetish-object of and for the mother. But it is the archaic mother, the reproductive/generative mother, who haunts the mise-en-scène of the film's first section, with its emphasis on different representations of the primal scene.

According to Freud, every child either watches its parents in the act of sexual intercourse or has fantasies about that act—fantasies that relate to the problem of origins. Freud left open the question of the cause of the fantasy but suggested that it may initially be aroused by "an observation of the sexual intercourse of animals."[9] In his study of "the Wolf Man," Freud argued that the child did not initially observe his parents in the act of sexual intercourse but that he witnessed the population of animals whose behavior he then displaced onto his parents. In situations where the child actually witnesses sexual intercourse between its parents, Freud argued that all children arrive at the same conclusion: "They adopt what may be called a *sadistic view of coition*."[10] If the child perceives the primal scene as a monstrous act—whether in reality or fantasy—it may fantasize animals or mythical creatures as taking part in the scenario. Possibly the many mythological stories in which humans copulate with animals and other creatures (Europa and Zeus, Leda and the Swan) are reworkings of the primal scene narrative. The Sphinx, with her lion's body and woman's face, is an interesting figure in this context. Freud suggested that the Riddle of the Sphinx was probably a distorted version of the great riddle that faces all children—where do babies come from? An extreme form of the primal fantasy is that of "observing parental intercourse while one is still an unborn baby in the womb."[11]

One of the major concerns of the sci-fi horror film (*Alien, The Thing, Invasion of the Body Snatchers, Altered States*) is the reworking of the primal scene in relation to the representation of other forms of copulation and procreation. *Alien* presents various representations of the primal scene. Behind each of these lurks the figure of the archaic mother, that is, the image of the mother in her generative function—the mother as the origin of all life. This archaic figure is somewhat different from the mother of the semiotic chora, posed by Kristeva, in that the latter is the pre-Oedipal mother who exists in relation to the family and the symbolic order. The concept of the parthenogenic, archaic mother adds another dimension to the maternal figure and presents us with a new way of understanding how patriarchal ideology works to deny the "difference" of woman in her cinematic representation.

The first birth scene occurs in *Alien* at the beginning, where the camera/spectator explores the inner space of the mother ship whose life-support system is a computer aptly named—"Mother." This exploratory sequence of the inner body of the "Mother" culminates with a long tracking shot down one of the corridors, which leads to a womblike chamber where the crew of seven are woken up from their protracted sleep by Mother's voice monitoring a call for help from a nearby planet. The seven astronauts emerge slowly from their sleep pods in what amounts to a rebirthing scene marked by a fresh, antiseptic atmosphere. In outer space, birth is a well-controlled, clean, painless affair. There is no blood, trauma, or terror. This scene could be interpreted as a primal fantasy in which the human subject is born fully developed—even copulation is redundant.

The second representation of the primal scene takes place when three of the crew enter the body of the unknown spaceship through a "vaginal" opening: the ship is shaped like a horseshoe, its curved sides like two long legs spread apart at the entrance. They travel along a corridor which seems to be made of a combination of inorganic and organic material—as if the inner space of this ship were alive. Compared to the atmosphere of the *Nostromo,* however, this ship is dark, dank, and mysterious. A ghostly light glimmers and the sounds of their movements echo throughout the caverns. In the first chamber, the three explorers find a huge alien life-form that appears to have been dead for a long time. Its bones are bent outward as if it exploded from the inside. One of the trio, Kane, is lowered down a shaft into the gigantic womblike chamber, in which rows of eggs are hatching. Kane approaches one of the eggs; as he touches it with his gloved hand, it opens out, revealing a mass of pulsating flesh. Suddenly, the monstrous thing inside leaps up and attaches itself to Kane's helmet, its tail penetrating Kane's mouth in order to fertilize itself inside his stomach. Despite the warnings of Ripley, Kane is taken back on board the *Nostromo,* where the alien rapidly completes its gestation processes inside Kane.

This representation of the primal scene recalls Freud's reference to an extreme primal scene fantasy where the subject imagines traveling back inside the womb to watch her/his parents having sexual intercourse, perhaps to watch her/himself being conceived. Here, three astronauts explore the gigantic, cavernous, malevolent womb of the mother. Two members of the group watch the enactment of the primal scene in which Kane is violated in an act of phallic penetration—by the father or phallic mother? Kane himself is guilty of the strongest transgression; he actually peers into the egg/womb in order to investigate its mysteries. In so doing, he becomes a "part" of the primal scene, taking up the place of the mother, the one who is penetrated, the one who bears the offspring of the union. The primal scene is represented as violent, monstrous (the union is between human and alien), and is mediated by the question of incestuous desire. All restagings of the primal scene raise the question of incest, as the beloved parent (usually the mother) is with a rival. The first birth scene, where the astronauts emerge from their sleep pods, could be viewed as a representation of incestuous desire par excellence: the father is completely absent; here, the mother is sole parent and sole life-support.

From this forbidden union, the monstrous creature is born. But man, not woman, is the "mother" and Kane dies in agony as the alien gnaws its way through his stomach. The birth of the alien from Kane's stomach plays on what Freud described as a common misunderstanding that many children have about birth, that is, that the mother is somehow impregnated through the mouth—she may eat a special food—and the baby grows in her stomach from which it is also born. Here, we have a third version of the primal scene.

A further version of the primal scene—almost a convention[12] of the science fiction film—occurs when smaller crafts or bodies are ejected from the mother ship into outer space; although sometimes the ejected body remains attached to the mother ship by a long life-line or umbilical chord. This scene is presented in two separate ways: one when Kane's body, wrapped in a white shroud, is ejected from the mother ship, and the second when the small space capsule, in which Ripley is trying to escape from the alien, is expelled from the underbelly of the mother ship. In the former, the "mother's" body has become hostile; it contains the alien whose one purpose is to kill and devour all of Mother's children. In the latter birth scene the living infant is ejected from the malevolent body of the "mother" to avoid destruction; in this scenario, the "mother's" body explodes at the moment of giving birth.

Although the "mother" as a figure does not appear in these sequences—nor indeed in the entire film—her presence forms a vast backdrop for the enactment of all the events. She is there in the images of birth, the representations of the primal scene, the womblike imagery, the long winding tunnels leading to inner chambers, the rows of hatching eggs, the body of the mother ship, the voice of the life-support system, and the birth of the alien. She is the generative mother, the prephallic mother, the being who exists prior to knowledge of the phallus.

Notes

1. Sigmund Freud, "Fetishism," in *On Sexuality* (Harmondsworth, U.K.: Penguin, 1981), 354.

2. Joseph Campbell, *The Masks of God: Primitive Mythology* (New York, Penguin, 1969), 73.

3. Sigmund Freud, "Medusa's Head," *Standard Edition* 18 (1964): 273–74.

4. Freud, 273.

5. Freud.

6. Julia Kristeva, *Powers of Horror: An Essay on Abjection* (New York: Columbia University Press, 1982). All page citations will be included in the text.

7. For a discussion of the way in which the modern horror film works upon its audience, see Philip Brophy, "Horrality—The Textuality of Contemporary Horror," *Screen* 27, no. 1 (1986): 2–13.

8. For a critique of *Powers of Horror,* see Jennifer Stone, "The Horrors of Power: A Critique of 'Kristeva,'" in *The Politics of Theory,* ed. F Barker, P Hulme, M Iversen, D Loxley (Colchester, U.K.: University of Essex, 1983), 38–48.

9. Sigmund Freud, "From the History of an Infantile Neurosis," in *Case Histories II* (Harmondsworth, U.K.: Penguin, 1981), 294.

10. Sigmund Freud, "On the Sexual Theories of Children," in *On Sexuality* (Harmondsworth, U.K.: Penguin, 1981), 198.

11. Sigmund Freud, "The Paths to the Formation of Symptoms," in *Introductory Lectures on Psychoanalysis* (Harmondsworth, U.K.: Penguin, 1981), 417.

12. Daniel Dervin argues that this structure does deserve the status of a convention. For a detailed discussion of the primal scene phantasy in various film genres, see his "Primal Conditions and Conventions: The Genres of Comedy and Science Fiction," *Film/Psychology Review,* Winter–Spring 1980, 115–47.

THE MONSTER AND THE HOMOSEXUAL

Harry Benshoff

IN THE 1970s, in a series of essays exploring the horror film, critic Robin Wood suggested that the thematic core of the genre might be reduced to three interrelated variables: normality (as defined chiefly by a heterosexual patriarchal capitalism), the Other (embodied in the figure of the monster), and the relationship between the two.[1] According to Wood's formulation, these monsters can often be understood as racial, ethnic, and/or political/ideological Others, while more frequently they are constructed primarily as sexual Others (women, bisexuals, and homosexuals). Since the demands of the classical Hollywood narrative system usually insist on a heterosexual romance within the stories they construct, the monster is traditionally figured as a force that attempts to block that romance. As such, many monster movies (and the source material they draw upon) might be understood as being "about" the eruption of some form of queer sexuality into the midst of a resolutely heterosexual milieu. By *queer*, I mean to use the word both in its everyday connotations ("questionable . . . suspicious . . . strange") and also as how it has been theorized in recent years within academia and social politics. This latter "queer" is not only what differs "in some odd way from what is usual or normal" but ultimately is what opposes the binary definitions and proscriptions of a patriarchal heterosexism. Queer can be a narrative moment, or a performance or stance which negates the oppressive binarisms of the dominant hegemony (what Wood and other critics have identified as the variable of "normality") both within culture-at-large and within texts of horror and fantasy. It is somewhat analogous to the moment of hesitation that demarcates Todorov's Fantastic, or Freud's theorization of the Uncanny: queerness disrupts narrative equilibrium and sets in motion a questioning of the status quo, and in many cases within fantastic literature, the nature of reality itself.[2]

Sociologically, the term *queer* has been used to describe an "oxymoronic community of difference,"[3] which includes people who might also self-identify as gay and/or lesbian, bisexual, transsexual, transvestite, drag queen, leather daddy, lipstick lesbian, pansy, fairy, dyke, butch, femme, feminist, asexual, and so on—any people not explicitly defining themselves in "traditional" heterosexual terms. Queer seeks to go beyond these and all such categories based on the concepts of normative heterosexuality and traditional gender roles to encompass a more inclusive, amorphous, and ambiguous contraheterosexuality (thus there are those individuals who self-identify as "straight queers"). Queer is also insistent that issues of race, gender, disability, and class be addressed within its politics, making interracial sex and sex between physically challenged people dimensions of queer sex also, and further linking the queer corpus with the figure of the Other as it has been theorized by Wood in the horror film. Queer activism itself has been seen as unruly, defiant, and angry: like the mad scientists of horror films, queer proponents do want to restructure society by calling attention to and eventually dismantling the oppressive assumptions of heterocentrist discourse. As one theorist has noted,

> the queer, unlike the rather polite categories of gay and lesbian, revels in the discourse of the loathsome, the outcast, the idiomatically proscribed position of same-sex desire. Unlike petitions for civil rights, queer revels constitute a kind of activism that attacks the dominant notion of the natural. The queer is the taboo-breaker, the monstrous, the uncanny. Like the Phantom of the Opera, the queer dwells underground, below the operatic overtones of the dominant; frightening to look at, desiring, as it plays its own organ, producing its own music.[4]

Queer even challenges "the Platonic parameters of Being—the borders of life and death."[5] Queer suggests death over life by focusing on nonprocreative sexual behaviors, making it especially suited to a genre that takes sex and death as central thematic concerns.

Earlier critical thinking on the monster movie frequently drew upon metaphysical or psychoanalytic concepts relating to the genre's twin obsessions, sex and death. Some earlier writing on the links between cinematic horror and (homo)sexuality used a Freudian model of repression as a theoretical rubric. In Margaret Tarratt's groundbreaking essay of the early 1970s, "Monsters from the Id," the

author examined Hollywood monster movies of the 1950s and persuasively postulated that the monster represented an eruption of repressed sexual desire.[6]
Thus, 1951's *The Thing (from Another World)* develops explicit parallels between
the monster in question and the libidinous nature of the film's male lead, Captain
Hendry. The monster serves as a metaphoric expression of Hendry's lusts; it is
a displaced and concretized figure of phallic desire. Even a cursory glance at the
monster movies of this era will repeatedly reveal this trope: *The Creature from the
Black Lagoon* (1954), *The Giant Gila Monster* (1959), and most of their scaly breth-
ren seem to "pop up" like clockwork whenever the hero and heroine move into a
romantic clinch. The ideas put forth by Tarratt became common and useful tools to
understanding the functioning of the genre, but what is perhaps less well known
was that her essay was initially published in the British journal *Films and Filming*,
which was produced and marketed primarily for and to a gay male readership.[7]

During the 1970s and 1980s, in a series of articles and books, Canadian film
scholar Robin Wood further developed Tarratt's ideas, expanding them generally
to all horror films, and specifically to the films of 1970s horror auteurs such as
Larry Cohen, Wes Craven, and Tobe Hooper. (Robin Wood is himself a gay man
who makes certain distinctions between his pre- and post-"coming out" work in
film criticism.)[8] Drawing on Herbert Marcuse's and Gad Horowitz's readings of
Marx and Freud (in *Eros and Civilization* and *Repression*, respectively),[9] Wood
invokes concepts of basic and surplus repression to sketch a model of life under
patriarchal capitalism. According to this model, society cannot be formed or continue to exist without a certain amount of basic repression. Surplus repression, on
the other hand, is used by those in control to keep all "Others" subjugated to the
dominant order. The Other reciprocally bolsters the image of "normality": as Simon
Watney has observed, "straight society needs us [homosexuals]. We are its necessary 'Other.' Without gays, straights are not straight."[10] According to Wood's readings of the American horror film, it is easy to see these Others cast in the role of the
monster: repressed by society, these sociopolitical and psychosexual Others are
displaced (as in a nightmare) onto monstrous signifiers, in which form they return
to wreak havoc in the cinema. While some have critiqued this model as essential-
ist, Wood did note the importance of historical parameters in understanding the
relationship between normality and monsters, asserting that "the monster is, of
course, much more protean, changing from period to period as society's basic
fears clothe themselves in fashionable or immediately accessible garments."[11]

For many, the repressive hypothesis explicit in Tarratt's and Wood's readings
of the genre was overturned by the work of the French theorist Michel Foucault,
who, in *The History of Sexuality* (1978), argued that sexuality is in fact not repressed
by society but rather explicitly constructed and regulated via a series of discourses
which include those of the medical, legal, religious, and media establishments.
While many of these discourses have the same effect on certain sectors of society

as might be argued under the repressive hypothesis (the exclusion from the public sphere, dehumanization, and monsterization of certain forms of sexuality), Foucault argues that "it is a ruse to make prohibition into the basic and constitutive element from which one would be able to write the history of what has been said concerning sex starting from the modern epoch."[12] In a by now famous turn of phrase, Foucault noted of "repression" that "there is not one but many silences."[13] (This does not mean that basic psychoanalytic concepts such as sexual repression and egodystonic homosexuality will not be discussed within the following pages. Indeed, homosexual repression—as it might exist within an individual psyche rather than within society at large—is still a potent formulation in how one might understand the homosexual and/or homophobic dynamics of many horror films.)

Like Wood, Foucault was a homosexual cultural critic who drew upon (and eventually expanded) a Marxist understanding of how society regulates human sexuality, developing a more precisely historicized formulation that examines how power and knowledge are embedded in the practice of social discourse. Shifting the debate from the repression of sex to the production of sexuality, Foucault noted that ours is now a culture wherein "the politics of the body does not require the elision of sex or its restriction solely to the reproductive function; it relies instead on a multiple channeling into the controlled circuits of the economy— on what has been called [by Marcuse] a hyper-repressive desublimation."[14] As sex and sexuality become more ever present in the public sphere, they are nonetheless regulated into certain cultural constructions through powerful social discourses. Yet, as Foucault further asserts,

> we must conceive discourse as a series of discontinuous segments whose tactical function is neither uniform nor stable. To be more precise, we must not imagine a world of discourse divided between accepted discourse and excluded discourse, or between the dominant discourse and the dominated one; but as a multiplicity of discursive elements that can come into play in various strategies.[15]

As British cultural theorists such as Stuart Hall have pointed out, the multiplicity of these discourses and their multiple sites of reception also allow for the active negotiation of these issues. Thus, when talking about a cultural product or "discursive object" such as a filmic genre system, one would be wise to take into consideration not only the historical discourses of production (where meanings are encoded) but also those of reception (where meanings are decoded according to a multiplicity of different reading positions).[16]

How actual practices of spectatorship interact with the narrative patterns of a genre system must then be considered when discussing the queer pleasures of a horror film text itself. Where does the viewer of monster movies position him-self or herself in relation to the text? The overtly heterosexualized couple of the classical horror film of the 1930s might be said to represent the most common (or intended?) site of spectatorial identification for these particular films, yet as many theorists have pointed out, it is more likely that specific shot mechanisms within the film's formal construction will link the spectator's gaze to that of the Gothic villain or monster.[17] Furthermore, there is more to the processes of spec-tatorial identification than patterns of subjective shots and cinematic suture.[18] For example, the heterosexualized couple in these films are invariably banal and underdeveloped in relation to the sadomasochistic villain(s), whose outrageous exploits are, after all, the raison d'être of the genre. To phrase it in Richard Dyer's terms, in the horror film, it is usually the heterosexualized hero and heroine who are stereotyped—painted with broad brush strokes—while the villains and mon-sters are given more complex, "novelistic" characterizations.[19] As the titular stars of their own filmic stories, perhaps it is the monsters that the audience comes to enjoy, experience, and identify with; in many films, normative heterosexuality is reduced to a trifling narrative convention, one that becomes increasingly unnec-essary and outmoded as the genre evolves across the years.

As I shall be arguing throughout this work, the cinematic monster's subjec-tive position is more readily acceded to by a queer viewer—someone who already situates himself or herself outside a patriarchal, heterosexist order and the pop-ular culture texts that it produces. . . . What does it mean if lesbians identify with the beautiful female vampires of *The Hunger* (1983), or if gay men go to see Tom Cruise bite Brad Pitt in *Interview with the Vampire* (1994)? In what ways does this happen, and what is the "price paid" in culture-at-large for yet another depiction of monstrous predatory homosexuals? Identification with the monster can mean many different things to many different people and is not necessarily always a negative thing for the individual spectators in question, even as some depictions of queer monsters undoubtedly conflate and reinforce certain sexist or homopho-bic fears within the public sphere. For spectators of all types, the experience of watching a horror film or monster movie might be understood as similar to that of the Carnival as it has been theorized by Bakhtin, wherein the conventions of normality are ritualistically overturned within a prescribed period of time in order to celebrate the lure of the deviant.[20] Halloween functions similarly, allowing otherwise "normal" people the pleasures of drag, or monstrosity, for a brief but exhilarating experience. However, while straight participants in such experiences usually return to their daylight worlds, both the monster and the homosexual are permanent residents of shadowy spaces: at worst caves, castles, and closets, and at best a marginalized and oppressed position within the cultural hegemony. Queer viewers are thus more likely than straight ones to experience the monster's plight in more personal, individualized terms.

What then exactly makes the experience of a horror film or monster movie gay, lesbian, or queer? There are at least four different ways in which homosexuality might intersect with the horror film. The first and most obvious of these occurs when a horror film includes identifiably gay and/or lesbian characters. These characters might be victims, passers-by, or the monsters themselves, although gay and lesbian people (to this point in time) have never been placed in the role of the normative hero or heroine.[21] Broadly speaking, the appearance of overtly homosexual film characters doesn't occur until the late 1960s and early 1970s, following the demise of the Production Code and its restrictions against the depiction of "sex perversion." Films such as *Blacula* (1972), *Theater of Blood* (1973), or *The Sentinel* (1977) fall into this category. In these films, gay or lesbian characters fall victim to the monster just as straight characters do, although somewhat disturbingly their fates are frequently deemed "deserved" by the films they inhabit, often solely on the basis of their characters' homosexuality. Other films such as *The Fearless Vampire Killers* (1967), *The Vampire Lovers* (1971), or *The Hunger* (1983) characterize their vampires as specifically homosexual or bisexual. These films have perhaps done much to cement into place the current social construction of homosexuals as unnatural, predatory, plague-carrying killers, even as they also might provide a pleasurable power–wish fulfillment fantasy for some queer viewers.

The second type of homo-horror film is one written, produced, and/or directed by a gay man or lesbian, even if it does not contain visibly homosexual characters. Reading these films as gay or lesbian is predicated upon (what some might call a debased) concept of the cinematic auteur, which would argue that gay or lesbian creators of film products infuse some sort of "gay sensibility" into their films either consciously or otherwise. Yet such questions of authorship, which are certainly important and hold bearing on this particular study (for example, the films of James Whale or Ed Wood), will herein be of lesser importance, since it is not necessary to be a self-identified homosexual or queer in order to produce a text that has something to say about homosexuality, heterosexuality, and the queerness that those two terms proscribe and enforce. A variation on the homo-horror auteur approach is that in which a gay or lesbian film star (whether "actually" homosexual or culturally perceived as such) brings his or her persona to a horror film. Classical Hollywood cinema is full of such performers, who, regardless of their offscreen lives, bring an unmistakable homosexual "air" to the characters they create: Eric Blore, Franklin Pangborn, Robert Walker, George Sanders, Judith Anderson, Eve Arden, Greta Garbo, and Marlene Dietrich, to name just a few. The characters created in 1930s horror films by Charles Laughton or by Vincent Price in the 1960s and early 1970s best typify this type of homo-horror film.

The third and perhaps most important way that homosexuality enters the genre is through subtextual or connotative avenues. For the better part of cinema's history, homosexuality onscreen has been more or less allusive: it lurks around the edges of texts and characters rather than announcing itself forthrightly. In films such as *White Zombie* (1932), *The Seventh Victim* (1943), or *How to Make a Monster* (1958), homosexuality becomes a subtle but undoubtedly present signifier that usually serves to characterize the villain or monster. This particular trope is not exclusive to the horror film. It has been pointed out in films noir, in action films, and in other films wherever homosexuality is used to further delineate the depravity of the villain.[22] Alexander Doty has argued against this model of connotation, suggesting that it keeps gay and lesbian concerns marginalized: "connotation has been the representational and interpretive closet of mass culture queerness for far too long. . . . [This] shadowy realm of connotation . . . allows straight culture to use queerness for pleasure and profit in mass culture without admitting to it."[23] Accordingly, in many of these films, queerness is reduced to titillation, frisson, fashion, or fad. The "love that dare not speak its name" remains a shadowy Other that conversely works to bolster the equally constructed idea of a normative heterosexuality.

But it is also precisely this type of connotation (conscious or otherwise) that allows for and fosters the multiplicity of various readings and reading positions, including what has been called active queer (or gay, or lesbian) reading practices. If we adopt Roland Barthes's model of signification wherein the denotative meaning of any signifier is simply the first of many possible meanings along a connotative chain, then we can readily acknowledge that a multitude of spectators, some queer, some not, will each understand the "denotative" events of a visual narrative in different ways. For Doty, then, there is the (fourth) sense that any film viewed by a gay or lesbian spectator might be considered queer. The queer spectator's "gay-dar," already attuned to the possible discovery of homosexuality within culture-at-large, here functions in relation to specific cultural artifacts. As such, "Queer readings aren't 'alternative' readings, wishful or willful misreadings, or 'reading too much into things' readings. They result from the recognition and articulation of the complex range of queerness that has been in popular culture texts and their audiences all along."[24] In the case of horror films and monster movies, this "complex range of queerness" circulates through and around the figure of the monster, and in his/her relation to normality.

These approaches to finding homosexuals in and around the text are hardly mutually exclusive—in fact, these factors usually work in some combination to produce a text which might easily be understood as being "about" homosexuality. James Whale's *The Old Dark House* (1932), directed by and starring homosexual men, would be one such film that combines these approaches: while it might be possible for some spectators to miss the homosexual undercurrents which fuel the plot (since no character is forthrightly identified as overtly homosexual), for other spectators these themes readily leap off the screen. Conversely, other films that have no openly homosexual input or context might still be understood as queer by virtue of the ways in which they situate and represent their monster(s) in relation to heterosexuality. Ultimately, then, this project rests upon the variable and intersubjective responses between media texts and their spectators, in this case spectators whose individualized social subjectivities have already prepared and enabled them to acknowledge "the complex range of queerness" that exists in the English-language monster movie.

A Short History of the Homosexual and the Monster

In many ways, the development of the Gothic form and the social understanding of homosexuality have followed concurrent and often commingling paths. Before the codification of the classical Hollywood horror film, and before the late nineteenth-century "invention" of the homosexual as a distinct type of person, it is apparent that Western and non-Western cultures alike had some sort of terminology for and/or knowledge of both the monstrous and same-sex love. In many cultures, such as that of ancient Greece, the two clusters of meaning had little in common; monsters were often terrible beasts encountered on perilous journeys, and (male) homosexual acts were an accepted element of the structuring patriarchy (although overtly sexualized monsters such as the incubus and succubus do date from these eras).[25] Out of necessity and prudence, this work focuses on the distinctly Western, modern/ist, nineteenth- and twentieth-century constructions of the monster and the homosexual, and their considerable overlap. The histories of these concepts are complex, but the origins of Western literary horror are usually traced to the mordant verses of the mid-eighteenth-century Graveyard Poets or the appearance of the "first" Gothic novel, The Castle of Otranto, in 1764. In that era, the term homosexuality was as yet unknown; if and when same-sex desire was acknowledged as a possible form of human sexuality, it was usually understood as a preference for a specific range of sexual behaviors and not as an entire identity. In many cultural artifacts of the time (including the early Gothic novels), contra-straight sexual behavior was often linked to members of the crumbling aristocratic class who had the means to indulge in whatever forms of pleasure they could imagine. Most significantly, when "homosexuality" (which appeared in the scientific lexicon in 1869) reached common English parlance in the 1880s and 1890s, Victorian England was in the middle of a Gothic renaissance whose legacy can still be felt in today's horror films.[26]

Still, even before this momentous cultural event, the confluence of contra-straight sexuality with the development of the Gothic, both in terms of its production and its thematic concerns, is striking. As Eve Kosofsky Sedgwick has noted, "the Gothic was the first novelistic form in England to have close, relatively visible links to male homosexuality."[27] She points to the fact that many of the writers of the first wave of Gothic novels (William Beckford, Matthew "Monk" Lewis, Horace Walpole) might be understood to have been homosexual by today's understanding of the word. A "case can be made about each that he was in some significant sense homosexual—Beckford notoriously, Lewis probably, Walpole iffily."[28] Horace Walpole, author of *The Castle of Otranto,* was certainly eccentric, if not forthrightly homosexual: his personal life exhibited tendencies that we might now view as indicative of a gay camp sensibility. One biographer describes the bachelor dandy as a "gentle, sickly, effeminate boy" who grew into a "whimsical man [who] found it difficult to avoid flights of fancy," such as spending most of his adult life constructing a mock medieval castle, a Gothic fantasy world, at his home, Strawberry Hill.[29] Whether or not Walpole was homosexual by today's understanding of the term remains unknowable; however, by virtue of his apparent gender-bending and his focus on the performative aspects of role-playing, he might more readily be called queer, a term more historically distant but perhaps more descriptively accurate.

Many of the Gothic works of this first wave (which were more or less satirized in Jane Austen's *Northanger Abbey,* written in 1797–98 but not published until 1818) focused on a young heroine and an older, sexualized male threat. Yet many also contained more obviously queer menaces, albeit in ways displaced through the Gothic signifiers of death, decay, and the double. William Beckford, who had been "hounded out of England in 1785 over charges involving a younger man,"[30] published *Vathek* in 1796, and this work can easily be read as an allegory about homosexual proclivity.[31] M. G. Lewis's *The Monk* (also published in 1796) found the form becoming increasingly explicit, and it garishly featured religiously repressed sexual hysteria and a transsexual demon. A few years later at the Villa Diodati, two of history's most enduring monsters entered the literary canon when a rather queer congress decided to write some ghost stories. The sexual eccentricities of John Polidori ("The Vampyre" [1819]), Lord Byron, Percy Bysshe Shelley, and Mary Wollstonecraft Shelley (*Frankenstein* [1818]) are well documented, and many read Polidori's sexually predatory Vampyre Lord Ruthven as a thinly disguised portrait of the bisexual libertine Lord Byron. *Frankenstein* itself has become something of a counterhegemonic classic; feminists and queers alike have plumbed its depths to underscore a scathing critique of male hubris in which the attempt to create life without the aid of procreative sexual union results in disaster for all. Though rarely filmed in any manner approaching the novel's complexity of metaphysical argument, this core idea—that of a mad, male, homosexual science giving birth to a monster—can be found to a greater or lesser degree in almost every filmic adaptation.

After several relatively dormant decades, Gothic writing flourished again during the latter half of the nineteenth century. Also at this time, homosexual "underworlds" began to be acknowledged in many European cities, and early sexologists such as Richard von Krafft-Ebing and Karl Heinrich Ulrichs began to argue that same-sex relations should be understood in terms medical rather than criminal. Ulrichs wrote essays on the natural etiology of same-sex feelings, arguing in 1862 that "Urnings" (his word for a passive, effeminate, male homosexual) were a biologically determined "Third Sex." Like the mad scientist of the Hollywood horror film, Ulrichs was interested in the effects of blood transfusion and wondered in print whether or not exchanges of bodily fluids might make an Urning into a "normal" man, and vice versa.[32] Ulrichs also perhaps unwittingly contributed to the monster–homosexual equation in 1869 when he wrote "Incubus: Urning-Love and Blood Lust" in response to a particularly violent rape and murder of a five-year-old boy.[33] While Ulrichs's aim was to explore and differentiate Urning love from murderous pederasty, the Zastrow case of 1869 (as it became known) and Ulrichs's discussion of it only helped to link same-sex relations with concepts of the monster both ages old (the Greek Incubus) as well as more modern (the sexual psychopath). For years after the trial, the common parlance of the day used the term "Zastrow" (the name of the accused murderer) in place of "Urning."[34] Also less well known is that toward the end of his career, Ulrichs wrote an explicitly homosexual vampire story entitled "Manor," which was published in 1885: true to what would become narrative convention, the story ends with its male lovers embracing, but only in death.

Like "Manor," the works of the late nineteenth century's Gothic renaissance were even more explicit than their predecessors regarding the conflation of the monstrous with some form of queer sexuality. J. Sheridan Le Fanu wrote his lesbian vampire tale "Carmilla" in 1872, and Robert Louis Stevenson published *The Strange Case of Dr. Jekyll and Mr. Hyde* in 1887. This latter tale has recently received an excellent queer exegesis from Elaine Showalter, who uses unpublished manuscripts to argue that Jekyll's repressed Mr. Hyde was meant to be read as homosexual.[35] Bram Stoker's *Dracula* (1897), which arguably created the most enduring of monsters, features an elegant and seductive count who preys not only upon the bodies of men and women, but also on the very *being* of his victims, transforming them into creatures as sexually monstrous as himself. This might be understood as mirroring the culture's invention of the homosexual: the vampire's victims not only indulge in vampiric sex but now become a new and distinct type of individual/monster themselves.[36]

Around this same time, the association of homosexual behavior with elitism, death, and decay existed dramatically in an entire movement of poets and painters who became known as the Decadents. Centering their work on abnormal loves, necrophilia, and the ever-present image of the woman's corpse, the school was simultaneously morbid and queer. As cultural historians have noted, the term *Decadence* itself became "a fin-de-siècle euphemism for homosexuality."[37] The (mostly) male Decadents celebrated themselves as pale, thin, delicate, aestheticized, and emotional creatures, turning upon one popular "scientific" construction of homosexuality at that time: that of gender inversion, "anima muliebris in corpore virili inclusa," a woman's soul trapped in a man's body. The Decadent monster queer is also invariably sad, like the tragic Gothic and Romantic heroes from whom he descends. This sad, young, slightly effeminate man can be found throughout the twentieth-century history of homosexuality and is a staple of horror films as well. In the 1950s this character was especially susceptible to the seductions of older, forthrightly "evil" men, and in the 1970s and 1980s he was often figured as an ostracized high school student and loner.

This image of the pathetic and slightly sinister homosexual dandy was perhaps cemented into place through the life and work of Oscar Wilde. Wilde was linked to the Decadents through social connections as well as through *The Yellow Book,* a literary magazine which was featured heavily in his 1895 trial for sodomy and itself became synonymous with homosexual scandal. But it is Wilde's 1891 book *The Picture of Dorian Gray* that contains the quintessential imagery of the monster queer—that of a sexually active and attractive young man who possesses some terrible secret which must perforce be locked away in a hidden closet. The common Gothic trope of the "unspeakable" was now (partially, incompletely) de-repressed; it had become, in the words of Wilde's young lover Lord Alfred Douglas, "the love that dare not speak its name."

Monsters, and especially the imagery of the vampire, continued to be linked with homosexuality during the early years of the twentieth century. *Der Eigene,* a German male homosexual magazine published between 1896 and 1931, "contained much vampire imagery in its fiction and at least one complete vampire story."[38] And Lillian Faderman has demonstrated how vampiric imagery crept into a slew of novels at this time in order to pathologize or "monsterize" women's "romantic friendships."[39] In the 1910s, when narrative cinema began to explore the monstrous, the Gothic literature of the nineteenth century was pressed into service. Edison filmed *Frankenstein* in 1910, and D. W. Griffith adapted Edgar Allan Poe's "The Tell-Tale Heart" as *The Avenging Conscience* in 1914. However, by far the most filmed horror story of the period was Oscar Wilde's *The Picture of Dorian Gray.* According to horror film historian Gregory William Mank, there were at least seven adaptations of the novel during the 1910s: "a 1910 Danish version; a 1913 US adaptation; a Russian film in 1915, as well as another American version; a British 1916 film, starring Henry Victor, with an appearance by 'the devil'; and, in 1917, versions from both Germany and Hungary (the latter possibly featuring Bela Lugosi)."[40] Whether or not these films (most of them are now lost) focused more on the novel's tropes of pictorial transformation or its thematic queerness, it is nonetheless clear that they did help to construct a very definite image of the monstrous male homosexual. For example, the poster for the 1917 German version of *The Picture of Dorian Gray* shows a figure consistent with that era's understanding of the male homosexual. Dorian Gray stands next to a vase filled with heart-shaped leaves; the figure himself wears a stylish tuxedo, patent leather slippers, bracelets, and makeup and has rounded hips, arms akimbo, with one on the pedestal and one on a hip, crossed legs, cocked head, flowered lapel, and a slightly bored, bemused expression on his face.[41]

It was the Germans who would ultimately create the distinctive "look" of the horror film by wedding its queer characters and occurrences to a visual style drawn from modernist painting, one that eventually became known as a cinematic style in its own right, German Expressionism.[42] The nightmarish subjectivity explored in the twisted and distorted mise-en-scène of these films proved to be a key visual analogue to the literature of horror and monsters, as well as to the hidden recesses of the human psyche and sexuality. Many of the German *Schauerfilme* of the era explored Gothic themes, such as the homosexual creation of life (*The Golem* [filmed in 1914 and 1920]), while others focused on homoerotic doubles and madness (*The Student of Prague* [1913], *The Picture of Dorian Gray* [1917], and perhaps most famously *The Cabinet of Dr. Caligari* [1919]). One of the leading filmic Expressionists of this era, F. W. Murnau, was homosexual; he made film versions of both *The Strange Case of Dr. Jekyll and Mr. Hyde* and *Dracula,* released in Germany as *Der Januskopf* (1920) and *Nosferatu* (1922).[43] German Expressionism and modern art in general was and still is frequently linked with homosexuality, not only through the historical sexuality of many of its practitioners but also through its subject matter and its opposition to "normality" as constructed through realist styles of representation. Nazi Germany made these links most clear in 1937 when it invited its citizens to denounce and mock modernist art at a Berlin exhibit snidely entitled *Degenerate Art*. The aim of the exhibit was to demonstrate how Aryan culture had been polluted by primitivism and the modernist style practiced (of course) by Jews, homosexuals, and other social deviants. By that time, however, many of Germany's artists had died or fled the continent. Filmmakers such as Karl Freund and Paul Leni (among many others) brought the German Expressionist style to America and specifically to the horror films of Hollywood's classical period. Once there, it helped to create some of the defining examples of cinematic horror, upon whose foundations almost all of Hollywood's later monster movies have been built.

In citing these historical "facts" I do not mean merely to suggest a rather coarse or knee-jerk auteurism (queer works are produced by queer authors) but rather to point out the confluence of contra-straight sexuality within the development of the Gothic/horror genre.

Notes

1. Many of these essays have been reworked and published in Robin Wood, *Hollywood: From Vietnam to Reagan* (New York: Columbia University Press, 1986), 79.

2. Tzvetan Todorov, *The Fantastic: A Structural Approach to a Literary Genre,* trans. Richard Howard (Ithaca, N.Y.: Cornell University Press, 1973), esp. 25–40; Sigmund Freud, "The Uncanny," *Standard Edition* 17 (1955): 219–52.

This trope of the genre has been theorized by a great many people in a variety of ways. For example, Noël Carroll has focused on rot, ooze, slime, and blood as generic motifs which suggest transition and transgression, concluding that "what horrifies is that which lies outside cultural categories"—in short, the queer. Carroll, *The Philosophy of Horror, or Paradoxes of the Heart* (New York: Routledge, 1990), 35.

3. Louise Sloan, "Beyond Dialogue," *San Francisco Bay Guardian Literary Supplement,* March 1991, quoted in Lisa Duggan, "Making It Perfectly Queer," *Socialist Review,* April 1992, 19.

4. Sue Ellen Case, "Tracking the Vampire," *differences* 3, no. 2 (1991): 3.

5. Case 3.

6. Margaret Tarratt, "Monsters from the Id," *Films and Filming* 17, no. 3 (1970): 38–42 and 17, no. 4 (1971): 40–42. Reprinted in Barry Keith Grant, ed., *Film Genre Reader* (Austin: University of Texas Press, 1986), 258–77.

7. For a brief narrative history of *Films and Filming,* see Anthony Slide, ed., *International Film, Radio, and Television Journals* (Westport, Conn.: Greenwood Press, 1985), 163–64. Slide notes the magazine's "definite homosexual slant" and also the mild controversy it caused in 1971 when some readers began to object. See also "Letters," *Films and Filming,* July 1971, 4.

8. See "Responsibilities of a Gay Film Critic," *Film Comment* 14, no. 1 (1978), Reprinted in Bill Nichols, ed., *Movies and Methods* (Los Angeles: University of California Press, 1985) 2:649–60. One might wonder as to the degree his thinking about and writing on the horror film were related to this process.

9. Herbert Marcuse, *Eros and Civilization: A Philosophical Inquiry into Freud* (Boston: Beacon Press, 1955); Gad Horowitz, *Repression: Basic and Surplus Repression in Psychoanalytic Theory: Freud, Reich, and Marcuse* (Buffalo: University of Toronto Press, 1977).

10. Simon Watney, *Policing Desire: Pornography, AIDS and the Media,* 2nd ed. (Minneapolis: University of Minnesota Press, 1987), 26.

11. Wood, *Hollywood,* 79.

12. Michel Foucault, *The History of Sexuality,* trans. Robert Hurley (New York: Vintage Books, 1978), 12.

13. Foucault, 27.

14. Foucault, 114. Compare these thoughts with those of Herbert Marcuse in "The Conquest of the Unhappy Consciousness: Repressive Desublimation," in *One-Dimensional Man: Studies in the Ideology of Advanced Industrial Society,* 56–83 (Boston: Beacon Press, 1964).

15. Foucault, *History of Sexuality,* 100.

16. For an overview of the theoretical arguments that developed within and from the Birmingham Centre for Contemporary Cultural Studies, see Graeme Turner, *British Cultural Studies: An Introduction* (Boston: Unwin Hyman, 1990). Many of the most important original essays are collected in Michael Gurevitch, Tony Bennett, James Curran, and Janet Woolacott, eds., *Culture, Society, and the Media* (New York: Methuen, 1982), and Stuart

Hall, Dorothy Hobson, Andrew Lowe, and Paul Willis, eds., *Culture, Media, Language* (London: Hutchinson, 1980).

17. Linda Williams, "When the Woman Looks," in *Re-Vision: Essays in Feminist Film Criticism,* ed. Mary Ann Doane, Patricia Mellencamp, and Linda Williams, 83–99 (Los Angeles, Calif.: University Publications of America, 1984).

18. For an exploration of some of these issues, see Nick Browne, "The Spectator-in-the-Text: The Rhetoric of *Stagecoach,*" in *Movies and Methods,* ed. Bill Nichols (Los Angeles: University of California Press, 1985), 2:458–75.

19. Richard Dyer, "The Role of Stereotypes," in *The Matter of Images: Essays on Representation,* 11–18 (New York: Routledge, 1993).

20. For a discussion of the Bakhtinian Carnival and how it relates to film (and briefly Halloween), see Robert Stam, "Film, Literature, and the Carnivalesque," in *Subversive Pleasures: Bakhtin, Cultural Criticism, and Film,* 85–121 (Baltimore: Johns Hopkins University Press, 1989). Although he doesn't specifically talk about horror films, several of the ten criteria he isolates for the cinematic expression of the Carnivalesque are highly relevant to the genre.

21. For an interesting account of how gay and lesbian actors get marginalized both within Hollywood narrative systems and industrial practice, see Patricia White, "Supporting Character: The Queer Career of Agnes Moorehead," in *Out in Culture: Gay, Lesbian, and Queer Essays on Popular Culture,* ed. Corey K. Creekmur and Alexander Doty, 91–114 (Durham, N.C.: Duke University Press, 1995).

22. See Dyer, "Homosexuality and Film Noir," in *The Matter of Images: Essays on Representations,* 62–72 (New York: Routledge, 1993).

23. Alexander Doty, *Making Things Perfectly Queer: Interpreting Mass Culture* (Minneapolis: University of Minnesota Press, 1993), xi–xii.

24. Doty, 16.

25. For a historical overview of these figures, see Nicolas Kiessling, *The Incubus in English Literature: Provenance and Progeny* (Seattle: Washington State University Press, 1977).

26. Elaine Showalter, *Sexual Anarchy: Gender and Culture at the Fin de Siècle* (New York: Penguin Books, 1990), 171.

27. Eve Kosofsky Sedgwick, *Between Men: English Literature and Male Homosocial Desire* (New York: Columbia University Press, 1985), 91.

28. Sedgwick, 92.

29. E. F. Bleiler, "Horace Walpole and *The Castle of Otranto,*" in *Three Gothic Novels: "The Castle of Otranto," "Vathek," and "The Vampyre,"* ed. E. F. Bleiler (New York: Dover, 1966), vii, x.

30. Sedgwick, *Between Men,* 92.

31. A fuller queer exegesis of *Vathek* was recently offered by Jason Tougaw in his paper "Owning Our Own Devils: Jeffrey Dahmer, *Vathek* and Gay Male Subjectivities," presented at Queer Frontiers: The Fifth Annual National Lesbian, Gay and Bisexual Graduate Student Conference, Los Angeles, Calif., 1995.

32. See Hubert Kennedy, *Ulrichs: The Life and Works of Karl Heinrich Ulrichs: Pioneer of the Modern Gay Movement* (Boston: Alyson, 1988), 77.

33. Kennedy, 136–44.

34. Kennedy, 138.

35. Showalter, *Sexual Anarchy*, 105–26.

36. For a fuller account of the novel's homoerotic aspects, see Christopher Craft, "'Kiss Me with Those Red Lips': Gender and Inversion in Bram Stoker's *Dracula*," *Representations* 8 (Fall 1984): 107–33.

37. Showalter, *Sexual Anarchy*, 171.

38. Reported in Richard Dyer, "Children of the Night: Vampirism as Homosexuality, Homosexuality as Vampirism," in *Sweet Dreams: Sexuality, Gender and Popular Fiction*, ed. Susanna Ranstone (London: Lawrence and Wishart, 1988), 48.

39. Lillian Faderman, *Surpassing the Love of Men* (New York: Marrow, 1981).

40. Gregory William Mank, *Hollywood Cauldron* (Jefferson, N.C.: Mcfarland, 1994), 298.

41. Reproduced in Phil Hardy, ed., *The Overlook Film Encyclopedia: Horror* (Woodstock, N.Y.: Overlook Press, 1986), 20. For a discussion of "arms akimbo" in relation to queer politics, both historically and today, see Thomas A. King, "Performing 'Akimbo': Queer Pride and Epistemological Prejudice," in *The Politics and Poetics of Camp*, ed. Moe Meyer, 23–50 (New York: Routledge, 1994).

42. See Lotte H. Eisner, *The Haunted Screen* (Los Angeles: University of California Press, 1969).

43. See Lotte H. Eisner, *Murnau* (Los Angeles: University of California Press, 1973).

THE UNDEAD

A Haunted Whiteness

Annalee Newitz

WHEN RACIAL DIFFERENCE cannot be talked about in a narrative—or is willfully ignored—one way it gets covertly described is as a difference between "dead" and "living" cultures, or more fantastically in the difference between dead bodies and animated ones. As anthropologist Marianna Torgovnick has pointed out, whites often distinguish themselves and their nations by laying claim to progress and the future, implicitly relegating the importance of all other racial groups to antiquity, the "savage" past, and dead civilizations.[1] This racist logic of progress holds that people of color are frozen in time, unchanged since the origins of human history. Hence, Torgovnick concludes, white anthropologists throughout the twentieth century claimed that African and Caribbean tribes should be studied for clues to the Euro-American past and that black and native bodies should be examined to explain their temporal inferiority.

In keeping with this anthropological tradition, popular tales that feature the undead often suggest a connection between certain racial identities and death. Toni Morrison's account of Edgar Allan Poe's "The Narrative of Arthur Gordon Pym" explores why this might be:

> [Because] images of impenetrable whiteness . . . appear almost always in conjunction with representations of black or Africanist people who are dead, impotent, or under complete control, these images of blinding whiteness

241

seem to function as both antidote to and meditation on the shadow that is companion to this whiteness—a dark and abiding presence that moves the hearts and texts of American literature with fear and longing. This haunting, a darkness from which our early literature seemed unable to extricate itself, suggests the complex and contradictory situation in which American writers found themselves.[2]

Morrison describes an "Africanist" presence in narrative that is "companion to" whiteness, but also "haunting" in a way that arouses both "fear and longing." These tensions—between companionship and haunting, fear and longing—are at the center of every undead tale. There is a kind of ghostly connection between whiteness and whatever racial group is cast as its opposite (Morrison places blacks in this position, but it is occupied just as often by natives, Asians, or Jews). Even the most triumphant, "impenetrable whiteness" cannot be understood without reference to a dead nonwhite body that haunts and taunts it, granting it a meaning that cannot always be controlled.

A great deal of literary and film criticism has suggested—occasionally in a persuasive way—that horror stories dealing with race always position whites as the human creatures who must battle supernaturalized minority groups.[3] But this is a dramatic oversimplification of the genre. Often whites cast themselves as the monsters in stories which suggest that their relationship to racism is, as Morrison suggests, "complex and contradictory." Stories about the undead are best understood in the context of anxieties about many kinds of race relationships that develop in the wake of colonialism. The undead are liminal beings who exist between the worlds of life and death. They represent the sorts of identities that erupt into being when different racial groups collide violently with one another and produce horrifying new cultures of deprivation and oppression.

In the first half of the twentieth century, stories about the undead are morbidly obsessed with colonialism and slavery. Pulp tales from this period, for example, associate the meeting of European and Caribbean cultures with the machinations of slimy, tentacled immortals who rise from watery tombs. Movies explore what happens when black voodoo priests gain the power to turn white women into zombies. Yet even the most simplistic and racist of these stories also reflects the moral confusion of a nation that feared, yet desired, an end to colonialism in the world and at home. Whites in these stories are haunted by knowledge of a distant past when people of color were free and powerful. And they anticipate a future where whites have become ghosts doomed to drift unsubstantially among formerly colonized people who have regained their sovereignty.

Undead narratives circulated before the 1960s and 1970s—before widespread political challenges to white supremacy—are filled with anxieties about what will happen to racial categories in the United States when colonialism dies out. Later in the century, as postcolonial writers and pundits begin to generate their own narratives about what bell hooks calls the "terrorism" of white power, the dead past that threatens to destroy our heroes is always associated with the colonial period.[4] Undead narratives of the 1980s, 1990s, and 2000s are preoccupied with the way anachronistic race relations exist alongside those of the present day, like zombies among the living.

Regardless of their historical period, undead stories share a common investment in the idea that communities murdered by colonialism can linger on, half-alive, and refuse to leave the living remainder alone. This half-alive fragment of a destroyed people is often associated with the mixed-race descendants of colonizer and colonized. Because miscegenation under colonialism is usually the result of rape or coercion, mixed-race coupling is generally regarded by these narratives as another form of violence and as a prelude to or outcome of racial extinction. Racial hybridity is a form of living death, and the desire for racial others is always tinged with fear and guilt.

I begin my exploration of the undead with the early twentieth-century colonial allegories of H. P. Lovecraft's Cthulhu tales and D. W. Griffith's story of "ghosts" in *The Birth of a Nation,* and I end with a series of post-1960s movies such as *Blacula, Tales from the Hood,* and *Bones.* I'll also chart the rise of a new breed of films, including *Blade* and *Underworld,* devoted to revaluing monstrosity as a kind of antiracist project. What is perhaps unsurprising is that in a group of narratives constructed around death and colonialism, whites are often the subjects and objects of haunting. Gradually emerging in this subgenre is a meditation on whether it is possible for any racial group—whether colonizer or colonized—to survive a racist history unscathed. Slavery and genocide may be part of the past, but they wreak havoc in the present. Zombies, vampires, and mummies bear in their half-alive bodies the signs of great social injustice whose effects cannot ever be entirely extinguished.

America's Weird Tale

Most accounts of the cinematic undead take Bram Stoker's novel *Dracula* to be the origin of modern stories about the walking dead. But to understand the particulars of the United States' obsession with racial identity and death, one must begin with tales of the undead in a pulp magazine whose star writer and sometime editor, H. P. Lovecraft, was steeped in American history. Founded in 1923, the pulp fiction magazine *Weird Tales* featured, in the words of its manifesto, "stories . . . taboo in the publishing world."[5] The manifesto goes on to explain that the weird tale is "the story of psychic phenomena or the occult story . . . [and] stories of advancement in the sciences and the arts to which the generation of the writer who creates them has not attained. All writers of such stories are prophets, and in the years to come, many of these prophesies will come true."[6] *Weird Tales* stories, especially those by H. P. Lovecraft and his disciples, took an ancient genre—stories of the dead returning—and modernized it to speak to twentieth-century preoccupations. Combining "occult" figures with science fiction–style "prophesies" about the future, weird fiction involves "crude physical horror"[7] and toys with the connections between eroticism, death, and racial identity. A common anecdote about the magazine is that it sold on the basis of its lurid covers, many of which featured semi-clad female demons and "savages," or women swooning in the arms of vampires and devils.[8] These images, with the stories they illustrated, were partly what made the weird tale "taboo." Especially in the hands of an author like Lovecraft, the weird tale evoked a pulp fiction–style dark side to American life which was explicitly linked to racial and sexual danger.[9] In Lovecraft's work, these dangers took on the aspect of "prophetic" writing in their attention to what he feared might be the future consequences of rampant fraternization between whites and other races.

Because race relations in the United States are deeply connected to class relations,[10] Lovecraft's work inevitably also captures the uneasiness of a nation witnessing the death throes of economic systems associated with imperialism and slavery. Often, the immortal and undead monsters in his stories are explicitly connected to the economic fate of an individual or community.

Lovecraft began writing for *Weird Tales* almost directly after it was founded and quickly became what S. T. Joshi terms a "fixture" of the publication.[11] Unlike most *Weird Tales* authors (with the possible exception of Robert Bloch), Lovecraft's writing has remained popular and in print throughout most of the twentieth century, experiencing a marked renaissance in the decades since the 1960s.[12] What George Wetzel calls Lovecraft's "Cthulhu Mythos"[13] is so influential that it has turned up in countless novels and movies, inspiring the work of authors from Stephen King to J. G. Ballard. Fans have even turned his stories into a series of role-playing games (Call of Cthulhu and Mythos) where one takes on the identity of a character battling monstrous forces from the pages of Lovecraft's short stories and novels.[14] Such an ongoing absorption with Lovecraft's writing in the United States is testimony to its continued relevance in the allegedly more enlightened eras of melting pots and multiculturalism.

Although not all of Lovecraft's stories and novels are about race relations and the undead, his typical Cthulhu Mythos formula involves both. In famous stories such as "The Call of Cthulhu," "The Dunwich Horror," "The Shadow over Innsmouth," "At the Mountains of Madness," and "The Horror at Red Hook," and in the novel *The Strange Case of Charles Dexter Ward*, the Cthulhu Mythos tells the secret history of planet Earth and introduces us to races of alien beings who populated it millions of years before human life existed.[15] Knowledge of this history, and of the aliens' influence over human affairs, is so horrifying that it drives humans utterly insane. "At the Mountains of Madness" provides us with an over-view of Lovecraft's prehuman history: a highly civilized race of Old Ones (who look like huge squash with starfish heads) arrives from the stars, populates the Earth, and later does battle with squid-like, seagoing "spawn of Cthulhu" and the "half-fungus, half-crustacean" Mi-Go. Long after all this is over, several explorers from Miskatonic University discover a lost city of the Old Ones in the mountains of the Antarctic. Art and writing on the walls of this city reveal the descent of a civilized culture into a "decadent" one, largely as a result of interspecies wars and a massive uprising among the Shuggoths, giant polymorphous beings who were used by the Old Ones as slave labor.[16]

Most of Lovecraft's Mythos stories focus on the lingering horrors of Shug-goths and Cthulhu's spawn, two alien races that have survived in a kind of suspended animation, occasionally managing to form ties with certain human communities and cults that have the power to awaken them. "The Dunwich Horror" and *The Strange Case of Charles Dexter Ward* feature Shuggoths con-jured through black magic, for instance, while "The Shadow over Innsmouth" and "The Call of Cthulhu" deal with the resurrection of Cthulhu and his spawn, who are busily mating with humans and ruling over cults which are "infinitely more diabolic than even the blackest of the African Voodoo circles."[17] Lovecraft's "diabolic" and hybridized alien races turn up in port towns, New York City, and nearly anywhere else in the United States that is associated with racial minorities and immigrant communities. The exalted Old Ones are totally extinct and appear mostly in references to the past or the dreams of white men.

Lovecraft writes in his autobiography, "I am an ultra-conservative socially, artistically and politically."[18] Of course we may say, in retrospect, that this con-servatism is obvious from his depictions of race relations. But Lovecraft's idea of conservatism is bound up in his fixation on "dead" historical periods, periods that haunt his stories both literally and figuratively. These periods, notably ancient Rome and the eighteenth century, are associated with vanished modes of produc-tion that depended on slave labor. You might say he's nostalgic for eras when one could easily tell the difference between masters and slaves. One of Lovecraft's basic projects is a kind of supernatural historical revisionism where he retells U.S. history as a weird tale, starting with occultists in colonial New England, moving through immortal Caribbean half-monsters spawned in the post–Civil War era, and ending in contemporary New York City, which is crawling with Cthulhu-worshiping illegal immigrants. What emerges is a portrait of how colonial rela-tionships transformed (often hideously) the Europeans who settled in America during his "favorite modern period . . . the eighteenth century."[19]

The Case of Charles Dexter Ward manages to capture white anxieties about what happens to white identity in a culture that cannot quite extricate itself from its colonial origins.[20] Charles Dexter Ward, a young antiquarian living in

Providence, Rhode Island, during the 1910s and 1920s, discovers that he is the descendant of Joseph Curwen, a powerful and wealthy man whose life story has been all but eradicated from local histories and landmarks. We begin the story knowing that Ward, by poring over Curwen's secret papers, has learned enough occult magic to resurrect the spirit of his dead ancestor in his own body.

But this shocking revelation is hardly the worst of it, as Ward's degeneration is simply a frame story for the more grotesque tale of Curwen's life as an eighteenth-century shipping magnate and summoner of the dead. Having educated himself in the sacred books of a non-Western culture, especially the "forbidden *Necronomicon* of the mad Arab Abdul Alhazred" (18), Curwen learns a way to reanimate the spirits of the dead using their powdered bones. Curwen has "a virtual monopoly of the town's trade in saltpetre, black pepper, and cinnamon," yet he is also known for "a freakish importation which could not conceivably have been destined for anyone else in the town" (30). This "freakish importation" is Curwen's other stock-in-trade: bones, mummies, chemicals, and "Guinea blacks . . . for whom he could produce [no] bona fide bills of sale" (21). Purchasing a farmhouse in Pawtuxet, a town outside Providence, Curwen brings startling numbers of slaves, cows, and books there to use in his "experiments," all of which he conducts in a vast underground network of caves.

Curwen has also discovered a way to become virtually immortal. His continued youth, along with his outsider status and escalating economic power, finally arouse the suspicion of several townspeople, especially Ezra Weeden. When Weeden discovers the extent of Curwen's "unholy" rituals, he leads a party—something like a lynch mob—out to the Pawtuxet farmhouse to destroy it and seal off the rooms below. Centuries later, Ward's friend Dr. Willett finds Weeden's journals in Ward's papers. Along with these are letters to Ward from Curwen's old friends, who are mysteriously still alive. Put together, these documents reveal the true horror at the heart of *The Case of Charles Dexter Ward*:

> There was, [Willett and Ward's father] conceded, a terrible movement alive in
> the world[;] . . . they were robbing the tombs of all the ages, including those of
> the wisest and greatest men. . . . A hideous traffic was going on among these
> nightmare ghouls, whereby illustrious bones were bartered with the calm
> calculativeness of schoolboys swapping books. (94)

Unlike most colonial traders of the period, Curwen isn't robbing the tombs of Africans or Indians for trinkets, nor is his "barter" in people restricted solely to these colonized groups. In fact, he and his friends are stealing the bones of Europeans, in particular the "greatest" of them, and causing the spirits of these dead men to be reawakened under their power. Using their bones, Curwen is able to keep spirits "prisoner" (28) and steal their knowledge. The "hideous traffic" in bones among Curwen and his colleagues is ultimately a form of white slavery:

white men are bought and sold, and used to serve their occult masters. The fear that white Europeans are just as easily enslaved as people from Africa, Asia, and pre-Columbian America is what haunts Lovecraft's story about the revolutionary period in U.S. history.

Curwen, whose house in the twentieth century is "now the abode of a Negro family much esteemed for occasional washing, house-cleaning and furnace-tending services" (49), is associated everywhere in the story with blacks, Jews, Indians, and of course the writings of "the mad Arab Abdul Alhazred."[21] So, one might plausibly argue that he is a stand-in for members of racial groups who had been oppressed—or disdained—by whites in the United States. But I would argue that Curwen is perhaps all the more frightening precisely because he is a white man who has chosen to use his own race for profit just as he uses his "Guinea blacks." He is the white man who refuses to respect the superiority of whiteness and is therefore chipping away at white sovereignty from the inside, revealing that whites are really no better or worse than racial "others." All races, for Curwen, are equal in their slavery to him after death.

"Dead Cthulhu Waits Dreaming"

The idea that whites can be destroyed by colonialism grows more elaborate in "The Shadow over Innsmouth" (1931), a story about the degeneration of a Massachusetts port town after the Civil War sends the local economy into a tailspin. Narrated by an unnamed young male antiquarian (much like Ward), the story begins with his travels through the Massachusetts countryside, where he happens upon the virtual ghost town of Innsmouth. People in neighboring towns have been warning him that Innsmouth is a very bad place to visit, but that the "way folks feel [about Innsmouth] is simply race prejudice."[22] What sort of race prejudice this might be is hinted at when a ticket seller tells the narrator about

> what a lot our New England ships used to have to do with queer ports in
> Africa, Asia, the South Seas, and everywhere else, and what kinds of people
> they sometimes brought back with 'em. . . . [Innsmouth people have] gotten to
> be about as bad as South Sea cannibals and Guinea savages. . . . I guess they're
> what they call "white trash" down South—lawless and sly, and full of secret
> things. (119–21)

Although currently filled with "white trash" in the fishing business, Innsmouth's economy was once based on shipping. After the War of 1812 and the Civil War ruined trade between those "queer ports" and the United States, Innsmouth was decimated financially, and even its best families "degenerated."

Once in Innsmouth, the narrator discovers that its inhabitants "did not look Asiatic, Polynesian, Levantine or negroid," but have "coarse-pored greyish cheeks," and "bulging, watery blue eyes … a flat nose, a receding forehead and chin, and singularly undeveloped ears" (126). Their religious culture is obviously non-European, too: their congregation is part of the wacky-sounding "Esoteric Order of the Dagon." Finally, the markedly white and aged town drunk, Zadok Allen, explains to the narrator what has happened to Innsmouth. In the 1830s, he says, the wealthy Captain Obed Marsh despaired of ever extricating the town from poverty. Then he journeyed to a South Sea island where the natives had fantastic luck with fishing. Their luck, apparently, came from having devoted themselves to the worship of what Zadok calls "some kind o' god-things that lived under the sea" (143). In desperation, Captain Obed decided to attempt the same kind of worship in Innsmouth. As any discerning Lovecraft reader would have expected, the "god-things" found in the South Seas turn out to be the Spawn of Cthulhu, and they demand human sacrifices in exchange for jewels and plentiful fishing.

But after 1846, things begin to change. As the country moves toward the Civil War, the "god-things" start demanding a higher price for their services: they want to mate with the humans, and in return they promise to grant their hybrid children eternal life under the sea. Tellingly, it's only after the Civil War that these mixed children are born and grow up, as if they represent the mixed-race "spawn" of a nation which has outlawed slavery and begun to acknowledge the humanity of blacks and colonized peoples. As Bennett Lovett-Graff argues, fears about the genetic disasters created through miscegenation had reached a fever pitch when Lovecraft published "The Shadow over Innsmouth." He notes that the story is heavily informed by popular notions about eugenics and Darwinism of the period, and that "[immigrants'] rate of reproduction … stands as the central threat to the purity of America's racial stock."[23]

But there is something in Innsmouth more menacing than the threat of black and immigrant breeds: whites who want to breed with them, and who flourish in the process. For it is strictly through the consent—indeed, the supplication—of whites that the Spawn of Cthulhu are brought from the South Seas to the shores of Massachusetts. While Lovecraft is careful to have his characters discuss the "revulsion" involved in mating with "fish-frogs," we are also given to understand that the children created are only ugly by human standards and that they enjoy rich, beautiful, eternal lives once they return to their "great palaces" beneath the ocean.

Our narrator discovers that he, too, is one of these hybrids and ultimately decides to join his kin beneath the sea. Like Curwen, he refuses to preserve the sanctity of whiteness and white privilege. Instead, he embraces a racial heritage—and an "eternal" racial future—which is flagrantly hybrid. It is also a future without death. This kind of white person, who dreams of escaping white America to live among "others," is what Lovecraft implies is the true outcome of the Civil War. It is an outcome both terrifying and hopeful—the future belongs to semi-dead monsters, but once viewed from the monsters' point of view, this isn't really so bad.

Commentators on Lovecraft's fiction often use the author's own life to explain his curious blending of fantasy and contemporary social preoccupations such as eugenics and immigration. Nowhere do the details of Lovecraft's life seem more relevant than in "The Horror at Red Hook," which can be read as a weird autobiography about Lovecraft's brief marriage to Sonia Greene, a Jewish merchant with whom he lived for a few years in New York.[24] Red Hook, the setting for his story, was close by one of the neighborhoods where Lovecraft and his wife lived at that time. Beyond his personal interest in a story of contemporary urban miscegenation, Lovecraft has a social interest in "The Horror at Red Hook": as an avowed "chalk-white" racist,[25] Lovecraft wants to demonstrate a connection between illegal immigration in the 1920s and supernatural evil. During his New York stint, Lovecraft wrote in his diary that Red Hook "is a maze of hybrid squalor."[26]

In "The Horror at Red Hook," he describes the region as "a hopeless tangle and enigma; Syrian, Spanish, Italian, and negro elements impinging upon one another. . . . It is a babel of sound and filth."[27] The story hinges on the discovery of a secret cadre of occultists, led by the wealthy Dutchman Robert Suydam, who are importing illegal immigrants into New York through a series of underground tunnels beneath the city. Police Inspector Malone, who is attempting to find out more about Suydam's whereabouts, accidentally happens upon an occult ceremony involving these illegals and several female demons. He witnesses a bizarre marriage ritual involving the recently dead body of Suydam and the undead demon Lilith, described as an "abominable naked phosphorescent thing" (88).

What is striking about this otherwise generic and critically maligned tale are Lovecraft's comments on the ancient historical tradition that informs Suydam's relationship to the immigrants and their religion.[28] On the street in New York, Malone observes, "They must be . . . the heirs of some shocking and primordial tradition. . . . There had survived among peasants and furtive folk a frightful and clandestine system of assemblies and orgies descended from dark religions antedating the Aryan world" (75). Later, Suydam explains to police that he needs to keep company with various minority groups because he is "engaged in the investigation of certain details of European tradition which required the closest contact with foreign groups and their songs and folk dances" (77). Here, Lovecraft suggests a direct connection between "European tradition" and "dark religions antedating the Aryan world." Not only is there a prehuman world, as we know from "At the Mountains of Madness," but there is a human world before whiteness, out of which whiteness has been born—and to which it is still profoundly attached. The dangerous and seductive heritage of a culture "antedating the Aryan world" is at the root of Lovecraft's weird fiction and permeates the twentieth- and early twenty-first-century genre of undead horror. Knowledge of such a culture is a reminder that there was once a thriving human culture without contemporary notions of racial distinction. As Lovecraft writes in his monograph *Supernatural Horror in Literature,*

> much of the power of Western horror-lore was undoubtedly due to the hidden but often suspected presence of a hideous cult of nocturnal worshipers whose strange customs—descended from pre-Aryan and pre-agricultural times when a squat race of Mongoloids roved over Europe with their flocks and herds— were rooted in the most revolting fertility-rites of immemorial antiquity.[29]

What is "hideous" here is not so much the fact that all people were once part of "a squat race of Mongoloids" but rather that there are still people whose "strange customs" recollect and celebrate that time. In short, Lovecraft's weird fiction is about the way this racial (or, interracial) heritage refuses to die. A "pre-Aryan" past is essentially a preracial past. Ultimately Lovecraft fears that this past might live again, become "reanimated," if the races mix to the point where distinguishing between them becomes impossible. This is certainly one motor driving the horror in *Case* and "Innsmouth."

Yet as Lovecraft's own marriage to a Jewish immigrant attests, the longing for sexual and social union with racial "others" can overwhelm even the most racist of individuals. It is that longing which Lovecraft chronicles in his infamous story "The Call of Cthulhu." Often hailed as his greatest work in the Mythos, this story is about the way human beings are constantly threatened with, and fascinated by, gaining access to a pre-Aryan and prehuman, past. The great god Cthulhu, awakened by accident during an earthquake, sends dreams out to people all over the world, filling their minds with images of alien cities, nonhuman architecture, and strange hybrid beings. Many of them experience an overwhelming flood of emotions, and hear the words, *"Ph'nglui mglw'nafh Cthulhu R'lyeh wgah'nagl fhtagn,"* which is translated to mean "In his house at R'lyeh dead Cthulhu waits dreaming."[30] Cthulhu is both "dead" and "dreaming," an undead alien who "waits" for a future when his spawn will walk the earth again. After we learn of several people who have sighted Cthulhu far out at sea and gone mad after attempting to sink him, the narrator speculates, "[Cthulhu] must have been trapped by the sinking . . . or else the world would by now be screaming with fright and frenzy. Who knows the end? What has risen may sink, and what has sunk may rise" (158). A pre-Aryan culture may yet rise again—especially if powerful whites like Curwen and Suydam keep fraternizing with Africans, Asians, and Middle Easterners. The language and icons of a preracial culture already exist in the unconscious minds of "Aryan" and "Mongolian" races alike. Indeed, as we know from "The Shadow over Innsmouth," for many people Cthulhu's existence is already an intimate reality.

In these ideas we find the terror, and the sexy "weirdness," that form the fantasy bedrock of undead stories that follow it. For Lovecraft, U.S. history—and the world's future—are about hybridization from beginning to end. The undead, in his stories, stand in for a kind of timeless, inextinguishable connectedness between whites and people of color, or "humans" and "aliens." Cthulhu's power, and the lure of his spawn, are a force that threatens white sovereignty not from the outside but from within: he is in the dreams of white men; he lurks at the heart of their cultural traditions; and his blood runs in what are supposed to be racially "pure" families. The monsters who haunt Lovecraft's weird tales are "undead" because they represent minority traditions that continue to live on in the United States, despite white domination. And their immortality is a prophesy of a world where new social relationships lead us into a post-Aryan future.

A Pair of Racial Ghost Stories

Two movies, one released slightly before Lovecraft began publishing and one released just a few years after his death, offer telling examples of the way Hollywood adopted many tropes of weird fiction to explain race war and U.S. colonialism. While *I Walked with a Zombie* falls within an identifiably "weird" genre, *The Birth of a Nation* is the kind of mainstream popular culture whose "realism" and "historical accuracy" managed to suggest—and perhaps inspire—the supernatural, pulp racism that *Weird Tales* made famous just seven years later. In spite of their distance from each other generically and historically, both movies are about how whites join the ranks of the undead while attempting to maintain their control over blacks. What is instructive about viewing them side by side is the chance to see how consistently the "racial undead" theme surfaces in what would appear to be quite different stories. In addition, *I Walked with a Zombie* gives us the opportunity to find out what happens to the theme after two decades of social transformations in the idea of "race."

The Birth of a Nation is famous both for its place in the history of early U.S. cinema and for being, in the words of Donald Bogle, "the most slanderous anti-Negro movie ever released."[31] Yet, like the weird tales of Lovecraft, this "anti-Negro" narrative turns out to be, in large part, about the degradation and interior horror of whiteness. Even a contemporary review of the film in the *New Republic* holds that *Birth* "degrades the censors that passed it and the white race that endures it."[32] Set during the Civil War period, *Birth* chronicles the personal and political repercussions of the fall of the Old South, following the tribulations of the Northern Stoneman family and the Southern Cameron family. At the center of the story is the "birth" of the Ku Klux Klan and its Aryan South.

The KKK's historical formation follows in the tradition of U.S. Revolutionary War militias and "vigilance committees" of various sorts. In *Birth*, it also follows the narrative tradition of "hunting parties" that band together in novels like *Dracula* and many subsequent movies to fight the undead. It is therefore no surprise that the movie itself acknowledges a connection between militias and the undead.

Ben Cameron, the "Little Colonel" whose love of the white South drives him to despair after Griffith's rabid, slovenly blacks have taken over, has the "inspiration" to form the KKK after watching two little white children play at being ghosts. Trying to scare some black children, they hide under a white sheet like a menacing spirit. The black children flee, screaming. Ben's eyes widen, and the intertitle proclaims, "The inspiration." Ben's militia will dress as the black South's worst nightmare. The result, however, at least metaphorically, is to convert the Aryan nation into a band of gun-toting, vengeful ghosts out to get the people who "killed" them.[33] Rather than placing blacks in the implicitly repulsive position of living death, *Birth* puts whites there. Not only is this an interesting reversal of the *Dracula* narrative—where living whites hunt down a bestial, undead Eastern European immigrant—but it also opens up a way for us to read the film as being about the death, rather than the birth, of whiteness.

Michael Rogin argues that *Birth* is haunted by a scene of castration which never appeared in the finished film: that of the mulatto Gus, who attempts to rape Ben's "pet sister" Flora. One witness claims that he saw an original print of the movie where members of the KKK graphically castrate Gus after the attempted rape, and we see a close-up of "his mouth flowing blood and his eyes rolling in agony."[34] Allegedly this castration scene was later edited out, although Linda Williams points out rightly that the evidence for its original existence is somewhat tenuous.[35] Regardless of whether an actual scene was edited out, or simply never represented (except obliquely), I think Rogin is correct to consider *Birth* as partly about Griffith's desire to assert the potency of fatherhood in patriarchal figures like Ben. He persuasively concludes that a nation of such fathers can be "born" in part when black men are castrated. "The nation was born in Gus's castration, from the wound that signified the white man's power to stop the black seed," he writes.[36] Yet a counterreading is also possible: Gus's castration never made it into the final cut, and the film as a whole was banned in several states as a result of vigorous NAACP protests. Moreover, every strong white man in the film chooses to represent himself as a ghost. Perhaps white patriarchy is established far more shakily than Rogin's analysis acknowledges.

I have written elsewhere about the connection between white supremacy and a fear of castration.[37] I argue that white supremacy can be understood as an unattainable ideal against which actually existing white people are measured and found lacking. Like the phallic power of men, it is constantly being contested, broken down, and sometimes utterly toppled by oppressed groups. Just as there can be no phallus without castration, there can be no white supremacy without white debasement. The peculiar uniforms of the KKK are almost a literal rendering of this principle: although they are symbolic of white supremacy, they are also symbols of white death. Ultimately, the Aryan South is populated by whites whose identities are half-dead.

Williams compares Griffith's KKK "ghost inspiration" scene to its historical antecedent (and inspiration) in *Uncle Tom's Cabin*. In the novel, cruel plantation owner Simon Legree never discovers that escaped slaves Cassy and Emmeline are hiding in his garret because the two women dress in white sheets and scare him away. Afraid that he's being haunted by the ghost of a slave he murdered, Legree never ventures into their secret sanctuary. "Haunting in Stowe's novel is the ingenious means by which Cassy saves Emmeline from rape by Legree while also avenging Legree's murder of Tom," Williams writes.[38] It is also a reminder that *Birth* is itself haunted by a previous melodrama of race relations, *Uncle Tom's Cabin,* which dramatizes the injustices of a white supremacist system.

While Williams reads the ghostly role reversal in *Birth* as creating a "newly configured spectre of white male rule" before which blacks "cower, cringe and disappear," I think it's equally plausible to view this change as a tacit admission that white power is not all it's cracked up to be. After all, Cassy and Emmeline's white-sheeted stunts are hardly the acts of empowered people: it is a desperate measure, performed by women whose lives are in danger, in a last-ditch effort to preserve their safety. To claim that Griffith's image of the KKK donning white sheets echoes this scene in *Uncle Tom's Cabin* is to admit that it is a depiction of "white male rule" in tremendous peril. Like Cassy and Emmeline, the Southern men of *Birth* are perched precariously on the edge of destruction and must pretend to be dead in order to protect themselves.

While this kind of against-the-grain reading reveals unconscious anxieties about white power, there can be no doubt that Griffith intended to portray blacks and mulattoes as the true monsters of his film. Ed Guerrero notes that it was the first film to introduce the stereotype "of the black as a brute and a vicious rapist."[39] Rather than being lazy, passive, or asexual "Uncle Toms," the black man in *Birth* is capable of politically organized brutality and is in direct sexual competition with white men for white women. We see several scenes of black armies terrorizing white Southerners, and follow the career of Silas Lynch, a mulatto politician in Washington who lusts after Elsie Stoneman, the white daughter of his liberal patron. In essence, we are watching the "black buck" stereotype transferred to celluloid for the first time, and it is interesting to note that cinematic images of powerful black men reemerge in the early 1970s with blaxploitation films featuring violent, seductive, black action heroes. I'll address the convergence of blaxploitation and weird fiction later; for now I would simply note that *Birth* was the first film to offer images of a sexually and socially potent black male that were later reclaimed and recuperated by blacks themselves. These erstwhile bucks later became the "badass motherfuckers" who challenge white authority and win.

Birth's most immoral and potent black male character, Silas Lynch, is a mulatto, and Griffith himself wrote after the movie's release that he knew the film was offensive to "prointermarriage" organizations like the NAACP and its leaders.[40] The mulatto is a figure who comes closest to embodying the forces that create an army of white male ghosts. For the mulatto, like Lovecraft's pre-Aryan civilization, hints at a racial identity that does not fall neatly into the binary white–not white, or superior–inferior. While we are supposed to associate Silas with blackness in *Birth*, he is also unforgettably marked as white: played by a white actor, promoted by a white politician, living among the white political elite, he is a reminder that after the Civil War, whiteness will never be the same. The KKK is an army of the undead because it is a militia dedicated to the preservation of a racial order that has already died. White supremacy has been challenged by blacks and whites alike. Whites may win a battle at the end of *Birth*, but they cannot ever win back their lives as uncontested masters of the South. Indeed, as I noted earlier, the absence of certain scenes in *Birth* underscores the degree to which contemporary audiences were aware that its racial politics were, or should be, archaic. Rarely does a history or treatment of this film neglect to mention the NAACP boycotts and protests of it. The film that epitomizes white triumph over black potency was itself censored—and this bit of narrative castration, however insignificant, remains material evidence of a challenge to white supremacy.

If we consider white supremacy to be what Antonio Gramsci would call "hegemonic," then Jacques Tourneur's *I Walked with a Zombie* is a movie about the way non-Western belief systems begin to challenge the hegemony of the white ruling class. Set during the early 1940s on a sugar plantation in the West Indies, *Zombie* offers us a fable of Gramsci's "crisis of hegemony," in which the plantation-owning Holland family suddenly finds that its "cultural, moral and ideological" leadership over the black population is no longer tenable.[41] Not only are the black servants and plantation workers disrespectful of the Hollands' authority, but we discover they have also converted the Holland matriarch to a belief in voodoo. With this movie, and many that come after it, we begin to see a kind of white ghost who is no longer powerful and vengeful, like those populating the KKK, but simply pathetic and lost. Challenges from the subordinate black population and internal instabilities within the Holland family result in the spectacular demise of white power and Western rationalism on the island of St. Sebastian. Using voodoo, and more importantly their knowledge of the Hollands' secret "shame and sorrow," the colonized population in *Zombie* finally declares itself supreme.

Betsy Connell arrives on St. Sebastian to nurse the ailing wife of Paul Holland, who lives in a state of gothic bitterness with his half-brother Wesley Rand and their mother, Mrs. Rand. As Betsy travels to their plantation, her black driver explains that the Hollands are one of St. Sebastian's oldest families, who "[brought] colored folks to the island," along with "Ti Misere," a figurehead of St. Sebastian from a slave ship that he describes as "one of the mothers of us all, chained to the bottom of the boat." Our introduction to the Rands is this story, told from the perspective of a man whose ancestors they enslaved. Later that night, she meets Paul's spectral wife, Jessica, wandering vacantly in a tower where we hear hidden women weeping. Paul explains to the startled Betsy that one of the servants has given birth. The women weep because for hundreds of years they lived in misery as slaves, and even today birth still seems a tragedy. In this tale, even whites openly admit that a heritage of black slavery bestows misery, implicitly blaming himself.

The next morning Betsy learns that Jessica may be a zombie, in part because Mrs. Rand, also a doctor, has become deeply involved in voodoo. Overhearing a local musician singing a ballad about the Hollands, Betsy learns that Paul's half-brother Wesley and Jessica fell in love, enraging Paul and leading to "shame and sorrow for the family." Knowing this, Betsy is more eager than ever to get to the bottom of Jessica's problem and please the brokenhearted Paul. Urged on by her maid Alma, Betsy seeks a cure for Jessica at a voodoo ritual, only to discover that the voodoo god "Danballa" is being channeled through Mrs. Rand. The matriarch eventually confesses that when she was possessed by Danballa, she wished to keep Jessica from fleeing the island and hurting Paul. Subsequently, Jessica was taken with fever and became a zombie.

Mrs. Rand is a kind of spiritual mulatto; she's a white woman who has taken on the belief system of the local black culture. And, one might argue, her miscegenated identity has led to the ruin of a white woman, Jessica—just as Silas Lynch nearly "ruins" Elsie. Yet the adulterous lust in *Zombie* comes from within the white family: Paul's half-brother Wesley desires Jessica, and therefore the sexual threat against white women is in fact from white men. Moreover, social power here comes from being literally possessed by blackness, the way Mrs. Rand is when she channels Danballa. Indeed, she admits that she originally began doing voodoo because she couldn't control the plantation workers after her husband died. Joining their voodoo rituals gave her the status she needed to diagnose illnesses and—presumably—to order blacks around. But now she is the puppet of a voodoo god, and her daughter-in-law is "living and dead," trapped between thwarted white desire and overwhelming black faith.

As the film draws to a close, we cut back and forth between a voodoo ritual and Jessica's incessant wandering—we discover that the ritual leaders have a voodoo doll of Jessica and are pantomiming drawing her toward them with a rope. To prevent her from leaving the plantation grounds once more, Wesley pulls one of the arrows from "Ti Misere" and kills her with it. At that moment, we see a pin enter the body of the white voodoo doll. Finally Wesley carries Jessica's body out to sea and drowns himself. This spectacular murder–suicide takes place entirely under the watchful eyes of a black zombie.

Michael Omi and Howard Winant have proposed that race relations involve constantly shifting categories, informed by a vast array of social forces, meanings, and events. They call this shifting set of forces "racial formation" to underscore the way race is most properly understood as the "sociohistorical process by which racial categories are created, inhabited, transformed, and destroyed." Importantly, a theory of racial formation holds that "race is a matter of both social structure and cultural representation."[42] Race, in other words, is an unstable category of identity associated with culture and with material life; hence, for example, race in *Zombie* is bound up in materialist economic relations between landholders and servants, but it is also depicted in the cultural clash between Western medicine and voodoo mysticism. What *Zombie* tracks are the profound, even violent, changes in the racial formations of whiteness and blackness as they move into a postcolonial era.[43] What we are left with is a portrait of crisis-ridden colonial relations on St. Sebastian: the masters are being destroyed by the slaves' tools.

Franz Fanon has explained that the social upheavals involved in decolonization do not generally lead to a cultural exchange or cross-racial communication, which is what we might be tempted to call Mrs. Rand's conversion to voodooism. Fanon writes,

> The natives' challenge to the colonial world is not a rational confrontation of points of view. . . . The violence with which the supremacy of white values is affirmed and the aggressiveness which has permeated the victory of these values over the ways of life and of thought of the native mean that, in revenge, the native laughs in mockery when Western values are mentioned in front of him. . . . In the period of decolonization, the colonized masses mock at these very values, insult them, and vomit them up.[44]

In this light, we can understand Mrs. Rand's "possession" by the culture of blackness on St. Sebastian to be a kind of violent revenge upon her family, which is so much a part of the island's colonial history. The voodoo worshipers are able to "insult" and "vomit . . . up" the economic and social misery visited on them by the Holland family: through their machinations, Wesley and Jessica die, and it appears that Betsy and Paul will leave the island to return to North America.

The former slaves' struggle to move St. Sebastian toward postcolonialism is also accompanied by wild fluctuations in the social and narrative meanings of whiteness and blackness. Where once Ti Misere was a sign of black sorrow, now it is a sign of white sorrow; where once Mrs. Rand and her Western medicine oversaw the plantation, now a black voodooist uses his magic to induce a crazed white man to murder his zombie lover and flee the shores of a West Indian land his family once colonized.

The kinds of changes in whiteness that are registered openly in *Zombie* are only hinted at in *Birth*. White power may be threatened in *Birth,* but the white citizens of the South are able to round up enough men to defeat the black military with ease. There is no defeating the colonized people in *Zombie,* however. Whites are driven from St. Sebastian with the same kind of violence they used to colonize it. White women in *Zombie* are vaguely incestuous, miscegenated sluts, whereas white women in *Birth* hurl themselves from precipices rather than have sex with a black man. Whiteness in *Zombie* is openly criticized; it's a social category nearly all the black characters legitimately contest. *Zombie*'s characterization of blacks as "savages," however, shares ideological terrain with *Birth.* Racist images and ideas did not disappear between the 1910s and 1940s, after all. The difference is that *Zombie* captures the anxieties of a Western imperialist force in retreat from morally justified, yet still menacing, colonized peoples. *Birth* merely registers the earliest intimations of such an anxiety.

Over Colonialism's Dead Body

Undead militias return full force in weird cinema after the 1960s. The single white zombie of *Zombie* is expanded a hundredfold in George Romero's *Night of the Living Dead,* while the idea of a vengeful colonized population is foregrounded quite explicitly in blaxploitation movies like *Blacula, Tales from the Hood,* and *Bones.* Other weird films—such as *The People under the Stairs* and *Nightbreed*—are contemporaneous with *Tales from the Hood* and reflect two profoundly different ways that the contemporary United States is still haunted by the colonial past. In all of these postcolonial era films, "undeath" is implicitly associated with colonial-era social and economic relationships, where one racial group engages in state-sanctioned subordination of others. Although all of these films are antiracist parables, they nevertheless rely heavily on narrative forms and figures first deployed in *Birth* and Lovecraft's weird fiction. Even as these stories embrace the power of formerly subordinated groups, such power is represented as monstrous; and even as the supremacy of whiteness seems about to rot away, it inexorably returns, sometimes with the power to pull the living from their present-day lives back into colonial hell.

Amy Kaplan's introductory essay in *Cultures of United States Imperialism* explains that U.S. culture, while overtly imperialistic, is rarely viewed in the context of colonial relationships. She notes that "imperialism" tends to get relegated to the international sphere; as a result, U.S. domestic culture appears somehow free of the kinds of issues that shape nations which were or are occupied by a colonizing force. Yet, she concludes, social relations within the United States are deeply bound up with struggles taking place beyond its borders. "Not only about foreign policy or international relations, imperialism is about consolidating domestic cultures and negotiating intranational relations," she writes.[45] National boundaries are far more porous than many people might like to imagine. While critics and politicians may attempt to locate imperialism elsewhere, the United States is nevertheless haunted by the kinds of violence and uneven power relations most often equated with colonial societies.

White people are the closest thing the United States has to a colonizing group. There are many disempowered whites, or what Roxanne Dunbar has called "colonial dregs,"[46] but whites have historically occupied the highest positions in the government and economy.[47] As pop theorist Jim Goad puts it, "there's a primitive, biblical, sins-o'-the-father notion that *all* American whites, by virtue of their birth alone, bear a stain on their souls for black slavery."[48] That "stain" is certainly what seems to have saturated the flesh of the rotting, cannibalistic, undead whites in George Romero's *Night of the Living Dead*. It is also what animates the KKK-esque militia that bands together to eradicate them.

Night is in many ways an updated version of *Birth,* except this time around the upwardly mobile black man is the film's hero, rather than its locus of evil and terror. Ben, the level-headed black protagonist of *Night,* is clearly marked as both middle class and a leader. Sporting a tidy haircut, loafers, and a cardigan, Ben immediately begins to delegate jobs to the other people hiding from the zombies with him in an abandoned house. Like Silas Lynch, Ben is a black man with power in a white-dominated society; he is also, like Silas, ultimately destroyed for it. But Ben's death, *Night* persuades us, is a result of white presumption, not righteousness. The befuddled, easily deceived whites who surround Silas in *Birth* reappear in *Night* as the proverbial selfish and hysterical victims of the late twentieth century slasher flick. As mysteriously reanimated dead bodies shamble toward the house where Ben and his white companions are holed up, we discover that *Night*'s zombies are all white folks, and their only interest is in eating the bodies of living people. Anyone killed by the living dead is shortly reanimated themselves, often in gory, dripping-bite-mark fashion.

Ben outmaneuvers the zombies at nearly every turn. His competence is contrasted sharply with that of Harry, a middle-aged white husband and father figure, who explodes in a rage when Ben insists that they not hide in a basement room with no escape routes. When Harry continues to complain and threaten Ben's leadership, Ben shoots him and throws him into the basement with his zombie daughter and soon-to-be-zombie wife. While Ben's actions are disturbing, they are at this point in the film clearly those of a soldier fighting for his life; Harry must be sacrificed for the survival of the group. There is heroism in Ben's violence. He fights to live, whereas Harry fights directionlessly, like a zombie.[49] As Richard Dyer explains, "in a number of places, the film shows that living whites are like, or can be mistaken for, the dead."[50] One might even go so far as to argue that whites like Harry are *asking* to be dead, since their survival instincts are so attenuated.

Meanwhile, a local militia is being organized by Sheriff McClelland, who tells a TV reporter that citizens dealing with the zombies should "beat 'em or burn 'em." Like the KKK in *Birth,* the militia in *Night* comprise ordinary white citizens who use privately owned firearms to protect their land and, implicitly, their country. As they fan out across the region, shooting and burning zombies, we begin to see the militia and zombies as caricatures of each other. The militia is full of cartoonish, mean rednecks, while the zombies act like stereotypes of drunken, shambling hillbillies with torn clothes and cannibalistic ways.[51] They are all preying on one another, seeming to take a kind of sport or pleasure in the activity of murder, and both groups move in what Gregory Waller calls "mass attack" formation.[52] This is the kind of self-defeating, dying whiteness that the KKK militia in *Birth* is supposed to fend off. Squabbling among themselves, these whites are so incompetent that they can only bumble into an act of white supremacy—killing Ben—that is more farcical than tragic.

Ben is shot when dawn breaks. McClelland's militia sees him from a distance in the house. Believing him to be a zombie, they shoot and kill him instantly. Audiences watching *Night* are strongly encouraged to understand Ben's death as horrifyingly ironic; the film's one heroic, intelligent character has been slaughtered by stupid white guys with guns. Ben's nobility, his classiness if you will, is actually heightened by the irony of his death. His identity—educated, middle class, alive—stands out in graphic relief against the hoards of undead, low-class white people. Where Silas Lynch's class position among whites marked him as little more than an "uppity nigger," Ben's class position makes him a better person. His death ultimately serves as a condemnation of brutal, mindless white society.

Yet Ben's racial identity is not entirely what's at stake here: he's a good guy because he behaves in an educated, authoritative, middle-class fashion. Ben's murder is staged intentionally to remind us of racist police attacks, and therefore it is easy to forget that he is the only black man killed during the entire film. Both the redneck militia and the hillbilly zombies are hell-bent on shooting and eating white folks. With *Night,* we find that class is changing the way audiences are invited to sympathize with the lot of the colonized. Whites are being criticized for their racism here, but also for a kind of general "low-class" ignorance. To put it differently: Ben is not just a black hero, he's a *middle-class* black hero. His racial heroism seems dependent upon class.

Blacula, a blaxploitation film released four years after *Night,* features another black hero whose class position determines how we evaluate whether he is superior to whites he meets in the United States. "Blacula," who prefers to go by his African name Mumawaldee, is an African prince who was turned into a vampire in 1780 while visiting Count Dracula. After Mumawaldee tells Dracula he wants to abolish slavery, Dracula shoots back that he thinks slavery is a good system, and proceeds to bite, curse, and imprison Mumawaldee. Stripped of his autonomy and nobility, Mumawaldee is chained in a coffin for almost two hundred years before being transported to New York by a gay couple from "the Village" who buy Dracula's mansion in the 1970s. They exclaim with swishy excitement that Dracula knickknacks are the "crème de la crème of camp" and vow to sell what they think is an empty coffin "back home." When they open the coffin, Mumawaldee jumps out and kills them instantly. These easily destroyed gay men—one white, one black—represent what the film understands as a form of "low" masculinity. Their strange entrance and exit from the film also tips us off to *Blacula*'s ensconcement in the weird genre: here we find racial anxieties, miscegenation, "deviant" sexuality, and the occult brought together in a morality tale that is finally about black manhood and class mobility.

Like Ben, the noble Mumawaldee dies—but his death is far from ironic. It is necessary for the sake of black social power. For unlike *Night, Blacula* offers a type of alternative black identity that is allowed to survive and flourish. Dr. Gordon Thomas, Mumawaldee's foil and pursuer, represents this kind of blackness. Like many heroes in blaxploitation films, such as *Shaft* (1971), Gordon has a professional job (as a New York police investigator) and is confidently, swaggeringly masculine.

Mumawaldee's presence is a threat not just to Gordon's life but also to his class position. Confronted with the ridiculousness of "an APB on a dead man," Gordon's colleague tells him to "forget [mass] hysteria" and worry about "mass unemployment starting with me." The Blacula case may cost Gordon his job and reputation as a good cop. Mumawaldee signals the potential return of colonial-style disenfranchised blackness, and tellingly, his character brings into focus the degree to which black heroism is linked to black economic power. He also demonstrates that a black man stripped of his rank is monstrous. Mumawaldee's undead body represents a fantastical form of slavery and reminds us of an imperial whiteness (Dracula) that is so powerful it can convert princes into monsters.

Thinking in these terms, it suddenly becomes clear why police officers blame Mumawaldee's first kills on "Panther activity," and why Gordon finds a den of largely black vampires led by what he calls "that faggot" who brought Mumawaldee back to New York in the first place. His crimes are being blamed on marginal blacks—ghetto militants and "faggots"—who are either socially or economically subordinated. Mumawaldee is feeding on, and appearing to emulate, a black "culture of poverty" characterized by violent crime and desperation. Gordon's desire to eliminate Mumawaldee is bound up with a desire to free blacks from the horror of marginality and from the kinds of people who perpetuate a ghetto status quo. Finally, it is as if Mumawaldee knows that Gordon and his community will be dragged backward with him into colonial conditions if he lives. Committing suicide, he frees both a woman he's seduced and the black community from his spell. Yet in spite of its triumphant finale, *Blacula* also acknowledges that many blacks continue to live in a state of powerlessness so extreme that they are no better than famished vampires, cursed by colonial-era whites to live forever in a state of perpetual need.

With movies like *Blacula,* we find the emergence of a theme that reappears in weird movies about minority cultures after the early 1970s, too: class divisions are refiguring racial identity in the postcolonial United States. Solidly middle-class, heroic, minority characters like Gordon are threatened by others who remain in an undeath of social and economic subjugation. Like the colonial economy itself, these subjugated minorities continue to live in spite of the fact that imperialism is officially dead.

There are two narrative tactics that emerge in response to what I'm calling the undeath of colonialism in U.S. culture. One, represented by Clive Barker's *Nightbreed,* invites audiences to sympathize with a group of racialized monsters who are being hunted by bigoted, Christian Right types. The other, which we find in Wes Craven's *The People under the Stairs,* tries to draw an explicit connection between class and racism on what amounts to a modern-day plantation in the ghetto. Both stories are grappling with the horror of colonial relations, yet they do not question the idea that colonized people are somehow inherently defective, monstrous, or socially crippled. The oppressed remain monstrous, but monsters are celebrated as being more sympathetic than the people who hunt them.

Rather than offering a socially palatable alternative to racial monstrosity in the figure of a Ben or a Gordon, *Nightbreed* instead traces the conversion of straight, white male Boone into an undead member of the tribal Nightbreed. Visually, the Nightbreed are unmistakably monsters: sporting tentacles, skinless faces, extra body parts, and markings that resemble aboriginal tattoos, they are almost a parody of "savage native" stereotypes. Living under a cemetery called Midian, the Nightbreed have haunted Boone's dreams for years because, as we discover later, he is a part of their destiny. Boone is "Cabal," the hero who will bring the Nightbreed out of their hiding place and help them evade their persecutors. As I noted earlier, these persecutors take the form of rural, Christian moralists who declare the Nightbreed "unnatural" and "unholy." Ultimately, they band together and form a truck-driving militia who attack Midian with dynamite and guns. Before this final confrontation, however, the audience follows Boone as he learns about the Nightbreed and their heritage as an ancient "tribe of the moon," oppressed and scapegoated by humans (which the Nightbreed call "naturals") throughout history.

Boone is also a victim of the "naturals." His demented psychiatrist is a serial killer who frames Boone for his own crimes and shoots him to cover up his guilt. Returning from the dead as a full member of the Nightbreed, Boone struggles to reevaluate these seemingly ugly, horrifying people and reconcile their culture with his own identity. Finally, he realizes that he and the Nightbreed share more than their undeath. They are both hunted by narrow-minded, sadistic humans who want to keep their species "pure" by killing anyone who seems different. When the townspeople come to destroy Midian, Boone helps leads the Nightbreed away from their burning cemetery to safety, bringing his human lover Lori along. We are led to understand that Boone's relationships with the Nightbreed and with Lori are a new beginning for the Nightbreed, a moment of reconciliation between their (un)lives and those of the "naturals." This ending amounts to a kinder, gentler form of ethnic separatism, which strongly echoes Lovecraft's "The Shadow over Innsmouth." But where Lovecraft's spawn of Cthulhu remain disturbing and unimaginable, Barker's Nightbreed are humanized and sympathetic. The Nightbreed are integrated further into human culture through Boone and Lori, whereas the narrator of "Innsmouth" plans to flee humankind for his family's underwater palace.

In spite of *Nightbreed*'s more minority-friendly tone, it remains heavily contained by the tropes of weird fiction, in which racial difference is tantamount to species difference. Here, as in Lovecraft, we find that social hierarchies proceed from nature. Because the Nightbreed are biologically "other," they are naturally victimized by humans. *Nightbreed* does not question the idea of racial monstrosity, but instead celebrates it as darkly beautiful and misunderstood. Even a much earlier film like *Zombie* offers audiences the possibility that what the whites considered "monstrous" about the blacks was actually a result of prejudice and imperial condescension. In *Nightbreed*, stereotypes of the colonized as unnatural, primitive, and helpless remain alive and well, permeating the film's representation of its undead minority.

The People under the Stairs presents us with monsters who are obviously socially constructed. Here the point of view is also firmly planted at the margins, and we view the "people under the stairs"—a band of cannibalistic, mutilated white boys—from the perspective of Fool, a black teenager who dreams of becoming a doctor and escaping from the ghetto. When Fool needs money to help his sick mother, his friend Leroy talks him into robbing their landlords, who own the local liquor store and, as Leroy puts it, "half the other houses in the ghetto." It turns out that their landlords are an incestuous, crazed brother and sister who live in a heavily fortified funeral home filled with their "sons"—white boys whom they have kidnapped, tortured, and locked in the basement. These boys look and act like zombies, feeding on the bodies of people "Daddy" has killed. Fool is trapped inside the house after "Daddy and Mommy" murder Leroy and then lock all the doors and windows. Having befriended Alice, their abused "daughter," and Roach, one of the boys who has escaped from the basement into the walls of the house, Fool manages to find the landlords' hidden cache of money, kill them, and set Alice and her brothers free.

Night of the Living Dead pitted a middle-class black man against low-class white zombies, but *People* suggests a possible alliance between these groups based on class. Alice and her brothers, who live in decayed parts of the house, exist in a kind of internal ghetto. They are white, but they are owned and held captive by

Daddy and Mommy, who threaten them with death if they do not obey. Alice and Roach instinctively help Fool, sensing that their relationships to Mommy and Daddy are basically the same as his. Rather than portraying its oppressed groups as monsters the way *Nightbreed* does, *People* casts the entire colonial system as populated by the undead: ghetto landlords (plantation owners) live in a funeral home, disenfranchised whites (sharecroppers) are zombified in their basement, and blacks (slaves) are trying to escape certain death. White power is quite literally a funeral home filled with money. When Fool blows the house up, a group of ghetto residents are protesting outside. Money released during the blast flies into the air and rains down on their heads. The wealth of the dead is redistributed among the living, and as we watch people of color gathering up armloads of money, we also see the white zombies running away penniless. Whites, in what critics have dubbed a ridiculously happy ending, are freed from their oppressive progenitors, and people of color are freed from poverty. Socioeconomic conditions make and unmake the monster, *People* seems to argue, whereas *Nightbreed* begs for conditions under which biological monsters are people too. Either way, somebody or something is always the monster; and colonialism lives on in its diabolical body.

In *Love and Theft: Blackface Minstrelsy and the American Working Class,* Eric Lott argues that colonial-era pop culture like minstrel shows dealt with changes in "the economics of race."[53] Lott's point is relevant here too. We are long past the era when slavery made a tradition out of minstrelsy, but bodies of all different colors become exchange values via the free market. This historical change in the economics of race means that class consciousness opens up the possibility for cross-racial alliances in the postcolonial era. It also generates mortal combat between members of the same racial group. Within the contemporary weird fiction tradition, this means that whites and people of color both attempt to reanimate imperialism's dead body. Formerly colonized racial groups begin to take on the characteristics of their former imperialist counterparts for economic and cultural gain.

"Welcome to Hell, Motherfuckers!"

Nowhere is this more obvious than in Rusty Cundieff's 1995 movie *Tales from the Hood.* A series of four short stories, Cundieff's film self-consciously parodies campy, weird horror movies like *Zombie* made in the 1930s and 1940s. Stealing tropes and images from an emphatically white-dominated period in weird fiction, Cundieff presents a morality tale about black male identity turned against itself in the postcolonial era. In a frame story, gangbangers Stack, Ball, and Bulldog plot to steal a stash of drugs from Mr. Simms, the owner of a local funeral parlor. Simms, maddened and menacing, greets them at the door and promises to give them "the shit" if they'll listen to some stories about how four of his corpses came to be that way. We hear about a black police officer pursued and killed by the ghost of a black man he allowed to be beaten to death by his white partners. Another dead black man has been literally crumpled into a ball by his abused stepson, who has miraculously developed psychic powers to defeat the monster beating him and his mother. A racist white senator with ties to the KKK is murdered by black voodoo dolls animated by the spirits of slaves who lived in the plantation house he now occupies. And finally, a black gangster who murders other black men is experimented on—and killed—by a mad scientist who tells him he's no better than a white supremacist who wants to destroy the black community. When this last tale ends, the black teenagers discover that *they* are the murdered gangsters of the final tale. Simms is, in fact, the devil. As flames leap up around them, Simms sprouts a forked tongue and screams, "Welcome to hell, motherfuckers!"

What is particularly interesting about Cundieff's *Tales* is that the movie unveils a form of guilt about racism that does not originate from white people. *Tales* is about black men whose desire for social and economic status forces them to recognize that they, too, might oppress blacks out of sheer, selfish greed. These men treat their black cohorts the way colonial whites once did: they abuse and murder them. As a result, they also experience a weird version of white guilt. After destroying their offspring and murdering their brothers, they cannot claim innocence in a postcolonial economic system that maintains ghettos and "undeveloped" nations for profit. Black men in *Tales* are pursued by angry black ghosts for the same reason the white racist politician is: for oppressing the black community. They're sent to hell by a black Satan for acting just like Simon Legree. Their desire for power rather than community, and death rather than cooperation, makes them shadow versions of white slave owners. More to the point, it makes them tools of a colonizing class. And that is a form of racial allegiance which, at least in Cundieff's version of the weird tale, makes them "motherfuckers" in search of "shit" on the road to "hell."

Another film that touches on many of the same themes as *Tales* is *Bones,* a classic story of revenge from beyond the grave. Jimmy Bones, played with wry dignity by rapper Snoop Dog, is a 1970s-era gangster with a heart of gold who is sold out to the cops by black friends who want to get out of the ghetto. Shot by corrupt police officers after he refuses to sell crack for them, Bones becomes an angry ghost who haunts the decaying mansion which was once the center of a thriving community and now looms over a ghetto wasteland. In the present day, a group of mixed-race young people decide to convert Bones's old pad into a dance club, and that's when the real haunting begins.

It turns out that two of the mansion's new owners, Patrick and Tia, are children of Jeremiah, one of the men who helped kill Bones. Jeremiah is now married to a white woman and living in suburbia. When he sees that his children have bought Bones's old house, he is filled with rage—he doesn't want them in the ghetto after he worked so hard to escape from it. When Patrick and Tia protest that they should be doing something about the conditions in the ghetto, he responds in a way that marks him as the narrative's guilty black man on the road to hell: "That place has already died and gone to hell," he says of the ghetto. But we know that the ghetto's spirit has been reanimated in Bones. And he's damn pissed.

Unlike *Tales, Bones* offers a sense of hope. Although Jeremiah is sucked into hell with Jimmy Bones, Patrick has started to date Cyn, Bones's daughter. Unlike his father, Patrick has a sense of responsibility toward the ghetto—he doesn't want to abandon it the way Jeremiah did. His relationship with Bones's old house and his daughter are indicative of a transformation in the relationships between blacks who want social power and those who have yet to achieve it. While the movie ends with a hokey last-minute scene where Cyn is possessed by her father's ghost, everything we've seen up to that point suggests that Patrick and Cyn's relationship represents a future where blacks will no longer be haunted by colonial history because they're forming alliances with each other across class lines.

Racists and Hybrids of the Future

Of course, old-school, white supremacist weird tales continue to find their way into pop culture. A perfect example is the wildly popular film *The Mummy,* a campy adventure flick where early twentieth-century white adventurers do battle with an ancient Middle Eastern mummy returned from the grave. Just in case you hadn't already picked up on how the depiction of monstrosity in such a film might fit nicely into current American international politics, the undead Arab of the film's title is also trying to take over the world. And he's fixated on making it with a white girl. It's a kind of cross between *Raiders of the Lost Ark* and *Birth of a Nation,* although I doubt the latter was brought up in pitch meetings.

What saves *The Mummy* from being a mere rehash of Lovecraftian racist fantasy is its wacky irony. Like *Tales from the Hood, The Mummy* steals its hamhanded style from early twentieth-century movies with a wink. Every character is a caricature. But unlike *Tales, The Mummy* doesn't offer us any twists on the old colonialist plot lines. Evil undead Arabs and simpering Egyptian servants are our enemies, and our hero is a muscular white guy who vanquishes what remains of an ancient culture—and of course, he keeps the white woman safe from Middle Eastern hands.

Before completely trashing *The Mummy* for its cartoony colonialist agenda, however, it's crucial to remember that the social and cinematic context of this film is hardly one of unquestioned white supremacy. Filmmakers of color can retaliate for something like *The Mummy* with movies of their own. Indeed, the Hughes

Brothers—filmmakers whose first effort, *Menace II Society,* was a stark and brutal reimagining of the blaxsploitation film—provide just such a corrective in their movie *From Hell.* This supernaturally inflected retelling of an old true crime tale, that of the serial killer known as Jack the Ripper, explores the way white aristo-crats terrorize nineteenth-century London.[54] Fred Abberline, a psychic, opium-addicted detective hired to find the Ripper, discovers that the killer is Sir William Gull, a possibly immortal demon who also serves as Queen Victoria's personal physician. *From Hell* could be described as the first-ever whitesploitation movie. Created by blacks, it's all about violent, drug-addicted, whoring white people and the criminal lives they lead. It's like a version of *Foxy Brown,* except this time around blacks are behind the camera and white culture is being mined and objec-tified for sensationalistic, entertaining excesses.

Representations of mixed-race people and miscegenation in the undead tale are also changing in the postcolonial period. As journalist Gregory Dicum has pointed out, a whole generation of mixed-race people—"originat[ing] in the cul-tural and sexual thaw of the 1960s"—has come of age in the United States. "Mixed parentage opens up all sorts of questions, particularly since many of our parents grew up in countries or colonies that no longer exist," he writes.[55] We see these questions answered after a fashion in *Blade* and *Blade II,* stories about a man known as the Daywalker, a half-breed vampire created when his mother was bitten by a vamp while she was still pregnant with him. Blade was born with vampire super-powers and a human's ability to survive in daylight. Sworn to avenge his mother's death, Blade stalks vamps from an ancient tribe of immortals who secretly rule human affairs Illuminati-style.

Both *Blade* and its far-superior sequel *Blade II* deal explicitly with what it means to have mixed blood and to be heir to what Dicum calls "colonies that no longer exist." In *Blade,* our hero tries to loosen the stranglehold that the "vampire council" has over humanity. Many of the council's members seem to be holdovers from the brutal period of colonial expansion in the ancient world; all they want to do is consolidate their wealth and occasionally feast on their human "cattle." Blade must mediate between his colonial-era ancestors and the humans whose blood also runs in his veins. Indeed, the entire plot winds up turning on the pre-ciousness of Blade's blood, which turns out to be the missing ingredient for a potion that will make one of the vampire council members into a god. The question seems to be who will control the Daywalker's blood. Blade must wrest control of his mixed blood from his supernatural ancestors—not without several sailing-through-the air fight scenes—in order to be at peace in the contemporary world.

Blade II finds Blade forging an alliance with the vampire council to bring down a rogue vamp who is genetically engineering super-vampires known as Reapers who eat vampires as well as humans. In a fiendish melding of the mad doctor subgenre with the undead, director Guillermo del Toro explores the difference between good mixed-blood creatures (the honorable Blade) and bad ones (the semi-cannibalistic Reapers). The difference between Blade and the Reapers is significant. Blade attempts to reconcile the different parts of his mixed heritage, although he is often bitter about it. But the Reapers go way beyond bitter: they were created to destroy their ancestors and rule the planet. They don't view themselves as a bridge between one culture and another, or between the past and the present. Reapers may be hybrid creatures, but they anticipate a future of rigid distinctions between masters and slaves, eater and eaten.

The blood of a hybrid is a precious commodity in another recent undead film, *Underworld*. An ancient, *Blade*-like family of vampires has been doing battle with an equally ancient tribe of werewolves for more than a thousand years. Selene, a vampire assassin who hunts werewolves (called Lycans), discovers that her family's ancient werewolf enemy Lucien has figured out a way to create a person who can become both werewolf and vampire. But to finish this mad experiment in miscegenation, Lucien must get blood from Michael, a dumb, hunky medical student whose extra-special hemoglobin comes to him from a medieval ancestor. As Selene races to stop Lucien's diabolical plot—and shares some improbable kisses with Michael in the process—she discovers that the feud between werewolves and vampires is not what she thought.

In a rather compelling plot twist, Lucien reveals to Michael that the werewolves were once the vampires' slaves. They guarded their masters during the day, and in return were treated with ruthless cruelty. During the Middle Ages, Lucien and the daughter of head vampire Viktor fell in love. Viktor was so horrified that his daughter was pregnant with a half-breed child that he murdered her and declared war on the Lycan. When Selene learns this, she realizes that the kindly father figure she once trusted is in fact a classic dead white male whose patriarchal, imperialist wrath knows no bounds. Both Lucien and Selene bite Michael, turning him into the vampwolf hybrid Viktor fears most. Then they slice the old colonial regime to bits with their ass-kicking mixed-blood powers.

While early twentieth-century stories about the undead are generally told from a white point of view, early twenty-first-century ones reflect the perspectives of people of color and racial hybrids. And yet certain tropes linger, their meaning transforming minutely as race relations change. The vengeful white ghosts of *Birth of a Nation* who strike terror into the hearts of "uppity" blacks are, roughly eighty years later, reimagined as the black ghost in *Bones*, who slaughters "uppity" blacks who betrayed him in order to escape from the ghetto. Both films solicit sympathy for their ghosts from the audience, and both use these ghosts to teach a lesson about whiteness. The lesson, however, has changed. The white ghosts of *Birth* tutor us in the supremacy of whiteness, while the black ghost in *Bones* has returned from the grave to purge his neighborhood of the white influences that destroyed it. Certainly the dead body of colonialism is still walking among the living, but colonized groups are not always at its mercy. As Toni Morrison argues, whiteness has been plagued by ghosts since the birth of U.S. literature. Now, in the nation's pop culture at the turn of the millennium, we are watching what happens when a haunting begins to transform the haunted.

Notes

1. Marianna Torgovnick, *Gone Primitive: Savage Intellects, Modern Lives* (Chicago: University of Chicago Press, 1990).

2. Toni Morrison, *Playing in the Dark: Whiteness and the Literary Imagination* (New York: Vintage, 1990), 33.

3. Skal offers an excellent analysis of how racial fears fit into stories about reanimating the dead, and here I'm thinking in particular of a passage where he compares the Frankenstein "angry mob" scene to a lynching. Tropes like this one abound in undead stories, and the crucial point is that they position the monster as a person of color besieged by white racists. See David J. Skal, *Screams of Reason: Mad Science and Modern Culture* (New York: W. W. Norton, 1998), 131.

4. bell hooks, "Whiteness in the Black Imagination," in *Cultural Studies,* ed. Lawrence Grossberg, Cary Nelson, and Paula Treichler (New York: Routledge, 1991).

5. Taken from "Why Weird Tales?," an editorial published in the *Weird Tales* anniversary issue of 1924. Otis Adelbert Kline has claimed to be its author. This editorial is reprinted in Robert Weinberg, *The Weird Tales Story* (West Linn, Oreg.: FAX Collectors Editions, 1977), 16.

6. Weinberg.

7. Colin Wilson uses this turn of phrase in his introduction to H. P. Lovecraft, *Crawling Chaos: Selected Works 1920–1935* (London: Creation Press, 1992), 9.

8. See Weinberg, *Weird Tales Story,* 62.

9. In his monograph *Supernatural Horror in Literature,* Lovecraft defines the three "terrors" that fuel the weird tale in America as a fear of the wilderness, a fear of Indians, and the repressive heritage of the Puritans. He was, in other words, quite conscious of the role played by racial others in his own weird fiction. It's also interesting to note that *Weird Tales* was host to the popular Conan the Barbarian stories of Robert E. Howard, which are almost entirely devoted to an exploration of what it would mean if whites were still "savage" peoples. See Lovecraft, *Supernatural Horror in Literature* (New York: Dover, 1973).

10. See, e.g., David Roediger's telling history of class warfare and racial identity in the United States in *The Wages of Whiteness: Race and the Making of the American Working Class* (New York: Verso Books, 1996). A second edition was released in 1999.

11. S. T. Joshi, *H. P. Lovecraft: A Life* (West Warwick, R.I.: Necronomicon Press, 1996), 268.

12. From Lin Carter, "Farewell to the Dreamlands," introduction to H. P. Lovecraft, *The Doom That Came to Sarnath and Other Stories,* ix–xiv (New York: Del Rey, 1971).

13. George T. Wetzel, "The Cthulhu Mythos: A Study," in *H. P. Lovecraft: Four Decades of Criticism,* ed. S. T. Joshi, 79–95 (Athens: Ohio University Press, 1980).

14. All these games are put out by a company called Chaosium (located in Oakland, California) devoted entirely to Lovecraftiana: they manufacture and sell fanzines, T-shirts, "Cthulhu for President" bumper stickers, and of course the extensive line of Call of Cthulhu game manuals, adventure modules, and character guides.

15. For the sake of brevity here, I'm not including a number of other important Mythos stories, most notably "The Dream-Quest of Unknown Kadath," which gives readers a detailed description of the more spiritual aspects of the Mythos. The Dreamlands of this work are the realm of the dead (which sleepers visit when they dream) and are also a kind of gateway to Nyarlathotep, the "crawling chaos" who is portrayed as a cruel, all-powerful, and indifferent force lurking over many of the Mythos tales.

16. H. P. Lovecraft, "At the Mountains of Madness" (1931), in *At the Mountains of Madness and Other Tales of Terror* (New York: Del Ray, 1971).

17. H. P. Lovecraft, *The Crawling Chaos: Selected Works 1920–1935* (London: Creation Press, 1992), 141.

18. H. P. Lovecraft, *Ec'h-Pi-El Speaks: An Autobiographical Sketch* (Saddle River, N.J.: Gerry de la Ree, 1972), 10.

19. It's also amusing to note that one of Lovecraft's favorite short stories was a work of horror by Arthur Machen called "The White People."

20. H. P. Lovecraft, *The Case of Charles Dexter Ward* (New York: Del Rey, 1941).

21. Curwen lives at Pawtuxet with only "a sullen pair of Narragansett Indians . . . probably [with] a mixture of Negro blood," and Lovecraft is careful to make Curwen's diabolical incantations sound very much like Hebrew. Ward raises the spirit of Curwen by chanting, in part, "Per Adonai Eloim, Adonai Jehova/Adonai Sabaoth." Lovecraft, 16, 66. As Levy notes, many of Lovecraft's magical formulas are written to sound as if they are in Hebrew. See Maurice Levy, *Lovecraft: A Study in the Fantastic* (Detroit, Mich.: Wayne State University Press, 1988), 93–94.

22. Lovecraft, "The Shadow over Innsmouth," in *The Lurking Fear and Other Stories* (New York: Del Rey, 1971), 119.

23. See Bennett Lovett-Graff's excellent article "Shadows over Lovecraft: Reactionary Fantasy and Immigrant Eugenics," *Extrapolation: A Journal of Science Fiction and Fantasy* 38 (1997): 175.

24. See Joshi, *H. P. Lovecraft*, and Levy, *Lovecraft*.

25. Lovecraft writes in a letter to Frank Belknap Long, "I am pretty well satisfied to be a Nordick, chalk-white from the Hercynian Wood and the Polar mists. . . . Our province is to found the cities and conquer the wilderness and people the waste lands—that, and to assemble and drive the slaves, who tell us stories and sing us songs and paint us pretty pictures. *We are the masters!*" Excerpted in August Derleth and Donald Wandrei, *H. P. Lovecraft: Selected Letters 1911–1924* (Sauk City, Wisc.: Arkham House, 1965), 276.

26. Quoted in Joshi, *H. P. Lovecraft*, 366.

27. Lovecraft, "The Horror at Red Hook," in *The Tomb and Other Tales* (New York: Del Rey, 1965), 73.

28. Peter Cannon remarks on the general incoherence of the story—and on many critics' agreement with his assessment—in *H. P. Lovecraft* (Boston: G. K. Hall, 1989), 56.

29. Lovecraft, *Supernatural Horror in Literature*, 18.

30. Lovecraft, "The Call of Cthulhu," in *The Crawling Chaos,* 143.

31. Donald Bogle, *Toms, Coons, Mulattoes, Mammies, and Bucks: An Interpretive History of Blacks in American Films* (New York: Continuum, 1973), 10.

32. Francis Hackett, "Brotherly Love," *New Republic* 7 (March 20, 1915), 185.

33. This theme is echoed in a number of B-grade films of the latter half of the twentieth century, perhaps most memorably in cult movie prince Herschel Gordon Lewis's *Two Thousand Maniacs!* (1964), where Southern ghosts reappear every year to torture and kill Northerners in memory of the Civil War.

34. This is a line from Griffith's screenplay, quoted in Michael Rogin, *Ronald Reagan: The Movie, and Other Episodes in Political Demonology* (Berkeley: University of California Press, 1987), 218.

35. Linda Williams, *Playing the Race Card: Melodramas of Black and White from Uncle Tom to O. J. Simpson* (Princeton, N.J.: Princeton University Press, 2001), 126–27.

36. Rogin, *Ronald Reagan,* 219. For simplicity's sake, I have singled out a specific thread in Rogin's rewardingly complex argument, which goes far more deeply into issues of gender, psychoanalysis, and Griffith's complete oeuvre than I do here.

37. Annalee Newitz, "White Savagery and Humiliation, or a New Racial Consciousness in the Media," in *White Trash: Race and Class in America,* ed. Matt Wray and Annalee Newitz (New York: Routledge, 1997).

38. Williams, *Playing the Race Card,* 129.

39. Ed Guerrero, *Framing Blackness: The African American Image in Film* (Philadelphia: Temple University Press, 1993), 13.

40. See D. W. Griffith, "Reply to the *New York Globe*," in Robert Lang, *The Birth of a Nation* (New Brunswick, N.J.: Rutgers University Press, 1994), 169.

41. For a discussion of the "crisis of hegemony" in which a ruling group is challenged by the subordinate classes, see excerpts from Antonio Gramsci's 1929–35 prison writings in "Hegemony, Relations of Force, Historical Bloc," in *A Gramsci Reader,* ed. David Forgacs (London: Lawrence and Wishart, 1988), 217–21.

42. Michael Omi and Howard Winant, *Racial Formation in the United States: From the 1960s to the 1990s* (New York: Routledge, 1994), 56.

43. When I use the term *postcolonial,* I intend it largely as a periodizing device, to denote the time period (roughly after 1960) when many formerly colonized states had either begun the decolonization process or were currently decolonizing. In a U.S. context, this time period would have begun after the civil rights movement and during the period in which practices of "cultural imperialism" began to operate where military imperialism seemed unethical or simply not feasible.

44. Franz Fanon, *The Wretched of the Earth* (New York: Grove Press, 1963), 41–43.

45. Amy Kaplan, "Left Alone with America," in *Cultures of United States Imperialism,* ed. Amy Kaplan and Donald E. Pease (Durham, N.C.: Duke University Press, 1993), 14.

46. Roxanne Dunbar, *Red Dirt: Growing Up Okie* (New York: Verso, 1997).

47. Of course, not all whites came from countries that colonized others. See Theodore Allen, *The Invention of the White Race* (New York: Verso, 1994), and Noel Ignatiev, *How the Irish Became White* (New York: Routledge, 1995), both of whom also explore quite fruitfully the way the Irish population is an exception to the rule that white bodies remind us

of imperial cultures. "Becoming white," for Irish immigrants to the United States, seemed to represent the promise of an imperial power they had been denied in their own land. Thus, although not literally true, "whiteness" was imaginatively cast as an identity shared by people from powerful, colonizing nations.

48. Jim Goad, *The Redneck Manifesto* (New York: Simon and Schuster, 1997), 52.

49. For more on Ben's heroism and the zombies' fighting style, see Gregory Waller's fascinating analysis of *Night of the Living Dead* in his *The Living and the Undead: From Bram Stoker's "Dracula" to Romero's "Dawn of the Dead"* (Urbana: University of Illinois Press, 1986), 272–322.

50. Richard Dyer, "White," *Screen* 29, no. 4 (1988): 59.

51. A complete discussion of these redneck stereotypes in film can be found in J. W. Williamson, *Hillbillyland: What the Movies Did to the Movies* (Chapel Hill: University of North Carolina Press, 1995).

52. Waller, *The Living and the Undead,* 294.

53. Eric Lott, *Love and Theft: Blackface Minstrelsy and the American Working Class* (New York: Oxford University Press, 1995), 59.

54. *From Hell* was originally a comic book written by Alan Moore. Interestingly, the Blade movies are also based on comic books, and it seems that *Underworld* was probably based on the White Wolf role-playing game. Postcolonial undead movies are no longer taking their cues from old pulp fiction and novels but instead from more contemporary forms of narrative.

55. Gregory Dicum, "Mutts at the Dog Show: Why Racial Categories Are Fading Away in America," *other* I (June 2003): 34–38.

INTOLERABLE AMBIGUITY
Freaks as/at the Limit

Elizabeth Grosz

But, I that am not shap'd for sportive tricks,
Nor made to court an amorous looking-glass;
I, that am rudely stamp'd, and want love's majesty
To strut before a wanton ambling nymph;
I, that am curtail'd of this fair proportion,
Cheated of feature by dissembling nature,
Deform'd, unfinish'd, sent before my time
Into this breathing world scarce half made up,
and that so lamely and unfashionable
That dogs bark at me as I halt by them—
   —Shakespeare, *King Richard III*, 1.1.14–23

ANY DISCUSSION OF FREAKS brings back into focus a topic that has had a largely underground existence in contemporary cultural and intellectual life, partly because it is considered below the refined sensibilities of "good taste" and "personal politeness" in a civilized and politically correct milieu, and partly because it has required a new set of intellectual tools, which are still in the process of development, to raise it above being an object of prurient speculation. I am interested in the question of human freaks not simply for voyeuristic reasons— although these must no doubt play a part—but also because I am interested in the psychical, physical, and conceptual *limits* of human subjectivity, that is, what the nature and forms of subjectivity consist in and the degree to which social, polit-ical, and historical factors shape the forms of subjectivity with which we are familiar; and the degree to which these factors are able to tolerate anomalies, ambiguities, and borderline cases, marking the threshold, not of humanity in itself, but of acceptable, tolerable, knowable humanity. Closely related to the question of the psychical conditions of subjectivity (a field that psychoanalytic theory has tended to dominate) is a concern about the corporeal limits of subjectivity. The ways in which the body is lived and represented, the inputs and effects of the subject's corporeality on its identity, seem crucial if usually underestimated fac-tors in any account of the subject.

I will explore some of the most severe and gross physical disorders afflicting those human beings who have been coarsely categorized as "freaks," "curiosi-ties," "prodigies," and "monstrosities," poor suffering individuals with observably disturbing bodily disorders, stunted limbs, distorted figures: Siamese twins, dwarfs, giants, hunchbacks, humans with parasitic or autositic attachments, so-called leg-less or armless wonders, half-creatures, hermaphrodites, rubber men, and so on. The simultaneous horror and fascination with these people, and the fact that many exist in the world of entertainment and gain their livelihood from being commercially exhibited, need to be explained. In the so-called normal subjects who constitute the paying audience for freak shows, this fascination amounts to both willingness and shame. The sometimes overpowering need to look and a horror of and pity toward what is seen are important elements in understand-ing the psychologies and the body-images of "normal" subjects, attesting to what is and is not tolerable or incorporable into normality. Moreover, in attempting to understand the freak's own body-image and psychological structure—the kinds of social, interpersonal, and narcissistic images freaks internalize and the ways in which their bodies are inscribed and made socially meaningful, medicalized, and rendered into a typology—may also prove invaluable to understanding subjectiv-ity and corporeality in their most general outlines, and in their most extreme forms.

First, however, it is necessary to specify what I mean by *freaks*. This is not an easy concept to define. I use this term in part, not as a description or a mode of moral evaluation, but as something of a political gesture. Like a series of other negative labels ("queer" comes most clearly to mind), it is a term whose use may function as an act of defiance, a political gesture of self-determination. For this reason I prefer it to euphemistic substitutes: it makes clear that there are very real and concrete political effects for those thus labeled, and a clear political reac-tion is implied by those who use it as a mode of self-definition. First, let me clarify what I do *not* mean by the term: I wish to exclude from my discussion the more commonplace bodily infirmities and deficiencies—those born with nonfunctional or improperly functional limbs and organs, the blind, those who are unable to walk, and those with cerebral palsy and other medical disorders. While these persons may be as or more disabled than those categorized as freaks, they do not exert the same ambivalent appeal. Nor do I wish to include those with congenital abnormalities in internal organs (heart, lung, kidney, etc.). Nor do I include the accidental tragedies in which individuals are maimed or wounded (e.g., amputees, brain damage cases, orthopedic problems). The term *freaks* does not simply refer to disabilities of either a genetic, developmental, or contingent kind. Indeed, some classified as freaks (such as the bearded lady or the human skeleton) are not necessarily physically incapacitated at all, although, of course, many are. All suffer a certain social marginalization. I also do not refer to those particularly gifted with unusual aptitudes, such as the athlete or technically skilled performer, although many freaks do fall into this category. Freaks are not just unusual or atypical; more than this is necessary to characterize their unique social position. The freak is thus neither unusually gifted nor unusually disadvantaged. He or she is not an object of *simple* admiration or pity but is a being who is considered simultaneously and compulsively fascinating and repulsive, enticing and sickening.

Many freaks are the result of genetic or hereditary factors: abnormal elasticity of the skin, albinism, the growth of human horns, microcephaly (pinheads), dwarfism or gigantism, multiple births, and so on are commonly observed in disproportionate numbers in certain families. Others, it seems, are the result of embryological or histological conditions, in which fetal development is hindered or altered in utero (e.g., conjoined twins and hermaphrodites). Others are the result of medical factors that emerge after birth: dwarfism is commonly the result of tumors on the pituitary gland; obesity and extraordinary thinness are usually the result of overeating or disgust of food. Some freaks are the result of conscious efforts on the part of individuals to maim, cripple, or distort the human body (there are many cases where limbs have been amputated by unscrupulous individuals, commonly parents, for profit or pity). Perhaps more alarmingly, some within the medical and veterinary sciences seem to have had a passion for experimentation in controlled mutation, cross-breeding, and genetic engineering in which, like Dr. Moreau, they create two-headed creatures, hermaphroditic cattle, freemartins,[1] and interspecies hybrids for (pseudo)scientific or perverse reasons.[2]

The freak is an object of simultaneous horror and fascination because, in addition to whatever infirmities or abilities he or she exhibits, the freak is an *ambiguous* being whose existence imperils categories and oppositions dominant in social life. Freaks are those human beings who exist outside and in defiance of the structure of binary oppositions that govern our basic concepts and modes of self-definition. They occupy the impossible middle ground between the oppositions dividing the human from the animal (Jo-Jo, the dog-faced boy; Percilla, the monkey girl; Emmitt, the alligator-skinned boy; the "wild man" or "geek"), one being from another (conjoined twins, "double-bodied wonders," two-headed or multiple-limbed beings), nature from culture (feral children, the "wild men of

Borneo"), one sex from the other (the bearded lady, hermaphrodites, Joseph–Josephines or Victor–Victorias), adults and children (dwarfs and midgets), humans and gods (giants), and the living and the dead (human skeletons). Freaks cross the borders that divide the subject from all ambiguities, interconnections, and reciprocal classifications, outside of or beyond the human. They imperil the very definitions we rely on to classify humans, identities, and sexes—our most fundamental categories of self-definition and boundaries dividing self from otherness.

The study of monstrosities, whether human or animal, has long preoccupied physicians, magicians, sages, and soothsayers. *Teratology,* the science of monsters, is almost as old as our culture itself, and the study of monstrosities has produced all sorts of peculiar associated knowledges, including fetomancy and teratoscopy, which regard monstrous births as omens or predictions of the future. The Greeks regarded minor and major terata with the greatest curiosity, holding them to be divine warnings of the future and/or symptoms of past indiscretions. Greek mythology abounds in representations of monsters, combinations of human and animal, centaurs and minotaurs, the cyclops, giants, and hermaphrodites. Empedocles, Democritus, Hippocrates, Aristotle, Galen, and Pliny all describe in considerable detail various human and animal deformities. Indeed, stories of double-monsters, individuals with two heads, and mixtures of animals and humans seem to litter the (pre)history of every race. Speculation that monstrosities were the result of carnal indulgences, and particularly of bestiality, was rife in the Middle Ages, when freaks and human monsters were regarded as divinations, forebodings, and examples of the wrath of God, as well as forms of glorification of God's might and power. These were usually seen as forms of divine punishment meted out to individuals, communities, or even nations.

Teratology was largely a mystic and superstitious doctrine until it was linked more closely to the medicalization of bodily regulation in the sixteenth century and became a *category* of illness for the first time. The management of teratology by medicine seems to have had a mysterious power to render what is horrifying and fascinating about such individuals into "neutral" facts, described in scientific terminology, as part of a meticulous classificatory system that explains anomalies and renders them more "normal," or at least places them within a broad continuum containing the "normal" as its ideal. Ambroise Paré classified and organized the monstrous in (pseudo)scientific form according to the (presumed) causes of terata. He postulated three major categories of monstrosities: anomalies of excess, of default, and of duplicity. This classificatory schema, with its impulse for tables, categories, forms, and order, was refined and augmented with medical descriptions only in the eighteenth century, and reached its pinnacle toward the end of the nineteenth century. In *Anomalies and Curiosities of Medicine* (1897), George M. Gould and Walter L. Pyle date the emergence of "modern" teratology in the nineteenth century from the work of Isidore Geoffroy Saint-Hilaire, who was committed not only to advancing a methodological study of human deformities but also to combating what he believed were the naive and superstitious myths surrounding them.[3]

Space permits me to concentrate on only two forms of monstrosity here, though I would have liked to discuss others. Nor can I direct adequate attention to the implications of medical discourse and practice in the simultaneous normalization and pathologization of the corporeally unclassifiable. I focus on those two examples of monstrosity that most tangibly present the human subject as ambiguously one identity and two, or one sex and the other: conjoined twins and hermaphrodites. Both are relatively regular occurrences today[4] and therefore are the continuing objects of medical investigation and surgical intervention. They are not usually subject to infantile euthanasia, as commonly occurs in other cases of gross deformity (which may explain the increasing rarity of so-called limbless wonders and other severely damaged individuals). And they continue to hold a place of public fascination, even if they are no longer exhibited in sideshows and as forms of public entertainment. This can be seen by the extensive coverage granted in the popular press to the birth of Siamese twins and hermaphrodites. In the last few years, for example, there have been detailed, globally circulated reports in newspapers on the birth or separation of conjoined twins, as well as on the medical interventions into the sexual typology of hermaphrodites.

Hermaphrodites have long been recorded in Western history and are referred to frequently in classical literature. Herodotus, for example, refers to the "Scythians," a race of soothsayers and prophets, comprising women-like men who predicted the future by reading the inner bark of the linden tree. Plato, by contrast, attributes no mythical or religious powers to an ambisexual tribe but regards them instead as the (mythical) origins of our own race. In *The Symposium,* he states, "The original human nature was not like the present, but different. In the first place the sexes were originally three in number, not as they are now; there was man, woman and the union of the two having a double nature; they once had a real existence, but it is now lost, and the name only is preserved as a term of reproach."[5]

The hermaphrodite was the child of Hermes (the god of invention, athletics, secret or occult philosophy) and Aphrodite (the goddess of love). In about 60 B.C.E., Diodorus speaks of Hermaphroditus "who was born of Hermes and Aphrodite, and received the name which was a combination of his parents. Some say that Hermaphroditus is a god ... [who] has a body which is beautiful and delicate like that of a woman, but has the masculine quality and vigor of a man, but some declare that such creatures of two sexes are monstrosities."[6] It seems clear from these and other accounts that ambisexual or intersexual individuals were a recognized, if not accepted, part of Greek and Roman life.

But it seems likely, given that there are many forms of hermaphroditism, that the Greeks and Romans were familiar with only one or two types, those in which the genitalia of one sex are coupled with the secondary sexual characteristics of the other in a visible, observable mismatch (Klinefelter's syndrome and testicular feminization). In the light of development in Mendelian genetics, and in view of more detailed studies of the nature of the sex chromosomes, it has become apparent that there are far more abnormalities of the sex chromosomes than are manifested in external sexual characteristics. It is now commonly accepted that the category of sex can be determined by at least six different criteria, which so-called normal subjects exist in agreement but intersexes or hermaphrodites exist in conflict with each other. There is genetic sex, which is the sex exhibited by the sexual chromosomes (XX in the case of females, XY in the case of males); gonadal structure (i.e., whether the organs of generation are testes, ovaries, or some other alternative, such as an ovotestis or a "streaklike" gonad); the morphology of external genitalia (which, incidentally, is the most common criterion for assigning sex to the newborn infant); the morphology of the internal genitalia (i.e., whether the wolffian ducts predominate as in males, or the müllerian ducts, as in females); hormonal constitution (in which the predominance of androgens, testosterone, or estrogen dictates secondary sexual characteristics); and the sex of rearing (which may confirm or conflict with the anatomical, hormonal, and functional aspects of the individual). John Money's various researches into intersexuality and sex change indicate that, paradoxically, the most difficult aspect of the individual's sexuality to change is the sex of rearing, and his advice to doctors and intersexed individuals is, where possible, to use surgical and hormonal procedures to approximate the sex of rearing rather than, as one would expect, change the sex of rearing to conform to the child's anatomical form or chromosomal structure—a point to which I will return later.[7] Wherever there is some discordance between any of these criteria, we are justified in talking about an intersexed subject, one who is anomalous in terms of our everyday conceptions of the clear-cut, binarily opposed notions of male and female.

Within the medical literature, sexual disorders are usually attributed to one or more of three possible causes: (1) errors present in the parents prior to conception (chromosomal anomalies); (2) errors that occur subsequent to conception, from the first division of cells to postnatal life (hormonal or gonadal anomalies); (3) errors in which sex determination is normal and sexual differentiation is abnormal (as in testicular feminization or gonadal dysgenesis). This leads to a variety of different types of intersexuality:

1. *Turner's syndrome,* in which the subject is chromosomally female but has primitive "streaklike" gonads in place of the ovaries. Here the subject is

generally of short stature, has neck webbing and immature development of breasts and genitals, and is infertile.

2. *Klinefelter's syndrome,* in which the subject is chromosomally male but may have undersized or nonfunctional testes. In this case as well, the subject is infertile. Occasionally there is also gynecomastia, meaning that breasts develop after puberty. This type is most commonly represented in popular images of the hermaphrodite—the subject who has both a penis and breasts.

3. *Chromosomal mosaics,* in which there is a shortfall in the number or quality of chromosomes (the normal complement is forty-six). Where the subject has forty-five chromosomes in some cells and forty-seven in others, we can speak of a mosaicism (XO/XXX). Here the subject's sexual phenotype is female, yet the external genitalia are undeveloped, the vagina is absent, and there is no breast development. (This type comes closest to an anatomical equivalent of the celibate—a "sexless" subject.)

4. *Testicular feminization,* in which genotypic males develop into female phenotypes. Here the chromosomal sex is female, but the subject has male gonads and, consequently, with the onset of puberty, becomes masculinized through increases in circulating male hormones, developing hirsutism and a deeper voice, with little or no breast development.

5. *Gonadal dysgenesis,* in which the subject is chromosomally female but the gonads are neither male nor female, instead exhibiting the streaklike characteristic already mentioned. The subject in this category is described as a tall, eunuchoid female, with primary amenorrhea and underdeveloped breasts and genitalia.

6. *"True" hermaphroditism,* in which the chromosomal sex is usually female but the subject has both testicular and ovarian tissue. Here there are a number of possibilities: the subject may have an ovary on one side of the body and a testis on the other. The testis may be undescended and undetected or may take up its place in the scrotal sac. Or the subject may have a combined ovotestis on one or both sides, or an ovotestis on one side and a primitive gonadal streak on the other.

In addition to these quite distinct types of hermaphroditism, there are also various gradations of intersexuality—depending on the strength, degree, and effectivity of hormonal, gonadal, and chromosomal anomalies—leading to a number of variations from "normal" sexual identity.

This has been an extremely brief overview of a complex set of categories common in the current medical literature, categories that are not without problems of their own. The effects of taxonomic schema on the groupings and regroupings of individual bodies is capable of catastrophic effects such as those outlined in Foucault's account of the reclassification of the hermaphrodite, Herculine Barbin: such reclassification has massive personal effects on the ways individuals live their bodies and their lives. Nevertheless, there are a number of points of interest

I would like to draw out of the various scientific and historical data available on the question of intersexuality.

First, what is normally seen as a sexual polarity, with the female at one extreme and the male at the other, could, based upon medical evidence and the existence of ambisexual subjects, be represented differently. Rather than presuming two binarily opposed sexes, sexed subjects could be seen to occupy a position within a sexual continuum. This spectrum would contain a broad range of different forms of sexuality, some located at the male and some at the female poles, with others occupying intermediary positions with varying mixtures of male and female attributes. Perhaps more accurately, rather than a continuum (which implies the smooth transition between intermediate categories), the sexes can be regarded as a (relatively discontinuous) *series*. There are *n*-sexes rather than two, but these *n*-sexes have only ever been defined relative to the two. Indeed, the series is established as such only *between* male and female, which continue to function as the limits within which anomaly is to be mapped.

Second, medically oriented studies of hermaphroditism have indicated that the primacy given to the visible or manifest differences between the sexes is biologically unwarranted. The morphology of external genitalia does not provide a clear-cut delineation of the differences between the sexes, even if it does provide the usual criterion for determining sex in the neonate. Sex is a multilayered phenomenon, in which a variety of different levels coalesce: these include organic, genetic, and somatic but also behavioral and psychological factors. Sex is thus a much more complicated matter than the information afforded by vision; yet our lived (as opposed to scientific) understanding of sexual difference is focused on the presence (or absence) of visible genitalia.

Third, there has been a remarkable medicalization of the hermaphrodite, so that today virtually the only discourses available on intersexuality are those provided by clinical and scientific disciplines. The mythical, religious, dramatic, and exhibitionistic context in which hermaphroditism has been positioned is a thing of the past. The awe and horror, the special privilege (in some cultures), and the very real dangers (in other cultures) facing the hermaphrodite are today neutralized and normalized through the processes of medicalization. In so positioning hermaphroditism, the question of medical intervention, "correction," is rendered predictable and necessary, and specific treatments can be prescribed.

It is therefore ironic, given the primacy accorded to medical discourses, and given medicine's recognition of the complex factors constituting a subject's sexuality, that nevertheless the primary concern of surgeons, pediatricians, endocrinologists, cytologists, and psychiatrists has been the surgical correction of the subject's nonconforming sexuality so that it comes to approximate one or the other category of sexual identity. Underneath its manifest or latent complexity, it is presumed that there is a true sexuality, which is simply inadequately formed, rather than an anomalous, nonconformist, or multiformed sexuality. One quote from recognized authorities on intersexuality will illustrate this:

> To visualise individuals who properly belong neither to one sex nor to the other is to imagine freaks, misfits, curiosities, rejected by society and condemned to a solitary existence of neglect and frustration. Few of these unfortunate people meet with tolerance and understanding from their fellows, and fewer still find even a limited acceptance in a small section of society: all are constantly confronted with reminders of their unhappy situation. The tragedy of their lives is the greater since it may be remediable; with suitable management and treatment, especially if this is begun soon after birth, many of these people can be helped to live happy well-adjusted lives, and some may even be fertile and be enabled to enjoy a normal family life.[8]

Finally, it is significant that there remains a wide schism between medical understandings and popularized representations of hermaphroditism: the most common sideshow and carnival images present a graphic, nongenital, lateral hermaphroditism by splitting the subject down the middle and dressing one-half as male and the other as female. The Victor–Victoria, John–Jane image has no known medical correlate: these individuals have probably had plastic surgery or wear implants on the one side (to create the impression of breasts) or have had one breast removed.[9] In other words, in popular, nonmedical discourses, there seems to be something intolerable, not about sexual profusion (a biological bisexuality that is fascinating and considered worth paying for by audiences), but about sexual *indeterminacy*: the subject who has clear-cut male and female parts seems more acceptable than the subject whose genitalia are neither male nor female. These subjects imperil the very constitution of subjectivity according to sexual categories. I will return to this.

I would like now to turn briefly to that category of monstrosity that is today named after its most famous examples, "Siamese" (or conjoined) twins, after Chang and Eng (who, incidentally, were Chinese, not Siamese). Born in Siam in 1811 of Chinese parents, the pair was discovered by the merchant Robert Hunter in 1824, who obtained the permission of their parents and the king to take them to the United States and Europe for exhibitions. Significantly, they were first exhibited before doctors (at Harvard University in 1829), legitimized and authenticated, and then exhibited before the general public. When they were forty-two, they took the name "Bunker," married two sisters, English women aged twenty-six and twenty-eight, and for a number of years lived together in one house. When their families became too large, they moved into separate residences, the twins spending three days with one woman then three with the other in alternation until their deaths. Between them, they had twenty-two children and more than two hundred grandchildren. Apparently their descendants now number several thousand, many of whom live in the same region today as the twins did.

Although they were examined by dozens of doctors, and in spite of the fact that as they grew older, they fought more and more bitterly, it was decided not to attempt to separate them. Conjoined twins had been successfully separated as early as 1690, when two Swiss sisters joined belly to belly were separated by ligature and a simple operation.[10] In Chang and Eng's case, however, it was decided that surgery would endanger the survival of both. Moreover, Chang and Eng were so dispirited by the idea of separation that, at least in the first forty years of their lives, they would weep if it was even mentioned. It is significant that today the lives of conjoined twins are considered tragic if the operation to separate them is not feasible. This does not always accord with the feelings of the conjoined twins themselves.

Conjoined twins are relatively rare, and first-person (singular or plural) accounts are even rarer, so it is difficult to know what the experience of a permanent coupling is like. There are now, in the late twentieth century, usually only two possible fates for conjoined twins: separation, with the attendant dangers it poses for the children's physical and emotional well-being, or isolation from society, either through institutionalization or through a kind of self-imposed segregation. Probably the most famous adult conjoined twins in recent times are the McCarther twins, Yvonne and Yvette, who were born in 1949 joined at the top of the head, and who died in 1992. Their story made newspaper headlines worldwide when they emerged from thirty-eight years of being housebound—as they put it "just (lying) around the house all day, watching TV and being worthless"— to enroll in college in Los Angeles.

The Siamese twins and the McCarther twins are the only conjoined twins I know of who have given some public indications of their psychical states of being. There are a number of striking similarities between them. It is clear for both sets of conjoined twins that they are two separate subjects, in the sense that they have different personalities, preferences, and styles. Yet it also seems evident that the usual hard-and-fast distinction between the boundaries of one subject and another are continually blurred: speech patterns and even sentences are shared; all their experiences are shared; they do not need to consult over decisions but make them in unison automatically. Chang and Eng, for example, even wrote their letters in the first-person singular, using "I" where others would have presumed a "we" was appropriate, and signing themselves in the joint name "ChangEng."

It seems to be an affront to the common sense of identity that two individuals, even identical twins, should submerge themselves so completely in an identification with another person as to lose all trace of their singularity. However, in the case of both of these sets of twins, every attempt to individuate them in terms of dress, appearance, and behavior was frustrated. It seems that both sets were more than happy to wear the same clothes, eat the same food, and do whatever they could to act and appear the same. Chang and Eng always bought their clothes at the same time, having two suits made in identical styles from the same materials. Admittedly, it would have been difficult for them not to at least shop at the same time, but their refusal, for example, to use up material that would have made a suit for one but not for two indicated that even where it may have been more convenient and cheaper to dress differently, they refused to do so. A *Los Angeles Times* article indicates that the same voluntary identification occurred with Yvonne and Yvette: "As usual, they dressed identically, from head to toe. Even their purses contain matching sets of everything from vitamin jars to wallets with exactly the same family photos." Ironically, the linkages between conjoined twins, which seem so pitiable and horrifying to us, are not considered problematic by the twins themselves. A contemporary report on Chang and Eng, from London's *Examiner*, succinctly puts the tragedy of their existence into words:

> It is a mournful sight, to behold two fellow-creatures thus fated to endure all the common evils of life, while they must necessarily be debarred from the enjoyment of many of its chief delights. The link which unites them is more durable than that of the marriage tie—no separation can take place, legal or illegal—no Act of Parliament can divorce them, nor can all the power of Doctors' Commons give them a release even from bed and board.[11]

However, the twins themselves seemed far more content than this, being limited more by the social necessity of their economic survival in a culture puzzled and horrified by them, and aware of their peculiarity only from others.

The conjunction of twins is made more stark, and the divisions between one existence and another more blurred, in the case of parasitic twins, where only one of the twins is fully formed and organically functional and the other is embedded in the body of the first. In such cases, it is exceedingly rare that the head of the parasitic twin is developed or formed; more commonly, the limbs exist in atrophied form, so that either a torso protrudes from the torso of the fully formed twin, or she or he has extra limbs in unexpected places. In such cases, it is no longer clear that there are two identities, even if the bodily functions of the parasitic twin occur independently of the will or awareness of the other. In such cases, is there one subject or two? If the subject is considered a single being, what kind of body-space does he or she occupy? Given that the sensations of the parasitic twin are not always perceived by the autositic twin, does the body-image include the parasitic body? What kind of body-image must it be if the body is to include sensations and experiences the subject cannot experience in the first person?

The presence of conjoined twins raises a number of points of interest, some of which are similar to those raised by hermaphrodites. First, just as sexuality is best regarded in terms of a series of sexual morphologies and positions, so, too, in the case of conjoined twins, there seems to be a continuum of identities, ranging from the so-called normal, individuated singular subject to a nonindividuated, collectivized multiple subject.

Second, the subject is not given an identity independent of his or her bodily morphology—either sexual or more broadly corporeal—but acquires an identity in the relation to the body. The range of peculiarities and biological anomalies to which the body is liable clearly make a difference to the kind of body-image and consequently to the kind of identity the subject (or subjects) attributes and finds others attributing to itself. If it is uncertain where one body ends and another begins, the subject's identity too must remain undecidably singular and plural, individual and collective.

Third, as in the case of hermaphroditism, it is significant that, in spite of the state of health of conjoined twins, there appears to be a medical imperative for surgical intervention and normalization, even if surgery may actually endanger lives that may otherwise remain healthy. It seems that the permanent conjunction of individuals is socially intolerable, and that it is unimaginable to others that these subjects themselves would not wish to be able to lead "normal" lives. Surgery, it is argued, provides the only hope of such a normality, and surgical intervention clearly functions more successfully the earlier it occurs: the younger the children are, the less formed their body-image is.

Finally, the existence of conjoined twins, whether autositic or parasitic, raises the question of the nature of bodily boundaries and the distinctions that separate one being from another. While psychologically distinct individuals, conjoined twins are nevertheless far closer than any other two beings ever could be, and while there are two identities, they are not sharply distinguished from each other. In separating conjoined twins, one does not thereby create two autonomous beings, only as close as identical twins; conjoined twins are bonded through the psychical inscription of their historical, even if not current, corporeal links. Those who have shared organs, a common blood circulation, and every minute detail of everyday life can never have this corporeal link effaced.

In conclusion, I would like to return to one of the concerns I mentioned at the beginning of this chapter: not to so-called freaks themselves but to what is freakish among those who are not freaks—that is, the dual horror and fascination others have toward those they label freaks. This mixture of reactions is a peculiar one that requires some kind of explanation. Why are people horrified at seeing deformities and human anomalies? Why do they classify such anomalies as freaks? What is so unsettling about freaks? I suggest that it is not gross deformity alone that is so unsettling and fascinating. Rather, there are other reasons for this curiosity and horror. First, it seems to me that the initial reaction to the freakish and the monstrous is a perverse kind of sexual curiosity. People think to themselves, "How do they do *it*?" What kind of sex lives are available to Siamese twins, hermaphrodites, bearded ladies, and midgets? There is a certain morbid speculation about what it would be like to be with such persons, or worse, to be them. It is not altogether surprising that a very large percentage of freaks I have researched were married or involved in sexual liaisons. As Victor Hugo writes in *The Man Who Laughs,* "You are not only ugly, but hideous. Ugliness is insignificant, deformity is grand. Ugliness is a devil's grin behind beauty; deformity is akin to sublimity."

The perverse pleasure of voyeurism and identification is counterbalanced by horror at the blurring of identities (sexual, corporeal, personal) that witness our chaotic and insecure identities. Freaks traverse the very boundaries that secure the "normal" subject in its given identity and sexuality. Monsters involve all kinds of doubling of the human form, a duplication of the body or some of its parts. The major terata recognized throughout history are largely monsters of excess, with two or more heads, bodies, or limbs, or with duplicated sexual organs. One might ponder why the excess of bodily parts is more discomforting than a shortage or diminution of limbs or organs. Perhaps our fear of the immersion or loss of identity with another is greater or more pervasive than our fear of bodily incompletion. This fear, like the fear and horror of ghostly doubles or *Doppelgänger,* is a horror at the possibility of our own imperfect duplication, a horror of submersion in an alien otherness, an incorporation in and by another.

The freak illustrates our so-called normal pleasure and fascination with our mirror images, a fascination with the limits of our own identities as they are witnessed from the outside. This is a narcissistic delight at the shape of our own externality, which is always inaccessible to us by direct means and is achievable only if we can occupy the perspective others have on us. The relation we bear to images of ourselves is drawn from this simultaneous and ambivalent reaction: the mirror image threatens to draw us into its spell of spectral doubling, annihilating the self that wants to see itself reflected. At the same time, it gains pleasure from the access it gives to the subject's exteriority, from an illusory mastery over its image. Fascination with the monstrous is testimony to our tenuous hold on the image of perfection. The freak confirms the viewer as bounded, belonging to a "proper" social category. The viewer's horror lies in the recognition that this monstrous being is at the heart of his or her own identity, for it is all that must be ejected or abjected from self-image to make the bounded, category-obeying self possible. In other words, what is at stake in the subject's dual reaction to the freakish or bizarre individual is its own narcissism, the pleasures and boundaries of its own identity, and the integrity of its received images of self.

Notes

This chapter was written in 1986, under the auspices of and with funding from the Humanities Research Centre, the Australian National University. It was published as "Freaks: An Exploration of Human Anomalies" in *Social Semiotics* 1, no. 2 (1991): 22–38. It has been rewritten for this collection.

1. A freemartin is a sterile twin in cattle, sheep, goats, and pigs, in which the female twin is masculinized when the male hormones secreted by the male twin enter the female twin through common blood circulation. See Ursula Mittwoch, *Genetics of Sexual Differentiation* (London: Academic Press, 1973), 60ff.

2. I was recently alarmed to read in my local newspaper a report on the experiments of scientists who, as part of the human genome project, are trying to map the genes relevant to sight. They have, through gene splicing, been able to induce the development of up to fourteen eyes on a single fly, in unlikely and dysfunctional sites (e.g., on the ends of antennae, on legs, on the thorax or back). Sadly, it seems, the more information about genetics and genetic manipulation is developed, the more bizarre and extreme are its experimental implications.

3. Geoffroy Saint-Hilaire's teratological classifications were as follows: CLASS I—Union of several fetuses. CLASS 2—Union of two distinct fetuses by a connecting band. CLASS 3—Union of two distinct fetuses by an osseous junction of cranial bones. CLASS 4—Union of two distinct fetuses in which one or more parts are eliminated by the junction. CLASS 5—Union of two fetuses by a bony union of the ischii. CLASS 6—Fusion of two fetuses below the umbilicus into a common lower extremity. CLASS 7—Bicephalic monsters. CLASS 8—Parasitic monsters. CLASS 9—Monsters with a single body and double lower extremities. CLASS 10—Diphallic terata. CLASS 11—Fetus in fetu, and dermoid cysts. CLASS 12—Hermaphrodites. Quoted in George M. Gould and Walter L. Pyle, *Anomalies and Curiosities of Medicine* (Philadelphia: W. B. Saunders, 1897), 167.

4. An estimated three hundred conjoined twins have survived beyond a few months of age in recorded history, although the success rate in separating conjoined twins is increasing with advances in the techniques of microsurgery. In the case of intersexuality, however, the rate is much more frequent, perhaps being one in two thousand.

5. Quoted in Howard W. Jones and William W. Scott, *Hermaphrodites, Genital Anomalies and Related Endocrine Disorders* (Baltimore: Williams and Wilkins, 1971), 3.

6. Quoted in Jones and Scott, 4.

7. See John Money, *Sex Errors of the Body: Dilemmas, Education, Counselling* (Baltimore: Johns Hopkins University Press, 1968).

8. Christopher J. Dewhurst and Ronald R. Gordon, *The Intersexual Disorders* (London: Baillière Tindall/Cassell, 1969), vii.

9. Significantly, probably the most striking mass culture representation of the hermaphrodite, in Federico Fellini's *Satyricon*, in which there is a closer correspondence with medicalized images, was played by a sexually immature boy who, through the help of makeup, was given the appearance of breasts.

10. Gould and Pyle, *Anomalies and Curiosities of Medicine*, 172.

11. Irving Wallace and Amy Wallace, *The Two* (London: Cassell, 1976), 80.

III
Monsters and Culture

MONSTERS AND THE MORAL IMAGINATION

Stephen T. Asma

MONSTERS ARE ON THE RISE. People can't seem to get enough of vampires lately, and zombies have a new lease on life. In 2009 and 2010, we had the release of the usual horror films like *Saw VI* and *Halloween II*; the campy mayhem of *Zombieland*; more-pensive forays like *9* (produced by Tim Burton and Timur Bekmambetov), *The Wolfman,* and *The Twilight Saga: New Moon*; and, more playfully, *Where the Wild Things Are* (a Dave Eggers rewrite of the Maurice Sendak classic).

The reasons for this increased monster culture are hard to pin down. Maybe it's social anxiety in the post-9/11 decade, or the conflict in Iraq—some think there's an uptick in such fare during wartime. Perhaps it's the economic downturn. The monster proliferation can be explained, in part, by exploring the meaning of monsters. Popular culture is reenchanted with meaningful monsters, and even the eggheads are stroking their chins—last month saw the seventh global conference on Monsters and the Monstrous at the University of Oxford.

The uses of monsters vary widely. In our liberal culture, we dramatize the rage of the monstrous creature—and Frankenstein's is a good example—then scold ourselves and our "intolerant society" for alienating the outcast in the first place. The liberal lesson of monsters is one of tolerance: we must overcome our innate scapegoating, our xenophobic tendencies. Of course, this is by no means the only interpretation of monster stories. The medieval mind saw giants and mythical creatures as God's punishments for the sin of pride. For the Greeks and Romans, monsters were prodigies—warnings of impending calamity.

After Freud, monster stories were considered cathartic journeys into our unconscious—everybody contains a Mr. Hyde, and these stories give us a chance to "walk on the wild side." But in the denouement of most stories, the monster is killed and the psyche restored to civilized order. We can have our fun with the "torture porn" of Leatherface and Freddy Krueger or the erotic vampires, but this "vacation" to where the wild things are ultimately helps us return to our lives of quiet repression.

Any careful reading of Bram Stoker's *Dracula,* for example, will reveal not only a highly sexualized description of blood drinking but an erotic characterization of the count himself. Even John Polidori's original 1819 vampire tale *The Vampyre* describes the monster as a sexually attractive force. According to the critic Christopher Craft, Gothic monster tales—*Frankenstein, The Strange Case of Dr. Jekyll and Mr. Hyde, Dracula,* Anne Rice's Vampire Chronicles—rehearse a similar story structure. "Each of these texts first invites or admits a monster, then entertains and is entertained by monstrosity for some extended duration, until in its closing pages it expels or repudiates the monster and all the disruption that he/she/it brings," he writes.

A crucial but often-ignored aspect of monsterology is the role those beasties play in our moral imaginations. Recent experimental moral psychology has given us useful tools for looking at the way people actually do their moral thinking. Brain imaging, together with hypothetical ethical dilemmas about runaway trolley cars, can teach us a lot about our real value systems and actions. But another way to get at this subterranean territory is by looking at our imaginative lives.

Monsters can stand as symbols of human vulnerability and crisis, and as such they play imaginative foils for thinking about our own responses to menace. Part of our fascination with serial-killer monsters is that we (and our loved ones) are potentially vulnerable to sadistic violence—never mind that statistical probability renders such an attack almost laughable. Irrational fears are decidedly unfunny. We are vulnerable to both the inner and the outer forces. Monster stories and films only draw us in when we identify with the persons who are being chased, and we tacitly ask ourselves: Would I board up the windows to keep the zombies out or seek the open water? Would I go down to the basement after I hear the thump, and if so, would I bring the butcher knife or the fireplace poker? What will I do when I am vulnerable?

The comedy writer Max Brooks understands that dimension of monster stories very well. In books like *The Zombie Survival Guide* and *World War Z,* Brooks gives us painstaking, haunting, and hilarious advice about how best to meet our undead foes. For its April Fools' edition, the otherwise serious journal *Archaeology* interviewed Brooks, asking him (tongue firmly in cheek), "Does the archaeological record hold any zombie-related lessons for us today? What can our ancestors teach us about meeting and, ultimately, defeating the undead menace?" Brooks replied, "The greatest lesson our ancestors have to teach us is to remain both vigilant and unafraid. We must endeavor to emulate the ancient Romans; calm, efficient, treating zombies as just one more item on a rather mundane checklist. Panic is the undead's greatest ally, doing far more damage, in some cases, than the creatures themselves. The goal is to be prepared, not scared, to use our heads, and cut off theirs."

Brooks is unparalleled in parodying a well-worn monster tradition, but he wouldn't be so funny if we weren't already using monster stories to imagine strategies for facing enemies. The monster is a virtual sparring partner for our imagination. How will I avoid, assuage, or defeat my enemy? Will I have grace under pressure? Will I help others who are injured? Or will I be that guy who selfishly goes it alone and usually meets an especially painful demise?

In a significant sense, monsters are a part of our attempt to envision the good life, or at least the secure life. Our ethical convictions do not spring fully grown from our heads but must be developed in the context of real and imagined challenges. In order to discover our values, we have to face trials and tribulation, and monsters help us imaginatively rehearse. Imagining how we will face an unstoppable, powerful, and inhuman threat is an illuminating exercise in hypothetical reasoning and hypothetical feeling.

You can't know for sure how you will face a headless zombie, an alien face-hugger, an approaching sea monster, or a chainsaw-wielding psycho. Fortunately, you're unlikely to be put to the test. But you might face similarly terrifying trials. You might be assaulted; be put on the front lines of some war; or be robbed, raped, or otherwise harassed and assailed. We may be lucky enough to have had no real acquaintance with such horrors, but we have all nonetheless played them out in our mind's eye. And though we can't know for sure how we'll face an enemy soldier or a rapist, it doesn't stop us from imaginatively formulating responses. We use the imagination in order to establish our own agency in chaotic and uncontrollable situations.

People frequently underestimate the role of art and imagery in their own moral convictions. Through art (e.g., Shelley's *Frankenstein,* Hitchcock's *Psycho,* King's and Kubrick's *The Shining*), artists convey moral visions. Audiences can reflect on them, reject or embrace them, take inspiration from them, and otherwise be enriched beyond the entertainment aspect. Good monster stories can transmit moral truths to us by showing us examples of dignity and depravity without preaching or proselytizing.

But imagining monsters is not just the stuff of fiction. Picture yourself in the following scenario. On the evening of August 7, 1994, Bruce Shapiro entered a coffee bar in New Haven, Connecticut. Shapiro and his friends had entered the café and were relaxing at a table near the front door. Approximately fifteen other people were scattered around the bar, enjoying the evening. One of Shapiro's friends went up to the bar to get drinks. "Suddenly there was chaos," Shapiro explained in the *Nation* the next year, "as if a mortar shell had landed." He looked up to see a flash of metal and people leaping away from a thin, bearded man with a ponytail. Chairs and tables were knocked over, and Shapiro protected one of his friends by pulling her to the ground.

In a matter of minutes, the thin man, Daniel Silva, had managed to stab and seriously injure seven people in the coffee shop. Using a six-inch hunting knife, Silva jumped around the room and attacked with lightning speed. Two of Shapiro's friends were stabbed. After helping some others, Shapiro finally escaped the café. "I had gone no more than a few steps," he recalled, "when I felt a hard punch in my back followed instantly by the unforgettable sensation of skin and muscle tissue parting. Silva had stabbed me about six inches above my waist, just beneath my rib cage."

Shapiro fell to the pavement and cried out, "Why are you doing this?" Standing over him, Silva plunged the knife into Shapiro's chest, beneath his left shoulder. "You killed my mother" was the incoherent response that Silva offered his victim. Silva then pulled the knife out of Shapiro and rode off on a bicycle. He was soon apprehended and jailed.

Was Silva a monster? Not exactly. He was a mentally ill man who snapped and seemed to think that his mother had been wronged and felt some obscure need to avenge her. (She was, in fact, in a nearby hospital at the time, being treated for diabetes.) But from the perspective of raw experience, this horrifying event shares many qualities with the imagined monster attack. Shapiro and his unfortunate company were suddenly presented with a deadly, irrational, powerful force that sent them reeling for mere survival. And yet the victims demonstrated an impressive ability to reach out and help each other. While the victims were leaping away from Silva's angry knife blade, I suspect that he was for them, practically speaking, a true monster. I would never presume to correct them on that account. In such circumstances, many of us are sympathetic to the use of the monster epithet.

One of the fascinating aspects of Shapiro's experience is how people responded to his story after the fact. I have been suggesting that monster stories are encapsulations of the human feeling of vulnerability—the monster stories offer us the "disease" of vulnerability and its possible "cures" (in the form of heroes and coping strategies). Few monster stories remain indefinitely in the "threat phase." When fear is at a fever pitch, they always move on to the hero phase. Hercules slays the Hydra, George slays the dragon, medicine slays the alien virus, the stake and crucifix slay the vampire. Life and art mutually seek to conquer vulnerability. "Being a victim is a hard idea to accept," Shapiro explained, "even while lying in a hospital bed with tubes in veins, chest, penis, and abdomen. The spirit rebels against the idea of oneself as fundamentally powerless."

This natural rebellion may have prompted the most repeated question facing Shapiro when he got out of the hospital. When people learned of Daniel Silva's attack on seven victims, they asked, "Why didn't anyone try to stop him?" Shapiro always tried to explain how fast and confusing the attack was, but people failed to accept this. Shapiro, who was offended by the question, says, "The question carries not empathy but an implicit burden of blame; it really asks 'Why didn't *you* stop him?' It is asked because no one likes to imagine oneself a victim." We like to see ourselves as victors against every threat, but of course that's not reality.

Believers in human progress, from the Enlightenment to the present, think that monsters are disappearing. Rationality will pour its light into the dark corners and reveal the monsters to be merely chimeric. A familiar upshot of the liberal interpretation of monsters is to suggest that when we properly embrace difference, the monsters will vanish. According to this view, the monster concept is no longer useful in the modern world. If it hangs on, it does so like an appendix—useful once but hazardous now.

I disagree. The monster concept is still extremely useful, and it's a permanent player in the moral imagination because human vulnerability is permanent. The monster is a beneficial foe, helping us to virtually represent the obstacles that real life will surely send our way. As long as there are real enemies in the world, there will be useful dramatic versions of them in our heads.

In 2006, four armed men in Kandahar, Afghanistan, broke into the home of an Afghan headmaster and teacher named Malim Abdul Habib. The four men held Habib as they gathered his wife and children together, forcing them to watch as they stabbed Habib eight times and then decapitated him. Habib was the headmaster at Shaikh Mathi Baba high school, where he educated girls along with boys. The Taliban militants of the region, who are suspected in the beheading, see the education of girls as a violation of Islam (a view that is obviously not shared by the vast majority of Muslims). My point is simply this: if you can gather a man's family together at gunpoint and force them to watch as you cut off his head, then you are a monster. You don't just seem like one; you are one.

A relativist might counter by pointing out that American soldiers at Abu Ghraib tortured some innocent people, too. That, I agree, is true and astoundingly shameful, but it doesn't prove there are no real monsters. It only widens the category and recognizes monsters on both sides of an issue. Two sides calling each other monsters doesn't prove that monsters don't exist. In the case of the American torturer at Abu Ghraib and the Taliban beheader in Afghanistan, both epithets sound entirely accurate.

My own view is that the concept of monster cannot be erased from our language and thinking. It cannot be replaced by other more polite terms and concepts, because it still refers to something that has no satisfactory semantic substitute or refinement. The term's imprecision, within parameters, is part of its usefulness.

Terms like *monster* and *evil* have a lot of metaphysical residue on them, left over from the Western traditions. But even if we neuter the term from obscure theological questions about Cain, or metaphysical questions about demons, the language still successfully expresses a radical frustration over the inhumanity of some enemy. The meaning of monster is found in its context, in its use.

So this Halloween season, let us, by all means, enjoy our fright fest, but let's not forget to take monsters seriously, too. I'll be checking under my bed, as usual. But remember, things don't strike fear in our hearts unless our hearts are already seriously committed to something (e.g., life, limb, children, ideologies, whatever). Ironically, then, inhuman threats are great reminders of our own humanity. And for that we can all thank our zombies.

INTRODUCTION TO *RELIGION AND ITS MONSTERS*

Timothy Beal

Genesis 1, Take Two

"To a new world of gods and monsters!" declares Dr. Pretorius in James Whale's 1935 movie *The Bride of Frankenstein.* Pretorius, eager to create a female counterpart for the first monster, is counting himself and his co-creator Henry Frankenstein among the gods, and their creations among the monsters. Pretorius makes his divine aspirations clear in biblical terms, identifying himself with God in the creation story of Genesis 1: "I also have created life, as we say, *in God's own image....* Follow the lead of nature, or God . . . *male and female created he them . . . be fruitful and multiply.*" Pretorius seems to have no problem telling who and what the gods are, and who and what the monsters are.

For the viewers, however, things are not so clear. We tend to identify with the unnamed monster played by Boris Karloff far more than we do with his creators and his killers. We understand the monster in a way that none of the characters in the movie do. When the monster declares "I love dead, hate living," for example, Pretorius hears only that the Creature wants a companion who is living-dead like himself. We, on the other hand, understand this statement also as a lament in which the Creature expresses his loathing of life in this world of gods and monsters and his longing for death. The creator god misses this more profound meaning, but we do not.

Indeed, everyone in *The Bride of Frankenstein* is caricatured *except* the monster. As they chase after him, the frenzied mob of would-be monster killers confirms Nietzsche's warning that "whoever fights monsters should see to it that in the process he does not become a monster."[1] As the monster is raised high on a stake, crucifixion-style, in order to be tried and executed, the camera closes in on his face. We can almost hear him saying "My God, my God, why have you forsaken me?" But the monster's creator god, Henry Frankenstein, is a more discomforting divine image than even Pretorius: an indecisive, self-absorbed, grave-robbing fool.

Like his far more eloquent counterpart in Mary Shelley's 1818 novel *Frankenstein; or, The Modern Prometheus,* Whale's god-forsaken, posthumous monster is something of a theologian—not a theologian with all the answers but one who raises profound questions, questions that survive their answers. By playing God, does one inadvertently end up playing monster? More radically, does *being* God end up being monstrous? Who is more monstrous, the creatures who must live through this vale of tears, or the creator who put them here? What does it mean to be "monstrous," anyway? Are we not all rendered monstrous under God? Is our monstrosity in the image of God? Where *is* God in all this?

Very quickly we find ourselves in deeply unsettling theological territory, a territory traditionally called theodicy. Theodicy concerns divine justice in the face of unjustifiable suffering. Why do the wicked prosper and the righteous suffer? In a world such as ours, how can we possibly conceive of a just God? Indeed, Shelley's novel begins with an epigraph from the quintessential English theodicy *Paradise Lost* by John Milton, whose explicit although inevitably unrealized aim is to "justify the ways of God to men." Shelley's epigraph draws us to the theodic question, which echoes far beyond any answer, and which will be posed again and again by the monster to Victor Frankenstein throughout the novel:

> Did I request thee, Maker, from my clay
> To mold Me man? Did I solicit thee
> From darkness to promote me?
>
> —*Paradise Lost* X.743–45[2]

The voice of the monster is the audacious voice of theodicy. It is addressed not only to the creator Frankenstein but also to the creator God. Why did you make me? Why did you put me here? What were you thinking? What kind of a world is this? What kind of divine justice is this? What kind of God are you? The monster in Shelley's novel, as in Whale's movie, stands for these questions and terrifying religious uncertainties. His questions pry at cracks in the world's foundations that open onto abysses of unknowing. In this unhallowed space of theodicy, opened by the creature's tragic appeals to its creator, clear distinctions between gods and monsters get awfully blurry. The horror of *Frankenstein* is a profoundly theological horror.

Religion and Its Monsters, Monsters and Their Religion

Most of us do not go to monster movies or read Gothic monster tales in search of religion, at least not consciously. Nor do we go to church or temple or ashram in search of monsters. Yet, as Frankenstein's monster has already begun to indicate, religion and monsters have more to do with each other than one might initially assume. Indeed, when it comes to gods and monsters, Pretorius's "new world" is not so new after all.

Paradox of the Monstrous

Monsters are in the world but not of the world. They are paradoxical personifications of *otherness within sameness*. That is, they are threatening figures of anomaly within the well-established and accepted order of things. They represent the outside that has gotten inside, the beyond-the-pale that, much to our horror, has gotten into the pale.

One helpful way of thinking about this paradoxical sense of the monster as a horrific figure of otherness within sameness is by way of Sigmund Freud's concept of the *unheimlich*, that is, the "unhomely" or "uncanny." If *heimlich* refers to that which belongs within the four walls of the house, inspiring feelings of restfulness and security, then *unheimlich* refers to that which threatens one's sense of "at-homeness," not from the outside but from *within* the house.[3] The *unheimlich* is in some sense what is in the house without belonging there, the outside that is inside. The horror of the unhomely experience, then, involves the awareness that something that should be outside the house is in it. It is an experience of otherness within sameness.

For Freud, "home" refers primarily to individual human consciousness. For our purposes, we may extend the sense of "home" in the idea of the *heimlich* to mean anything from self to society to cosmos. That is, this *heimlich* feeling of security and "at-homeness" may refer to one's confidence in the meaning, integrity, and well-being of oneself as a subject (the body or self as "house"). Or it may refer to one's confidence in the meaning, integrity, and well-being of one's society or culture (the "house of culture," as Herbert Marcuse puts it).[4] Or it may refer to one's confidence in the meaning, integrity, and well-being of the entire cosmos (the world ecology as "house"). Taken in this very broad way, the *unheimlich* is that which invades one's sense of personal, social, or cosmic order and security—the feeling of being at home in oneself, one's society, and one's world. The *unheimlich* is the other within, that which is "there" in the house but cannot be comprehended by it or integrated into it.

Monsters are personifications of the *unheimlich*. They stand for what endangers one's sense of at-homeness, that is, one's sense of security, stability, integrity, well-being, health, and meaning. They make one feel *not at home at home*. They are figures of chaos and disorientation *within* order and orientation, revealing deep insecurities in one's faith in oneself, one's society, and one's world.

Demonizing and Deifying

In his glory days as the vampire in *Dracula,* Bela Lugosi was a celebrity icon, idolized by fans from Broadway to Hollywood. He was not a monster, but he played one on stage and screen. In his last years, the aging star became, as they say, a *monstre sacré*. Still later, after his death and his burial in full Dracula costume and makeup, Goth bands like Bauhaus canonized him as their sacred icon, the ultimate incarnation of Count Dracula for a new generation of monster devotees. Thus Lugosi, like the monster he played, has become a *monstre sacré* in more ways than one.

In what ways can a monster be, or become, sacred?

We humans respond to the monster as a personification of the *unheimlich*, of otherness within sameness, and our responses range from demonization to deification. Often we *demonize* the monster as a threat not only to "our" order but also to the order of the gods or God. In this way the monstrous other who threatens "us" and "our world" is represented as an enemy of God and then is exorcized from the right order of things and sent to some sort of Hell. "Our" order is identified with the sacred order against a diabolically monstrous chaos. Such is the fate of Apophis in Egyptian tradition and of the sea monster Leviathan in Psalm 74 and Isaiah 27. Think also of the fate of the vampire in Bram Stoker's *Dracula,* as well as of many other monsters from the past century of horror novels and movies. By demonizing our monsters, we keep God on our side.

In other cases, however, the monster is *deified* as a revelation of sacred otherness. Its coming into the world is represented as a *hierophany*, that is, a revelation of the holy. Here the monster is an envoy of the divine or the sacred as radically other than "our" established order of things. It is an invasion of what we might call *sacred chaos* and disorientation within self, society, and world. Such is the case with Tiamat in the Babylonian *Enuma Elish* as well as with Leviathan and Behemoth in the divine speech from the whirlwind in the book of Job. Such is also the case, I propose, with the vampire in F. W. Murnau's film *Nosferatu,* as well as with Cthulhu and other monster gods in the stories of H. P. Lovecraft. If demonizing the monster keeps God on our side, then deifying it often puts us in a world of religious disorientation and horror.

Often what we find is not simply one reaction or the other but both. The monster is often *both* demonized and deified, revealing a deep sense of ambivalence about the relation between the monstrous and the divine, and intensifying the sense of paradox.

Monstrum Tremendum, Mysterium Tremendum

We are less accustomed to thinking of the monstrous as a figure of divine revelation or an envoy of the sacred than we are to thinking of it as demonic or "evil." Yet the monster's religious import is rooted in the word itself: *monster* derives from the Latin *monstrum,* which is related to the verbs *monstrare* ("show" or "reveal") and *monere* ("warn" or "portend"), and which sometimes refers to a divine portent that reveals the will or judgment of God or the gods. In this sense a *monstrum* is a message that breaks into this world from the realm of the divine. Even in the ancient and cruel notion of "monstrous births" as revelations of divine judgment, the otherness of the monster is considered not only horrifically *unnatural* but also horrifically *supernatural,* charged with religious import.[5]

Likewise, the *experience* of horror in relation to the monstrous is often described in terms reminiscent of religious experience. Both are often characterized as an encounter with mysterious otherness that elicits a vertigo-like combination of both fear and desire, repulsion and attraction. Both religious experience and horror are characterized as encounters with something simultaneously awesome and awful—a feeling captured in the older spelling, "aweful," which still retains its sense of awe. Nowhere is the affinity between horror and religious experience drawn out more fully than in Rudolph Otto's *The Idea of the Holy* (*Das Heilige,* 1917). Working from the idea of the sublime in Immanuel Kant and Edmund Burke, Otto describes religious experience as an encounter with the *mysterium tremendum,* that is, a radically other mystery that brings on a stupefying combination of fascination and terror, wonder and dread. It is "something inherently wholly other, whose kind and character are incommensurable with our own, and before which we therefore recoil in a wonder that strikes us chill and numb."[6] For Otto, "the monstrous" (*das Ungeheuere*), like the "uncanny" (*unheimlich*), is "a fairly exact expression for the numinous in its aspects of mystery, awefulness, majesty, augustness and 'energy'; nay, even the fascination is dimly felt in it."[7] For him the monster is an aweful *monstrum tremendum.* Indeed, Otto interprets the monsters Leviathan and Behemoth in the book of Job as quintessential representations of the monstrous as a figure for the wholly other.

Of course, Otto (and others who have read horror as religious experience à la Otto) presumes that there is such a transcendent wholly other, a sacred that is not reducible to a cultural or psychological phenomenon. You need not agree. Although Otto, in his introduction to *The Idea of the Holy,* discourages readers from reading his book if they have not had such an experience of the sacred, I do not. This book is not an altar call to the church of the monstrous. The connections we make between the monstrous and the divine, and between horror and religious experience, do not necessarily mean that we have to *confess* monsters as revelations of the divine or the sacred. Because they are sometimes represented as such does not mean that we have to believe in them. Indeed, we may decide instead, following Freud, that the horror inspired by the monstrous, like other experiences of the *unheimlich,* is best explained as the *return of the repressed.* Whereas for Otto, the *unheimlich* is an experience of the radically transcendent other, a completely unhomely experience of the *mysterium* that has broken into the home from a wholly other realm, for Freud, there is no such thing as wholly otherness or radical transcendence. What Otto calls "wholly other" Freud would call "other" only insofar as it has been repressed. For Freud the *unheimlich* is only "outside the house" (the house of the self, the house of culture, the house of the cosmos) insofar as it is hidden within the house. It is a revelation not of the wholly other but of a repressed otherness within the self.[8] The monster, as personification of the *unheimlich,* stands for that which has broken out of the subterranean basement or the locked closet where it has been banished from consciousness.

My interest here is not in determining what the monstrous *really* is (whether an envoy of the sacred, the returned of the repressed, or both, or something else). Rather, I want to explore those places where representations of the monstrous and the religious converge. In those points of convergence, the monstrous becomes a site for religious reflection. I am not so much constructing a theology of the monstrous as I am exploring the monstrous as a form of theological expression. What, for example, can we learn about theological discourse in biblical literature when we approach it through its monsters? By the same token, how does the ostensibly nonreligious popular culture of horror often become a venue for doing theology?

Both monsters and religions are always culturally specific. There are only particular religions, and particular monsters, and no one book can hope to be comprehensive of all that gets called religion and all that gets called monstrous. How do monsters and religion converse in other cultural fields? How are they related, for example, in Japanese graphic novels (mangas) and animation? My aim is not only to rethink the monstrous in terms of religion, however, but also to rethink religion in terms of the monstrous. It strikes me that exploring religion via its monsters presents a challenge to the common conception of religion as being exclusively about the establishment of order against chaos. This conception was given its classic (that is, normative) formulation in Mircea Eliade's *The Sacred and the Profane,* a book that has exercised powerful influence over many scholars and innumerable college students in Introduction to Religion courses over the past half-century. Eliade describes religion as essentially *cosmogonic,* or world creative. Religion is about creating and maintaining a sacred cosmic order against chaos.[9] Religion is about establishing and maintaining sacred space and sacred time against the "formless expanse" of chaos surrounding it:[10]

> The former is the world (more precisely, our world), the cosmos; every thing outside it is no longer a cosmos but a sort of "other world," a foreign, chaotic

space, peopled by ghosts, demons, "foreigners." . . . It is not difficult to see why the religious moment [i.e., the manifestation of the sacred] implies the cosmogonic moment. The sacred reveals absolute reality and at the same time makes orientation possible; hence it founds the world in the sense that it fixes the limits and establishes the very order of the world.[11]

Later Eliade reiterates this idea of religion in language that indicates where he sees the monsters in this scenario of sacred order against demonic chaos: "An attack on 'our world' is equivalent to an act of revenge by the mythical dragon, who rebels against the work of the gods, the cosmos, and struggles to annihilate it. 'Our' enemies belong to the powers of chaos."[12] Here religion is about the sacred and the sacred is about order, foundation and orientation over against chaos and disorientation, which are demonized. Certainly this is one aspect of religion in many cultural contexts, and we will see it operative in those instances when the monstrous is demonized as a force of chaos that threatens "our" sacred order. One of those instances is the vision of the great dragon in the Apocalypse of John in the New Testament. In fact, this is the fallen angel turned diabolic dragon to which Eliade is referring in the passage above. Much of contemporary horror functions in just the same way, as a shoring up and consecration of the established order of things (especially social orders that distinguish "us" from "them," self from other). Yet there are other cases in which the monstrous-chaotic is *identified with* the divine or the sacred against cosmic order. So it is in a number of ancient Near Eastern religious texts, as well as in some biblical texts about Leviathan, and throughout contemporary horror literature and film. As we get to know these monsters, what they often reveal is a divinity or a sacredness that is, like many of our religions and like many of ourselves, caught in endless, irreducible tensions between order and chaos, orientation and disorientation, self and other, foundation and abyss.

Religion is never without its monsters. Whether demonized or deified or both, no matter how many times we kill our monsters, they keep coming back for more. Not just Dracula but all monsters are undead. Maybe they keep coming back because they still have something to say or to show us about our world and ourselves. Maybe that is the scariest part.

Notes

1. Friedrich Nietzsche, *Beyond Good and Evil: Prelude to a Philosophy of the Future,* trans. Walter Kaufman (New York: Random House, 1966), section 146.

2. Mary Wollstonecraft Shelley, *Frankenstein; or, The Modern Prometheus,* ed. M. K. Joseph (Oxford: Oxford University Press, 1969), 1.

3. Sigmund Freud, "The Uncanny," *Standard Edition* 17 (1955): 222, 226.

4. Herbert Marcuse, *Eros and Civilization: A Philosophical Inquiry into Freud* (Boston: Beacon, 1955), 72.

5. On early conceptions of the idea of "monstrous births" (*teras* in Greek, *monstrum* in Latin), see Marie-Hélène Huet, *Monstrous Imagination* (London: Harvard University Press, 1993), whose larger focus is on the closely related history of the idea that "monstrous births" were divine revelations of the mother's imagination, especially of her unfulfilled desires (esp. 1–10, 61–78). This led to ideas about art as the offspring of an artist's monstrous imagination.

6. Rudolph Otto, *The Idea of the Holy: An Inquiry into the Non-Rational Factor in the Idea of the Divine and Its Relation to the Rational,* 2nd ed., trans. John W. Harvey (New York: Oxford University Press, 1950), 28. Otto's essay has had tremendous influence in studies of horror as religious experience. See, e.g., S. L. Varnado, *Haunted Presence: The Numinous in Gothic Fiction* (Tuscaloosa: University of Alabama Press, 1987). See also the critical discussion of this trend in Noël Carroll, *The Philosophy of Horror or Paradoxes of the Heart* (New York: Routledge, 1990), 165–67.

7. Otto, *Idea of the Holy,* 40.

8. Freud, "The Uncanny," 241. There are many recent studies of modern horror as the return of the repressed, including, most recently, Valdine Clemens, *The Return of the Repressed: Gothic Horror from "The Castle of Otranto" to "Alien"* (New York: SUNY Press, 1999); see also Eve Kosofsky Sedgwick, *The Coherence of Gothic Conventions* (New York: Methuen, 1986). In film studies, particular attention has been paid to horror as the return of repressed sexuality that threatens established social norms of heterosexuality, monogamy and family. Robin Wood, in "An Introduction to the American Horror Film," in *Planks of Reason: Essays on the Horror Film,* ed. Barry Keith Grant (Metuchen: Scarecrow Press, 1984), summarizes the sociological implications: "that in a society built on monogamy and family there will be enormous surplus of sexual energy that will have to be repressed; and that what is repressed must always strive to return" (177). See also Wood, "Return of the Repressed," *Film Comment* 14 (July–August 1978). A particularly influential psychoanalytic study of the horror of abjection is Julia Kristeva, *Powers of Horror: An Essay on Abjection,* trans. Leon S. Roudiez (New York: Columbia University Press, 1982).

9. Mircea Eliade, *The Sacred and the Profane: The Nature of Religion,* trans. Willard R. Trask (New York: Harcourt Brace, 1959).

10. Eliade, 20.

11. Eliade, 29–30.

12. Eliade, 48.

THE SELF'S CLEAN AND PROPER BODY

Margrit Shildrick

I N ORDER TO SHED MORE LIGHT on the predicament of the monstrous in
Western thought, my purpose in this chapter is to investigate further the precarious place of the body, and to bring it into relation with dominant conceptions
of the self. During the last few years, both feminist scholarship and postmodernist philosophy have opened up afresh an interest in monstrous corporeality that
moves far beyond a well-established clinical concern—where therapeutic modification is the major issue—to an altogether more discursive reading. Like the
well-established configuration of matter and mother, to which it is also supple-
mental in the Derridean sense, the monstrous is somehow both excessive to and
yet, as I shall show, embedded in the structuration of the Western logos. What is
at stake is not only the categorical integrity of bodies that matter but also the
hitherto taken for granted stability and autonomy of the singular human subject
as the center of the logos, of a self that is foundational without being embodied,
and a body whose integrity is so unquestioned that it may be forgotten, transcended.
Against this, the confused and essentially fluid corporeality of monsters, makes
them an ideal location for an enquiry into the closure of both subjects and bodies
that characterizes modernist philosophical discourse. As I have suggested elsewhere, the issue "is one of leaky boundaries, wherein the leakiness of the logos . . .
is mirrored by the collapse of the human itself as a bounded being."[1]

It is not, of course, that modernist philosophy has shown any great interest
in the organic substantial body as such but rather in the human as the abstract

universal marker of the site of foundational voice, vision, and vitality. In one major tradition, the body itself is simply the mechanical housing of the subject, and as such may be bracketed out, unrepresented, transcended. As Descartes puts it in the *Meditations,* "although the whole mind seems to be united to the whole body, yet, if a foot, or an arm, or any other part, is separated from my body, it is certain that, on that account, nothing has been taken away from my mind."[2] The mind, in short, is an indivisible thinking substance, exempt from the laws of natural science that determine the nature of the body. The human has been of interest then not as a biologically defined category but only to the extent that the term is elided with that of *person*—the possessor, conventionally, in a Lockean formulation, of a sense of self as a continuing subject of its own experiences.[3] I will not rehearse here the by now well-known arguments identifying the subject of the Western logos with the human male[4] but will simply mark that insofar as their difference is specified, women are the nonsubject other, the excluded, the embodied, the monstrous. As the masculinist subject surveys his world, he sees only that which reflects his own self-presence, the confirmation of his own wholeness and completion.

As one alternative among the multiple histories of thinking ontology, the underlying question of what it is to be a subject, and experience oneself and the world as such, is addressed increasingly through a phenomenological approach, which is perhaps more in keeping with our commonsense understanding of our embodied selves. Unlike the mind–body split effected by the Cartesian tradition, in phenomenology, abstract selfhood is seen as inseparable from material being-in-the-world. The two are intertwined such that it is in the spatial and temporal extension of our bodies that we become our selves. It is a model that calls for a radical rethinking of the concept of embodiment. Moreover, as Merleau-Ponty understands it, perception is no longer the inner representation of an outer world in the mind of a distinct perceiver but is constituted in the "organic relationship" between the self and the world.[5] In consequence, the order of perception is from the first an interdependent relation between the perceiver and the perceived, in which the seeing "I" is decentered. More important, Merleau-Ponty stresses the reversibility of every body as a visible-seer or tangible-toucher; in other words, the status of the self as a sensible-sentient being collapses the rigid distinctions both between mind and body, and between subject and object. Above all, it is in the application of corporeal schema—habitual ways of seeing, touching, and listening—that the body is constituted as meaningful and integral to our sense of self.

Although in our active relation to the world we remain open in principle to transformation, there is nonetheless a certain solidification of perception such that we can reflexively experience our embodied selves in more or less consistent ways. What matters is the practical competence in relation to our material context that enables us to *act* appropriately prior to conscious reflection or intent. As

I read to the end of a page, for example, I turn it without thought. Yet, even when our own bodies are taken as that of which we can be most certain, the finite material site of the bounded individual, and the point of interface with a social world, there remains a breach between self and body to the extent that the latter can betray us as that which is beyond logic and reason. Even in the phenomenological tradition of Merleau-Ponty which stresses in particular the unity of matter and mind expressed through the dynamic being-in-the-world of bodies, the healthy body—as I have analyzed in more detail elsewhere—far from being consistently present to us, is scarcely experienced at all.[6] It is what Drew Leder refers to as "the absent body."[7] Once, however, it is broken—that is, diseased, damaged, or otherwise unwhole—the body forces itself into our consciousness and that comfortable absence is lost. The body is now perceived but is experienced as other. As Leder puts it, "the body is no longer alien-as-forgotten, but precisely as remembered, a sharp searing presence threatening the self."[8] In consequence, there is a sense in which embodiment, in being symbolically associated with the disruption of the subject, runs the same risk of being ontologically devalued, being seen as potentially monstrous, in phenomenology as it does in more conventional philosophies.

There is too a related problem in that despite the nature of embodiment being a fundamental component of phenomenology, the method nonetheless assumes as standard a "normal" model of corporeal development, and finds it difficult to theorize from the grossly disordered body. I don't mean to suggest that the phenomenological perspective has not already figured prominently in staging the ontological and epistemological consequences of corporeal anomalies—be they the result of illness, trauma or congenital disorders—but rather that the integrated and fully functioning body remains an implicit standard. In other words, marked differences in embodiment are seen a priori as deviations from a singular model rather than as equally valid alternatives. Clearly there are many corporeal forms which signal an acute loss of previous bodily integrity and corresponding function, but in the case of congenital conditions in particular, negative comparison to a putative model of normality seems more a matter of disciplinary regulation and control than of pragmatic value. But what if the focus were on the "abnormal," on the explicitly monstrous? At this point, it is not my intention to offer a phenomenological account, but just as feminist phenomenologists such as Iris Marion Young and Ros Diprose have moved to disrupt the assumption of a gender-neutral, ageless, and universalized body as the center of lived experience, so too we may gain further insights by theorizing nonnormative morphology, not as a failure of form (inviting therapeutic modification), but as an-other way of being.[9] The existence of monstrosity may serve to define by comparison and opposition the delimited corporeality and secure subjectivity of the majority, but what is important is the realization that the standard is not normal but normative.

The question that haunts the Western imagination—"Who am I?"—and its implicit companion—"Where did I come from?"—has been answered conventionally by reference to a sense of self having a transcendent detachment from the material business of the world, or at least effective autonomy within it. To be a self is above all to be distinguished from the other, to be ordered and discrete, secure *within* the well-defined boundaries of the body rather than actually being the body. Although from time to time we may experience ourselves out-of-body, what rarely happens—and then it is defined as a special type of madness—is that we should either inhabit the body of another or find our own bodies shared—invaded we would say—by another.[10] And while the narcissistic pleasure to be derived from perceiving our image from the outside, most commonly in the mirror, may also evoke the sensation of strangeness and misrecognition, it is the unfamiliarity of the material body and the space it occupies that strikes us, not the perception that another subject might occupy that body. In short, though the *integration* of mind and body may be contested by a Western discourse of transcendent subjectivity, there are few doubts as to which minds and bodies go together. Self-identity may always and necessarily be a case of misrecognition as Lacan would say, but it is precisely the mapping of the boundaries between singular selves and bodies and those of others that authorizes our being-in-the-world as subjects. Moreover, the inherent exclusivity of such a closure is marked, as I have noted already, by the realization that the sovereign "I," who defines himself against the other, the nonself, describes an intrinsically masculine subject.

Given that the Western logos is at best ambivalent about the ontological status of the body, the putative split between mind and body that it puts into play has not resulted in disinterest in or disengagement from questions of corporeal being. Contra Descartes, we are obsessed with bodies, such that the desire to know oneself, to establish identity, involves always both the interface between singular bodies and the "difficult, even intractable, relations between self and body."[11] To the extent that the Western notion of subjectivity in general is both guaranteed and contested by those who do not, indeed cannot, unproblematically occupy the subject position, the self-present subject who defines himself against all that is nonself need scarcely acknowledge his own corporeality. The assumption is that if sovereign minds are housed in appropriate bodies, then those who are "inappropriate/d others" cannot occupy unproblematically the subject position. It is not, then, normative morphology that engages the greatest attention, but those bodily forms—the monstrous, the physically vulnerable, the disabled, the congenitally different like conjoined twins or hermaphrodites[12]—which most clearly challenge the distinctions both between mind and body and between body and body.

In terms of modernist ontology, epistemology and ethics, the ideal parameters of thought and action in the social world point to an inviolable self/body that is secure, distinct, closed, and autonomous. In setting up a model of such invulnerability, it is inevitable that for all of us there is a struggle to maintain the necessary boundaries, while for a substantial minority who experience some form of corporeal breakdown or congenital anomaly, the ideal is beyond reach. Despite such a plethora of antithetical lived forms, however, morphological difference continues to figure the monstrous. What happens, in effect, is that normative discourse, which is propelled by the notion of discrete and autonomous sites of being and agency, sets itself against such a blurring of distinctions and attempts to maintain physical and moral detachment from those for whom the boundaries of embodied selfhood are uncertain or plainly breached. Now those lines of separation are not merely symbolic, but are realized quite literally in the material of the body. Accordingly, as the most visible boundary of all, the skin is both the limit of the embodied self and the site of potentially transgressive psychic investments. In consequence, any compromise of the organic unity and self-completion of the skin may signal monstrosity. Many fairly common congenital conditions are counted as deformities precisely because they breach the external margins of the body. Spina bifida, cleft palate, and exomphalos, for example, are all the result of a lack of material closure, the more serious arising initially from the failure of the infolding primitive streak to establish ever new but securely consolidated boundaries in the increasingly complex organization of the early embryo. What is more notable, however, is that the nonnormative development of the surface phenomenon can be taken to denote, both in the present day and historically, a far more significant disturbance to the structure of being.

One need only look at the many representations of the Monster of Cracow (Figure 16.1)—a sixteenth-century favorite displaying both excess and displacement—to appreciate how violently monstrosity might breach the borders of humanity. The human-born infant is beset not only with manifold excrescences which burst through the surface membrane, but by an inhuman mix of fur, horn, skin, and scale. It is, in other words, indiscriminately transspecies in appearance. Moreover, the deformities constitute a multiplicity of additional orifices, the creature being described as having apes' faces instead of breasts, dogs' heads at both elbows and knees, toads' feet, and cats' eyes under the navel.[13] The emphasis on the points of exchange between inner and outer marks the creature's monstrosity as a matter of being as much as of appearance. Although it plays no part in the Cracow monster's form, it is perhaps worthy of note that racial difference too has often been reduced to a focus on the sites of the body where there is an open intersection between inside and outside. The attention given to the forms of the mouths, noses, breasts and genitalia[14] may well speak, in its concentration on erogenous zones, to an eroticization of the racial other, but I would suggest that even more is at stake. As breaches in the body's surfaces—points of vulnerability for us all—such sites, in their evident or supposed difference, mark an uncertainty

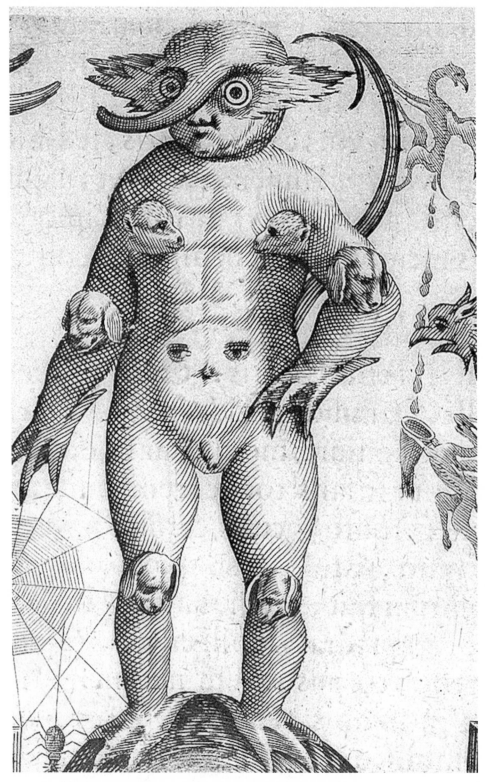

Figure 16.1. The Monster of Cracow in *De monstrorum natura, caussis et differentis* (Licetus 1634).

about the putatively self-contained human being. Moreover, as with the Monster of Cracow, their contaminatory potential is clear.

That unusual bodily form has a long history of provoking fear, repugnance, and frequently condemnation is widely evidenced in a variety of Western texts. I am not suggesting that those are the only responses but rather that whatever other explanations and interests are predominant at any particular time and cultural location, there does seem to be a continuous thread of anxiety. The elision of ethical and physical affronts to the norms of human being has its roots in classical antiquity. If Aristotelian virtue is that which strikes the harmonious balance between the vices of excess and deficiency, the very same characteristics by which Aristotle defines monstrosity, then it is a simple step to corporeal disorder inviting moral condemnation, and indeed the institutional, as well as individual, response of erasure. In his history of the monstrous races, for example, Friedman cites customary Roman law, which states, "A father shall immediately put to death a son recently born, who is a monster, or who has a form different from that of members of the human race,"[15] while wonder books and broadside ballads give endless accounts of infants being destroyed at birth, sometimes along with their mothers. As we have seen, for medieval Christianity, with its belief in human descent from the bodily perfection of the single progenitor, Adam, morphological difference represented the corruption of the species either by miscegenation, or as a result of divine punishment for collective or individual sin. In Bateman's account of the Monster of Cracow he makes clear that the creature is born to "honest and gentle" parents, thus allaying the suspicion of parental transgression. Nonetheless, the monstrous birth has portentous value in that it warns of the general dangers of sin, and reminds the sixteenth-century viewers of the coming judgment of the Lord. And despite the partial turn in subsequent centuries toward more scientific forms of knowledge, those exist alongside a persistent belief that nonnormative bodies of all kinds are marked by moral deficiency.

Given the highly negative historical value accorded the monstrous, the term may be suppressed today as an explicit description while still functioning implicitly in relation to those whose bodies transgress normative standards. The inference that people with disease or disabilities are morally at fault is clearly evident in the blame and stigma attached, for example, to cancer and subsequently to HIV/AIDS in the twentieth century.[16] In the case of AIDS in particular, the initial widespread public reception of the condition as figuring a gay plague, from which blameless heterosexuals were exempt, speaks to the notion that those affected were paying for sins in their past. The disruption of corporeal integrity and the open display of bodily vulnerability is always a moment for anxiety and very often for hostility. Where disabled people in contemporary developed societies are, more generally, accorded all sorts of legal and social rights which overtly challenge discrimination against them, there is nevertheless a persistent unease occasioned by corporeal difference. That such differences are more likely to be addressed by measures that are designed to minimize or cover over their effects, rather than by full acknowledgment of them, does little to allay dis-ease. It is as though the characteristic split between mind and body that marks modernist discourse enables us to bracket out the lived materiality of the flesh, especially when it threatens our sense of what Kristeva calls "the self's clean and proper body."[17] Yet the divisions which operate between body and body and between mind and body are under pressure from the very liminality of the monster—in whatever form it might take—and by its refusal to stay in the place of the other. For all that the monster may be cast as a figure vulnerable in its own right by reason of its own lack of fixed form and definition and its putative status as an outsider, what causes anxiety is that it threatens to expose the vulnerability at the heart of the ideal model of body/self.

Although we might think of the Monster of Cracow, for example, as a semi-mythological construct that stands in contradistinction to the "natural" possibilities of the human body, it should be recalled that *techne* is never absent from the construction of monsters, and indeed from bodies more generally. As a model of the proper in which everything is in its place and the chaotic aspects of the natural are banished, the so-called normal and natural body—and particularly its smooth and closed-up surface—always remains to be realized. The task, as Bakhtin describes it, is one of normalization: "That which protrudes, bulges, sprouts or branches off . . . is eliminated, hidden, or moderated. All orifices of the body are closed. The basis of the image is the individual, strictly limited mass, the impenetrable façade."[18] In short, the normal body is materialized through a set of reiterative practices that speak to the instability and leakiness of the singular standard. The monster, then, rather than being simply an instance of otherness, reminds us always of what must be abjected from the self's clean and proper body. Even the Monster of Cracow's gross violation of external order, its suturing together of surfaces that should remain apart, its excrescences and orifices that "lead . . . beyond the body's limited space or into the body's depths," cannot disguise its claim on the human.[19] It remains a figure of both horror and fascination. And as Kristeva makes clear, the abject is never completely externalized: alongside their external manifestation, monsters leave a trace embedded within. In collapsing the distinctions between self and other, monsters constitute an undecidable absent presence at the heart of human being.[20]

The monstrous may of course be the openly crafted result of techno-organic creation like Haraway's cyborg or of intentionally transgressive conjunctions and displacements of body parts, as in the novel *Geek Love,* but for the remainder of this chapter I want to look at the epistemological and ontological status of wholly organic, unquestionably human, beings whose difference is always already evident.[21] The monstrosity they evidence is not, then, the result of accident, degeneration or disease, nor yet of self-willed modification, but rather the very condition of life. Nonetheless, such congenital monstrosity—especially as it pertains to my later focus on conjoined twins—facilitates an understanding of the processes of normalization that underpin the so-called natural body. As I understand it, the concept of corporeal modification implies reference to a biological given that might be denaturalized, or at very least to the notion of a standard morphology which might then be altered or transgressed. But once such a standard of bodyliness is understood as an impossible ideal in itself—as something to be achieved rather than as a given—then it makes good sense to take the monstrous as the starting point rather than the end point of any enquiry into the lived body. I shall be looking, then, at the issue of body modification as an intervention into the always already unstable corpus, whereby what is intended is not the practice of transgression, but is on the contrary a matter of managing—often clinically—what is inherently unruly. It is a process of normalization, albeit one fraught with anxieties.

The clinical encounter, then, though putatively directed toward the relief of supposedly fragile bodies—those affected by viral illnesses, disabilities, or the breakdown of autoimmunity, for example—is at least as much concerned with the restoration of normative forgetfulness. Indeed, it is hardly the broken body that is fragile and vulnerable, though clearly that may be perceived as monstrous—as the metaphors of cancer and AIDS in particular make clear—but the "normal" body itself. Although the monstrosity of chronic disease or disability overtly undermines any notion of a securely embodied subject, that ordinary body is not given but is always an achievement. It is a body that requires constant maintenance and/or modification to hold off the ever-present threat of disruption: extra digits are excised at birth, tongues are shortened in Down's syndrome children, noses are reshaped, warts removed, prosthetic limbs fitted, "healthy" diets recommended, HRT prescribed. And in such cases, it is the *unmodified* body that is seen as unnatural, in need of "corrective" interventions. In short, the normal body is materialized through a set of reiterative practices that speak to the instability of the singular standard. That the standard may be achieved, or at least approximated, by material intervention is of course highly dependent on levels of technological expertise developed during the last hundred years, but there is already evident in historical texts an understanding that regular morphology could not be simply taken for granted. Writing in the seventeenth century, Thomas Bedford argued that what is demonstrated by "monstrous and misfeatured births" is "that it is a singular mercy of God when the births of the womb are not misformed, when they receive their fair and perfect feature."[22] In the modern day we are less likely to attribute flawless morphology to God, but we may well expect the gynecologist or surgeon to eliminate or tidy up any defects which offend against the narrow canons of normality.

The construction and maintenance of the self's clean and proper body is not, however, a matter of material practice alone but is fully imbricated with the discursive mechanisms that constitute psychic unity. As I have indicated already, the security of human being is unsettled constantly by what Kristeva calls the abject, which she defines as "what disturbs identity, system and order. What does not respect boundaries, positions, rules. The in-between, the ambiguous, the composite."[23] Human monsters, then, both fulfill the necessary function of the binary opposite that confirms the normality and centrality of the accultured self, and at the same time threaten to disrupt that binary by being all too human. Although the monstrous may provoke both the fascination and horror accorded the absolute other, that response is never unproblematic but spills over into the anxiety and repulsion that are occasioned by the violation of internal order. And as Kristeva makes clear, that which is abjected is never completely externalized. It is, then, in their failure to wholly and only occupy the place of the other that such monsters betray the fragility of the distinctions by which the human subject is fixed and maintained as fully present to itself and autonomous. In collapsing the boundaries between self and other, monsters constitute an undecidable absent presence at the heart of human being. Alongside their external manifestation, they also leave a trace embedded within, that, in Derridean terms, operates as the signifier not of difference but of *différance*. What is at stake throughout is the risk of indifferentiation. In illustration of the operation and force of such theoretical considerations, I want to look specifically at a set of embodied forms which radically challenge normative standards of human selfhood.

The phenomenon of conjoined twins has been recorded throughout history, and it is estimated that, even prior to the development of present-day surgical techniques of separation, several hundred have lived to adulthood.[24] As a thread that runs through the sociohistory of monstrosity and teratology, the material manifestation of the body that is not one—whether as functioning adults or dying neonates—demands specific epistemological and ontological reflection in which the issue of the boundaries of subjecthood, and in earlier periods of a soul, is particularly acute. I will leave aside the very many recorded instances of the supposed conjunction of human and animal bodies to concentrate on what remains to this day an area of deep-seated fascination. Unlike the hybrid variety which leaves room for a wholly exclusionary approach, the incidence of corporeal doubling in which both bodies are visibly human is highly disruptive to Western notions of individual agency and personal identity. Rather than such twins being absolutely other to ourselves—and that response as I have indicated is in any case finally untenable—they are in effect the manifestation of the mirroring process that underlies and founds identity in the doubling of the selfsame.[25] Textual evidence suggests that conjoined twins have always counted among the monstrous, though their portentous value was sometimes positive rather than negative.[26]

Although most undoubtedly died at birth or soon after, they are often portrayed in archival texts as fully formed children or adults, thus throwing up not simply the urgent question of which twin has the soul but also whether one or both should be considered autonomous persons. Medieval and early modern theologians adopted a kind of fail-safe with regard to baptism, which required the priest to baptize one, and then turn to the other head or body with the words: "If you are baptised, I do not baptise you, but if you are not yet baptised, I baptise you."[27] It remains unclear how great a degree of separation was required for the formula to be invoked, but the doubling of limbs alone was not sufficient. Excess is merely monstrous, whereas the conjunction of that which could and should be separate invites and requires discursive normalization.

The significance of morphology, and the relationship between the body and the subject, is put center stage by the wide range of forms that conjoined twins may take. The simplest from the point of view of understanding them as separate individuals are those whose bodies appear relatively self-complete externally, albeit joined by fleshy material and shared circulation, though they might also lack two complete sets of internal organs. The anomaly of conjunction is overridden in such cases by the commonsense judgment that in all other respects such twins *are* two autonomous beings. The famous nineteenth-century Siamese twins Chang and Eng, for example, were indeed sufficiently independent of each other to contract marriage to two sisters and for each to father several children. The conjunction of Chang and Eng was relatively simple, consisting of a five-inch band of cartilaginous material between their chests, with the liver as the only shared internal organ—although even that was not apparent until postmortem examination (Figure 16.2). Although surgical intervention was considered and rejected as too dangerous, it is not surprising that they were each accorded full social and legal identity. Nonetheless, despite such strategies of normalization, the unmodified corporeal excessiveness of the twins' condition labeled them as freaks, who existed only as a unit, and they were frequently exhibited as such. The fascination for the viewing public, and for the wider media who followed Chang and Eng throughout their long life, was the simultaneous possibility of objectifying them as the monstrous other and identifying with them—in their role as upright American citizens—as the same. The twins themselves on the one hand endured conjunction and are known to have insisted on the semblance of autonomy, by maintaining two marital households for example, yet on the other they were so identified with one another that the idea of separation is said to have filled them with dread.

The perception that separation is in the best interests of conjoined twins rests on the prior assumption that two distinct persons with distinct identities have, as it were, become trapped in a single morphology. Whatever the visual form, there is an overriding need to find distinctive selves. As Hillel Schwartz writes,

Figure 16.2. Chang and Eng, the Siamese twins, photographed in 1860. Source unknown.

"That it or he or she or they might be neither exactly one nor exactly two [is] too logically distressing or emotionally unsatisfying to be true."[28] In the nonclinical sphere, even a writer as nonjudgmental as Fiedler seems to concur with the common cultural anxiety of losing individuality. Of Chang and Eng he remarks, "nothing but death could deliver them from this lifelong bondage";[29] and of Daisy and Violet Hilton, the conjoined vaudeville and film stars of the early twentieth century, "they remained slaves to each other to the end of their lives."[30] Modern medicine wholly reflects such attitudes, and the issue of surgical intervention and modification is taken as settled in principle, and subject only to technical feasibility, as though there is nothing at stake except an inappropriate body. But what is not taken into account is the complex interrelationship of body and self, the phenomenological sense of being-in-the-world, in which corporeal extension is indivisible from subjecthood and identity. In short, there is no clear distinction to be made between corporeal exteriority and psychical inferiority. Nonetheless, in Western discourse, the evident privileging of singularity and autonomy implicitly premised on the bodily separation, and the value accorded bodily self-determination combine to erase any consideration that there might be other ways of being. I am not suggesting that conjoined twins, and others whose morphology defies normative categories of embodiment, should be denied personhood; rather it is the defining parameters of the self, still more of the subject, that are inadequate to embodied difference. Moreover, the question of *identity*, which is commonly taken to indicate what is the unique core of each person, may equally well express that which is the same.

In any case, if, as Merleau-Ponty asserts, identity is realized only as the lived body is immersed in the lived bodies of others, then concorporation is scarcely hostile to that model.[31] In contrast, the dominant discourse of the singular and bounded subject, together with the privileging of corporeal self-completion, where exclusive property rights in one's own body stage the meeting with the other, enact a closure that suspends more open and ambiguous modes of existence. Though in the majority of cases the drive is to see conjoined twins as two persons, it might be more appropriate to say instead that the symbolic distinction between self and other that is taken to found identity in difference is deferred by the persistence of identification. For conjoined twins, the other-self is indivisible, not just as a facet of early infanthood, but as the very texture of experiential being. And where in general the Lacanian mirror stage marks "the assumption of the armour of an alienating identity" and inaugurates an illusory corporeal integrity and singularity,[32] for conjoined twins the undecidable other-self is figured in a very different kind of reflection. The (mis)recognition of the mirror stage is in a sense the permanent condition of such twins, with the evident difference that in that moment they may refuse identity in its symbolic sense and choose identification. What conjoined twins have in common with other monozygotic twins is not that they are visually identical, for many are not, but that they cannot be told apart. For external observers, the in-common materiality of such twins disconcerts the discriminating gaze, but what is equally confusing is that they may, in both types, experience a kind of internal merging.[33]

Given that twin studies have often been notorious for their question-begging assertions of mental and behavioral coincidence which seem to point to some peculiar quasi-telepathic power, they should be approached with some caution. Dorothy Burlingham's psychoanalytically based study, for example, which followed the lives of three sets of identical twins in a wartime boarding nursery over a period of many months, is rigorous in its observation of behavior, without ever adequately addressing the issue of whether family-based pairs might produce different results.[34] In being separated from their mothers, it seems highly likely that close siblings would forge substitute relationships with each other in which both intense love and hate formed a large part. Burlingham does record, nevertheless, an exceptional number of instances where an individual twin seems genuinely uncertain as to his or her own unique identity. Mirror images are especially confusing to them. Most telling of all is that despite episodes of intense anger and (self) rejection, all the twins are unable to cope with separation. Burlingham herself is in no doubt that the twin relationship is every bit as important as the mother–child bond. Even though some of it may be scientifically dubious, there is here and elsewhere plenty of evidence that monozygotic twins in general habitually blur the boundaries between one and the other—simultaneously thinking the same thoughts, making the same choices, speaking together as one—and it should not be surprising that conjoined twins, who share experiential being, do not make the separations that are commonly taken for granted.[35] If being-in-the-world, and still less identity, is not a given, then might not a different morphology ground other ontological and ethical relationships between self and other?

In nonautobiographical accounts of conjoined twins, both modern historical and contemporary, the one consistent factor that overrides differences in morphology is the reiteration of their essential separateness.[36] Clinical understanding is far from decisive, however, and as the *Encyclopaedia Britannica* puts it, "such double malformations probably arise following the less than complete separation of the halves of the early embryo, or from partial separation at later stages."[37] What this suggests to me is a difference between putative twins who remain anomalously joined at birth, and a putative singleton whose body has unfortunately begun to divide prenatally. What is at stake with the latter case is perhaps even more ontologically disruptive than the former, and I have yet to see the implications of such specificity addressed. Instead, the question with regard to all conjoined twins is rarely if they should be separated but rather how and how soon. As Schwartz puts it, "the pressure to cleave them is not narrowly medical; it is broadly cultural."[38] The expected birth of conjoined twins in Manchester in 1996 was, for example, the occasion for a spate of articles reviewing similar cases and looking at the prospects of the present pair. Most telling of all were the attempts of the prospective parents to normalize the birth. The father is quoted as saying, "We have made up our minds to look on the bright side and focus on having two lovely girls who will eventually lead *normal separate* lives."[39] Quite clearly, and understandably, he and the medical advisers could conceive of the twins' lives only as being on hold until they were separated, stripped as it were of their power to disrupt. So deeply is the ideal of corporeal and mental autonomy written into the Western understanding of what it is to be a person that any suggestion that the infants could function as a merged unit was swiftly rejected.

A similar emphasis is evident in a 1999 BBC documentary entitled *Separate Lives*. The program focuses on a pair of Pakistani twins, Hira and Nida, who, we are told and shown, are joined at the scalp in such a way that they are unable to stand upright. Right from the beginning the commentary sets the tone with the assurance that "they had come halfway across the world . . . for the chance of a normal life." The stress on such factors cannot but carry, I feel, certain racist overtones both in terms of the superior civilization of the west, and in the implicit allusion to the racialized chain of being that moves from apes through stooping black bodies to the upstanding white figure, which in turn evokes the Christian notion of the human being as "upright, erect." In contradistinction to the acceptance shown by the girls' mother who expresses her joy at seeing them laugh and play together, and their father when he says "I see them as one life that God has given to two children," the Canadian neurosurgeon who examines the twins treats them primarily as a clinical problem, albeit one with an interwoven but unacknowledged value judgment: "There's a possibility of cutting *this* into two normal children" (my emphasis). Ironically his desire to construct "normal functioning" is spoken over shots of the twins playing happily with building bricks, just as other children of their age might do. In the view of the medical specialists, however, the strain on the kidneys and the heart in "Hira's" body which are doing the work for both twins is sufficient in itself to justify surgical intervention. In the absence of any real discussion of the ethical issues of separation surgery itself, the major question that they must consider is the bioethical and legal one of whether Hira, as a child, can donate a living organ (a kidney) to her sister. This is indeed a pertinent consideration, which raises the issue of whether the twins can be regarded as one or two, but it is couched in the characteristically Western terms of the ownership of body parts. As an audience we are implicitly invited to empathize with the professionals' dilemma in their treatment of a perplexing vulnerability in the body of the other, but not to reflect on the phenomenological difference of such a body. When Nida fails to survive separation ("her brain was not enough . . . to keep her alive as an individual"), the commentary reassures viewers, without any sense of doubt, that Hira is thriving. The clear implication is that where no properly constituted subject could exist in the unmodified twin body, at least there is now one.[40]

I want now to look in greater detail at the story of the Irish conjoined twins Katie and Eilish, whose early childhood and subsequent separation features in two television documentaries shown initially in 1993 and 1995. The twins' body is merged from the upper thoracic area, giving them just two legs and two functioning arms—with two other residual upper limb stumps having been already excised in the expectation of future separation surgery. There are separate hearts and lungs, but all other organs are single. What is at stake throughout for both the parents and the medical team is how best to balance the risk of separation—and it is made clear that the twins' degree of conjunction exceeds any in which surgical intervention has been previously attempted—with the normative desire that each should have a functionally autonomous existence. The issue of corporeal normalization, is, however, clearly distinct from a more complex and contradictory understanding of what constitutes normality in the specific case of the twins. For the parents, Katie and Eilish already operate as two "normal" children, having individual personalities which they do much to encourage; while for his part, the consultant surgeon is constrained to stress that he cannot promise the twins a "normal" life if they are separated. The characteristic Western split between mind and body is mirrored in the assumption of an existential normality that is merely obstructed by the abnormal morphology of the children. As they are not one, then they must become two. The voice-over suggestion that "although we value individuality, they might not value it. They might prefer togetherness" is, then, both a disturbing glimpse of other ways of being, and a reminder of what the normative regime of individuality must repudiate.[41]

Although at that moment the commentary may reveal an unresolved tension in our response to the normative operation of self and other, its reflection of a nostalgia for togetherness does not challenge what we take to be a developmentally necessary split. It is not, I think, that there is any recognition that the concorporation of the twins might speak to new and more fluid forms of embodied subjectivity but rather that the ideal of the autonomous subject is contested by the twins' concurrent and cooperative intentionality. Their successful negotiation of their environment largely depends on their acting as one, even in such small matters as unscrewing a bottle. Nonetheless, the sense that being-in-the-world might imbricate with body and environment is not explored; to those who must decide their future, the discrete subjectivities of the twins are already given and simply awaiting release. The twins' embodiment is, then, a monstrous insult to the norms of human corporeality, an other mode of being that defies the binary of sameness and difference into which medical intervention is designed to recuperate them. Although both parents and doctors are sensitive to the implicitly ethical question of potentially disrupting the twins' current contentment, the phenomenological and epistemological questions remain unexplored in the face of an overriding concern with the material risks of surgery. Following a visit to some "successfully" separated conjoined twins, matters of procedure become paramount. The operation is undertaken with some real confidence, but although Eilish recovers, Katie unexpectedly dies.

The point of turning to this often very moving narrative is not so much to critique the current medical practice—for in this case the participants, whether detached professionals or closest family, are all properly caring and reflective[42]—but to illustrate the power of ontological anxiety. Against the corporeal excessiveness of Katie and Eilish, the attempt to radically reconstruct their bodies speaks eloquently to the notions of closure and containment assumed to be at the heart of being. What is finally unacceptable about the twins is not the degree of their disability—and indeed it is uncertain that a successful outcome would have increased function—but the ambiguity of their concorporation. For all the discursive efforts to normalize their life in terms of assigning dual individuality, it remains undecidable whether they are one or two. In contrast, the conventional understanding of the only proper form of subjectivity requires a clarity of boundaries between self and other, an affective and effective autonomy that is fully realized only by singular embodiment. Despite the death of Katie, then, the father of the twins is constrained to justify the operation by remarking on the surviving twin's enhanced quality of life after separation: "She's free of being joined to another human-being."[43] In fashioning Eilish's body so that she may comply with normative ideals, she is realized as an intelligible subject, and a body that matters. The impossibility of the ideal is made clear, however, in the acknowledgment that for Eilish, body modification must be continued throughout life: her prosthetic leg and body harness must be periodically replaced to ensure scopic normalization. It is ironic that although no one seems able to articulate the real extent of Eilish's corporeal disruption, the doctor worries that in losing her first prosthesis, she will think some part of her is being taken away. For her own part, Eilish renames her new leg "Katie," in recognition of the absent presence of her self/other.

The phenomenological specificity of concorporate being-in-the-world is addressed by no adult in the films, except perhaps in the psychologist's half-recognition that Katie is still incorporated into the life of her surviving twin. At bedtime, Eilish gets what she calls her "Katie kisses," but even that observation is normalized in the remark that the ritual happens "in a healthy way, not in any way that is holding Eilish back."[44] That implicit rewriting of the twin relationship as obstructive is reiterated in an interchange between Eilish and her sisters. When asked what she remembers of her sister, Eilish replies, "She used to bring me round everywhere," only to be interrupted by an older sibling, who declares, "Eilish couldn't go wherever she wanted." What matters to the family is that Eilish should be well adjusted, and indeed, despite the four months spent in hospital postoperatively in which she is described as traumatized, she does appear happy and talkative in the second documentary shot over the next two years. For her parents, her social and physical recovery is a matter of relief, but it is evident too that for Eilish herself, the splitting of her (subject) body has produced an effect somewhat akin to the phenomenon of the phantom limb. As Merleau-Ponty explains it, to experience such a phantom is to remain open to the presence of what is lost.[45] The wound she experiences, unacknowledged, is as much psychical as material, a severe disruption to the unified, albeit imaginary, body map that founds the ego.[46] When Teresa, the elder sister, says of Katie, "She had freckles," the response from Eilish is both confused and defiant: "So did I, so do I, [pushes Teresa], I still do." Katie both is and is not there, a shifting body memory and continued inscription on the flesh of her twin.

What these stories emphasize is a dominant post-Enlightenment discourse in which our psychic investment in the corporeal is covered over by the illusion that the body is merely instrumental, a source only of impediment or advantage to the subject. Biomedicine in particular proceeds on the basis that any intervention into the materiality of the body can be divorced from the patient's own sense of self and from her phenomenological engagement with the world. The clarity of corporeal boundaries is what grounds existential and moral personhood, while the meeting with the other is premised on bodily self-determination and property rights in one's own body. The conjunction of two consciousnesses is characterized only in terms of a meeting of self and other, properly mediated by contract or the calculation of individual best interests. What separation surgery attempts then—aside from cases where it is medically indicated to preserve life— is a reconstitution of autonomous subjecthood as the only proper way of being-in-the-world. In a move that strongly calls to mind Foucault's theorization of *assujettissement,* it is the very subjection of the body to the forces of normalization which enables the emergence of the subject herself.[47] But for conjoined twins, the other is also the self—a transgressive and indeterminate state in which corporeal, ontological and ultimately ethical boundaries are distorted and dissolved. As Clark and Myser put it, the assumption is "that conjoined life, precisely because of its imagined phenomenological *un*intelligibility must be intolerable."[48] And one might add, intolerable to society rather than to the twins themselves. There is no sense here that corporeality might constitute the subject, only that a somehow foundational subject—or rather two—is thwarted by a monstrous body.

I want finally to look briefly at other forms of concorporate twins whose monstrous bodies do not afford the contemplation, theoretical or material, of separation into self and other, although less radical modification may be possible. The horror of losing one's singular identity to a parasitic other is a powerful motif in monster narratives of all kinds, and is, Judith Halberstam claims in her book

Skin Shows, paramount within the genre of Gothic monster fiction. What the trope of parasitism expresses is an ever-present threat within, "an internal not an external danger that Gothic identifies and attempts to dispel."[49] It is a moment of semiotic confusion in which inner and outer are indistinguishable, bodies are both doubled and diminished, and meanings flow into one another. In nonliterary sources, the same concerns are in operation with regard to concorporation, particularly in extreme instances. Of the cases of monstrous excess considered here, one is specifically called parasitic twinning, where the very naming speaks to a putative insult to an ideal of bodily self-determination; the other concerns the mirroring of heads on a singular body.[50] In both instances the infants involved survived birth and lived for several years in a state of monstrosity. The appearances of the seventeenth-century Coloredo brothers—the wholly formed Lazarus and his parasitic twin John Baptista—are extremely well documented in popular histories, contemporary ballads, and official documents (Figure 16.3). Although for the most part they were viewed benignly as marvels, the existence of so extraordinary a body raised worrying questions. The following is an account from a pamphlet of 1640 referring to Lazarus, who

> from one of his sides hath a twin brother growing, which was borne with
> him, and living still; though having sence and feeling, yet destitute of reason
> and understanding: whence methinks a disputable question might arise,
> whether[,] as they have distinct lives, so they are possessed of two souls; or
> have but one imparted betwixt them both.[51]

The second case was even more extraordinary, the more so in that the child involved survived until he was four years old, when he was killed, reputedly, by a cobra bite. The so-called Bengali boy was born with two heads—not unusual within the context of conjoined twins, except that the second head grew not from his neck but was attached upside down and back-to-front on the top of the child's scalp (Figure 16.4). The bone casing of the craniopagus skull, as it was known, was fused where crown met crown and, as a contemporary postmortem report to the Royal Society put it, "the two brains were . . . separate and distinct, having a complete partition between them."[52] Moreover, the bodiless head during life was not in itself unusual in appearance, having well-formed facial features, ears, and a crop of hair, and separate affect. Nonetheless, the anxiety that such an occurrence might be expected to generate was effaced by regarding the skull, not as the site of contested subjecthood, but merely as an object of biomedical enquiry. The significance of the craniopagus skull to the British scientific community of the day was not, as it might have been in the past, an occasion for reflection on the notion of maternal imagination—though the initial report from the East India Company was clearly obliged to assert that the mother had suffered no fright or accident during her pregnancy—but rather as ammunition in a wholly medicalized controversy

Figure 16.3. Lazarus and John Baptista Coloredo from *The Gentlemen's Magazine* (1777).

regarding the process of evolutionary development. As Evelleen Richards notes in her detailed analysis of that debate, "historical monsters . . . may be understood at one and the same time both as anatomical objects and as the embodiments of different strategies of power."[53] In her understanding of what she calls "political anatomy" Richards is reluctant to pursue a Foucauldian deconstruction of what she sees as "concrete historical events," but nonetheless her account does point up the discursive construction of the meanings inscribed on the monstrous body. The widespread scientific interest excited by the craniopagus skull, which became and remains a prize exhibit in the Hunterian Museum, indicates too that by the rationalist mid-eighteenth century, monsters were—as before—a primary ground for competing discourses, but stripped now of questions of personal agency. For my own part, however, I want to return to those very questions.

If the issue of subjectivity or identity is at very least problematized in the indistinct corporeality of those conjoined twins with two relatively well-formed bodies, both internal and external, or more remarkably where two heads append the same body, then it is radically challenged by such incomplete instances of doubling. In her essay entitled "Freaks," Elizabeth Grosz remarks, "It is no longer

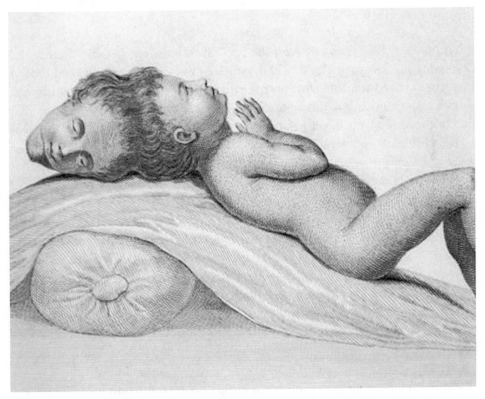

Figure 16.4. The Bengali Boy (Basire) from *The Philosophical Transactions of the Royal Society* 80 (1790).

clear that there are two identities, even if the bodily functions of the parasitic twin occur independently of the will or awareness of the other. In such cases, is there one subject or two?"[54] The question haunts the historical accounts of the cases I have mentioned. Contemporary descriptions of the Coloredo brothers often touch on such a point, and, like the distinctive affect of the two heads of the Bengali boy which Everard Home recorded, make frequent reference to the independent physical sensitivity of the parasitic body. The inherent confusion of embodied identity is apparent in William Turner's depiction which describes first the "little brother":

> his left foot alone hung downwards; he had two Arms, only three Fingers upon each Hand: Some appearance there was of the Secret Parts; he moved his Hands, Ears, and Lips, and had a little beating in the Breast. This little Brother voided no Excrements but by the Mouth, Nose, and Ears, and is nourished by that which the greater takes: He has distinct Animal and Vital parts from the greater; since he sleeps, sweats, and moves, when the other wakes, rests, and sweats not. . . . Lazarus is of a just Stature, a decent Body, courteous Deportment, and gallantly Attired; he covers the Body of his Brother with his Cloak: Nor could you think a Monster lay within at your first Discourse with him.[55]

What marks a difference between the two cases, however, is that whereas the Coloredos are always referred to and named as two distinct people, and indeed each was baptized according to report, the Bengali boy is already singular. Although surgical intervention was not a possibility in either case, a discursive normalization of the excessive subject has taken place. That the singularity of all subject bodies is similarly constructed and reiterated by regimes of normalization that defer the slippage of excessive embodiment is obscured by the insistence that monstrosity is radically other, the exceptional case that secures the normative standard.

So what type of subjectivity or identity could fit such a range of differences, and how does the monstrous corporeality of my examples imbricate with the sense of self? Where Elizabeth Grosz, in her paper "Freaks," posits a continuum of identity—ranging from the autonomous, self-complete and individuated subject, which Western discourse assumes as the standard for all, to a nondifferentiated, quasi-collective subject in which the symbolic moment of distinction between self and other is endlessly deferred—I am inclined to caution. The desire for full self-presence is, I think, never realized, and results only in a phantasmatic structure of subjectivity. As I understand it, monsters both define the limits of the singular embodied subject, and reflect our own ultimately insecure and unstable identities. As Rosi Braidotti puts it, "the monstrous other is both liminal and structurally central to our perception of normal human subjectivity."[56] And it is the move to forcibly impose the norm of one body/one mind, the move to erase difference either by exclusion or by processes of normalization, that underlines the instability of the ideal. Where monsters blatantly blur the parameters of being, they invoke in us all—and this seems particularly true of the doubling of twinned bodies—both a nostalgia for identification and the horror of incorporation. They demonstrate that the relation between self and other, as with body and body, is chiasmatic, precisely insofar as corporeality and subjectivity—body and mind—are themselves folded back into each other, overflowing, enmeshed and mutually constitutive.

Though bodily modification may hope to avert the overtly transgressive, its very practice alerts us to the crisis at the boundaries of the body which is never one. As the in-between, as *différance,* the monstrous shows us that neither the one nor the two is proof against deconstruction. Promise and risk lie equally in the move beyond/before—it is undecidable—the one that determines ontological and corporeal unity, or the two that mark difference as opposition and relationship as the quasi-contractual exchange between autonomous beings. It is the necessarily incomplete abjection of monstrosity that guards against the successful closure of what Derrida has called "an illegitimately delimited subject."[57] If, then, such closure is merely a myth of modernity, the attempted limitation of the monstrous body by both surgical and discursive means is doubly doomed to failure. Rather than attempting to recuperate the monstrous, might we not refigure it as an alternative, but equally valuable, mode of being, an alterity that throws doubt on the singularity of the human and signals other less restrictive possibilities? As such, the monster might be the promising location of a reconceived ontology and an ethics centered on a relational economy that has a place for radical difference.

Notes

1. Margrit Shildrick, "Posthumanism and the Monstrous Body," *Body and Society* 2, no. 1 (1996): 1.

2. René Descartes, "Meditations on First Philosophy," in *Discourse on Method and "The Meditations,"* trans. F. E. Sutcliffe (Harmondsworth, U.K.: Penguin Books, 1968), 164.

3. See John Locke, *An Essay Concerning Human Understanding,* ed. P. H. Nidditch (Oxford: Clarendon Press, 1975).

4. The argument is established in feminist critique as diverse as Genevieve Lloyd's *The Man of Reason: "Male" and "Female" in Western Philosophy* (London: Methuen, 1984), and Luce Irigaray's *Speculum of the Other Woman,* trans. G. C. Gill (Ithaca, N.Y.: Cornell University Press, 1985).

5. See Maurice Merleau-Ponty, *The Phenomenology of Perception* (London: Routledge and Kegan Paul, 1962).

6. See Margrit Shildrick, *Leaky Bodies and Boundaries: Feminism, Postmodernism and (Bio)ethics* (London: Routledge, 1997).

7. See Drew Leder, *The Absent Body* (Chicago: University of Chicago Press, 1990).

8. Leder, 91.

9. See Iris Marion Young, *Throwing Like a Girl and Other Essays in Feminist Social Theory* (Bloomington: Indiana University Press, 1990), and Rosalyn Diprose, *The Bodies of Women: Ethics, Embodiment and Sexual Difference* (London: Routledge, 1994).

10. This is no small matter, for invasion, either corporeal or psychic, is one of our greatest fears. Indeed the whole genre of horror stories, to which the monstrous is clearly related, might be said to be fundamentally about invasion. As Barbara Creed puts it in *The Monstrous-Feminine,* "the possessed or invaded being is a figure of abjection in that the boundary between self and other has been transgressed." Creed, *The Monstrous-Feminine: Film, Feminism, Psychoanalysis* (London: Routledge, 1993), 32. It will strike us, nonetheless, that there is something odd about a fear that effectively denies the maternal–fetal connection. We all once were concorporate with another, and some of us, as mothers, have experienced the sharing of bodies in pregnancy. Yet it is precisely that archaic link that constitutes the abject.

11. Julia Epstein, *Altered Conditions: Disease, Medicine and Storytelling* (London: Routledge, 1995), 4.

12. Julia Epstein offers an extensive discussion of the significance of hermaphrodism and related genital "disorders" in the early modern period. See *Altered Conditions.*

13. Stephen Bateman, *The Doome Warning All Men to the Iudgemente: Wherein are contained for the most parte all the straunge Prodigies hapned in the Worlde* (London: Ralphe Nubery, 1581), 337.

14. See Londa Schiebinger, *Nature's Body: Gender in the Making of Modern Science* (Boston: Beacon Press,1993), on the social and medical fascination with such differences in the context of racial categorization.

15. John Block Friedman, *The Monstrous Races in Medieval Art and Thought* (Cambridge, Mass.: Harvard University Press, 1981), 179.

16. See Susan Sontag, *Illness as Metaphor and AIDS and Its Metaphors* (New York: Doubleday, 1990).

17. Julia Kristeva, *The Powers of Horror: An Essay on Abjection* (New York: Columbia University Press, 1982), 71.

18. Mikhail Bakhtin, *Rabelais and His World* (Bloomington: Indiana University Press, 1984), 320.

19. Bakhtin, 318.

20. See Kristeva, *Powers of Horror.*

21. See Donna Haraway, "A Manifesto for Cyborgs: Science, Technology and Socialist Feminism in the 1980s," in *Feminism/Postmodernism,* ed. Linda Nicholson (London: Routledge, 1990), and Katherine Dunn, *Geek Love* (New York: Warner, 1989).

22. Thomas Bedford, *A True and Certain Relation of a Strange Birth which was Born at Stonehouse in the Parish of Plymouth, the 20th of October, 1635* (London: Anne Griffin, 1635), n.p.

23. Kristeva, *Powers of Horror,* 4.

24. Estimates of the incidence of conjoined twins vary from one in fifty thousand to 1 in one hundred thousand. The first successful operation in which both twins survived was not carried out until 1953 in the United States.

25. See Jacques Lacan, "The Mirror Stage as Formative of the Function of the I," in *Écrits: A Selection,* trans. Alan Sheridan (New York: W. W. Norton, 1977).

26. Aristotle implies in *De generatione animalium* that all twins are monstrous. In justification of this apparently extreme position, J. M. Thijssen reminds us, "By monsters, Aristotle does not just mean creatures which, due to some pathological process, are misshapen, but, much more generally, all creatures which are out of the ordinary in the sense that they are not the result of the common course of Nature." Thijssen, "Twins as Monsters: Albertus Magnus's Theory of the Generation of Twins and its Philosophical Context," *Bulletins of the History of Medicine* 61 (1987): 240. Surprisingly, then, the Biddenden Maids—reputedly born in Kent in 1100—may be the exception to the rule that conjoined twins are certainly monstrous. Tradition has it that they led an exemplary Christian life and, on their death at the age of thirty-four, endowed a charity for the needy of the parish. It should be remembered, too, that the monstrous does not always imply negativity. Edward Fenton's reference to a child with doubled limbs is, for example, entitled "A Wonderful Historie of a monstrous childe, which was borne the same day that the Genervois and Venicians were reconciled," in *Certaine Secrete Wonders of Nature, containing a Description of Sundry Strange Things* (London: Henry Bynneman, 1569), 135. In a similar vein, Thomas Bedford's sermon on the birth of conjoined twins eulogises their metaphorical relation to the Christian body: "Surely these are not more nearly conjoined in breast and belly than christians ought to be in heart and affection." Bedford, *A True and Certain Relation.*

27. Quoted in Friedman, *Monstrous Races,* 180.

28. Hillel Schwartz, *The Culture of the Copy: Striking Likenesses, Unreasonable Facsimiles* (New York: Zone Books, 1996), 52.

29. Leslie Fiedler, *Freaks: Myths and Images of the Secret Self* (Harmondsworth U.K.: Penguin Books, 1981), 217.

30. Fiedler, 209.

31. See Maurice Merleau-Ponty, *The Primacy of Perception* (Evanston, Ill.: Northwestern University Press, 1964).

32. Lacan, "Mirror Stage," 4. Merleau-Ponty in *The Primacy of Perception* takes a less deterministic view of the mirror stage, in which the inauguration of difference is always offset by a continuing mutuality of being-in-the-world with others.

33. Interestingly, what Hillel Schwartz labels "the myth of the vanished twin . . . the notion that each of us may once have had a living copy," in *Culture of the Copy,* 24, appears to have some clinical justification. Schwartz indicates research that suggests that as many as a quarter of singleton births may originally have been twin conceptions (20), with the possibility that the weaker fetus is absorbed into its twin in the early stages of pregnancy. Indeed, the idea of bodies that leak and flow into one another is a familiar part of the modern language of embryology and is only gradually displaced by reference to the apparent certainty of organic boundaries.

34. See Dorothy Burlingham, *Twins: A Study of Three Identical Twins* (London: Imago, 1952).

35. Although on one level the oneness of such twins may appall, on another they may be an attractive, albeit uneasy, reminder of the lost presubjectal plenitude of undifferentiated infant–maternal corporeality.

36. In analyzing a number of recent accounts of conjunction and concorporation, I am aware that my approach traverses ground that will have highly personal meanings to surviving twins and their families. None of the material I use is outside the public domain, and some has been very deliberately given wide circulation, but in addition to safeguards already incorporated into the original texts, I have taken the step of withholding potentially identifying surnames. Nonetheless, I remain conscious that the significances I wish to elicit may be in tension with authorized interpretations and want to stress that my primary concern is not with the specific material circumstances of the twins as such. Emphatically, the issue is not to offer judgment on any of those involved in the varying accounts but to investigate the nature of the ontological and ethical responses.

37. "Biological Growth and Development," s.v. *New Encyclopaedia Britannica*.

38. Schwartz, *Culture of the Copy*, 61.

39. "Medical Team Standing By for Siamese Twins Birth," *Guardian*, September 11, 1996, 5, emphasis mine.

40. Since I finished this chapter, the highly publicized case of the Maltese conjoined twins, born in the United Kingdom in 2000, has brought some of the issues I discuss to a wider audience. Known as Jodie and Mary, the pair have been consistently treated as separate beings, despite an extensive degree of concorporation. The "need" for separation surgery in this case, nonetheless, has been widely debated—both in lay and legal contexts—not for reasons of doubt about the ontological status of the infant body but because it was clear that Mary was parasitic on Jodie and would inevitably die if she were unable to share her twin's vital functions. At the same time, it was calculated that failure to operate would result in the deaths of both after a few months. (The operation did in fact go ahead in November 2000.) The situation was, then, extremely complex, and I do not presume to judge it. The point I would make, however, is that the debate was conducted in almost exclusively modernist terms, hinging on the right to life, and/or to self-defence, and the disputed rights of the parents, while professional bioethicists added in cost–benefit considerations. The question of what constitutes a self and its relation to the body was not addressed.

41. *Katie and Eilish: Siamese Twins,* Yorkshire Television, Network First, 1993.

42. For a rather different documentary narrative of medical intervention, in which the concerns of the clinic were overriding, and for which the filming itself realized "a certain technologized medical gaze," see David L. Clark and Catherine Myser's account of the separation of the Thai conjoined twins Dao and Duan: "Being Humaned: Medical Documentaries and the Hyperrealisation of Conjoined Twins," *Freakery: Cultural Spectacles of the Extraordinary Body*, ed. Rosemarie Garland Thomson (New York: New York University Press, 1996).

43. *Eilish: Life without Katie,* Yorkshire Television, Network First, 1995.

44. *Eilish: Life without Katie.*

45. Merleau-Ponty, *Phenomenology of Perception*, 80–86.

46. In psychoanalytic terms, the mirroring process (both literal and metaphorical), by which the infant comes to see itself as separate and distinct allows accession to a self-image of corporeal unity that covers over the reality of the fragmentary and uncoordinated motor experiences of the child. See Lacan, "Mirror Stage." As an ego ideal, however, the

resultant body map is precarious, having, as Elizabeth Grosz explains, "a psychical interior, which requires continual stabilization, and a corporeal exterior which remains labile, open to many meanings." Grosz, *Volatile Bodies: Toward a Corporeal Feminism* (Bloomington: Indiana University Press, 1994), 38.

47. See Michel Foucault, *Discipline and Punish: The Birth of the Prison*, trans. Alan Sheridan (London: Allen Lane, 1977).

48. Clark and Myser, "Being Humaned," 351.

49. Jack Halberstam (writing as Judith), *Skin Shows: Gothic Horror and the Technology of Monsters* (Durham, N.C.: Duke University Press, 1995), 15.

50. Neither of these cases is in any way unique. Parasitic twinning, and to a lesser extent supernumerary heads, feature in many early "monster" books and are described by Conrades Lycosthenes in *Prodigiorum ac ostentorum chronicon quae praeter naturae ordinem* (Basle: H. Petri, 1557), Pierre Boaistuau in *Histoires prodigieuses les memorables qui ayent esté observees, depuis la nativité de Jesus Christ, jusques a nostre siècle* (Paris: Vincent Sertenas, 1560), Ambroise Paré in *Des monsters tant terrestres que marins, avec leurs Portrais* (Paris, 1573), Fortunius Licetus in *De Monstrorum Natura, Caussis, et Differentis* (Padua: P. Frambotti, 1634), Ulyssis Aldrovandus in *Monstrorum Historia cum paralipomenis historiae omnium animalium* (Bononia: Nicolai Teraldini,1642), and Thomas Bartholinus in *Historiarum anatomicarum rariorum* (London: Francis Leach, 1654), among others. C. J. S. Thompson details many other occurrences, traced through handbills, eyewitness accounts, and personal appearances, as for example in Barnum's freak shows. Thompson, *The Mystery and Lore of Monsters* (London: Williams and Northgate, 1930).

51. The pamphlet, *A Certain Relation of the Hog-Faced Gentlewoman*, is quoted in Hyder E. Rollins, *The Pack of Autolycus* (Cambridge, Mass.: Harvard University Press, 1927), 8.

52. Everard Home, "Some Additions to a Paper, Read in 1790, on the Subject of a Child with a Double Head," *Philosophical Transactions of the Royal Society* 89 (1799): 30.

53. Evelleen Richards, "A Political Anatomy of Monsters, Hopful or Otherwise: Teratogeny, Transcendentalism, and Evolutionary Theorising," *Isis* 85 (1994): 405.

54. Elizabeth Grosz, "Freaks," *Social Semiotics* 1, no. 2 (1991): 34.

55. William Turner, *A Compleat History of the Most Remarkable Providences* (1697; repr. London: John Dunton, 1967), 8.

56. Rosi Braidotti, "Signs of Wonder and Traces of Doubt: On Teratology and Embodied Difference," in *Between Monster, Goddesses and Cyborgs: Feminist Confrontations with Science, Medicine and Cyberspace*, ed. Nina Lykke and Rosi Braidotti (London: Zed Books, 1996), 141.

57. Jacques Derrida, "'Eating Well,' or the Calculation of the Subject: An Interview with Jacques Derrida," in *Who Comes after the Subject?*, ed. Eduardo Cadava, Peter Connor, and Jean-Luc Nancy (London: Routledge, 1991), 108.

HAUNTING MODERNITY

Tanuki, *Trains, and Transformation in Japan*

Michael Dylan Foster

I N FRONT OF RESTAURANTS, BARS, AND SAKÉ SHOPS throughout Japan, one often finds a ceramic statuette of a wide-eyed, cheerful beast known as a *tanuki*. Standing upright and adorned with a straw hat, the *tanuki* is portrayed as a jovial hedonist; he has a rotund belly, a jug of saké in one hand, and is particularly distinguished—if you look carefully—by an enormous scrotum. On the streets of a modern city, the *tanuki* radiates a sense of good-natured camaraderie and traditional welcome.[1] But the ubiquitous, lighthearted image of the *tanuki* is only one manifestation of this particular *yōkai*, or supernatural creature; the *tanuki* also has a long history as a common character in folktales, legends, local beliefs, and, more recently, all sorts of commercial iconography. Since at least the Kamakura period (1185–1333), narratives have featured the *tanuki* as a trickster who enjoys causing mischief, and sometimes mayhem, in the human world.

Zoologically, the *tanuki* is a real animal, a small, generally nocturnal, omnivorous mammal that looks somewhat like a raccoon crossed with a possum. In English the *tanuki* is sometimes referred to as a badger, but "raccoon dog" is perhaps a more accurate label, at least in terms of its Linnaean classification as a canid.[2] The *tanuki* is found throughout East Asia, and in the twentieth century it was introduced into the former Soviet Union because of the value of its fur; it reproduced rapidly and now inhabits Scandinavia and much of northern Europe. In addition to its high rate of reproduction, one reason for the *tanuki*'s success is

330

its ability to live in relatively close proximity to humans and eat human-made foods.[3] That is, similar to raccoons, possums, foxes, and coyotes in other parts of the world, the *tanuki* is a wild animal that occasionally makes mischievous forays into areas inhabited by humans. It is a beast of the borders, ecologically skirting the line between culture and nature. Folklorically, too, *tanuki* are commonly depicted as liminal creatures, simultaneously of this world and the other world.

It is not my intention here to present a comprehensive survey of the enormous amount of folklore concerning the *tanuki*.[4] Rather, I will briefly introduce the creature and then focus on one cycle of *tanuki*-related narratives that emerged at a particular time of transition soon after the Meiji Restoration (1868), as Japan embarked on its frantic rush into modernity. This moment of intense cultural, political, and economic flux provides insight into the intersection, and occasional collision, of the natural world with the human world, and concomitantly of folk belief with the modern desires of a nation-state experiencing rapid industrialization and urbanization. I do not argue that modernity and scientific rationalization caused an attenuation of the importance of *tanuki* and other folk creatures; rather, I suggest that the familiar character of the *tanuki* and the motifs surrounding it were readily adapted for a new set of narratives through which anxieties about modernity, and the way modernity was reshaping the geographical and cultural landscape, could be voiced. If we listen carefully to a cycle of *tanuki* legends that circulated at this time, we hear a counternarrative to the hegemonic story of progress and modernity: through the din of industrialization, urbanization, and modern science, tales of *tanuki* voice a subtle ideological resistance. From the vantage point of the present, we can see how often overlooked folklore can articulate critical concerns that fly below the radar of conventional histories.

I also want to push this analysis one step further, and consider these counternarratives as narratives of *haunting*, in which restless memories of the past disturb the easy flow of the present. Haunting, of course, is commonly expressed in frightening stories of ghosts and revenants; most of the *tanuki* legends I relate here are not explicitly frightening, but they reflect a similar disjuncture between time and space that is, I suggest, characteristic of haunting narratives. Moreover, within their particular historical context, the haunting of modernity represented by these *tanuki* tales assumes not only an affective quality, but political and ideological shades as well.

A Very Brief History of Shape-shifting

Although the *tanuki* (or a related/conflated creature called a *mujina*) makes its earliest documented appearance in one of the oldest extant texts in Japan, the mythohistorical *Nihon shoki* of 720, it is not until a *setsuwa* (short tale) from the thirteenth-century *Uji shūi monogatari* that we find what one scholar has

Figure 17.1. A ceramic figurine of a *tanuki* outside a restaurant in Nagano Prefecture. (The sign hanging from his nose indicates that the shop is closed for a regular holiday.) Photograph by the author.

Figure 17.2. *Tanuki*. Photograph by the author.

called the first recorded *tanuki* "haunting."[5] The *setsuwa* tells of a mountain hermit who, after years of deep devotion, begins to receive nightly visits from the Bodhisattva Fugen on his white elephant. A hunter who brings the hermit food is invited to stay to witness the holy vision. But when Fugen appears, radiating a beautiful light, the hunter is suspicious. Why would he, a killer of animals, be permitted this vision of the divine? And so, to test its veracity, he duly fits an arrow to his bow and lets fly at the image. The light goes out and a crashing sound is heard. In the morning, the hunter and the hermit follow a trail of blood to the bottom of a ravine where they find a dead *tanuki* with an arrow in its chest.[6]

Historically, the image of the *tanuki* is often combined with that of the fox, or *kitsune*, and sometimes legends associated with the two creatures are interchangeable. Indeed, a common term for the two together was *kori* (Ch. *huli*), a combination of the two Chinese characters that came to refer to all manner of supernatural or mysterious occurrences. While it is difficult to generalize, *kitsune*-related narratives and belief—often directly influenced from Chinese folk and literary motifs—tend to portray a seductive, sly, and dangerous creature. Often a *kitsune* will take the shape of a woman, seducing a man away from his wife and dangerously disrupting family or village life. Fox possession of a person or a place was a well-known problem; even until the early twentieth century, certain types of illnesses or erratic personal behavior might be diagnosed as possession by a fox.[7]

Broadly speaking, *tanuki* tended to be more bumbling than foxes, and were not as commonly implicated in the possession of humans. As in the medieval-period narrative related above, they often end up dead, despite the temporary magnificence of their transformations. Whereas the sleek body of the *kitsune* translates into a sharp and deviously deceptive shape-shifter, the *tanuki* came gradually to be characterized as a more comical and ribald trickster, sometimes assuming the human form of a pudgy, Falstaffian Buddhist monk. As lore relating to the *tanuki* continued to develop during the long Edo period (c. 1600–1868), a time of relative political stability in Japan, the lighthearted image of a somewhat inept shape-shifter could be found, for example, in the famous folktale of the *Bunbuku-chagama,* in which the *tanuki* is unable to sustain a transformation into a teapot—a dilemma that made for all sorts of wonderful imagery in woodblock prints and other visual forms.[8]

I would be amiss not to mention here the fact that the *tanuki*'s magic is often performed through the machinations of its gigantic scrotum—numerous woodblock prints and other images attest to the protean abilities of this magnificent physical feature. With such paraphernalia, it is not surprising that one of the many roles the *tanuki* plays in contemporary Japan is that of fertility symbol in the realm of commerce, a function transferred into a sign of prosperity and good fortune as he stands in front of restaurants and shops throughout the country. While this chapter does not focus on the dynamics and origins of the *tanuki*'s magical equipment, I would note only that his gigantic scrotum becomes—in imagery and legendry throughout the Edo period—a fertile symbol of shape-shifting itself, a completely mutable, flexible instrument through which the *tanuki* changes his own shape.

But the *tanuki*'s shape-shifting abilities are not limited to self-transformation; they extend to a power to reshape the landscape. Many a local legend is told of somebody eager to get home after a night of saké drinking only to become hopelessly lost in terrain magically defamiliarized by the antics of playful *tanuki*. Such defamiliarization may be caused by optical illusion—the creation of *fata morgana*—or just as likely by mischievous behavior: an early twentieth-century legend, for example, tells of "a *tanuki* who is in the habit of throwing sand. When a person is passing through at night, the *tanuki* will rain down so much sand that the person will lose his way, and then the *tanuki* will guide him to a river or waterside and cause him to fall in."[9] *Tanuki* are also adept at leading people astray by imitating sounds, creating what we might call sonic mirages; they are particularly notorious for making an uncanny drumming noise by thumping their bellies (*hara tsuzumi*).[10]

The Edo period witnessed the efflorescence of a rich visual and print culture of woodblock prints, *kabuki* drama, *bunraku* puppet theater, and numerous forms of graphic literature, such as the *kibyōshi* that featured lighthearted, often satirical stories, complete with detailed illustrations. In these formats, folklore relating to the *tanuki* (and other *yōkai*) intersected dynamically with popular cultural concerns, veiled political sentiments, and commercial and artistic interests. At the same time, this period also witnessed numerous scholarly attempts to organize both the natural and human-made world, and we find a proliferation of almanacs, travel guides, natural history texts, and encyclopedias. The *tanuki* duly makes an appearance in these venues as well: for example, in the *Kinmō zui*, an exceedingly popular illustrated encyclopedia published in 1666, the *tanuki* appropriately shares a page with the *kitsune*.[11] And in a later, more detailed encyclopedia, the *Wakan sansai zue* (circa 1713), an extended entry on the *tanuki* describes its appearance and habitat, and then, very casually, mentions that, "Just like *kitsune*, old *tanuki* will often change their shape [*henshin*] and become monsters [*yōkai*]. They always hide in a hole in the ground and emerge to steal and eat grains, fruits, chickens and ducks. . . . And also, they enjoy themselves by thumping on their bellies."[12]

Even as we get this sort of encyclopedic description, however, the *tanuki* continues to appear as a common character in *kaidan*, or spooky narratives, often related in tale-telling sessions known as *Hyaku monogatari kaidan kai*. Here, for example, is one from a 1677 collection called *Shokoku hyaku monogatari*:

> In Bishū, a samurai with a salary of two thousand *koku* had lost his wife. Every night she was all he could think about. Then one night, when he set down his light and nodded off, his dead wife, beautifully made up and appearing exactly as she had in life, came to his bedroom. She looked [at him] longingly and made to get under the covers. Surprised, the samurai said, "Is it possible for a dead person to come back?" He grabbed her, pulled her toward him, and he stabbed her three times with his sword: she disappeared into thin air. His retainers rushed in, lit torches, and searched everywhere, but there was nothing. When morning broke, they discovered a trace of blood on the hole of the door latch. Thinking this was very strange indeed, they searched and found a hole in a grove located at the northwest corner of the property. They dug this up and found an aged *tanuki*, stabbed three times and lying dead.[13]

Much could be said about this short narrative, but I will note only a few elements that will resurface again later. First, just as in the earlier tale in which the *tanuki* appears to a devout hermit as the Bodhisattva Fugen, here too the *tanuki* takes on the shape of the protagonist's deepest desire. In this case, he (literally) embodies the samurai's longing for his dead wife. Of course, we cannot read the *tanuki*'s intentions—whether his objective is simple mischief or perhaps even an expression of pity—but certainly he disrupts the *present* by appearing as something from the *past*, a projection of the samurai's desperate longing for what is lost and irrecoverable. Second, we see here the trumping of desires and dreams by reason and

Figure 17.3. Illustrated entries for *kitsune* (top) and *tanuki* (bottom) from *Kinmō zui* encyclopedia (1666). From the Japanese collection at Stanford University Libraries.

reality. In a shockingly sudden move, the samurai violently stabs the image of his wife. Whether this can be interpreted as his private coming to terms with the irreversibility of his wife's demise or as an expression of samurai stoicism, it is through this bold action that the samurai reunifies real time (that is, a time in which his wife is dead) with physical space (his room where he sleeps alone).

This is just one brief narrative; tales of *tanuki* are too varied and numerous to generalize beyond noting that in the popular imagination of Edo period Japan, the *tanuki* was a common everyday animal with fantastic and supernatural potential. Sometimes the *tanuki* is fleshed out, so to speak, in narratives like the one above, but often it simply serves as a kind of numinous scapegoat, a default explanation for the otherwise unexplainable—odd sounds in the forest, a sense of being watched, strange occurrences of all sorts. In many cases, the term invoked is *kori*, again, a combination of *kitsune* and *tanuki* that simply connotes the mysterious forces found in the natural environment.

The Train Arrives

Against this Edo period backdrop, what happens to the *tanuki* when the nation becomes possessed by the ideology of modernity? In Japan, modernization, both in theory and practice, was rapid and transformative. With the advent of the Meiji period (1868–1912), a relatively isolated nation was abruptly flooded with fresh ideas and new technologies, in large part inspired by direct contact with the West. The capital was officially moved to Tokyo and the disparate provinces of Japan were politically reconsolidated under a new government. During this period of radical transition, one of the clearest symbols of the linking together of the nation, and of modernity itself, was the steam train. If the *tanuki* is one protagonist in my story, the train is the second.

On October 14, 1872, the nation's first railroad line, an eighteen-mile stretch between Shinbashi and Yokohama, was officially opened. Government employees were given the day off, citizens lined the rails, the military fired salutes on land and sea, and Japanese officials and foreign dignitaries gathered at both stations to honor this monumental technological achievement.[14] The next several decades witnessed the rapid diffusion of a network of rails throughout the country; by 1889, a thousand miles of track had already been laid[15] and by 1907 almost five thousand.[16] More and more people were coming in contact with this fantastic new invention: from 1890 to 1900, the number of rail passengers increased from 23 million to a staggering 114 million.[17] As the train became a common sight, tunneling through mountainsides, slithering along riverbanks, thundering through rice fields, it was celebrated in newspapers, magazines, books, travel literature, woodblock prints, songs, and even games, as a glorious symbol of *bunmei kaika* or "civilization and enlightenment," one of several slogans "repeatedly wielded as emblems and instruments of national policy" from the 1870s on.[18] The railroad was both a sign of modernity and modernity itself, the superlative metonym of this age of rapid transition; as historian Steven J. Ericson puts it, "for the Japanese of Meiji . . . the steam locomotive was the quintessential symbol of progress and civilization, the very epitome of modern industrial power."[19]

The train literally reshaped the landscape, carving passages through mountains and across rivers, and creating new routes to previously hard-to-reach places. People traveled. Community boundaries were suddenly more permeable. Local identities and traditions were exposed to distant influences. Nature itself was changed forever, and the human relationship with the environment was indelibly altered.[20] In pre-Meiji folklore, mountains and forests—the no-man's land between village boundaries—were commonly portrayed as otherworldly, mysterious places where one might run into a troublesome, supernatural presence. It was often in these very in-between spaces that *tanuki* would work their mischief, causing the wayfarer to get lost. As the train made progressively deeper inroads into previously mysterious terrain, perhaps it was inevitable that this metonym for modernity and industrialization, this new shape-shifter, would clash with that older icon of tradition and nature, the *tanuki*.

Death of the *Tanuki*

This clash was narrativized in numerous memorates and legends similar to this one from the Tokyo region:

> Now there's reclaimed land in the area around Shinagawa, but in those days the waves ran against the shore, making a sound like *pashan pashan*. It was a lonely place, and there were a lot of *tanuki* and *kitsune* there as well.
>
> At night, when the train would run through [the area], they would hear a sound, *shu shu po po po* coming from the other direction, and they'd hear a steam whistle blowing, and they'd say "a train is coming!" At first, even the conductor was thinking, "we're going to crash," and he would stop his own train and have a look around.
>
> But the train from the other direction never came. "This is strange," they'd think, and then one night as always, the *shu shu po po po* sound came, and they could hear the steam whistle, and this time they thought, "let's not worry about it," and they gave it more speed and went straight ahead.
>
> . . . Everybody expected a head-on collision—but they just went right on with no problem.
>
> When dawn broke, along the tracks at the foot of Mt. Yatsu, they found a big *tanuki* lying there dead. Back in the days of the steam engines, there was only one track so there was no way a train could randomly come from the

other direction. Well, of course, it was just that *tanuki* really enjoy imitating things.[21]

This is but one version of what would come to be known as the legend of the *nise kisha,* the "counterfeit steam train" legend or, more poetically, the "phantom train legend" (also called the *yūrei kikansha,* or "ghost train"). The putative father of Japanese folkloristics, Yanagita Kunio (1875–1962), mentions the legend in a 1918 essay;[22] Sasaki Kizen (1886–1933), folklorist and Yanagita's source for his famous *Tōno monogatari,* also writes about the narrative;[23] and in a more recent collection, children's author and folklorist Matsutani Miyoko (b. 1926) presents more than forty examples of creatures imitating trains from prefectures throughout Honshu, Kyushu, and Shikoku, and suggests that some form of the legend probably existed as early as 1878.[24] Certainly real dead *tanuki* were found wherever railroad tracks were laid, and with them these phantom train narratives proliferated; Matsutani notes that by 1910 the legend had spread throughout Japan.[25] Sasaki also alludes to the ubiquity of the narrative, commenting in 1926 that "probably everybody has heard this story somewhere at least once."[26]

Beyond Matsutani's collection, scholarly focus on the legend has been relatively limited. Yanagita emphasizes the comic nature of the narrative and references it as an example of the *tanuki*'s penchant for imitating sounds.[27] Sasaki explains that, "It seems we have recognized the legend of ghost ships (*funa yūrei*) since a long time ago. But the phantom train appears to be only a very recent story, the oldest [version going back to] sometime between 1879–1880 and around 1887. Despite this [relative newness], the narrative has been distributed far and wide, spreading along with the railroad."[28] Sasaki also makes the point that, unlike earlier ghost ship legends, the train narratives are not "mystical"; rather they contain "humor" and generally end with a laugh on the part of the raconteur.[29] He concludes his analysis by noting that this "new interesting legend" has even been found in recently settled areas of Hokkaido and does not seem to be fading—though he does not know why.[30]

I would suggest that one reason for the legend's resilience during the early years of the twentieth century is that on a metaphorical level it betrays deep ambivalence about modernity, and a sense of loss for the natural environment and local traditions that the train, as the vehicle of progress, would destroy. The legend expresses concern about the unstoppable forces of industrialized modernity that were everywhere changing the land and its traditions; the *tanuki* is a small, native animal, made of flesh and blood, who futilely resists the encroachment into its territory of a huge, foreign-inspired monster made of iron. If the mountains and forests were otherworldy regions in which a person en route from one village to another might encounter a supernatural force, the phantom train legends creatively document the destruction of these liminal zones; the steam train tied together villages in a whole new way, taking the mystery and danger from these otherworldly spaces.

The legends can be interpreted as allegorical on many levels—culture versus nature, industry versus environment, foreign versus native, dominant technologies versus local knowledge—and it is perhaps not surprising that they accompanied, as a kind of counterpoint, the network of rails expanding from region to region. If the hegemonic narrative of Meiji was *bunmei kaika,* then these legends speak of resistance to the tales of progress told of (and by) a nation becoming modern. They lament the indelible changes to the physical and cognitive landscape; the train is a monster of modernity rampaging through traditional community life—defended in vain by the human's proxy, the native, old-fashioned *tanuki.* The legends present the possibility of a counternarrative to the glorious and romantic official story of modernity.

Historians have suggested that some rural villages actively resisted the incursion of the train, forcing stations to be built on the outskirts of town. In some cases there may have been an economic rationale for this opposition: hotel owners and workers felt that the train, passing quickly through, would reduce the number of travelers spending the night. There were also fears that the smoke might affect mulberry trees and damage silk production, or that the noise would cause chickens to stop laying eggs,[31] and in at least one instance, a rumor circulated that the sound of the train whistle would shorten the hearer's life.[32] The actual prevalence of local opposition movements is a matter of dispute; one scholar adamantly argues that there is no historical evidence for these "legends of refusal" (*kyōhi densetsu*).[33] Ultimately, however, whether local opposition to the railway was historical fact or not, the very development of "legends of refusal" indicates real anxiety about the changes the railroad, and its inexorable penetration throughout the land, might bring.

Resistance to the train was also found in the literature of the time. Japan's most influential novelist and literary theorist of the early twentieth century, Natsume Sōseki (1867–1916), for example, repeatedly "uses the motion of trains as a metaphor for rapid national changes that have not been fully understood by the individuals they affect" and "implicitly critiques Japan's state-sponsored capitalist development, imperialism and war, all of which were predicated on the mobility of goods and people."[34] In novels such as *Sanshirō* (1908), railroads (steam trains and street cars) represent violent forces that not only cause characters to feel anxious and disoriented but sometimes literally lead to death through suicide or accident.[35]

Despite this strain of critical commentary, as railroads became more and more ubiquitous, the dominant attitude, both in official and popular culture, was acceptance and celebration. "For the vast majority of the population," Ericson suggests, "darker images paled before the bright symbol of the railroad as the engine of civilization and enlightenment." Negative "perceptions were," he explains, "largely confined to the world of disaffected novelists, agrarian ideologues, and rural story-tellers."[36] But indeed, this is my point: as lingering tales of resistance, the phantom train legends provide insight into the sentiments of the people who felt dispossessed by Japan's modernity.

Moreover, such sentiments represented more than just apprehension about a new technology with the potential to destroy the environment. Historian Carol Gluck has noted that the two most powerful symbols of modern Japan were the railroad and the emperor, a correlation that is only fitting, for the train and the emperor are both part of the received narrative of modern Japanese nationhood.[37] It is no coincidence that the Meiji Emperor was the star passenger on that official inaugural journey between Tokyo and Yokohama. And by the early 1900s, almost all railway lines in Japan were state owned.[38] Furthermore, during this same period of intensive railroad building at home, Japan was engaged in violent imperialist ventures abroad, including the first Sino-Japanese War (1894–95), the Russo-Japanese War (1904–5), and the annexation of Korea (1910); trains were deeply implicated in (and also symbolic of) these colonialist incursions.[39] In short, the railroad and the imperial nation-state were one and the same during this period; the train signified not only the destructive potential of industrial technology itself, but also the consolidation of nationhood and the imperial expansion that such technologies made possible.

Within this context, the phantom train narratives can be read as, to invoke James C. Scott's term, "hidden transcripts," in which people openly, yet in "disguised form . . . insinuate a critique of power."[40] Quietly but incisively the legends comment on the binding together, through train and emperor, of metropole and periphery into a single imagined community. The *tanuki* may seem like a passive victim in this national, industrial expansion, but by confronting the progress of the steam train, often through sound, he voices a sentiment counter to the modern, homogenizing project. As in the earlier examples—whether the *tanuki* poses as Fugen or as the wife of a samurai—the narrative hinges on the trope of transformation and mischievous mimicking. But in this instance, when confronting a pervasive symbol of modernity, the trope functions not only as a comic or affective narrative device, but also articulates a political critique. The *tanuki* deploys his traditional skills of deception just as he has always done, but by targeting the train, he enacts an ideological offensive against everything the railroad stands for: industrial modernity, the destruction of nature, and the dissolution of rural community structures.

It is, therefore, all the more significant that the legends end with the *tanuki*'s death. When he stands up to the train, his small voice is tragically silenced, his old magic squelched by a new industrial magic that permanently alters his traditional territory. The *tanuki*'s imitation of a train is a plaintive cry to halt the progress of the modern; though it gives the engineers pause for a moment, eventually they choose to ignore the sound and, come what may, go full steam ahead. Like the samurai of the earlier narrative, their bold decision brings them back to reality. In the morning light, the *tanuki*'s dead body—mundane, bloody, bereft of magic—signifies the futility of trying to retain the old landscape. The legends may reflect disillusionment with the train and all that it signifies, but also, more devastatingly, they reflect an *acceptance* of the inevitability of this destruction, and ultimately the futility of fighting against it. In the wake of progress, it seems, there is always a dead body, and the *tanuki*'s corpse becomes a metonym for those things—nature, tradition, magic—that the narrative of modernity destroys.[41]

The Politics of Haunting

If there is political and ideological conflict voiced in the phantom train legends, we can extend this analysis one step further to explore how these counternarratives can be understood as tales of *haunting* we can also, therefore, gesture to how tales of haunting might be read as political or ideological critiques. I suggest that we can think of "haunting" as a kind of contextual error in which the past articulates itself uncomfortably, threateningly, into the present. This does not mean that haunting has anything to do with a lack of rationality on the part of the teller or listener; indeed, memorates such as the phantom train legends are often flush with evidentiary details—from specific locations, to the body of the dead *tanuki* themselves—that serve the cause of believability. In a sense, in fact, these tales thematize the triumph of modern sensitivities over the supernatural; they are all about getting to the truth behind the illusion, causing the deceptive shape-shifter to reveal its true form.[42]

I am more interested in thinking about how these narratives are structured around the persistence of something from one time into another time; their plots are driven by intrusive anachronism. In the samurai narrative recounted earlier, for example, the wife in her living form is a vision *from the past*; therefore her embodied appearance *in the present* is inappropriate: it is, as it were, out of time. Only through a powerful act of will, as the samurai thrusts his sword into his wife's body, can the past be banished from the present. Etymologically, the notion of a *haunt* or *haunting* comes from the French and refers not—as in contemporary vernacular discourse—to something spooky, but rather to the notion of habituating or frequenting a place or a practice. Even today, of course, we speak of our old "haunts." The kind of haunting I am concerned with here, then, is the possibility of a "thing" that frequented a particular place in the past continuing to frequent that same place in the present. Of course, this is to a certain extent the mechanism of memory itself: all memories hinge on the existence of the past in the present.

But a haunting is a pathological experience of memory; it signifies the subject's inability to retain a memory *as* just a memory. The past is perceived as real, but in the wrong place.[43]

We see this with the phantom train legend. The time of modernity, as manifest by the train, is in the process of claiming the landscape. That is, the train is in the present time and the *tanuki* can, only for a moment, use their old powers of transformation and imitation to thwart this forward progress. Ultimately, however, the *tanuki*'s appearance is only a temporary imposition of the past on the reality of the present. Here is another version of the legend, this one reported in the *Tōō Nippō* newspaper on May 3, 1889:

> Just before arriving in Okegawa one evening, a steam train that had left: Ueno [in Tokyo] encountered another train, with its steam whistle blowing, advancing along the same tracks from the opposite direction. The train driver was surprised; he hastily reduced his speed and blew his whistle wildly. The oncoming train did the same, blowing its whistle insistently. However, the train that had appeared close [at first], did not seem to come any closer. When he fixed his eyes on it, the train seemed to be there but it also seemed not to be there; it was very unclear, so he increased his speed so much that he was going to crash into the other train. But the other train just disappeared like smoke, leaving not a trace. However, where it had been, two old *tanuki* the size of dogs were found lying dead on the tracks, having been hit by the train. Thinking they were terrible nuisances and now they would get their comeuppances, the driver skinned them and used the meat for *tanuki* soup. What a surprise that such a thing could occur these days, during the Meiji period.[44]

There are many familiar elements here, including the decision to go full speed ahead, and the tragicomic ending in which the *tanuki* ends up as dinner, but I want to focus on the reporter's last line. "What a surprise," he says, "that such a thing could occur these days, during the Meiji period." The narrative itself emerges from this surprise—from the disjuncture between the industrial, institutional, modern(izing) time of Meiji and the still mysterious spaces of the countryside. This disjuncture is the catalyst for the feeling of haunting.

Bakhtin famously coined the term *chronotope* for what he describes as "the intrinsic connectedness of temporal and spatial relationships." He explains that in the chronotope, "spatial and temporal indicators are fused into one carefully thought-out, concrete whole," and that "time, as it were, thickens, takes on flesh, becomes artistically visible; likewise space becomes charged and responsive to the movements of time, plot and history."[45] While Bakhtin is writing specifically about literary narratives, the basic concept of the *connectedness* of time and place is a good starting point for exploring the *disconnectedness,* or incongruity, of temporal and spatial relationships that characterizes the phantom train narratives, and many other narratives of haunting.[46]

When I speak of *time* in this context, I am referring to what I will call "indexical time." In contrast (or in addition) to scientific time or calendrical time, indexical time reflects a sense of time in one place in reference to time in another place. Indexical time hinges on the fact of history as a narrative of sociocultural change and continuity: modernity, with all its accoutrements and defining characteristics, is distinguished as a particular historical moment in a particular place in contrast to—that is, having an indexical relationship with—historical moments that come before and after it. The phenomenon of simultaneously being *physically present in one time but affectively connected to another time* can cause the cognitive and contextual disorientation of haunting. In other words, haunting articulates an impossible copresence; it is the bewilderment a subject feels when two times are simultaneously experienced in the same place. If Bakhtin's notion of chronotope suggests that a particular place is linked to a particular time, then the phenomenology of haunting complicates the logic of this indexicality: time is out of place, or place is out of time. Put another way, we can say that if chronotopes themselves are historical constructs, then the changes wrought by the train ruptures chronotopic unity—and the disorientation of this movement gives rise to hauntings.[47]

Speed, Loss, Desire, Nostalgia

During the Meiji period, the train was the literal vehicle through which modern regularized (urban) time was introduced into the countryside. It not only provided access to other villages and to once distant cities, but it also standardized schedules, creating set timetables regardless of season and climate. The extent of these changes cannot be overemphasized: before the Meiji period, for example, such fine calibrations of time as the "minute" did not exist because that level of exactitude was not necessary in daily life. "Through the opening of the railways," historian Harada Katsumasa explains bluntly, "people had to learn new units of time measurement."[48]

The railroad also simply made things faster. The locomotive embodied speed, altering relationships between once disparate places through its steam-driven velocity, bringing them closer together in time and imagination. The spatial disorientation caused by speed was a notorious effect of trains everywhere; in 1843, for example, German poet Heinrich Heine (1797–1856) commented simply that "space is killed by the railways."[49] In Meiji Japan, the average train speed was only about twenty miles an hour, but even this pace triggered cognitive disjunctions with regard to place and time. The technology of the train ruptured the "traditional space-time continuum" which was "organically embedded in nature."[50] A possibly apocryphal, though nonetheless significant, story recounts one of the first railroad journeys from Shinbashi to Yokohama. The passengers, it is said, refused to deboard after arriving in Yokohama because they simply could not grasp the fact that they had arrived at their destination so quickly. How could they possibly have covered the distance of a full day's walk in little more than an hour?[51] With the advent of the train, traditional human perceptions of time-space relations were rapidly and shockingly altered.[52]

The phantom train legends play with this temporal and spatial reshaping, narrating the disorienting experience of rapid travel between city centers. In a sense, railroad time does not even allow space to exist between cities: "the railroad," Wolfgang Schivelbusch points out, "knows only points of departure and destination."[53] When traversing the traditionally liminal spaces of rural Japan, therefore, travelers enter not only another space, but also another time—a time from the past in which *tanuki* can still enact mystery and danger. Significantly, in this in-between (and therefore nonexistent) space, the train drivers overcome the illusion of the *tanuki* by trusting their own sensibilities as modern men and using the violent technology at hand to go forward at full throttle. Like the hunter's arrow shot or the samurai's sword thrust, the burst of full steam ahead pierces the veil of illusion. It brings the timeless space of the wild countryside into the same time zone as the cities, a time-space in which the *tanuki* is nothing more than a flesh and blood animal fit for soup.

As with much folklore collected during this period, it is difficult to know the context in which the phantom train narratives were related, but their abundance and the relatively long period in which they circulated suggest that they clearly had resonance with a great many people. While I have argued that they represent an expression of resistance to the inevitability of modernization, one might argue inversely that the *tanuki*'s constant failure suggests that the tales express complicity with the modern project. They do, in one sense, fit the mold of so-called *yōkai taiji*, traditional narratives in which a (usually) human hero triumphs over a troublesome or dangerous monster. In this case the question may be which is the monster, the *tanuki* or the train?[54] Ultimately, we can say that even as the phantom train narratives are about resistance to modernity, they are also about the inevitability of its triumph; even as they are about complicity with progress, they document a longing for the things destroyed in its wake. In short, whether the teller/listener cheers for the *tanuki* or for the train, the popularity and ubiquity of these narratives reflects ambivalence to the changes that were occurring throughout the nation; the *tanuki*—even as he is killed—is a symbol of the sacrifices made for the sake of modernity. The phantom train narratives are about loss.[55]

Just as the *tanuki* in the samurai story mentioned earlier represents the physical embodiment of the samurai's personal longing, the *tanuki* protagonist of the phantom train tales enacts a desire for that prelapsarian moment before the radical shifts of modernity, when *tanuki* still had agency in, and on, the landscape. The longing in this case is not personal, but ideological, a desire to counter with equal power the forward movement of the train, to reverse the flow of time;

the *tanuki*'s inevitable death articulates the futility, the already-too-lateness, of such an emotion. His corpse lying on the side of the tracks embodies the impossibility of longing for a time already no longer possible.[56]

In a sense, then, the narratives articulate nostalgia at a moment of profound change. The word *nostalgia* derives from Greek and literally combines grief or pain (*algia*) with the notion of returning home (*nostos*). In contemporary discourse, of course, it has come to encompass a range of feelings concerning "the juxtaposition of an idealized past with an unsatisfactory present."[57] In addition to the homesickness felt on leaving one's native place, nostalgia can also be experienced when the place that *was* home changes beyond recognition. That is, the desire to go back home can indicate a desire to go back in time. In this way, we can affiliate the concept of *nostos* with the chronotope, the fusion of time and place, to signal that the telling of these tales emerges from a longing for a "concrete whole," as Bakhtin puts it, in which temporal and spatial vectors are fused, or rather, when the subject feels a sense of unity or wholeness between time and space.[58] The phantom train narratives circulate only when the past is already impossible to (re)claim because it no longer exists or, more likely, never did. And the *tanuki* represents this desire given form; as revenants of the past they haunt the modern lives of the people who tell their tales.[59]

Modernity Haunting

But in times of rapid flux and cultural change, it is not only the past that haunts the present. The desire for the future, for an impossible modernity, can be just as disorienting. I would like to complicate the phantom train legends now by introducing another similar narrative originally told in the 1920s and 1930s, toward the end of the period during which the phantom train legends were most prevalent. The narrative is not set in one of Japan's expanding conurbations, but on a small island where there has never been a train. Shimo-Koshikijima is situated about twenty-five miles off the west coast of Kagoshima Prefecture in southwestern Japan, hundreds of miles from the large urban centers of the Tokyo and Osaka regions. In the 1930s, the population of Teuchi the community in which the narrative takes place, was probably no more than four thousand people. But even in a place like this, excitement about the steam train infected the residents.

In 2001, an islander named Torii Keijirō, then in his late sixties, recounted to me this legend he had heard as a small child. The protagonist is a man from the island, recently married. In my slightly abbreviated translation here, I have tried to replicate, as much as possible, Torii-san's words and style:

> Of course, there's absolutely no way there can be a train on this island [*aru-wake wa nai*]. But in spite of that, this guy's asleep and, you know, in those

days bathrooms were outside, so you had to put on *geta* [wooden clogs] and go outside or you couldn't use the toilet. . . . So this guy wakes up in the middle of the night and goes out to the toilet . . . and he hears the *chīn chīn* sound of a train. He's never seen a train before, never even heard the *chīn chīn* sound of a train before. Only maybe he's heard about it in rumor [*seken kara*]—that the train goes *chīn chīn* . . . you know, he's just heard people talking about it. So he hears *chīn chīn* and believe it or not [*masa ni*] a train comes along. This guy lived in an area called Amida-zo; he hears, "This is Amida-zo Station." And he thinks, "Wow, that's a train" . . . and he runs and leaps aboard . . . and then the train gradually goes along the coast, and [the announcement] says, "This is Jugoya-baba; are there any departing passengers?" . . . The guy thinks, I'm already [*sekkaku*] on board so I may as well ride on to the last station . . . the next stop is Kunboigawa, so the [announcement] says, "This is Kunboigawa [*koko wa Kunboigawa desu* . . .]," and you know there's a place called Shirakihama, so when they get there it says "This is Shirakihama." . . . And then there's that shrine, Suwa-jinja, and they arrive there and it says, "Last stop, Suwa-jinja." In the old days there was a rocky shore there, so they get to the shore, and then the guy gets off and arranges the area, making a nice spot for himself.

Meanwhile, his wife [back home] is thinking, he went out for a piss and he hasn't come home yet. . . . And they were just newlyweds, so she's wondering what could have happened, where could he have gone? So she calls the fire department and the search begins. The firemen search throughout the village, and when they find the guy, he tells them proudly, "Hey, I came out here by train."

That's the story. When was it? Probably from the fourth or fifth year of Shōwa, so a pretty recent story, not all that old. . . . Nobody's sure what it was, but it was probably a *tanuki* [*sore wa tanuki deshō*]. There are a lot of people tricked by *tanuki*, so it was most likely a *tanuki* for sure.[60]

The narrative makes clear that even on an island where there was no train, the romance and excitement of the modern affected the psychic worlds of the residents. There is also a distinct emphasis on sound here. Although he says nothing of the visual aspects of the *tanuki* train, Torii-san very vividly describes the *chīn chīn* sound and performs the station-stop announcements.

Moreover, within the story, the *tanuki* lives up to its traditional function as a shape-shifter renowned, as Torii-san reminds us, for tricking people. Becoming a train, or the illusion of a train, the creature causes the man to interact with familiar terrain in an entirely new way, ironically performing a function similar to real trains on the mainland that were defamiliarizing geographies and altering human relationships to time and space. In fact, residents would know the actual placenames mentioned in the narrative and realize that a distance of hardly one hundred meters separates each station stop and that the entire distance traveled by the *tanuki* train is probably no more than two kilometers. These distances do not require a train—the scale is wrong. So while the plot itself is driven by an error of perception, for those aware of the geographical setting and spatial context, the humor of the narrative is derived from a disjuncture of distances.

Considered within its historical context, the legend suggests a local desire to be one with the modernity of the nation—separated by water, perhaps, yet linked in terms of progress and potential, part of the broader, expanding Japanese nation-state. But the message is ambiguous, even cynical; its humor is based on the fact that unity with the rest of the nation is ultimately nothing more than a dream, the product of an over-excited imagination, and that the island has already been left behind as Japan moves forward. In the guise of the *tanuki,* the specter of modernity, like a ghost of the future, haunts the island, poking fun at its desire to have what it cannot have. On one level, the tale is nothing more than a humorous narrative about a country bumpkin longing to have what he thinks they have in the city, a self-critical commentary about a desire to keep up with the rest of the nation. More poignantly, however, it also critiques the effects of modernity itself, the way scales of consumption leave some people and places behind—to live, as it were, in a different time zone.[61]

It is significant also that, unlike the newspaper reporter's conclusion earlier—"What a surprise that such a thing could occur these days"—Torii-san ends by noting, with no surprise at all, that this was a "recent story" and "it was most likely a *tanuki* for sure." The implication is that on the island in the 1930s, *tanuki* were not anachronistic; it was only natural that they would practice their traditional antics. Furthermore, the *tanuki* in this story does not end up dead, but, in a sense, continues to haunt the island. In fact, if we return to the notion of haunting here, we find that this narrative represents a converse form of the other tales we have looked at. In the phantom train legends, the *time* of modernity is real, but the *landscape* is distant and imaginary—an idealized space of supernatural possibility disconnected from the temporal world of the Meiji period. Inversely, in Shimo-Koshikijima the landscape is real, but the modernity imposed upon it in the guise of the train represents, for the islanders, an imagined time in which trains might actually have a relevant function. Within the narrative, the real space of the village is overlaid by a temporal world of the future, an image fashioned from a longing for a time not available on the island. A real place and a desired time are fused to create an idealized but impossible narrative. The *tanuki* enacts this desire, enchanting the islanders with the specter of a modernity in which they cannot fully participate.[62]

Death of the *Tanuki*: Redux

This brings me to a final, much more contemporary, example: the animated film *Heisei tanuki gassen Ponpoko,* known in English simply as *Pom Poko,* directed by

Takahata Isao of Studio Ghibli (1994). The story is set in the late 1960s and revolves around the plight of a tribe of *tanuki* living in the Tama Hills on the outskirts of Tokyo. Humans are planning to build a new suburb, destroying the *tanuki*'s native home. In a desperate attempt to thwart the encroachment of human civilization, the older *tanuki* teach the younger *tanuki* the shape-shifting magic of old. Together they create illusions and roadblocks in order to stop the construction of the suburb and the destruction of their traditional habitat. Here we have a vivid, animated representation of ideological clash and a storyline uncannily reminiscent of the phantom train legends.

Without going into details, suffice it to say that the *tanuki* eventually fail in their efforts. The film evokes the same comic-tinged pathos of the phantom train legends, and articulates the same sense of resignation to the futility of struggling against the hegemonic narrative of progress. Toward the end of the film, the *tanuki*

Figure 17.4. *Tanuki,* looking back. Photograph by the author.

marvel at the fact that humans are the ones doing all the transforming of the landscape, when this had always been their own traditional role. In a final gesture of defiance—though they know it will be futile—the *tanuki* muster up their abilities for one last, temporary transformation. In this extended scene, they cause a landscape from the past to reassert itself into the present: buildings drop away to reveal pristine forests and tranquil rice paddies, with children and *tanuki* alike playing in this pastoral world. For the *tanuki,* as well as for the human residents of the new suburb, it is an intensely nostalgic moment—an overlaying of the present with the memories of the past. It is a haunting scene.

Of course, all the tales I have discussed here—whether related by word of mouth, print, or film—are created by humans and reflect very human feelings of desire. By halting the forward movement of the locomotive, even for just a night or two, the *tanuki* of the phantom train narratives express a human longing for the tranquility of the rapidly disappearing premodern landscape, for "those days," as the narrator says, when "waves ran against the shore." The *tanuki* haunts the modern Japanese citizen with a visceral reminder of a place, and a way of being, already no longer possible. In the Shimo-Koshikijima narrative, the *tanuki*-as-train enacts a dream of a modernity coeval to, and connected with, that of the mainland, a local desire to be integrated into the broader Japanese nation. Here the *tanuki* is an enchanted projection of modern time onto an unchanged landscape. These narratives of haunting are alternately informed by a desire to return to the past and a longing for an impossible future. Either way, time and place are, momentarily, out of sync with each other. As the narrative vehicle through which these desires are enacted, the *tanuki* ultimately becomes a powerful symbol of the futility of such desires.

Yanagita Kunio suggests that by the modern period, when the phantom train narratives proliferated, the *tanuki* had already descended into a comic role in which it retained only the power to cause surprise (*odorokasu*), but nothing more.[63] But I would argue that even, or especially, as a lighthearted character, the *tanuki* can critique the hegemonic narrative of the moment. It is exactly by performing the role of bumbling trickster that the *tanuki* articulates an ideological counternarrative, a hidden transcript, against the rapid rush of human historical change.

By situating the phantom train narratives within a time-space structure of haunting, I have also tried to gesture more generally to ways of reading narratives of haunting as forms of political or ideological critique. The disconnect between the temporal and spatial dimensions that gives rise to the fantasy of haunting so often indicates a very real, and likely unvoiced, site of anxiety or discontent. And just as these sites themselves change from period to period, so too the role of the *tanuki* is constantly remediated, from late nineteenth-century legend to late twentieth-century animated film. During different historical moments, these shape-shifting creatures voice the conflicting desires of the humans who tell their tales, commenting critically about the time and place in which they live, and die.

Notes

I presented earlier versions of this essay at Indiana University, University of Maryland, Willamette University, the Ohio State University, University of Colorado, and the 2009 American Folklore Society annual meeting. I am grateful for the perceptive questions, comments, and enthusiasm of participants at these events. The essay has also benefited immensely from the suggestions and insights of three anonymous reviewers and the editors of *Asian Ethnology*. My greatest thanks, as always, goes to Michiko Suzuki.

1. The image described here is generally associated with the Shigaraki pottery style from Shiga Prefecture; although many of these features have long been associated with the *tanuki*, the ubiquity of the Shigaraki figurine is a twentieth-century phenomenon. Walker suggests that the figurine can be interpreted as saying "Come inside, and be reassured that what you will find in this place is 'traditional' and 'Japanese.'" Brett L. Walker, "Introduction: Japanimals: Entering into Dialogue with Japan's Nonhuman Majority," in *Japanimals: History and Culture in Japan's Animal Life*, ed. Gregory M. Plugfelder and Brett L. Walker (Ann Arbor: Center for Japanese Studies, University of Michigan, 2005), 4.

2. Linnaean classification *Nyctereutes procyonoides*. Three subspecies have been identified: *Nyctereutes procyonoides procyonoides* and *N. p. ussuriensis* in continental Asia, and *N. p. viverrinus* in Japan. See Kaarina Kauhla, "The Raccoon Dog: A Successful Canid," *Canid News*, 1994, 37–40, http://www.canids.org/PUBLICAT/CNDNEWS2/racoondg .htm; Oscar G. Ward and Doris H. Wurster-Hill, "Nyctereutes procyonoides," *Mammalian Species* 358 (1990): 1–5; Nakamura Teiri, *Tanuki to sono sekai* [Tanuki and their world] (Tokyo: Asahi shinbunsha. Nomura Jun'ichi, 1990), 236–44; and Inoue Tomoji, *Tanuki to Nihonjin* [*Tanuki* and the Japanese] (Nagoya: Reimei shobō, 1980), 106–12.

3. Kauhla, "Raccoon Dog."

4. For a brief review of *tanuki* lore, see Violet Harada, "The Badger in Japanese Folklore," *Asian Folklore Studies* 35 (1976): 1–6. For in-depth overviews of *tanuki*-related lore and history, see Nakamura, *Tanuki to sono sekai,* and Inoue, *Tanuki to Nihonjin*.

5. M. W. De Visser, "The Fox and Badger in Japanese Folklore," *Transactions of the Asiatic Society of Japan* 36 (1908): 41. The relationship between the *mujina* and *tanuki* is often confusing. In contemporary biological terms, the *mujina* generally refers to an *anaguma*, or badger, also native to parts of Japan. In some regions of Japan, however, *tanuki* were also called *mujina,* and the two are often conflated in folklore. See Murakami Kenji, *Yōkai jiten* [Monster/*yōkai* dictionary] (Tokyo: Mainichi Shinbunsha, 2000), 236; Nakamura, *Tanuki to sono sekai,* 236–44; Inoue, *Tanuki to Nihonjin,* 57–61.

6. The tale is found in the *Uji shūi monogatari* vol. 8, tale 6. For English translations, see Royall Tyler, *Japanese Tales* (New York: Pantheon Books, 1987), and D. E. Mills, *A Collection of Tales from Uji: A Study and Translation of Uji shūi monogatari* (Cambridge: Cambridge University Press, 1970). See also Michelle Osterfeld Li, *Ambiguous Bodies: Reading the Grotesque in Japanese Setsuwa Tales* (Stanford, Calif.: Stanford University Press, 2009),

192–233, for an important contextualized discussion of this tale and similar animal-related *setsuwa*.

7. Research on *kitsune* is extensive and often considers the fox's ability to possess humans; see, e.g., Hiruta Genshirō, "Kitsune tsuki no shinseishi" [Spiritual history of fox possession], in *Tsukimono*, ed. Komatsu Kazuhiko (Tokyo: Kawade shobō shinsha, 2000), 67–90. *Tanuki* possession was not as common as fox possession. For a brief discussion of *kitsune* lore, see Komatsu Kazuhiko, *Nihon yōkai ibunroku* [Record of strange things heard about Japanese monsters/*yōkai*] (Tokyo: Shōgakukan, 1995), 44–79. For English-language discussions of the fox in history and religion, see Carmen Blacker, *The Catalpa Bow: A Study of Shamanistic Practices in Japan* (London: George Allen and Unwin, 1986), 51–68; Michael Bathgate, *The Fox's Craft in Japanese Religion and Folklore: Shapeshifters, Transformations, and Duplicities* (New York: Routledge, 2004); Karen Smyers, *The Fox and the Jewel: Shared and Private Meanings in Contemporary Japanese Inari Worship* (Honolulu: University of Hawai'i Press, 1999); and Thomas Johnson, "Far Eastern Fox Lore," *Asian Folklore Studies* 33 (1974): 35–68. For a thorough early discussion of both *tanuki* and *kitsune*, see De Visser, "Fox and Badger in Japanese Folklore." De Visser suggests that in Chinese texts the term *kori* referred exclusively to foxes (1); he also notes that it is not until the early thirteenth-century *Gukanshō* that the term appears in a Japanese text (41). See also U. A. Casal, "The Goblin Fox and Badger and Other Witch Animals of Japan," *Folkore Studies* 18 (1959): 1–93, and Michael Dylan Foster, "Strange Games and Enchanted Science: The Mystery of Kokkuri," *Journal of Asian Studies* 65 (2006): 251–75.

8. Inoue, *Tanuki to Nihonjin*, 106–12. Although it is fair to say that the *tanuki* image from the Edo period onward was generally a lighthearted one, such comicality is not ubiquitous. Particularly in the famous folktale of *Kachi kachi yama*, the *tanuki* is portrayed as vicious and dangerous; however, even this decidedly nasty *tanuki* dies in the end. For a brief outline in English of this tale and similar types, see Seki Keigo, "Types of Japanese Folklore," *Asian Folkore Studies* 25 (1966): 39–40.

9. Konno Ensuke, *Nihon kaidan shū, yōkai hen* [Collected scary tales of Japan: Monster/*Yōkai* division] (Tokyo: Shakai shisōsha, 1999), 144.

10. The *tanuki*'s particular ability to deceive with sound has been noted by Yanagita Kunio, "*Tanuki* to demonoroji" [The *tanuki* and demonology], *Yanagita Kunio zenshū* 25 (Tokyo: Chikuma Shobō, 2000), 314; see also Konno Ensuke, *Nihon kaidan shū, yūrei hen* [Collected scary tales of Japan: Ghost/*yūrei* division] (Tokyo: Shakai shisōsha, 1999), 236–37. Matsutani Miyoko also notes the *tanuki*'s long association with mimicking sounds. Matsutani *Gendai minwa kō* [Considerations of modern folktales] (Tokyo: Rippū shobō, 1985), 3:14–15.

11. Asakura Haruhiko, ed., *Kinmō zui shūsei* [Illustrated collections to instruct the unenlightened] (Tokyo: Ōzorasha, 1998).

12. Terajima Ryōan, *Wakan sansai zue* [Illustrated encyclopedia of Japan and China] (Tokyo: Heibonsha, 1994), 6:92–93. One of the remarkable qualities of this description is the way it oscillates seamlessly between details that we would currently consider zoological (eating of grains) and those that we might think of as slightly fabulous (belly-thumping) all the way to the blatantly magical (ability to change shape). The entry goes on to describe ways *tanuki* can be cooked and various uses for *tanuki* skin (particularly good for making

bellows). Unless otherwise noted, translations from written and oral sources in Japanese are my own.

13. Tachikawa Kiyoshi, ed., *Collection of 100 Tales of the Strange* (in Japanese) (Tokyo: Kokusho kankōkai, 1995), 81. From *Shokoku hyaku monogatari* [*Hyaku monogatari* of the various provinces], compiled by an unknown editor in 1677; see Higashi Masao, *Hyaku monogatari no hyakukai* [One hundred mysteries of one hundred tales] (Tokyo: Dōhōsha/ Kadokawa shoten, 2001), 85. For more on the *Hyaku monogatari* genre of tale-telling, see Higashi, *Hyaku monogatari no hyakukai*; Noriko T. Reider, "The Emergence of Kaidan-shū: The Collection of Tales of the Strange and Mysterious in the Edo Period," *Asian Folklore Studies* 60 (2001): 79–99; and Michael Dylan Foster, *Pandemonium and Parade: Japanese Monsters and the Culture of e ani* (Berkeley: University of California Press, 2009), 52–55.

14. Steven J. Ericson, *The Sound of the Whistle: Railroads and the State in Meiji Japan* (Cambridge, Mass.: Harvard University Press, 1996), 61–62. Technically, this was not the first run of a railway line in Japan: a portion of the same track, from Shinagawa through Yokohama, had already been opened for daily usage in June of the same year; see Harada Katsumasa, *Nihon no tetsudō* [Japanese railways] (Tokyo: Yoshikawa kōbunkan, 1991), 17.

15. Aoki Eiichi, *Tetsudō kihi densetsu no nazo: Kisha ga kita machi, konakatta machi* [The riddle of the train refusal legend: Towns to which the steam train came, towns to which it did not come] (Tokyo: Yoshikawa kōbunkan, 2009), 3.

16. Ericson, *Sound of the Whistle*, 9.

17. Ericson, 68.

18. Carol Gluck, *Japan's Modern Myuths: Ideology in the Late Meiji Period* (Princeton, N.J.: Princeton University Press, 1985), 18.

19. Ericson, *Sound of the Whistle*, 3. For more on the early trains in Japanese popular culture, see Ericson, 54–55, and Alisa Freedman, *Tokyo in Transit: Japanese Culture on the Rails and Road* (Stanford, Calif.: Stanford University Press, 2011), 38–46.

20. On the radical shifts in consciousness and society caused by the railroad during the Victorian period in Britain and the United States, see Michael Freeman, *Railways and the Victorian Imagination* (New Haven, Conn.: Yale University Press, 1999).

21. Matsutani, *Gendai minwa kō*, 3:34–35. This was related by the son of the man who experienced it in early Meiji. Incidents of *kitsune* and *tanuki* causing mischief along the train tracks were widely distributed. See Matsutani, *Gendai minwa kō*, 3:13–47, and Nomura Jun'ichi, *Edo-Tōkyō no uwasa-banashi: "Konna ban" kara "Kuchi-sake-onna" made* [Rumor tales from Edo-Tokyo: From "Konna ban" to "Kuchi-sake-onna"] (Tokyo: Taishūkan shoten, 2005), 200–210.

22. Yanagita Kunio, "Tanuki to demonorojī," 310–16.

23. Sasaki Kizen, *Tōō ibun* [Strange things heard from the eastern depths] (Tokyo: Sakamoto Shoten Shuppan, 1926), 157–64.

24. Matsutani, *Gendai minwa kō*, 3:13–47.

25. Matsutani, 3:15.

26. Sasaki, *Tōō ibun*, 157. Although I focus on *tanuki* here, in some cases, including many of Matsutani's and Sasaki's examples, the protagonist is a *kitsune*. See also Inoue, *Tanuki to Nihonjin*, 72–75. Kenseiji (temple) in the Katsushika Ward of Tokyo has a *mujina tsuka* (*mujina* mound) dedicated to a *mujina* killed after imitating a train. The general structure

of the narrative is similar regardless of whether the animal in question is a *tanuki, kitsune,* or *mujina.* Some motifs associated with the phantom train legend are Ki887 (illusory sounds), Ki886 (illusions in landscape), and F491.1 (spirit leads person astray). Also, there is a correlation here to D420 (transformation: animal to object) in Hiroko Ikeda, *A Type and Motif Index of Japanese Folk-Literature* (Helsinki: Suomalainen tiedeakatemia, 1971).

27. See Yanagita, "Tanuki to demonoroji̅," 310–16.

28. Sasaki, *Tōō ibun,* 157.

29. Sasaki, 162.

30. Sasaki, 163. There is no clear date at which point the phantom train legends disappear, though they seem to have become less and less prevalent in the 1930s. But the association of the train as a vehicle at odds with the natural and supernatural world persisted at least into the late twentieth century. When the Sanyō Shinkansen (bullet train) was opened in the 1970s and 1980s, passengers noticed a loud booming sound coming from the mountains; explanations were offered that the "mountain gods were angry at the construction, or that this was the work of a *tanuki,*" and in some cases it was said that you could see a ghost through the window when traveling through a tunnel. It was later determined that the sounds were caused by air compression as the train shot rapidly through tunnels. See Ogano Minoru, *Omoshiroi hodo yoku wakaru shinkansen* [The bullet train understood well enough to be interesting] (Tokyo: Nihon bungeisha, 2010), 204.

31. Nagata Hiroshi, ed., *Meiji no kisha: Tetsudō sōsetsu 100 nen no kobore banashi kara* [Steam trains of Meiji: Stories from the hundred years since the founding of the railways] (Tokyo: Kōtsū Nihonsha, 1964), 99.

32. Ericson, *Sound of the Whistle,* 59. Not surprisingly, the early trains were frightening to behold; a young spectator standing along the tracks at the opening ceremonies in 1872 described the train as "a monster . . . leaping at me" and noted that many people "covered their ears with both hands, shut their eyes, and faced downward as if waiting for a frightening thing to pass" (61–62).

33. Aoki, *Tetsudō kihi densetsu no nazo.*

34. Freedman, *Tokyo in Transit,* 70.

35. For a detailed analysis of the role of trains in *Sanshirō* and other fiction at this time, see Freedman, 68–115.

36. Ericson, *Sound of the Whistle,* 57.

37. Gluck, *Japan's Modern Myths,* 101.

38. For more on the nationalization of the railroads, see Harada, *Nihon no tetsudō,* 50–58, and Ericson, *Sound of the Whistle,* 375–79.

39. Harada Katsumasa, *Nihon no tetsudō* [Japanese railways] (Tokyo: Yoshikawa kōbunkan, 1991), 42–54.

40. James C. Scott, *Domination and the Arts of Resistance: Hidden Transcripts* (New Haven, Conn.: Yale University Press, 1990), xiii.

41. As mentioned earlier, iconography associated with the *tanuki* is often lighthearted; in the phantom train narratives, too, the creature's death may be tragic in its inevitability but it is also somewhat comically anticlimactic. Yanagita suggests that the "demonology" of the *tanuki* can be divided into three historical epochs. In the first, *tanuki* have the power to possess [*tsuku*] people; in the second, they can only deceive [*taburakasu*]; in the third,

they only have the power to startle [*odorokasu*]. "Demonology," Yanagita says, "declines inversely to the evolution of civilization." Yanagita, "*Tanuki* to demonorojī," 310. The phantom train legend is told within the third epoch—the historical juncture of modernity—when *tanuki* have lost the power to do anything more than startle. Yanagita's thinking reflects the social-Darwinistic mind-set of the early twentieth century when he wrote this essay (1918); yet his point that the *tanuki*'s powers devolve in inverse proportion to the advances of modernity is useful for considering the way in which *tanuki* tales gesture toward a resistance to the master narrative of progress.

42. On the rhetorical strategies invoked by tellers of supernatural tales, see Diane E. Goldstein, "Scientific Rationalism and Supernatural Experiences," in *Haunting Experiences: Ghosts in Contemporary Folklore,* ed. Diane E. Goldstein, Sylvia Ann Grider, and Jeannie Banks Thomas, 70–78 (Logan: Utah State University Press, 2007). While my own analysis of haunting may differ from folkloric interpretations that focus on issues of belief, I share a similar concern with highlighting often forgotten or overlooked ways of knowing; as Motz suggests about "practices of belief," stories of haunting are "there but not there, seen but unseen, said but unsaid, floating just out of reach as a ghostly reminder of tasks left undone, insights unnoticed, omissions uncorrected." Marilyn Motz, "The Practice of Belief," *Journal of American Folklore* 3 (1998): 341.

43. Perhaps we can draw an instructive analogy between the haunting of a narrative and the growth of weeds in a garden. A weed, most simply defined as a "plant growing in the wrong place," is ultimately a social and cultural construct determined by the expectations and needs of the gardener or farmer. See Richard Mabey, *Weeds: In Defense of Nature's Most Unloved Plants* (New York: HarperCollins, 2010), 5. By persistently appearing in the "wrong place" (or at the wrong time) weeds not only obstruct or make chaotic the growth of the garden but also bring attention to the cultural parameters that define the garden *as* a garden in the first place—that is, to the worldview that determines what kind of plants are supposed to be there. Similarly, a haunting figure such as the *tanuki* reveals the assumptions and structures of the hegemonic paradigm that define it as something in the "wrong place."

44. "Kori no kisha" reprinted in Yumoto Koichi, ed., *Meijiki kaii yōkai kiji shiryō shūsei* [Collection of articles concerning strange and monstrous phenomena during the Meiji period] (Tokyo: Kokusho kankōkai, 2009), 209. In another version of the legend from Yamagata Prefecture, railroad workers similarly dine on soup made from the carcass of the mischievous *tanuki*. See Matsutani, *Gendai minwa kō,* 3:21–22.

45. M. M. Bakhtin, *The Dialogic Imagination: Four Essays by M. M. Bakhtin,* ed. Michael Holquist, trans. Caryl Emerson and Michael Holquist (Austin: University of Texas Press, 1981), 84.

46. The notion of the chronotope is notoriously complex; my own invocation here is necessarily limited. As Morson and Emerson note, "characteristically for Bakhtin, he never offers a concise definition. Rather he offers some initial comments, and then repeatedly alternates concrete examples with further generalizations. In the course of this exposition, the term turns out to have several related meanings" (366–67). For an analysis of these related meanings, see Gary Saul Morson and Caryl Emerson, *Mikhail Bakhtin: Creation of a Prosaics* (Stanford, Calif.: Stanford University Press, 1990), 366–432.

47. See Morson and Emerson, 369.

48. Harada Katsumasa, *Tetsudō to kindaika* [Railways and modernization] (Tokyo: Yoshikawa kōbunkan, 1998), 6s. In the pre-Meiji system, the smallest measurement commonly used was a segment of approximately fifteen minutes. For details, see Harada, 63–66. The modern mode of time standardization associated with the railroads is reminiscent of what Benedict Anderson famously describes as "'homogeneous, empty time, in which simultaneity is, as it were, transverse, cross-time, not marked by prefiguring and fulfillment, but by temporal coincidence, and measured by clock and calendar." See Benedict Anderson, *Imagined Communities: Reflections on the Origins and Spread of Nationalism,* rev. ed. (London: Verso, 1991), 24, 187–88. Anderson derives this concept from Walter Benjamin, *Illuminations,* ed. Hannah Arendt (New York: Schocken Books, 1968), 262–63.

49. Heine, quoted in Wolfgang Schivelbusch, *The Railway Journey: The Industrialization of Time and Space in the Nineteenth Century* (Berkeley: University of California Press, 1986), 37.

50. Schivelbusch, 36.

51. Ericson, *Sound of the Whistle,* 69–70.

52. For more on the space-time compression caused by the train, see Harada, *Nihon no tetsudō,* 57–59, and Harada, *Tetsudō to kindaika,* 51–66; see also the classic analysis by Schivelbusch, *Railway Journey.*

53. Schivelbusch, *Railway Journey,* 38.

54. While introducing the phantom train legend, Sasaki Kizen also significantly includes a tale about an old woman who sees a train approaching from the distance and mistakes it for a smoke-belching "black monster" [*makkuro na kaibutsu*]; even after she eventually gets accustomed to seeing trains, she cannot help but think of the locomotive as a "living thing." Sasaki, *Tōō ibun,* 160–61.

55. In her analysis of the relationship between modernity, folklore studies, and the uncanny, Marilyn Ivy notes of Yanagita Kunio's *Tōno monogatari,* "written at a moment (1909–1910) when it has become inescapably clear that western industrial capitalism would not only bring civilization and enlightenment but would efface much of an older Japanese world, *The Tales of Tōno* thematized this effacement in its description of Tōno, an obscure region in northeastern Japan." Ivy, *Discourses of the Vanishing: Modernity, Phantasm, Japan* (Chicago: University of Chicago Press, 1995), 72. The phantom train legends similarly thematize a loss of an older world, but through a less literary and more widely distributed form of popular narrative.

56. One anonymous reader of this essay noted that the *tanuki*'s lonely struggle against modernity is akin to the human heroes, "who waged their forlorn struggle against overwhelming odds," discussed in Ivan Morris's classic analysis in *The Nobility of Failure: Tragic Heroes in the History of Japan* (New York: Farrar Straus Giroux, 1975), xxii.

57. George K. Behlmer, introduction to *Singular Continuities: Tradition, Nostalgia, and Identity in Modern British Culture,* ed. George K. Behlmer and Fred M. Leventhal (Stanford, Calif.: Stanford University Press, 2000), 7.

58. Bakhtin, *Dialogic Imagination,* 84.

59. *Gendai minwa kō,* 3:18. Matsutani notes that the very earliest steam trains were driven by British engineers, who never reported the phantom train legend. The British workers, of course, had no memories of a pre-railroad Japan for which to long.

60. Mini disk recording by author in Teuchi, Shimo-Koshikijima, Kagoshima Prefecture, January 17, 2001. In a follow-up interview on April 4, 2012, Torii-san calculated that this incident itself would have occurred approximately ninety years ago, in the early 1920s, and then circulated as a "true story" [*jitsuwa*] for years afterward. Although there are probably no *tanuki* currently living on the island, older residents confirm that they used to be the go-to explanation for all manner of strange occurrences.

61. The narrative here is just one articulation of the stark distinction between island life and urban Japan. Recently, for example, a resident in her eighties explained to me that when she first came to the island from Tokyo after the end of World War II, she was considered exotic, and islanders flocked to get a glimpse of her. For her part, she was stunned at how "primitive" life was on the island at that time. Interview in Teuchi, Shimo-Koshikijima, Kagoshima Prefecture, January 24, 2012.

62. Perhaps we can loosely characterize *haunting* as the return of the past and *enchantment* as a projection of the future—*enchantment* implies hope and optimistic longing rather than the sad longing of the haunt.

63. Yanagita, "*Tanuki* to demonoroji," 310.

INVISIBLE MONSTERS

Vision, Horror, and Contemporary Culture

Jeffrey Andrew Weinstock

I T TAKES A VILLAGE TO MAKE A MONSTER.

By this, I mean that nothing or no one is intrinsically or "naturally" monstrous. Instead, as Jeffrey Jerome Cohen points out in "Monster Culture (Seven Theses)," the monster's body is always "pure culture," the embodiment of culturally specific fears, desires, anxieties, and fantasies.[1] What follows from this is that ideas of monstrosity and the forms that monsters take will differ across time and from place to place. This stands to reason—what scared people (and what they hoped for) in, say, twelfth-century Slovenia will obviously differ from what scares people (and what they hope for) in twenty-first-century America. We inevitably make our own monsters with the ingredients we have on hand, so the recipe keeps changing—even when the monsters themselves have been passed down from generation to generation.

The implications of the shifting social constructions of ideas of monstrosity are particularly significant when one bears in mind that what is monstrous is always defined in relation to what is human. The monster is, as Cohen appreciates, "difference made flesh";[2] it is the other, the "not us," that which a culture rejects, disowns, disavows, or, to borrow from Julia Kristeva, "abjects."[3] What this means is that to redefine monstrosity is simultaneously to rethink humanity. When our monsters change, it reflects the fact that we—our understanding of what it means to be human, our relations with one another and to the world around us, our conception of our place in the greater scheme of things—have changed as well.

This chapter will discuss a sequence of interrelated trends governing contemporary Western ideas and representations of monstrosity. While there is of course some continuity between present-day representations of monstrosity and those of previous generations, the differences are telling and offer provocative insight into culturally specific anxieties and desires. To consider our current monsters is to reflect on how we think about ourselves and our relation to the world. I will begin by observing the contemporary disconnection of monstrosity from physical appearance. Beginning with the nineteenth-century Romantics and acquiring a substantial degree of momentum in the twentieth century—especially from post–Second World War reconsiderations of ethnic and racial difference—one significant trend in representing the monster has been to decouple physical abnormality from assumptions about intelligence, character, or morals. As presented in Mary Shelley's *Frankenstein* (1818) and elaborated on in Tim Burton's updated version of Shelley's seminal Gothic tale, *Edward Scissorhands* (1990), looking different is no longer sufficient to categorize a creature as monstrous. Instead, such narratives shift the emphasis onto oppressive cultural forces that unjustly ostracize or victimize those who are physically divergent. When the "monster" becomes the protagonist and culture becomes the antagonist, ideas of normality and monstrosity must be reconsidered. This trend of "sympathy for the devil" culminates in contemporary narratives such as the Twilight series (both book and film) in which one aspires toward monstrosity as an escape from the stultification of hegemonic social forces of normalization.

What follows from this decoupling of monstrosity from appearance is an important cultural shift that aligns monstrosity not with physical difference but with antithetical moral values. Monstrosity thus is reconfigured as a kind of invisible disease that eats away at the body and the body politic and manifests visibly through symptomatic behavior. I will suggest here that this reconfiguration of monstrosity surfaces in contemporary cultural narratives in four connected ways: (1) through the psychopath (and his first cousin, the terrorist) who lives among us and could be anyone; (2) through the faceless corporation or government agency that finds its impetus in greed and corruption, and sends forth its tendrils into the cracks and crevices of everyday life; (3) through the virus that silently infiltrates and infects the body; and (4) through the conceit of the revenge of an anthropomorphized nature that responds to human despoilment of the environment in dramatic and deadly ways. What links these four related manifestations of contemporary monstrosity is their invisibility and potential ubiquity, and the response that they elicit is a form of paranoia most evident in contemporary conspiracy theories.

I will then conclude this discussion of present-day monstrosity with some consideration of one form that the response to the fear that monsters are everywhere takes—what I will refer to as "rational irrationalism" or the construction of nonsensical origins. These are horror stories and monster movies that, to a certain extent circling around to my initial discussion of "sympathy for the devil," go back in time in the attempt to explain the origins of the monster. The attempt here is to offer a rational explanation for irrational behavior by inserting that behavior into a familiar narrative framework, be it childhood neglect and abuse, scientific hubris, or magic. These narratives, however, ultimately offer only a semblance of logic while in actuality failing to demystify anything. The monster, as Cohen notes, always escapes,[4] can never finally be known or captured fully—which is part of its monstrosity.

Sympathy for the Devil

Representations of monsters in mainstream media arguably vacillate back and forth between general cycles of identification and nonidentification that develop out of and respond to specific cultural conditions. For example, many of the classic horror movies of the 1930s, such as *Frankenstein* (1931), *The Mummy* (1932), and *King Kong* (1933), offer the viewer sympathetic monsters victimized by cultural forces that reflect the shared senses of alienation and persecution felt by those traumatized by the Great Depression, while monster movies of the 1950s, giving shape to cultural anxieties about communism and atomic energy, offer creatures such as giant irradiated ants (*Them!*, 1954) and the Blob (*The Blob*, 1958), for which it is difficult to feel anything other than loathing.[5] Despite these localized cycles, however, the overall trend in monstrous representation across the twentieth century and into the twenty-first has been toward not just sympathizing with but empathizing with—and ultimately aspiring to be—the monster. Touchstone twentieth-century texts demonstrating this shift in response to established categories of monstrosity are John Gardner's novel *Grendel* (1971), a retelling of the Beowulf myth from the monster's perspective, and Anne Rice's Vampire Chronicles series, featuring her vampire heroes Louis and Lestat, which present to the reader a very attractive representation of the vampire. Twenty-first-century mainstream representations of monsters, most notably animated films oriented toward children, such as *Shrek* (2001) and *Monsters, Inc.* (2001), and vampire narratives, such as the Home Box Office (HBO) adaptation of the Charlaine Harris Sookie Stackhouse novels, *True Blood,* and the Stephenie Meyer *Twilight* franchise, forcefully develop this trend of asking the audience to identify with and even esteem the traditional monster while resisting or reviling the cultural forces that define monstrosity based on nonnormative appearance or behavior. The result is a reversal of polarities in which evil is associated not with physical difference but with cultural forces that constrain personal growth and expression.

John Gardner's 1971 novel *Grendel,* which arguably initiated the current trend of first-person monster narratives, is a retelling of the Anglo-Saxon epic poem *Beowulf* from the perspective of its antagonist, the monster Grendel. It is, however, much more than this, as it constitutes an extended meditation on the power and seduction of narrative, the pain of isolation, and what existentialist Jean-Paul Sartre refers to as our "monstrous freedom"—the fact that we alone are responsible for our choices.[6] In contrast to many of the autobiographical accounts told by monsters that follow in its wake, *Grendel* arguably does not ask the reader to sympathize with its main character. The reader comes to understand Grendel and his evil nature more fully, but as Matthew Scott Winslow observes in his online review, his behavior is never justified, and he is perhaps to be pitied but not liked.[7] What subsequent monster narratives rendered from the monster's point of view do tend to share with *Grendel*—and which Gardner's novel articulates more clearly than any of them—is a sense of the confusion and meaninglessness of existence. *Grendel* in essence asks the reader to consider not just what makes a monster but if there is a difference between a man and a monster at all.

The attempts to understand what it means to exist and what the implications of existing are can also be found at the heart of Anne Rice's Vampire Chronicles, and these questions are emphasized most fully in the first novel in the series, *Interview with the Vampire* (1976), which introduces the reader to Louis, the angst-ridden vampire protagonist, and Lestat, his charismatic and devil-may-care companion. Rice, despite the commonly held misconception, was not the first author to feature the vampire telling his own story—that achievement arguably lies with Fred Saberhagen's *The Dracula Tape,* a novel published one year prior to *Interview* that features Dracula, depicted as the historical figure Vlad Țepeș, telling his own story and coming off decidedly better than Van Helsing and the bungling vampire hunters whom he thwarts. Rice's achievement, however, is to create a rich, sensual world in which the traditional monster, the vampire, emerges as the complex and conflicted hero. Gifted with immortality, physical beauty, extraordinary speed and strength, and even the ability to fly, Rice's vampires are essentially transformed into superheroes. At the end of *Interview with the Vampire,* the young interviewer, Daniel, seduced by the power the vampire possesses, encapsulates the thrust of much post-1970s monster fiction by desiring to *become* a vampire. He aspires to escape the world of the mundane by becoming monster.

Jumping ahead to the twenty-first century, this reversal of polarities, in which the traditional monster becomes the hero, is explicitly combined with an interrogation of the social construction of ideas of normality in works such as *Shrek, Monsters, Inc., Twilight,* and *True Blood. Shrek* and *Monsters, Inc.,* animated films ostensibly for children but appealing to adults, vigorously decouple monstrosity from physical appearance. The hero of *Shrek* is a traditional fairytale villain, an ogre. His eventual love-interest, Princess Fiona, is a sort of were-ogre—

human during the day, ogre at night—and, running contrary to conventional narrative expectations, when presented with the option, she ultimately chooses to remain in her ogre form and to surrender her human one. The villain in the first Shrek film is the existing power structure as represented by Lord Farquaad, the diminutive ruler of the kingdom of Duloc. Conventional expectations are reversed even more fully in *Shrek 2* (2004), in which the villains are the physically attractive but morally bankrupt Fairy Godmother and Charming, her vain, spoiled, and egotistical son (who is also the villain in the third *Shrek* incarnation, *Shrek the Third* [2007]). *Monsters, Inc.* presents an even more straightforward disconnection of appearance from monstrosity and interrogation of normality as it presents a world of monsters—most notably kindly monsters Sully (voiced by John Goodman) and Mike (voiced by Billy Crystal)—who are scared of humans. *Monsters, Inc.* is thus entirely the product of contemporary cultural relativism—the awareness that what one culture considers normal may be considered exotic by another.

The Shrek films and *Monsters, Inc.* teach the lesson that it is moral values and behavior, not physical appearance, that define monstrosity. The hip HBO series *True Blood,* targeted at a more mature audience, adds to this contemporary awareness of cultural relativism attentiveness to the ways in which monstrosity is a socially constructed category used to police behavior and empower the arbiters of right and wrong. The premise of the series is that, co-opting a metaphor from the gay rights movement, vampires—who have always lived among humans—have decided to "come out of the coffin" and reveal their existence to the world. The push for "vampire rights" prompts a conservative backlash, as expressed in the opening credits of each episode by a billboard reading "God hates fangs," a tongue-in-cheek parody of evangelical homophobia. By paralleling vampires with homosexuals, each group unjustly demonized by a society with narrow ideas of socially correct behavior, the series prompts the awareness not just of the ways in which the term "monster" has functioned as a convenient catch-all rubric for any individual, group, race, or culture whose appearance, behavior, or values run contrary to prevailing social norms in a given time and place, but also of how the deployment of the term *monster* is a powerful political tool for the furthering of particular political designs. Expressed in *True Blood,* as in other contemporary revisions of traditional monster narratives, is the suspicion that it is those who refer to others as monsters who are most deserving of the label.

The contemporary reversal of values, in which traditional monsters and individuals with nonnormative appearances are recast as heroes, is at the center of any number of modern literary and cinematic narratives—most notably comic books and their cinematic adaptations, such as the Hellboy films (*Hellboy* [2004], *Hellboy II: The Golden Army* [2008]) featuring a demon fighting on behalf of good; the X-Men stories, in which "mutants" advocate for their freedom from conservative forces of bigotry; *The League of Extraordinary Gentleman* (2003), which features Mr. Hyde cast in an heroic role and Mina Harker from Bram Stoker's *Dracula* (1897) as both a vampire and a hero; the Incredible Hulk stories, and so on—but nowhere is the attractiveness of monstrosity more vividly illustrated than in the novels and film adaptations of Stephenie Meyer's Twilight series, in which vampires and werewolves are presented as powerful and beautiful. As anyone with even a passing familiarity with these narratives is aware, at the center of the series is protagonist Bella, who falls in love with, essentially, the perfect man, Edward (played by Robert Pattinson in the films), who turns out to be a vampire—albeit a "vegetarian" one who resists drinking human blood. Although a monster as conceived of in traditional thinking, Edward in the Twilight narratives is represented as more angelic than demonic: he is powerful, immortal (barring certain forms of physical violation), handsome, caring, and faithful; and, as if that were not enough, he can read the minds of everyone, except for Bella. He is the apotheosis of the modern sensitive man rather than a repellent monster, and he offers to Bella love, excitement, protection, and escape from the mundane.

The Monster among Us: The Psychokiller

What first-person narrative accounts told from the monster's perspective and monster tales highlighting cultural relativism effectively assert is that, while we still recognize and refer to traditional monsters as such, the idea of monstrosity has been decoupled from physical appearance and today refers first and foremost to the intention and desire to do harm to the innocent. This redefinition of monstrosity, however, creates a conundrum for contemporary citizens: how does one remain safe in a world in which anyone could be a monster? This is the powerful epistemological anxiety underpinning the popularity of contemporary crime programs like the CSI: Crime Scene Investigation franchise, narratives of psychopaths and serial killers, and in a twist with very practical "real-world" implications, paranoia concerning terrorists. What Shrek and Sully and Lestat and Edward Cullen present to us are traditional monsters that act humanely—that demonstrate the care and concern for others and the range of emotional responses which we currently define as characteristic of humanity; what *Psycho*'s Norman Bates (1960), and his figurative offspring, *American Psycho*'s Patrick Bateman (book, 1991; film, 2000), *The Silence of the Lambs*' Hannibal Lecter (book, 1988; film, 1991), to a certain extent the Showtime series *Dexter*'s eponymous antihero, and popular conceptualizations of terrorists such as the September 11 hijackers all have in common is that they look human while in reality being, from the contemporary perspective, monsters. Through his antisocial actions, the psychopath and the murderous terrorist make visible the internal lack of humanity obscured by their human facades—they are monsters on the inside.

Norman Bates, the antagonist of Alfred Hitchcock's film *Psycho,* famously played by Anthony Perkins, is arguably the poster boy for contemporary monstrosity. What is so disconcerting about Norman is just how *normal* and average he appears. Clean-cut, polite, and diffident, Norman disarms those whom he encounters with the appearance of wholesomeness. What the viewer dramatically discovers at the end of the film, however, is that Norman is not one person, but two—he suffers from multiple personality disorder and has internalized his "mother," who refuses to allow him to express adult male sexuality and instead orders him to kill any woman who arouses his lust. Norman thereby defies the conventional expectation that an individual personality be singular and coherent. He is in a sense possessed, compelled by a demonic force within to commit monstrous acts. The result is a disconnection between his external wholesomeness and his internal diseased state. He is a monster whose monstrousness only becomes visible through his actions.

The shock of *Psycho* is the revelation of Norman's mental disorder. Bret Easton Ellis tips his hat to *Psycho* both through the title of his novel, *American Psycho,* and through the name of his antihero protagonist, Patrick *Bate*man. Ellis, however, in curious ways inverts *Psycho.* To begin with, the narrative is a first-person account told from Bateman's perspective, in which he first reveals his obsessive materialist "yuppie" concerns with wealth and status, and then increasingly details his sadistic murders involving rape, torture, cannibalism, and necrophilia. Who the murderer is in *American Psycho* is not concealed and, as a result, the narrative suspense is shifted to when and whether he will be caught. In the end, though, Ellis undercuts the reader's expectations by raising questions as to whether Bateman has actually committed the horrendous acts that he narrates or rather if they were all in his mind—sick fantasies. Like Norman Bates, however, Patrick Bateman presents a facade of normality that obscures his monstrous, sadistic desires, and, again like Norman, Patrick is clearly mentally deranged. Whether a murderer in fact or in fantasy, Patrick nevertheless is a Harvard-educated Wall Street monster whose monstrosity defies easy visual detection.

In contrast to Norman Bates and Patrick Bateman, who are made easy to revile in the end, Thomas Harris's creation, Hannibal Lecter, and Dexter of the Showtime series of the same name, based on the novels by Jeff Lindsay, are especially interesting—and troubling—manifestations of the psychopathic serial killer, as each is presented to varying degrees as simultaneously monstrous and heroic. Hannibal Lecter is a brilliant, soft-spoken, and cultured psychologist—which jars greatly with his murderous and cannibalistic impulses. As with Norman Bates and Patrick Bateman, one wouldn't know Lecter for the monster he is were his psychotic tendencies not explained to the viewer and then revealed through his actions. Nevertheless, despite knowing Lecter for a monster—indeed, in *Silence of the Lambs'* most brutal sequence, the viewer observes Lecter reveal himself from beneath the flayed face of one of his guards that he has used to disguise himself— the narrative still manages to present Lecter as an attractive and compelling force. Because he is cultured; because his foil in villainy, Buffalo Bill, is so repulsive; because of the bond he forms with Detective Starling (Jodie Foster), whom he assists; and because he is so vastly more interesting than the repressive system of law and order that underestimates him, our sympathies are strangely enlisted on behalf of Lecter.

Showtime's Dexter, who is essentially Hannibal Lecter with a stricter moral system, engages those same sympathies. Dexter is the monster aware of his own monstrosity—he takes pains to hide it but cannot suppress it entirely. As revealed in the series, Dexter is a sociopath who was taught by his adoptive police officer father to direct his murderous tendencies only toward other killers. Dexter must have proof that an individual is guilty of murdering an innocent person, lacks remorse, and intends to kill again before he murders the murderer. Dexter (who in interesting ways seems indebted to Kevin Spacey's character John Doe in *Se7en* [1995], who is a sociopath who kills those he considers reprehensible) is the dark side to the superhero narrative—he is essentially Batman if Batman did not only brutally apprehend villains but also intentionally killed them. And the trick of the series is to seduce the viewer into not just excusing but indeed sanctioning Dexter's "eye-for-an-eye" system of justice that allows him to be both hero and murderer. What Dexter, however, has in common with almost all accounts of serial killers and psychopaths is that, on the surface, he looks like a normal, average person. His monstrosity is an internal, irresistible force that compels him to harm others.

Monsters, as I have suggested above, give shape to culturally specific anxieties and desires. It is no surprise then that, in the wake of the contemporary decoupling of appearance from monstrosity, concerns that anyone could be a monster and monsters could be anywhere should find, in our post-9/11 world, especially compelling embodiment in the figure of the terrorist. The terrorist— more a convention of the action genre in film and literature than horror—is essentially the sociopath with a focused and often more political impetus for his monstrous desire to do harm, and as such, terrorist narratives are often more explicitly ideological than conventional monster narratives. When Jack Bauer (Kiefer Sutherland) saves the president and the United States from violent extremists on *24*, he is supporting a particular set of beliefs and way of life. The problem for Jack Bauer and Homeland Security, and citizens riding the New York subway, however, is that—racial profiling notwithstanding—the terrorist, like the serial killer, presents no obvious external markers of his monstrosity. This is why old women and young children must go through metal detectors at airports. All of

us are potentially psychopathic terrorists. We are subjected to these visual pros-
theses because vision is not enough to separate out the monsters from the rank
and file of humanity. We no longer recognize a monster when we see one.

The Monster Is Everywhere: Corporations, Governments, and Conspiracy Theories

It is really only a small step from the concern that anyone could be a monster and
the monster could be anywhere to the paranoiac fantasy that *everyone* is a monster and the monster is *everywhere*. The invisibility of the monster allows it to
infiltrate the city, the countryside, even the intimate domestic space of the home.
In her recent study of monsters, *Pretend We're Dead: Capitalist Monsters in American Pop Culture,* Annalee Newitz surveys contemporary manifestations of a particular monster narrative, stories in which capitalism transforms human beings
into monsters that cannot distinguish between commodities and people.[8] In the
course of her analysis, she considers serial killers, mad doctors, the undead, robots,
and—curiously—people involved in the media industry. What she omits from her
discussion are corporate and government officers dedicated to furthering the
greed-driven, insidious ambitions of power-hungry, capitalist organizations.

In the 1950s—as expressed in "Red Scare" monster movies such as *The Thing
from Another World* (1951) and *Invasion of the Body Snatchers* (1956)—the anxiety
that "communism" was infecting American democracy was rife. The problem
with a communist—like a sociopath or terrorist—is that he is not immediately
visually distinguishable. You could have Bolsheviks in your company washroom,
as the famous propaganda poster states, and not even know it! Following the
Vietnam War and the Watergate scandal—as well as the dissolution of the USSR
and the fall of the Berlin Wall—social anxieties shifted from concerns about communist infiltration to concerns about corporate and government encroachment
into everyday life, and these concerns have found expression in science fiction,
fantasy, and horror narratives from *Alien* (1979) to *Avatar* (2009), and most notably in *The X-Files* television series which ran from 1993 until 2002, which are all
linked by an emphasis on the monstrousness of capitalist corporations and corrupt government organizations.

The ostensible monster in *Alien* and its various sequels is obviously the night-
marish double-mouthed extraterrestrial designed by H. R. Giger. Just as monstrous and more insidious, however, is the corporation (unnamed in the first film
but subsequently identified in later films as the "Weyland-Yutani Corporation")
that desires a specimen of the alien life-form and considers the crew expendable
in achieving this objective. In *Alien,* the agent of the corporation is the android,
Ash (Ian Holm). In the 1986 sequel, *Aliens,* the corporate agent is Carter Burke
(Paul Reiser at his most smarmy), a human. Both, however, have been "programmed" by the corporation to disregard human life and safety if it promotes

the corporation's capitalist agenda. The Alien films thus essentially have two monsters—the alien itself and the bigger monster, the monstrous corporation, that just as clearly feeds off the lives of the human characters.

This monsterization of the corporation (with an eco-friendly twist) becomes the motor force propelling the blockbuster *Avatar* (2009)—which, in keeping with the decoupling of appearance from monstrosity addressed above, casts the "traditional" monsters in the roles of sympathetic victims and heroes. *Avatar* is about a rapacious corporation conducting mining operations on the distant planet Pandora inhabited by the Na'vi, ten-foot-tall, blue-skinned sapient humanoids who live in harmony with nature. When the RDA Corporation discovers a huge mineral deposit under the massive tree which constitutes the Na'vi home, the Na'vi are attacked and forced to leave, the tree is destroyed, and the area is despoiled. Eventually, the Na'vi—led by human Jake Sully, a paraplegic former marine whose consciousness animates an "avatar" Na'vi body—band together and, assisted by other Pandoran creatures, fight back and successfully repel the human invaders. The heroes in this film, upending the conventions of science fiction, are giant blue extraterrestrials. The monster is the human-run RDA Corporation—especially as represented by the head of RDA's private security force, Colonel Miles Quaritch (Stephen Lang)—which has no compunction about displacing and killing the Na'vi and destroying both their way of life and their planet.

Post-Watergate suspicion of the government as a monster furthering its own clandestine and menacing agenda without regard for the health or welfare of the general populace is the recurring theme of any number of films, including *Three Days of the Condor* (1976), *JFK* (1991), and *Enemy of the State* (1998), but finds its fullest expression through the hit 1990s television series *The X-Files*. One of the primary slogans of the program (flashed during the opening credits of each episode), "Trust No One," clearly indicates the disposition of the program's primary detective, Fox Mulder (David Duchovny), who believes that a vast government conspiracy to hide evidence of extraterrestrial contact has occurred and that the U.S. government is conspiring with aliens and other governments on a range of sinister projects. While approximately two out of every three *X-Files* episodes were stand-alone, in which Mulder, together with his partner, the skeptic Dana Scully (Gillian Anderson), investigated bizarre cases involving paranormal phenomena, the main story arc involving government conspiracy and a shadowy division of the government called "The Syndicate"—represented by the Smoking Man (William B. Davis), a merciless killer and masterful political strategist—effectively characterized the government itself as the series's most ruthless and craftiest monster.

As is the case in narratives about serial killers and terrorists, what is most unsettling in stories of corporate greed and government conspiracy is that the monster defies visual identification. And it is not just that hidden behind the facades of business executives and government officers lurk consuming lusts for power and wealth; beyond this, what is most disturbing about such narratives is the diffuse nature of the Kafka-esque monster that cannot be located, much less killed. Like a classical monster, the hydra, corporations and governments have many heads, and if *The X-Files* teaches us anything, it is that for every "Smoking Man" apprehended, two more spring up in his place.

The Monster Is Inside Us: The Virus

If the monster can be everywhere by virtue of its invisibility, if the snaky tendrils of corporate greed or government manipulation can bypass one's defenses and penetrate the intimate spaces of one's life, the logical final extension of this infiltration is the possibility that the invisible monster (invisible, at least, to the naked eye) is already within us. This fear is at the heart of the subgenre of film (also generalizable to literature) that Murray Pomerance has referred to as the "infection film"—films governed by the "omnipresent suggestion that the body (a body politic, a body of cultural wisdom, and most essentially, of course, a protagonist's [usually beautiful] personal body) has been surreptitiously invaded, and that defenses treated in some central way as 'natural' and hegemonic have been outwitted, outmanned, outperformed, overrun, or bypassed."[9] The monster in such narratives is microscopic and the threat it presents is generally either death—often on a massive scale—or monstrous transformation. The virus as bringer of death is the underlying premise of films such as *The Andromeda Strain* (book, 1969; film, 1971) and *Outbreak* (1995). The virus as agent of monstrous transformation is the recurring premise of many zombie and vampire films such as *28 Days Later* (2002) and *I Am Legend* (2007).

The Andromeda Strain interestingly shares a basic conceit with the seminal zombie horror movie, *Night of the Living Dead,* released only one year prior to Michael Crichton's novel—that of extraterrestrial infection. In George A. Romero's *Night of the Living Dead,* the reanimation of the recently deceased and their cannibalistic appetite is credited to radiation released by the explosion of a returning space probe in the Earth's atmosphere. In *The Andromeda Strain,* the concern is over an extraterrestrial microorganism returned to Earth on a military satellite. The microorganism, dubbed the "Andromeda Strain," fatally clots human blood in most people, while causing suicidal or psychotic behavior in others, and the basic plot of both book and film is to isolate the organism, keep it from spreading, and develop a cure. In Wolfgang Petersen's *Outbreak*—which derives its impetus from the late twentieth-century AIDS pandemic—the culprit is a lethal virus originating in Africa. Combining the infection theme with the government conspiracy theme, the revelation in *Outbreak* is that the military discovered the virus thirty years prior to the California-based epidemic and has been experimenting with it as a form of germ warfare. *Outbreak,* like *Alien,* thus has two monsters: the virus itself and the military, especially as represented by Major General Donald McClintock (Donald Sutherland), who is willing to bomb the infected town of Cedar Creek to cover up his culpability in the viral epidemic and to continue his weapons development unimpeded.

In *28 Days Later* and *I Am Legend,* scientific experimentation goes horribly awry. In *28 Days Later,* animal rights activists break into a scientific research facility to free chimpanzees being used for medical research. In the process, they become infected with a disease referred to only as "Rage," which turns individuals psychotic. (While not technically a zombie film, the movie is often classified as such, given the resemblance of the infected to the living dead.) The virus spreads quickly throughout England, and the plot centers on the struggle of the main characters to survive in a postapocalyptic landscape. The plot of *I Am Legend*—the most recent adaptation of Richard Matheson's 1954 novel of the same name—is similar. A reengineered strain of measles virus, developed as a treatment for cancer, mutates and becomes lethal, killing 90 percent of the world's population. Of those remaining, most are transformed into animalistic, aggressive creatures intolerant of sunlight. (Matheson's novel actually has vampires in it; the 2007 film adaptation does not.) The plot of the film concerns U.S. Army virologist Lieutenant Colonel Robert Neville's (Will Smith) dual quests to stay alive and to develop a cure for the virus.

All four films are representative of contemporary infection paranoia in which the virus takes center stage as a modern variant of the monster. Such films clearly reflect contemporary anxieties concerning both germ warfare and pandemics such as AIDS, the Ebola virus, Bird Flu, and Swine Flu. By virtue of its invisibility to the naked eye, not only does the virus have the potential to be everywhere and to bypass all boundaries but the real concern is that we may already be infected without knowing it. The monster may not only be lurking without, but within, defying visibility until its horrific effects occur.

Reaping What We Have Sown: Nature as Monster

Closely related to the viral pandemic is the recurring contemporary nightmare of nature's revenge. Indeed, in monster virus narratives such as *I Am Legend,* the holocaust is often shown to be the product of man's tampering with nature— human hubris, sometimes with benevolent intentions, sometimes not, results in tragedy. In these instances, we literally make our own monsters. This is essentially the same story that gets played out in eco-disaster films in which human beings must contend for survival against an anthropomorphized mother nature. In films such as *The Day after Tomorrow* (2004) and most interestingly in M. Night Shyamalan's *The Happening* (2008), nature becomes monster as it actively—and with seeming intentionality—threatens human survival.

The Day after Tomorrow offers the most vivid representation of nature's revenge through its depiction of the catastrophic effects of global warming. What takes place in *The Day after Tomorrow* is a sequence of extreme weather events—including snowstorms in India, devastating hail in Japan, monster tornadoes in Los Angeles, and a massive super-hurricane that swamps New York with a forty-foot storm surge—all of which culminate in the ushering in of a new ice age. In this film, nature is the enemy—a monster of irresistible force seemingly punishing the human race for its failure to care for the environment. The thrust of the film, therefore, is that—just like any mad scientist in the typical "overreacher" horror film—humanity's overstepping of natural boundaries gives rise to the monster that wreaks its bloody revenge upon its arrogant creator. The nature-as-monster plot takes the idea of the monster being everywhere to its fullest possible expression: the world as monster bent on human destruction.

In *The Happening,* writer and director M. Night Shyamalan combines the themes of nature as monster and virus as monster to give us one of the most unsettling portrayals of the potential consequences of human alteration of the environment. The plot of the film is, in keeping with disaster films in general, the struggle for survival of a small group of people in a decimated landscape. In this instance, the struggle is against a mysterious neurotoxin that is carried by the wind and causes those infected to commit suicide. While there is no definitive explanation for the existence of the neurotoxin, the primary hypothesis presented in the film is that it is being released by trees and other plants that have developed a capacity to defend themselves against human encroachment. At the end of the film, the pandemic gripping the East Coast of the United States abruptly abates, but an expert on television, comparing the outbreak to a red tide (aquatic algal blooms of harmful phytoplankton), warns that the epidemic may have just been a first sally, as plants respond to the human threat to the planet by releasing toxins. The film then concludes with a recurrence of the pandemic beginning in Paris.

What stands out about *The Happening* is the literal form of intentionality attributed to nature. The proposition presented in the film is that nature is aggressively responding to human desecration of the environment by fighting back in a particularly dramatic and perversely poetic way—we are literally killing ourselves, stresses the film, as a result of destroying nature. Of particular note within the film are shots that normally would be considered pastoral and soothing—of the wind blowing across fields of grass, for example, and of trees swaying in the breeze—that are infused by the plot with a sense of dread and fear. As Eliot (Mark Wahlberg), Alma (Zooey Deschanel), and Jess (Ashlyn Sanchez) attempt to flee nature's wrath, nature itself seems consciously to be pursuing them with the intention of killing them. But how does one run from the wind, and where can one hide when the monster is the earth itself?

Rational Irrationalism or the Search for False Origins

The progression that this chapter has charted in terms of conceiving present-day monstrosity is one that has moved from the idea that, in the wake of decoupling monstrosity from appearance, anyone could be a monster (the psychopath), to the concern that everyone is a monster (the corporate or governmental conspiracy), to the concern that the monster is everywhere, including potentially within us (the virus and nature as antagonists). What links these four manifestations of contemporary monstrosity (psychopath, corporation, virus, nature) is epistemological anxiety related to visibility. We used to be able to recognize a monster when we saw one and therefore to act accordingly in the name of self-preservation. But how do you avoid a monster that you cannot see? How do you identify the monster when it could be anyone or anywhere? The recurring concern underlying contemporary monster narratives is that, through a sort of retroactive causality, we can now only determine the monster's presence through its effects. We know a serial killer is on the loose, that a corporation has prioritized wealth over health, that a deadly virus is spreading, or that nature is "angry" only after people start dying and the bodies begin to pile up—and the casualties then continue to mount as the protagonist is forced to determine who the monster is and how to combat it (assuming resistance is even possible).

I would like to suggest as a conclusion to this chapter that one cultural response to the epistemological barrier erected by invisibility and the anxiety attending it is the attempt to extend vision temporally and to augment it prosthetically so as to define, situate, and comprehend monstrosity and thus to be able to predict it. The attempt is to create narratives that allow us to see the invisible—to determine the origins of the monster and thus to understand, to see, what we are dealing with. More often than not, however, rather than producing actual understanding, the monster is inserted into a familiar, but nonsensical, narrative—an origin story that presents the semblance of logic but under closer scrutiny is revealed to explain very little at all. Norman Bates's murderous inclinations in *Psycho* are revealed to be the product of a controlling mother, and the psychologist at the end of *Psycho* presents a compelling narrativization of Norman's psychoses, but what, in fact, is actually explained? Similarly, the hypothesis in *The Happening* is that nature is responding to human encroachment by producing deadly neurotoxins—an explanation that makes a kind of narrative sense, but very little from a scientific perspective. This is what I call *rational irrationalism*—a logical narration of nonsensical origins that has three significant effects: it responds to the reader's or viewer's desire to make sense of what is taking place; however, it does not fully satisfy this desire, and it therefore leaves a residue of mystery and a sense of unease that allows for further elaboration in a sequel.

Vampire narratives in particular tend to be obsessed with making visible the invisible and providing origin stories that make no actual sense. One sees this in Rice's Vampire Chronicles when the origins of the vampire are traced back to ancient Egypt and demonic possession. One sees it repeatedly in vampire films, such as *Blade* (1998), that attempt to offer a veneer of scientific plausibility, as well as in infection films, through the now-iconic shot of the scientist looking through the microscope and observing infected blood cells, indicating the presence of different or diseased blood. And one sees it in Romantic horror films, such as Francis Ford Coppola's *Bram Stoker's Dracula* (1992), which trace the origins of the vampire back to heresy, magic, and the "true love conquers all" narrative; since this movie offers the most explicit example of what I am calling rational irrationalism, I would like to close by focusing on it in a bit more detail.

Bram Stoker's novel *Dracula* provides no explanation for the vampire's existence. In the 1992 film adaptation, however, Coppola felt the need to supply one and thus invented a beginning that, while explaining the vampire's existence, in actuality explains nothing. What the viewer learns is that, in 1462, Vlad Dracula, aka Vlad Țepeș, returned from battling the Turks to discover that his wife and the love of his live, Elisabeta, had committed suicide after receiving false reports of his death. Enraged by this ironic twist of fate, Dracula desecrates a chapel and renounces God, as blood dramatically wells up from candles, the communion font, and the heart of a large cross that he stabs with his sword. Developing this thwarted love plot further, the film then has the infamous Count stalking Mina Harker because he believes her to be the reincarnation of his lost love, Elisabeta.

Despite being titled *Bram Stoker's Dracula*, this origin story for Dracula and the explanation of his pursuit of Mina finds no basis in Stoker's narrative. Rather, it is Coppola's invention and satisfies the modern desire for explanations. It tells the viewer how and why Dracula transformed into a monster, what animates him, and why he pursues Mina Harker in the way that he does. It makes the monster comprehensible by inserting him into the familiar narrative paradigm "love never dies." This is, of course, the same underlying explanatory framework that structures a large number of ostensible "monster" movies; from tales of the mummy, in which the animated mummy pursues the reincarnation of his ancient bride, to ghost stories such as the paradigmatic *Ghost* (1990), starring Patrick Swayze and Demi Moore, in which the murdered Sam Wheat (Swayze) hovers around his wife, Molly (Moore), until she is out of danger and his murderers are brought to justice, the desire to believe that departed loved ones are still "out there," looking out for us, is powerful indeed. The narrative is comforting because it is familiar, but in actuality it makes sense of nothing. The "logical" origin story that it conveys remains irrational, but it does powerful ideological work in supporting the cultural investment in the ideas of marriage, monogamous love, and divine justice, so it is received as making sense.

In *Bram Stoker's Dracula,* Mina recalls her previous life as Elisabeta; in *Ghost,* Molly "sees" Sam through the mediation of the psychic Oda Mae Brown (Whoopi Goldberg); in *Blade,* we see the vampire blood cells; in *Dexter,* we learn how Dexter became what he is. In other contemporary horror films centered on invisibility and vision—such as *Predator* (1987), in which the alien monster has a cloaking device, and *Pitch Black* (2000), in which the monsters only come out at night and when an eclipse is looming—the drive is toward visualization, both figurative and literal. Recalling the repeated mantra of *Avatar,* the "I see you" expression of love, the attempt is again and again to *see* our monsters for what they are, to bring them into view, to understand them, and thus to gain some control over them. Underlying this obsessive emphasis on the visual, including the rational irrationalism of familiar but illogical origin stories, is the deeply seated contemporary anxiety that our monsters are no longer visible until they kill. In the wake of the modern decoupling of monstrosity from appearance, the monster can be anyone and anywhere, and we only know it when it springs upon us or emerges from within us.

Notes

1. Jeffrey Jerome Cohen, ed., *Monster Theory: Reading Culture* (Minneapolis: University of Minnesota Press, 1996), 4.

2. Cohen, 7.

3. Julia Kristeva, *The Powers of Horror: An Essay on Abjection,* trans. Leon S. Roudiez (New York: Columbia University Press, 1982), 1.

4. Cohen, *Monster Theory,* 4.

5. Inasmuch as these monsters from the 1950s are thinly veiled metaphors for communism, they are on some level "human." Nevertheless, while we may recognize them as such, the films prevent us from overcoming our fundamental aversion to them.

6. On the idea of monstrous freedom, see Jean-Paul Sartre's *The Family Idiot: Gustave Flaubert 1821–1857* (Chicago: University of Chicago Press, 1989), 22.

7. Matthew Scott Winslow, review of John Gardner's *Grendel,* in *The Greenman Review,* http://www.greenmanreview.com/book/book_gardner_grendel.html.

8. Annalee Newitz, *Pretend We're Dead: Capitalist Monsters in American Pop Culture* (Durham, N.C.: Duke University Press, 2006), 2.

9. Murray Pomerance, "Whatever Is *Happening* to M. Night Shyamalan: Meditation on an 'Infection' Film," in *Critical Approaches to the Films of M. Night Shyamalan: Spoiler Warnings,* ed. Jeffrey Andrew Weinstock (New York: Palgrave Macmillan, 2010), 205.

MONSTER, TERRORIST, FAG

*The War on Terrorism and the Production of
Docile Patriots*

Jasbir K. Puar and Amit S. Rai

H OW ARE GENDER AND SEXUALITY central to the current "war on terrorism"? This question opens on to others: How are the technologies that
are being developed to combat "terrorism" departures from or transformations
of older technologies of heteronormativity, white supremacy, and nationalism?
In what way do contemporary counterterrorism practices deploy these technologies, and how do these practices and technologies become the quotidian framework through which we are obliged to struggle, survive, and resist? Sexuality is
central to the creation of a certain knowledge of terrorism, specifically that branch
of strategic analysis that has entered the academic mainstream as "terrorism
studies." This knowledge has a history that ties the image of the modern terrorist to a much older figure, the racial and sexual monsters of the eighteenth and
nineteenth centuries. Further, the construction of the pathologized psyche of the
terrorist-monster enables the practices of normalization, which in today's context often means an aggressive heterosexual patriotism.

As opposed to initial post–September 11 reactions, which focused narrowly
on "the disappearance of women," we consider the question of gender justice and
queer politics through broader frames of reference, all with multiple genealogies—indeed, as we hope to show, gender and sexuality produce both hypervisible

icons and the ghosts that haunt the machines of war. Thus, we make two related arguments: (1) that the construct of the terrorist relies on a knowledge of sexual perversity (failed heterosexuality, Western notions of the psyche, and a certain queer monstrosity) and (2) that normalization invites an aggressive heterosexual patriotism that we can see, for example, in dominant media representations (for example, *The West Wing*), and in the organizing efforts of Sikh Americans in response to September 11 (the fetish of the "turbaned" Sikh man is crucial here).[1] The forms of power now being deployed in the war on terrorism in fact draw on processes of quarantining a racialized and sexualized other, even as Western norms of the civilized subject provide the framework through which these very same others become subjects to be corrected. Our itinerary begins with an examination of Michel Foucault's figure of monstrosity as a member of the West's "abnormals," followed by a consideration of the uncanny return of the monster in the discourses of "terrorism studies." We then move to the relationship between these monstrous figures in contemporary forms of heteronormative patriotism. We conclude by offering readings of the terrorism episode of *The West Wing* and an analysis of South Asian and Sikh American community-based organizing in response to September 11.

The Monster and the Terrorist

To begin, let us consider the monster. Why, in what way, has monstrosity come to organize the discourse on terrorism? First, we could merely glance at the language used by the dominant media in its interested depictions of Islamic militancy. So, as an article in the *New York Times* points out, "Osama bin Laden, according to Fox News Channel anchors, analysts and correspondents, is 'a dirtbag,' 'a monster' overseeing a 'web of hate.' His followers in Al Qaeda are 'terror goons.' Taliban fighters are 'diabolical' and 'henchmen.'"[2] Or, in another web article, we read, "It is important to realize that the Taliban does not simply tolerate the presence of bin Laden and his terrorist training camps in Afghanistan. It is part and parcel of the same evil alliance. Al-Qa'ida and the Taliban are two different heads of the same monster, and they share the same fanatical obsession: imposing a strict and distorted brand of Islam on all Muslims and bringing death to all who oppose him."[3]

In these invocations of terrorist-monsters, an absolute morality separates good from a "shadowy evil."[4] As if caught up in its own shadow dance with the anti-Western rhetoric of radical Islam,[5] this discourse marks off a figure, Osama bin Laden, or a government, the Taliban, as the opposite of all that is just, human, and good. The terrorist-monster is pure evil and must be destroyed, according to this view.[6] But does the monster have a mind? This begs another question: Do such figures and such representational strategies have a history? We suggest this language of terrorist-monsters should be read by considering how the monster has been used throughout history in Western discourses of normality. We could begin by remembering, for instance, that the monster was one of three elements that Foucault linked to the formation of the "abnormals":

> The group of abnormals was formed out of three elements whose own formation was not exactly synchronic. 1. The human monster. An Ancient notion whose frame of reference is law. A juridical notion, then, but in the broad sense, as it referred not only to social laws but to natural laws as well; the monster's field of appearance is a juridico-biological domain. The figures of the half-human, half-animal being . . . , of double individualities . . . , of hermaphrodites . . . in turn represented that double violation; what makes a human monster a monster is not just its exceptionality relative to the species form; it is the disturbance it brings to juridical regularities (whether it is a question of marriage laws, canons of baptism, or rules of inheritance). The human monster combines the impossible and the forbidden. . . . 2. The individual to be corrected. This is a more recent figure than the monster. It is the correlative not so much of the imperatives of the law as of training techniques with their own requirements. The emergence of the "incorrigibles" is contemporaneous with the putting into place of disciplinary techniques during the seventeenth and eighteenth centuries, in the army, the schools, the workshops, then, a little later, in families themselves. The new procedures for training the body, behavior, and aptitudes open up the problem of those who escape that normativity which is no longer the sovereignty of the law.[7]

According to Foucault, the monster can be both half an animal and a hybrid gender (later in this text Foucault will go on to position the onanist as the third of the abnormals). But crucially, the monster is also to be differentiated from the individual to be corrected on the basis of whether power operates on it or through it. In other words, the absolute power that produces and quarantines the monster finds its dispersal in techniques of normalization and discipline. What Foucault does, we believe, is enable an analysis of monstrosity within a broader history of sexuality. This genealogy is crucial to understanding the historical and political relays, reinvestments, and resistances between the monstrous terrorist and the discourse of heteronormativity. And that is because monsters and abnormals have always also been sexual deviants. Foucault tied monstrosity to sexuality through specific analyses of the deployment of gendered bodies, the regulation of proper desires, the manipulation of domestic spaces, and the taxonomy of sexual acts such as sodomy. As such, the sexualized monster was that figure that called forth a form of juridical power but one that was tied to multiform apparatuses of discipline as well.[8]

We use Foucault's concept of monstrosity to elaborate what we consider to be central to the present war on terrorism: monstrosity as a regulatory construct of modernity that imbricates not only sexuality, but also questions of culture and race. Before we tie these practices to contemporary politics, let us note two things. First, the monster is not merely another; it is one category through which a multiform power operates. As such, discourses that would mobilize monstrosity as a screen for otherness are always also involved in circuits of normalizing power as well: the monster and the person to be corrected are close cousins. Second, if the monster is part of the West's family of abnormals, questions of race and sexuality will have always haunted its figuration. The category of monstrosity is also an implicit index of civilizational development and cultural adaptability. As the machines of war begin to narrow the choices and life chances people have here in America and in decidedly more bloody ways abroad, it seems a certain grid of civilizational progress organized by such keywords as *democracy, freedom,* and *humanity* have come to superintend the figure of the monster. We turn now to this double deployment of the discourse of monstrosity in "terrorism studies."

Terrorism Studies

Today, we find the two figures of the monster and the person to be corrected in some ways converging in the discourse of the terrorist-monster. Which is to say that the terrorist has become both a monster to be quarantined and an individual to be corrected. It is in the strategic analyses of terrorism that these two figures come together. For the past thirty years, since 1968, the Western academy has been involved in the production and implementation of a body of knowledge that took the psyche of the terrorist as its object and target: "terrorism studies." The strategic analysis of what in the intelligence community is known as "violent substate activism" is at the moment a highly sought-after form of knowledge production. And it has direct policy relevance; hence its uneven integration into the broader field of what Edward Said once named as the disciplinary home of Orientalism: "policy studies."[9] Our own analysis has been usefully informed by the pioneering work of scholars and activists such as Said, Cynthia Enloe, Ann Tickner, Noam Chomsky, Shirin M. Rai, Edward Herman, Helen Caldicott, Philip Agee, Talal Asad, and others.[10] These writers have opened a space of critique that brings the epistemological and ethical claims of terrorism studies to crisis; their rigorous and impassioned interrogation of U.S. foreign policy has not only enabled subsequent writers to make connections to ongoing domestic wars against people of color and the working poor but, crucially, their critiques have enabled the countermemory of other genealogies, histories, and modes of power: for example, sexuality, colonialism, and normalization. So, for instance, in the discourse of counterterrorism the shared modernity of the monster and the delinquent comes together in the knowledge of cultures, nations, and races. As one editorial in the magazine *Foreign Policy* put it, "the Global Positioning System, unmanned drones, unrivaled databases, and handheld computers—much has been made of the technological resources available to the U.S. military and diplomatic establishments. But what do you do if you're trying to wage war in or against a country where you don't know the locals, can't speak the language, and can't find any reliable maps? Welcome to the front lines of the war against terrorism, likely to be waged primarily in 'swamp states' about which the United States knows little."[11] The writer ends the piece by drawing a particular lesson from Sun Tzu's *The Art of War*: "'If you know yourself but not the enemy, for every victory gained you will also suffer a defeat.' If any war on terrorism is to succeed, the United States has some serious learning to do."

Terrorism studies is at the forefront of this knowledge production. In an article in the RAND Corporation–funded journal *Studies in Conflict and Terrorism,* Richard Falkenrath notes:

> The literature on terrorism is vast. Most of this work focuses on the practitioners of terrorism, that is, on the terrorists themselves. Different strands within terrorism studies consider, for example, the motivations or belief systems of individual terrorists; the external strategies or . . . internal dynamics of particular terrorist organizations; or the interaction of terrorist movements with other entities, such as governments, the media, or social sub-groups. . . . Terrorism studies aspires not just to scholastic respectability but to policy relevance. . . . It has helped organize and inform governmental counterterrorism practices.[12]

Counterterrorism is a form of racial, civilizational knowledge, but now also an academic discipline that is quite explicitly tied to the exercise of state power. This knowledge, moreover, takes the psyche as its privileged site of investigation. As another article in *Studies in Conflict and Terrorism* put it:

> Models based on psychological concerns typically hold that "terrorist" violence is not so much a political instrument as an end in itself; it is not contingent on rational agency but is the result of compulsion or psychopathology. Over the years scholars of this persuasion have suggested that "terrorists" do what they do because of (variously and among other things) self-destructive urges, fantasies of cleanliness, disturbed emotions combined with problems with authority and the Self, and inconsistent mothering. Articulate attempts at presenting wider, vaguer, and (purportedly) generalizable psychological interpretations of terrorism have been made by, among others, Jerrold M. Post, who has proposed that ". . . political terrorists are driven to commit acts of violence as a consequence of psychological forces, and . . . their special psychologic is constructed to rationalize acts they are psychologically compelled to commit."[13]

We should note how white mythologies such as "inconsistent mothering" (and hence the bad family structure apparently common in the East) are presented as psychological compulsions that effectively determine and fix the mind of the terrorist.

In this way, psychologists working within terrorism studies have been able to determine and taxonomize the terrorist mind. In a recent article in the journal *Analyses of Social Issues and Public Policy,* Charles L. Ruby has noted that there are two dominant frameworks in the interpretation of the terrorist "mindset": "The first camp includes theories that portray terrorism as the result of defects or disorders in one's personality structure. This first group of theories uses a broadly psychodynamic model. The second camp consists of theories that approach the phenomenon of terrorist behavior as a form of political violence perpetrated by people who do not have sufficient military resources to carry out conventional forms of political violence."[14] The personality defect model of terrorism holds that terrorists have fundamental and pathological defects in "their personality structure, usually related to a damaged sense of self." Moreover, these defects result from "unconscious forces in the terrorist's psyche." And, of course, the psyche is the site of a familiar family romance: "Terrorism is a reflection of unconscious feelings of hostility toward parents and . . . this feeling is an outgrowth of childhood abuse or adolescent rebellion. The terrorist's hostile focus is so great during childhood and adolescence that it continues into adulthood and becomes very narrow and extreme, ostensibly explaining the terrorist's absolutist mindset and dedication."

As a leading light in the constellation of "terrorism experts," Jerrold Post has proposed that terrorists suffer from pathological personalities that emerge from negative childhood experiences and a damaged sense of self.[15] Post argues for two terrorist personality types, depending on the specific quality of those childhood experiences. First, Post suggests, there is the "anarchic-ideologue." This is the terrorist who has experienced serious family dysfunction and maladjustment, which lead to rebellion against parents, especially against the father. Anarchic-ideologues fight "against the society of their parents . . . an act of dissent against parents loyal to the regime." Second, there is the terrorist personality type known as the "nationalist-secessionist"—apparently the name indicates "a sense of loyalty to authority and rebellion against external enemies." During childhood, a terrorist of this personality type experienced a sense of compassion or loyalty toward his or her parents. According to Post, nationalist-secessionists have pathologically failed to differentiate between themselves and the other (parental object). Consequently, they rebel "against society for the hurt done to their parents . . . an act of loyalty to parents damaged by the regime." Both the anarchic-ideologue and nationalist-secessionist find "comfort in joining a terrorist group of rebels with similar experiences."[16] The personality defect model views terrorists as suffering from personality defects that result from excessively negative childhood experiences, giving the individual a poor sense of self and a resentment of authority. As Ruby notes, "its supporters differ in whether they propose one (Kaplan), two (Post and Jones & Fong), or three (Strentz) personality types."[17]

What all these models and theories aim to show is how an otherwise normal individual becomes a murderous terrorist, and that process time and again is tied to the failure of the normal(ized) psyche. Indeed, an implicit but foundational supposition structures this entire discourse: the very notion of the normal psyche, which is in fact part of the West's own heterosexual family romance—a narrative space that relies on the normalized, even if perverse, domestic space of desire supposedly common in the West. Terrorism, in this discourse, is a symptom of the deviant psyche, the psyche gone awry, or the failed psyche; the terrorist enters this discourse as an absolute violation. So when Billy Collins (the 2001 poet laureate) asserted on National Public Radio immediately after September 11 that "now the U.S. has lost its virginity," he was underscoring this fraught relationship between (hetero)sexuality, normality, the nation, and the violations of terrorism.

Not surprisingly, then, coming out of this discourse, we find that another very common way of trying to psychologize the monster-terrorist is by positing a kind of failed heterosexuality. So we hear often the idea that sexually frustrated Muslim men are promised the heavenly reward of sixty, sixty-seven, or sometimes even seventy virgins if they are martyred in jihad. But As'ad Abu Khalil has argued, "in reality, political—not sexual—frustration constitutes the most important factor in motivating young men, or women, to engage in suicidal violence. The tendency to dwell on the sexual motives of the suicide bombers belittles these socio-political causes."[18] Now of course, that is precisely what terrorism studies intends to do: to reduce complex social, historical, and political dynamics to various psychic causes rooted in childhood family dynamics. As if the Palestinian Intifada or the long, brutal war in Afghanistan can be simply boiled down to bad mothering or sexual frustration! In short, these explanatory models and frameworks function to (1) reduce complex histories of struggle, intervention, and (non)development to Western psychic models rooted in the bourgeois heterosexual family and its dynamics; (2) systematically exclude questions of political economy and the problems of cultural translation; and (3) attempt to master the fear, anxiety, and uncertainty of a form of political dissent by resorting to the banality of a taxonomy.[19]

Our contention is that today the knowledge and form of power that are mobilized to analyze, taxonomize, psychologize, and defeat terrorism have a genealogical connection to the West's abnormals, and specifically those premodern monsters that Western civilization had seemed to bury and lay to rest long ago. The monsters that haunt the prose of contemporary counterterrorism emerge out

of figures in the eighteenth and nineteenth centuries that have always been racialized, classed, and sexualized. The undesirable, the vagrant, the Gypsy, the savage,
the Hottentot Venus, or the sexual depravity of the Oriental torrid zone shares a
basic kinship with the terrorist-monster. As we know, in the twentieth century,
these disparate monsters became case studies, objects of ethnographies, and interesting psychological cases of degeneracy. The same Western, colonial modernity
that created the psyche created the racial and sexual monster. In other words,
what links the monster-terrorist to the figure of the individual to be corrected is
first and foremost the racialized and deviant psyche. Isn't that why there is something terrifyingly uncanny in the terrorist-monster? As one specifically liberal
article in the RAND journal put it, "members of such groups are not infrequently
prepared to kill and die for their struggles and, as sociologists would attest, that
presupposes a sort of conviction and mindset that has become uncommon in
the modern age. Thus, not only the acts of 'terrorism' but also the driving forces
behind them often appear incomprehensible and frightening to outsiders. Terrorism studies emerged as a subcategory within the social sciences in the early
1970s seeking to explain the resurgence of the seemingly inexplicable."[20]

It is the figure of the inexplicable that continues to haunt all the civilizational
grids that the Western war machine would deploy in its attempt to "understand
the terrorist psyche." We now turn to consider more explicitly the relationship
between this will to knowledge and the practices and rituals of heteronormativity.

Heteronormativity and Patriotism

We start by simply noting some obvious factors that constitute the heteronormative character of American nationalism that have been exacerbated in the current
political climate. These include, but are not limited to, heterosexual family narratives of trauma and grief (the images of the Cantor Fitzgerald wives come to
mind, as well the "families" who are petitioning the government for increased
bereavement funds); the problems gay survivors are having accessing relief and
disaster funds; "sexually active" gay men being banned from donating blood; the
lauding of national "gay heroes" such as Mark Bingham by lesbian–gay–bisexual–
transgender–queer conservatives such as Andrew Sullivan; the reevaluation of the
"Don't Ask, Don't Tell" policy in the face of military action and enlistment; and
finally, even the Miss America beauty pageant, which took place just a few weeks
after September 11, emphasized the national pride of the contestants ("There's so
much ugliness in the world, we need to see beauty").

Yet again, we could interrogate the way in which patriotism has activated
and transformed the historical memory of a militarist, racist, and class-specific
masculinity. In the days and weeks following the September 11 attacks on the
World Trade Center and the Pentagon, a rapid proliferation of mocking images

circulated of a turbaned Osama bin Laden, not to mention of the turban itself. In a photomontage from Stileproject.com, even George Bush has been depicted sporting a bin Ladenesque turban. Another internet favorite is a picture of bin Laden superimposed into a 7-Eleven convenience store scene as a cashier (harking back to, among others, Apu of *The Simpsons*).

Posters that appeared in midtown Manhattan only days after the attacks show a turbaned caricature of bin Laden being anally penetrated by the Empire State Building. The legend beneath reads, "The Empire Strikes Back" or "So you like skyscrapers, huh, bitch?" Or think of the website where, with a series of weapons at your disposal, you can torture Osama bin Laden to death, the last torture being sodomy; or another website that shows two pictures, one of bin Laden with a beard, and the other without—and the photo of him shaven turns out to be O. J. Simpson.[21] What these representations show, we believe, is that queerness as sexual deviancy is tied to the monstrous figure of the terrorist as a way to otherize and quarantine subjects classified as "terrorists," but also to normalize and discipline a population through these very monstrous figures.

Though much gender-dependent "black" humor describing the appropriate punishment for bin Laden focuses on the liberation of Afghan women (liberate Afghan women and send them to college or make bin Laden have a sex change operation and live in Afghanistan as a woman—deeply racist, sexist, and homophobic suggestions), this portrayal suggests something further still: American retaliation promises to emasculate bin Laden and turn him into a fag. This promise not only suggests that if you're not for the war, you're a fag; it also incites violence against queers and specifically queers of color. And indeed, there have been reports from community-based organizations throughout New York City that violent incidents against queers of color have increased. So on the one hand, the United States is being depicted as feminist and gay-safe by this comparison with Afghanistan, and on the other hand, the U.S. state, having experienced a castration and penetration of its capitalist masculinity, offers up narratives of emasculation as appropriate punishment for bin Laden, brown-skinned folks, and men in turbans.

It seems to us that what we see happening in America is the active promotion of self-righteous aggression and murderous violence, which have achieved almost holy status in the speeches and comments of our recently enthroned president, George W. Bush (let us not forget the 5–4 Supreme Court decision that gave him the presidency). What all these examples show is that the historical connections between heteronormativity as a process and the monstrous terrorist as an object of knowledge have been obfuscated, and in some cases severed: indeed, aspects of "homosexuality" have come within the purview of normative patriotism after September 11. In other words, what we see in the deployment of heteronormative patriotism is, on the one hand, the quarantining of the terrorist-monster-fag using the bodies and practices of a queered other, and on the other, the incorporation of aspects of queer subjectivity into the body of the normalized nation.

This dual process of incorporation and quarantining involves as well the articulation of race with nation. M. Jacqui Alexander has written that the "nation disallows queerness," and V. Spike Petersen locates "nationalism as heterosexism"; yet it is certainly the case that within a national as well as transnational frame, some queers are better than others.[22] The dearth of (white) queer progressive/Left voices is perhaps due to safety issues and real fears that many have about offering up dissenting voices; at the same time, racism and unexamined notions of citizenship seem to be operative here also.[23] Queer Left voices have also pointed out that the treatment of women by the Taliban extends to homosexuality, which is punishable by public stoning in Afghanistan.[24] When a U.S. Navy bomb aboard the USS *Enterprise* had scrawled upon it "Hijack This Fags," national gay and lesbian rights organizers objected to the homophobia of this kind of nationalist rhetoric, but not to the broader racist war itself.[25]

Clearly, a hegemonic struggle is being waged through the exclusionary and normative idioms of patriotism, humanitarianism, and, yes, even feminism. In this context, we see how the dominant media are using the figure of the *burkha*-ed woman in what are often racist and certainly chauvinistic representations of the Middle East. These representations, we should remember, have a very old colonial legacy, one that Gayatri Spivak once characterized as "white men saving brown women from brown men."[26] Furthermore, the continuities between Bush's agenda and queer Left, feminist, and South Asian diasporic and even South Asian queer diasporic positions are rather stunning, especially in the use of "culture" and "cultural norms" to obscure economic and political histories, much in the way that terrorism studies positions the relationship of the psyche to the terrorist.

Now suddenly condemning the Taliban for their treatment of women, Bush's administration has in essence occupied the space of default global feminists in an uncanny continuity with Western liberal feminists, who also have been using Afghan women as an "easy icon" in need of feminist rescue (as the successor to female genital surgery). The Feminist Majority (headed by Eleanor Smeal), along with First Lady Laura Bush and the former Duchess of York Sarah Ferguson, represent liberal feminist human rights practices that are complicit with U.S. nationalism as well as older forms of colonialist missionary feminist projects.[27] While initially Afghan women were completely absent from media representation and discussion, now RAWA (Revolutionary Afghan Women's Association) is being propped up as the saved/savior other: on a speaking tour throughout the United States, fully sponsored and paid for by the National Organization of Women, led by Executive Director Patricia Ireland. (This is not to minimize the work of RAWA, but to point out that the fetishizing of RAWA erases other women's groups in the region, ignores the relative privilege and access of resources that RAWA's members have in relation to the majority of women in Afghanistan, and obscures the network of regional and international political and economic interests that govern such organizations as NOW or even RAWA.)[28]

Another historical memory must organize our practice. As we begin to unearth these historical and discursive reticulations, we must not lose sight of the shared histories of the West's abnormals. All of these examples, and more, function to delimit and contain the kinds of responses that LGBTQ (lesbian, gay, bisexual, transgender, queer) communities can articulate in response to September 11. If we are to resist practically the "war effort" and the Us/Them and "you're either with us or against us" rhetoric, we must disarticulate the ties between patriotism and cultural and sexual identity. We must pose questions that allow us to construct practical solidarities with domestic and international communities and movements. If Western feminism has been complicit with certain forms of imperial and nationalist domination, how can feminists of color in the United States as well as "Third World" feminists (such as RAWA) undermine and displace these dominant agendas? If certain forms of queer and progressive organizing remain tied to forms of nationalist and imperial domination, how can queers of color both here and across the globe disrupt the neat folding in of queerness into narratives of modernity, patriotism, and nationalism?

Docile Patriots I: *The West Wing*

Here are two examples of contemporary cultural and community politics that speak to the network of discourses and practices we have analyzed. We have seen thus far that the terrorist-monster has a history, and through that history we can interrogate the norms and practices that aim to quarantine, know, eliminate, and correct the monster. This brings us to our next point: the monstrous terrorist, once quarantined in secret military courts, in prisons, in cells, in caves, in besieged cities or forts—this figure also provides the occasion to demand and instill a certain discipline on the population. This discipline aims to produce patriotic, docile subjects through practices, discourses, images, narratives, fears, and pleasures. One of the central sites for the construction of these docile patriots is the dominant televisual media. On CNN, FOX News, BBC, or ABC, we hear terrorist experts, psychiatrists, state officials, and journalists use the figure of the terrorist-monster as a screen to project both the racist fantasies of the West and the disciplining agenda of patriotism. Infantilizing the population, they scream with what seems to be at times one voice: "The terrorist is a monster. This monster is the enemy. The enemy must be hunted down to protect you and all those women and children that you do not know, but we know."

We can see this dual infantilization of the citizenry and production and quarantining of the monster on TV shows that have aired or are going to air in response
to September 11. These sitcoms, serials, and dramas are in fact more ideologically diverse than the mainstream news media, which have egregiously failed to
inform the public of the racist backlash against Arab American and South Asian
American communities, as well as antiwar activism. As one *USA Today* article
noted:

> producers have been rapidly churning out scripts for future episodes based
> on the aftermath of last month's attacks, following an October 3 episode of
> NBC's *The West Wing* that attracted the White House drama's biggest audi-
> ence yet. *Ally McBeal* will take an allegorical approach in a Christmas episode
> written by David E. Kelley in which a Massachusetts town official tries to
> block a holiday parade after a tragedy in which firefighters are lost, and the
> residents argue whether it is acceptable to be festive. *The Practice*'s law firm
> represents an Arab-American who argues that he is being unfairly held as a
> material witness in a fictional terrorist act in an episode of the ABC drama
> due later this fall. Popular new CBS series *The Guardian* plans a December
> storyline about a Middle Eastern family in Pittsburgh whose restaurant is
> vandalized by a white youth. "There's a lot of knee-jerk rage," says series
> creator David Hollander. "I want to touch on the reality that there's an
> incredible irrational fear." CIA-blessed drama *The Agency* originally planned
> to air a fictional anthrax attack last winter, but pulled the episode two days
> before it was scheduled to air due to anti-terrorist sentiments. And CBS has
> been pitched a new romantic comedy about a couple who lost their spouses
> in the World Trade Center attacks, says network president Les Moonves,
> who hasn't ruled out the idea. The interest marks a stark departure from the
> days immediately after September 11, when anxious censors rushed to excise
> any signs of the Trade Center or references to planes or terrorists from TV
> shows. Military drama *JAG* plans references to Afghanistan, and an episode
> about covert operations there, but producer Don Bellisario is treading
> carefully.[29]

Consider, as the first of such takes on September 11 to be aired, the October 3
episode of *The West Wing.* "The episode, entitled 'Isaac and Ishmael,' was written
by the show's creator Aaron Sorkin, and was completed in less than three weeks.
The script made no reference to the events which inspired its creation."[30] The
story line places the show's fictitious White House staff in a lock-out crisis mode
following a "crash" (which "means there has been some kind of security break:
no one in or out of the White House"; the Secret Service feared a suspected terrorist might actually be on the premises). We cut to an Arab American man, a
White House staff member, smoking a cigarette out of a window in the Old Executive Building; a group of armed white Secret Service agents break down the door

and, with guns drawn, arrest him on suspicion of plotting some kind of terrorist activity (he is later found to be innocent). Meanwhile, Josh Lyman, the deputy chief of staff, finds himself locked in a cafeteria with a group of visiting high school children who had won a trip to the White House. According to the BBC web review, "They look to him for answers to questions similar to those asked by many Americans over the past few weeks."

Most of the episode takes place in one of two rooms. In the White House mess, "gifted" high school students ask questions of various staff members. Simultaneously, the interrogation of the "terrorist" goes on in a darkened room somewhere in the Old Executive Building. The show consists of intercutting between the interrogation of the man—whose name, Raqim Ali, matches one of the aliases used by a terrorist who has just entered the United States—and "the heavy-duty chat session in the mess."[31] Students ask such questions as "What's the deal with everybody trying to kill you?" Josh turns the conversation into an interrogation, or better, translation, of the "nature" of the Taliban. He asks the students, "Islamic extremists are to Islam as ____ is to Christianity." After hearing from the students, Josh writes down his answer: "KKK." He says, "It's the Klan gone medieval and global. It couldn't have less to do with Islamic men and women of faith of whom there are millions and millions. Muslims defend this country in the Army, Navy, Air Force, Marine Corps, National Guard, Police and Fire Department." When it seems he is running out of things to say, other White House staff members join the question-and-answer session. Toby Zeigler (Richard Schiff), the president's speechwriter, champions freedom of religion and equates the people of Afghanistan with European Jews under Hitler. "There's nothing wrong with a religion whose laws say a man's got to wear a beard or cover his head or wear a collar. It's when violation of these laws become a crime against the state and not your parents that we're talking about lack of choice. . . . The Taliban isn't the recognized government of Afghanistan. The Taliban took over the recognized government of Afghanistan. . . . When you think of Afghanistan, think of Poland. When you think of the Taliban, think of the Nazis. When you think of the people of Afghanistan, think of Jews in concentration camps." Toby then tells these very attentive students a story he once heard from a friend who had been in a Nazi concentration camp. "He said he once saw a guy at the camp kneeling and praying. He said, 'What are you doing?' The guy said he was thanking God. 'What could you possibly be thanking God for?' 'I'm thanking God for not making me like them.'" Inexplicably, Toby concludes, "Bad people can't be recognized on sight. There's no point in trying."

At least one reviewer of the episode bristled at what he argued were unAmerican messages hidden in the dialogue of the episode. For this reviewer, the show's creator Aaron Sorkin was entirely to blame. Writing in the *Washington Post*, Tom Shales lambasted the show for its "tone of moral superiority":

Terrorism is definitely bad. That was established by the talk with the students. It was pointed out that . . . Islamic extremists are to Islam what the Ku Klux Klan is to Christianity. But the main thrust of the episode was summarized in another line: "Bad people can't be recognized on sight. There's no point in trying." What if they're carrying guns and have bombs strapped to each limb? That wasn't asked or answered. What was really on Sorkin's mind was the mistreatment of the apparently guiltless American-born Muslim who, as played by Ajay Naidu, maintained a tone of suffering moral superiority throughout. Ali, it was revealed, had once been arrested for taking part in demonstrations against the presence of U.S. troops in Saudi Arabia, but he was indignant—and Sorkin was indignant—that investigating such a thing might be considered appropriate for a person working in the same building as the president of the United States. How dare they?

For Shales, "discrimination against Arab Americans and against people who even just look Arabic has been a serious problem in the wake of the terrorist attacks. And is to be deplored and, one hopes, stopped. But the attention given that problem by the *West Wing* episode, as well as by some talk shows and news-casts, seems to suggest that it's the major issue arising out of the attacks. Viewers of MTV, for instance, have heard more condemnation of discrimination ('Fight for your rights') than of terrorism itself." This passing nod to the massive suspension of constitutional rights for immigrants and noncitizens is overshadowed by Shales's insistence that not only did Sorkin miss the central moral to be learned from September 11 (terrorism demands a new security state, and true patriots—even when they are the targets of that state, will stand by it, come what may), but that his is not a legitimate voice of morality in the first place. Shales concludes, "It is fair to note that in April, Sorkin was arrested at Burbank Airport and charged with two felony counts of drug possession when cocaine, hallucinogenic mush-rooms and pot were found in his carry-on bag. This would seem to have some bearing on his status as moral arbiter for the nation. . . . The implications are un-settling—that even in this moment of pain, trauma, heartbreak, destruction, assault and victimization, Hollywood liberals can still find some excuse to make America look guilty. For what it's worth, that's crap."

Such responses oblige us to recognize that in a moment of what is termed "national crisis," even platitudinous dissent is beyond the pale of the proper. How does a drug charge disallow a subject from speaking from a space that is morally legitimate—how does any kind of impropriety disqualify a subject who would dissent from the norm? But what this reviewer's diatribe points to is the subtle and not so subtle forms of normalization that the new patriotism demands of us all. Consider, then, the show's double frame itself as a kind of technology that is supposed to manage dissent, a technology that demands allegiance even as it pro-duces pluralism. For we see a double-framed reality. On the one side, brightly lit and close to the hearth (invoking the home and the family), is the classroom, a racially and gender-plural space. A space where normal, docile, but heterogeneous psyches are produced, in opposition to the terrorist-monster-fag. A space where the president as Father enters and says that what we need right now are heroes; where the first lady as Mother tells the precocious and sometimes troublesome youngsters a kind of bedtime story of two once and future brothers, Isaac (the Jews) and Ishmael (the Arabs); where male experts regale them with fantastic facts concerning the first acts of terrorism committed back in the tenth century by drug frenzied Muslims; where one woman staff member (C. J. Cregg, played by Allison Janney) declares, "We need spies. Human spies. . . . It's time to give the intelligence agencies the money and the manpower they need"; and finally, where Josh's parting advice to the students on how to relate to the terrorists is: "Remember pluralism. You want to get these people? I mean, you really want to reach in and kill them where they live? Keep accepting more than one idea. It makes them absolutely crazy."

On the other side of the frame, a dimly lit room, an enclosed, monitored space, managed entirely by white men, at the center of which is a racially and sexually ambiguous figure, a subject who at one and the same time is a possible monster and a person to be corrected. A tiny, darkened stage where the ritual of the examination, of the interrogation, is enacted on and through a subject who must perform both his racial and cultural difference and his normality. A subject quarantined, and so secluded, but whose testimony becomes a spectacle through which power will work. A subject whose greatest moment, it seems, comes when, after being terrorized at gunpoint, racially profiled, and insulted, he goes back to work. His interrogator, after stumbling through a kind of apology for his earlier racist remarks, looks back over his shoulder and says, "Hey kid, way to be back at your desk."

This double frame stages the two forms of power that we have been marking here: to quarantine and to discipline. It is we who are the schoolchildren who must be taught why "War means Peace" in Afghanistan, and certainly some of us match the profile of the monster to be quarantined, corrected, and neutralized. Let us remember that a Hindu South Asian (Ajay Naidu) plays the Arab Muslim in *The West Wing*. We can see the ways in which sexuality, gender, deviancy, normality, and power are knotted together in this TV drama: sometimes in explicit ways, as in the exchange between the interrogator and the Arab American man, or in Shales's diatribe against the immorality of Sorkin. But what we are in fact suggesting is that the entire double frame comes out of racial and sexual genealogies that imbricate the production of the radical other, as monster, to the practice of producing normalized and docile patriots. These practices, justified in the name of a Holy Crusade against Evil and legitimized through a knowledge of the psyche, follow a simple rule: "Know Thine Enemy."[32] It recalls what Sigmund Freud once wrote in his famous essay "Thoughts on War and Death." We should recall these words written in the midst of war, 1915:

> The individual in any given nation has . . . a terrible opportunity to convince himself of what would occasionally strike him in peace-time—that the state has forbidden to the individual the practice of wrong-doing, not because it desired to abolish it, but because it desires to monopolize it like salt and tobacco. The warring state permits itself every such misdeed, every such act of violence, as would disgrace the individual man. It practices not only the accepted stratagems, but also deliberate lying and deception against the enemy; and this, too, in a measure which appears to surpass the usage of former wars. The state exacts the utmost degree of obedience and sacrifice from its citizens, but at the same time treats them as children by maintaining an excess of secrecy, and censorship of news and expressions of opinion that renders the spirits of those thus intellectually oppressed defenceless against every unfavourable turn of events and every sinister rumour. It absolves itself from the guarantees and contracts it had formed with other states, and makes unabashed confession of its rapacity and lust for power, which the private individual is then called upon to sanction in the name of patriotism.[33]

In the name of patriotism, a double-framed reality and a double movement of power tie together the production of docile patriots: those monsters who must be quarantined, whose psyches offend the norms of domesticity, of the properly masculine or feminine. Such monsters, through their very example, provide patriotism with its own pedagogies of normalization. And then we have the space of the national family, inhabited by a plurality of subjects who find their proper being in the heterosexual home of the nation: these subjects are called forth, given being even, by the very figure of the monster, and they are called upon to enact their own normalization—in the name of patriotism. These docile patriots, committed to the framework of American pluralism, are themselves part of a history of racialization that is simply assumed. In our last section, we contextualize both this history and the subjectivities it engenders.

Docile Patriots II: Sikhs and Racial Formation

If in the name of patriotism, a certain docility is being demanded of us, we would like to end this essay with a consideration of how communities of color can begin to reframe these discourses, and so articulate the complex pragmatics of solidarity politics. Recent immigration policy and the discourse surrounding it have had an impact on the production of "docile patriotism." How did the state and its ideological apparatuses prepare "us" for the aftermath of the events of September 11?

In response to increasing mobility of capital across national borders, the anti-immigrant agenda serves to psychically as well as materially prevent the further contamination of the nation. The absence of a concretized external other once embodied by the Soviet Union and other Communist states marks the prime setting for targeting internal others for expulsion or normalization. In advocating the sanctity of the national body through policing of individual bodies, 1990s anti-immigrant sentiment has been primarily and perniciously fueled by conservative American "family values" rhetoric, aided by the figure of the colored welfare mother as embodying failed heterosexuality as well as compromised production capacity. In fact, many feminist scholars have pointed to the patriarchal family as foundational to the appearance of national belonging as "natural," much as familial attachments are conceptualized. In the example of post–September 11 organizing by Sikh Americans, once again we see that the underpinnings of nationalism and patriotism are composed not only of demands to produce "good citizenship" status vis-à-vis outlawed undocumented immigrants but also of heteronormativity.

In the racist backlash of the immediate aftermath of September 11, turban-clad Sikhs were "mistaken" for the kin and national compatriots of Osama bin Laden. In fear of being the targets of racist backlash against Muslims and Arab Americans, Sikhs who wear turbans (albeit, as has been repeatedly pointed out by spokespersons for Sikh advocacy groups, not the type worn by bin Laden) have discovered various counternarratives of respectable turban-hood. Many Sikhs, hearing early reports of turban grabbing and the fatal shooting of turbaned Sikh gas station owner Balbir Singh Sodhi in Mesa, Arizona, have simply abandoned their turbans, for the same reasons that many Sikhs abandoned them when they first migrated to the United States. While turbaned individuals in multicultural America have often been referred to as "towelheads," the repertoire of sophisticated references has expanded further still: on September 17, U.S. Representative John Cooksey explained to a network of Louisiana radio stations that anyone "wearing a diaper on his head" should expect to be interrogated as a possible suspect in the investigations of the terrorist attacks.[34]

Others have contributed to the current fervor of American patriotic/ multicultural exceptionalism by donning red, white, and blue turbans. Organizations such as SMART (Sikh Mediawatch and Resource Task Force, a Sikh American civil rights advocacy group) have released statements, "Talking Points," and photos explaining the differences between "those" turbans and Sikh turbans.[35] Sikhs are being stopped at airport security and asked to take off their turbans so they can be checked for knives. For this Sikhs are directed by SMART to patiently educate: "The turban is not a hat. It is a mandatory symbol of the Sikh religion. I cannot simply remove it; it must be unwrapped."[36]

To the average uninterested American eye, however, a turban is just a turban. And it symbolizes the revived, erect, and violent patriarchy of the East, of Islam, and of the Taliban; the oppression of Afghan women; the castration and the penetration of white Western phallic power by bad brown dick and its turban. (Lest one think that the backlash is "over" and that Americans are now educated about Sikhs, a *gurudwara* [temple] in upstate New York that was burned to the ground a few days before Thanksgiving was declared to be arson.)[37]

The turban is a complicated and ambivalent signifier of both racial and religious community as well as of the power of masculine heteronormativity (the shaving of the heads and beards of the suspected Taliban and al-Qaeda nonlegal combatants before being brought to Camp X-Ray at Guantánamo Bay, Cuba, is one indication of just how powerful). As such, we are as troubled by the increasing forms of turban profiling and its consequences as we are about the reemergence of cultural nationalism in Sikh and South Asian communities, which often obscures issues of gender and sexuality (for example, the ongoing violence against women in the domestic spheres and the racist backlash against women wearing the hijab). The turban becomes a contested symbol for remasculinization and nationalization in the strategies of numerous middle-class Sikh communities. Such strategies, we should note, respond to and are in conversation with the initial emasculation of the white male state (signaled by the castration of the trade towers on September 11) and the ongoing remasculinization through the war on terrorism.

What these strategies of resistance collude with, however, is precisely the "good psyche" (as opposed to the terrorist psyche) that values and legitimates middle-class domesticity, heteronormativity, and the banal pluralism of docile patriotism. Much mainstream Sikh response has focused on getting the attention of white America, intent on renarrating themselves through American nationalism as respectable, exemplary, model minority citizens who have held vigils, donated blood and funds to the Red Cross, and were quick to cover their *gurudwaras* in American flags. Many national Sikh media outlets, attempting to counter the "mistaken identity" phenomenon, have put out messages to the effect of "we are not them" (Muslims), encouraging Sikhs to use this opportunity to educate people about the peaceful Sikh religion. They are also sending an endless stream of lawyers to Washington, D.C., to meet with senators and other public officials to expound upon Sikh commitments to American civic life.[38] Sikh *gurudwaras* across the country are hiring public relations firms to "deal with this misunderstanding among the American public." While much of this "damage control" colludes with Hindu nationalist agendas to discredit Muslims and Pakistan, Indian prime minister Vajpayee was actually reprimanded by Sikh groups for both suggesting that women wear bindis in order to pass as Hindus and also for asking the U.S. government to protect Sikhs against hate crimes while not mentioning the need to protect Muslim Americans.[39]

There is a complex history that ties Sikh communities to the discourse of terrorism. As is well known, the Indian state throughout much of the 1980s was involved in a massive ideological labor as well as bloody police repression that sought to mark off Sikh groups in Punjab and in the diaspora as terrorist, and to contain the movement for Khalistan (a separatist Punjab). This history positions Sikh identity in an ambivalent relationship to the current war on terrorism: on the one hand, Sikhs in India and in the diaspora, especially *gurudwara* communities, face severe repercussions from the antiterrorist act (known as the USA PATRIOT Act);[40] on the other hand, their self-positioning as victims of both state-sponsored terrorism (for example, of the 1984 riots in New Delhi) and, as American patriots, victims of the "Islamic" terrorism of September 11 simultaneously invokes a double nationalism—Sikh and American. For example, Sikhs are holding vigils to mourn September 11 in conjunction with the pogroms of 1984—in other words, to unite with Americans under the rubric of "victims of terrorist attacks."[41] In this way, we can see how Sikh Americans face the threat of being quarantined as the terrorist-monster by refashioning themselves as docile patriots.

While the revival of Sikh middle-class "good citizenship" nationalist pride threatens to hinder possible coalitions across class, race, and sexuality, South Asian queer organizations have been relatively quiet about the racist backlash. Turbans have never been viewed as very queer-friendly, at least not in the diaspora. Community-based antibacklash/war organizing efforts—for example, a recent vigil in Jackson Heights, New York, organized by International South Asia Forum— have been conspicuously "straight." Religious differences have remained largely unaddressed in South Asian queer diasporic organizing contexts, which historically have been predominantly Hindu (and Indian). Unresolved issues of "difference" (class, immigration status, religion, caste) are now coming back to haunt the diaspora, while at the same time, clearly fear around the backlash, outing, and for some, immigration status may prevent many South Asian queers from organizing.

Within the spectrum of towelheads, diapers, and faggotry, the turban is a powerful reminder of the constructions of racial and sexual difference that inform both U.S. discourses of pluralism and South Asian, Middle Eastern, and Arab American community formations. The current climate is an opportunity for Sikhs to rethink the historical fissures among Hindus and Muslims while building stronger coalitions with other communities of color and for South Asian queers to address the pervasive Hindu-centric nature of diasporic organizing in the United States. It is unfortunate, of course, that the class specificity and specifics of violence against brown people are rarely discussed, nor is the perpetuation of this violence by other people of color available for much comment. In light of the fact that Arab Americans historically have not had a racial categorization and as such are coded as white by default, are there new racial formations emerging in response to September 11? What kinds of historically specific racial formations emerging out of model minority/postcolonial privilege and American pluralism and citizenship are South Asians struggling to hold on to or contest?[42]

Conclusion: Monster-Terrorist-Fag

In the contemporary discourse and practice of the war on terrorism, freedom, democracy, and humanity have come to frame the possibility of thinking and acting within and beyond the nation-state. We have sought to show how the uncanny monster-terrorist-fag is both a product of the anxieties of heteronormative civilization and a marker of the noncivilized—in fact, the anxiety and the monster are born of the same modernity. We have argued that the monster-terrorist-fag is reticulated with discourses and practices of heteronormative patriotism but also in the resistant strategies of feminist groups, queer communities, and communities of color. We suggest that all such strategies must confront the network of complicities that structure the possibilities of resistance: we have seen how docile patriots, even as they refuse a certain racist positioning, contribute to their own normalization and the quarantining of those they narrate themselves against. This genealogy takes on a particular urgency given the present disarray of the antiwar Left, as well as the lack of communication, debate, and connections between white progressives and communities of color, especially those implicated by changing immigration laws, new "border" hysteria, the USA PATRIOT Act, and the widespread detention of noncitizens.[43]

Moreover, these questions of discipline and normalization serve to foreclose the possibilities of solidarities among and within communities of color, for instance, between Sikhs and Muslims or among Sikhs who inhabit different class locations. So that even if the longtime surveillance of African American and Caribbean American communities might have let up a bit after September 11, what we see is the legitimation and expansion of techniques of racial profiling that were in fact perfected on black bodies. If contemporary counterterrorism discourses deploy tropes and technologies with very old histories rooted in the West's own anxieties of otherness and normality, what transformations are we witnessing in the construction of the terrorist-monster? What innovations and reelaborations open new vistas to dominant and emergent forces in the hegemonic politics of the war on/of terrorism? The return of the monster today has enabled a multiform power to reinvest and reinvent the fag, the citizen, the turban, and even the nation itself in the interests of another, more docile modernity.

Notes

1. While we are critical of the circulation of imagery that produces the turban as the fetishized signifier of the terrorist, effacing the subjectivities of women and the multiple acts of veiling and unveiling that have predominated media representation of the war in Afghanistan, we acknowledge that in some part we reinscribe this erasure in our attempts to deconstruct the heteronormative masculinities of patriotism. We thank Negar Mottahedeh for her astute observations regarding this point. In future analyses we intend to

draw on Frantz Fanon's "Unveiling Algeria" to further elaborate on these complex relations of gender.

2. Jim Rutenberg, "Fox Portrays a War of Good and Evil, and Many Applaud," *New York Times,* December 3, 2001.

3. Rand Green, "Taliban Rule in Afghanistan Is a Horrible Reign of Terror," September 24, 2001, http://www.perspicacityonline.com/109/Talibanrule10924.htm. In a review of a recent art exhibition on the monstrous at the DeCordova Museum, Miles Unger glosses why a meditation on monstrosity is timely: "Having been thrust into a context never imagined by its organizers may perhaps work to the show's advantage, throwing into bold relief many aspects of the monstrous that might otherwise have remained harder to detect. Now, more than ever, it seems important not to neglect our fears and to inspect by daylight the demons that always hide in the recesses of the mind. Psychologists have often suggested a therapeutic role for tales of horror, which allow us to acknowledge real fears in a form made manageable through narrative conventions." Miles Unger, "When Horror Can Be Healthy," *New York Times,* October 28, 2001.

4. In his Christmas address to the armed forces, Defense Secretary Donald Rumsfeld "drew a comparison between the members of today's armed forces and those who served during earlier wars, such as World War II. 'Like those heroes of that earlier era, you too stand against evil—the shadowy evil of terrorism,' Rumsfeld said. 'And like them, you also will be victorious. Of that, there is no doubt.' He said the hearts and prayers of Americans are with them, according to his statement on the Pentagon's Web site. In his holiday message to the troops, General Richard Myers, chairman of the Joint Chiefs of Staff, said Americans count the members of the armed forces among the blessings they have 'rediscovered' since September 11." CNN on the Web, Washington, D.C., Bureau, December 25, 2001, http://www.cnn.com/.

5. As Negri put it in a recent interview, "indeed this confrontation is being played out between those who are in charge of Empire and those who would like to be. From this point of view it can be asserted that terrorism is the double of Empire. The enemy of both Bush and Bin Laden is the multitude." "An Interview with Toni Negri by Giuseppe Cocco and Maurizio Lazzarato," trans. Thomas Seay and Hydrarchist, *Multitudes* 7 (December 2001), http://www.samizdat.net/multitudes.

6. Michael Hardt and Antonio Negri have remarked on how the deployment of the "human" and the demarcation of the "terrorist enemy" always seem to be the prelude to American police intervention: "Moral intervention serves as the first act that prepares the stage for military intervention. In such cases, military deployment is presented as an internationally sanctioned police action. Today military intervention is progressively less a product of decisions that arise out of the old international order or even U.N. structures. More often it is dictated unilaterally by the United States, which charges itself with the primary task and then subsequently asks its allies to set in motion a process of armed containment and/or repression of the current enemy of Empire. These enemies are most often called terrorist, a crude conceptual and terminological reduction that is rooted in a police mentality." Hardt and Negri, *Empire* (Durham, N.C.: Duke University Press, 2000), 37. In many ways, we find Hardt and Negri's argument prescient. Yet we also take issue with their own at times profoundly reductive and grossly overgeneralizing framework: we argue

that, far from a "crude conceptual and terminological reduction," the term *terrorist* today references a heterogeneous, meticulous, and multiform tactic of power.

7. Michel Foucault, "The Abnormals," trans. Robert Hurley, in *Ethics: Subjectivity and Truth*, ed. Paul Rabinow (New York: New Press, 1997), 51–52.

8. We would add that our analysis of multiform apparatuses is also indebted to network metaphors—for example, Gilles Deleuze and Félix Guattari's "rhizome"—to situate varied bodies such as the al-Qaeda network of terrorist cells or even the rituals of the body associated with anthrax spores that suggest contamination, penetration, and contact. Thanks to Patricia Clough for foregrounding these connections for us.

9. As Said put it in *Orientalism*, "Modern Orientalists—or area experts, to give them their new name—have not passively sequestered themselves in language departments. . . . Most of them today are indistinguishable from other 'experts' and 'advisers' in what Harold Lasswell has called the policy sciences." Edward Said, *Orientalism* (New York: Pantheon, 1979), 107. See Harold Lasswell, *The Political Writings of Harold D. Lasswell* (Glencoe, Ill.: Free Press, 1951); Harold Lasswell, *A Pre-View of Policy Sciences* (New York: American Elsevier, 1971); and Daniel Lerner, ed., *The Policy Sciences: Recent Developments in Scope and Method* (Stanford, Calif.: Stanford University Press, 1951). Later in his critique of Orientalism, Said remarks on how monstrosity was used by such "biological speculators" as Isidore and (his father) Etienne St. Hilaire in the first half of the nineteenth century in France. "Not only were Etienne and Isidore legatees of the tradition of 'Romantic' biology, which included Goethe and Cuvier . . . but they were also specialists in the philosophy and anatomy of monstrosity—teratology, as Isidore called it—in which the most horrendous physical aberrations were considered a result of internal degradation within the species-life." Such anomalies (whether physical or linguistic, let us keep in mind) "confirm the regular structure binding together all members of the same class" (144–45). One can, therefore, link monstrosity to nineteenth-century projects of physical anthropology and comparative linguistics that integrated concerns for "regular" structure within an overall framework of the intrinsic coherence of nature.

10. See Said, *Orientalism*; Edward Said, *Covering Islam: How the Media and the Experts Determine How We See the Rest of the World* (New York: Pantheon, 1981); Philip Agee, *Inside the Company: CIA Diary* (New York: Stonehill, 1975); Edward S. Herman, *The Terrorism Industry: The Experts and Institutions That Shape Our View of Terror* (New York: Pantheon Books, 1989); Edward S. Herman, *The Real Terror Network: Terrorism in Fact and Propaganda* (Boston: South End, 1982); Noam Chomsky, *Pirates and Emperors: International Terrorism in the Real World* (New York: Claremont Research, 1986); Talal Asad, ed., *Anthropology and the Colonial Encounter* (Ithaca, N.Y.: Cornell University Press, 1971); Cynthia Enloe, *Maneuvers: The International Politics of Militarizing Women's Lives* (Berkeley: University of California Press, 2000); Shirin M. Rai, ed., *International Perspectives on Gender and Democratization* (New York: St. Martin's, 2000); Helen Caldicott, *The New Nuclear Danger: George W. Bush's Military-Industrial Psychosis* (New York: New Press, 2002). See also Ann Tickner, "Feminist Perspectives on Security in a Global Economy," in *Globalization, Human Security, and the African Experience*, ed. Caroline Thomas and Peter Wilkin (Boulder, Colo.: Lynne Rienner, 1999), 42. The human security framework emergent in UN forums and human rights discourses seeks a new discourse that shifts emphasis

from the security of states to the security of persons and that provides a framework for analysis of the obligations of states to ensure "human" security in a context that includes the "globalization" of problems across borders and boundaries. Feminist scholars are beginning to articulate a multifaceted gendered analysis of human security.

11. "Know Thine Enemy," *Foreign Policy*, November–December, 2001, 2.

12. Richard Falkenrath, "Analytic Models and Policy Prescription: Understanding Recent Innovation in U.S. Counter terrorism," *Studies in Conflict and Terrorism* 24 (2001): 162. The RAND Corporation's website explains, "Our job is to help improve policy and decision making through research and analysis. We do that in many ways. Sometimes, we develop new knowledge to inform decision makers without suggesting any specific course of action. Often, we go further by spelling out the range of available options and by analyzing their relative advantages and disadvantages. On many other occasions, we find the analysis so compelling that we advance specific policy recommendations. In all cases, we serve the public interest by widely disseminating our research findings. RAND (a contraction of the term research and development) is the first organization to be called a 'think tank.' We earned this distinction soon after we were created in 1946 by our original client, the U.S. Air Force (then the Army Air Forces). Some of our early work involved aircraft, rockets, and satellites. In the 1960s we even helped develop the technology you're using to view this web site." http://www.rand.org/about/.

13. David Brannan, Philip Esler, and N. T. Anders Strindberg, "Talking to 'Terrorists': Towards an Independent Analytical Framework for the Study of Violent Substate Activism," *Studies in Conflict and Terrorism* 24 (2001): 6.

14. Charles L. Ruby, "Are Terrorists Mentally Deranged?," *Analyses of Social Issues and Public Policy* (2002): 16.

15. Jerrold Post, "Notes on a Psychodynamic Theory of Terrorist Behaviour," *Terrorism: An International Journal* 7 (1984): 243. Accounts of Osama bin Laden's childhood and his psychological makeup reiterate such frameworks even as they defy them. See, e.g., Mary Ann Weaver, "The Real bin Laden: By Mythologizing Him, the Government Has Made Him Even More Dangerous," *New Yorker*, January 24, 2000.

16. Post, "Notes on a Psychodynamic Theory." Like Post, Strentz also has offered a personality grid for terrorist psychopathology. Strentz's first type of terrorist is the leader. Such a person has the overall vision and intellectual purpose of the terrorist group. He or she understands the theoretical underpinnings of the group's ideology. Strentz proposes that such a person projects a sense of personal inadequacy onto society (thus the belief that society is inadequate and in need of change). The leader is suspicious, "irrationally dedicated," and uses "perverted logic." T. Strentz, "The Terrorist Organization Profile: A Psychological Role Model," in *Behavioral and Quantitative Perspectives on Terrorism* (New York: Pergamon, 1981), 88. The narcissist and paranoid personality is attracted to this terrorist position. The second of Strentz's roles is that of the opportunist. Such a person has technical know-how and is the group's "muscle." Strentz suggests such a person has a criminal history that predates involvement in the terrorist group. According to Strentz, the antisocial personality is drawn to the opportunist role. Lastly, there is the idealist. This is the young person who is never satisfied with the status quo and who has a naive view of

social problems and social change. Strentz claims that an inadequate personality best describes the person who is attracted to this role.

17. Ruby, "Are Terrorists Mentally Deranged?"

18. As'ad Abu Khalil, "Sex and the Suicide Bomber," November 13, 2001, professors_for_peace@yahoogroups.com (originally published on Salon.com).

19. The questions that are posed in this literature are, "Why does terrorism occur? What motivates terrorists? What strategies and tactics do terrorists employ to achieve their goals? How do terrorists perceive their external environment? Under what conditions will terrorists abandon their violent struggle? The success of the terrorism studies literature in answering these questions is uneven. . . . The most powerful analyses of the origins of terrorism tend to be highly specific, applying only to a single terrorist movement of an individual terrorist, and rooted in particular social and psychological circumstances." Richard Falkenrath, "Analytic Models and Policy Prescription: Understanding Recent Innovation in U.S. Counterterrorism," *Studies in Conflict and Terrorism* 24 (2001): 164. We would also add that recent articles in this journal do not indicate a monovocal diatribe against the "terror from the East." For instance, Peter Chalk, in his "Separatism and Southeast Asia: The Islamic Factor in Southern Thailand, Mindanao, and Aceh," argues rightly, we think: "The force of modernization pursued so vigorously by Southeast Asian states has, in many respects, aggravated the situation by undermining [older forms of horizontal community solidarity and hierarchical patriarchal sociality] traditional authority and socio-economic structures. This is especially true in remote, outlying areas that have suffered from administrative neglect and, in some cases outright exploitation, as a result of development programs whose prime purpose has been to further the interests and preferences of the dominant community. For these regions, the unifying ethos of secular modernization has not only acted as a major stimulant for the basis of a new sense of communal identity (ethnic, religious, or both); it has also worked to reinforce the separatist 'credentials' of local rebel groupings. The tendency of Southeast Asian governments to periodically crack down on outbursts of communal identity with draconian countermeasures . . . has merely served to further heighten this sense of regional alienation." *Studies in Conflict and Terrorism* 24 (2001): 242.

20. Brannan et al., "Talking to 'Terrorists,'" 4.

21. See http://www.gzero.net/osamatron/osamatron.html and http://www.funblaze.com/media/osama/osama.shtml.

22. See M. Jacqui Alexander, "Not Just (Any)*Body* Can Be a Citizen: The Politics of Law, Sexuality, and Postcoloniality in Trinidad and Tobago and the Bahamas," *Feminist Review* 48 (Autumn 1994): 5–23; and V. Spike Petersen, "Sexing Political Identities: Nationalism as Heterosexism," *International Feminist Journal of Politics* 1 (June 1999): 34–65. For a discussion of how queerness is produced for and through the nation-state, see Jasbir Puar, "Transnational Configurations of Desire: The Nation and Its White Closets," in *The Making and Unmaking of Whiteness,* ed. Birgit Brander Rasmussen et al. (Durham, N.C.: Duke University Press, 2001), 167–83.

23. See http://www.andrewsullivan.com/, Daily Dish, for responses to Mark Bingham's heroism as well as the "Don't Ask, Don't Tell" policy of the military. For example, one gay man wrote, "You see, whether I admitted it consciously or not, one of my problems with

gays in the military was not only the unit cohesion issue, but also the sense that gays just couldn't cut it. Well, as we found out last week, Mark Bingham could cut it. He's a hero, plain and simple. I simply can't say to myself anymore that gays have no place in the military" (September 22, 2001). On September 14, 2001, Bush authorized but did not compel the secretary of defense to consider a "stop-loss" order that could potentially suspend gay discharges. The "Don't Ask, Don't Tell, Don't Pursue, Don't Harass" order was never repealed or suspended.

24. See, e.g., Michelangelo Signorile, "Like the Taliban, America's Issues Middle East Allies Tyrannize Gays and Women Hate Crimes," http://villagevoice.com/issues/0140/signorile.php.

25. For example, GLAAD protested the homophobic caption but neglected to voice any concern for the racist implications of the image. See http://www.GLAAD.org/.

26. Gayatri Chakravorty Spivak, "Can the Subaltern Speak?," in *Marxism and the Interpretation of Culture,* ed. Cary Nelson and Lawrence Grossberg (Urbana: University of Illinois Press, 1988), 271–313. The irony, if not hypocrisy, of George W. Bush coming out against the misogyny of the Taliban has been pointed out by Barbara Ehrenreich in her article "Veiled Threat": "Feminists can take some dim comfort from the fact that the Taliban's egregious misogyny has finally been noticed. For years, the oppression of Afghan women was a topic for exotic Listservs and the occasional forlorn Internet petition. As recently as May 2001, for example, President Bush congratulated the ruling Taliban for banning opium production and handed them a check for $43 million—never mind that their regime accords women a status somewhat below that of livestock" (http://www.latimes.com/news/opinion/la-110401ehrenreich.story). In this article, Ehrenreich puts forward a number of explanatory models to account for the misogyny of "Islamic fundamentalism." She notes that the increase of women in unskilled, low-waged labor under globalization and the consequent mass "lumpenization" of men in developing countries have led to a global crisis in masculinity. She argues, rightly, that it would be a mistake to take Islamic fundamentalism out of the context of other fundamentalisms, such as Hindu, Christian, or Jewish, where we can see a reaction to a global, Western modernity that always in specific ways targets women.

27. See Elisabeth Bumiller, "First Lady to Speak about Afghan Women," *New York Times,* November 16, 2001. In a similar vein, Global Exchange is now offering, in celebration of International Women's Week, a special tour by and for women to Afghanistan called "Courage and Tenacity: A Women's Delegation to Afghanistan." One can meet with Afghan women in refugee camps, visit the underground schools for girls and the newly reopened women's bathhouses, and meet with female professionals such as doctors and government officials. See http://www.globalexchange.org/.

28. For an astute analysis of the complexities of feminist organizing, see Sharon Lerner, "What Women Want: Feminists Agonize over War in Afghanistan," *Village Voice,* November 6, 2001. See also Sonera Thobani, "War Frenzy"; and Paola Bacchetta et al., "Transnational Feminist Practices against War," both in "Creating an Archive: September 11: A Feminist Archive," *Meridians: Feminism, Race, Transnationalism* 2 (March 2002): 250–315.

29. Gary Levin, "More TV Shows Work Attacks into Plots," *USA Today,* October 17, 2001, http://www.usatoday.com/life/enter/tv/2001-10-16-plotlines.htm.

30. *"West Wing* Airs Attacks Show," http://news.bbc.co.uk/hi/english/entertainment/ tv_and_radio/newsid_1579000/1579439.stm; see also Tom Shales, *"The West Wing* Assumes the Role of Moral Compass," *Washington Post,* October 5, 2001.

31. Shales, *"West Wing."*

32. As in the title of the article cited above.

33. Sigmund Freud, "Thoughts on War and Death," trans. E. Colburn Mayne, in *Collected Papers,* ed. Joan Riviere (New York: Basic Books, 1959), 4:293–94.

34. See Joan McKinney, "Cooksey: Expect Racial Profiling," *Advocate,* September 19, 2001, http://www.theadvocate.com/news/story.asp?storyID=24608. McKinney writes, "U.S. Rep. John Cooksey, R-Monroe, told a network of Louisiana radio stations Monday that someone 'wearing a diaper on his head' should expect to be interrogated in the investigation of terrorist attacks on the Pentagon and New York City." Apparently Cooksey did not retract his remarks, stating, "If I see someone [who] comes in that's got a diaper on his head and a fan belt wrapped around the diaper on his head, that guy needs to be pulled over." See also "SMART Calls for Action against Cooksey," http://www.sikh mediawatch.org/, reporting a national letter-writing and telephone campaign protesting Cooksey's remarks. SMART (the Sikh Mediawatch and Resource Task Force), founded in 1996 to promote the fair and accurate portrayal of Sikh Americans and the Sikh religion in American media and society, is a nonprofit, nonpartisan, membership-based organization. Its mission is to combat bigotry and prejudice, protect the rights and religious freedoms of Sikh Americans, and provide resources that empower the Sikh American community.

35. See "Understanding Turbans," http://seattletimes.nwsource.com/news/lifestyles/ links/turbans_27.html.

36. See "SMART Initiates Airport Educational Campaign, Requests Community Involvement"; and "SMART Encourages Community Members to Educate Local Airport Security Personnel about Sikhs," November 16, 2001, http://www.Sikhnet.com/s/Attack onAmerica. Stating that many cases of "turban-removal have occur red at small or mid-size airports" like Raleigh-Durham, Albany, and Phoenix, but also at larger airports such as JFK, SMART urges Sikhs to initiate educational forums for security personnel and airline employees about turbans and Sikhism and has developed presentations and other resources for this purpose. See also "Federal Aviation Administration to Ensure New Security Procedures That Preserve and Respect the Civil Rights of All Americans," November 19, 2001, http://www.Sikhnet.com/. The FAA (Federal Aviation Administration) issued a set of directives detailing methods for conducting airport security based on information presented by the Sikh Coalition and other Sikh organizations (SCORE, Sikh Communications, SMART, and USSA) "about the racial profiling that has caused turban-wearing Sikh Americans to be denied air transportation while being publicly humiliated and embarrassed." "This kind of treatment to loyal Americans makes many feel humiliated, naked in public, victimized and most important, unwelcome in the country that many of us were born in," said Harpreet Singh, director of community relations of the Sikh Coalition. "It is especially upsetting since terrorists take great pains to wear typical American clothing in

order to not stand out. We are grateful that the FAA has taken such a firm stand against this type of racial profiling as it is against everything America and Americans stand for." See also http://www.sikhcoalition.org/FAAGuidelines.pdf; www.sikhcoalition.org/airports .ppt; and "Your Rights and Avenues of Action as a Victim of Airport Profiling," http://www.sikhcoalition.org/AirportProfiling.pdf.

37. For example, the Sikhs of Richmond Hill held a parade (Nagar Kirtan) on December 1, 2001, stating, "After September 11, 2001, many people have mistaken Sikhs for Muslims and Arab Americans with the attacks on New York and Washington. This is one way for Sikh Americans to educate their communities about themselves and Sikhism." See "National Sikh Group Adds to Reward," Associated Press state and local wire, November 29, 2001: "A national Sikh organization has added $5,000 to a reward fund in the case of a Sikh temple destroyed by arson. The money from the Washington, D.C.–based Sikh council brings to $15,000 a reward fund for information leading to an arrest and conviction in the case. The main building of the religious center, a 100-year-old converted farmhouse, was destroyed by fire early November 18. Officials last week determined the fire was deliberately set and are considering the fire a possible hate crime, a federal offense." Since September 11, the Justice Department's Civil Rights Division, the FBI, and U.S. attorneys' offices have investigated more than 250 "backlash" incidents involving violence or threats against Arab Americans, Muslim Americans, Sikh Americans, South Asian Americans, and individuals perceived to be members of these communities. As of December 3, there were 217 pending FBI investigations—121 (56 percent) were incidents that had occurred within the first seven days after September 11, and 179 (82 percent) within the first eighteen days after September 11. In the month of November, there were only four reported incidents that resulted in FBI investigations. See http://www.usdoj.gov/crt/nordwg.html for other information on the division's Initiative to Combat Backlash Discrimination and http://www.eeoc.gov/ for statements from the participants at the Equal Employment Opportunity Commission's public hearing on employment discrimination since September 11. See also Orith Goldberg, "Valley Sikh's Beating Branded as Hate Crime," *LA Daily News,* December 8, 2001.

38. See "Sikh Representatives Meet U.S. Congressional Leaders," http://www.sikhnet .com/s/SikhMemorialDC. On December 11, three months to the day after the tragedy, Sikh leadership from the across the United States and Canada gathered under the dome of the U.S. Capitol building for the first annual "One Nation United Memorial Program" sponsored by the Washington-based Sikh Council on Religion and Education. The program included senators, members of Congress, government officials, and top leadership from commerce, labor, and the interfaith communities. This was the first event of its kind hosted by the Sikh community in Washington. New York senator Hillary Rodham Clinton stated, "We will always remember the sacrifices that were made by the Sikh Community in the wake of the terrible terrorist attacks of September 11. No community suffered greater loss as a reaction to the terrible losses" of September 11.

39. For examples of Hindu nationalist lobbying against financial aid to Pakistan, see Online Resource for Indian-Americans, http://www.indiatogether.org/us/lobby.htm. See also http://www.usindialobby.net. "Sikhs Respond to Representative Saxby Chambliss

on Bigoted Comments," December 22, 2001, http://www.sikhnet.com/s/Chambliss.Sikh net, Sikh American Association, Sikh Coalition, Sikh Council on Religion and Education (SCORE), SMART, and the Sikh Communications Council state: "As Sikhs and as Americans, we are deeply distressed about the comments that Representative Saxby Chambliss made November 19 to a group of law enforcement officers in Valdosta, Georgia. He alluded to 'turning the Sheriff loose to arrest every Muslim that crosses the state line.' We in America look to our elected officials for responsible leadership and guidance." About SCORE: Founded in 1998, the Sikh Council on Religion and Education, a think tank based in Washington, represents Sikhs in various forums and venues. From the group's inception, its leadership has been invited repeatedly by the White House, Congress, and various nongovernmental organizations to present the Sikh perspective. The Sikh Council fosters understanding through education and interfaith relations, promoting the concept of community and working to secure a just society for all.

40. "Anti-Terrorism Bill Could Impact Nonprofits," November 14, 2001, http://www.ombwatch.org/article/articleview/288/1/18. The USA PATRIOT Act (PL 107-56) could pose big problems for nonprofits, especially those that advocate changes in U.S. foreign policy or provide social services to individuals who become targets of government investigations. The central problem is a vague, overbroad definition of a new crime, "domestic terrorism." In addition, greatly expanded search and surveillance powers can be invoked under a lowered threshold, requiring only that investigators assert that the information sought is relevant to a foreign intelligence investigation. For praise of the USA PATRIOT Act by Sikh organizations, see http://www.Sikhnet.com/ (October 31, 2001); and "Measure Supporting Sikh Americans Becomes Law," http://www.sikhcoalition.org/. This law states, "The Civil Rights and Civil Liberties of All Americans, Including Sikh Americans, Should Be Protected." S. Con. Res. 74 and H. Res. 255 condemn crimes against Sikh Americans in the wake of the September 11 terrorist attacks and mandate that acts of violence against Sikh Americans are to be prevented and prosecuted. "This law represents a significant milestone for Sikh Americans as it addresses the unique nature of the issues faced by Sikhs in the aftermath of September 11, and calls for protection of our civil liberties, along with those of all Americans," said Gurpreet Singh Dhillon, member of the advisory board of the Sikh American Association. (About the Sikh Coalition: "The Sikh Coalition was started as an effort to educate the greater North American community on Sikhs and Sikhism, the coalition seeks to safeguard the rights of all citizens as well as to promote the Sikh identity and communicates the collective interests of Sikhs to the community at large. The coalition serves as a resource for all organizations and individuals as well as a point of contact to Sikh people.")

41. USSA held a candlelight vigil in memory of the 1984 pogroms and September 11 on December 8, 2001, at Madison Square Park, New York City. See http://www.sikh.org/vigil; "Are Kashmiri Sikhs Next on India's Hit List—Again?," August 7, 2001, *Khalistan Calling*, http://www.khalistan-affairs.org/main/k_calling/kc08072001.htm; and "Thirty-Five Sikhs Murdered in Chitthisinghpura, Kashmir, by the Indian Army," March 21, 2000, http://www.khalistan-affairs.org/main/k_calling/kc03212000.htm.

42. On South Asian racial formation, see Vijay Prashad, *The Karma of Brown Folk* (Minneapolis: University of Minnesota Press, 2000). For more nuanced analyses of gender,

sexuality, and transnationalism, see Inderpal Grewal, *South Asian Transnationalities: Gender, Class, Ethnicity, and Diaspora* (Durham, N.C.: Duke University Press, 2002).

43. On the detainees and the connections between the 1996 Detention Act and the USA PATRIOT Act, see Mark Dow, "The New Secret War against Immigrants," January 30, 2002, http://www.gothamgazette.com/citizen/feb02/haiti-progres.shtml, as well as a special edition of *ColorLines,* "War on Terrorism: Profiled and Punished" (December 2001).

ZOMBIE TROUBLE

Zombie Texts, Bare Life, and Displaced People

Jon Stratton

T HIS ESSAY IS ABOUT THE RELATIONSHIP BETWEEN zombies and displaced people, most obviously refugees, asylum-seekers, and illegal immigrants. It is founded on a realization that the underlying characteristics of zombies are similar to those attributed to displaced people: that is, people predominantly from non-Western states striving for entry into Western states. The essay begins from the recognition that during the 2000s, there has been a tremendous increase in the number of films released featuring zombies. At the same time, zombies have begun to appear in other media. A video game series called *Resident Evil,* which includes biologically mutated flesh-eating undead, founded a genre now called "survival horror." Released originally for Sony PlayStation in 1996, by September 30, 2004, the various forms of the game had sold more than twenty-five million units, and in 2002 it spawned a film also called *Resident Evil.*[1] The film became the fourteenth highest grossing R-rated film in the United States that year and the fiftieth highest grossing film globally.[2] There are now two sequels. In 2009, Quirk Books released *Pride and Prejudice and Zombies,* a "mash-up" in which author Seth Grahame-Smith introduced zombies into Jane Austen's 1813 Romance novel. The book became an instant success. In April it had reached the third spot on the *New York Times* best-seller list, and by the end of the year it had sold more than seven hundred thousand copies.[3] Such was the success of the revisioned novel that Quirk Books were inspired to commission a prequel, Steve Hockensmith's *Pride and Prejudice and Zombies: Dawn of the Dreadfuls.*

During this same period, since the 1990s, there has been an increasing anxiety in Western countries over the numbers of displaced people attempting to gain entry across their borders (the reasons for this are many, but beyond the scope of this chapter). Certainly there has been an overall increase in refugee numbers. One set of figures released by the United Nations High Commissioner for Refugees (UNHCR) tells us that whereas in 1980 there were slightly over ten million people classified as refugees, in 2007 the number was closer to sixteen million.[4] However, most of these refugees are situated in countries outside the developed West. Anxieties over border protection in all countries, but especially in the West, were heightened in the wake of the 2001 attacks on the World Trade Center in New York. The link between these anxieties and concerns over displaced people attempting to gain entry to Western countries was made in, for example, *Children of Men,* which was released in 2006 and set in 2027. Directed by Alfonso Cuarón, who also cowrote the screenplay, the backdrop to the film's ostensible concern with global infertility is a Great Britain in which the increase in unsanctioned immigration is such that asylum-seekers are placed in cages on London's streets, and Bexhill-on-Sea on the south coast has been turned into a massive detention camp.[5]

I will be arguing that in many of the recent zombie texts, the zombie threat can be read in terms of the fears of many members of Western countries about being overwhelmed by displaced people. What might be the justification for this connection between zombies and displaced people? The recent renaissance in zombie films lifts off from the revision of zombies in Western popular culture that is traced to George A. Romero's now-classic 1968 film *Night of the Living Dead.* This film began what is now colloquially called the zombie apocalypse trope, in which entire communities, whole countries, and even the world are subject to destruction by increasing numbers of zombies that appear from nowhere, often originating as a consequence of radiation from outer space—that is, if any rationale for their existence is proffered. In these films the zombie presence is qualitatively different from the earlier zombie trope, derived from claims about the existence of zombies in Haiti in which witches or evil scientists turned individuals into zombies as a means of controlling them. Nevertheless, the foundational idea of the zombie as a dead person resurrected to a state that remains nearer death than life is a constant.

What I will be arguing is that what audiences find most frightening in the zombie idea is not the resurrection from death but the state of living death that is the fate of the zombie. Indeed, in some films that are identified as a part of the zombie genre, such as *28 Days Later* (dir. Danny Boyle, 2002), the person does not even die before turning into what is now being described as a zombie. In this case, if the key to the identification of a zombie is the interstitial state of being between life and death, then the zombie takes on the characteristic of what Giorgio Agamben calls "bare life."[6] Bare life is difficult to define because it has two aspects. The first is (for want of a better word) social. In setting up his discussion of the relationship between bare life and aesthetics, Anthony Downey writes:

> Lives lived on the margins of social, political, cultural, economic and geographical borders are lives half lived. Denied access to legal, economic and political redress, these lives exist in a limbo-like state that is largely preoccupied with acquiring and sustaining the essentials of life. The refugee, the political prisoner, the disappeared, the victim of torture, the dispossessed— all have been excluded, to different degrees, from the fraternity of the social sphere, appeal to the safety net of the nation-state and recourse to international law. They have been outlawed, so to speak, placed beyond recourse to law and yet still in a precarious relationship to law itself.[7]

Members of all these groups, including displaced people, can be thought of as experiencing bare life in its modern form.

The second describes the existential state of a person placed in this circumstance. Following Agamben, I argue elsewhere that the typifying existential state is that to which many Jews were reduced in the concentration and death camps of Nazi Germany: a person in this condition was called in many camps a *Muselmann*.[8] This state, often described as a living death, closely resembles that of the zombie—the difference being that zombies, living after death, are portrayed as fundamentally threatening to the living, while the *Muselmänner* lived only until their transformation into the dead was complete. The point here is twofold: that excluded from the rights and privileges of the modern state, those displaced people are positioned legally as bare life; and that in this legal limbo, these people can be treated in a way that enables them to become associated with a condition mythically exemplified in the zombie. The consequence is that not only can the zombie texts of films and other media be read as reproducing this connection, drawing on present-day anxieties to increase the terror produced by these texts, but displaced people are characterized using the same terminology that describes the threat that zombies generate in zombie apocalypse texts.

The Popularity of Zombies

Through the first decade of the twenty-first century, there has been a very significant increase in the cultural presence of zombies.[9] In January 2006, Steven Wells, in an article in the *Guardian,* wrote that "there were zombies everywhere in 2005."[10] That same year in March, Warren St. John commented in the *New York Times* that "in films, books and video games, the undead are once again on the march, elbowing past werewolves, vampires, swamp things and mummies to become the post-millennial ghoul of the moment."[11] What St. John's remark signals is something quite important, that it is not just that there has been an increase in visibility of zombies as a consequence of their appearance in an increased number of texts, but that this increase outstrips other conventional horror characters such as werewolves and vampires.

It is worth noting that vampires also have recently enjoyed a renaissance in popularity. In the late 1990s, Angel and Spike appeared in *Buffy the Vampire Slayer*. They helped to start a shift to more humanized vampires that could be love objects. Since then, vampires have appeared in the four Twilight books by Stephenie Meyer, the first of which was published in 2005, and the immensely popular film of the same name, made from the books, was released in 2008, with a sequel, *The Twilight Saga: New Moon,* being released the following year. In 2008 *Twilight* was the seventh highest grossing film in the United States.[12] Among other recent texts, vampires feature in a number of television series. *Moonlight* ran for one season in late 2007 and early 2008. The protagonist was a private investigator who was also a vampire. His love interest was a mortal woman who was a reporter. The show achieved a cult following and was very successful with adults in the eighteen to forty-nine range. *The Vampire Diaries,* in which a mortal woman becomes romantically entangled with vampires, began in September 2009 on CW. It rapidly won its timeslot for a female viewing audience aged up to thirty-four. In these texts vampires, which used to suggest forbidden sexual desire, now constitute the love interest in a more liberated time.[13] An early example of this genre was the 1983 cult film *The Hunger* (dir. Tony Scott), which starred Catherine Deneuve, Susan Sarandon, and David Bowie, although crucially in this film the vampire is a woman. In addition, vampires are a key character component of the HBO cable television network's *True Blood* series, which is based on Charlaine Harris's The Southern Vampire Mysteries novels, first published in 2001. In these texts, vampires either are the source of forbidden romance or are integrated problematically into everyday society, or both. Vampires, then, have lost their traditional fear factor and are positioned more as strange Others who have different cultural ways and are sometimes still a threat, especially to the one that loves them, but one that is generally manageable. Coming out of an American society dealing with major changes in its racial profile, and in a country where marriage between the races has become acceptable only relatively recently, these vampire texts suggest among others a racial reading, one in which the dominant society is struggling to come to terms with a rapidly changing racial order.[14] As we shall see, zombies can be read racially, but this reading places them as a racial threat to Western civilization.

There is nothing benign about zombies. In short, as Simon Pegg, the writer of and actor in *Shaun of the Dead,* a British zombie film released in 2004, remarks, "as monsters from the id, zombies win out over vampires and werewolves when it comes to the title of Most Potent Metaphorical Monster."[15] It needs to be noted that Pegg has an ahistorical view of these monsters:

> Where their pointy-toothed cousins are all about sex and bestial savagery, the zombie trumps all by personifying our deepest fear: death. Zombies are our destiny writ large. Slow and steady in their approach, weak, clumsy, often absurd, the zombie relentlessly closes in, unstoppable, intractable.[16]

As I have argued, the sex and bestial savagery of vampires have now been tamed into a disturbing and disruptive cultural difference, fear transformed into a romantic frisson, within a cultural pluralist multiculturalism. The fear of zombies is now not so much about death as of those excluded from Western societies who seem to be threatening civilization as we know it in the West.

Thus zombies have become the most important mythic monster at the present time. In an astute discussion of the zombie phenomenon, Peter Dendle writes about "the resurgence of zombie movie popularity in the early 2000s."[17] For him, this "has been linked with the events of September 11, 2001."[18] Making a different but still generalizing claim to Pegg's, Dendle goes on to argue that

> apocalypticism has always been ingrained into the archetypal psyche of any society defining itself—as all human endeavours must—in the context of history and time. The possibility of wide-scale destruction and devastation which 9–11 brought once again into the communal consciousness found a ready narrative expression in the zombie apocalypses which over thirty years had honed images of desperation subsistence and amoral survivalism to a fine edge.[19]

Following Dendle, Kyle Bishop makes a similar point:

> Although the conventions of the zombie genre remain largely unchanged, the movies' relevance has become all the more clear—a post-9/11 audience cannot help but perceive the characteristics of zombie cinema through the filter of terrorist threats and apocalyptic reality.[20]

Both Dendle and Bishop argue that 9/11 had a considerable impact on the American national imaginary, and that this is expressed in the way that Americans make and read zombie films.

However, films made outside the United States, and even a recent American zombie film such as Romero's *Land of the Dead,* released in 2005, show evidence of quite a different anxiety. To understand this, we need to begin with a discussion of what constitutes a zombie. As Dendle argues:

the essence of the "zombie" at the most abstract level is supplanted, stolen, or effaced consciousness; it casts allegorically the appropriation of one person's will by another. It is no coincidence that the creature flourished in the twentieth century, a century whose broad intellectual trends were preoccupied with alienation.[21]

Here, Dendle is extrapolating from a history that refers back to the zombie as a characteristic of Haitian voodoo. In doing so he elides the recognition that, often, the zombies of the zombie apocalypse films after Romero's *Night of the Living Dead* are not created by someone. They do not have will, but they are not in somebody's control. Indeed, this is one of things that make them so frightening—their existence is entirely alien.

Dendle traces the American popular cultural interest in zombies to the American occupation of Haiti between 1915 and 1934. He writes:

Ghosts and revenants are known world-wide, but few are so consistently associated with economy and labour as the shambling corpse of Haitian vodun, brought back from the dead to toil in the fields and factories by miserly land-owners or by spiteful *houngan* or *bokor* priests. . . . The zombie, a soulless hulk mindlessly working at the bidding of another, thus records a residual communal memory of slavery: of living a life without dignity and meaning, of going through the motions.[22]

Dendle links the rise of American interest in zombies to the Great Depression and the crisis of labor. It is an important point. In post–*Night of the Living Dead* zombie apocalypse films, the link between the zombie and slavery, and by extension the worker in a capitalist economy, has been repressed. As we shall see, in the films where the zombies can be read as displaced people, this connection is reappearing.

Joan Dayan, an anthropologist, provided this description of the zombie:

Born out of the experience of slavery and the sea passage from Africa to the New World, the zombie tells the story of colonization: the reduction of human into thing for the ends of capital. For the Haitian no fate is to be more feared.[23]

Dayan goes on to explain that, in the present day,

in a contemporary Caribbean development of American style, the zombi phenomenon obviously goes beyond the machinations of the local boco. As Depestre puts it, "This fantastic process of reification and assimilation means the total loss of my identity, the psychological annihilation of my being, my zombification." And Laënnec Hurbon explains how the zombi stories produce and capitalize on an internalization of slavery and passivity, making the victims of an oppressive social system the cause: "The phantasm of the zombi . . .

does nothing but attest to the fulfilment of a system that moves the victim to internalize his condition."[24]

Dayan's purpose is to explain how, in the present Haitian context, the zombie functions as an explanation for the destruction of Haitian culture by American colonialism disguised as development. The mindless zombie, laboring for another, becomes a way of understanding the impact of American capital on Haiti, and the Caribbean more generally.

Jean Comaroff and John Comaroff make a similar point about the rise in zombie stories in South Africa:

> There can be no denying the latter-day preoccupation with zombies in rural South Africa. Their existence, far from being the subject of elusive tales from the backwoods, of fantastic fables from the *veld,* is widely taken for granted. As a simple matter of fact. In recent times, respectable local newspapers have carried banner headlines like "Zombie Back from the Dead" illustrating their stories with conventional, high-realist photographs.[25]

The Comaroffs argue that the zombie narrative is a useful way for people who do not understand the complexities of international, neoliberal capitalism to account for how some people apparently become rich very quickly without doing any visible work: they create zombies who work for them and do not have to be paid. Looking over the history of zombies in Africa, the Comaroffs state:

> Zombies themselves seem to be born, at least in the first instance, of colonial encounters, of the precipitous engagement of local worlds with imperial economies that seek to exert control over the essential means of producing value, means like land and labor, space and time.[26]

In other words, at a conceptual level, zombies are a local response of the colonized to the impact of colonial capitalism, a way of understanding how those capitalist practices produce wealth for some and immiseration for others.

From *Pride and Prejudice* to *Pride and Prejudice and Zombies*

At this point we can return to the Caribbean. Two years before Romero's *Night of the Living Dead* revisioned the zombie trope, Jean Rhys published a book in England that is now written about as a key postcolonial novel. *Wide Sargasso Sea* is a kind of answer text, which Bill Ashcroft, Gareth Griffiths, and Helen Tiffin (1989) describe as a literary work that writes back to the book that inspired it, illuminating the colonizing assumptions that underpin the earlier novel. In this case that novel is Charlotte Brontë's *Jane Eyre*. Published in 1847, thirty-four years after *Pride and Prejudice*, *Jane Eyre* tells the story of a young woman's rise from a straightened childhood eventually to marry Edward Rochester, the owner of Thornfield Hall. What Jane does not know until the day that she is supposed to marry Rochester is that he is already married. He keeps his first wife, whom he regards as mad, locked in the attic under the ministrations of Grace Poole. This wife is Bertha Mason, the Creole woman from Jamaica whose dowry of thirty thousand pounds is the source of Rochester's wealth. Unable to marry, Jane refuses to cohabit with Rochester and leaves. Later, Bertha escapes her prison and sets fire to the house, committing suicide by jumping from the roof. Rochester loses his sight and his left hand in trying to save her. Finally, Jane and Rochester are able to marry.

What Rhys divined was that behind this romance lay the story of an abused first wife, married for her colonial wealth and then discarded. *Wide Sargasso Sea* tells Bertha's story. In this novel we find that Bertha was originally named Antoinette, and that it is Rochester who renames her. Rhys's narrative highlights the power imbalance between the Caribbean colonies and Britain while also showing how, at the time of the novel, much of the wealth on which Britain's gentry depended came from these colonies in which slavery had only been abolished in 1834, and many remained slaves for a further six years. In a discussion of the novel, Thomas Loe has argued that the zombie is "an extremely potent central image associated with Antoinette."[27] One of its purposes would seem to be to give an exotic quality to the Caribbean, compared to the mundane realism of Rochester's England. However, the zombie motif does other work. Loe argues that Antoinette's mother is made into a zombie, that Antoinette tries to zombify Rochester in the hope of keeping his love, and that most important of all for my purpose here, Rochester attempts to turn Antoinette into a zombie. For Loe,

> the figure of the zombie provides Rhys with an astonishingly appropriate metaphor for dramatizing her vision of the powerless and displaced woman against [what Judith Gardiner calls] the "unified ideology" of "capitalism, colonialism, and patriarchal domination."[28]

Rochester tries to transform Antoinette while moving her to England, attempting to remake her as a woman of the gentry, even going so far as to change her name from the French-influenced Antoinette to the solidly English Bertha. He does not succeed. Instead, Antoinette becomes "mad," a victim of a failed zombification, displaced from her Jamaican home to an England she neither likes nor understands, caught between two cultures.

We can now turn to *Pride and Prejudice and Zombies*.[29] Austen's *Pride and Prejudice* remains her most popular book. It is a romance that is also a comedy of manners about the early nineteenth-century English landed gentry, and its setting is restricted to England. Stimulated by the work of Edward Said, there has been some debate over Austen's awareness of the slavery in the colonial Caribbean, the plantations of which provided some of the wealth which made the life of the

English gentry possible. In 1772, Lord Mansfield's judgment in the case of a recaptured runaway slave owned by a man from Boston visiting England, known after the slave's name as the *Somersett* case, established the basis for ending slavery in England. However, as I have already mentioned, slavery in the British colonies continued until the Emancipation Act came into force in 1834. Austen published *Pride and Prejudice* in 1813 and *Mansfield Park* in 1814.

In *Mansfield Park*, the wealth that sustains Sir Thomas Bertram and his family at the home that bears the name of the man who ended slavery in England derives from Sir Thomas's plantation in Antigua. There are problems on the plantation that require his presence. Commenting on the narrative, Said remarks:

> Whatever was wrong there—and the internal evidence garnered by Warren
> Roberts suggests that economic depression, slavery, and competition with
> France were at issue—Sir Thomas was able to fix thereby maintaining his
> control over his colonial domain.[30]

I do not want to enter the debate as to whether or not Austen approved of slavery.[31] Said explains that

> the Bertrams could not have been possible without the slave trade, sugar,
> and the colonial planter class; as a social type Sir Thomas would have been
> familiar to eighteenth- and early nineteenth-century readers who knew the
> powerful influence of this class through politics, plays . . . and many other
> public activities (large houses, famous parties and social rituals, well-known
> commercial enterprises, celebrated marriages).[32]

In his history of British colonial slavery, Robin Blackburn argues that the wealth derived from New World slavery formed the necessary basis for the Industrial Revolution.[33]

Austen's indication of the presence of slavery in the colonies, and its importance, occurs in the novel following *Pride and Prejudice*. As Suvendrini Perera remarks:

> this growing visibility of the navy in *Mansfield Park* supplements the increas-
> ing presence of empire at the edges of Austen's texts; progressively, her "3 or
> 4 Families in a Country Village" . . . come to encompass and incorporate more
> extensive portions of the globe.[34]

Only a decade earlier, in 1804, the slaves of Haiti had completed a successful rebellion against the French and, as Perera suggests, "the terrifying possibility of a Haiti-style rebellion in the English slave colonies had instantly become a national obsession."[35]

What, then, are we to make of the zombies that increasingly threaten the social life of the gentry in *Pride and Prejudice and Zombies*? As is usual in zombie apocalypse texts, we are not told whence they came. In this text, Elizabeth Bennett and her sisters are trained in martial arts so that they can act as vigilantes, killing zombies. They have visited China, where they learned Kung Fu from Shaolin monks. What we do know is that zombies have been roaming the English countryside for a generation or more. We know that London has been walled and that the army moves from area to area of England, trying to keep the zombies under control. We know also that zombies are comparable to "savages" because Mr. Darcy remarks to Sir William Lucas that "every savage can dance. Why, I imagine that even zombies could do it with some degree of success."[36] Zombies, then, have some similarity with the black slaves who were thought of as savages, who work the colonial Caribbean plantations that supply the wealth which supports the lifestyle of the gentry.[37]

Zombies do not appear to infest anywhere but England—or possibly Britain. With the connection between slavery and zombies that we have already established, we can now understand the zombie threat as a return of the repressed. Whether we read the text literally in terms of a slave revolt that has spread to England or metaphorically as an expression of the vengeance of the enslaved Africans on which the gentry's wealth was built, what we have is a movement of the displaced from the Caribbean colonies to England. It is a zombie apocalypse set in the early nineteenth century that can be read as making clear the connections between English wealth and colonial slavery which, in this early novel at least, Austen had elided.

Zombies and the Displaced

The narrative of *Night of the Living Dead* centered on a group of humans attempting to defend themselves in a house by stopping it from being overrun by marauding zombies. Romero's second zombie film, *Dawn of the Dead* (1978), had the human survivors holed up in a shopping mall. The trope of a group of humans defending a space from threatening zombies has become common in zombie apocalypse texts, and it is now even more open to be read in terms of the threat considered to be posed by illegal immigrants than in Romero's first film. In Romero's fourth zombie film, *Land of the Dead,* released in 2005, the parallel between the zombie siege of Pittsburgh and the fear over illegal entry to the United States across the Mexican border is easily made:

> To ensure the status quo, Dennis Hopper's Kaufman, the self-appointed leader of Pittsburgh, constructs the world's most extreme border security—blown up and barricaded bridges make the rivers impassable, and electric fences and armed guards protect the area from any intrusion; in an extreme example of xenophobia, soldiers shoot any invaders on sight. These forms of immigration control have become even more jarringly familiar with recent debates about erecting a fence between the United States and Mexico and the redeployment

of National Guard troops to guard the United States' southern border during George W. Bush's presidency.[38]

Here, the zombies can be easily read as illegal migrants threatening traditional American society. With this reading, the zombie acquires again its earlier reference: a worker who either is, or is able to be worked into, a comatose state. Indeed, the worker with no protection can become a slave.

In zombie films made outside the United States, this reading is more available. In *Shaun of the Dead*, with the sudden transformation of people into zombies, Shaun and his white friends make for their local pub, the Winchester, as the most defensible place he can think of. In British films, the pub is historically the place of community, as it is for example in *Passport to Pimlico* (dir. Henry Cornelius, 1949). By extension, in *Shaun of the Dead*, the pub is a synecdoche for a white England under siege from a range of illegal immigrants, asylum-seekers, and so forth, all trying to breach the pub's defenses. Finally, the British army comes to the rescue of Shaun and his friends, killing off the besieging zombies.

Dead Set was made in England during summer 2008 and shown on television as a series of five episodes. In the narrative, a group of reality show contestants secured in a *Big Brother*-style house find themselves threatened by zombies who appear to have taken over the rest of the country. Davina McCall, who presented the British *Big Brother* series, appears in *Dead Set* as herself and is transformed into a zombie. As the series proceeds, the zombies gradually overwhelm the occupants of the house. In this narrative, the zombies are triumphant. *Dead Set* was nominated for a British Academy of Film and Television Arts (BAFTA) award for Best Drama Serial. As in *Shaun of the Dead*, the horror of the zombie threat is increased by the ease with which the zombies can be read as illegal immigrants—or, indeed, legal immigrants from elsewhere in the European Union who are often identified as overwhelming British society.

In his *Guardian* article quoted earlier, Pegg comments on his dislike of Charlie Brooker's use of "fast" zombies—that is, zombies that walk and run, rather than stagger slowly, in *Dead Set*. In what one presumes is supposed to be read as a jokey riposte, Brooker responds: "Simon: your outright rejection of running zombies leaves you exposed, in a very real and damning sense, as a terrible racist."[39] If zombies stand for those displaced people attempting to enter Britain, then they are indeed mostly nonwhite. The immiseration of the displaced people at the border is expressed in the bare life that is represented in the zombies. The racialized difference of those people is metaphorized in the zombies' difference from humans.

With this in mind we should not be surprised that, in a voice-over at the end of *Shaun of the Dead* that tells us what happens after the zombie threat has been quelled, we are told that the few remaining zombies are used as game show participants and domestics. Domestic work is characteristic labor for illegal immigrants across the West. *Shaun of the Dead* can be read analogically, whereas *Children of Men* presents a literal image of Britain falling to the pressure of displaced people entering the country.

In *Fido* (dir. Andrew Currie), a Canadian zombie film released in 2006, zombies are fitted with a specially invented collar that renders them harmless to humans.[40] They can be used for menial work, and any household that does not have at least one zombie domestic is considered to be socially embarrassed. *Fido* goes even further in the development of the zombie–displaced people connection. Set in a 1950s America after the Zombie Wars, towns are fenced off from the Wild Zone where the zombies without collars still prowl, attempting to enter the areas where humans live. In an information film that we see at the beginning made by ZomCom, the company that makes the zombie collars, we are told, in rhetoric which echoes anxieties over border security that stretch from illegal immigrants to terrorists, that the advent of the zombies meant that "we were forced to defend our homeland . . . mankind pitted against legions of the undead." ZomCom also "built security systems like the perimeter fence that encloses our towns in a wall of protective steel." The film's title comes from the name that Timmy, the Robinsons' young son, gives the zombie that his mother acquires for their home. It is, of course, a name that is typically given to a dog, although nobody in the film acknowledges this. When Timmy plays baseball with Fido, he acts toward him in the way that black servants historically were treated, for example, by telling him to get the ball: "Go fetch it, boy!" These zombies are marked as racially different and, indeed, not human. In these films, but especially in *Fido,* the zombie as bare life is linked with the zombie as unenfranchised worker.

An Australian low-budget film, *Undead* (dir. Michael and Peter Spierig, 2003), was made over a number of years and is perhaps one of the stranger recent additions to the zombie genre.[41] The film includes both zombies and an alien visitation from space. A small town in Queensland is the focus of a zombie outbreak caused by something raining down from outer space. Marion is a survivalist who has been affected by this development before, when the fish he was catching turned into zombies. He is convinced that the aliens are a part of the zombie threat. When asked by Sallyanne "Have you ever seen anything like this before?" he answers, "I have. It's an invasion. The end of life as we know it." The police are shown to be incompetent and unable to understand what to do in the new circumstance. Marion takes charge of protecting the small group of people who have escaped transformation into zombies. He is a characteristic figure in recent Australian film. Similar to Mick Taylor, the kangaroo shooter and serial killer in *Wolf Creek* (dir. Greg McLean, 2005), and the unnamed kangaroo shooter in *Lucky Miles* (dir. Michael Rowland, 2007), who both appear to be patrolling Australia's border, Marion attempts to protect the village from what he thinks are the depredations of the aliens.[42] By the end of the film, it turns out that the aliens are actually try-ing to stop the zombie plague and return everybody to being human. Thinking that they have succeeded, they leave. Unfortunately, one of the townsfolk, who has been bitten by a zombie, escapes confinement and infects the rest of Austra-lia. This time, the aliens do not return.

This somewhat confusing combination of zombie apocalypse and sci-fi film can make sense in the context of John Howard's government ramping up the Australian population's anxieties about asylum-seekers in the early 2000s. In 2001, the government refused entry to shipwrecked asylum-seekers picked up by the *MV Tampa,* started the so-called Pacific Solution, where asylum-seekers were sent to detention camps in other countries in the Pacific region while they waited to be processed, and altered Australia's migration zone to exclude the Australian islands around the north of the country. Also in 2001, shortly before a federal election, the Howard government promoted the idea that asylum-seekers on a boat had been threatening to throw their children overboard. The practical consequence of these and other acts by the government was that the general pop-ulation became increasingly concerned about the threat posed by asylum-seekers and voted the government back into power. The more general consequence was an increase in Australians' xenophobic fear of illegal immigration.

With this history we are now better able to read *Undead.* Here again, the zombie threat is a translation of the fear generated by, in this Australian case, specifically asylum-seekers attempting to find a home in Australia. In this film, it seems, nothing can stop them, certainly not the police or even the local survival-ist, except aliens. We now need to think about these aliens. They emit light, they wear what look like cassocks with cowls, and, as they cure people of zombification, those people are taken into the clouds until the aliens have eradicated the zombie scourge. The Christian connotations are spelled out by Rene near the end of the film, when she is trying to convince Marion that he has been wrong about the aliens' intentions. She says, "Aliens are the saviors. It's not us." It seems that "we" are simply not powerful enough to save Australia from the zombies. At one point in the film, when Rene is shooting down zombies in the town's general store, she has the Australian flag behind her. We, the white Australians, need God, or some Christian force allied to God, to save us. When that is no longer available, Austra-lia is overrun. It is easy to see how *Undead*'s zombies can stand in for asylum-seekers at a time when Australian anxiety over asylum-seekers had been ramped up to extreme levels.

Rhetoric

That *Fido* can make such a clear analogy between displaced people and zombies is because the same rhetoric is used for each. Zombies provide a monster for our time because they express our anxieties over the relationship between bare life and the modern state. As I have noted previously, zombies are an expression of bare life. From the viewpoint of the members of those countries of the West, the displaced people attempting to enter them are also bare life. They have no protection from any state. This underlying similitude enables the same metaphors to be used for both zombies and displaced people. Where zombies appear as a remorseless threat laying siege to wherever humans manage to collect to defend themselves, displaced people are constructed in the same way, as a threat at the border of the state. In an article on the way that Austrian newspapers write about asylum-seekers, Elisabeth El Refaie describes how "Kurdish refugees are quite regularly represented as an 'army' on the point of 'invading' Europe, and their arrival is often referred to as an *Ansturm* [onslaught] or *Invasion* [invasion]."[43] She quotes from a newspaper article that writes of "new hordes of applicants for asylum."[44] While an onslaught or invasion might conjure up an image of an organized, rational army, *horde* implies a disorganized, irrational mass. El Refaie explains:

> In other articles, the "war" metaphor is also evoked by verbs, which describe the refugees as "forcing their way" *(drängen)* over the border into Europe, of "invading" *(eindringen)* Germany and of "storming" *(stürmen)* Fortress Europe.[45]

All these metaphors suggest that Europe is under siege from a mindless throng.

In describing the language used in Australia, Sharon Pickering lists some of the terms that she found in the *Brisbane Courier Mail* and the *Sydney Morning Herald* between 1997 and 1999 to describe the threat posed by asylum-seekers:

> "we" are soon to be "awash," "swamped," "weathering the influx," of "waves," "latest waves," "more waves," "tides," "floods," "migratory flood," "mass exodus" of "aliens," "queue jumpers," "illegal immigrants."[46]

Terms such as wave and flood use the water reference to conjure up some overwhelming and amorphous force. They are dehumanizing expressions that identify the asylum-seekers as a mass rather than as individuals. These people are "aliens" constructed, as Pickering points out, in a system of binary logic "which routinely renders one normal and the other strange/other."[47] Thinking of the zombie as bare life, this is the binary Other of the humanizing effect of membership of modern society.

As in zombie films, Pickering shows that it is the human members of the Australian state who are the ones under siege, their civilized existence always at threat from the zombified bare life attempting to enter the protected space. As Pickering states:

> in the case of asylum seekers, the boundaries [between "us" and "them"] are easily identified by the discrete nation state—not only fixed national

and geographic boundaries in the case of Australia but also those of race. In "record arrest," "swoop," "incident," "criminal gangs" and "illegal run," criminal justice discourse becomes interwoven with that of war: "incursion," "sustained assault on Australian shores," "gathering to our north," "massing in Indonesia," all to invade the "land of hope."[48]

Here again, this "war" that Australia is fighting is actually a siege in which the country is being defended against the invasion of a racial Other that is disorganized, massified, and relentless. They appear, like apocalyptic zombies, as a faceless, unthinking mass of less-than-human people that accumulates at the border, threatening to overwhelm the state's defenses by their sheer pressure and destroy the human beings and the social order inside.

These examples are drawn from work studying the rhetoric used for asylum-seekers in Austria and Australia, and the same terms are used across the West. As mentioned previously, displaced people—that is, those officially classified as illegal immigrants, asylum-seekers, refugees, and the like—are bare life striving to enter states where they will be given protection. Those states experience them as an unregulated threat to life within the border. As Aihwa Ong writes, "in camps of the disenfranchised or displaced, bare life becomes the ground for political claims, if not for citizenship, then for the right to survive."[49] At the same time, in the modern state, bare life is the basis for the treatment even of citizens of the state. The zombie is the mythic expression of racialized bare life striving to enter the state, but at the same time, the zombie is the condition that awaits all of us from whom the state withdraws protection. The zombies besieging the places of sanctuary in zombie apocalypse films can be read as displaced people seeking recognition from the countries of the West. As *Pride and Prejudice and Zombies* makes clear, they bear the histories of the enslaved whose labor enabled the quality of life at the heart of the colonial empires and provided the wealth for the Industrial Revolution. However, the zombies are also an image of what we—members of the modern state—might become. In the modern state, bare life founds the political order. In the neoliberal version of that state, where rights are dependent on what people within the border of the state can offer to its economic well-being, the degree to which one is reprieved from bare life depends on one's economic worth. In this way, within the state, labor returns as an inverse measure of zombification, while without the protection of the state, bare life equates with the most menial and unprotected forms of labor, exemplified in the zombie as domestic.

Conclusion

As I have explained previously, bare life has a dual meaning. In the first place it refers to lack of legal protection by the state. Without that protection, the person reduced to bare life can become transformed into the second understanding of bare life: the liminal condition of death-in-life. Indeed, such a person can become one of the living dead. This is the existential condition represented in the zombie. The equation of the zombie and the displaced person occurs through the construction of bare life in both aspects of the term. The new fascination with zombie apocalypse texts can be understood in relation to, but of course is not limited to, the increasing anxiety of members of Western states founded in the threat that these states feel is posed by racialized, displaced people. Both manifestations of bare life are described using the same discursive terms. The fear of what is perceived to be an external threat from the zombie Other helps those who live in Western states to repress awareness of how easily their own existence can become reduced to bare life.

Notes

1. "Capcom's Million-Selling Series, Resident Evil, Expanding to the Nintendo Game-Cube and Sony PlayStation2!," November 1, 2004, http://www.capcom.co.jp/ir/english/news/pdf/e041101.pdf.

2. "*Resident Evil,*" Box Office Mojo, 2002, http://www.boxofficemojo.com/movies/?id=residentevil.htm.

3. Stephanie Merritt, "*Pride and Prejudice and Zombies* by Jane Austen and Seth Grahame-Smith," *Observer,* December 6, 2009, http://www.guardian.co.uk/books/2009/dec/06/pride-prejudice-zombies-grahame-smith.

4. UNHCR Statistics Team, "Are Refugee Numbers the Highest Ever?," UNHCR Blogs, https://www.unhcr.org/blogs/statistics-refugee-numbers-highest-ever/.

5. See Jon Stratton, "'Welcome to Paradise': Asylum Seekers, Tourists and Deaths," in *Our Patch: Enacting Australian Sovereignty Post-2001,* ed. Suvendrini Perera, 167–96 (Perth, Wash.: Network Books, 2007).

6. See Giorgio Agamben, *Homo Sacer: Sovereign Power and Bare Life* (Palo Alto, Calif.: Stanford University Press, 1995).

7. Anthony Downey, "Zones of Indistinction: Giorgio Agamben's Bare Life and the Politics of Aesthetics," *Third Text* 233, no. 2 (2009): 109.

8. Jon Stratton, "Trouble with Zombies: Muselmänner, Bare Life and Displaced People," *Somatechnics* 1, no. 1 (2011).

9. I even have a T-shirt, made in the United States, bearing the legend "Zombie Outbreak Response Team." It includes the slogan "Shoot Them in the Head; They Stay Dead."

10. Wells, quoted in Kyle William Bishop, "Dead Man Still Walking: Explaining the Zombie Renaissance," *Journal of Popular Film and Television* 37, no. 1 (2009): 19.

11. St. John, quoted in Bishop, 19.

12. "*Twilight,*" Box Office Mojo, 2008, http://boxofficemojo.com/movies/?id=twilight08.htm.

13. David Punter and Glennis Byron in *The Gothic* write that "early vampires are not only aristocrats, but also seducers, and from the start the vampire has been associated with sexuality." Punter and Byron, *The Gothic* (Malden, Mass.: Blackwell, 2004), 269.

14. In the United States, interracial marriage was legalized across the country by a 1967 Supreme Court decision. It was only in 2000 that the census allowed respondents to claim two or more racial backgrounds.

15. Simon Pegg, "The Dead and the Quick," *Guardian,* November 3, 2008, https://www.theguardian.com/media/2008/nov/04/television-simon-pegg-dead-set.

16. Pegg.

17. Peter Dendle, "The Zombie as Barometer of Cultural Anxiety," in *Monsters and the Monstrous: Myths and Metaphors of Enduring Evil,* ed. Niall Scott (Amsterdam: Rodophi, 2007), 54.

18. Dendle, 54.

19. Dendle, 54.

20. Bishop, "Dead Man Still Walking," 24.

21. Dendle, "Zombie as Barometer," 47–48.

22. Ibid., 47.

23. Joan Dayan, "Vodoun, or the Voice of the Gods," in *Sacred Possessions: Vodou, Santeria, Obeah, and the Caribbean,* ed. Margarite Fernández Olmos and Lizabeth Paravisini-Gebert (New Brunswick, N.J.: Rutgers University Press, 1997), 33.

24. Dayan, 33.

25. Jean Comaroff and John Comaroff, "Alien Nation: Zombies, Immigrants, and Millennial Capitalism," *South Atlantic Quarterly* 101, no. 4 (2002): 786–87.

26. Comaroff and Comaroff, 795.

27. Thomas Loe, "Patterns of the Zombie in Jean Rhys's *Wide Sargasso Sea*," *Journal of Postcolonial Writing* 31, no. 1 (1991): 35.

28. Loe, 41.

29. Seth Grahame-Smith and Jane Austen, *Pride and Prejudice and Zombies* (Philadelphia: Quirk Books, 2009).

30. Edward Said, *Culture and Imperialism* (London: Chatto and Windus, 1993), 87.

31. Although it seems to me that the evidence points to her disapproval of it; see Susan Fraiman, "Jane Austen and Edward Said: Gender, Culture, and Imperialism," *Critical Inquiry* 21, no 4 (1995): 805–21.

32. Said, *Culture and Imperialism,* 94.

33. See Robin Blackburn, *The Making of New World Slavery: From the Baroque to the Modern 1492–1800* (London: Verso, 1997).

34. Suvendrini Perera, *Reaches of Empire: The English Novel from Edgeworth to Dickens* (New York: Columbia University Press, 1991), 47.

35. Perera, 20.

36. Grahame-Smith, *Pride and Prejudice and Zombies,* 22.

37. On the eighteenth-century understanding of slaves as savages, see J. Robert Constantine, "The Ignoble Savage: An Eighteenth-Century Literary Stereotype," *Phylon* 27, no. 2 (1966): 171–79. Constantine argues that "the ignoble savage stereotype came to be used as a basic factor in the defense of slavery and slave trading" (171).

38. Bishop, "Dead Man Still Walking," 24.

39. Charlie Brooker, "Is Obama Really President or Am I Just Watching a Fantasy? It's Almost Too Good to Be True," *Guardian*, November 10, 2008.

40. For reviews of *Fido*, see, e.g., Steve Biodrwoski, "Fido—A Boy and His Zombie," *Hollywood Gothique*, June 12, 2007, http://new.hollywoodgothique.com/fido-a-boy-and -his-zombie/.

41. It is not the first Australian zombie film; that would seem to be *Zombie Brigade*, released in 1986. In this film the zombies are Vietnam War veterans risen from the dead to take revenge on the attempt by Japanese developers to build a theme park on the site of the war memorial. The anxieties here would seem to connect with long-standing Australian fears of Asian invasion.

42. See Jon Stratton, "Dying to Come to Australia" as well as Jon Stratton, "'Welcome to Paradise.'"

43. Elisabeth El Refaie, "Metaphors We Discriminate By: Naturalized Themes in Austrian Newspaper Articles about Asylum Seekers," *Journal of Sociolinguistics* 5, no. 3 (1995): 364.

44. Ibid., 364.

45. Ibid., 364–65.

46. Sharon Pickering, "Common Sense and Original Deviancy: News Discourses and Asylum Seekers in Australia," *Journal of Refugee Studies* 14, no. 2 (2001): 172.

47. Ibid., 172.

48. Ibid., 174.

49. Aihwa Ong, "Mutations in Citizenship," *Theory, Culture, and Society* 23, no. 2–3 (2006): 501.

IV
The Promises of Monsters

BEASTS FROM THE DEEP

Erin Suzuki

W HY DO SO MANY MONSTERS ply the deep waters of the Pacific? The Pacific has been a breeding ground for all kinds of fictional beasts bearing apocalyptic significance, from Moby Dick to Godzilla. While Cold War–era monster movies spoke to historically specific anxieties around nuclearization, imperialism, and containment, spectacle-driven summer blockbusters from the early 2010s—specifically Peter Berg's *Battleship* (2012), Guillermo del Toro's *Pacific Rim* (2013), and Gareth Edwards's remake of *Godzilla* (2014)—revisit these monster-movie tropes not only to reconsider such issues in a twenty-first-century context but to overcome them with future promises of transpacific partnership between the United States and Asian nations.

Scholarship in Asian Americanist and science fiction studies has begun to theorize these interconnections between transpacific economics, politics, and the increasingly global production and circulation of contemporary pop culture. The critical focus on "techno-orientalism," a term originally coined by David Morley and Kevin Robins to describe changing U.S./Western attitudes toward Japan as it emerged as a technological and economic superpower in the 1970s and 1980s, addresses how transpacific perceptions of Asia as a site of technological advancement and economic speculation have expressed themselves in narrative and formal aesthetics of speculative fiction and film.[1] Contemporary critics working on techno-Orientalism (such as David Roh, Betsy Huang, Greta Niu, and Jane Park) note that while this particular narrative/aesthetic style certainly works to construct a "collusive, futurized Asia that affirms the West's centrality," it also presents an "opportunity for critical reappropriations in texts that self-referentially engage with Asian images," particularly when deployed in the work of Asian and Asian American cultural producers.[2] Yet as Aimee Bahng points out, the very flexibility of these techno-Orientalist motifs also speak to the proliferation and adaptability of neoliberal subjectivities across the Asia-Pacific region. In this context, a critical approach to Asian futurity would not only address the reappropriation of racist discourses that circulate in Western media but also seek to "intervene in neoliberal orientations of 'the good life.'"[3]

While Bahng draws out the connections between transpacific financial speculation—particularly the trading in economic "futures"—and the political and cultural narratives that posit Asian nations and Asian peoples as having a special relationship to futurity, Joseph Jeon has analyzed the relationship between financial speculation and digital media technologies in order to explore the *formal* dimensions of this "speculative digital capital."[4] Focusing on the algorithmic code used in software that supports both financial speculations and computer-generated imagery (CGI), Jeon argues that CGI monsters in contemporary Korean science fiction films like *The Host* (2006) and *D-War* (2007) function as an allegory for both U.S. militarization and neoliberal capitalism by revealing the "invisible forces that work behind the scenes of everyday life in an age of financialization."[5] Building on these readings of the monstrous intersections of neoliberalism, militarization, and technology, I posit that the oceanic beasts prominently featured in *Battleship, Pacific Rim,* and the 2014 version of *Godzilla* not only work to represent or allegorize the militarization and economic liberalization of the "Pacific Rim" nations whose economies have come to dominate the region but also assert the inextricable entanglement of these neoliberal projects from the chaotic and unpredictable crises that they purport to solve or prevent. For not only do these beasts, as Jeon notes, "make visible" the financial instruments, technologies, and philosophies that both compose and construct the infrastructures that support transpacific trade but they also operate as figures of chaos, ambivalence, and transgressive connections that cannot be fully suppressed or contained by these neoliberal architectures.

As a political and economic metaphor, these beasts' oceanic origins also speak to the absent presence of indigenous Pacific histories and epistemologies within the construction of contemporary transpacific networks. It is not insignificant that the monsters tied most closely to the geography and ecology of the Pacific Ocean—Pacific Rim's *kaiju* and the eponymous Godzilla—are also implicitly tied to the history of nuclear tests on the Pacific Islands; indeed, the opening sequence of Edwards's film implies that the tests at Bikini Atoll were intended not to promote a policy of Cold War containment but to put an end to Godzilla. These references to nuclear testing and island territories gesture at the environmental and cultural damage created by the settler colonial legacies that have provided the material basis for the military, technological, and economic infrastructures that support contemporary visions of transpacific futurity—as is perhaps made most explicit in Peter Berg's *Battleship,* set in Hawai'i's Pearl Harbor (Pu'uloa). My analysis of these films therefore also borrows from both ecocritical and indigenous critiques of settler colonial futurity, focusing particularly on the way that concepts of intersubjectivity and relationality engage with the neoliberal architectures that are simultaneously allegorized and destroyed by these beasts from the deep.

In late 2011, as direct U.S. military involvement in Iraq and Afghanistan was beginning to wind down, the Obama administration announced their intent to shift the focus of U.S. foreign policy from the Middle East to Asia. Although the U.S. Department of Defense had been planning a significant "realignment" of their forces in the region since at least 2006, the official announcement of this "pivot to Asia" in the period immediately following the assassination of Osama bin Laden and the capture of other key figures in al-Qaeda's terrorist network was intended to signal both a geographic change in American foreign policy and military interests and a paradigm shift in terms of the concept of securitization. In a speech delivered at the 2011 Asia-Pacific Economic Cooperation summit in Honolulu, Hawai'i, then secretary of state Hillary Clinton predicted that going forward, "the world's strategic and economic center of gravity will be the Asia Pacific. . . . And one of the most important tasks of American statecraft over the next decades will be to lock in a substantially increased investment—diplomatic, economic, strategic, and otherwise—in this region." Clinton went on to proclaim that "the twenty-first century will be America's Pacific Century, a period of unprecedented outreach and partnership in this dynamic, complex, and consequential region."[6]

Clinton's deployment of the language of partnership to connect the maintenance of U.S. hegemony in the region to a vision of peaceful neoliberal futurity is echoed in much of the Obama administration's public statements in support of the Trans-Pacific Partnership (TPP), a multistate agreement that would liberalize trade between its partner nations. Yet the very use of the term *partnership* in this context carries with it an unresolved tension regarding America's future stake in the region. While the deployment of *partnership* is certainly a euphemistic way of describing a U.S.-led economic coalition intended to contain Chinese influence, it also betrays a genuine anxiety about a globalizing world in which the United States is not (yet) presumed to have the ability to direct the region's future path.[7] That is, the language of *partnership* includes a clear awareness that the United States cannot act unilaterally in order to create the "mature security and economic architecture" needed to secure a U.S.-led vision of the future that will "promote security, prosperity, and universal values."[8]

While the primary goal of the United States' renewed commitment to building partnerships in the Pacific region may be to isolate and compete with China politically and economically, another less immediate but equally important goal is to address and combat environmental crises that require multilateral actions. Particularly in the wake of the 2011 Daiichi Fukushima nuclear disaster in Japan, and with a rising awareness of the way that climate change, overfishing, and human-created waste are negatively affecting sea levels, ocean temperatures, and sea life, nations in and around the Pacific are certainly aware of how their populations are increasingly vulnerable to drastic environmental change. Yet the proposed U.S. actions to limit climate change and other potential ecological disasters are, like their discussions on transpacific trade, couched in terms of *containing* and *managing* the threat. While not limited to discussions of proposed environmental policies for the Asia-Pacific alone, the political practice of articulating policies that seek to mitigate environmental change in terms of "targets," "offsets," and "sustainability"—all terms that blend seamlessly into the language of both economics and military strategy—speaks to a framework of what Robert Marzec has called *environmentality,* or the transformation of the natural environment itself into a security concern.[9] While *environmentality* has been used by other critics to address the intersections of environmental policy with economic and ecofeminist politics, Marzec's deployment of the term focuses on how nature itself is viewed as an entity that must be secured, capitalized upon, and potentially deployed in the interests of a security society.[10] This society is not limited to the borders and boundaries of the U.S. nation-state but expands to include a global community connected by shared investments in a mode of rationalist modernity that associates both economic and personal security with standardization, strategy, and surveillance. In this context, the increasing concern for environmental and ecological sustainability in U.S. public policy operates alongside the "pivot to Asia" as another way of attempting to stay ahead of, and manage, the evolving threats of both economic competition and ecological catastrophe.

Against these projected visions of a region secured against economic and environmental threat, the subterranean "beasts" in the three movies explored here represent the chaotic and unforeseeable consequences that haunt these optimistic projections of transpacific partnership and its role in securing an American-dominated vision of neoliberal futurity. *Battleship* (2012), *Pacific Rim* (2013), and *Godzilla* (2014) are all summer blockbuster-style movies released in the years immediately following the spate of 2011 announcements of the U.S. "pivot to Asia." While these three films were designed primarily as eye-catching entertainment, it is nevertheless still indicative of a trending transpacificism that all three films feature as their primary antagonists a series of terrifyingly adaptive alien monsters whose very presence mobilizes a transpacific partnership between American and Asian allies. If the ocean is, as Chris Connery has claimed, "capital's favored myth-element," these beasts from the deep speak to deep-seated anxieties about disruptions to the militarized transpacific architectures that facilitate the flow of global capital as well as to the kinds of monstrous disruptions that are in turn created by them.[11] Thus, while Peter Berg's *Battleship* (2012) foregrounds and celebrates the history of American militarization in the Pacific, its ambivalent stance on military technology also operates as a critique of an increasingly militarized future. Conversely, although Gareth Edwards's *Godzilla* (2014) is represented as a force of nature that easily overpowers—and remains relatively indifferent to—American military infrastructures, the film's monster-versus-monster showdown problematically renders the human (and specifically U.S. military) contributions to environmental destruction less visible. Finally, while Guillermo del Toro's monster-versus-machine showdown *Pacific Rim* (2013) ends with a decisive victory of transpacific technologies over the shifting and unpredictable threat posed by aquatic alien bodies, the film's subplot involving black-market trafficking in alien biomaterials works to uncannily and uncomfortably connect the human to the alien through military science and the "dirty" underbelly of capitalism. In what follows, I unpack the contradictions and critiques of the concept of transpacific futurity articulated by these three films and also explore potential sites for thinking through alternative modes of transpacific relation that might exist outside of militarized or neoliberal models of partnership.

In an early scene from Peter Berg's science fiction film *Battleship* (2012), a nervous NASA scientist—who has just been informed that his group will be engaged with sending out a communications signal to contact potential life-forms out in deep space—mutters to his colleague, "This could be like Columbus and the Indians. Except we're the Indians." Although this was intended as a throwaway line, the scientist's fear that humankind will be decimated by a technologically superior and warlike alien race carries unintended and ironic resonances with the movie's setting in Hawai'i, a site where the indigenous occupants were themselves displaced (and rendered mostly invisible in the film) by the very military–industrial systems and technologies that are the formal and narrative centerpieces of the film. This tension between past, present, and future provides a constant undercurrent throughout the movie: while the attacking aliens and their explosive, CGI-enhanced weaponry provide the film with a futuristic, science fictional sheen, the heart of the film is firmly rooted in its nostalgia for the period when U.S. military power established itself as a powerful global force. In many ways, *Battleship*'s narrative incoherence emerges out of the contradiction between its celebration of America's military past and its fear of the nation's militarized future. The film's mid-Pacific setting is not incidental but absolutely crucial to its ambivalent approach to transpacific histories, alliances, and futurities.

Directed by the son of a naval historian and produced with the support and approval of the U.S. Navy, *Battleship*'s plot revolves around an alien attack that takes place during an international naval exercise happening just off the coast of O'ahu. Before the aliens arrive, a heated rivalry develops between the American and Japanese sailors. However, when an amphibious alien warship attacks, they end up working together to defeat this common threat to humanity. The alien mothership creates a force field that seals off a perimeter around Hawai'i; meanwhile, amphibious fighter ships burst out from beneath the waves to disable and destroy the few naval ships that have been trapped within the perimeter. (While the aliens are amphibious, and appear on both land and water, I'm classifying them here as "beasts from the deep" because their submarine seacraft play such a central role not only in the visual iconography of the movie but also in the film's rather tenuous tie-in with the Hasbro game.) Although one ship is briefly successful in pinpointing the aliens' position by tracking wave patterns, it is also ultimately destroyed, and its crew are left with no choice but to use the decommissioned World War II battleship ("The Mighty Mo") docked at Pearl Harbor. Using this technologically outdated battleship, the human crews are able to both knock out the force field isolating the islands *and* destroy the satellite array on O'ahu, eliminating the aliens' ability to communicate with their home planet. Once the force field is dismantled, the rest of the fleet arrives to dismantle the remaining alien warships—and humanity is presumably saved.

As this synopsis suggests, *Battleship*'s narrative relies heavily, if rather crudely, on World War II history and iconography. From the surprise attack on Pearl Harbor through the resurrection of the USS *Missouri,* the very battleship on which Japan formally surrendered to the United States, the movie taps into the nostalgia for a period when U.S. military actions appeared to be relatively clear-cut and morally righteous, as opposed to the drawn-out hostilities of the "cold" wars in Korea and Vietnam and the messy, ambiguous, and open-ended enterprises in which the modern American military finds itself currently enmeshed. Yet by recasting the enemy as an alien race whose strength lies in their superior technology and whose weakness is their eyes (both their physical inability to see in the sunlight as well as their overreliance on visual perception to give them a strategic edge), *Battleship*'s primary antagonist operates as science fictional analogy for the very military–technological–industrial complex that helped to bring the film into being. Here I refer not only to the U.S. Navy's participation in the film's production but also to the way that, as Paul Virilio and others have argued, military technologies and film technologies have increasingly operated in tandem with one another to construct a "global vision" of militarized surveillance since World War II: together, both have been responsible for creating a significant shift in the perception of warfare, so that it appears not so much as an *exceptional* mode of struggle or conflict as a natural part of everyday life.[12] Thus, while *Battleship*'s use of the historically resonant site of Pearl Harbor deliberately engages with a nostalgic form of American wartime patriotism, the narrative arc of its plot simultaneously promotes a certain degree of skepticism or suspicion regarding the visualizing technologies upon which much of modern military strategy and weaponry relies. Indeed, by placing the technologically outdated "Mighty Mo" at the emotional and narrative center of the film, *Battleship* illustrates a sense of longing for the U.S. military past that operates as subtle critique of its militarized present.

Battleship deploys the competition and eventual reconciliation between American and Japanese naval officers to recall the bilateral dynamic of the World War II in an attempt to both transcend and transform it for this new era of global warfare. Although the initially threatening Japanese captain Nagata becomes familiarized and domesticated through his eventual alliance with the American hero, *Battleship* rehearses the trope of an Orientalized enemy that is aligned not with Asian *bodies* but with technology itself. This "techno-Orientalism," as David Morley and Kevin Robins have called it, emerges out of the rise of industrial economies out of East Asian nations such as Japan (but also Hong Kong, Taiwan, and South Korea) in the late twentieth century, a global shift that has worked to make technology and (post)modernity synonymous with Asia, and vice versa, in the American imagination. In this context, the very concept of technology becomes invested with "Oriental" qualities.[13] Thus, while there is nothing phenotypically Asiatic about the *Battleship* aliens, they are nevertheless framed by an Orientalist *discourse* that conveniently positions them—via their association with advanced technologies—as destructive forces to be overcome.

This discursive positioning becomes more obvious when read against the initial passivity of the "invading" alien force. There is nothing overtly threatening about the aliens at first, aside from their status as nonhuman entities. In their initial encounter with humankind, they do not attack until they are fired upon by the navy ships; moreover, throughout the film, they appear to be more interested in dismantling infrastructure and weaponry than in attacking human beings. The aliens refrain from attacking persons or things that do not register as aggressive, armed, or hostile: while they swiftly destroy loaded guns, armed choppers, and freeway infrastructures, they avoid directly attacking unarmed human beings. Furthermore, the aliens' motives are never really known: although the movie's hero has a brief, nightmarish vision of interstellar destruction when he accidentally touches one of the aliens, it's never clear if these particular aliens were the initiators or the victims of that violence. Nevertheless, the subsequent action of the film relies upon the characters' (and the audience's) eagerness to force these inscrutable aliens into familiar "yellow peril" tropes borrowed from both the first and last decades of the twentieth century. Whatever their motives may be, the *Battleship* aliens engage fears of a terrifying immigrant "horde" capable of destroying the local population with their resource-devouring numbers, and threaten to render all of humankind obsolete by dint of their unmatched technological superiority.[14]

Yet if militarized technology and the hubristic blindness that comes with it is reconfigured as the enemy, what might this imply about America's military presence in the Pacific? Beginning with the analogy drawn in the opening comparison of humankind to "Indians" and the aliens to "Columbus," the conflict that *Battleship* stages between a low-tech, "indigenous" fighting force and a technologically superior colonizer would seem not so much to celebrate American militarization as to render it, paradoxically, more alien. The film glosses over both the historical and the ongoing colonial implications of the U.S. military's current presence in the Pacific—not only the extant presence of the massive military and technological infrastructure in Hawai'i but also the most current buildup of bases on the U.S. island territory of Guam following the 2006 realignment treaty with Japan.[15] Yet viewed against the grain, it certainly invokes such parallels: both Hawai'i and Guam were strategically located territories that were acquired by or ceded to the United States through the use of military force in the late nineteenth century, and both continue to be strategically significant to the transpacific architectures for trade and security constructed and sustained through the U.S. military's war and surveillance technologies.[16] In addition, beneath the film's apparent cheerleading for the U.S. armed forces and their transpacific partners, *Battleship* belies a supreme sense of unease regarding militarized technologies that can be detached from human control: in terms of not only the aliens' destructive drones but also the visualizing and targeting systems used by the modern U.S. Navy ships. The film's signature sequence—where a modern battleship has its networked tracking systems knocked out and must detect the alien ships using only grid coordinates—uses wave displacement measurements sent by tsunami buoys on a radio frequency. "We've been doing it to America for twenty years," sniffs the Japanese captain, implying that Americans' overreliance on more visually based technologies has allowed them to overlook this relatively low-tech maneuver.

In this context, it is not entirely surprising that overreliance on visual technologies turned out to be the downfall of not only the antagonists in the film, but the film itself. *Battleship* was, predictably, condemned by critics for both the excesses of its production—particularly its heavy use of CGI—and the silliness of its narrative; however, it also failed at the box office, earning only twenty-five million dollars in its opening weekend in the United States.[17] Unlike Universal Studios' previous Hasbro tie-in movie, *Transformers*—which had also been panned by critics—*Battleship* did not manage to resonate with the viewing public at home or abroad, and its failure to do so quickly scuttled any plans to turn the film into a franchise series.[18] However, this would not be the case with the next summer's CGI-laden, Pacific-themed blockbuster, Guillermo del Toro's *Pacific Rim*.

Although *Pacific Rim*, like *Battleship*, did not fare well in the domestic marketplace, the movie's less explicitly American focus and shrewd international marketing transformed it from big-budget flop to an unexpected success story.

Although it only grossed around one hundred million dollars in U.S. theaters, it grossed four hundred million worldwide—quite enough for the film's production company, Legendary, to consider the movie a success and initiate plans for a sequel.[19] This market positioning did not escape some of the film's reviewers: writing for the *Atlantic,* Christopher Orr noted that *Pacific Rim*'s "greatest breakthrough may be that it's the first Hollywood blockbuster to sport a title less descriptive of its plot than its intended market."[20] The *New Yorker*'s Anthony Lane likewise highlighted the film's nakedly global ambitions, noting that the consumer market invoked by the film's title "account[s] for an ever-swelling proportion of Hollywood's box office. . . . It is possible to applaud 'Pacific Rim' for the efficacy of its business model while deploring the tale that has been engendered."[21]

However, the plot of the movie *Pacific Rim* and the narratives driving the "business models" that define the market region cannot be so neatly separated. In the movie, human civilization is being threatened by *kaiju,* which are shapeshifting, adaptable, and swiftly evolving alien beasts who emerge from a transdimensional crack in the Pacific seafloor. To combat this threat, mankind creates jaegers, giant robotic cyborgs controlled by two human copilots who are sent out to fight the kaiju as they emerge from the seas. In the film's main action sequences, we see four different teams sent out to subdue the kaiju menace: first, Chinese and Russian jaeger teams are sent out and destroyed; then, a jaeger team comprising Australian and British copilots heroically sacrifice themselves so that the final jaeger, steered by an American man and Japanese woman, can unleash the nuclear payload that destroys the last of the kaiju and seals the transdimensional portal—at least for now. This narrative sequence of events—the fall of the Cold War communist bloc as represented by China and Russia, followed by the emergence of a powerful U.S.–Japanese union leading the way with the support and assistance of the Commonwealth nations—is not dissimilar to contemporary narratives of renewal and trade partnership that have shaped contemporary "Pacific Rim" economic policies, at least from the point of view of the United States. In the post–Cold War context in which both cinematic and politico-economic Pacific Rims are constructed, the focus is not so much on containing an established threat as on developing and evolving technologies and strategic alliances to master and outmaneuver an ever-changing economic environment.

Yet if the military triumphalism of *Pacific Rim*'s explosive conclusion optimistically gestures toward the success of flexible, technology-driven transpacific architectures in staying ahead of the amorphous threat (and black-market profits) that the kaiju represent, the film also offers up an alternative possibility in one of its side plots, where a human scientist figures out how to "drift," or mind-meld, with one of the alien creatures. First, we learn that after kaiju are defeated, their bodies are harvested by scientists seeking answers—and black-market dealers seeking riches—in the alien biomatter. In a moment of crisis, a scientist decides to attempt a "drift" with one of the harvested brains of a dead kaiju, which un-expectedly reveals important information on how to defeat the kaiju once and for all. However, the film also reveals that the neural connection goes both ways: the humans can learn about the kaiju, but the kaiju can learn about humans, too. There is an implication that both participants in the "drift" state are themselves altered and hybridized: after mind-melding with the kaiju, the human scientist begins bleeding from the nose and eyes, marking him out as physically, as well as psychically, changed by the experience. Moreover, in the aftermath of his experiment, the other kaiju are drawn irresistibly toward him, since he has been incorporated into their hive mind. While the film does not push this plot much further, it is certainly tempting to speculate about how else this newly hybridized human subject may have been altered by his transgressive experience with an alien being. Besides opening the door for a potential movie sequel, the sequence also opens up important questions of how the "clean" global capitalism repre-sented by the jaeger squad cannot ultimately be disentangled from the "dirty" black market represented by the kaiju.

In this sense, the oceanic setting of *Pacific Rim* is particularly apt. As *Battleship* clearly illustrates, the Pacific figured as a theater of war in the U.S. imagina-tion for a large part of the twentieth century, but in recent political discourse, it has been invoked primarily as an economic zone. As such, it has been constructed as an area of both promise—in the optimistic language of shared economic bene-fit and transpacific partnership—and peril, as fears emerge about how the influ-ence of transnational corporations and powerful overseas economies may work to override or dissolve member states' national interests and policies. Conveniently, the oceanic ecology of the Pacific itself serves as both metaphor *and* material for these contradictory ideologies. Placing the symbolic equivalence of oceans and capital into an ecological context, Stefan Helmreich points out how the biomate-rials that emerge or are harvested out of oceanic environments have been con-structed, in the context of a late capitalist environment, as both resources and threats.[22] In both popular and policy discourses, the ocean environment is con-structed as a boundless and biodiverse resource with the promise of renewable biotechnologies to help heal and sustain the Earth and its human populations. But at the same time, it is also represented as a threateningly alien, terrifyingly fecund culture for the spread of contamination, pollution, or bacteria. As dis-putes over oceanic territory—illustrated by China's construction of a number of man-made islands in the South China Sea within maritime space also claimed by the Philippines, Malaysia, Taiwan, and Vietnam—have shown, the struggle for control over these threatening/promising oceanic resources has become a point of heightened interest in the negotiation of transpacific trade and economic and political partnerships in the region, not only for the United States but for all nations with a stake in the region.

This "double vision"[23] of Pacific ocean ecologies and the transpacific trade it is intimately entangled with finds cinematic expression in the 2014 reboot of Toho Studio's most famous creation, *Godzilla*. In the original 1954 film, directed by Ishiro Honda, Godzilla operates as a metaphor for postwar Japanese anxieties about nuclear weaponry. Awakened by nuclear testing in the Pacific, Godzilla emerges from the ocean to wreak havoc on Tokyo and can be destroyed only by a weapon so powerful that its creator sacrifices himself to make sure it can never be used again. While the original *Godzilla* foregrounds this parallel between the destructive powers of its imaginary, prehistoric beast and the destructive powers of human invention, the most recent reboot of the franchise—directed by American Gareth Edwards and released in theaters this past summer—reimagines this beast from the deep as less of an antagonist than a force of nature. Like the ocean whence he comes, Godzilla has the ability to both destroy and preserve. In this version of *Godzilla,* human experiments with nuclear power are once again responsible for the rise of a bestial threat: in this case, MUTOs (massively unidentified terrestrial organisms), ancient monsters that feed off of the nuclear radiation that humans have produced. Although a pan-Pacific partnership of scientists and military strategists attempts to stop the MUTOs as they make their way from Japan to Hawai'i to San Francisco, it is ultimately Godzilla who takes center stage as the true hero, balancing the scales by hunting down and destroying the MUTOs before they can repopulate. Despite the beautifully shot action sequences showing troops parachuting into the San Francisco Bay in an attempt to fight both sets of monsters, the humans in the film are ultimately sidelined in favor of a monster-versus-monster showdown. Unlike *Pacific Rim* and *Battleship,* which depended on the establishment of transpacific military alliances to defeat an alien threat, Edwards's *Godzilla* embraces the alien nature of the beast itself, against whose might human strategy, alliances, and technologies mean very little.

Yet, in so doing, this film also falls short of recognizing the complex interrelationship between human intervention and the chaos represented by Godzilla and the MUTOs. Reviewing the film for the *New Jersey Star-Ledger,* Priscilla Wald notes that "if chastened respect for the power and danger of science is the message of the original 'Godzilla,' Edwards' reboot tells us to be more humble before nature. It also tells us to get out of the way: Nature will restore its own balance."[24] However, Wald notes that when transferred to the real world, this message is in itself deeply problematic, as it removes the human responsibility to respond to ecological disasters such as climate change—making us, in practice, as "dangerous as the MUTOs" in their blatant disregard for the human cost of their actions.[25] In this sense, the most current rendering of *Godzilla*—particularly the film's overly sentimental portrayal of this massive and unpredictable superpredator at the story's conclusion—supports Frederick Buell's contention that the idea of apocalypse has itself become naturalized and, in a sense, domesticated. Buell argues that in the present day, the ever-present threat of ecological crisis, far from being perceived as a threat to be averted, in fact works to shape "construct society's sense of daily normality"; even though that concept of "normality," as Buell is quick to point out, is based not necessarily on *engagement* with these environmental problems but rather on a *denial* of them.[26] Precisely because the average American has not yet directly experienced the negative consequences of climate change or other environmental crises, many have come to the conclusion that the apocalyptic rhetoric of an earlier era has been overblown—and that nature, after all, can take care of itself.

The world's oceans in particular appear to be a relatively self-regulating environment in this way, and certainly Godzilla's oceanic origins may have contributed to his (or her) representation as an indomitable and unconquerable force of nature. Stacy Alaimo points out that, like Godzilla, the absolute alien otherness of ocean ecologies, particularly in their benthic (or deep-sea) zones, contributes to the popular cultural conception of the oceans as a space that is "so enormous, so powerful, so abundantly full of life that it is impervious to human harm," a mind-set that often results in the practice of dumping "garbage, sewage, weapons, toxic chemicals, and radioactive waste" into the world's oceans with the idea that they will disperse in the oceans and effectively disappear.[27] Yet such practices overlook the myriad ways that the ocean environments shape human ones, and how such wastes return through currents, tides, and the food chain to affect human life. Building on theories of intersubjectivity developed by Donna Haraway, Bruno Latour, and others, Alaimo argues that adopting a "trans-corporeal" framework to explore the "material interchanges between human bodies, animal bodies, and the wider material world" would work to render the idea of the human subject as permeable rather than isolated—as stewards as well as consumers. Like the scientist-and-kaiju drift pairing from *Pacific Rim,* this type of trans-corporeal perspective requires participants to confront the way that both human and environmental subjects mutually shape one another.

While this concept of trans-corporeality draws from an ecocritical genealogy, a more immediate and local context for such intersubjective relationality would be the indigenous cultures, histories, and epistemologies that have been largely evacuated from all three films, as well as much of the critical discourse around them. For example, J. Kēhaulani Kauanui points out that not only did Native Pacific kinship practices encompass both human and natural worlds; they were also "a product of one's specific *relational* history," which means that Native genealogies and epistemologies are not based on the kind of strict or static biological essentialism demanded by a racialized, statist discourse.[28] Instead, they operate as dynamic, historical constructions that are "strategic, always partial, and shifting depending on one's current set of relationships and perspectives."[29] In a way that prefigures and anticipates the paired "drift" state deployed in *Pacific*

Rim (and, to a lesser extent, the one brief moment of physical human–alien contact in *Battleship*), the threat that this radical relationality poses to the construction of transpacific futurities is its embrace of the contingent and shifting nature of any given partnership, as opposed to attempting to pin it down with legal or financial instruments.

Native Pacific approaches to environmental stewardship in particular have also long modeled an alternative, relational perspective that can be applied equally to transpacific political, economic, and cultural alliances.[30] As Paul Lyons and Ty Kāwika Tengan note, Native Pacific models for "being in the world" take a relational approach to the oceanic environment—a respectful and careful observation of its patterns, tides, and currents—that operates as both "practical advice and philosophy for approaching challenging environments" both inclusive of and beyond the natural world.[31] In a world where everything from scientific technology to military strategy to financial markets is defined not so much by classification and certainty as by narratives of hybridity, risk, and indeterminacy, the concept of "drift," a term that also speaks to oceanic concepts of currents and circulation, gestures toward an alternative mode of transnational and transpacific connection, one that puts pressure on the binary logic of "us-vs-them," "man-vs-nature," "man-versus-monster," or "jaeger-vs-kaiju."

While the flexible strategies of modern militarization have also been central to the establishment of neoliberalism in and across the Pacific, a "drift"-like acceptance of the unknown differs from the practice of *managing* it by hedging or redistributing risk—the purpose toward which many contemporary transpacific alliances and architectures have been erected. As Edward LiPuma and Benjamin Lee note, these neoliberal practices tend to simultaneously objectify both concrete and abstract concepts of risk in order to transform them into commodities that may be traded and circulated on a global market.[32] Moreover, such global circulations have a tendency to redistribute risk in a manner that tends to follow a "racial and colonial logic" where the material consequences of such risk tend to disproportionately affect racialized and/or colonized communities that have already been marked as "other."[33]

By contrast, a "drift" approach requires a radical openness to alien otherness and the potential for chaos. It operates as a call to recognize the mutual weight of risk and responsibility that affects all participants in transpacific environmental and economic networks alike. At the very least, this openness to uncertainty focuses on the ways that what may seem like momentary stability nevertheless always comes with some kind of cost. Produced in the wake of the renewed U.S. interest in the Asia-Pacific—which in many ways represents an attempt or desire to both imagine and manage impending environmental, economic, and political crises—*Battleship, Pacific Rim,* and *Godzilla* speak to a globalizing world where the consequences of distributing risk are still making themselves known. While one form of apocalypse may have been subverted, we may want to consider what new conditions have been created to engender new forms of chaos that lie just out of sight, lurking like beasts in the deep.

Notes

1. See David Morley and Kevin Robins, *Spaces of Identity: Global Media, Electronic Landscapes, and Cultural Boundaries* (London: Routledge, 1995).

2. See David S. Roh, Betsy Huang, and Greta A. Niu, eds., *Techno-Orientalism: Imagining Asia in Speculative Fiction, History, and Media* (New Brunswick, N.J.: Rutgers University Press, 2015), 7.

3. Aimee Bahng, "The Cruel Optimism of Asian Futury and the Reparative Practices of Sonny Liew's *Malinky Robot*," in Roh et al., *Techno-Orientalism*, 165.

4. Joseph Jeon, "Neoliberal Forms: CGI, Algorithm, and Hegemony in Korea's IMF Cinema," *Representations* 126 (2014): 88.

5. Jeon, 89.

6. Hillary Clinton, "America's Pacific Century," speech, Asia-Pacific Economic Cooperation Summit, East-West Center, Honolulu, November 10, 2011. Many sections of this speech were also reprinted in slightly altered form in the *Foreign Policy* op-ed by the same name.

7. This shift in rhetoric can be traced back to the late Cold War period, when the concept of the region as a "Pacific Rim" with no hegemonic center was introduced. See Chris Connery, "Pacific Rim Discourse: The US Global Imaginary in the Late Cold War Years," *Boundary 2* 21 (1994): 30–56.

8. Clinton, "America's Pacific Century."

9. Robert Marzec, *Militarizing the Environment: Climate Change and the Security State* (Minneapolis: University of Minnesota Press, 2016), 4.

10. See, e.g., Timothy W. Luke, "On Environmentality: Geo-power and Eco-knowledge in Discourses of Contemporary Environmentalism," *Cultural Critique* 31 (Autumn 1995): 57–81; also see Arun Agrawal, *Environmentality: Technologies of Government and the Making of Subjects* (Durham, N.C.: Duke University Press, 2005).

11. Connery, "Pacific Rim Discourse," 56.

12. See Paul Virilio, *War and Cinema: The Logistics of Perception* (New York: Verso, 1989), 1. For an analysis of war technologies and perception in an explicitly transpacific context, see Rey Chow, *Age of the World Target: Self-Referentiality in War, Theory, and Comparative Work* (Durham, N.C.: Duke University Press, 2006).

13. As Morley and Robins note, "the dynamism of technological innovation has appeared to move eastwards, so have these postmodern technologies become structured into the discourse of Orientalism." David Morley and Kevin Robins, "Techno-Orientalism: Japan Panic," in *Spaces of Identity*, 169.

14. For more on the legacy of "yellow peril" discourse in techno-Orientalism, see Roh et al., *Techno-Orientalism*.

15. The United States–Japan Roadmap for Realignment Implementation, signed in May 2006 by former secretary of state Condoleezza Rice, was an agreement for the United

States to move more than eight thousand troops currently stationed in Okinawa to new bases that would be built up on the U.S.-held territory of Guam by 2014.

16. See Keith Camacho and Setsu Shigematsu, "Militarized Currents, Decolonizing Futures," in *Militarized Currents: Toward a Decolonized Future in Asia and the Pacific,* ed. Keith Camacho and Setsu Shigematsu (Minneapolis: University of Minnesota Press, 2010), xv–xlvii.

17. To give just a few examples, *Rolling Stone*'s Peter Travers writes that "*Battleship* is all noise and crashing metal, sinking to the shallows of Bay's *Armageddon* and then digging to the brain-extinction level of the *Transformers* trilogy," while NPR's Bob Mondello says, more charitably, that "the story, by brothers Erich and Jon Hoeber . . . is cleverer and quippier than it has any reason to be, even if it makes not the remotest sense." Travers, "Battleship," *Rolling Stone,* May 17, 2012, http://www.rollingstone.com/movies/reviews/battleship-20120517; Mondello, "Board Game + Explosions + Aliens = Battleship," May 17, 2012, http://www.npr.org/2012/05/17/152674665/board-game-explosions-aliens-battleship.

18. Writing for the *Daily Variety,* Andrew Stewart noted that although Universal and Hasbro had invested heavily in movie tie-in merchandise, *Battleship*'s disappointing box office performance was likely to render "downstream revenues . . . questionable." Stewart, "Half the Battle," *Daily Variety,* May 21, 2012. In *Forbes,* John Gaudiosi speculated that the film's unpopularity was likely to carry over to the video game release as well. Gaudiosi, "$220 Million Battleship Flop Sinks Not Only Universal Pictures, but Activision Game," *Forbes,* May 20, 2012, https://www.forbes.com/sites/johngaudiosi/2012/05/20/220-million-battleship-flop-sinks-not-only-universal-pictures-but-activision-game/#83e8a5c33a14.

19. While Legendary Pictures, this time in conjunction with Universal Studios, had originally planned to release a *Pacific Rim* sequel in the summer of 2017, the project has been reportedly tabled indefinitely. See Mia Galuppo, "It's Official: Universal Takes 'Pacific Rim 2' Off of the Release Calendar," *Hollywood Reporter,* September 29, 2015.

20. Christopher Orr, "A Beautiful, Disappointing *Pacific Rim,*" *Atlantic,* July 12, 2013, http://www.theatlantic.com/entertainment/archive/2013/07/a-beautiful-disappointing-i-pacific-rim-i/277746/.

21. Anthony Lane, "Grim Tidings," *New Yorker,* July 22, 2013, http://www.newyorker.com/magazine/2013/07/22/grim-tidings.

22. Stefan Helmreich, *Alien Ocean: Anthropological Voyages in Microbial Seas* (Berkeley: University of California Press, 2008).

23. Helmreich, 14.

24. Priscilla Wald, "Man vs Nature Is 'Godzilla's' Message, Then and Now: Opinion," *New Jersey Star-Ledger,* May 24, 2014, http://www.nj.com/opinion/index.ssf/2014/05/man_vs_nature_godzillas_message_then_and_now_opinion.html.

25. Wald.

26. Frederick Buell, *From Apocalypse to Way of Life: Environmental Crisis in the American Century* (New York: Routledge, 2004), xviii.

27. Stacy Alaimo, "Dispersing Disaster: The Deepwater Horizon, Ocean Conservation, and the Immateriality of Aliens," in *American Horizons: Climate, Culture, Catastrophe,* ed. Christof Mauch and Sylvia Mayer (Heidelberg: Universitätsverlag, 2012), 181–82.

28. See J. Kēhaulani Kaunaui, *Hawaiian Blood: Colonialism and the Politics of Sovereignty and Indigeneity* (Durham, N.C.: Duke University Press, 2008), 51.

29. Kaunaui, 51.

30. Several Pacific studies scholars and artists have explored the relationships between indigenous epistemologies and environmental awareness/stewardship. To list just a few: Kauanui, *Hawaiian Blood*; Haunani-Kay Trask, *From a Native Daughter: Colonialism and Sovereignty in Hawai'i* (Honolulu: University of Hawai'i Press, 1999); ku'ualoha ho'omanawanui, "'This Land Is Your Land, This Land Was My Land': Kanaka Maoli versus Settler Representations of 'Āina in Contemporary Literature of Hawai'i," in *Asian Settler Colonialism: From Local Governance to the Habits of Everyday Life in Hawai'i*, ed. Candace Fujikane and Jonathan Okamura (Honolulu: University of Hawai'i Press, 2008); Dina El Dessouky, "Activating Voice, Body, and Place: Kanaka Maoli and Ma'ohi Writings for Kaho'olawe and Moruroa," in *Postcolonial Ecologies: Literatures of the Environment,* ed. Elizabeth DeLoughrey and George B. Handley (New York: Oxford University Press, 2011).

31. Paul Lyons and Ty P. Kāwika Tengan, "Introduction: Pacific Currents," *American Quarterly* 67, no. 3 (2015): 545–46.

32. Edward LiPuma and Benjamin Lee, *Financial Derivatives and the Globalization of Risk* (Durham, N.C.: Duke University Press, 2004).

33. Paula Chakravartty and Denise DaSilva, "Accumulation, Dispossession, and Debt: The Racial Logic of Global Capital—An Introduction," *American Quarterly* 64, no. 3 (2012): 363.

OF SWAMP DRAGONS

Mud, Megalopolis, and a Future for Ecocriticism

Anthony Lioi

I N HER CLASSIC *Purity and Danger,* anthropologist Mary Douglas defines ritual pollution as "matter out of place" and concludes that such pollution can be a door to whole cosmologies: "Where there is dirt, there is a system."[1] Accordingly, she distinguishes between "dirt-affirming" and "dirt-rejecting" cultures based on their reaction to ritual pollution.[2] To affirm dirt is to recognize that impurity is inevitable, and to offer it a carefully defined place that recognizes and contains its power. To reject dirt is to imagine that it can be separated from what is sacred, and to finalize that separation by annihilating pollution from the cosmic order itself. I want to suggest that despite its desire to affirm Earth, much of ecocritical culture has been dirt-rejecting. In our quest to promote wildness and nonanthropocentric cosmologies, ecocritics have shunned texts and places compromised by matter-out-of-place, the ritual uncleanness of cities, suburbs, and other defiled ecosystems. Though I am not the first to notice this problem, the pattern of dirt-denying has continued. Therefore, we must consciously construct a symbolic place in ecocriticism for dirt and pollution, an alias or icon that allows us to give dirt its due. I suggest that American ecocritics consider the figure of the swamp dragon—embodying elemental mixture, ethical impurity, and serpentine wisdom—as an alternative to the posture of prophet and judge, the arbiters of purity and righteousness.[3] The critic need not always stand on a mountaintop, declaiming. Before I explain further, however, we need to take a short trip into the slippery terrain of disciplinary flux.

A glance at recent publications reveals that ecocriticism is entering a moment of transfiguration. Though ecocritics have been asking ourselves what methods and canons constitute the field for as long as the field has existed, the last five years offer signs that this questioning has entered a peculiarly intense phase. As ecocriticism moves out of the margins of literary studies, as the founders of the field acquire tenure, departmental chairs, and emeritus positions, it becomes possible to transform as well as defend the field. Evidence of this change can be seen even in a brief list of works that seek to expand the domain of ecocriticism and to question its founding assumptions: Karla Armbruster and Kathleen R. Wallace structured *Beyond Nature Writing: Expanding the Boundaries of Ecocriticism* to encompass nations, genres, traditions, and periods beyond American nature writing of the past two centuries, as did Patrick Murphy in *Farther Afield in the Study of Nature-Oriented Literature*. Lawrence Coupe's *The Green Studies Reader* attempted with great success to reverse-engineer the theoretical foundations of the field to include British and Continental philosophy and more recent work in cultural studies. Steven Rosendale, in *The Greening of Literary Scholarship: Literature, Theory, and Environment*, mixed old and new texts and approaches, balancing our traditional strengths with original directions. In the first summa since Cheryll Glotfelty's *Ecocriticism Reader*, Michael P. Branch and Scott Slovic edited *The "ISLE" Reader: Ecocriticism, 1993–2003*, representing a more assured critical center culled from our flagship journal. More radical challenges appeared as well. Joni Adamson, Mei Mei Evans, and Rachel Stein edited *The Environmental Justice Reader* to recenter the discipline on activism and non-Anglo, non-middle-class texts and cultures, while Dana Phillips's *The Truth of Ecology: Nature, Culture, and Literature in America* issued a challenge to rethink what we know about ecology as a science and its relationship to literary-critical method. Finally, Lawrence Buell, long the defender of the Thoreauvian center of green letters, moved decisively toward the literature of environmental crisis in *Writing for an Endangered World*. In the midst of these magisterial contributions, I offer a more modest rubric for critical transfiguration at the beginning of a new century.[4]

My investigation of the swamp dragon as a figure for ecocritical work begins in the swamps of home. Growing up in New Jersey, I always wondered what "purple mountains' majesty" of "America the Beautiful" was: my mountains, in the Kittatinny Range, are green and not exactly majestic. As many friends from the West have said, "Those aren't really mountains," meaning that the Appalachians lack the grandeur of the Rockies and the Cascades.[5] They are not the summit of a sublime landscape. They are not the mountains from which the law is given to the people, not the setting for a Mosaic environmentalism.[6]

Thus I became slowly aware that my allegiances to the land are different than the ecocritical norm and that my land is often a wetland: Burnt Fly Bog, the Superfund site two miles from my childhood home; the Raritan River, just recovering from centuries of industrial use; and the cedar-water streams of the Pine Barrens that stain white clothes wood-brown.[7] These places are damaged and unspectacular, even ugly, when your standards of loveliness are Mount Hood and the Sierra Madres. They have nonetheless provoked a blaze of environmentalist work, as in the late 1960s, when the core of the Barrens was preserved against plans for a second international airport for Philadelphia, and more recently when Raritan Riverkeeper became an integral part of the national Waterkeeper Alliance. But if sublime beauty is not the heart of such efforts, what is? I suggest that a swamp dragon moves through these regions, that the unlovely worlds where water and land meet spawned a spirit to which ecocritics must pay attention, if we are to sway the millions of people who live in the East, where very little is pure and high, and the distant hope of repristination cannot be the foundation of environmentalist devotion.

The East and its landforms have fared about as well in the annals of ecocriticism—Walden Pond and Tinker Creek are the exceptions that prove the rule. Michael Bennett's analysis of the "cultural geography" of ecocriticism in "From Wide Open Spaces to Metropolitan Places: The Urban Challenge to Ecocriticism" still holds true: though the encounter with urban nature has begun, most ecocritics still identify with wilderness and the West.[8] Conversely, the East is categorized in the ASLE Bibliography as a regional subtopic while there is no corresponding category for "West," because the West is everywhere.[9] The presence of Bennett's article in the *"ISLE" Reader* demonstrates an awareness of this problem, and the proliferation of ecocritics in the East is a hopeful sign. However, more will need to be done, and at a deeper level, if the cultural geography of the discipline is to include the Norport Megalopolis, as the Maine-to-Virginia sprawl has been called, not to mention the rest of the East. We can see the need for deeper thought in the name of ASLE's first conference east of the Mississippi in June 1999: "What to Make of a Diminished Thing."[10] Thomas Bailey, the organizer of the conference, explained the meaning of the name:

> "We have seen a real ecological crisis come upon us in the last 35 years. The East doesn't have the natural world it once did, hence the 'diminished thing,'" Bailey explains, noting this is the first time the ASLE conference has been held east of the Mississippi. "When it comes to nature, there's a big difference between East and West. Natural descriptions of the East are less rhetorical than those of the West as well. We have hills, not grand mountains; woods, not forests. But our nature is just as complex and worthy of study."[11]

Let me be clear that one would easily understand from the conference's promotional materials in the *ASLE Newsletter* and from the conference website that its name was meant to evoke the practice of ecological restoration.[12] Nonetheless, even as apologia, Bailey's explanation expresses a number of attitudes that need to be overcome: the sense that the East is ruined; that it is "diminished," like a musical chord, by minor materials at its core; and that even before ecological crisis, it was literally diminutive, suggesting lesser value or interest.

There is, however, some comfort in this discourse: it explains why I shuddered when I first heard the name of the conference, which confirmed the attitudes I felt were implicit in American ecocriticism in the 1990s. This compensatory sense that the East is not as good as the West is, perhaps, understandable, given that ecocriticism braced itself against an urban hegemony in literary studies.[13] It is understandable, but unsustainable: one cannot decide how to care for a place while calling it diminished, because condescension cannot be the basis for love or respect.

In many ways, the swamp is the exemplary figure in the American semiotics of place for chaos, desecration, and diminishment, and these associations began long before ecocriticism. As David C. Miller points out in *Dark Eden: The Swamp in Nineteenth-Century American Culture,* love and respect were not the traditional European sentiments attached to the swamp: "Its associations had been traditionally tied to theological and folkloric contexts: It was the domain of sin, death, and decay; the stage for witchcraft; the habitat of weird and ferocious creatures."[14] Swamps were both the land of death and a traditional image of Hell.[15] This attitude began to change in 1850s America, however, and the swamp began also to represent a "matrix of transformation"[16] that sheltered a variety of rebels, including slaves, Native Americans, and white southerners,[17] coming to symbolize, as Victorianism progressed into Modernism, unconscious mental processes, repressed matriarchy, and anarchism.[18] In *Postmodern Wetlands: Culture, History, Ecology* the Australian critic Rod Giblett points to several non-American parallels to this tradition of the swamp as site of political resistance and repressed psychic materials: the English Fens, the Mekong Delta of Vietnam, and the wetlands of Perth, Australia, which were cartographically erased as part of the symbolic progress of white settlement.[19] In a memorable sentence, Ingrid Bartsch, Carolyn DiPalma, and Laura Sells describe how this historical set of wetland dynamics iterated into a contemporary bureaucratic context: "Wetlands are literally and figuratively a terrain of struggle for government agencies, developers, environmentalists, scientists, and ducks, all of whom have competing interests in questions of definition, jurisdiction, regulation, and control."[20] As ecologist Ralph W. Tiner demonstrates exhaustively with *In Search of Swampland: A Wetland Resource and Field Guide,* the commonsense definition of a wetland as land-covered-in-water-some-of-the-time is complicated by the needs of farmers, for whom swamps and other wetlands were obstacles to agriculture; by the taxonomy of ecology, which makes fine distinctions among swamps, marshes, bogs, and vernal pools; and by state and federal agencies engaged in a rearguard effort to protect remaining American wetlands from corporate development.[21]

These historical, symbolic, and political tangles return us to the swamps of home. The Great Swamp National Wildlife Refuge, located in Basking Ridge, New Jersey, about twenty-five miles west of Manhattan, is a remnant of Lake Passaic, which formed after the Wisconsin glaciation retreated ten thousand years ago and left much of northeastern New Jersey covered in freshwater. Lake Passaic finally drained into Newark and Raritan bays, leaving the marshes and swamps that would become, among other things, the Meadowlands, where the New Jersey Nets basketball team plays. In the mid-1990s, just as ecocriticism was getting off the ground, the Nets did an unexpected thing: they considered changing their name to the New Jersey Swamp Dragons, in a bid, I think, to seem more local, much as New Jersey's professional hockey team had done by employing the folklore of the Jersey Devil. The Nets never did change their name, perhaps because the native swamp dragon was already taken, but I found the possibility of such a thing intriguing.[22] As I walked through the Great Swamp one bright day in fall not too long ago, I thought about what it might mean to know or become a swamp dragon.

Drakon and *draco* mean "serpent" in Greek and Latin; the root of these words means "to watch" or "to guard with a sharp eye," a hopeful etymology, environmentally.[23] The winged serpent appears across classical world cultures, often in the shape of messenger or wisdom divinities such as Isis, Hermes, and Quetzalcoatl. In the Hippocratic tradition of medicine, the serpent is a power of healing, and in Indian yogic disciplines, *shakti* coils up and around the spine as the force of enlightenment. In many Greek and Hebrew texts, however, the serpent is demonized in narratives of patriarchal defeat of chaos. Zeus, for instance, must fight Typhon, a chaos-dragon, before he can ascend to the throne of the gods, and the hero Perseus must rescue the princess Andromeda from Cetus as it prepares to devour her at the ocean's edge. Likewise, Leviathan, the great sea monster of Hebrew scripture, is portrayed, in Job and the Psalms, as a power of watery chaos that God has subdued. Leviathan is related to the waters God divides in Genesis 1:6–7, and these waters, *tehom* or the Deep, according to strong scholarly consensus, are a memory of the water dragon Tiamat, the mother goddess who is killed by her grandson Marduk in the Babylonian creation story, the *Enuma Elish*.[24] In *Face of the Deep*, feminist theologian Catherine Keller demonstrates an enduring "tehomophobia," or fear of the sea as a power of chaos, pervading Hebrew and Christian scripture, finally manifesting in the book of Revelation as the defeat of Satan-as-dragon and the drying up of the sea.[25] In Christian legend, both Saint Michael and Saint George slay dragons; this conflict is feminized in Catholic iconography in the figure of Mary, Queen of Heaven, who crushes the serpent underfoot and tames the waters as Our Lady, Star of the Sea. My attempt to rehabilitate the swamp dragon as a positive figure must admit openly to this phobic history. I see it as an advantage, however; truly to accord a proper place to pollution, ecocritics must retain a sense of pollution's danger, and our own connection to it, rather than reduce its power through domestication.

The danger of the dragon of waters is more than symbolic: it has manifested in the history of the Great Swamp as a Superfund site. The dumping of industrial pollutants into a wetland suggests the dragon of unrestrained corporate capitalism guarding its filthy horde amidst the suffering of others. This is the dragon out of European folk tradition, typified in contemporary Anglophone literature by Smaug, the central monster in J. R. R. Tolkien's *The Hobbit*. To a native New Jerseyan, such a dragon poses an important problem: how to love the land that has been poisoned, and may be poisoning you. Here, the other dragon comes in: the dragon of wisdom, once native to Asia but now part of New Jersey through the influence of Taiwanese, Cantonese, and other East Asian immigrants. The *long*-dragon, whose snakelike body and crested head are familiar throughout the Chinese diaspora, is a hydrological power of oceans, clouds, and rivers.[26] This dragon is culturally impure in diaspora: most people would know it from Chinatown New Year's celebrations, through its appropriation in *Dungeons and Dragons,* from album covers in the era of progressive rock, and in Ursula K. Le Guin's Taoist-influenced *Tehanu* and *The Other Wind*.[27] Nonetheless, the dragon of wisdom has not been absent from the Great Swamp. Getting into the Halloween spirit, the staff at the visitor center once mounted a display, at once poignant and farcical, of the tombstones of extinct and endangered species. Approaching the center entrance, one could not avoid the names "Passenger Pigeon," "Bog Turtle," "Right Whale," and many others. Surrounded by the brilliant gold and scarlet of fall foliage, the viewer could not remain innocent of the swamp's function as refuge or the environmental crisis that created the need for refuge in the first place. While many people come to the Great Swamp for its spectacular birding, the permanent park apparatus—constructed paths across the water, signage, bird blinds—forces visitors to see that the swamp has to be protected from us as much as we have to be guided through it. This apparatus, along with the more ephemeral tombstones, suggested the workings of ecological wisdom, of dragons moving through clouded waters.

I want to hold out the figure of the swamp dragon as a new model for ecocritical activity that does not shun compromised places and the politics of poison but encompasses the ironies of diminishment under the aegis of critical affection. The dragon can be an alias insofar as we assume its role in critical practice; it can be an icon insofar as it provides an ideal image for contemplation of these new values.[28] A swampy, draconian criticism will require a new practice of reading, a new attitude toward canon formation, and the consideration of compromised texts as well as compromised environments. As a beginning, I turn toward two contemporary books, Susan Griffin's *Woman and Nature: The Roaring inside Her* and Robert Sullivan's *The Meadowlands: Wilderness Adventures on the Edge of a City,* in an attempt to discern a swampy hermeneutics, a heuristic for swamp dragons, under the surface of the text.[29]

The Lyric Swamp: The Undoing of Dualism in Woman and Nature

The lyric swamp—the wetland figured as the fusion of intelligence and passion, body and mind, matter and spirit—is the alternative offered by Susan Griffin in *Woman and Nature* to the tradition of swamp-as-disease-and-damnation. Griffin is a poet, essayist, playwright, and activist who has been publishing since the late 1960s. Though her work has continued to win literary prizes and is widely anthologized, *Woman and Nature* is her most famous and influential book. It was published in 1979, when the idea of ecofeminism had already arisen in Western Europe and the United States, but it was widely hailed by radical feminists as a theoretical and artistic breakthrough.[30] It is a beautiful and difficult work. Though there is a plot, the book is also hypertextual: it can be read by jumping in nonlinear fashion from any section to any other section. Because every section of the book is a comment on, addition to, or explanation of what happens in the others, because the sections depend on one another but do not require one way of reading, it can be characterized as an *ecological hypertext,* a form of writing that tries to mimic the physics of biological communities as the metaphysics of discourse. This is one reason, I think, for the confusion that so characterizes the interpretation of *Woman and Nature*: more than most essayistic prose, it requires the reader to move through it as a process and to hold seemingly contradictory positions without immediate resolution. Her method is not accidental: as many critics have pointed out, the aim of *Woman and Nature* is to undo the hierarchical dualisms of Western thought, which Griffin believes to be the origin of the political oppression of women and nature.[31] This principle, that a world gendered into master–slave opposites must be remade, may fairly be said to be the central tenet of contemporary Anglophone ecofeminism.

It is equally fair to say that ecofeminism is having a hard time undoing dualism in the intellectual and political realms. Why should this be the case? A clue appears in Myra Jehlen's 1981 essay "Archimedes and the Paradox of Feminist Criticism," where Jehlen points out the difficulty of establishing a new ground for the lever of feminist criticism:

> Reconsideration of the relation between female and male can be a way to reconsider that between intuition and reason and ultimately between the whole set of such associated dichotomies: heart and head, nature and history. But it also creates unusual difficulties. Somewhat like Archimedes, who to lift the earth with his lever required someplace else on which to locate himself and his fulcrum, feminists questioning the presumptive order of both nature

and history—and thus proposing to remove the ground from under their own feet—would, appear to need an alternative base. For as Archimedes had to stand somewhere, one has to assume something in order to reason at all. So if the very axioms of Western thought already incorporate the sexual teleology in question, it seems that, like the Greek philosopher, we have to find a stand-point off this world altogether.[32]

What seems to be required is a discourse that would allow us to be in several worlds at once, such that the history of culture and nature is not ignored, as if we were not ourselves a product of it, even as we stand in the place of a new fulcrum, intent upon moving the world we still inhabit. I believe that *Woman and Nature* is designed, in structure and content, to further this project of walking in many worlds, to provide for the lever of feminist cosmology a ground that is simultane-ously inside and outside the old world of dualism. Griffin is a keen observer who wants a feminist empiricism, a contemplative who wants to change the world, a seeker after ecstatic union with otherkind who seeks to preserve its autonomy. *Woman and Nature* is built, therefore, on strategies of critique and reconstruction, separation and reunion, dialectical movements through previously polarized ideas and events. The goal of this movement is not an absolute holism in which Many become One forever; instead, it is a dynamic interrelationship among the elements of a cosmos, neither unchanging order nor random chaos. It should come as no surprise that Griffin embodies this idea in the figure of the swamp, a local manifes-tation of the cosmic music that only the spheres used to sing, a swamp that shines with the light of the stars.

It is ironic, then, that Dante's *Comedy* is a crucial intertext to *Woman and Nature,* because Dante casts many parts of Hell as wetland. The central pattern of the *Comedy*—a pilgrimage through suffering, purgation, and redemption—is also the pattern of Griffin's book, with the delusions of patriarchy standing in for the Wood of Error. *Woman and Nature* does not, however, follow the plot of verti-cal ascent of the *Comedy,* which is governed by a Neoplatonic logic of the Great Chain of Being and identifies the lowest part of the universe, Hell, with absolute matter, and the highest part, Heaven, with absolute Spirit. Instead, Griffin begins and ends with sections called "Matter," but these sections are not equivalent, so the book's structure is not quite circular. While the first "Matter" section is a critique and rejection of materialism and its obverse, idealism, the final section, "Matter: How We Know," is an intensely lyrical account of a nondualistic cosmos as experienced from the inside, or, perhaps, from a place where inside and out-side are no longer halves of a dualism.

The beginning of "Matter: How We Know" is a kind of manifesto and an inter-pretive key for the rest of the section. It does not appear, at first, to be a manifesto; rather, it appears to be a poetic meditation on the continuity of the human and the natural. Because it is poetic, it appears to be unphilosophical, because poetry and philosophy are opposed in Anglophone cultures. But in accordance with her nondualistic agenda, Griffin brings poetry and philosophy together, resulting in a sensual and imagistic prose that resembles the work of Loren Eiseley and Annie Dillard in particular.[33] Here is the beginning:

> Because we know ourselves to be made from this earth. See this grass. The patches of silvers and brown. Worn by the wind. The grass reflecting all that lives in the soil. The light. The grass needing the soil. With roots deep in the earth. And patches of silver. Like the patches of silver in our hair. Worn by time. This bird flying low over the grass. Over the tules. The cattails, sedges, rushes, reeds, over the marsh. Because we know ourselves to be made from this earth. Temporary as this grass. Wet as this mud. Our cells filled with water. Like the mud of this swamp. Heather growing here because of the damp. Sphagnum moss floating on the surface, on the water standing in these pools. Places where the river washes out. Where the earth was shaped by the flow of lava. Or by the slow movements of glaciers. Because we know ourselves to be made from this earth, and shaped like the earth, by what has gone before.[34]

This passage is lyric in the most direct way: it is structured like a song; it could be separated into stanzas and a refrain. The refrain "because we know ourselves to be made from this earth" is perhaps the most famous line of ecofeminist literature and certainly one of the most famous lines in contemporary nature writing. But why should that be? Griffin seems to have gone out of her way to avoid the sublime here, identifying earth with a quotidian marsh scene: grass, mud, water, birds. It seems we are not made of very elevated stuff at all, and that is exactly the point. This opening is the start of a manifesto because Griffin's strange singing about marshes and mud and birds is pointed right at the heart of dualism in Western culture. It is pointed at Plato's Allegory of the Cave, which teaches suspicion of the senses, and the seeking of a light that comes from outside of material existence; at Descartes's *Discourse on Method*, which posits a fundamental ontological split between living mind and dead matter; and at every version of Christianity that identifies the Kingdom of God with a disembodied realm.[35] (This is why Griffin allies herself with Dante, who understood that a Neoplatonic heaven that lasted forever was a contradiction of a final resurrection of the faithful in their bodies.) So instead of seeking the light from a changeless world, Griffin has returned to matter to write an account of it as the source of the light itself. This is signaled by the continuity of the section title with the refrain: the question of "how we know" is answered by "because we are made from this earth." This is both a metaphysical and an epistemological argument with the idealist tradition. If the light of the Divine Mind flows into the object-world of matter as its motive force and principle of consciousness, the light is fundamentally unlike matter, and consciousness points outside of the created universe to a space of the Absolute that is finally self-sufficient and self-justifying. But in Griffin's account, the light is part of the grass's reflection of everything that lives in the soil. The light is not opposed to the soil or the grass but implies and is implied by them. Griffin does not use the technical term *photosynthesis* to ground her claim in science itself, but she could: it is literally true that the chloroplasts of plants use the light of the sun to drive metabolism. This is what the "cattails, sedges, rushes, [and] reeds" are all doing. Griffin indicates that she understands the connections of her claims to cellular biology by drawing the analogy between "Our cells full of water" and the muddy swamp: the cell is a swamp, the swamp is a cell, we are made of cells and thus made of swamps. This celebration of our connection to wetlands that move and change and age and die is a transvaluation of values, a shifting of loyalties from the old order that valued transcendence, changelessness, and control to a new order that finds the transcendence of light inside the material world, eternity in the flux of matter, and distance as a sign of respect for the autonomy of otherkind. The last phrase of the book, "and I long to tell you, you who are earth too, and listen *as we speak to each other of what we know: the light is in us,*" signifies this transformation (emphasis in original). The light, which at the beginning of the book was said to be outside of the world entirely, is now in the narrator and the entire cosmos. The knowledge of light-in-the-world is no longer a special possession of the narrator but dwells in the reader as well. This is Griffin's new order, the world for the fulcrum of ecofeminism: a swamp that sings.

The Comedic Swamp: The Irony of Urban Wilderness in *The Meadowlands*

In his classic analysis of American pastoral literature and ideology, *The Machine in the Garden*, Leo Marx describes the intrusion of industrial technology as "noise clashing through harmony,"[36] and nothing in *Woman and Nature* would disrupt that idea. Indeed, Griffin's organic cosmology drove Donna Haraway to declare, "I would rather be a cyborg than a goddess."[37] It may be, as Haraway argues, that a model of nondualism that does not address the dualism of human and machine is not nondualistic enough: the next step would be to accept the machine into the garden.[38] This problem is implicit in what Michael Bennett has called "Deep Eco-criticism," after Deep Ecology: the claim that only pristine wilderness is enough to unite humanity and nature.[39] In *The Meadowlands: Wilderness Adventure on the Edge of a City*, Robert Sullivan addresses this problem directly by writing a parodic adventure narrative about exploring the New Jersey Meadowlands, perhaps the most thoroughly polluted wetland on the planet, which I first mentioned as the direct inspiration for the idea of the swamp dragon. That Sullivan knows he is engaged in a parody of adventure narrative—specifically, a parody of pioneering in the West—becomes clear almost immediately, when he describes people in Newark Airport

> with travel books or maybe brand-new water-repellent hiking clothes or Powerbars and polypropylene underwear [who are] heading West to travel and explore. But I am creeping slowly back East, back to America's *first* West—making a reverse commute to the already explored land that has become, through negligence, through exploitation, and through its own chaotic persistence, explorable again.[40]

There are multiple levels of parody here: a sarcastic lighting out for the territories, which diminishes into a "reverse commute," but also a parody of contemporary eco-adventuring, known well to Sullivan in his work for *Outside* magazine. Even deeper is the practice of self-parody, repeated throughout the book, in which Sullivan himself appears most ridiculous for embarking on a "wilderness adventure" in New Jersey when he is coming from Portland, Oregon, one of the jewels of Ecotopia. But all of this perversity leads to something impossible in the diminished-thing paradigm, namely, an assertion of the agency of the Meadowlands themselves, which become "explorable again" in part through their own stubbornness. This is where many supportive reviewers have it wrong: *The Meadowlands* is not merely an entertainment but a postmodern *Walden* for a toxic age.[41] Sullivan is not just a raconteur—though his wit illuminates even the most frightening details—but an advocate and philosopher. His humor is not gratuitous but a studied response to the hopelessness that polluted landscapes inspire. His writing is "postnatural" nonfiction in Cynthia Deitering's sense, inscribing an awareness of toxicity as environmental norm, and akin to Don DeLillo's *White Noise* and John Updike's *Rabbit at Rest* in the realm of the novel.[42]

Sullivan's attachment to Thoreau is especially strong; he refers to Thoreau directly many times, especially in the chapter called "Walden Swamp," which contains a parody of *Walden*'s supply list, including a compass, insect repellent, beef jerky, the ubiquitous Powerbars, water filtration kits, and an appropriately named "Mad River" canoe.[43] The visual joke is funny—Sullivan has gone to some lengths to reproduce the appearance of Thoreau's list—but the underlying message is clear: the Meadowlands are, through no fault of their own, far more deadly than a Concord pond and could kill the narrator just through skin-to-water contact. This setting is even deadlier in its own way than the typical western river-with-rapids that populates so many eco-adventure stories, in that rapids can be shot with the proper level of skill, whereas no one is sure whether Sullivan's detoxification and antimicrobial kits will allow him to drink the swamp water safely. In fact, pollution and microbial activity surface again and again, indicating not only the writer's careful research into the ecology of garbage but also his awareness of the conventions of American nature writing. Here, for instance, Sullivan presents a set piece on anaerobic decomposition, with sinister results:

> The big difference between the garbage hills and the real hills in the Meadow-
> lands is that the garbage hills are alive. In some completely peopleless areas of
> the swamp, there are billions of microscopic organisms thriving underground
> in dark, oxygen-free communities. They multiply and even evolve so that they
> can more readily digest the trash at their disposal. It can take a team of three
> organisms to finish off a dump-buried piece of cellulose in a bit of newspaper
> too small to even see. Eventually, there are whole suites of organisms in each
> hill, as if each hill were a bacterial high-rise. After having ingested the tiniest
> portion of New Jersey or New York, these cells then exhale huge underground
> plumes of carbon dioxide and of warm moist methane, giant stillborn tropical
> winds that seep through the ground to feed the Meadowlands fires, or creep
> up into the atmosphere, where they eat away at the Earth-protecting layer of
> ozone.[44]

This passage turns the lyricism of Griffin's swamp-song on its head, even as it participates in a related rhetoric. There is a kind of Morlock appeal to Sullivan's account of the garbage hill ecosystem; it is, as he points out, more alive than the blasted wrecks of the original hills. However, no sooner do we admire the virtuosity of microbial teamwork and the conviviality of the anaerobic world than we see the hellish results: garbage decomposition feeds swamp fires and the destruction of the ozone layer (not to mention contributing to global warming, not quite the issue in 1998 that it would soon become). Suddenly, the swamp is demonic again, though its malignity is domestic rather than alien. After Griffin's triumphant revision of Dante's *Comedy,* this vision is more sobering. Though the Meadowlands were once a fine cedar swamp, human abuse has turned them into an engine of Hell, complete with wildfires from Central Casting.

It is fascinating to note, however, that passages like this one made *The Meadowlands* an immensely popular text in a course on nature writing I taught at Rutgers University, New Brunswick, New Jersey, in 2001—far more popular than its Thoreauvian ur-text. Mostly from Cook College, the agricultural-biotechnical wing of Rutgers, and highly literate environmentally, my students found Thoreau prissy and moralistic, but in Sullivan they found a kindred spirit (Puck rather than Ariel) who approached environmental disaster with something like our native attitude. Had Sullivan simply made fun of the swamp, or of New Jersey as a stinking pit, he would have joined the chorus of disdain my students had heard since childhood and would have been ignored. Instead, by finding a way into the Meadowlands physically, Sullivan found a way into local culture rhetorically. Like the people of North Jersey he encounters throughout his travels, Sullivan manifests disgust and awe at the presence of the swamps, which are friend and enemy, refuge and prison, victim and perpetrator. In his own way, he enacts an undoing of dualism that makes such undoing a realistic project for the people of the Meadowlands: the possibility of a Manichean destruction of the "bad side" of swamps is disavowed. If Griffin creates an ideal landscape to contain matter's own light, Sullivan shows how light and darkness, survival and destruction, coinhere in a postindustrial swamp. For this reason, my students embraced *The Meadowlands* as a model of nature writing that did not alienate them from their native place.

One student, a fan of *Walden* who despaired of writing like Thoreau because, as he put it, "Jersey isn't like that," found a way to talk about his East Brunswick pond and its waterfowl by using Sullivan's tone as a model. East Brunswick, a Central Jersey suburb bisected by the Turnpike, is less compromised than the Meadowlands but nothing like the western ideal of text-worthy land. The student was trying to describe an experience of love and loyalty inspired by "a crappy little pond and some ducks," and though *Walden* fueled a desire to write, it failed to provide a rhetoric that could encompass affection and disdain, attachment and revulsion, at the same time. Ironically, Sullivan's smart-ass routine allowed this student to narrate the very mystical oneness that his neighbor in Princeton, Joyce Carol Oates, decried in "Against Nature," which the class also read. In that essay, Oates substitutes an attack of tachycardia for an Emersonian eyeball-experience, taking nature writers to task for their limited set of responses to a morally ambiguous world. My students thoroughly agreed with her—they too were tired of reverence as the only option—but Oates failed to produce an alternative to cynicism, which they already had in abundance. Sullivan, on the other hand, revealed irony as a vehicle of love, when the object of love, like Socrates in Plato's *Symposium,* is a pug-nosed thing that shines with divine light from within.

It is appropriate, then, when Sullivan, after a book full of muckraking, allows himself an indulgence—a fantasy of resurrection for the crucified land at the start of a chapter called "Digging":

> If, by magic or the assistance of angels or with the help of a grant awarded
> through the Federal Enterprise Zone program, I could turn the bottom of
> the Meadowlands to the top and restore what was thrown into the muck
> to its pristine predumped condition, the place would be instantly de-
> wastelandized. I'd sit on Snake Hill and watch as Swartwout's old muskrat-
> chewed dikes restored themselves and his farm returned and prospered
> and he danced in his fields with his family. I'd watch demolished buildings
> reassembled in the pristine marsh. I'd see barrels of toxic waste rise from
> the no-longer-polluted water and levitate harmlessly above the ground.
> Among the most enthusiastic of reanimated items would be the small bands
> of executionees, roaming together—their hands patting their chests, pinching
> their cheeks in wonderment—each clumsy step rousing a pheasant or a wild
> turkey.[45]

With all the moxie of Donne's "Holy Sonnets," this passage imagines what Eliot's "The Waste Land" tithes to caution: the Final Trumpet blowing, and the swamp with all its lost denizens arising in their proper forms in a New Jerusalem. There is in this passage a Catholic-boyishness—Gerard Manley Hopkins's "God's Grandeur" is one of the book's epigraphs—that infuses much charm into otherwise disturbing stories. Unfortunately, the larger function of this vision, in a chapter devoted to finding Jimmy Hoffa's body, is to insist on its own impossibility: no power, human or angelic, will ever separate all the toxic waste from the swamp bottom, and the other miracles are likewise impossible.

Sullivan thereby demands that the Meadowlands be taken as they are, or not at all. This, too, bespeaks a kind of sacramental consciousness: the world is flawed but good and must be loved as a broken embodiment of the grandeur of God. It is not permissible to despair of it permanently, and not even the Meadowlands may be abandoned. This consciousness is the center of the tough talk, the sweetness at the core of Sullivan's humor. Literary criticism calls it "cosmic irony" when the universe turns out to be hiding the opposite of its surface contents, though critics are more used to the Thomas Hardy version, in which defeat is snatched from the jaws of ambiguity. Hardy may not know why his "Darkling Thrush" sings through the bitter cold, but Sullivan does, and therein lies his value for aspiring swamp dragons. Though he is disgusted by the Meadowlands, he does not turn away; though his fear is justified, it does not drive him out. Persisting until it finds a hidden loveliness, Sullivan's parody turns in on itself to become a real adventure and revelation. Having chosen one of the most abused places for his experiment, Sullivan overcomes the logic of diminishment and finds his way past Snake Hill to a serpentine wisdom.

Horror of Horrors, or Becoming a Swamp Dragon

In his indispensable guide to the semiotics of swamps, *Postmodern Wetlands*, Rod Giblett points out that just as the swamp has been a locus of death and decay in traditional Western cultures, so it has been the lair of something even worse: "As the marsh or swamp itself is often represented as a place of horror, the swamp serpent is doubly horrific, the horror of horrors."[46]

So now I must admit that the swamp dragon is not just an atavism of nerdy childhood, a piece of folklore, or even a mild bit of Orientalism but the advocacy of our own nightmares. By asking ecocritics to consider the swamp dragon as a new identity or an icon for further work, I am asking us to do something terrifying: to become the monster under the bed, the thing we dare not touch, the evil bent upon the destruction of civilization.[47] I do so in part because Susan Griffin and Robert Sullivan traveled into the nightmares of philosophy and the ruins of industry and returned with a stronger way to love the world we actually live in.

Learning to love a postlapsarian world is not just a countermove to pastoral retreat but an anodyne for injury we did not prevent.[48] As the environmental justice movement reminds us, white, middle-class environmentalism in the United States has often been guilty of protecting wilderness and its charismatic megafauna while ignoring the suffering of urban ecologies. The logic of the swamp dragon is a way out of this dilemma. Impure and defiled, both literally and figuratively, the swamp dragon is uncharismatic but still alive, an ecstatic identification with a beleaguered cosmos. It prevents the idealization of nature *or* culture and thereby avoids traditional dualism *and* its reversal, which Karla Armbruster and Kathleen Wallace have warned us against.[49] In a political landscape ruled by the sublime, by the "enchantment of distance," as Rick van Noy has said,[50] swamp dragon offers the enchantment of proximity and proximity's curse: a view of the damage to the world that cannot be completely undone.

What would the rubric of the swamp dragon do for ecocriticism as a literary discipline? First, it would focus our attention on the stakes of our game. In his moving foreword to *The Greening of Literary Scholarship,* Scott Slovic tells the story of his lost dog, Sally, hit by a truck one day while he was at work. Sally's tragedy, he thinks, is that she did not see the truck coming and never knew what hit her.[51] A swampy, dragonlike ecocriticism would keep its hundred eyes of Argus on the monsters around us to understand better the dangers we face; it would also admit that we are partially monstrous ourselves, not quite separable from the oncoming truck, transforming the guilt of complicity into an appreciation of finitude and impurity. At the same time, the swamp dragon is a figure of resistance from a land of refuge. If Griffin's swamp exudes a cosmic music, so might we; if the Meadowlands survived its own destruction with stubbornness and humor, the ends of comedy might be our ends, too. As arbiters of the canon, ecocritics might choose, then, to counter the matter of environmental crisis with the matter of restoration, as Bill McKibben has already done in his own work, balancing *The Ends of Nature* with *Hope, Human and Wild.*[52] We might, like Sue Hubbell in *Waiting for Aphrodite,* encourage our students to become experts on some part of the nonhuman world—even to make their own homes speakable, as in the case of my students at Rutgers—knowing that amateurs are sometimes the best, and the only, naturalists where certain places and creatures are concerned. Finally, the swamp dragon is a figure of guile and nonlinear connection, which ecocritics might apply to ourselves and our institutional alliances.[53] ASLE has been very good at creating structures where no structures existed before, such as mentoring programs for graduate students and communal bibliographies. What if we extended that work to combine the powers of institutions that do not normally talk to each other—community colleges and state schools with elite, private universities, technical schools with environmental liberal arts colleges—in bioregional consortiums and networks of networks? Serpentine alliances like these might stand a chance of countering the logic of academic competition and harnessing the swamps of bureaucracy for our own ends. By thinking of ourselves in collective terms and working toward collective goals, by becoming a swamp dragon en masse, ecocritics might wield the influence we all hope for in the name of conservation and restoration, survival and flourishing.

Notes

I would like to thank my ecocritical colleagues, and two anonymous readers, for the opportunity to present and discuss earlier drafts of this material. I would also like to thank Kristen Abbey, Aryana Bates, Lauren Butcher, John Fitzgerald, Marc Manganaro, Leo Marx, Mary Ellen O'Driscoll, Jim Paradis, Jun Ho Son, Mary Beth Son, Adam W. Sweeting, and the Woonasquatucket River Watershed Council of Providence, Rhode Island, for their help, interest, and encouragement. Finally, I dedicate this essay to Itzam Ka, a green iguana I once knew—a very good dragon indeed.

1. Mary Douglas, *Purity and Danger: An Analysis of the Concepts of Pollution and Taboo* (New York: Taylor and Francis, 2003), 44.

2. Douglas, 202.

3. Prophet, judge, serpent: those who see a biblical typology here are not mistaken. It would be surprising if American ecocritics, as heirs to a tradition of sermon and jeremiad, never took up rhetorical postures with biblical roots. I leave it to ecocritics from other national/rhetorical traditions—and American ecocritics of nonbiblical backgrounds—to ponder their own rhetorical archetypes.

4. Kathleen R. Wallace and Karla Armbruster, "Introduction: Why Go beyond Nature Writing, and Where To?," in *Beyond Nature Writing: Expanding the Boundaries of Ecocriticism,* ed. Karla Armbruster and Kathleen R. Wallace, 1–25 (Charlottesville: University of Virginia Press, 2001); Patrick D. Murphy, *Farther Afield in the Study of Nature-Oriented Literature* (Charlottesville: University of Virginia Press, 2000); Lawrence Coupe, ed., *The Green Studies Reader: From Romanticism to Ecocriticism* (London: Routledge, 2000); Steven Rosendale, ed., *The Greening of Literary Scholarship: Literature, Theory, and Environment* (Iowa City: University of Iowa Press, 2002); Cheryll Glotfelty, ed., *The Ecocriticism Reader: Landmarks in Literary Ecology* (Athens: University of Georgia Press, 1996); Michael P. Branch and Scott Slovic, eds., *The "ISLE" Reader: Ecocriticism, 1993–2003* (Athens: University of Georgia Press, 2003); Joni Adamson, Mei Mei Evans, and Rachel Stein, eds., *The Environmental Justice Reader: Politics, Poetics and Pedagogy* (Tucson: University of Arizona Press, 2003); Dana Phillips, *The Truth of Ecology: Nature, Culture, and Literature in America* (Oxford: Oxford University Press, 2003); Lawrence Buell, *Writing for an Endangered World: Literature, Culture, and Environment in the US and Beyond* (Cambridge, Mass.: Harvard University Press, 2001).

5. This is ironic, given that the name "Kittatinny" means "Biggest Mountain," according to local accounts of Lenape/Delaware place-names. The highest point in the New Jersey Kittatinnies is about eighteen hundred feet above sea level.

6. This problem is related to American ecocriticism's largely uncritical appropriation of an Anglo-Protestant righteousness, of which it should become more aware, particularly

in the Muirish heritage of nineteenth-century conservationism. How different would American ecocriticism be if it transcended the logic of purity versus pollution in the valuation of environments? That question, however, is the project of another essay.

7. The Superfund is a program administered by the federal government to clean up toxic waste sites. The official EPA home page for Burnt Fly Bog is http://www.epa.gov/superfund/sites/npl/mar72.htm. More information about the Raritan's recovery is available through Raritan Riverkeeper, http://www.nynjbaykeeper.org/riverkeeper/riverkeep er%20open.htm. The New Jersey Pinelands Commission home page is http://www.state .nj.us/pinelands.

8. Michael Bennett, "From Wide Open Spaces to Metropolitan Places: The Urban Challenge to Ecocriticism," in Branch and Slovic, The "ISLE" Reader, 296–317. Two helpful volumes in this regard are Michael Bennett and David W. Teague, eds., The Nature of Cities: Ecocriticism and Urban Environments (Tucson: University of Arizona Press, 1999), and William Cronon, ed., Uncommon Ground: Toward Reinventing Nature (New York: W. W. Norton, 1995). For an explanation of urban nature that traces the connections between polis and region, see William Cronon, Nature's Metropolis: Chicago and the Great West (New York: W. W. Norton, 1991).

9. It is sometimes difficult to say exactly where the East is, however. For my purposes, the East excludes the Midwest and the South, which might be considered eastern by westerners, because they are both culturally and geographically distinct from what most people mean by "East" in the pejorative sense: the area bounded by Maryland in the south, Pennsylvania in the west, and Maine in the north. I therefore make no attempt here to account for the lakes of Minnesota or the Florida Everglades, though these places might be eastern in other accounts. This problem of regional boundaries is explored from the other direction in Michael E. McGerr, "Is There a Twentieth-Century West?," in Under an Open Sky: Rethinking America's Western Past, ed. William Cronon, George Miles, and Jay Gitlin, 239–56 (New York: W. W. Norton, 1992).

10. The title of the conference is a quotation from Robert Frost's sonnet "The Oven Bird," which itself presents a curious theory of summer as the diminishment of spring: "He says the leaves are old and that for flowers / Mid-summer is to spring as one to ten." Frost anticipates the ironic posture of Robert Sullivan's The Meadowlands: Wilderness Adventure on the Edge of a City (New York: Scribner, 1998), examined later in this essay, toward lyric pastoralism, because the bird's sense of diminishment is directly connected to its unbirdlike suspicion of singing: "The bird would cease and be as other birds / But that he knows in singing not to sing. / The question that he frames in all but words / Is what to make of a diminished thing." The fact that the bird is singing near a highway, of course, is directly related to the East's diminished condition in the early twentieth century.

11. Thomas Bailey, "Nature Writers Come to Kalamazoo," ASLE News: A Biannual Publication of the Association for the Study of Literature and Environment 11, no. 1 (1999): n.p.

12. "The Third Biennial ASLE Conference," update in ASLE News: A Biannual Publication of the Association for the Study of Literature and Environment 11, no. 1 (1999): 3.

13. This hegemony is by no means overthrown; however, megalopolitan ecocritics should not be assumed to support or accommodate it. For a brief but revealing account of the history of the West's resentment against eastern capitalism and cultural elitism, see

Clyde A. Milner II, "The View from Wisdom: Four Layers of History and Regional Identity," in *Under an Open Sky: Rethinking America's Western Past,* ed. William Cronon, George Miles, and Jay Gitlin, 203–22 (New York: W. W. Norton, 1992).

14. David C. Miller, *Dark Eden: The Swamp in Nineteenth-Century American Culture* (Cambridge: Cambridge University Press, 1989), 3.

15. Miller, 47.

16. Miller, 23.

17. Miller, 8.

18. Miller, 8.

19. Rod Giblett, *Postmodern Wetlands: Culture, History, Ecology* (Edinburgh: Edinburgh University Press, 1996), 203–27.

20. Ingrid Bartsch, Carolyn DiPalma, and Laura Sells, "The Jeremiad's Promise: Cyborg Wetlands and Vampire Practices," *Intertexts* 3, no. 2 (1999): 27.

21. Ralph W. Tiner, *In Search of Wetlands: A Wetland Resource and Field Guide* (New Brunswick, N.J.: Rutgers University Press, 1999), 3–13.

22. The Jersey Devil has certain draconian characteristics, such as bat wings, a pointy tail, claws, and an elongated, reptilian face. For a summary of the relevant folklore, see http://njfolkfest.rutgers.edu/devil.htm.

23. The Online Etymology Dictionary (http://www.etymonline.com) derives the word from the Greek "*drak-*, the strong aorist stem of *derkesthai,* 'to see clearly.'" The *American Heritage Dictionary,* 4th edition, notes its relationship to *derk-,* the Indo-European root for "to see." Both sources suggest that the intended meaning is something like "beast with the sharp glance" or "creature with the evil eye."

24. The rewriting of the Babylonian creation story by the priestly writer of the Torah is now so conventional an idea that it is included prominently in the notes to many popular Bible editions in English. See, for instance, *The HarperCollins Study Bible: New Revised Standard Version,* ed. Wayne Meeks (New York: HarperCollins, 1993), 6–8, notes on Genesis 1.1–2.7.

25. Catherine Keller, *Face of the Deep: A Theology of Becoming* (New York: Routledge, 2003), 27–28.

26. Roy Bates, *Chinese Dragons* (New York: Oxford University Press, 2002), 14.

27. This diasporic figure has manifested recently on television in the Disney Channel's show *Jake Long: American Dragon.* Here the grandson of Chinese immigrants, and later his little sister, inherit the power of the *long*-dragon to fight magical evil and to assert a continued, if transformed, ethnic identity inside American culture.

28. Here I am drawing upon the tradition of Greek Orthodox Christianity, in which icons of Christ, Mary, and the saints are gazed upon as gateways to the spiritual realm.

29. Susan Griffin, *Woman and Nature: The Roaring Inside Her* (San Francisco: Sierra Club Books, 2000); Sullivan, *The Meadowlands.*

30. The most important critic to analyze *Woman and Nature* is Alicia Ostriker, who, in *Stealing the Language: The Emergence of Women's Poetry in America* (London: Women's Press, 1986), characterizes Griffin's logic as separatist, at least in certain passages (231). Ostriker offers the most convincing argument for the book as an artifact of a moment in Second Wave feminism that imagined men as too violent to be trusted.

31. Karla Armbruster offers the most convincing argument about Griffin's anti-dualism, in which she claims that *Woman and Nature* works strongly against dualism while not entirely escaping it. See Karla Armbruster, "'Buffalo Gals Won't You Come Out Tonight': A Call for Boundary-Crossing in Ecofeminist Literary Criticism," in *Ecofeminist Literary Criticism: Theory, Interpretation, Pedagogy*, ed. Greta Gaard and Patrick Murphy, 97–122 (Urbana: University of Illinois Press, 1998).

32. Myra Jehlen, "Archimedes and the Paradox of Feminist Criticism," in *Feminisms: An Anthology of Literary Theory and Criticism*, rev. ed., ed. Robyn Warhol and Diana Price Herndl (New Brunswick, N.J.: Rutgers University Press, 1997), 192.

33. Griffin thanks Dillard in the acknowledgments, and Eiseley was one of Dillard's own models as an essayist.

34. Griffin, *Woman and Nature*, 223. Italics in original.

35. In this sense, Griffin is allied with Latin American liberation theology and North American feminist theology, which see the Kingdom of God as a this-worldly phenomenon.

36. Leo Marx, *The Machine in the Garden: Technology and the Pastoral Ideal* (New York: Oxford University Press, 1967), 17.

37. Donna J. Haraway, *Simians, Cyborgs, and Women: The Reinvention of Nature* (New York: Routledge, 1991), 181.

38. By this I do not mean that it should be impossible to ban snowmobiles in a national park but rather that the exclusion of postindustrial technology from the traditional cosmos of pastoralism forces people to choose between modernity and cosmic harmony, excluding the possibility that the machine might participate in such harmony.

39. Michael Bennet, "From Wide Open Spaces to Metropolitan Places: The Urban Challenge to Ecocriticism," in Branch and Slovic, *The ISLE Reader*, 297–302.

40. Sullivan, *The Meadowlands*, 14–15.

41. Here I have in mind the reviewers on the back of the original hardcover edition, who, with the exception of Frank McCourt, emphasize the book's value as a good read.

42. Cynthia Deitering, "The Postnatural Novel: Toxic Consciousness in the Fiction of the 1980s," in Glotfelty, *The Ecocriticism Reader*, 196–97.

43. Sullivan, *The Meadowlands*, 77.

44. Sullivan, 96.

45. Sullivan, 141–42.

46. Giblett, *Postmodern Wetlands*, 179.

47. David E. Jones, in *An Instinct for Dragons* (London: Routledge, 2000), theorizes that the universality of the dragon image across cultures may be the result of an atavistic conflation of the raptor, the big cat, and the serpent, enemies of our primate relatives and our anthropoid ancestors (23–38).

48. I have no quarrel with a dialectical mode of retreat, such as Thoreau practiced at Walden, in which one moves away from society for a time as one step in a synthesis of contemplation and action. However, a model of pastoralism in which the goal is to escape, as permanently as possible, all involvement with the human world in the name of ethical purity is elitist at best and delusional at worst. It fosters a fall-of-Rome mentality in which the spiritual elite flee to the desert to await the collapse of the corrupt empire. It could never be practiced even by a significant minority of megalopolitan citizens without enormous

destruction of local environments. The suspicion that such exclusion may be precisely the point of radical green praxis leads to the fear that ecocriticism is not merely ecocentric but misanthropic.

49. Wallace and Armbruster, "Introduction," 4.

50. Rick van Noy, "Surveying the Sublime: Literary Cartographers and the Spirit of Place," in Rosendale, *Greening of Literary Scholarship*, 182–83.

51. Scott Slovic, foreword to Rosendale, *Greening of Literary Scholarship*, vii–xi.

52. Bill McKibben, *Hope, Human and Wild: True Stories of Living Lightly on the Earth* (Minneapolis, Minn.: Milkweed Editions, 2007).

53. Sue Hubbell, *Waiting for Aphrodite: Journeys into the Time before Bones* (New York: Houghton Mifflin, 2000).

THE PROMISES OF MONSTERS

A Regenerative Politics for Inappropriate/d Others

Donna Haraway

If primates have a sense of humor, there is no reason why intellectuals may not share in it.

—William Plank[1]

A Biopolitics of Artifactual Reproduction

"The Promises of Monsters" will be a mapping exercise and travelogue through mindscapes and landscapes of what may count as nature in certain local/global struggles. These contests are situated in a strange, allochronic time—the time of myself and my readers in the last decade of the second Christian millennium—and in a foreign, allotopic place—the womb of a pregnant monster, here, where we are reading and writing. The purpose of this excursion is to write theory, i.e., to produce a patterned vision of how to move and what to fear in the topography of an impossible but all-too-real present, in order to find an absent, but perhaps possible, other present. I do not seek the address of some full presence; reluctantly, I know better. Like Christian in *Pilgrim's Progress*, however, I am committed to skirting the slough of despond and the parasite-infested swamps of nowhere to reach more salubrious environs.[2] The theory is meant to orient, to provide the roughest sketch for travel, by means of moving within and through

459

a relentless artifactualism, which forbids any direct si(gh)tings of nature, to a science fictional, speculative factual, SF place called, simply, elsewhere. At least for those whom this essay addresses, "nature" outside artifactualism is not so much elsewhere as nowhere, a different matter altogether. Indeed, a reflexive artifactualism offers serious political and analytical hope. This essay's theory is modest. Not a systematic overview, it is a little siting device in a long line of such craft tools. Such sighting devices have been known to reposition worlds for their devotees—and for their opponents. Optical instruments are subject-shifters. Goddess knows, the subject is being changed relentlessly in the late twentieth century.

My diminutive theory's optical features are set to produce not effects of distance but effects of connection, of embodiment, and of responsibility for an imagined elsewhere that we may yet learn to see and build here. I have high stakes in reclaiming vision from the technopornographers, those theorists of minds, bodies, and planets who insist effectively—i.e., in practice—that sight is the sense made to realize the fantasies of the phallocrats.[3] I think sight can be remade for the activists and advocates engaged in fitting political filters to see the world in the hues of red, green, and ultraviolet, i.e., from the perspectives of a still possible socialism, feminist and anti-racist environmentalism, and science for the people. I take as a self-evident premise that "science is culture."[4] Rooted in that premise, this essay is a contribution to the heterogeneous and very lively contemporary discourse of science studies *as* cultural studies. Of course, what science, culture, or nature—and their "studies"—might mean is far less self-evident.

Nature is for me, and I venture for many of us who are planetary fetuses gestating in the amniotic effluvia of terminal industrialism,[5] one of those impossible things characterized by Gayatri Spivak as that which we cannot not desire. Excruciatingly conscious of nature's discursive constitution as "other" in the histories of colonialism, racism, sexism, and class domination of many kinds, we nonetheless find in this problematic, ethno-specific, long-lived, and mobile concept something we cannot do without but can never "have." We must find another relationship to nature besides reification and possession. Perhaps to give confidence in its essential reality, immense resources have been expended to stabilize and materialize nature, to police its/her boundaries. Such expenditures have had disappointing results. Efforts to travel into "nature" become tourist excursions that remind the voyager of the price of such displacements—one pays to see funhouse reflections of oneself. Efforts to preserve "nature" in parks remain fatally troubled by the ineradicable mark of the founding expulsion of those who used to live there, not as innocents in a garden, but as people for whom the categories of nature and culture were not the salient ones. Expensive projects to collect "nature's" diversity and bank it seem to produce debased coin, impoverished seed, and dusty relics. As the banks hypertrophy, the nature that feeds the storehouses "disappears." The World Bank's record on environmental destruction is exemplary in this regard. Finally, the projects for representing and enforcing human "nature" are famous for their imperializing essences, most recently reincarnated in the Human Genome Project.

So, nature is not a physical place to which one can go, nor a treasure to fence in or bank, nor an essence to be saved or violated. Nature is not hidden and so does not need to be unveiled. Nature is not a text to be read in the codes of mathematics and biomedicine. It is not the "other" who offers origin, replenishment, and service. Neither mother, nurse, nor slave, nature is not matrix, resource, or tool for the reproduction of man.

Nature is, however, a *topos,* a place, in the sense of a rhetorician's place or topic for consideration of common themes; nature is, strictly, a commonplace. We turn to this topic to order our discourse, to compose our memory. As a topic in this sense, nature also reminds us that in seventeenth-century English the "topick gods" were the local gods, the gods specific to places and peoples. We need these spirits, rhetorically if we can't have them any other way. We need them in order to reinhabit, precisely, *common* places—locations that are widely shared, inescapably local, worldly, enspirited, i.e., topical. In this sense, nature is the place to rebuild public culture.[6] Nature is also a *trópos,* a trope. It is figure, construction, artifact, movement, displacement. Nature cannot preexist its construction. This construction is based on a particular kind of move—a *trópos* or "turn." Faithful to the Greek, as *trópos,* nature is about turning. Troping, we turn to nature as if to the earth, to the primal stuff—geotropic, physiotropic. Topically, we travel toward the earth, a commonplace. In discoursing on nature, we turn from Plato and his heliotropic son's blinding star to see something else, another kind of figure. I do not turn from vision, but I do seek something other than enlightenment in these sightings of science studies as cultural studies. Nature is a topic of public discourse on which much turns, even the earth.

In this essay's journey toward elsewhere, I have promised to trope nature through a relentless artifactualism, but what does artifactualism mean here? First, it means that nature for us is *made,* as both fiction and fact. If organisms are natural objects, it is crucial to remember that organisms are not born; they are made in world-changing technoscientific practices by particular collective actors in particular times and places. In the belly of the local/global monster in which I am gestating, often called the postmodern world,[7] global technology appears to *denature* everything, to make everything a malleable matter of strategic decisions and mobile production and reproduction processes.[8] Technological decontextualization is ordinary experience for hundreds of millions if not billions of human beings, as well as other organisms. I suggest that this is not a *denaturing* so much as a *particular production* of nature. The preoccupation with productionism that has characterized so much parochial Western discourse and practice seems to have hypertrophied into something quite marvelous: the whole world is remade in the image of commodity production.[9]

How, in the face of this marvel, can I seriously insist that to see nature as artifactual is an *oppositional,* or better, a *differential* siting?[10] Is the insistence that nature *is* artifactual not more evidence of the extremity of the violation of a nature outside and other to the arrogant ravages of our technophilic civilization, which, after all, we were taught began with the heliotropisms of enlightenment projects to dominate nature with blinding light focused by optical technology?[11] Haven't eco-feminists and other multicultural and intercultural radicals begun to convince us that nature is precisely *not* to be seen in the guise of the Eurocentric productionism and anthropocentrism that have threatened to reproduce, literally, all the world in the deadly image of the Same?

I think the answer to this serious political and analytical question lies in two related turns: (1) unblinding ourselves from the sun-worshiping stories about the history of science and technology as paradigms of rationalism and (2) refiguring the actors in the construction of the ethnospecific categories of nature *and* culture. The actors are not all "us." If the world exists for us as "nature," this designates a kind of relationship, an achievement among many actors, not all of them human, not all of them organic, not all of them technological.[12] In its scientific embodiments as well as in other forms, nature is made, but not entirely by humans; it is a co-construction among humans and nonhumans. This is a very different vision from the postmodernist observation that all the world is denatured and reproduced in images or replicated in copies. That specific kind of violent and reductive artifactualism, in the form of a hyperproductionism actually practiced widely throughout the planet, becomes *contestable* in theory and other kinds of praxis, without recourse to a resurgent transcendental naturalism. Hyperproductionism refuses the witty agency of all the actors but One; that is a dangerous strategy—for everybody. But transcendental naturalism also refuses a world full of cacophonous agencies and settles for a mirror-image sameness that only pretends to difference. The commonplace nature I seek, a public culture, has many houses with many inhabitants which/who can refigure the earth. Perhaps those other actors/actants, the ones who are not human, are our topick gods, organic and inorganic.[13]

It is this barely admissible recognition of the odd sorts of agents and actors which/whom we must admit to the narrative of collective life, including nature, that simultaneously, first, turns us decisively away from enlightenment-derived modern and postmodern premises about nature and culture, the social and technical, science and society, and, second, saves us from the deadly point of view of productionism. Productionism and its corollary, humanism, come down to the story line that "man makes everything, including himself, out of the world that can only be resource and potency to his project and active agency."[14] This productionism is about man the tool-maker and -user, whose highest technical production is himself, i.e., the story line of phallogocentrism. He gains access to this wondrous technology with a subject-constituting, self-deferring, and self-splitting entry into language, light, and law. Blinded by the sun, in thrall to the father, reproduced in the sacred image of the same, his reward is that he is self-born, an autotelic copy. That is the mythos of enlightenment transcendence.

Let us return briefly to my remark above that organisms are not born, but they are made. Besides troping on Simone de Beauvoir's observation that one is not born a woman, what work is this statement doing in this essay's effort to articulate a relentless differential/oppositional artifactualism? I wrote that organisms are made as objects of knowledge in world-changing practices of scientific discourse by particular and always collective actors in specific times and places. Let us look more closely at this claim with the aid of the concept of the apparatus of bodily production.[15] Organisms are *biological* embodiments; as natural-technical entities, they are not preexisting plants, animals, protistes, etc., with boundaries already established and awaiting the right kind of instrument to note them correctly. Organisms emerge from a discursive process. Biology is a discourse, not the living world itself. But humans are not the only actors in the construction of the entities of any scientific discourse; machines (delegates that can produce surprises) and other partners (not "pre- or extra-discursive objects" but partners) are active constructors of natural scientific objects. Like other scientific bodies, organisms are not *ideological* constructions. The whole point about discursive construction has been that it is *not* about ideology. Always radically historically specific, always lively, bodies have a different kind of specificity and effectivity—and so they invite a different kind of engagement and intervention.

Elsewhere, I have used the term *material-semiotic actor* to highlight the object of knowledge as an active part of the apparatus of bodily production, without *ever* implying immediate presence of such objects or, what is the same thing, their final or unique determination of what can count as objective knowledge of a biological body at a particular historical juncture. Like Katie King's objects called "poems," sites of literary production where language also is an actor, bodies as objects of knowledge are material-semiotic generative nodes. Their boundaries materialize in social interaction among humans and nonhumans, including the machines and other instruments that mediate exchanges at crucial interfaces and that function as delegates for other actors' functions and purposes. "Objects" like bodies do not preexist as such. Similarly, "nature" cannot preexist as such, but neither is its existence ideological. Nature is a commonplace and a powerful discursive construction, effected in the interactions among material-semiotic actors, human and not. The siting/sighting of such entities is not about disengaged discovery but about mutual and usually unequal structuring, about taking risks, about delegating competences.[16]

The various contending biological bodies emerge at the intersection of biological research, writing, and publishing; medical and other business practices; cultural productions of all kinds, including available metaphors and narratives; and technology, such as the visualization technologies that bring color-enhanced killer T cells and intimate photographs of the developing fetus into high-gloss art books, as well as scientific reports. But also invited into that node of intersection is the analogue to the lively languages that actively intertwine in the production of literary value: the coyote and protean embodiments of a world as witty agent and actor. Perhaps our hopes for accountability for technobiopolitics in the belly of the monster turn on revisioning the world as coding trickster with whom we must learn to converse. So while the late-twentieth-century immune system, for example, is a construct of an elaborate apparatus of bodily production, neither the immune system nor any other of biology's world-changing bodies—like a virus or an ecosystem—is a ghostly fantasy. Coyote is not a ghost, merely a protean trickster.

This sketch of the artifactuality of nature and the apparatus of bodily production helps us toward another important point: the corporeality of theory. Overwhelmingly, theory is bodily, and theory is literal. Theory is not about matters distant from the lived body—quite the opposite. Theory is *anything* but disembodied. The fanciest statements about radical decontextualization as the historical form of nature in late capitalism are tropes for the embodiment, the production, the literalization of experience in that specific mode. This is not a question of reflection or correspondences but of technology, where the social and the technical implode into each other. Experience is a semiotic process—a semiosis.[17] Lives are built; so we had best become good craftspeople with the other worldly actants in the story. There is a great deal of rebuilding to do, beginning with a little more surveying with the aid of optical devices fitted with red, green, and ultraviolet filters.

Repeatedly, this essay turns on figures of pregnancy and gestation. Zoe Sofia taught me that every technology is a reproductive technology.[18] She and I have meant that literally; ways of life are at stake in the culture of science. I would, however, like to displace the terminology of reproduction with that of generation. Very rarely does anything really get *reproduced*; what's going on is much more polymorphous than that. Certainly people don't reproduce, unless they get themselves cloned, which will always be very expensive and risky, not to mention boring. Even technoscience must be made into the paradigmatic model not of closure but of that which is contestable and contested. That involves knowing how the world's agents and actants work, how they/we/it come into the world, and how they/we/it are reformed. Science becomes the myth not of what escapes agency and responsibility in a realm above the fray but rather of accountability and responsibility for translations and solidarities linking the cacophonous visions and visionary voices that characterize the knowledges of the marked bodies of history. Actors, as well as actants, come in many and wonderful forms. And best of all, "reproduction"—or less inaccurately, the generation of novel forms—need not be imagined in the stodgy bipolar terms of hominids.[19]

If the stories of hyperproductionism and enlightenment have been about the reproduction of the sacred image of the same, of the one true copy, mediated by the luminous technologies of compulsory heterosexuality and masculinist self-birthing, then the differential artifactualism I am trying to envision might issue in something else. Artifactualism is askew of productionism; the rays from my optical device diffract rather than reflect. These diffracting rays compose *interference* patterns, not reflecting images. The "issue" from this generative technology, the result of a monstrous[20] pregnancy, might be kin to Vietnamese American filmmaker and feminist theorist Trinh Minh-ha's "inappropriate/d others."[21] Designating the networks of multicultural, ethnic, racial, national, and sexual actors emerging since World War II, Trinh's phrase referred to the historical positioning of those who cannot adopt the mask of either "self" or "other" offered by previously dominant, modern Western narratives of identity and politics. To be "inappropriate/d" does not mean "not to be in relation with"—i.e., to be in a special reservation, with the status of the authentic, the untouched, in the allochronic and allotopic condition of innocence. Rather, to be an "inappropriate/d other" means to be in critical, deconstructive relationality, in a diffracting rather than reflecting (ratio)nality—as the means of making potent connection that exceeds domination. To be inappropriate/d is not to fit in the *taxon,* to be dislocated from the available maps specifying kinds of actors and kinds of narratives, not to be originally fixed by difference. To be inappropriate/d is to be neither modern nor postmodern, but to insist on the *a*modern. Trinh was looking for a way to figure "difference" as a "critical difference within" and not as special taxonomic marks grounding difference as apartheid. She was writing about people; I wonder if the same observations might apply to humans and to both organic and technological nonhumans.

The term *inappropriate/d others* can provoke rethinking social relationality within artifactual nature—which is, arguably, global nature in the 1990s. Trinh Minh-ha's metaphors suggest another geometry and optics for considering the relations of difference among people and among humans, other organisms, and machines than hierarchical domination, incorporation of parts into wholes, paternalistic and colonialist protection, symbiotic fusion, antagonistic opposition, or instrumental production from resource. Her metaphors also suggest the hard intellectual, cultural, and political work these new geometries will require. If Western patriarchal narratives have told that the physical body issued from the first birth, while man was the product of the heliotropic second birth, perhaps a differential, diffracted feminist allegory might have the "inappropriate/d others" emerge from a third birth into an SF world called elsewhere—a place composed from interference patterns. Diffraction does not produce "the same" displaced, as reflection and refraction do. Diffraction is a mapping of interference, not of replication, reflection, or reproduction. A diffraction pattern does not map where differences appear but rather maps where the *effects* of difference appear. Tropically, for the promises of monsters, the first invites the illusion of essential, fixed position, while the second trains us to more subtle vision. Science fiction is generically concerned with the interpenetration of boundaries between problematic selves and unexpected others and with the exploration of possible worlds in a context structured by transnational technoscience. The emerging social subjects called "inappropriate/d others" inhabit such worlds. SF—science fiction, speculative futures, science fantasy, speculative fiction—is an especially apt sign under which to conduct an inquiry into the artifactual as a reproductive technology that might issue in something other than the sacred image of the same, something inappropriate, unfitting, and so, maybe, inappropriated.

Within the belly of the monster, even inappropriate/d others seem to be interpellated—called through interruption—into a particular location that I have learned to call a cyborg subject position.[22] Let me continue this travelogue and inquiry into artifactualism with an illustrated lecture on the nature of cyborgs as they appear in recent advertisements in *Science,* the journal of the American Association for the Advancement of Science. These ad figures remind us of the corporeality, the mundane materiality, and the literality of theory. These commercial cyborg figures tell us what may count as nature in technoscience worlds. Above all, they show us the implosion of the technical, textual, organic, mythic, and political in the gravity wells of science in action. These figures are our companion monsters in the *Pilgrim's Progress* of this essay's travelogue.

Consider Figure 23.1, "A Few Words about Reproduction from a Leader in the Field," the advertising slogan for Logic General Corporation's software duplication system. The immediate visual and verbal impact insists on the absurdity of separating the technical, organic, mythic, textual, and political threads in the semiotic fabric of the ad and of the world in which this ad makes sense. Under the unliving, orange-to-yellow rainbow colors of the earth–sun logo of Logic General, the biological white rabbit has its (her? yet, sex and gender are not so settled in this reproductive system) back to us. It has its paws on a keyboard, that inertial, old-fashioned residue of the typewriter that lets our computers feel natural to us, user-friendly, as it were.[23] But the keyboard is misleading; no letters are transferred by a mechanical key to a waiting solid surface. The computer–user interface works differently. Even if she doesn't understand the implications of her lying keyboard, the white rabbit is in her natural home; she is fully artifactual in the most literal

We don't believe the facts about diskette reproduction should be left to rumor and streetcorner conversation. So here's the straight talk about software duplication from the experts at Logic General.

Logic General can satisfy software duplication orders of literally any size and complexity at a most competitive cost. Our years of experience as a leading distributor and duplicator of magnetic media, combined with the latest automated high-speed production equipment, give us the edge.

Our synergistic approach to software duplication, a real partnership with each client, helps us tailor each order to cost, performance and system parameters with unique flexibility and precision.

And the accuracy, reliability and quality of each Logic General-duplicated diskette is guaranteed, 100%.

Of course, this isn't the whole story. To learn more, call Logic General. Where all software is re-created equal.

LOGIC GENERAL CORPORATION
31999 Aurora Road
Cleveland, OH 44139

A FEW WORDS ABOUT REPRODUCTION FROM AN ACKNOWLEDGED LEADER IN THE FIELD.

Call toll-free: (800) 321-8908. In Ohio, (216) 349-2800.

CIRCLE 106

Figure 23.1

sense. Like fruit flies, yeast, transgenic mice, and the humble nematode worm, *Caenorhabditis elegans,*[24] this rabbit's evolutionary story transpires in the lab; the lab is its proper niche, its true habitat. Both material system and symbol for the measure of fecundity, this kind of rabbit occurs in no other nature than the lab, that preeminent scene of replication practices.

With Logic General, plainly, we are not in a biological laboratory. The organic rabbit peers at its image, but the image is not her reflection, indeed, *especially* not her reflection. This is not Lacan's world of mirrors; primary identification and maturing metaphoric substitution will be produced with other techniques, other writing technologies.[25] The white rabbit will be translated, her potencies and competences relocated radically. The guts of the computer produce another kind of visual product than distorted, self-birthing reflections. The simulated bunny peers out at us face first. It is she who locks her/its gaze with us. She, also, has her paws on a grid, one just barely reminiscent of a typewriter, but even more reminiscent of an older icon of technoscience—the Cartesian coordinate system that locates the world in the imaginary spaces of rational modernity. In her natural habitat, the virtual rabbit is on a grid that insists on the world as a game played on a chesslike board. This rabbit insists that the truly rational actors will replicate themselves in a virtual world where the best players will not be Man, though he may linger like the horse-drawn carriage that gave its form to the railroad car or the typewriter that gave its illusory shape to the computer interface. The functional privileged signifier in this system will not be so easily mistaken for any primate male's urinary and copulative organ. Metaphoric substitution and other circulations in the very material symbolic domain will be more likely to be effected by a competent mouse. The if-y femaleness of both of the rabbits, of course, gives no confidence that the new players other to Man will be women. More likely, the rabbit that is interpellated into the world in this nonmirror stage, this diffracting moment of subject constitution, will be literate in a quite different grammar of gender. *Both* the rabbits here are cyborgs—compounds of the organic, technical, mythic, textual, and political—and they call us into a world in which we may not wish to take shape, but through whose "Miry Slough" we might have to travel to get elsewhere. Logic General is into a very particular kind of *écriture.* The reproductive stakes in this text are future life-forms and ways of life for humans and unhumans. "Call toll-free" for "a few words about reproduction from an acknowledged leader in the field."

Ortho-mune's monoclonal antibodies expand our understanding of a cyborg subject's relation to the inscription technology that is the laboratory (Figure 23.2). In only two years, these fine monoclonals generated more than one hundred published papers—higher than any rate of literary production by myself or any of my human colleagues in the human sciences. But this alarming rate of publication was achieved in 1982, and has surely been wholly surpassed by new generations

Ortho-mune* monoclonal antibodies in only two years generated more than 100 published papers

In a way, this is a tribute to Köhler and Milstein. Because they're the ones who gave us the idea. But the scientists and engineers at Ortho deserve credit, too, for making it happen.

It started, of course, with monoclonal antibodies. Six years ago, when George Köhler and Cesar Milstein showed the world how hybridomas could be made to produce antibodies against specific immunogens, there was no way to predict exactly which questions the new technology would answer.

OKT*: WELL-CHARACTERIZED MONOCLONAL ANTIBODIES†

The questions we had at Ortho were immunological ones. Our researchers were particularly interested in human lymphocytes. We developed a series of monoclonal antibodies directed against purified human T cells and called them the OKT panel.

Then the real work began. Because clear-cut results can come only from well-characterized reagents, scientists at Ortho put a lot of emphasis on defining the specificity of each clone. Input also came from scientists outside Ortho who worked with the OKT reagents. And as more has been published about the reagents, they've become more and more useful.

New potential applications came to mind. It began to look like the OKT reagents could

standardize T lymphocyte subset analysis. Some immune deficiency disease states turned out to be associated with abnormal ratios of T cell subsets. Research oncologists have now begun using the OKT reagents to characterize proliferative lymphocytic disease states, and they have been used to study immune responses to renal transplantation.

MONOCYTES AND Ia-POSITIVE CELLS

We continued to develop more monoclonal antibodies. The new ones could differentiate monocytes and Ia-positive cell subsets. More applications were developed—sorting human peripheral blood cells, elimination of cell populations by complement lysis, studies on cytotoxicity and histochemical staining of tissue sections.

*Trademark

†For research use only.
Not to be used for diagnostic procedures.

Figure 23.2

of biotech mediators of literary replication. Never has theory been more literal, more bodily, more technically adept. Never has the collapse of the "modern" distinctions between the mythic, organic, technical, political, and textual into the gravity well, where the unlamented enlightenment transcendentals of Nature and Society also disappeared, been more evident.

LKB Electrophoresis Division has an evolutionary story to tell, a better, more complete one than has yet been told by physical anthropologists, paleontologists, or naturalists about the entities/actors/actants that structure niche space in an extra-laboratory world: "There are no missing links in MacroGene Workstation" (Figure 23.3). Full of promises, breaching the first of the ever-multiplying final frontiers, the prehistoric monster *Ichthyostega* crawls from the amniotic ocean into the future, onto the dangerous but enticing dry land. Our no-longer-fish, not-yet-salamander will end up fully identified and separated, as man-in-space, finally disembodied, as did the hero of J. D. Bernal's fantasy in *The World, the Flesh, and the Devil*.[26] But for now, occupying the zone between fishes and amphibians, *Ichthyostega* is firmly on the margins, those potent places where theory is best cultured. It behooves us, then, to join this heroic reconstructed beast with LKB, in order to trace out the transferences of competences—the metaphoric-material chain of substitutions—in this quite literal apparatus of bodily production. We are presented with a travel story, a *Pilgrim's Progress,* where there are no gaps, no "missing links." From the first nonoriginal actor—the reconstructed *Ichthyostega*—to the final printout of the DNA homology search mediated by LKB's software and the many separating and writing machines pictured on the right side of the advertisement, the text promises to meet the fundamental desire of phallologocentrism for fullness and presence. From the crawling body in the Miry Sloughs of the narrative to the printed code, we are assured of full success—the compression of time into instantaneous and full access "to the complete GenBank . . . on one laser disk." Like Christian, we have conquered time and space, moving from entrapment in body to fulfillment in spirit, all in the everyday workspaces of the Electrophoresis Division, whose Hong Kong, Moscow, Antwerp, and Washington phone numbers are all provided. Electrophoresis: *pherein*—to bear or carry us relentlessly on.

Bio-Response, innovators in many facets of life's culture, interpellates the cyborg subject into the barely secularized, evangelical, Protestant Christianity that pervades American technoculture: "Realize the potential of your cell line" (Figure 23.4). This ad addresses us directly. We are called into a salvation narrative, into history, into biotechnology, into our true natures: our cell line, ourselves, our successful product. We will testify to the efficacy of this culture system. Colored in the blues, purples, and ultraviolets of the sterilizing commercial rainbow—in which art, science, and business arch in lucrative grace—the viruslike crystalline shape mirrors the luminous crystals of New Age promises. Religion, science,

There are no missing links in a MacroGene Workstation

The short-legged fish on the facing page is Ichthyostega, the oldest known four-footed animal. Until fossils of this meter-long creature were found, he was one of evolution's missing links. Too bad there's none of its DNA to analyze. On LKB's new MacroGene Workstation, his evolutionary relationships could be evaluated quickly with the sequence information on the unique CD-ROM Laser Reference Disk.

Not only does the LKB MacroGene Workstation let you study intergenic relationships easily — it is fully equips you to achieve optimum results at every step in DNA sequencing. From start to finish.

You can cast flawless ultrathin and wedge-shaped gels, as thin as 0.1 mm, in seconds. Maximize both resolution and the number of readable bases by drying your gels down to a very thin film. Carry out dideoxy reactions in a single dish. Load radioactive samples into 0.2 mm gel slots, with no risk of breaking a tip.

You can also read a longer DNA sequence rapidly and transfer it directly to your personal computer for analysis with user-friendly DNASIS* software.

DNASIS has all the functions needed to manipulate and evaluate large amounts of data in little time at all. It enables maximum matching, auto-connection of shotgun sequence fragments, control element search, automatic generation of restriction maps from gel data, reformatting of external files, and scores of other routines. And DNASIS alone offers you instantaneous access to the complete GenBank and NBRF databases, both on one laser disk.

MacroGene is the only DNA sequencing system you can buy which has no missing links. See for yourself! Ask your nearest LKB representative today for a MacroGene brochure and a DNASIS demonstration disk.

*For casting and moulding sequencing gels: the LKB MacroMould™ System.**

For sequencing reactions: the 60-well LKB MicroSample Plate.

For heat control: the LKB Thermostatic Plate or Isothermal Plate.

For loading: the LKB Sequencing Syringe, with unbreakable, exchangeable needle.

For fast data output: the LKB MacroRead™ Digitizer and Light Table.

For analysis and comparison. DNASIS software and the compact laser disk.

LKB

Electrophoresis Division

Pharmacia LKB Biotechnology AB, Box 305, S-16126 Bromma, Sweden, Tel. 08-799 6000, telex 10492.

DNASIS is a trademark of Hitachi Software Engineering Co. Ltd.
**MacroMould is based on an invention of Dr. W.Ansorge.

Circle No. 57 on Readers Service Card

390

Above: A reconstruction of Ichthyostega, the "missing link" between fishes and amphibia. Left: An example of a MacroGene homology search with DNASIS software and a CD-ROM disk. In the LKB MacroGene Workstation, there are no "missing links."

Figure 23.3

and mysticism join easily in the facets of modern and postmodern commercial bioresponse. The simultaneously promising and threatening crystal/virus unwinds its tail to reveal the language-like icon of the Central Dogma, the code structures of DNA that underlie all possible bodily response, all semiosis, all culture. Gem-like, the frozen, spiraling crystals of Bio-Response promise life itself. This is a jewel of great price—available from the Production Services office in Hayward,

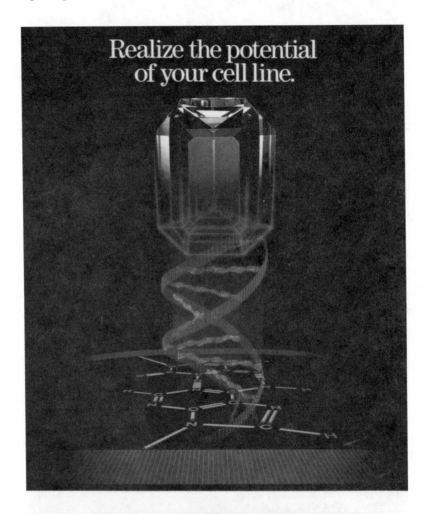

Figure 23.4

California. The imbrications of layered signifiers and signifieds forming cascading hierarchies of signs guide us through this mythic, organic, textual, technical, political icon.[27]

Finally, the advertisement from Vega Biotechnologies graphically shows us the final promise, "the link between science and tomorrow: Guaranteed. Pure" (Figure 23.5). The graph reiterates the ubiquitous grid system that is the signature and matrix, father and mother, of the modern world. The sharp peak is the climax of the search for certainty and utter clarity. But the diffracting apparatus of a monstrous artifactualism can perhaps interfere in this little family drama, reminding us that the modern world never existed and its fantastic guarantees are void. Both the organic and computer rabbits of Logic General might reenter at this point to challenge all the passive voices of productionism. The oddly duplicated bunnies might resist their logical interpellation and instead hint at a neo-natalogy of inappropriate/d others, where the child will not be in the sacred image of the same. Shape-shifting, these interfering cyborgs might craft a diffracted logic of sameness and difference and utter a different word about reproduction, about the link between science and tomorrow, from collective actors in the field.

II. The Four-Square Cyborg: Through Artifactualism to Elsewhere

It is time to travel, therefore, with a particular subset of shifted subjects, Cyborgs for Earthly Survival,[28] into the mindscapes and landscapes indicated at the beginning of this essay. To get through the artifactual to elsewhere, it would help to have a little travel machine that also functions as a map. Consequently, the rest of the "Promises of Monsters" will rely on an artificial device that generates meanings very noisily: A. J. Greimas's infamous semiotic square. The regions mapped by this clackety, structuralist meaning-making machine could never be mistaken for the transcendental realms of Nature or Society. Allied with Bruno Latour, I will put my structuralist engine to amodern purposes: this will not be a tale of the rational progress of science, in potential league with progressive politics, patiently unveiling a grounding nature, nor will it be a demonstration of the social construction of science and nature that locates all agency firmly on the side of humanity. Nor will the modern be superseded or infiltrated by the postmodern, because belief in something called the modern has itself been a mistake. Instead, the amodern refers to a view of the history of science as culture that insists on the absence of beginnings, enlightenments, and endings: the world has always been in the middle of things, in unruly and practical conversation, full of action and structured by a startling array of actants and of networking and unequal collectives. The much-criticized inability of structuralist devices to provide the narrative of diachronic history, of progress through time, will be my semiotic square's greatest virtue. The shape of my amodern history will have a different geometry, not of

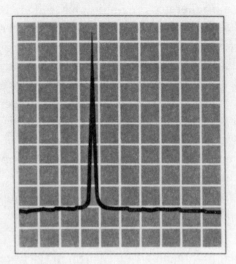 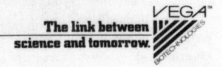
Figure 23.5

progress, but of permanent and multipatterned interaction through which lives and worlds get built, human and unhuman. This *Pilgrim's Progress* is taking a monstrous turn.

I like my analytical technologies, which are unruly partners in discursive construction, delegates who have gotten into doing things on their own, to make a lot of noise, so that I don't forget all the circuits of competences, inherited conversations, and coalitions of human and unhuman actors that go into any semiotic excursions. The semiotic square, so subtle in the hands of a Fredric Jameson, will be rather more rigid and literal here.[29] I only want it to keep four spaces in differential, relational separation, while I explore how certain local/global struggles for meanings and embodiments of nature are occurring within them. Almost a joke on "elementary structures of signification" ("Guaranteed. Pure."), the semiotic square in this essay nonetheless allows a contestable collective world to take shape for us out of structures of difference. The four regions through which

The Promises of Monsters
Through Artifactualism to Elsewhere . . .
A regenerative politics for inappropriate/d others

A	B
Real Space: Earth	**Out Space:** The Extraterrestrial
"Understanding is everything" neo-natology of the collective	"The choice is the universe or nothing" neo-natology of ETs and Earthlings
Gombe saving nature	**One Small Step . . .** HAM and the right stuff
Amazonia social nature	**Love Your Mother** Western Shoshone lands and the State of Nevada

Ā	B̄
Virtual Space: SF	**Inner Space:** The Biomedical Body
"If you wish to know more, press Enter ▮" neo-natology of inappropriate/d other	"The stuff of the stars has come alive" neo-natology of the body
Lisa Foo rereading the collective	**Fetus** spaceman vs. relational personhood
Cyborg a rainbow semiotics	**Immune System** viral invaders + smart missiles vs. IS grammar + ACT UP

Figure 23.6

we will move are A, Real Space or Earth; B, Outer Space or the Extraterrestrial; not-B, Inner Space or the Body; and finally, not-A, Virtual Space or the SF world oblique to the domains of the imaginary, the symbolic, and the real (Figure 23.6).

Somewhat unconventionally, we will move through the square clockwise to see what kinds of figures inhabit this exercise in science studies as cultural studies. In each of the first three quadrants of the square, I will begin with a popular image of nature and science that initially appears both compelling and friendly but quickly becomes a sign of deep structures of domination. Then I will switch to a differential/oppositional image and practice that might promise something else. In the final quadrant, in virtual space at the end of the journey, we will meet a disturbing guide figure who promises information about psychic, historical, and bodily formations that issue, perhaps, from some other semiotic processes than the psychoanalytic in modern and postmodern guise. Directed by John Varley's story of that name, all we will have to do to follow this disquieting, amodern Beatrice will be to "Press Enter."[30] Her job will be to instruct us in the neo-natology of inappropriate/d others. The goal of this journey is to show in each quadrant, and in the passage through the machine that generates them, metamorphoses and boundary shifts that give grounds for a scholarship and politics of hope in truly monstrous times. The pleasures promised here are not those libertarian masculinist fantasmics of the infinitely regressive practice of boundary violation and the accompanying *frisson* of brotherhood but just maybe the pleasure of regeneration in less deadly, chiasmatic borderlands.[31] Without grounding origins and without history's illuminating and progressive tropisms, how might we map some semiotic possibilities for other topick gods and common places?

A. Real Space: Earth

In 1984, to mark nine years of underwriting the National Geographic Society's television specials, the Gulf Oil Corporation ran an advertisement entitled "Understanding Is Everything" (Figure 23.7). The ad referred to some of the most watched programs in the history of public television—the nature specials about Jane Goodall and the wild chimpanzees in Tanzania's Gombe National Park. Initially, the gently clasped hands of the ape and the young white woman seem to auger what the text proclaims—communication, trust, responsibility, and understanding across the gaps that have defined human existence in Nature and Society in "modern" Western narratives. Made ready by a scientific practice coded in terms of "years of patience," through a "spontaneous gesture of trust" *initiated by the animal,* Goodall metamorphoses in the ad copy from "Jane" to "Dr. Goodall." Here is a natural science, coded unmistakenly feminine, to counter the instrumentalist excesses of a military–industrial–technoscience complex, where the code of science is stereotypically anthropocentric and masculine. The ad invites the

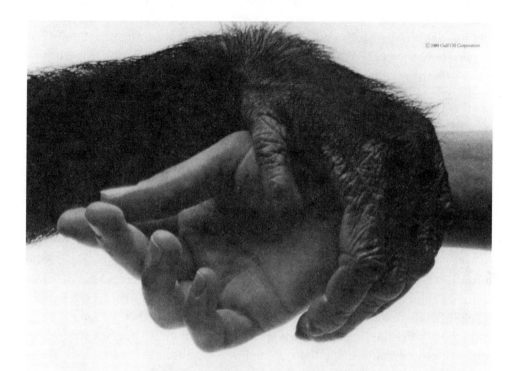

Understanding is everything.

In a spontaneous gesture of trust, a chimpanzee in the wilds of Tanzania folds his leathery hand around that of Jane Goodall – sufficient reward for Dr. Goodall's years of patience.

The moment occurred in one of the National Geographic Specials, a series underwritten throughout its nine consecutive years on public television by the Gulf Oil Corporation.

In a sense, it symbolizes what the whole series is about.

Dr. Goodall's quiet triumph grew slowly over years of studying the chimpanzee: from curiosity, to observation and learning, to understanding.

Gulf underwrites the National Geographic Specials in the belief that the same sequence can occur within the vast PBS audience. Our goal is to provoke curiosity about the world and the fragile complexity of its natural order; to satisfy that curiosity through observation and learning; to create an understanding of man's place in the ecological structure, and his responsibility to it— on the simple theory that no thinking person can share in the destruction of anything whose value he understands.

It's an ambitious goal, but we have embraced that challenge. Since 1975, when we helped bring the National Geographic Specials to PBS, the series has become one of the most watched in public-television history. It has earned eight Emmy awards, an Oscar nomination, and the coveted George Foster Peabody Award for "unsurpassed excellence in documentaries."

Association with the National Geographic Society and the television specials is only one aspect of Gulf's lively concern for the environment. But it is an especially proud one.

Gulf Oil Corporation

Figure 23.7

viewer to forget Gulf's status as one of the Seven Sisters of big oil, ranking eighth among the Forbes 500 in 1980 (but acquired by Chevron by the end of the decade's transnational capitalist restructuring). In response to the financial and political challenges mounted in the early 1970s by the Organization of Oil Exporting Countries (OPEC) and by ecological activism around the globe, by the late 1970s the scandal-ridden giant oil corporations had developed advertising strategies that presented themselves as the world's leading environmentalists—indeed, practically as the mothers of eco-feminism. There could be no better story than that of Jane Goodall and the chimpanzees for narrating the healing touch between nature and society, mediated by a science that produces full communication in a chain that leads innocently "from curiosity, to observation, to learning, to understanding."[32] Here is a story of blissful incorporation.

There is another repressed set of codes in the ad as well, that of race and imperialism, mediated by the dramas of gender and species, science and nature. In the National Geographic narrative, "Jane" entered the garden "alone" in 1960 to seek out "man's" closest relatives, to establish a knowing touch across gulfs of time. A natural family is at stake; the PBS specials document a kind of inter-species family therapy. Closing the distance between species through a patient discipline, where first the animals could only be known by their spoor and their calls, then by fleeting sightings, then finally by the animal's direct inviting touch, after which she could name them, "Jane" was admitted as "humanity's" delegate back into Eden. Society and nature had made peace; "modern science" and "nature" could coexist. Jane/Dr. Goodall was represented almost as a new Adam, authorized to name not by God's creative hand but by the animal's transformative touch. The people of Tanzania disappear in a story in which the actors are the anthropoid apes and a young British white woman engaged in a thoroughly modern sacred secular drama. The chimpanzees and Goodall are both enmeshed in stories of endangerment and salvation. In the post–World War II era the apes face biological extinction; the planet faces nuclear and ecological annihilation; and the West faces expulsion from its former colonial possessions. If only communication can be established, destruction can be averted. As Gulf Oil insists, "Our goal is to provoke curiosity about the world and the fragile complexity of its natural order; to satisfy that curiosity through observation and learning; to create an understanding of man's place in the ecological structure, and his responsibility to it—on the simple theory that no thinking person can share in the destruction of anything whose value he understands." Progress, rationality, and nature join in the great myth of modernity, which is so thoroughly threatened by a dozen looming apocalypses. A cross-species family romance promises to avert the threatened destruction.

Inaudible in the Gulf and National Geographic version, communication and understanding are to emerge in the communion between Jane/Dr. Goodall and the spontaneously trusting chimpanzee at just the historical moment when dozens of African nations are achieving their national independence, fifteen in 1960 alone, the year Goodall set out for Gombe. Missing from the family romance are such beings as Tanzanians. African peoples seek to establish hegemony over the lands in which they live; to do that the stories of the natural presence of white colonists must be displaced, usually by extremely complex and dangerous nationalist stories. But in "Understanding Is Everything," the metonymic "spontaneous gesture of trust" from the animal hand to the white hand obliterates once again the invisible bodies of people of color who have never counted as able to represent humanity in Western iconography. The white hand will be the instrument for saving nature—and in the process be saved from a rupture with nature. Closing great gaps, the transcendentals of nature and society meet here in the metonymic figure of softly embracing hands from two worlds, whose innocent touch depends on the absence of the "other world," the "third world," where the drama actually transpires.

In the history of the life sciences, the great chain of being leading from "lower" to "higher" life-forms has played a crucial part in the discursive construction of race as an object of knowledge and of racism as a living force. After World War II and the partial removal of explicit racism from evolutionary biology and physical anthropology, a good deal of racist and colonialist discourse remained projected onto the screen of "man's closest relatives," the anthropoid apes.[33] It is impossible to picture the entwined hands of a white woman and an African ape without evoking the history of racist iconography in biology and in European and American popular culture. The animal hand is metonymically the individual chimpanzee, all threatened species, the third world, peoples of color, Africa, the ecologically endangered earth—all firmly in the realm of Nature, all represented in the leathery hand folding around that of the white girl-woman under the Gulf sun logo shining on the Seven Sisters' commitment to science and nature. The spontaneous gesture of touch in the wilds of Tanzania authorizes a whole doctrine of representation. Jane, as Dr. Goodall, is empowered to speak for the chimpanzees. Science speaks for nature. Authorized by unforced touch, the dynamics of representation take over, ushering in the reign of freedom and communication. This is the structure of depoliticizing expert discourse, so critical to the mythic political structures of the "modern" world and to the mythic political despair of much "postmodernism," so undermined by fears about the breakdown of representation.[34] Unfortunately, representation, fraudulent or not, is a very resilient practice.

The clasping hands of the Gulf ad are semiotically similar to the elution peak in the Vega ad of Figure 23.5: "Guaranteed. Pure."; "Understanding Is Everything." There is no interruption in these stories of communication, progress, and salvation through science and technology. The story of Jane Goodall in Gombe, however, can be made to show its conditions of possibility; even in the footage of the National Geographic specials we see the young woman on a mountain top at night eating from a can of pork and beans, that sign of industrial civilization so crucial to the history of colonialism in Africa, as Orson Welles's voice-over speaks of the lonely quest for contact with nature! In one of Goodall's published accounts of the early days at Gombe, we learn that she and her mother, en route to the chimpanzee preserve, were stopped on the shores of Lake Tanganyika in the town of Kigoma, across from the no-longer-Belgian Congo, as *uhuru,* freedom, sounded across Africa. Goodall and her mother made two thousand spam sandwiches for fleeing Belgians before embarking for the "wilds of Tanzania."[35] It is also possible to reconstruct a history of Gombe as a research site in the 1970s. One of the points that stands out in this reconstruction is that people—research staff and their families, African, European, and North American—considerably outnumbered chimpanzees during the years of most intense scientific work. Nature and Society met in one story; in another story, the structure of action and the actants take a different shape.

It is hard, however, to make the story of Jane Goodall and the wild chimpanzees shed its "modern" message about "saving nature," in both senses of nature as salvific and of the scientist speaking for and preserving nature in a drama of representation. Let us, therefore, leave this narrative for another colonized tropical spot in the Real/Earth quadrant in the semiotic square—Amazonia. Remembering that all colonized spots have, euphemistically stated, a special relation to nature, let us structure this story to tell something amodern about nature and society—and perhaps something more compatible with the survival of all the networked actants, human and unhuman. To tell this story, we must disbelieve in both nature and society and resist their associated imperatives to represent, to reflect, to echo, to act as a ventriloquist for "the other." The main point is there will be no Adam—and no Jane—who gets to name all the beings in the garden. The reason is simple: there is no garden and never has been. No name and no touch is original. The question animating this diffracted narrative, this story based on little differences, is also simple: is there a consequential difference between a political semiotics of articulation and a political semiotics of representation?

The August 1990 issue of *Discover* magazine has a story entitled "Tech in the Jungle." A one-and-one-half-page color photo of a Kayapó Indian, in indigenous dress and using a videocamera, dramatically accompanies the opening paragraphs. The caption tells us the man is "tap[ing] his tribesmen, who had gathered in the central Brazilian town of Altamira to protest plans for a hydroelectric dam on their territory."[36] All the cues in the *Discover* article invite us to read this photo as the drama of the meeting of the "traditional" and the "modern," staged in this popular North American scientific publication for audiences who have a stake in maintaining belief in those categories. We have, however, as disbelieving members of those audiences, a different political, semiotic responsibility, one made easier by another publication, Susanna Hecht and Alexander Cockburn's *The Fate of the Forest* through which I propose to suggest articulations and solidarities with the *filming practice* of the Kayapó man, rather than to read the *photograph of him*, which will not be reproduced in this essay.[37]

In their book, which was deliberately packaged, published, and marketed in a format and in time for the 1989 December gift-giving season, a modest act of cultural politics not to be despised, Hecht and Cockburn have a central agenda. They insist on deconstructing the image of the tropical rain forest, especially Amazonia, as "Eden under glass." They do this in order to insist on locations of responsibility and empowerment in current conservation struggles, on the outcome of which the lives and ways of life for people and many other species depend. In particular, they support a politics not of "saving nature" but of "social nature," not of national parks and walled-off reserves, responding with a technical fix to whatever particular danger to survival seems most inescapable, but of a different organization of land and people, where the practice of justice restructures the concept of nature.

The authors tell a relentless story of a "social nature" over many hundreds of years, at every turn co-inhabited and co-constituted by humans, land, and other organisms. For example, the diversity and patterns of tree species in the forest cannot be explained without the deliberate, long-term practices of the Kayapó and other groups, whom Hecht and Cockburn describe, miraculously avoiding romanticizing, as "accomplished environmental scientists." Hecht and Cockburn avoid romanticizing because they do not invoke the category of the modern as the special zone of science. Thus, they do not have to navigate the shoals threatening comparisons of, according to taste, mere or wonderful "ethnoscience" with real or disgusting "modern science." The authors insist on visualizing the forest as the dynamic outcome of human as well as biological history. Only after the dense indigenous populations—numbering from six to twelve million in 1492—had been sickened, enslaved, killed, and otherwise displaced from along the rivers could Europeans represent Amazonia as "empty" of culture, as "nature," or, in later terms, as a purely "biological" entity.

But, of course, the Amazon was not and did not become "empty," although "nature" (like "man") is one of those discursive constructions that operates as a technology for making the world over into its image. First, there are indigenous people in the forest, many of whom have organized themselves in recent years into a regionally grounded, world-historical subject prepared for local/global interactions, or, in other terms, for building new and powerful collectives out of humans and unhumans, technological and organic. With all of the power to reconstitute the real implied in discursive construction, they have become a new discursive subject/object, the Indigenous Peoples of the Amazon, made up of national and tribal groups from Colombia, Ecuador, Brazil, and Peru, numbering about one million persons, who in turn articulate themselves with other organized groups of the indigenous peoples of the Americas. Also, in the forest are about two hundred thousand people of mixed ancestry, partly overlapping with the indigenous people. Making their living as petty extractors—of gold, nuts, rubber, and other forest products—they have a history of many generations in the Amazon. It is a complex history of dire exploitation. These people are also threatened by the latest schemes of world banks or national capitals from Brasilia to Washington.[38] They have for many decades been in conflict with indigenous peoples over resources and ways of life. Their presence in the forest might be the fruit of the colonial fantasies of the *bandeirantes,* romantics, curators, politicians, or speculators; but their fate is entwined intimately with that of the other always historical inhabitants of this sharply contested world. It is from these desperately poor people, specifically the rubber tappers union, that Chico Mendes, the world-changing activist murdered on December 22, 1988, came.[39]

A crucial part of Mendes's vision for which he was killed was the union of the extractors and the indigenous peoples of the forest into, as Hecht and Cockburn argue, the "true defenders of the forest." Their position as defenders derives not from a concept of "nature under threat," but rather from a *relationship* with "the forest as the integument in their own elemental struggle to survive."[40] In other words, their authority derives *not* from the power to represent from a distance, *nor* from an ontological natural status, but from a constitutive social relationality in which the forest is an integral partner, part of natural/social embodiment. In their claims for authority over the fate of the forest, the resident peoples are articulating a social collective entity among humans, other organisms, and other kinds of nonhuman actors.

Indigenous people are resisting a long history of forced "tutelage," in order to confront the powerful representations of the national and international environmentalists, bankers, developers, and technocrats. The extractors, for example, the rubber tappers, are also independently articulating their collective viewpoint. Neither group is willing to see the Amazon "saved" by their exclusion and permanent subjection to historically dominating political and economic forces. As Hecht and Cockburn put it, "the rubber tappers have not risked their lives for extractive reserves so they could live on them as debt peons."[41] "Any program for the Amazon begins with basic human rights: an end to debt bondage, violence, enslavement, and killings practiced by those who would seize the lands these forest people have occupied for generations. Forest people seek legal recognition of native lands and extractive reserves held under the principle of collective property, worked as individual holdings with individual returns."[42]

At the second Brazilian national meeting of the Forest People's Alliance at Rio Branco in 1989, shortly after Mendes's murder raised the stakes and catapulted the issues into the international media, a program was formulated in tension with the latest Brazilian state policy called Nossa Natureza. Articulating quite a different notion of the first person plural relation to nature or natural surroundings, the basis of the program of the Forest People's Alliance is control by and for the peoples of the forest. The core matters are direct control of indigenous lands by native peoples; agrarian reform joined to an environmental program; economic and technical development; health posts; raised incomes; locally controlled marketing systems; an end to fiscal incentives for cattle ranchers, agribusiness, and unsustainable logging; an end to debt peonage; and police and legal protection. Hecht and Cockburn call this an "ecology of justice" that rejects a technicist solution, in whatever benign or malignant form, to environmental destruction. The Forest People's Alliance does not reject scientific or technical know-how, their own and others'; instead, they reject the "modern" political epistemology that bestows jurisdiction on the basis of technoscientific discourse. The fundamental point is that the Amazonian Biosphere is an irreducibly human/nonhuman collective entity.[43] There *will be* no nature without justice. Nature and justice, contested discursive objects embodied in the material world, will become extinct or survive together.

Theory here is exceedingly corporeal, and the body is a collective; it is an historical artifact constituted by human as well as organic and technological unhuman actors. Actors are entities which do things, have effects, build worlds in concatenation with other *unlike* actors.[44] Some actors, for example specific human ones, can try to reduce other actors to resources—to mere ground and matrix for their action; but such a move is contestable, not the necessary relation of "human nature" to the rest of the world. Other actors, human and unhuman, regularly resist reductionisms. The powers of domination do fail sometimes in their projects to pin other actors down; people can work to enhance the relevant failure rates. Social nature is the nexus I have called artifactual nature. The human "defenders of the forest" do not and have not lived in a garden; it is from a knot in the always historical and heterogeneous nexus of social nature that they articulate their claims. Or perhaps, it is within such a nexus that I and people like me narrate a possible politics of articulation rather than representation. It is our responsibility to learn whether such a fiction is one with which the Amazonians might wish to connect in the interests of an alliance to defend the rain forest and its human and non-human ways of life—because assuredly North Americans, Europeans, and the Japanese, among others, cannot watch from afar as if we were not actors, willing or not, in the life-and-death struggles in the Amazon.

In a review of *Fate of the Forest,* Joe Kane, author of another book on the tropical rain forest marketed in time for Christmas in 1989, the adventure trek *Running the Amazon,*[45] raised this last issue in a way that will sharpen and clarify my stakes in arguing against a politics of representation generally, and in relation to questions of environmentalism and conservation specifically. In the context of worrying about ways that social nature or socialist ecology sounded too much like the multiuse policies in national forests in the United States, which have resulted in rapacious exploitation of the land and of other organisms, Kane asked a simple question: "[W]ho speaks for the jaguar?" Now, I care about the survival of the jaguar—and the chimpanzee, and the Hawaiian land snail, and the spotted owl, and a lot of other earthlings. I care a great deal; in fact, I think I and my social groups are particularly, but not uniquely, *responsible* if jaguars, and many other nonhuman, as well as human, ways of life should perish. But Kane's question seemed wrong on a fundamental level. Then I understood why. His question was precisely like that asked by some pro-life groups in the abortion debates: Who speaks for the fetus? What is wrong with both questions? And how does this matter relate to science studies as cultural studies?

Who speaks for the jaguar? Who speaks for the fetus? Both questions rely on a political semiotics of representation.[46] Permanently speechless, forever requiring the services of a ventriloquist, never forcing a recall vote, in each case the object or ground of representation is the realization of the representative's fondest dream. As Marx said in a somewhat different context, "they cannot represent themselves; they must be represented."[47] But for a political semiology of representation, nature and the unborn fetus are even better, epistemologically, than subjugated human adults. The effectiveness of such representation depends on distancing operations. The represented must be disengaged from surrounding and constituting discursive and nondiscursive nexuses and relocated in the authorial domain of the representative. Indeed, the effect of this magical operation is to disempower precisely those—in our case, the pregnant woman and the peoples of the forest—who are "close" to the now-represented "natural" object. Both the jaguar and the fetus are carved out of one collective entity and relocated in another, where they are reconstituted as objects of a particular kind—as the ground of a representational practice that *forever* authorizes the ventriloquist. Tutelage will be eternal. The represented is reduced to the permanent status of the recipient of action, never to be a co-actor in an articulated practice among unlike, but joined, social partners.

Everything that used to surround and sustain the represented object, such as pregnant women and local people, simply disappears or reenters the drama as an agonist. For example, the pregnant woman becomes *juridically* and *medically,* two very powerful discursive realms, the "maternal environment."[48] Pregnant women and local people are the *least* able to "speak for" objects like jaguars or fetuses because they get discursively reconstituted as beings with opposing "interests." Neither woman nor fetus, jaguar nor Kayapó Indian, is an actor in the drama of representation. One set of entities becomes the represented, the other becomes the environment, often threatening, of the represented object. The *only* actor left is the spokesperson, the one who represents. The forest is no longer the integument in a co-constituted social nature; the woman is in no way a partner in an intricate and intimate dialectic of social relationality crucial to her own personhood, as well as to the possible personhood of her social—*but unlike*—internal co-actor.[49] In the liberal logic of representation, the fetus and the jaguar must be protected precisely from those closest to them, from their "surround." The power of life and death must be delegated to the epistemologically most disinterested ventriloquist, and it is crucial to remember that all of this *is* about the power of life and death.

Who, within the myth of modernity, is less biased by competing interests or polluted by excessive closeness than the expert, especially the scientist? Indeed, even better than the lawyer, judge, or national legislator, the scientist is the perfect representative of nature, that is, of the permanently and constitutively speechless objective world. Whether he be a male or a female, his passionless distance is his greatest virtue; this discursively constituted, structurally gendered distance legitimates his professional privilege, which in these cases, again, is the power to testify about the right to life and death. After Edward Said quoted Marx on representation in his epigraph to *Orientalism,* he quoted Benjamin Disraeli's *Tancred,* "The East is a career."[50] The separate, objective world—non-social nature—is a career. Nature legitimates the scientist's career, as the Orient justifies the representational practices of the Orientalist, even as precisely "Nature" and the "Orient" are the *products* of the constitutive practice of scientists and orientalists.

These are the inversions that have been the object of so much attention in science studies. Bruno Latour sketches the double structure of representation through which scientists establish the objective status of their knowledge. First, operations shape and enroll new objects or allies through visual displays or other means called inscription devices. Second, scientists speak as if they were the mouthpiece for the speechless objects that they have just shaped and enrolled as allies in an agonistic field called science. Latour defines the actant as that which is represented; the objective world *appears* to be the actant solely by virtue of the operations of representation.[51] The authorship rests with the representor, even as he claims independent object status for the represented. In this doubled structure, the simultaneously semiotic and political ambiguity of representation is glaring. First, a chain of substitutions, operating through inscription devices, relocates power and action in "objects" divorced from polluting contextualizations and named by formal abstractions ("the fetus"). Then, the reader of inscriptions speaks for his docile constituencies, the objects. This is not a very lively world, and it does not finally offer much to jaguars, in whose interests the whole apparatus supposedly operates.

In this essay I have been arguing for another way of seeing actors and actants—and consequently another way of working to position scientists and science in important struggles in the world. I have stressed actants as collective entities doing things in a structured and structuring field of action; I have framed the issue in terms of articulation rather than representation. Human beings use names to point to themselves and other actors and easily mistake the names for the things. These same humans also think the traces of inscription devices are like names—pointers to things, such that the inscriptions and the things can be enrolled in dramas of substitution and inversion. But the things, in my view, do not preexist as ever-elusive, but fully prepackaged, referents for the names. Other actors are more like tricksters than that. Boundaries take provisional, never-finished shape in articulatory practices. The potential for the unexpected from unstripped human and unhuman actants enrolled in articulations—i.e., the potential for generation—remains both to trouble and to empower technoscience. Western philosophers sometimes take account of the inadequacy of names by stressing the "negativity" inherent in all representations. This takes us back to Spivak's remark cited early in this chapter about the important things that we cannot not desire, but can never possess—or represent, because representation depends on possession of a passive resource, namely, the silent object, the *stripped* actant. Perhaps we can, however, "articulate" with humans and unhumans in a social relationship, which for us is always language-mediated (among other semiotic, i.e., "meaningful," mediations). But, for our unlike partners, well, the action is "different," perhaps "negative" from our linguistic point of view, but crucial to the generativity of the collective. It is the empty space, the undecidability, the wiliness of other actors, the "negativity," that gives me confidence in the *reality* and therefore ultimate *unrepresentability* of social nature and that makes me suspect doctrines of representation and objectivity.

My crude characterization does not end up with an "objective world" or "nature," but it certainly does insist on the *world*. This world must always be articulated, from people's points of view, through "situated knowledges."[52] These knowledges are friendly to science but do not provide any grounds for history-escaping inversions and amnesia about how articulations get made, about their political semiotics, if you will. I think the world is precisely what gets lost in doctrines of representation and scientific objectivity. It is *because* I care about jaguars, among other actors, including the overlapping but nonidentical groups called forest peoples and ecologists, that I reject Joe Kane's question. Some science studies scholars have been terrified to criticize their constructivist formulations because the only alternative seems to be some retrograde kind of "going back" to nature and to philosophical realism.[53] But above all people, these scholars should know that "nature" and "realism" are precisely the consequences of representational practices. Where we need to move is not "back" to nature but *elsewhere,* through and within an artifactual social nature, which these very scholars have helped to make expressable in current Western scholarly practice. That knowledge-building practice might be articulated to other practices in "pro-life" ways that aren't about the fetus or the jaguar as nature fetishes and the expert as their ventriloquist.

Prepared by this long detour, we can return to the Kayapó man videotaping his tribesmen as they protest a new hydroelectric dam on their territory. The National Geographic Society, *Discover* magazine, and Gulf Oil—and much philosophy and social science—would have us see his practice as a double boundary crossing between the primitive and the modern. His representational practice, signified by his use of the latest technology, places him in the realm of the modern. He is, then, engaged in an entertaining contradiction—the preservation of an unmodern way of life with the aid of incongruous modern technology. But, from the perspective of a political semiotics of articulation, the man might well be forging a recent collective of humans and unhumans, in this case made up of the Kayapó, videocams, land, plants, animals, near and distant audiences, and other constituents; but no boundary violation is involved. The way of life is not unmodern (closer to nature); the camera is not modern or postmodern (in society). Those categories should no longer make sense. Where there is no nature and no society, there is no pleasure, no entertainment to be had in representing the violation of the boundary between them. Too bad for nature magazines, but a gain for inappropriate/d others.

The videotaping practice does not thereby become innocent or uninteresting; but its meanings have to be approached differently, in terms of the kinds of collective action taking place and the claims they make on others—such as ourselves, people who do not live in the Amazon. We *are all* in chiasmatic borderlands, liminal areas where new shapes, new kinds of action and responsibility, are gestating in the world. The man using that camera is forging a practical claim on us, morally and epistemologically, as well as on the other forest people to whom he will show the tape to consolidate defense of the forest. His practice invites further articulation—on terms shaped by the forest people. They will no longer be represented as Objects, not because they cross a line to represent themselves in "modern" terms as Subjects but because they powerfully form articulated collectives.

In May 1990, a week-long meeting took place in Iquitos, a formerly prosperous rubber boomtown in the Peruvian Amazon. COICA, the Coordinating Body for the Indigenous Peoples of the Amazon, had assembled forest people (from all the nations constituting Amazonia), environmental groups from around the world (Greenpeace, Friends of the Earth, the Rain Forest Action Network, etc.), and media organizations (*Time* magazine, CNN, NBC, etc.) in order "to find a common path on which we can work to preserve the Amazon forest."[54] Rain forest protection was formulated as a necessarily joint human rights–ecological issue. The fundamental demand by indigenous people was that they must be part of *all* international negotiations involving their territories. "Debt for nature" swaps were particular foci of controversy, especially where indigenous groups end up worse off than in previous agreements with their governments as a result of bargaining between banks, external conservation groups, and national states. The controversy generated a proposal: instead of a swap of debt-for-nature, forest people would support swaps of debt-for-indigenous-controlled territory, in which non-indigenous environmentalists would have a "redefined role in helping to develop the plan for conservation management of the particular region of the rain forest."[55] Indigenous environmentalists would also be recognized not for their quaint "ethnoscience" but for their *knowledge*.

Nothing in this structure of action rules out articulations by scientists or other North Americans who care about jaguars and other actors; but the patterns, flows, and intensities of power are most certainly changed. That is what articulation does—it is always a noninnocent, contestable practice; the partners are never set once and for all. There is no ventriloquism here. Articulation is work, and it may fail. All the people who care, cognitively, emotionally, and politically, must articulate their position in a field constrained by a new collective entity, made up of indigenous people and other human and unhuman actors. Commitment and engagement, not their invalidation, in an emerging collective are the conditions of joining knowledge-producing and world-building practices. This is situated knowledge in the New World; it builds on common places, and it takes unexpected turns. So far, such knowledge has not been sponsored by the major oil corporations, banks, and logging interests. That is precisely one of the reasons why there is so much work for North Americans, Europeans, and Japanese, among others, to do in articulation with those humans and nonhumans who live in rain forests and in many other places in the semiotic space called earth.

B. Outer Space: The Extraterrestrial

Since we have spent so much time on earth, a prophylactic exercise for residents of the alien "First World," we will rush through the remaining three quadrants of the semiotic square. We move from one topical commonplace to another, from earth to space, to see what turns our journeys to elsewhere might take.

An ecosystem is always of a particular type, for example, a temperate grassland or a tropical rain forest. In the iconography of late capitalism, Jane Goodall did not go to that kind of ecosystem. She went to the "wilds of Tanzania," a mythic "ecosystem" reminiscent of the original garden from which her kind had been expelled and to which she returned to commune with the wilderness's present inhabitants to learn how to survive. This wilderness was close in its dream quality to "space," but the wilderness of Africa was coded as dense, damp, bodily, full of sensuous creatures who touch intimately and intensely. In contrast, the extra-terrestrial is coded to be fully general; it is about escape from the bounded globe into an anti-ecosystem called, simply, space. Space is not about "man's" origins on earth but about "his" future, the two key allochronic times of salvation history. Space and the tropics are both utopian topical figures in Western imaginations, and their opposed properties dialectically signify origins and ends for the creature whose mundane life is supposedly outside both: modern or postmodern man.

The first primates to approach that abstract place called "space" were monkeys and apes. A rhesus monkey survived an eighty-three-mile-high flight in 1949. Jane Goodall arrived in "the wilds of Tanzania" in 1960 to encounter and name the famous Gombe Stream chimpanzees introduced to the National Geographic television audience in 1965. However, other chimpanzees were vying for the spotlight in the early 1960s. On January 31, 1961, as part of the U.S. man-in-space program, the chimpanzee HAM, trained for his task at Holloman Air Force Base, twenty minutes by car from Alamogordo, New Mexico, near the site of the first atom bomb explosion in July 1945, was shot into suborbital flight (Figure 23.8). HAM's name inevitably recalls Noah's youngest and only black son. But this chimpanzee's name was from a different kind of text. His name was an acronym for the scientific–military institution that launched him, Holloman Aero-Medical; and he rode an arc that traced the birth path of modern science—the parabola, the conic section. HAM's parabolic path is rich with evocations of the history of Western science. The path of a projectile that does not escape gravity, the parabola is the shape considered so deeply by Galileo, at the first mythic moment of origins of modernity, when the unquantifiable sensuous and countable mathematical properties of bodies were separated from each other in scientific knowledge. It describes the path of ballistic weapons, and it is the trope for "man's" doomed projects in the writings of the existentialists in the 1950s. The parabola traces the path of Rocket Man at the end of World War II in Thomas Pynchon's *Gravity's Rainbow*.[56] An understudy for man, HAM went only to the boundary of space, in suborbital flight. On his return to earth, he was named. He had been known only as #65 before his successful flight. If, in the official birth-mocking language of the Cold War, the mission had to be "aborted," the authorities did not want the public worrying about the death of a famous and named, even if not quite human, astronaut. In fact, #65 did have a name among his handlers, Chop Chop Chang, recalling the stunning racism in which the other primates have been made to participate.[57] The space race's surrogate child was an "understudy for man in the conquest of space."[58] His hominid cousins would transcend that closed parabolic figure, first in the ellipse of orbital flight, then in the open trajectories of escape from earth's gravity.

HAM, his human cousins and simian colleagues, and their englobing and interfacing technology were implicated in a reconstitution of masculinity in Cold War and space race idioms. The movie *The Right Stuff* (1985) shows the first crop of human astronau(gh)ts struggling with their affronted pride when they realize their tasks were competently performed by their simian cousins. They and the chimps were caught in the same theater of the Cold War, where the masculinist, death-defying, and skill-requiring heroics of the old jet aircraft test pilots became obsolete, to be replaced by the media-hype routines of projects Mercury, Apollo, and their sequelae. After chimpanzee Enos completed a fully automated orbital flight on November 29, 1961, John Glenn, who would be the first human American astronaut to orbit earth, defensively "looked toward the future by affirming his belief in the superiority of astronauts over chimponauts." *Newsweek* announced Glenn's orbital flight of February 20, 1962, with the headline, "John Glenn: One Machine That Worked without Flaw."[59] Soviet primates on both sides of the line of

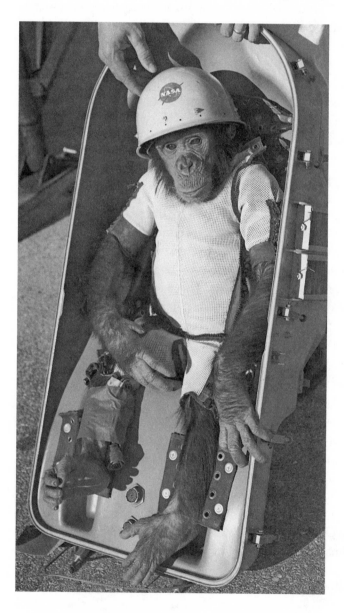

Figure 23.8. HAM awaits release in his couch aboard the recovery vessel LSD *Donner* after his successful Mercury Project launch. Photograph by Henry Borroughs.

hominization raced their U.S. siblings into extraterrestrial orbit. The space ships, the recording and tracking technologies, animals, and human beings were joined as cyborgs in a theater of war, science, and popular culture.

Henry Burroughs's famous photograph of an interested and intelligent, actively participating HAM, watching the hands of a white, laboratory-coated, human man release him from his contour couch, illuminated the system of meanings that binds humans and apes together in the late twentieth century.[60] HAM is the perfect child, reborn in the cold matrix of space. *Time* described chimponaut Enos in his "fitted contour couch that looked like a cradle trimmed with electronics.[61] Enos and HAM were cyborg neonates, born of the interface of the dreams about a technicist automaton and masculinist autonomy. There could be no more iconic cyborg than a telemetrically implanted chimpanzee, understudy for man, launched from earth in the space program, while his conspecific in the jungle, "in a spontaneous gesture of trust," embraced the hand of a woman scientist named Jane in a Gulf Oil ad showing "man's place in the ecological structure." On one end of time and space, the chimpanzee in the wilderness modeled communication for the stressed, ecologically threatened and threatening, modern human. On the other end, the ET chimpanzee modeled social and technical cybernetic communication systems, which permit postmodern man to escape both the jungle and the city, in a thrust into the future made possible by the social-technical systems of the "information age" in a global context of threatened nuclear war. The closing image of a human fetus hurtling through space in Stanley Kubrick's *2001: A Space Odyssey* (1968) completed the voyage of discovery begun by the weapon-wielding apes at the film's gripping opening. It was the project(ile) of self-made, reborn man, in the process of being raptured out of history. The Cold War was simulated ultimate war; the media and advertising industries of nuclear culture produced in the bodies of animals—paradigmatic natives and aliens—the reassuring images appropriate to this state of pure war.[62]

In the aftermath of the Cold War, we face not the end of nuclearism but its dissemination. Even without our knowing his ultimate fate as an adult caged chimpanzee, the photograph of HAM rapidly ceases to entertain, much less to edify. Therefore, let us look to another cyborg image to figure possible emergencies of inappropriate/d others to challenge our rapturous mythic brothers, the postmodern spacemen.

At first sight, the T-shirt worn by antinuclear demonstrators at the Mother's and Others' Day Action in 1987 at the United States' Nevada nuclear test site seems in simple opposition to HAM in his electronic cradle (Figure 23.9). But a little unpacking shows the promising semiotic and political complexity of the image and of the action. When the T-shirt was sent to the printer, the name of the event was still the "Mother's Day Action," but not long after some planning participants objected. For many, Mother's Day was, at best, an ambivalent time for a women's action. The overdetermined gender coding of patriarchal nuclear culture all too easily makes women responsible for peace while men fiddle with their dangerous war toys without semiotic dissonance. With its commercialism and multileveled reinforcement of compulsory heterosexual reproduction, Mother's Day is also not everybody's favorite feminist holiday. For others, intent on reclaiming the holiday for other meanings, mothers, and by extension women in general, do have a special obligation to preserve children, and so the earth, from military destruction. For them, the earth is metaphorically mother and child and, in both figurations, a subject of nurturing and birthing. However, this was not an all-women's (much less all-mothers') action, although women organized and shaped it. From discussion, the designation "Mother's and Others' Day Action" emerged. But then, some thought that meant mothers and men. It took memory exercises in feminist analysis to rekindle shared consciousness that mother does not equal woman, and vice versa. Part of the day's purpose was to recode Mother's Day to signify men's obligations to nurture the earth and all its children. In the spirit of this set of issues, at a time when Baby M and her many debatable—and unequally positioned—parents were in the news and the courts, the all-female affinity group which I joined took

Figure 23.9. Mother's Day 1987 Nevada Test Site Action T-shirt.

as its name the Surrogate Others. These surrogates were not understudies for man but were gestating for another kind of emergence.

From the start, the event was conceived as an action that linked social justice and human rights, environmentalism, antimilitarism, and antinuclearism. On the T-shirt, there is, indeed, the perfect icon of the union of all issues under environmentalism's rubric: the "whole earth," the lovely, cloud-wrapped, blue planet earth is simultaneously a kind of fetus floating in the amniotic cosmos and a mother to all its own inhabitants, germ of the future, matrix of the past and present. It is a perfect globe, joining the changeling matter of mortal bodies and the ideal eternal sphere of the philosophers. This snapshot resolves the dilemma of modernity, the separation of Subject and Object, Mind and Body. There is, however, a jarring note in all this, even for the most devout. That particular image of the earth, of Nature, could only exist if a camera on a satellite had taken the picture, which is, of course, precisely the case. Who speaks for the earth? Firmly in the object world called nature, this bourgeois, family-affirming snapshot of mother earth is about as uplifting as a loving commercial Mother's Day card. And yet, it *is* beautiful, and it is ours; it must be brought into a different focus. The T-shirt is part of a complex collective entity, involving many circuits, delegations, and displacements of competencies. Only in the context of the space race in the first place, and the militarization and commodification of the whole earth, does it make sense to relocate that image as the special sign of an antinuclear, antimilitaristic, earth-focused politics. The relocation does not cancel its other resonances; it contests for their outcome.

I read Environmental Action's "whole earth" as a sign of an irreducible artifactual social nature, like the Gaia of SF writer John Varley and biologist Lynn Margulis. Relocated on this particular T-shirt, the satellite's-eye view of planet earth provokes an ironic version of the question, Who speaks for the earth (for the fetus, the mother, the jaguar, the object world of nature, all those who must be represented)? For many of us, the irony made it possible to participate—indeed, to participate as fully committed, if semiotically unruly, eco-feminists. Not everybody in the Mother's and Others' Day Action would agree; for many, the T-shirt image meant what it said: love your mother, who is the earth. Nuclearism is misogyny. The field of readings in tension with each other is also part of the point. Eco-feminism and the nonviolent direct action movement have been based on struggles over differences, not on identity. There is hardly a need for affinity groups and their endless process if sameness prevailed. Affinity is precisely *not* identity; the sacred image of the same is not gestating on this Mother's and Others' Day. Literally, enrolling the satellite's camera and the peace action in Nevada into a new collective, this Love Your Mother image is based on diffraction, on the processing of small but consequential differences. The processing of differences, semiotic action, is about ways of life.

The Surrogate Others planned a birthing ceremony in Nevada, and so they made a birth canal—a sixteen-foot-long, three-foot-diameter, floral polyester-covered worm with lovely dragon eyes. It was a pleasingly artifactual beast, ready for connection. The worm-dragon was laid under the barbed-wire boundary between the land on which the demonstrators could stand legally and the land on which they would be arrested as they emerged. Some of the Surrogate Others conceived of crawling through the worm to the forbidden side as an act of solidarity with the tunneling creatures of the desert, who had to share their subsurface niches with the test site's chambers. This surrogate birthing was definitely not about the obligatory heterosexual nuclear family compulsively reproducing itself in the womb of the state, with or without the underpaid services of the wombs of "surrogate mothers." Mother's and Others' Day was looking up.

It wasn't only the desert's nonhuman organisms with whom the activists were in solidarity as they emerged onto the proscribed territory. From the point of view of the demonstrators, they were quite legally on the test-site land. This was so not out of some "abstract" sense that the land was the people's and had been usurped by the war state but for more "concrete" reasons: all the demonstrators had written permits to be on the land signed by the Western Shoshone National Council. The 1863 Treaty of Ruby Valley recognized the Western Shoshone title to ancestral territory, including the land illegally invaded by the U.S. government to build its nuclear facility. The treaty has never been modified or abrogated, and U.S. efforts to buy the land (at 15 cents per acre) in 1979 were refused by the only body authorized to decide, the Western Shoshone National Council. The county sheriff and his deputies, surrogates for the federal government, were, in "discursive" and "embodied" fact, trespassing. In 1986 the Western Shoshone began to issue permits to the antinuclear demonstrators as part of a coalition that joined antinuclearism and indigenous land rights. It is, of course, hard to make citizens' arrests of the police when they have you handcuffed and when the courts are on their side. But it is quite possible to join this ongoing struggle, which is very much "at home," and to articulate it with the defense of the Amazon. That articulation requires collectives of human and unhuman actors of many kinds.

There were many other kinds of "symbolic action" at the test site that day in 1987. The costumes of the sheriff's deputies and their nasty plastic handcuffs were also symbolic action—highly embodied symbolic action. The "symbolic action" of brief, safe arrest is also quite a different matter from the "semiotic" conditions under which most people in the United States, especially people of color and the poor, are jailed. The difference is not the presence or absence of "symbolism" but the force of the respective collectives made up of humans and unhumans, of people, other organisms, technologies, institutions. I am not unduly impressed with the power of the drama of the Surrogate Others and the other affinity groups, nor, unfortunately, of the whole action. But I do take seriously the work to relocate, to diffract, embodied meanings as crucial work to be done in gestating a new world.[63] It is cultural politics, and it is technoscience politics. The task is to build more powerful collectives in dangerously unpromising times.

Not-B. Inner Space: The Biomedical Body

The limitless reaches of outer space, joined to Cold War and post–Cold War nuclear technoscience, seem vastly distant from their negation, the enclosed and dark regions of the inside of the human body, domain of the apparatuses of biomedical visualization. But these two quadrants of our semiotic square are multiply tied together in technoscience's heterogeneous apparatuses of bodily production. As Sarah Franklin noted, "the two new investment frontiers, outer space and inner space, vie for the futures market." In this "futures market," two entities are especially interesting for this essay: the fetus and the immune system, both of which are embroiled in determinations of what may count as nature and as human, as separate natural object and as juridical subject. We have already looked briefly at some of the matrices of discourse about the fetus in the discussion of earth (who speaks for the fetus?) and outer space (the planet floating free as cosmic germ). Here, I will concentrate on contestations for what counts as a self and an actor in contemporary immune system discourse.

The equation of Outer Space and Inner Space, and of their conjoined discourses of extraterrestrialism, ultimate frontiers, and high-technology war, is literal in the official history celebrating one hundred years of the National Geographic Society.[64] The chapter that recounts the magazine's coverage of the Mercury, Gemini, Apollo, and Mariner voyages is called "Space" and introduced with the epigraph "The Choice Is the Universe—or Nothing." The final chapter, full of stunning biomedical images, is titled "Inner Space" and introduced with the epigraph "The Stuff of the Stars Has Come Alive."[65] The photography convinces the viewer of the fraternal relation of inner and outer space. But, curiously, in outer space, we see spacemen fitted into explorer craft or floating about as individuated cosmic fetuses, while in the supposed earthy space of our own interiors, we see nonhumanoid strangers who are the means by which our bodies sustain our integrity and individuality, indeed our humanity in the face of a world of others. We seem invaded not just by the threatening "non-selves" that the immune system guards against but more fundamentally by our own strange parts.

Lennart Nilsson's photographs, in the coffee table art book *The Body Victorious* (1987) as well as in many medical texts, are landmarks in the photography of the alien inhabitants of inner space (Figure 23.10).[66] The blasted scenes, sumptuous textures, evocative colors, and ET monsters of the immune landscape are simply *there,* inside *us.* A white extruding tendril of a pseudopodinous macrophage ensnares bacteria; the hillocks of chromosomes lie flattened on a blue-hued moonscape of some other planet; an infected cell buds myriads of deadly virus particles into the reaches of inner space where more cells will be victimized; the autoimmune disease–ravaged head of a femur glows against a sunset on a dead world; cancer cells are surrounded by the lethal, mobile squads of killer T cells that throw chemical poisons into the self's malignant traitor cells.

A diagram of the "Evolution of Recognition Systems" in a recent immunology textbook makes clear the intersection of the themes of literally "wonderful"

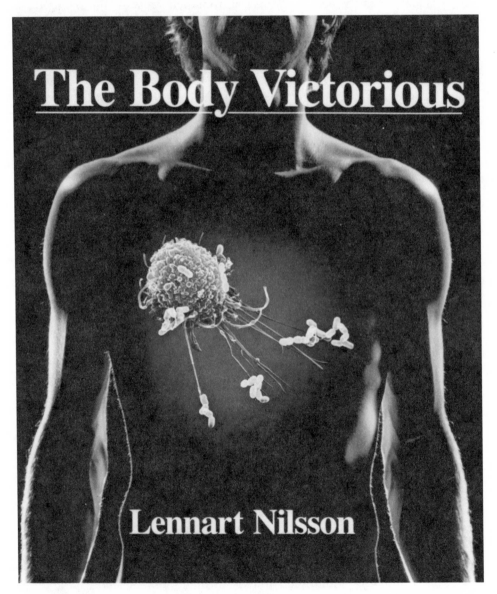

Figure 23.10. Cover design for Lennart Nilsson book.

diversity, escalating complexity, the self as a defended stronghold, and extraterrestrialism in inner space (Figure 23.11). Under a diagram culminating in the evolution of the mammals, represented without comment by a mouse and a *fully-suited spaceman,* is this explanation: "From the humble amoeba searching for food (top left) to the mammal with its sophisticated humoral and cellular immune mechanisms (bottom right), the process of 'self versus non-self recognition' shows a steady development, keeping pace with the increasing need of animals to maintain their integrity in a hostile environment. The decision at which point 'immunity' appeared is thus a purely semantic one."[67] These are the "semantics" of defense and invasion. The perfection of the fully defended, "victorious" self is a chilling fantasy, linking phagocytotic amoeba and space-voyaging man cannibalizing the earth in an evolutionary teleology of postapocalypse extraterrestrialism. When is a self enough of a self that its boundaries become central to institutionalized discourses in biomedicine, war, and business?

Images of the immune system as a battlefield abound in science sections of daily, newspapers and in popular magazines, e.g., *Time* magazine's 1984 graphic for the AIDS virus's "invasion" of the cell-as-factory. The virus is a tank, and the viruses ready for export from the expropriated cells are lined up ready to continue

Evolution of recognition systems

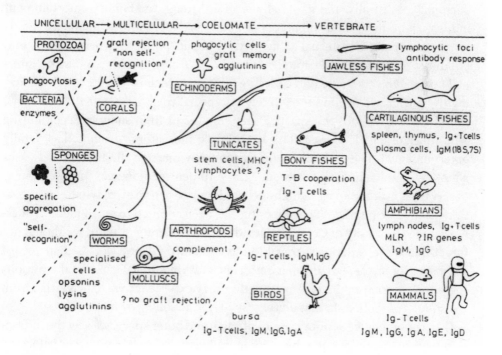

Figure 23.11. "Evolution of recognition systems," from a recent immunology textbook.

their advance on the body as a productive force. *National Geographic* explicitly punned on Star Wars in its graphic called "Cell Wars."[68] The militarized, automated factory is a favorite convention among immune system technical illustrators and photographic processors. The specific historical markings of a Star Wars–maintained individuality are enabled by high-technology visualization technologies, which are also basic to conducting war and commerce, such as computer-aided graphics, artificial intelligence software, and specialized scanning systems.

It is not just imagers of the immune system who learn from military cultures; military cultures draw symbiotically on immune system discourse, just as strategic planners draw directly from and contribute to video game practices and science fiction. For example, arguing for an elite special force within the parameters of "low-intensity conflict" doctrine, a U.S. army officer wrote, "The most appropriate example to describe how this system would work is the most complex biological model we know—the body's immune system. Within the body there exists a remarkably complex corps of internal bodyguards. In absolute numbers they are small—only about one percent of the body's cells. Yet they consist of reconnaissance specialists, killers, reconstitution specialists, and communicators that can seek out invaders, sound the alarm, reproduce rapidly, and swarm to the attack to repel the enemy. . . . In this regard, the June 1986 issue of *National Geographic* contains a detailed account of how the body's immune system functions."[69]

The circuits of competencies sustaining the body as a defended self— personally, culturally, and nationally—spiral through the fantasy entertainment industry, a branch of the apparatus of bodily production fundamental to crafting the important consensual hallucinations about "possible" worlds that go into building "real" ones. In Epcot Center of Walt Disney World, we may be interpellated as subjects in the new Met Life Pavilion, which is "devoted to dramatizing the intricacies of the human body." A special thrill ride, called Body Wars, promises that we will "experience the wonders of life," such as encountering "the attack of the platelets."[70] This lively battle simulator is promoted as "family entertainment." The technology for this journey through the human body uses a motion-based simulator to produce three-dimensional images for a stationary observer. As in other forms of high-tech tourism, we can go everywhere, see everything, and leave no trace. The apparatus has been adopted to teach medical anatomy at the University of Colorado Health Sciences Center. Finally, we should not forget that more Americans travel to the combined Disney worlds than voyage in most other myth-realizing machines, like Washington, D.C.[71] Met Life cautions those who journey on Body Wars that they may experience extreme vertigo from the simulated motion. Is that merely "symbolic action" too?

In the embodied semiotic zones of earth and outer space, we saw the diffraction patterns made possible by recomposed visualizing technologies, relocated circuits of competencies that promise to be more user-friendly for inappropriate/d others. So also, the inner spaces of the biomedical body are central zones of tech-noscientific contestation, i.e., of science as culture in the amodern frame of social nature. Extremely interesting new collectives of human and unhuman allies and actors are emerging from these processes. I will briefly sketch two zones where promising monsters are undergoing symbiogenesis in the nutrient media of tech-noscientific work: (1) theories of immune function based on laboratory research and (2) new apparatuses of knowledge production being crafted by Persons with AIDS (PWAs) and their heterogeneous allies. Both sets of monsters generate distinctly diffracted views of the self, evident in beliefs and practices in relation to vulnerability and mortality.

Like nonviolent direct action and environmentalism, immune system discourse is about the unequally distributed chances of life and death. Since sickness and mortality are at the heart of immunology, it is hardly surprising that conditions of battle prevail. Dying is not an easy matter crying out for "friendly" visualization. But battle is not the only way to figure the process of mortal living. Persons coping with the life-threatening consequences of infection with HIV have insisted that they are *living* with AIDS, rather than accepting the status of *victims* (or prisoners of war?). Similarly, laboratory scientists also have built research programs based on nonmilitaristic, relational embodiments rather than on the capabilities of the defended self of atomic individuals. They do this in order to construct IS articulations more effectively, not in order to be nice folks with pacifist metaphors.

Let me attempt to convey the flavor of the artifactual bodily object called the human immune system, culled from major textbooks and research reports published in the 1980s. These characterizations are part of working systems for interacting with the immune system in many areas of practice, including business decisions, clinical medicine, and lab experiments. With about ten to the twelfth cells, the IS has two orders of magnitude more cells than the nervous system. IS cells are regenerated throughout life from pluripotent stem cells. From embryonic life through adulthood, the immune system is sited in several morphologically dispersed tissues and organs, including the thymus, bone marrow, spleen, and lymph nodes; but a large fraction of its cells are in the blood and lymph circulatory systems and in body fluids and spaces. If ever there were a "distributed system," this is one! It is also a highly adaptable communication system with many interfaces.

There are two major cell lineages to the system. (1) The first comprises the *lymphocytes,* which include the several types of T cells (helper, suppressor, killer, and variations of all these) and the B cells (each type of which can produce only one sort of the vast array of potential circulating antibodies). T and B cells have particular specificities capable of recognizing almost any molecular array of the right size that can ever exist, no matter how clever industrial chemistry gets. This specificity is enabled by a baroque somatic mutation mechanism, clonal selection, and a polygenic receptor or marker system. (2) The second immune cell lineage is the *mononuclear phagocyte system*, including the multitalented macrophages, which, in addition to their other recognition skills and connections, also appear to share receptors and some hormonal peptide products with neural cells. Besides the cellular compartment, the immune system comprises a vast array of circulating acellular products, such as antibodies, lymphokines, and complement components. These molecules mediate communication among components of the immune system but also between the immune system and the nervous and endocrine systems, thus linking the body's multiple control and coordination sites and functions. The genetics of the immune system cells, with their high rates of somatic mutation and gene product splicings and rearrangings to make finished surface receptors and antibodies, makes a mockery of the notion of a constant genome even within "one" body. The hierarchical body of old has given way to a network body of amazing complexity and specificity. The immune system is everywhere and nowhere. Its specificities are indefinite if not infinite, and they arise randomly; yet these extraordinary variations are the critical means of maintaining bodily coherence.

In the early 1970s, winning a Nobel Prize for the work, Niels Jerne proposed a theory of immune system self-regulation, called the network theory, which deviates radically from notions of the body victorious and the defended self. "The network theory differs from other immunological thinking because it endows the immune system with the ability to regulate itself using only itself."[72] Jerne proposed that any antibody molecule must be able to act functionally as both antibody to some antigen *and* as antigen for the production of an antibody to itself, at another region of "itself." These sites have acquired a nomenclature sufficiently daunting to thwart popular understanding of the theory, but the basic conception is simple. The concatenation of internal recognitions and responses would go on indefinitely, in a series of interior mirrorings of sites on immunoglobulin molecules, such that the immune system would always be in a state of dynamic internal responding. It would never be passive, "at rest," awaiting an activating stimulus from a hostile outside. In a sense, there could be no *exterior* antigenic structure, no "invader," that the immune system had not already "seen" and mirrored internally. Replaced by subtle plays of partially mirrored readings and responses, self and other lose their rationalistic oppositional quality. A radical conception of *connection* emerges unexpectedly at the core of the defended self. Nothing in the model prevents therapeutic action, but the entities in the drama have different kinds of interfaces with the world. The therapeutic logics are unlikely to be etched into living flesh in patterns of DARPA's latest high-tech tanks and smart missiles.

Some of those logics are being worked out in and by the bodies of persons with AIDS and ARC. In their work to sustain life and alleviate pain in the context of mortal illness, PWAs engage in many processes of knowledge building.

These processes demand intricate code switching, language bridging, and alliances among worlds previously held apart. These "generative grammars" are matters of life and death. As one activist put it, "ACT UP's humor is no joke."[73] The AIDS Coalition to Unleash Power (ACT UP) is a collective built from many articulations among unlike kinds of actors—for example, activists, biomedical machines, government bureaucracies, gay and lesbian worlds, communities of color, scientific conferences, experimental organisms, mayors, international information and action networks, condoms and dental dams, computers, doctors, IV drug users, pharmaceutical companies, publishers, virus components, counselors, innovative sexual practices, dancers, media technologies, buying clubs, graphic artists, scientists, lovers, lawyers, and more. The actors, however, are not all equal. ACT UP has an animating center—PWAs, who are to the damage wrought by AIDS and the work for restored health around the world as the indigenous peoples of the Amazon are to forest destruction and environmentalism. These are the actors with whom others must articulate. That structure of action is a fundamental consequence of learning to visualize the heterogeneous, artifactual body that is our "social nature," instead of narrowing our vision that "saving nature" and repelling alien invaders from an unspoiled organic Eden called the autonomous self. Saving nature is, finally, a deadly project. It relies on perpetuating the structure of boundary violation and the falsely liberating *frisson* of transgression. What happened in the first Eden should have made that clear.

So, if the tree of knowledge cannot be forbidden, we had all better learn how to eat and feed each other with a little more savvy. That is the difficult process being engaged by PWAs, Project Inform, ACT UP, NIH, clinical practitioners, and many more actors trying to build responsible mechanisms for producing effective knowledge in the AIDS epidemic.[74] Unable to police the same boundaries separating insiders and outsiders, the world of biomedical research will never be the same again. The changes range across the epistemological, the commercial, the juridical, and the spiritual domains. For example, what is the status of knowledge produced through the new combinations of decision-making in experimental design that are challenging previous research conventions? What are the consequences of the *simultaneous* challenges to expert monopoly of knowledge *and* insistence on both the rapid improvement of the biomedical knowledge base and the equitable mass distribution of its fruits? How will the patently amodern hybrids of healing practices cohabit in the emerging social body? And who will live and die as a result of these very noninnocent practices?

Not-A. Virtual Space: SF[75]

Articulation is not a simple matter. Language is the effect of articulation, and so are bodies. The articulata are jointed animals; they are not smooth like the perfect spherical animals of Plato's origin fantasy in the *Timaeus*. The articulata are cobbled together. It is the condition of being articulate. I rely on the articulata to breathe life into the artifactual cosmos of monsters that this essay inhabits. Nature may be speechless, without language, in the human sense; but nature is highly articulate. Discourse is only one process of articulation. An articulated world has an undecidable number of modes and sites where connections can be made. The surfaces of this kind of world are not frictionless curved planes. Unlike things can be joined—and like things can be broken apart—and vice versa. Full of sensory hairs, evaginations, invaginations, and indentations, the surfaces that interest me are dissected by joints. Segmented invertebrates, the articulata are insectoid and wormlike, and they inform the inflamed imaginations of SF filmmakers and biologists. In obsolete English, to articulate meant to make terms of agreement. Perhaps we should live in such an "obsolete," amodern world again. To articulate is to signify. It is to put things together: scary things, risky things, contingent things. I want to live in an articulate world. We articulate; therefore, we are. Who "I" am is very limited, in the endless perfection of (clear and distinct) Self-contemplation. Unfair as always, I think of it as the paradigmatic psycho-analytic question. "Who am I?" is about (always unrealizable) identity; always wobbling, it still pivots on the law of the father, the sacred image of the same. Since I am a moralist, the real question must have more virtue: who are "we"? That is an inherently more open question, one always ready for contingent, friction-generating articulations. It is a remonstrative question.

In optics, the virtual image is formed by the apparent, but not actual, convergence of rays. The virtual seems to be the counterfeit of the real; the virtual has effects by seeming, not being. Perhaps that is why "virtue" is still given in dictionaries to refer to women's chastity, which must always remain doubtful in patriarchal optical law. But then, "virtue" used to mean manly spirit and valor too, and God even named an order of angels the Virtues, though they were of only middling rank. Still, no matter how big the effects of the virtual are, they seem somehow to lack a proper ontology. Angels, manly valor, and women's chastity certainly constitute, at best, a virtual image from the point of view of late twentieth-century "postmoderns." For them, the virtual is precisely *not* the real; that's why "postmoderns" *like* "virtual reality." It seems transgressive. Yet, I can't forget that an obsolete meaning of "virtual" was having virtue, i.e., the inherent power to produce effects. "Virtue," after all, is excellence or merit, and it is still a common meaning of virtue to refer to having efficacy. The "virtue" of something is its "capacity." The virtue of (some) food is that it nourishes the body. Virtual space *seems* to be the negation of real space; the domains of SF *seem* the negation of earthly regions. But perhaps this negation is the real illusion.

"Cyberspace, absent its high-tech glitz, is the idea of virtual consensual community. . . . A virtual community is first and foremost a community of belief."[76]

For William Gibson, cyberspace is "consensual hallucination experienced daily by billions . . . unthinkable complexity."[77] Cyberspace seems to be the consensual hallucination of too much complexity, too much articulation. It is the virtual reality of paranoia, a well-populated region in the last quarter of the Second Christian Millennium. Paranoia is the belief in the unrelieved density of connection, requiring, if one is to survive, withdrawal and defense unto death. The defended self reemerges at the heart of relationality. Paradoxically, paranoia is the condition of the impossibility of remaining articulate. In virtual space, the virtue of articulation—i.e., the power to produce connection—threatens to overwhelm and finally to engulf all possibility of effective action to change the world.

So, in our travels into virtual space, if we are to emerge from our encounter with the artifactual articulata into a livable elsewhere, we need a guide figure to navigate around the slough of despond. Lisa Foo, the principal character in a Hugo and Nebula award-winning short story by John Varley, will be our unlikely Beatrice through the System.

"If you wish to know more, press enter."[78]

With that fatal invitation, Varley's profoundly paranoid story begins and ends. The Tree of Knowledge is a Web, a vast system of computer connections generating, as an emergent property, a new and terrifyingly unhuman collective entity. The forbidden fruit is knowledge of the workings of this powerful Entity, whose deadly essence is extravagant connection. All of the human characters are named after computers, programs, practices, or concepts—Victor Apfel, Detective Osborne, and the hackers Lisa Foo and Charles Kluge. The story is a murder mystery. With a dubious suicide note, called up by responding to the command "press enter" on the screen of one of the dozens of personal computers in his house, which is also full of barrels of illicit drugs, Kluge has been found dead by his neighbor, Apfel. Apfel is a reclusive middle-aged epileptic who had been a badly treated prisoner of war in Korea, leaving him with layers of psychological terror, including a fear and hatred of "orientals." When Los Angeles homicide Detective Osborne's men prove totally inept at deciphering the elaborate software running Kluge's machines, Lisa Foo, a young Vietnamese immigrant, now a U.S. citizen, is called in from Cal Tech, and she proceeds to play Sherlock Holmes to Osborne's Lestrade. The story is narrated from Apfel's point of view, but Foo is the tale's center and, I insist, its pivotal actor.

Insisting, I wish to exercise the license that is built into the anti-elitist reading conventions of SF popular cultures. SF conventions invite—or at least permit more readily than do the academically propagated, respectful consumption protocols for literature—rewriting as one reads. The books are cheap; they don't stay in print long; why not rewrite them as one goes? Most of the SF I like motivates me to engage actively with images, plots, figures, devices, linguistic moves, in short, with worlds, not so much to make them come out "right," as to make them move "differently." These worlds motivate me to test their virtue, to see if their artic-ulations work—and what they work for. Because SF makes identification with a principal character, comfort within the patently constructed world, or a relaxed attitude toward language, especially risky reading strategies, the reader is likely to be more generous and more suspicious—*both* generous and suspicious, exactly the receptive posture I seek in political semiosis generally. It is a strategy closely aligned with the oppositional and differential consciousness theorized by Chela Sandoval and by other feminists insistent on navigating mined discursive waters.

Our first view of Lisa Foo is through Apfel's eyes; and for him, "leaving out only the moustache, she was a dead ringer for a cartoon Tojo. She had the glasses, ears, and the teeth. But her teeth had braces, like piano keys wrapped in barbed wire. And she was five-eight or five-nine and couldn't have weighed more than a hundred and ten. I'd have said a hundred, but added five pounds for each of her breasts, so improbably large on her scrawny frame that all I could read of the message on her T-shirt was 'POCK LIVE.' It was only when she turned sideways that I saw the esses before and after."[79] Using such messages among the many other languages accessed by this intensely literate figure, Foo communicated constantly through her endless supply of T-shirts. Her breasts turned out to be silicone implants, and as Foo said, "I don't think I've ever been so happy with anything I ever bought. Not even the car [her Ferrari]."[80] From Foo's childhood perspective, "the West . . . [is] the place where you buy tits."[81]

When Foo and Apfel became lovers, in one of the most sensitively struc-tured heterosexual, cross-racial relationships in print anywhere, we also learn that Foo's body was multiply composed by the history of Southeast Asia. Varley gave her a name that is an "orientalized" version of the computer term "fu bar"—"fucked up beyond all recognition." Her Chinese grandmother had been raped in Hanoi by an occupying Japanese soldier in 1942. In Foo's mother's Vietnam, "being Chinese was bad enough, but being half Chinese and half Japanese was worse. . . . My father was half French and half Annamese. Another bad combina-tion."[82] Her mother was killed in the Tet Offensive when Foo was ten. The girl became a street hustler and child prostitute in Saigon, where she was "protected" by a pedophilic white U.S. major. Refusing to leave Saigon with him, after Saigon "fell," Foo ended up in Pol Pot's Cambodia, where she barely survived the Khmer Rouge work camps. She escaped to Thailand, and "when I finally got the Ameri-cans to notice me, my Major was still looking for me."[83] Dying of a cancer that might have been the result of his witnessing the atom bomb tests in Nevada early in his career, he sponsored her to the United States. Her intelligence and hustling got her "tits by Goodyear,"[84] a Ferrari, and a Cal Tech education. Foo and Apfel struggle together within their respective legacies of multiple abuse, sexual and otherwise, and crisscrossing racisms. They are both multitalented, but scarred, survivors. This story, its core figure and its narrator, will not let us dodge the scary issues of race/racism, gender/sexism, historical tragedy, and technoscience within the region of time we politely call "the late twentieth century." There is no safe place here; there are, however, many maps of possibility.

But, there is entirely *too much* connection in "Press Enter," and it is only the beginning. Foo is deeply in love with the power-knowledge systems to which her skills give her access. "This is money, Yank, she said, and her eyes glittered."[85] As she traces the fascinating webs and security locks, which began in military computer projects but which have taken on a vastly unhuman life of their own, her love and her skills bring her too deep into the infinitely dense connections of the System, where she, like Kluge before her, is noticed. Too late, she tries to withdraw. Soon after, a clearly fake suicide note appears on her T-shirt on her ruined body. Investigation showed that she had rewired the microwave oven in Kluge's house to circumvent its security checks. She put her head in the oven, and she died shortly after in the hospital, her eyes and brain congealed and her breasts horribly melted. The promise of her name, "fu bar," was all-too-literally fulfilled—fucked up beyond all recognition. Apfel, who had been brought back into articulation with life in his love with Lisa Foo, retreated totally, stripping his house of all its wiring and any other means of connecting with the techno-webs of a world he now saw totally within the paranoid terms of infinite and alien connection. At the end, the defended self, alone, permanently hides from the alien Other.

It is possible to read "Press Enter" as a conventional heterosexual romance, bourgeois detective fiction, technophobic-technophilic fantasy, dragon-lady story, and, finally, white masculinist narrative whose condition of possibility is access to the body and mind of a woman, especially a "Third World" woman, who, here as elsewhere in misogynist and racist culture, is violently destroyed. Not just violently—superabundantly, without limit. I think such a reading does serious violence to the subtle tissues of the story's writing. Nonetheless, "Press Enter" induces in me, and in other women and men who have read the story with me, an irreconcilable pain and anger: Lisa Foo should not have been killed that way. It really is not all right. The text and the body lose all distinction. I fall out of the semiotic square and into the viciously circular thing-in-itself. More than anything else, that pornographic, gendered and colored death, that excessive destruction of her body, that total undoing of her being—that extravagant final connection—surpasses the limits of pleasure in the conventions of paranoid fiction and provokes the necessity of active rewriting as reading. I cannot read this story without rewriting it; that is one of the lessons of transnational, intercultural, feminist literacy. And the conclusion forces rewriting not just of itself, but of the whole human and unhuman collective that is Lisa Foo. The point of the differential/oppositional rewriting is not to make the story come out "right," whatever that would be. The point is to rearticulate the figure of Lisa Foo to unsettle the closed logics of a deadly racist misogyny. Articulation must remain open, its densities accessible to action and intervention. When the system of connections closes in on itself, when symbolic action becomes perfect, the world is frozen in a dance of death. The cosmos is finished, and it is One. Paranoia is the only possible posture; generous suspicion is foreclosed. To "press enter" is, in that world, a terrible mistake.

The whole argument of "The Promises of Monsters" has been that to "press enter" is not a fatal error but an inescapable possibility for changing maps of the world, for building new collectives out of what is not quite a plethora of human and unhuman actors. My stakes in the textual figure of Lisa Foo, and of many of the actors in Varley's SF, are high. Built from multiple interfaces, Foo can be a guide through the terrains of virtual space, but only if the fine lines of tension in the articulated webs that constitute her being remain in play, open to the unexpected realization of an unlikely hope. It's not a "happy ending" we need but a non-ending. That's why none of the narratives of masculinist, patriarchal apocalypses will do. The System is not closed; the sacred image of the same is not coming. The world is not full. The final image of this excessive essay is *Cyborg*, a 1989 painting by Lynn Randolph in which the boundaries of a fatally transgressive world, ruled by the Subject and the Object, give way to the borderlands, inhabited by human and unhuman collectives (Figure 23.12).[86] These borderlands suggest a rich topography of combinatorial possibility. That possibility is called the Earth, here, now, this elsewhere, where real, outer, inner, and virtual space implode. The painting maps the articulations among cosmos, animal, human, machine, and landscape in their recursive sidereal, bony, electronic, and geological skeletons. Their combinatorial logic is embodied; theory is corporeal; social nature is articulate. The stylized DIP switches of the integrated circuit board on the human figure's chest are devices that set the defaults in a form intermediate between hardwiring and software control—not unlike the mediating structural-functional anatomy of the feline and hominid forelimbs, especially the flexible, homologous hands and paws. The painting is replete with organs of touch and mediation, as well as with organs of vision. Direct in their gaze at the viewer, the eyes of the woman and the cat center the whole composition. The spiraling skeleton of the Milky Way, our galaxy, appears behind the cyborg figure in three different graphic displays made possible by high-technology visualizing apparatuses. In the place of virtual space in my semiotic square, the fourth square is an imaging of the gravity well of a black hole. Notice the tic-tac-toe game, played with the European male and female astrological signs (Venus won this game); just to their right are some calculations that might appear in the mathematics of chaos. Both sets of symbols are just below a calculation found in the Einstein papers. The mathematics and games are like logical skeletons. The keyboard is jointed to the skeleton of the planet Earth, on which a pyramid rises in the left mid-foreground. The whole painting has the quality of a meditation device.

The large cat is like a spirit animal, a white tiger perhaps. The woman, a young Chinese student in the United States, figures that which is human, the universal, the generic. The "woman of color," a very particular, problematic, recent collective identity, resonates with local and global conversations.[87] In this painting, she embodies the still oxymoronic simultaneous statuses of woman, "Third World" person, human, organism, communications technology, mathematician, writer,

Figure 23.12. Lynn Randolph, *Cyborg* (1989).

worker, engineer, scientist, spiritual guide, lover of the Earth. This is the kind of "symbolic action" transnational feminisms have made legible. S/he is not finished.

We have come full circle in the noisy mechanism of the semiotic square, back to the beginning, where we met the commercial cyborg figures inhabiting technoscience worlds. Logic General's oddly recursive rabbits, forepaws on the keyboards that promise to mediate replication and communication, have given way to different circuits of competencies. If the cyborg has changed, so might the world. Randolph's cyborg is in conversation with Trinh Minh-ha's inappropriate/d other, the personal and collective being to whom history has forbidden the strategic illusion of self-identity. This cyborg does not have an Aristotelian structure; and there is no master–slave dialectic resolving the struggles of resource and product, passion and action. S/he is not utopian or imaginary; s/he is virtual. Generated, along with other cyborgs, by the collapse into each other of the technical, organic, mythic, textual, and political, s/he is constituted by articulations of critical differences within and without each figure. The painting might be headed "A few words about articulation from the actors in the field." Privileging the hues of red, green, and ultraviolet, I want to read Randolph's *Cyborg* within a rainbow political semiology, for wily transnational technoscience studies as cultural studies.

Notes

1. William Plank, "Ape and *Ecriture*: The Chimpanzee as Post-Structuralist," paper presented at the meetings of the Society for Literature and Science, Ann Arbor, Mich., September 21–24, 1989.

2. "They drew near to a very Miry Slough. . . . The name of this Slow was Dispond." John Bunyan, *Pilgrim's Progress*, 1678, quoted in the *Oxford English Dictionary*. The nonstandardization of spelling here should also mark, at the beginning of the "Promises of Monsters," the suggestiveness of words at the edge of the regulatory technologies of writing.

3. Sally Hacker, in a paper written just before her death ("The Eye of the Beholder: An Essay on Technology and Eroticism," manuscript, 1989), suggested the term *pornotechnics* to refer to the embodiment of perverse power relations in the artifactual body. Hacker insisted that the heart of pornotechnics is the military as an institution, with its deep roots and wide reach into science, technology, and erotics. "Technical exhilaration" is profoundly erotic; joining sex and power is the designer's touch. Technics and erotics are the crosshairs in the focusing device for scanning fields of skill and desire. See also Sally Hacker, *Pleasure, Power, and Technology: Some Tales of Gender, Engineering, and the Cooperative Workplace* (Boston: Unwin Hyman, 1989). Drawing from Hacker's arguments, I believe that control over technics is the enabling practice for class, gender, and race supremacy. Realigning the join of technics and erotics must be at the heart of anti-racist feminist practice. See Donna Haraway, "Technics, Erotics, Vision, Touch: Fantasies of the Designer Body," talk presented at the meetings of the Society for the History of Technology,

October 13, 1989; see also Carol Cohn, "Sex and Death in the Rational World of Defense Intellectuals," *Signs* 12, no. 4 (1987): 687–718.

4. See the provocative publication that replaced *Radical Science Journal, Science as Culture,* Free Association Books, 26 Freegrove Rd., London N7 9RQ, England.

5. This incubation of ourselves as planetary fetuses is not quite the same thing as pregnancy and reproductive politics in post-industrial, post-modern, or other posted locations, but the similarities will become more evident as this essay proceeds. The struggles over the outcomes are linked.

6. Here I borrow from the wonderful project of the journal *Public Culture,* now published by Duke University Press. In my opinion, this journal embodies the best impulses of cultural studies.

7. I demure on the label "postmodern" because I am persuaded by Bruno Latour that within the historical domains where science has been constructed, the "modern" never existed, if by modern we mean the rational, enlightened mentality (the subject, mind, etc.) actually proceeding with an objective method toward adequate representations, in mathematical equations if possible, of the object—i.e., "natural"—world. Latour argues that Kant's *Critique,* which set off at extreme poles Things-in-Themselves from the Transcendental Ego, is what made us believe ourselves to be "modern," with escalating and dire consequences for the repertoire of explanatory possibilities of "nature" and "society" for Western scholars. The separation of the two transcendences, the object pole and subject pole, structures "'the political Constitution of Truth.' I call it 'modern,' defining modernity as the complete separation of the representation of things—science and technology—from the representation of humans—politics and justice." See Bruno Latour, "One More Turn after the Social Turn . . . Easing Science Studies into the Non-Modern World," in *The Social Dimension of Science,* ed. Ernan McMullin, 272–92 (South Bend, Ind.: Notre Dame University Press, 1992).

Debilitating though such a picture of scientific activity should seem, it has guided research in the disciplines (history, philosophy, sociology, anthropology), studying science with a pedagogical and prophylactic vengeance, making culture seem other to science; science alone could get the goods on nature by unveiling and policing her unruly embodiments. Thus, science studies, focused on the edifying object of "modern" scientific practice, has seemed immune from the polluting infections of cultural studies—but surely no more. To rebel against or to lose faith in rationalism and enlightenment, the infidel state of respectively modernists and postmodernists, is not the same thing as to show that rationalism was the emperor that had no clothes, that never was, and so there never was its other either. (There is a nearly inevitable terminological confusion here among *modernity,* the *modern,* and *modernism.* I use *modernism* to refer to a cultural movement that rebelled against the premises of modernity, while *postmodernism* refers less to rebellion than loss of faith, leaving nothing to rebel against.) Latour calls his position *a*modern and argues that scientific practice is and has been amodern, a sighting that makes the line between real scientific (West's) and ethnoscience and other cultural expressions (everything else) disappear. The difference reappears, but with a significantly different geometry—that of scales and volumes, i.e., the size differences among "collective" entities made of humans and nonhumans—rather than in terms of a line between rational science and ethnoscience.

This modest turn or tropic change does not remove the study of scientific practice from the agenda of cultural studies and political intervention but places it decisively on the list. Best of all, the focus gets fixed clearly on inequality, right where it belongs in science studies. Further, the addition of science to cultural studies does not leave the notions of culture, society, and politics untouched, far from it. In particular, we cannot make a critique of science and its constructions of nature based on an ongoing belief in culture or society. In the form of social constructionism, that belief has grounded the major strategy of left, feminist, and anti-racist science radicals. To remain with that strategy, however, is to remain bedazzled by the ideology of enlightenment. It will not do to approach science as cultural or social construction, as if culture and society were transcendent categories, any more than nature or the object is. Outside the premises of enlightenment—i.e., of the modern—the binary pairs of culture and nature, science and society, the technical and the social all lose their co-constitutive, oppositional quality. Neither can explain the other. "But instead of providing the explanation, Nature and Society are now accounted for as the historical consequences of the movement of collective things. All the interesting realities are no longer captured by the two extremes but are to be found in the substitution, cross over, translations, through which actants shift their competences." Bruno Latour, "Postmodern? No, Simply Amodern! Steps towards an Anthropology of Science," *Studies in the History and Philosophy of Science* 21, no. 1 (1990): 170. When the pieties of belief in the modern are dismissed, both members of the binary pairs collapse into each other as into a black hole. But what happens to them in the black hole is, by definition, not visible from the shared terrain of modernity, modernism, or postmodernism. It will take a super-luminal SF journey into elsewhere to find the interesting new vantage points. Where Latour and I fundamentally agree is that in that gravity well, into which Nature and Society as transcendentals disappeared, are to be found actors/actants of many and wonderful kinds. Their relationships constitute the artifactualism I am trying to sketch.

8. See N. Katherine Hayles, *Chaos Bound: Orderly Disorder in Contemporary Literature and Science* (Ithaca, N.Y.: Cornell University Press, 1990).

9. For quite another view of "production" and "reproduction" than that enshrined in so much Western political and economic (and feminist) theory, see Marilyn Strathern, *The Gender of the Gift* (Berkeley: University of California Press, 1988), 290–308.

10. Chela Sandoval develops the distinctions between oppositional and differential consciousness in her doctoral dissertation. See Sandoval, "Oppositional Consciousness in the Postmodern World: United States Third World Feminism, Semiotics, and the Methodology of the Oppressed" (PhD diss., University of California, Santa Cruz, 1993). See also Sandoval, "Feminism and Racism," in *Making Face, Making Soul: Haciendo Caras,* ed. Gloria Anzaldúa, 55–71 (San Francisco: Aunt Lute, 1990).

11. My debt is extensive in these paragraphs to Luce Irigaray's wonderful critique of the allegory of the cave in *Spœculum de l'autre femme* (Paris: Minuit, 1974), translated by G. Gill as *Speculum of the Other Woman* (Ithaca, N.Y.: Cornell University Press, 1985). Unfortunately, Irigaray, like almost all white Europeans and Americans after the mid-nineteenth-century consolidation of the myth that the "West" originated in a classical Greece unsullied by Semitic and African roots, transplants, colonizations, and loans, never questioned the "original" status of Plato's fathership of philosophy, enlightenment, and

rationality. If Europe were colonized first by Africans, that historical narrative element would change the story of the birth of Western philosophy and science. Martin Bernal's extraordinarily important book *Black Athena,* Vol. 1, *The Fabrication of Ancient Greece, 1785–1985* (London: Free Association Books, 1987), initiates a groundbreaking reevaluation of the founding premises of the myth of the uniquenes and self-generation of Western culture, most certainly including those pinnacles of Man's self-birthing, science and philosophy. Bernal's is an account of the determinative role of racism and Romanticism in the fabrication of the story of Western rationality. Perhaps ironically, Martin Bernal is the son of J. D. Bernal, the major pre–World War II British biochemist and Marxist whose four-volume *Science in History* movingly argued the superior rationality of a science freed from the chains of capitalism. Science, freedom, and socialism were to be, finally, the legacy of the West. For all its warts, that surely would have been better than Reagan's and Thatcher's version! See Gary Wersky, *The Invisible College: The Collective Biography of British Socialist Scientists in the 1930s* (London: Allen Lane, 1978).

Famous in his own generation for his passionate heterosexual affairs, J. D. Bernal, in the image of enlightenment second birthing so wryly exposed by Irigaray, wrote his own vision of the future in *The Word, the Flesh, and the Devil* as a science-based speculation that had human beings evolving into disembodied intelligences. See John Desmond Bernal, *The World, the Flesh, and the Devil: An Enquiry into the Future of the Three Enemies of the Rational Soul* (1929; repr., New York: Verso, 2018). In her unpublished manuscript "Talking about Science in Three Colors: Bernal and Gender Politics in the Social Studies of Science" (May 1990), Hilary Rose discusses this fantasy and its importance for "science, politics, and silences." J. D. Bernal was also actively supportive of independent women scientists. Rosalind Franklin moved to his laboratory after her nucleic acid crystallographic work was stolen by the flamboyantly sexist and heroic James Watson on his way to the immortalizing, luminous fame of the *Double Helix* of the 1950s and 1960s and its replicant of the 1980s and 1990s, the Human Genome Project. The *story* of DNA has been an archetypical tale of blinding modern enlightenment and untrammeled, disembodied, autochthonous origins. See Ann Sayre, *Rosalind Franklin and DNA* (New York: W. W. Norton, 1975); Mary Jacobus, "Is There a Woman in This Text?," *New Literary History* 14 (1982): 117–41; and Evelyn Fox Keller, "From Secrets of Life to Secrets of Death," in *Body/Politics: Women and the Discourse of Science,* ed. Mary Jacobus, Evelyn Fox Keller, and Sally Shuttleworth (New York: Routledge, 1990), 171–91.

12. For an argument that nature is a *social* actor, see Elizabeth Bird, "The Social Construction of Nature: Theoretical Approaches to the History of Environmental Problems," *Environmental Review* 11, no. 4 (1987): 255–64.

13. Actants are not the same as actors. As Terence Hawkes put it in his introduction to Greimas, actants operate at the level of function, not of character. See Terence Hawkes, *Structuralism and Semiotics* (Berkeley: University of California Press, 1977), 89. Several characters in a narrative may make up a single actant. The structure of the narrative generates its actants. In considering what kind of entity "nature" might be, I am looking for a coyote and historical grammar of the world, where deep structure can be quite a surprise, indeed, a veritable trickster. Nonhumans are not necessarily "actors" in the human sense, but they are part of the functional collective that makes up an actant. Action is not so

much an ontological as a semiotic problem. This is perhaps as true for humans as non-humans, a way of looking at things that may provide exits from the methodological individualism inherent in concentrating constantly on who the agents and actors are in the sense of liberal theories of agency.

14. In this productionist story, women make babies, but this is a poor if necessary substitute for the real action in reproduction—the second birth through self-birthing, which requires the obstetrical technology of optics. One's relation to the phallus determines whether one gives birth to oneself, at quite a price, or serves, at an even greater price, as the conduit or passage for those who will enter the light of self-birthing. For a refreshing demonstration that women do not make babies everywhere, see Strathern, *Gender of the Gift,* 314–18.

15. I borrow here from Katie King's notion of the apparatus of literary production, in which the poem congeals at the intersection of business, art, and technology. See King, "A Feminist Apparatus of Literary Production," *Text* (1990): 91–103. See also Donna Haraway, *Simians, Cyborgs, and Women: The Reinvention of Nature* (New York: Routledge, 1991), chapters 8–10.

16. Latour has developed the concept of delegation to refer to the translations and exchanges between and among people doing science and their machines, which act as "delegates" in a wide array of ways. Marx considered machines to be "dead labor," but that notion, while still necessary for some crucial aspects of forced and reified delegation, is too unlively to get at the many ways that machines are part of *social* relations "through which actants shift competences." See Latour, "Postmodern? No, Simply Amodern!," 170. See also Bruno Latour, "One More Turn after the Social Turn." Latour, however, as well as most of the established scholars in the social studies of science, ends up with too narrow a concept of the "collective," one built up out of only machines and scientists, who are considered in a very narrow time and space frame. But circulations of skills turn out to take some stranger turns. First, with the important exception of his writing and teaching in collaboration with the primatologist Shirley Strum, who has fought hard in her profession for recognition of primates as savvy social actors, Latour pays too little attention to the non-machine, *other* nonhumans in the interactions. See Strum, *Almost Home: A Journey into the World of Baboons* (New York: Random House, 1987).

The "collective," of which "nature" in any form is one example from my point of view, is always an artifact, always social, not because of some transcendental Social that explains science or vice versa, but because of its heterogeneous actants/actors. Not only are not all of those actors/actants people; I agree there *is* a sociology of machines. But that is not enough; not all of the other actors/actants were *built* by people. The artifactual "collective" includes a witty actor that I have sometimes called coyote. The interfaces that constitute the "collective" must include those between humans and artifacts in the form of instruments and machines, a genuinely *social* landscape. But the interface between machines and *other* nonhumans, as well as the interface between humans and *nonmachine* nonhumans, must also be counted in. Animals are fairly obvious actors, and their interfaces with people and machines are easier to admit and theorize. See Donna Haraway, *Primate Visions: Gender, Race, and Nature in the World of Modern Science* (New York: Routledge, 1989), and Barbara Noske, *Humans and Other Animals: Beyond the Boundaries of Anthropology* (London: Pluto Press, 1989). Paradoxically, from the perspective of the kind of artifactualism I am trying to sketch, animals lose their *object* status that has reduced them to things in so much Western philosophy and practice. They inhabit neither nature (as object) nor culture (as surrogate human), but instead inhabit a place called elsewhere. In Noske's terms, they are other "worlds, whose otherworldliness must not be disenchanted and cut to our size but respected for what it is" (xi). Animals, however, do not exhaust the coyote world of nonmachine nonhumans. The domain of machine and nonmachine nonhumans (the unhuman, in my terminology) joins people in the building of the artifactual collective called nature. None of these actants can be considered as simply resource, ground, matrix, object, material, instrument, frozen labor; they are all more unsettling than that. Perhaps my suggestions here come down to reinventing an old option within a non-Eurocentric Western tradition indebted to Egyptian Hermeticism that insists on the active quality of the world and on "animate" matter. See Bernal, *Black Athena*, 121–60, and Frances Yates, *Giordano Bruno and the Hermetic Tradition* (London: Routledge, 1964). Worldly and enspirited, coyote nature is a collective, cosmopolitan artifact crafted in stories with heterogeneous actants.

But there is a second way in which Latour and other major figures in science studies work with an impoverished "collective." Correctly working to resist a "social" explanation of "technical" practice by exploding the binary, these scholars have a tendency covertly to reintroduce the binary by worshipping only one term—the "technical." Especially, *any* consideration of matters like masculine supremacy or racism or imperialism or class structures are inadmissible because they are the old "social" ghosts that blocked real explanation of science in action. See Latour, *Science in Action.* As Latour noted, Michael Lynch is the most radical proponent of the premise that there is no social explanation of a science but the technical content itself, which assuredly includes the interactions of people with each other in the lab and with their machines, but excludes a great deal that I would include in the "technical" content of science if one really doesn't want to evade a binary by worshipping one of its old poles. See Lynch, *Art and Artifact in Laboratory Science: A Study of Shop Work and Shop Talk in a Research Laboratory* (London: Routledge1985); see also Latour, "Postmodern? No, Simply Amodern!," 169. I agree with Latour and Lynch that practice creates its own context, but they draw a suspicious line around what gets to count as "practice." They *never* ask how the *practices* of masculine supremacy, or many other systems of structured inequality, get *built* into and out of working machines. How and in what directions these transferences of "competences" work should be a focus of rapt attention. Systems of exploitation might be crucial parts of the "technical content" of science. But the SSS scholars tend to dismiss such questions with the assertion that they lead to the bad old days when science was asserted by radicals simply to "reflect" social relations. But in my view, such transferences of competences, or delegations, have nothing to do with reflections or harmonies of social organization and cosmologies, like "modern science." Their unexamined, consistent, and defensive prejudice seems part of Latour's stunning misreading of several moves in Sharon Traweek's *Beam Times and Life Times: The World of High Energy Physicists* (Cambridge, Mass.: Harvard University Press, 1988). See Latour, "Postmodern? No, Simply Amodern!," 164–69. See also Hilary Rose, "Science in Three Colours: Bernal and Gender Politics in the Social Studies of Science," unpublished manuscript, May 2, 1990.

The same blind spot, a retinal lesion from the old phallogocentric heliotropism that Latour *did* know how to avoid in other contexts, for example, in his trenchant critique of the modern and postmodern, seems responsible for the abject failure of the social studies of science as an organized discourse to take account of the last twenty years of feminist inquiry. What counts as "technical" and what counts as "practice" should remain far from self-evident in science in action. For all of their extraordinary creativity, so far the mappings from most SSS scholars have stopped dead at the fearful seas where the worldly practices of inequality lap at the shores, infiltrate the estuaries, and set the parameters of reproduction of scientific practice, artifacts, and knowledge. If only it were a question of reflections between social relations and scientific constructions, how easy it would be to conduct "political" inquiry into science! Perhaps the tenacious prejudice of the SSS professionals is the punishment for the enlightenment transcendental, the social, that did inform the rationalism of earlier generations of radical science critique and is still all too common. May the topick gods save us from both the reified technical and the transcendental social!

17. See Teresa de Lauretis, *Alice Doesn't: Feminism, Semiotics, Cinema* (Bloomington: Indiana University Press, 1984).

18. See Zoe Sofia, "Exterminating Fetuses: Abortion, Disarmament, and the Sexo-Semiotics of Extraterrestrialism," *Diacritics* 14, no. 2 (1984): 47–59.

19. See Lynn Margulis and Dorion Sagan, *Origins of Sex: Three Billion Years of Genetic Recombination* (New Haven, Conn.: Yale University Press, 1986). This wonderful book does the cell biology and evolution for a host of inappropriate/d others. In its dedication, the text affirms "the combinations, sexual and parasexual, that bring us out of ourselves and make us more than we are alone" (v). That should be what science studies as cultural studies do, by showing how to visualize the curious collectives of humans and unhumans that make up naturalsocial (one word) life. To stress the point that all the actors in these generative, dispersed, and layered collectives do not have human form and function—and should not be anthropomorphized—recall that the Gaia hypothesis with which Margulis is associated is about the tissue of the planet as a living entity, whose metabolism and genetic exchange are effected through webs of prokaryotes. Gaia is a society; Gaia is nature; Gaia did not read the *Critique*. Neither, probably, did John Varley. See his Gaea hypothesis in the SF book *Titan* (New York: Berkeley Books, 1979). Titan is an alien that is a world.

20. Remember that *monsters* have the same root as *to demonstrate*; monsters signify.

21. See Trinh T. Minh-ha, ed., "She, the Inappropriate/d Other" (special issue), *Discourse* 8 (1986–87); see also her *Woman, Native, Other: Writing Postcoloniality and Feminism* (Bloomington: Indiana University Press, 1989).

22. Interpellate: I play on Althusser's account of the call which constitutes the production of the subject in ideology. Althusser is, of course, playing on Lacan, not to mention on God's interruption that calls Man, his servant, into being. Do we have a vocation to be cyborgs? Interpellate: *Interpellatus,* past participle for "interrupted in speaking"—effecting transformations like Saul into Paul. Interpellation is a special kind of interruption, to say

the least. Its key meaning concerns a procedure in a parliament for asking a speaker who is a member of the government to provide an explanation of an act or policy, usually leading to a vote of confidence. The following ads interrupt us. They insist on an explanation in a confidence game; they force recognition of how transfers of competences are made. A cyborg subject position results from and leads to interruption, diffraction, reinvention. It is dangerous and replete with the promises of monsters.

23. In *King Solomon's Ring,* trans. Marjorie Kerr Wilson (London: Methuen, 1961), Konrad Lorenz pointed out how the railroad car kept the appearance of the horse-drawn carriage, despite the different functional requirements and possibilities of the new technology. He meant to illustrate that biological evolution is similarly conservative, almost nostalgic for the old, familiar forms, which are reworked to new purposes. Gaia was the first serious bricoleuse.

24. For a view of the manufacture of particular organisms as flexible model systems for a universe of research practice, see Barbara R. Jasny and Daniel Koshland Jr., eds., *Biological Systems* (Washington, D.C.: AAAS Books, 1990). As the advertising for the book states, "the information presented will be especially useful to graduate students and to all researchers interested in learning the limitations and assets of biological systems currently in use." Advertisement in *Science* 248 (1990): 1024. Like all forms of protoplasm collected in the extra-laboratory world and brought into a technoscientific niche, the organic rabbit (not to mention the simulated one) and its tissues have a probable future of a particular sort—as a commodity. Who should "own" such evolutionary products? If seed protoplasm is collected in peasants' fields in Peru and then used to breed valuable commercial seed in a "First World" lab, does a peasant cooperative or the Peruvian state have a claim on the profits? A related problem about proprietary interest in "nature" besets the biotechnology industry's development of cell lines and other products derived from removed human tissue, e.g., as a result of cancer surgery. The California Supreme Court recently reassured the biotechnology industry that a patient whose cancerous spleen was the source of a product, Colony Stimulating Factor, that led to a patent that brought its scientist-developer stock in a company worth about $3 million did not have a right to a share of the bonanza. Property in the self, that lynchpin of liberal existence, does not seem to be the same thing as proprietary rights in one's body or its products—like fetuses or other cell lines in which the courts take a regulatory interest. See Marcia Barinaga, "A Muted Victory for the Biotech Industry," *Science* 249 (July 20, 1990): 239.

25. Here and throughout this essay, I play on Katie King's play on Jacques Derrida's *Of Grammatology.* See King, "A Feminist Apparatus of Literary Production." See also Katie King, *Theory in Its Feminist Travels: Conversations in U.S. Women's Movements* (Bloomington: Indiana University Press, 1995), where she develops her description, which is also a persuasive enabling construction, of a discursive field called "feminism and writing technologies."

26. See Bernal, *The World, the Flesh, and the Devil.*

27. Roland Barthes, *Mythologies,* trans. Annette Lavers (London: Cape, 1972), is my guide here and elsewhere.

28. Peace activist and scholar in science studies Elizabeth Bird came up with the slogan and put it on a political button in 1986 in Santa Cruz, California.

29. See A. J. Greimas, *Sémantique Structurale* (Paris: Larousse, 1966), and Fredric Jameson, *The Prison-House of Language* (Princeton, N.J.: Princeton University Press, 1972).

30. John Varley, "Press Enter," in *Blue Champagne* (New York: Berkeley Books, 1986).

31. I am indebted to another guide figure throughout this essay, Gloria Anzaldúa, *Borderlands, La Frontera: The New Mestiza* (San Francisco, Calif.: Spinsters/Aunt Lute, 1987), and to at least two other travelers in embodied virtual spaces: Ramona Fernandez, "Trickster Literacy: Multiculturalism and the (Re) Invention of Learning," Qualifying Essay, History of Consciousness, University of California, Santa Cruz, 1990, and Allucquére R. Stone, "Following Virtual Communities," unpublished essay, History of Consciousness, University of California, Santa Cruz. The ramifying "virtual consensual community" (Sandy Stone's term in another context) of feminist theory that incubates at UCSC densely infiltrates my writing.

32. For an extended reading of National Geographic's Jane Goodall stories, *always to be held in tension with other versions of Goodall and the chimpanzees at Gombe,* see Haraway, "Apes in Eden, Apes in Space," in *Primate Visions,* 133–95. Nothing in my analysis should be taken as grounds to oppose primate conservation or to make claims about the other Jane Goodalls; those are complex matters that deserve their own careful, materially specific consideration. My point is about the semiotic and political frames within which survival work might be approached by geopolitically differentiated actors.

33. My files are replete with recent images of cross-species ape–human family romance that fail to paper over the underlying racist iconography. The most viciously racist image was shown to me by Paula Treichler: an ad directed to physicians by the HMO, Premed, in Minneapolis, from the *American Medical News,* August 7, 1987. A white-coated white man, stethoscope around his neck, is putting a wedding ring on the hand of an ugly, very black, gorilla-suited female dressed in a white wedding gown. White clothing does not mean the same thing for the different races, species, and genders! The ad proclaims, "If you've made an unholy HMO alliance, perhaps we can help." The white male physician (man) tied to the black female patient (animal) in the inner cities by HMO marketing practices in relation to Medicaid policies must be freed. There is no woman in this ad; there is a hidden threat disguised as an ape female, dressed as the vampirish bride of scientific medicine (a single white tooth gleams menacingly against the black lips of the ugly bride)—another illustration, if we needed one, that black women do not have the *discursive* status of woman/human in white culture. "All across the country, physicians who once had visions of a beautiful marriage to an HMO have discovered the honeymoon is over. Instead of quality care and a fiscally sound patient-base, they end up accepting reduced fees and increased risks." The codes are transparent. Scientific medicine has been tricked into a union with vampirish poor black female patients. Which risks are borne by whom goes unexamined. The clasped hands in this ad carry a different surface message from the Gulf ad's, but their enabling semiotic structures share too much.

34. At the oral presentation of this essay at the conference on "Cultural Studies Now and in the Future," Gloria Watklins/bell hooks pointed out the painful current U.S. discourse on African American men as "an endangered species." Built into that awful metaphor is a relentless history of animalization and political infantilization. Like other "endangered species," such people cannot speak for themselves but must be spoken for. They must be

represented. Who speaks for the African American man as "an endangered species"? Note also how the metaphor applied to black *men* justifies antifeminist and misogynist rhetoric about and policy toward black women. They actually become one of the forces, if not the chief threat, endangering African American men.

35. Jane Goodall, *In the Shadow of Man* (Boston: Houghton Mifflin, 1971), 27.

36. Carl Zimmer, "Tech in the Jungle," *Discover,* August 1990, 42–45.

37. Susanna Hecht and Alexander Cockburn, *The Fate of the Forest: Developers, Destroyers, and the Defenders of the Amazon* (New York: Verso, 1989); see also T. Turner, "Visual Media, Cultural Politics, and Anthropological Practice: Some Implications of Recent Uses of Film and Video among the Kaiapo of Brazil," *Commission on Visual Anthropology Review,* Spring 1990. Committing only a neo-imperialist venial sin in a footnote, I yield to voyeuristic temptation just a little: in *Discover* the videocam and the "native" have a relation symmetrical to that of Goodall's and the chimpanzee's hands. Each photo represents a touch across time and space, and across politics and history, to tell a story of salvation, of saving man and nature. In this version of cyborg narrative, the touch that joins portable high technology and "primitive" human parallels the touch that joins animal and "civilized" human.

38. It is, however, important to note that the present man in charge of environmental affairs in the Amazon in the Brazilian government has taken strong, progressive stands on conservation, human rights, destruction of indigenous peoples, and the links of ecology and justice. Further, current proposals and policies, like the government's plan called Nossa Natureza and some international aid and conservations organizations' activities and ecologists' understandings, have much to recommend them. In addition, unless arrogance exceeds all bounds, *I* can hardly claim to adjudicate these complex matters. The point of my argument is not that whatever comes from Brasília or Washington is bad and whatever from the forest residents is good—a patently untrue position. Nor is it my point that nobody who doesn't come from a family that has lived in the forest for generations has any place in the "collectives, human and unhuman," crucial to the survival of lives and ways of life in Amazonia and elsewhere. Rather, the point is about the self-constitution of the indigenous peoples as *principal* actors and agents, with whom others must interact— in coalition and in conflict—not the reverse.

39. For the story of Mendes's life work and his murder by opponents of an extractive reserve off limits to logging, see Andrew Revkin, *The Burning Season* (New York: Houghton Mifflin, 1990).

40. Hecht and Cockburn, *Fate of the Forest,* 196.

41. Hecht and Cockburn, 202.

42. Hecht and Cockburn, 207.

43. Similar issues confront Amazonians in countries other than Brazil. For example, there are national parks in Colombia from which native peoples are banned from their historical territory but to which loggers and oil companies have access under park multiuse policy. This should sound very familiar to North Americans as well.

44. Revising and displacing his statements, I am again in conversation with Bruno Latour here, who has insisted on the social status of both human and nonhuman actors. "We use actor to mean anything that is made by some other actor the source of an action. It is in no

way limited to humans. It does not imply will, voice, self-consciousness or desire." Latour makes the crucial point that "figuring" (in words or in other matter) nonhuman actors as if they were like people is a semiotic operation; non-figural characterizations are quite possible. The likeness or unlikeness of actors is an interesting problem opened up by placing them firmly in the shared domain of social interaction. See Latour, "Where Are the Missing Masses? Sociology of a Few Mundane Artifacts," in *Shaping Technology/Building Society: Studies in Sociotechnical Change,* ed. Wiebe Bijker and John Law 225–59 (Cambridge, Mass.: MIT Press, 1992).

45. Joe Kane, *Running the Amazon* (New York: Knopf, 1989). Kane's review appeared in the *Voice Literary Supplement,* February 1990, and Hecht and Cockburn replied under the title "Getting Historical," *Voice Literary Supplement,* March 1990, 26.

46. My discussion of the politics of representation of the fetus depends on twenty years of feminist discourse about the location of responsibility in pregnancy and about reproductive freedom and constraint generally. For particularly crucial arguments for this essay, see Jennifer Terry, "The Body Invaded: Medical Surveillance of Women as Reproducers," *Socialist Review* 19, no. 3 (1989): 13–43; Valerie Hartouni, "Containing Women: Reproductive Discourse in the 1980s," in *Technoculture,* ed. Constance Penley and Andrew Ross (Minneapolis: University of Minnesota Press, 1991): 27–56; and Rosalind Pollock Petchesky, "Fetal Images: The Power of Visual Culture in the Politics of Reproduction," *Feminist Studies* 13, no. 2 (1987): 263–92.

47. *The Eighteenth Brumaire of Louis Bonaparte.* Quoted in Edward Said, *Orientalism* (New York: Random House, 1978), xiii, as his opening epigraph.

48. See Ruth Hubbard, *The Politics of Women's Biology* (New Brunswick, N.J.: Rutgers University Press, 1990).

49. Marilyn Strathern describes Melanesian notions of a child as the "finished repository of the actions of multiple others," and not, as among Westerners, a resource to be constructed into a fully human being through socialization by others. Strathern, "Between Things: A Melanesianist's Comment on Deconstructive Feminism," unpublished manuscript. Western feminists have been struggling to articulate a phenomenology of pregnancy that rejects the dominant cultural framework of productionism/reproductionism, with its logic of passive resource and active technologist. In these efforts the woman–fetus nexus is refigured as a knot of relationality within a wider web, where liberal individuals are not the actors, but where complex collectives, including nonliberal social persons (singular and plural), are. Similar refigurings appear in eco-feminist discourse.

50. See Said, *Orientalism.*

51. Bruno Latour, *Science in Action: How to Follow Scientists and Engineers through Society* (Cambridge, Mass.: Harvard University Press, 1987), 70–74, 90.

52. See Donna Haraway, "Situated Knowledge," *Feminist Studies* 14, no. 3 (1988): 575–99, and Haraway, *Simians, Cyborgs, and Women.*

53. See the fall 1990 newsletter of the Society for the Social Study of Science, *Technoscience* 3, no. 3, pp. 20, 22, for language about "going back to nature." A session of the 4S October meetings is titled "Back to Nature." Malcolm Ashmore's abstract "With a Reflexive Sociology of Actants, There Is No Going Back" offers "fully comprehensive insurance against going back," instead of other competitors' less good "ways of not going back to

Nature (or Society or Self)." All of this occurs in the context of a crisis of confidence among many 4S scholars that their very fruitful research programs of the last ten years are running into dead ends. They are. I will refrain from commenting on the blatant misogyny in the Western scholar's textualized terror of "going back" to a fantastic nature (figured by science critics as "objective" nature. Literary academicians figure the same terrible dangers slightly differently; for both groups such a nature is definitively presocial, monstrously not-human, and a threat to their careers). Mother nature always waits, in these adolescent boys' narratives, to smother the newly individuated hero. He forgets this weird mother is his creation; the forgetting, or the inversion, is basic to ideologies of scientific objectivity and of nature as "Eden under glass." It also plays a yet-to-be-examined role in some of the best (most reflexive) science studies. A theoretical gender analysis is indispensible to the reflexive task.

54. James Arena-DeRosa, "Indigenous Leaders Host U.S. Environmentalists in the Amazon," *Oxfam America News,* Summer/Fall 1990, 1–2.

55. Arena-DeRosa, 1.

56. See Thomas Pynchon, *Gravity's Rainbow* (New York: Viking, 1973).

57. *Time,* February 10, 1961, 58. The caption under HAM's photograph read "from Chop Chop Chang to No. 65 to a pioneering role." For HAM's flight and the Holloman chimps' training, see Kenneth Weaver, "Countdown for Space," *National Geographic* 119, no. 5 (1961): 702–34, and *Life,* February 10, 1961. *Life* headlined "From Jungles to the Lab: The Astrochimps." All were captured from Africa; that means many other chimps died in the "harvest" of babies. The astrochimps were chosen over other chimps for, among other things, "high IQ." Good scientists all.

58. Sarel Eimerl and Irven Devore, *The Primates* (New York: Time Inc., 1965), 173.

59. *Time,* December 8, 1961, 50; *Newsweek,* March 5, 1962, 19.

60. Weaver, "Countdown for Space," 702–34.

61. *Time,* December 8, 1961, 50.

62. Paul Virilio and Sylvere Lotriunger, *Pure War* (New York: Semiotext(e), 1983). See also Chris Gray, "Postmodern War," Qualifying Exam, History of Consciousness, University of California, Santa Cruz, 1988.

63. For indispensable theoretical and participant-observation writings on eco-feminism, social movements, and nonviolent direct action, see Barbara Epstein, *Political Protest and Cultural Revolution: Nonviolent Direct Action in the 1970s and 1980s* (Berkeley: University of California Press, 1993).

64. C. Bryan, *The National Geographic Society: 100 Years of Adventure and Discovery* (New York: Abrams, 1987).

65. For a fuller discussion of the immune system, see Haraway, "The Biopolitics of Postmodern Bodies," in *Simians, Cyborgs, and Women.*

66. Lennart Nilsson, *The Body Victorious: The Illustrated Story of Our Immune System and Other Defenses of the Human Body* (New York: Delacourt, 1987). Recall that Nilsson shot the famous and discourse-changing photographs of fetuses (really abortuses) as glowing back-lit universes floating free of the "maternal environment." See Lennart Nilsson, *A Child Is Born* (New York: Dell, 1977).

67. J. Playfair, *Immunology at a Glance,* 3rd ed. (Oxford: Blackwell, 1984).

68. Peter Jaret, "Our Immune System: The Wars Within," *National Geographic* 169, no. 6 (1986): 701–35.

69. Col. Frederick Timmerman, "Future Warriors," *Military Review* 67 (September 1987): 52.

70. Advertising copy for the Met Life Pavilion. The exhibit is sponsored by the Metropolitan Life and Affiliated Companies. In the campground resort at Florida's Walt Disney World, we may also view the "endangered species island," in order to learn the conventions for "speaking for the jaguar" in an Eden under glass.

71. Ramona Fernandez, "Trickster Literacy," Qualifying Exam, History of Consciousness, University of California, Santa Cruz, 1990, wrote extensively on Walt Disney World and the multiple cultural literacies required and taught on-site for successfully traveling there. Her essay described the visualizing technology and medical school collaboration in its development and use. See *Journal of the American Medical Association* 260, no. 18 (1988): 2776–783.

72. See Edward Golub, *Immunology: A Synthesis* (Sunderland, Mass.: Sinauer, 1987), and Niels Jerne, "The Generative Grammar of the Immune System," *Science* 229 (1985): 1057–59. Building an unexpected collective, Jerne drew directly from Noam Chomsky's theories of structural linguistics. The "textualized" semiotic body is not news by the late twentieth century, but what kind of textuality is put into play still matters!

73. Douglas Crimp and Adam Rolston, *AIDS Demo Graphics* (Seattle, Wash.: Bay Press, 1990), 20. See also Crimp, "On the Museum's Ruins," in *The Anti-Aesthetic: Essays on Postmodern Culture,* ed. Hal Foster, 43–56 (Port Townsend, Wash.: Bay Press, 1983).

74. See, e.g., the recent merger of Project Inform with the Community Research Alliance to speed the community-based testing of promising drugs—and the NIH's efforts to deal with these developments: *PI Perspective,* May 1990. Note also the differences between President Bush's secretary of health and human services, Lewis Sullivan, and director of the National Institute of Allergy and Infectious Diseases, Anthony Fauci, on dealing with activists and PWAs. After ACT UP demonstrations against his and Bush's policies during the secretary's speech at the AIDS conference in San Francisco in June 1990, Sullivan said he would have no more to do with ACT UP and instructed government officials to limit their contacts. (Bush had been invited to address the international San Francisco conference, but his schedule did not permit it. He was in North Carolina raising money for the ultra-reactionary senator Jesse Helms at the time of the conference.) In July 1990, at the ninth meeting of the AIDS Clinical Trials Group (ACTG), at which patient activists participated for the first time, Fauci said that he would work to include the AIDS constituency at every level of the NIAID process of clinical trials. He urged scientists to develop the skills to discuss freely in those contexts. See "Fauci gets softer on activists," *Science* 249 (1990): 244. Why is constructing this kind of scientific articulation "softer"? I leave the answer to readers' imaginations informed by decades of feminist theory.

75. This quadrant of the semiotic square is dedicated to A. E. Van Vogt's *Players of Null-A* (New York: Berkeley Books, 1974), for their non-Aristotelian adventures. An earlier version of "The Promises of Monsters" had the imagination, not SF, in virtual space. I am indebted to a questioner who insisted that the imagination was a nineteenth-century faculty that is in political and epistemological opposition to the arguments I am trying to

formulate. As I am trying vainly to skirt psychoanalysis, I must also skirt the slough of the romantic imagination.

76. Allucquére R. Stone, "Following Virtual Communities," unpublished manuscript, History of Consciousness, University of California, Santa Cruz, 1990.

77. William Gibson, *Neuromancer* (New York: Ace, 1986), 51.

78. Varley, "Press Enter," 286. Thanks to Barbara Ige, graduate student in the Literature Board, University of California, Santa Cruz, for conversations about our stakes in the figure of Lisa Foo.

79. Varley, 241–42.

80. Varley, 263.

81. Varley, 263.

82. Varley, 275.

83. Varley, 276.

84. Varley, 275.

85. Varley, 267.

86. Oil on canvas, 36 by 28 inches, photo by D. Caras. In conversation with the 1985 essay "A Manifesto for Cyborgs" (in Haraway, *Simians, Cyborgs, and Women*), Randolph painted her *Cyborg* while at the Bunting Institute and exhibited it there in a spring 1990 solo exhibition titled *A Return to Alien Roots*. The show incorporated, from many sources, "traditional religious imagery with a postmodern secularized context." Randolph paints "images that empower women, magnify dreams, and cross racial, class, gender, and age barriers" (exhibition brochure). Living and painting in Texas, Randolph was an organizer of the Houston Area Artists' Call against U.S. Intervention in Central America. The human model for *Cyborg* was Grace Li, from Beijing, who was at the Bunting Institute in the fateful year of 1989.

87. I borrow this use of "conversation" and the notion of transnational feminist literacy from Katie King's concept of women and writing technologies. See King, *Theory in Its Feminist Travels*.

POSTHUMAN TERATOLOGY

Patricia MacCormack

THIS CHAPTER WILL EXPLORE ways of thinking posthuman teratology. Teratology has referred to the study of monsters and monstrosity in all epistemic incarnations, though most often in medicine and physiology. Two inclinations resonate with two effects encountered in relations with monsters. Irrefutable and irresistible wonder and terror have led, in the life sciences, to a compulsion to cure or redeem through fetishization, making sacred or simply sympathetic. The effect that monstrosity has upon the "nonmonstrous" is an inherently ambiguous one, just as monsters themselves are defined, most basically, as ambiguities. The hybrid and the ambiguous hold fascination for the "nonmonster" because they show the excesses, potentialities, and infinite protean configurations of form and flesh available in nature even while human sciences see them as unnatural. Human sciences' study of and quest for cures for monstrosity are less about monstrosity and more about preserving the myth and integrity of the base level zero, normal human.

Monsters are only ever defined contingent with their time and place; they are never unto themselves. It could be argued that monstrosity is only a failure of or catalyst to affirm the human. Can we even ask what a monster *is*? Configured as "subjects" who fail to fulfill the criteria of human subjects, monstrosity points out the human as the icon of what is normal, and thus the monster as what is not human. For this reason, the monster has an ideal and intimate relationship with the concept of the posthuman. Posthuman theory developed as a result of the deconstruction of meta-discourses such as science, history, and transcendental philosophy that had worked to attain and maintain the meaning, truth, and status of what defines the human.[1] It does not come after humanism but interrogates the conditions of possibility of being and knowing the human while offering examples from all discourses of how there is always something more in the human that delimits its parameters and possibilities. In this sense the posthuman emphasizes that we are all, and *must* be, monsters because none are template humans. The human is an ideal that exists only as a referent to define what deviates from it. Just as the monster is predicated on a judgment based upon what defines a normal human, so too, the human is a conceptualized idea that can be figured as a referent defined only through that which deviates from it. Through teratology we discover in the posthuman what can be thought as ethical, material, experimental, creative, and yet which escapes definition—the inhuman, the a-human, the nonhuman. In the most reduced sense, then, through concepts of adaptability and evolution itself, all organisms are unlike—we are all, and must be, monsters because nothing is ever like another thing, nor like itself from one moment to the next.

While immediately associated with human sciences, teratological studies frequently glean their names from both animality and myth—the Elephant Man/ Protean syndrome being one example that includes both animal and ancient monstrous-man figure. Myth, symbolic use of animals, fiction, and fable coalesce in hypertrichotic "werewolf" syndrome. These are two of many examples that show that the monster unifies disparate fields of study and the residue of myth, fantasy, fear, and hybrid aberration that is maintained in science. This chapter will explore ways in which monstrosity works alongside and inflects with the posthuman, and will also inflect science with myth and the actual with the fictive to emphasize the established relationship between these different orders of knowledge that seem to already form a hybrid—even monstrous—foundation of studies in monstrosity.

I consistently use the term *the monster*. This tactical use should be qualified in two ways. First, it is clear that there is no single taxonomical category of monster; second, I use this term not to describe a thing but more to name a catalyst toward an encounter. *The monster* refers to the element outside the observer that sparks and creates an event of perception that necessitates the participation of two unlike entities. The monster can simultaneously refer to anything that refuses being *the human* and that which makes the person who encounters it posthuman. There are a number of ways by which we can conceive this kind of monster. Importantly, it emphasizes that referring to a monster only ever refers to an encounter with alterity. This is so even if both entities could be described (or describe themselves) as monsters because monsters are as unlike each other as they are the nonmonstrous.

Why a Posthuman Teratology?

Posthumanism has become a field of investigation that incites excitation due to its unapologetic refusal to quicken to a hermeneutic epistemology or an ontological project: inherent in this play with the basic parameters and goals of discovery and analysis is the subject of the posthuman itself. Where humanism has sought to empirically and philosophically reduce the concept of being to a transcendental essence, so posthumanism seeks to open out the field of study of its "object" as an infinite refolding and metamorphic mobilization of its subject and thus its nature of enquiry. In spite of its name, the posthuman must not be understood as coming after the human. Inherent in posthumanism is the very notion of narrative time or causality as being arbitrary—both are taken as expressions of power rather than necessary elements of logic. The question for the posthuman becomes not "what is the posthuman?" but "why is it necessary?" and analyses ask "how does it emerge?" Before any exemplifications of the posthuman emerge, posthuman philosophy has taken as its task the ethical and creative need to rethink the category of human, both as an object of study and as a discursive technique of categorization where it is not so much what one is but *where* one is in the taxonomical hierarchy that matters and, indeed, where one's matter is created. Humanism allows investigation to collapse all differing systems of knowledge into an essentially unified consistency of value. The elements that measure value are deferred to an isomorphic system where alterity comes more from what one is not than what one is. Alterity is thus conceived as failure. The paradigmatic nature of philosophy, science, and other epistemologies means that certain qualities are consistently desired over others on the objects of analysis of each, but more so certain tendencies of modes of conception underpin the way that these objects are able to emerge at all.

The posthuman challenges not only qualities that make up the human—as an organism and a cultural, reflective, knowing subject (including knowledge of self)—but qualities that compel the paradigms by which things are perceived to be able to be known. These include organism or object discretion, the possibility of essence, the promise of investigation being exhausted when the object is known absolutely, belief in the myth of objectivity or the possibility of the observer being entirely extricated from the observed, and adherence to established, agreed modes of perception constituted by maintaining traditionally accepted techniques of experimentation and study. The posthuman does not therefore depose the human, nor come after it, but allows access to and celebrates the excesses, conundrums, jubilant failures, and disruptive events which are already inherent in any possibility of contemplation. Shifting possibility to potentiality, the posthuman spatially encourages an address to the multiple within a dividuated organism and the organism as part of a teeming series of relations with its inextricable environment, both conceptual and material (but of course no longer bifurcated). Temporally, the post-human is past, present, and future contracted into immanent entity, emergent without arrival and fled before it is complete. We can invoke certain words that persist in encounters with the posthuman—the multiple, the transformative, the space between, the manifold, the other—but one term that is particularly reso-nant with the posthuman, sharing its tentative qualities, its failure to be majori-tarian and most importantly, its ethical urgency, is *the monster.*

Majoritarian does not refer to the majority of people, nor the majority of beliefs, truths and such. Majoritarianism is a compulsion to reiterate certain modes of thinking rather than thoughts themselves. Majoritarian thinking is knowledge as absolute (or the possibility of it being such). Majoritarian knowl-edge anchors on a master discourse where it is not so much that things are mon-sters but certain traits, forms, and ways of negotiating the world are considered the only ways, based on the privileging of concepts such as objectivity and logic. Historically, then, majoritarians have been white, able-bodied, heterosexual, edu-cated males, but all people who participate in these ways of thinking are majori-tarian in spite of their corporeal status.

Teras means both monster and marvel. Immediately one is struck with an inherent contradiction. The aberrant as marvelous points to the crucial role that desire plays in thinking both the posthuman and monsters. Where the posthuman is scary because it eviscerates absolute knowledge as an impossible goal, mon-sters are scary because they do not fit into the classifications we create in order for something to exist at all.[2] The monster is not a being unto itself; it is a failure to be a proper being. In 1831, Cambridge University professor of medicine W. Clark wrote a treatise based on transactions of the Cambridge Philosophical Society. Clark commented on the fascination that monsters elicit: "Of late years no sub-ject has more incessantly occupied the labours of learned continental Anatomists than the investigation of the steps by which the rudimentary organs of embryos advance to their perfect form."[3] Here temporality is configured in an early herald-ing of evolution where the form at which one arrives, as well as the comparative place that form will occupy in relation to others, are "results" of stages toward perfection. Being a being is a finite goal in this configuration, creating resonances of the organic with the increments of knowledge one must take to arrive at a concept of one's self philosophically and the ultimate arrival where man attains God, through access to truth, absolutism, and, most importantly, likeness to God. The human template, the micro-God, is both that which nature seeks in order to create proper healthy, normal human life, and that which science seeks to know in order to match it elegantly with more esoteric or philosophical notions of what it means to be a living human. This template is seemingly basic and straight-forward but actually an impossible concept of singularity, showing that any organ-ism only ever exists as a version of an ideal that, by its very nature, is immaterial and fantasmatic. The focus on elements of disambiguation and temporal trans-formation is key in theories of the posthuman, where plethora replaces persona and being becomes becoming.

The monster reminds us of the ethical importance inherent in thinking about posthuman aberration. A key factor in posthumanism in relation to teratol-ogy is that teratology brings us back to history as a remembered present while it seeks the future-now upon which much posthuman theory focuses. Exchang-ing history for individual memories means that the past does not affirm the pres-ent and guarantee a future, as posthumanism opens up potentialities rather than repeating forms. However, it acknowledges the suffering, objectification, and effects of being named monster that cannot be denied. A remembered present asks "how does experience of the past effect present modes of being"? For the mon-ster it validates experience as other; for the objectifier it demands accountability.

My positing posthuman teratology will not focus on the more obvious exam-ples of the posthuman, the primary one of which is the techno-posthumanism. Perhaps the most famous theorist of the cyborg, Donna Haraway, created a con-nection between woman as the first step away from the "human"—correctly the Man masquerading gender specificity with all its associated powers of significa-tion as neutrality—and technology. What she emphasized was that technology persists in the compulsion of majoritarian paradigms, which operate primar-ily through the production of meaning as "binary dichotomisation."[4] If the pre-human was nature to culture, the posthuman in the context of techno-biopolitics is culture to future while simultaneously a collapse between the most basic biol-ogy and the most refined technology. The persistence of the binary system is the issue here, as it shows that the quality of an event of the human cannot be posthu-man if it stands in opposition to a less attractive, oppressed, or suppressed other who both threatens to reemerge in order to subsume it and also reminds it of the irrefutable necessity for dominance in the quest for liberation from the flesh. It is the very flesh of the other that is usually subjugated (this is especially so for xeno-biology in animal organ harvest experiments for transplantation). A system of equivalence sits side by side with that of accumulation. As animal is to human, and woman is to man, so man is to cyborg. The first term in each dyad is one from which the majoritarian flees but also which it needs in order to oper-ate a structure of proportion—definition based on difference as only success or failure at resemblance. In a seeming contradiction, the cyborg as a posthuman future reminds us that the "natural" flesh, particularly the animal and woman, is the most monstrous. A troubling appendix to this series of proportion is the cur-rent tendency to equate brains with computers, yet it is most often the computer system that is seen to offer an insight into the brain, while the brain's complexity finds its greatest power in its capacity to be synthetically constructed in cyborg consciousness. But neurophysiologist Rodney Cotterill emphasizes that it is

rather unlikely that computers as such could be given consciousness merely
through the use of a specific type of software. There would have to be something that is likened to a body, equipped with counterparts of our muscle-
moving apparatus. . . . Given that thought is essentially stimulation of the
body's interactions with the environment, as I have said, this would mean that
the computer would be simulating simulation . . . we humans appear to be
mesmerised by the prospect of artificially producing copies of ourselves.[5]

Cyborg and simulated consciousness technology has come a long way since
Cotterill's text; however, what remains the same is the desire to reactivate qualities associated with human-yet-transcendental subjectivity.

Is simulation empty copying, an elliptical compulsive return to the human,
or is it a virtualization of potentiality that goes beyond the paradigms that allow
traditional coveted qualities of idealized humanity to operate?[6] Two intriguing
issues arise in Cotterill's lament—the first is the inextricability of identity from
environment, the second the necessity of flesh or something akin to it. Consciousness is flesh, and vice versa. A Cartesian extrication of consciousness from flesh
compels many cyborg theories, while a more Spinozan understanding of expressions, relations, and affects between entities, environment, subject, thought, and
(inter) act(ion) haunts its as yet impossibility. Spinoza states that "matter is everywhere the same, parts are distinguished in it only insofar as we conceive matter
to be affected in different ways, so that its parts are distinguished only modally."[7]
Robert Pepperell's seminal posthuman manifesto states, "The idealists think that
the only things that exist are ideas, the materialists think that the only thing that
exists is matter. It must be remembered that ideas are not independent of matter
and that matter is just an idea."[8]

Pepperell emphasizes that posthumanity is liberated from binary dichotomization, an anchoring of ideas into virtualities that must be actualized in order
to be (that is, they are neither transcendental nor independent from other ideas
from all fields, particularly the inextricability of science and philosophy). Yet
there still resonates a fear of matter because, as will be explored below, through
posthuman ethical philosophy, matter may be emergent as a negotiated concept
through being an idea, but there is nonetheless matter beyond and independent of (because always within) simply being "just" an idea. Pain, actual suffering, experiments on nonconsenting flesh, or the results of technologies of combat
show us not an "idea" of matter but matter's ubiquitous all. I am not suggesting
here that matter creates ideas, per se, or lurks beneath them, waiting to pounce
out to destroy us by reminding us that we cannot be without a body, but in order
to think an ethics of biopolitics, the future-now needs to acknowledge what we
cannot get rid of, either through technology or through signification. Knowledge
of matter is just matter as an idea, but matter for itself is not.

Dysfunctional Cyborg Dreams

While the cyborg body is constituted by defining qualities of monstrosity—hybridity, negotiating binaries such as flesh–technology, nature–future and experimentation, on which an enormous amount has been written—I would argue this has been to the detriment of certain ways in which we can, or *should,* think posthumanism as now and as a field that should not place itself in a future without a past or residue. Critically, cyborgism can tend to a hyperevolutionary obsession where the only way to be posthuman is to collapse the technology created by man to manipulate life with the organism, lamentably for cyborgs, as which we still persist to exist, with all our frailties and failures. Cyborgism has promises of enhancement toward immortality and a God-scientist who can create and extend life and become the ultimate self-authorizing identity, no longer in need of the physiology alienated from his will that threatens to destroy him through age and disease. Cyborgism can be experimental, playful, and hold much promise, but teratology reminds us that the negotiation of volition and self-expression that underpins cyborgism has too frequently been denied monsters, be they anatomical congenital aberrations, transgressives, or bodies at the most basic level of alterity from the majoritarian understanding of the human. Additionally, perhaps contentiously, should not monsters in their posthuman incarnations, by their very aberrant definition, ethically and politically challenge the structures that underpin dominant powers? C. Ben Mitchell et al. write:

> Some individuals even call themselves "transhumanist," explicitly promoting the re-engineering of humankind into some form or forms of "posthuman" being. Even the US government has invested in a controversial project to reengineer human beings.[9] Yet even if not adopting such an extreme view or goal it would seem a large number of individuals in the United States and around the world are enticed by all the potential technologies of "enhancement." The desires for modification may be rooted in wishes for fashioning oneself into a more socially acceptable image, attempting to improve self-esteem through reengineering, or making oneself more competitive in business, the professions, academia, or athletics. Unfortunately the motivations behind these desires are usually socially driven fears, experiences of rejection or failure, or just plain greed, and they may reflect a social rather than biological pathology.[10]

While vaguely theological, this criticism elucidates the point that we cannot find the posthuman as a liberating concept in what it is but in what it does to majoritarian systems of control, social hierarchies, and the obsessions with an extension or enhancement of the same old power enforcements taken to their longed-for eternity. The question with cyborgism is "enhancing what?" Artistic and conceptual-performance cyborgism, such as the work of Stelarc, which makes

up a considerable component of cyborg incarnations and biotechnological experiments, may find itself aligned more with traditional teratology than with cyborg
theory, per se. Stelarc's third arm project formed a disambiguation of the bina-
rization of two arms (and even the healthy human baby as two arms, two legs)
and the conceptualization of limb movement as volitional and organic, as the arm
was manipulated by interface users. His third ear transplanted onto his forearm
exhibited an organ with no use and redefined through its proximity with a non-
compatible organ (itself relatively rudimentary, the forearm apprehended as a
vista of skin rather than an organ with a function per se).

Relationality as Hybridity

Covertly, I could make the same argument against the fetishization of animality in certain becomings, where the posthuman collapses animality with human
form brought out in experiments with body modification—the implantation of
certain animal elements such as stripes, whiskers, fangs, and horns. Here, alterity
has become oversignified as a liberatory regression or devolution. Such examples include Dennis Avner the Stalking Cat and Eric Sprague the Lizard Man.[11]
Rather than entering into their own becomings, however, both have rented themselves out, in that Sprague is a "freak show" performer and Avner performs personal narrativizations in public appearances, which suggests seeking to reify his
being rather than explore his becomings. For this reason, while I invoke these
figures, I use them as illustrative risks setting down a template as to what does
or does not constitute a becoming-animal.[12] Where the cyborg is the future-
human-now, the becoming-animal of certain posthumans is the past-reclaimed.[13]
Many teratological conditions have been named such because aberrant traits are
perceived as animal qualities—elephant men, wolf children, mermaid (thus fish)
syndrome. Becomings-animal in certain body modifications directly refuse being
named as a failure by presenting as a volitional way to rename oneself via qualities which are considered liberating rather than devolutionary. The power of
naming and the myth of compulsory humanness are taken from majoritarian systems, and so is the belief that being human is the most desirable state of subjectivity. Although offering fascinating examples of the inherent hybridity of
any attempt to become something else, in a sense, some of these animal-humans
want to become, not animals, but irreducibly human perceptions of animals.
An animal—and what is (or is not) an animal—is no less nor more "natural" than
a human. The animal-human's seeking origin positions itself in a parabolic configuration with the cyborg's seeking eternity. Thinking the animal ethically—which
may confess to not thinking it at all beyond thinking through grace as the pure
allowance of the other to be, without intervention—gives way to idealizing and
fetishizing.

More problematic than the animal aims of modifiers is the increasing collapse of possible resonances of biology, from testing to transplantation, where the subjugated element is not technically apprehended as living being but as living material. Theories of the posthuman are increasingly questioning the meaning of "life." The multiple in the singular may seem all-too posthuman—the pig's heart transplanted into the human body, the animal used for performances as some symbiotic claim (such as Monika Oeschler's Eagle Project)[14]—but these fail to encounter an animal as a consistency of (its own owned) life, let alone animality. It is fine for the human to question his own human status through experiments with hybridity, multiplicity, and symbiosis with alterity, but the seeking of these forms of the posthuman involves another element, and that element, when animal, even in the most seemingly benevolent circumstances, but certainly not those involving pain or death, is incapable of consent, is simply a return to the absolute power that the concept of being human perpetuates and vindicates. Beyond thinking that the impossibility of animal consent is something that comes solely from a linguistic system, the very notion of the right to "use" fantasizes that there is an appropriate field of operations where the human has both the right to intervene (including the symbolic or the performative) in animal life and the opposing view that they do not. While the latter does acknowledge that the incapacity to consent should mean a refusal to compel, both impose an assimilating regime upon the animal nonetheless. The radical and uncomfortable issue is that we exist within purely human discourse, with all its ambiguities, temporal and spatial contingencies, and to attempt to operate outside these is itself a human project. The question is not one of purely linguistic or structural questioning of animal–human relations, though this is perhaps whence it begins, but the right to consider difference at all if it is irreducible difference without negotiation.

Cary Wolfe states two factors that have made theories of animality become so prevalent in recent years. The first is the crisis in humanism in philosophy; the second, which inflects animality as a primal form of life toward the futures that techno-biopolitics promise, is that the animal has found its presence most in nonhumanities epistemes.[15] Both are human-to-human tendencies, whatever that means beyond meaning incapable of encountering the extra-human. The question of who we are now that we are no longer human is counteracted by the question, What can we do with animals to make us live longer? Both uses of animals, however, persist in binary dichotomization, as they necessitate animals as nothing more than not human. Resemblance through metaphor and arrogant use through biological harvesting affirm that "it was as a comment on *human* nature that the concept of 'animality' [and so too monster] was devised."[16]

Cyborgism can facilitate our escape from just being animals, while using animals insinuates that we are not animals but a somehow higher form of life.

Where, in poststructuralism, epistemes collide, these two claims cannot coexist. Giorgio Agamben calls this the ironic anthropomorphic machine of humanism: "You can degenerate into the lower things, which are brutes; you can regenerate, in accordance with your soul's decision, into the higher things which are divine. . . . The humanist discovery of man is the discovery that he lacks himself."[17] Posthumanism, neither a before nor an after, is the *crisis* of the end of the myth of man. Questions such as what can we do to extend the human, or what the animal means, essentially ask one single question, which is the "what now?" of the human.

While, once again, I am adamantly not claiming that cyborg and animal posthumans are always resonating with humanistic tendencies, what teratology reminds us is that the monster as aberration is that which is traditionally and historically denied volition or any sense of self-authorization. Defined through this word *marvel*, teratology describes a study of *relation* more than of an object. Rather than I "am" a cyborg project or becoming-animal, monstrosity is an encounter. The subject in proximity with the monster must be accountable for subjects' mode of perception; the monster is nothing unto itself except aberrant to the other. The other is just as easily able to be monstrous to the monster. What is emphasized is the space between. Monstrosity is the event; thus, teratologically speaking, posthumanism is neither a natural object nor a volitional refusal of the human but the creation of a multiple through the desire to marvel at that which cannot be perceived via traditional modes of signification and apprehension. There is no resolution, no finality, no knowledge of, just the consistency of being as a being in relation with, and the incited thoughts, creative perceptions, and imagined potentiality that comes from this marvelous encounter where both and thus neither are aberrations except to one another, beyond scientific or philosophical humanist reduction or deferral to the already established categories of the human. "I find the other in me (it is always concerned with showing how the other, the distant, is always the near and the same). It resembles exactly the invagination of a tissue in embryology, or the act of doubling in sewing: twist, fold, stop and so on."[18] Shifting the earlier critique of the manipulated posthuman, we can find in our most humble and ordinary bodies radical possibilities when we are liberated from taxonomy.

Monstrous Metamorphoses

The primary element that defines monsters is that they are not not-monsters, not us, not normal. They have no category of their own by which they may be recognized and thus removed. To have an object (monsters are objectified, never subjects unto themselves) that cannot be described and placed into a category alongside other like objects is the primary concept that structures all other elements of monstrosity—that is the ambiguous, the neither-neither—neither this, nor that, but not "not" these things. Monsters when they are formed from human matter are never entirely independent from the human form. The very problem comes from their uncanny redistribution of human elements into aberrant configurations. It is the part we recognize as made strange, or in proximity with a part with which it should not sit side by side, that makes monsters monstrous. Like the posthuman, the monster is neither before nor beyond the human but an interrogation of the myths of human integrity, biologically and metaphysically. A monster is not a classified object nor a self-authorized subject but more the result of an act of being named such. So the next circle of ambiguity and relation after that which recognized the monster as familiar and unfamiliar is the relation between the monster and the nonmonster who names it. Again, this involves the element of the familiar, here normal, with the unfamiliar and indefinable, the monster. Both in itself and in its relation with the not-monster, the monster operates through this system of hybridity. We cannot speak of monsters. We speak only of examples of the plasticity and creativity that is inherent in all concepts, including those formed to describe and know biological phenomena. Ambiguous hybridity of form and encounter spatially locate the monster. Temporally, the monster is constituted through metamorphosis and distortion. While the form of a monster may not necessarily undergo perceptible alteration any more than all bodies are in constant state of change, the way the monster is perceived does—historically, monsters have been encountered first as abominations, then with sympathy, then as projects to fix. Again we see that it is the structure of relation with the monster that creates its meaning, rather than the quality or nature of the monster itself.

Monsters in themselves are created through a bordering and create bordering encounters. Within monstrous "identity," therefore, there is already more-than-one, and relating with the monster mirrors this multiplicity within the singular. There is no evidence of discrete identity, not even bad identity. Resonating with the turn to animality in posthuman theory, the monster is often a hybrid of "animal" and "human." But another way to utilize animality in posthuman teratology without assimilation or fetishization comes from fabulations of impossible combinations created not through sutured forms but through intermingling intensities. For example, in fiction, myth, and popular culture we find the werewolf and the vampire. Werewolves are part man, part wolf, without being examples of either. The werewolf is rather the "wolfing" of man. It is defined by its temporal transformations and instability. Additionally, werewolves are frequently characterized by their tragic benevolence and horror at wolfing, so they cannot be reduced to a single expression of intent or nature. The vampire mingles dead with living undead; it becomes bat, wolf, even molecules of fog. The vampire does not metamorphosize; it is itself a metamorphosis. Covert to the tragically benevolent werewolf, the vampire is unapologetically horrifying and seductive precisely for being such. We cannot ask what a werewolf or vampire is, as each is always changing. In a contradictive conundrum, they are defined by instability, mingling of different forms, and invoking violent aggression in sympathy and irresistible desire in repulsion. "The abnormal can be defined only in terms of character-istics, specific or generic; but the anomalous is a position or set of positions in relation to a multiplicity. . . . It is always with the anomalous . . . that one enters into alliance with becoming animal."[19]

In a posthuman project toward becoming-animal (where the venture, the *becoming*, is the focus, and the final form never arrives), ironically the fictive animal becomes more real than any becoming based on intimate knowledge of zoology. Just as teratology risks fetishizing the monster, as sacred, as victim, as repulsive, through claims that absolute knowledge will mean absolute capacity to name and describe the limits and meanings of the monster, so zoology's study of animals to the most refined molecular point creates a phantasy of understand-ing an animal and thus being ethically vindicated in co-opting one, be it through consumption, experimentation, or just idealized symbolicization. The fictive fab-ulation animals that Deleuze and Guattari mention are those that demand creation and imagination—encounters that ignite thought rather than promise knowledge and its associated powers. As imaginary concepts, most frequently found in art, literature, and film, fabulation animal-monsters such as werewolves and vampires cannot be co-opted, as they exist only as demands for relations of othering. We can never "know" that which does not exist, but, like all art and fiction, it does not mean that our ideologies, paradigmatic tendencies, and responses are not affected by experiences of these entities. Posthuman tribal totems are not those of "prim-itive" culture, nor even of the use of animals as symbols in modernity, but strange, taxonomically impossible creatures that are us, and *not* us, which move us to dif-ferent positions. The werewolf is man and beast, the vampire inherently meta-morphic to the limit of being gaseous, a future of postdeath rather than eternal, technologically facilitated life. Both are fleshy, furred, corroded, showing differ-ent conditions of the smooth, hard flesh of normal humanity and its ambition toward being impervious cyborg metal. Yet both are recognizably human. Most importantly, both infect and exist in packs. By very virtue of being infective, vam-pires must form packs, even if they are disparate. Indeed the idea that one belongs to a pack although one may never see one's fellow pack mates exemplifies the oxymoronic status of these monstrous evocations. This means that the only way to access these monsters is to be part of them—the encounter is the concept itself. The enigmatic nature of these monsters is eternal but notably popular in con-temporary culture. This shows that they are not abject abnormal creatures to be put away, made sacred or profane, but always externalized. They are seductive present promises of extending thoughts of human potentiality, and we enter into an internal teratological realm. Emphasizing the marvelous, fascinating etymol-ogy of the word, fabulated monsters can only be encountered by becoming with them. While each emergence of werewolf and vampire is unique, the packs that they create are communities of those who are not common to each other, as much of a seeming contradiction as monsters themselves.

Toward an Ethics of Posthuman Monstrosity

There may seem to be a problem here with the possibility of ignoring "real-life" monsters, entities both human and animal that have been forced to suffer through oppression catalyzed by their alterity. The function of fiction here does not oppose that of reality, but it breaks down the binary itself. Fiction requires a belief in the unbelievable. While readers are aware of the fictive form, the affects and intensities incited in the imagination are real and have direct effects on the subjectivity of the reader, just as all fictive art affects the self beyond the fiction, and all science of the real operates via beliefs in what kinds of knowledge are possible and acceptable, the belief in which is its own fiction. Modes of perception are neither fictive nor true. They are constructs of possibilities of ideas. This means that all encounters with alterity will create a choice—to turn away by knowing the other as abnormal and therefore affirming the self as normal, or to enter into a bordering or pack with the monstrous, creating a revolutionary hybridity of two who were already hybrids, and so forth. This bordering is as relevant for political activism as it is for dreams of wolfing and vampirism. Foucault states of power, "That's just like you, always with the same *incapacity* to *cross the line,* to pass over to the other side . . . it is always the same choice, for the side of power, for what power says or what it causes to be said."[20] It is just as easy for the fictive to incite reiterations of oppressive power—the hybrid must be punished, the abnormal is evil—as it is for the limitless potentials of fiction to exploit those elements that are unthinkable outside of literature and all art. As it is more difficult to imagine the becoming-vampire of everyday subjectivity, so it is more important in reference to the need to think the fact of everyday monstrosity as that which proves the infinite differentiations of the myth of the static human as a single possibility of expression whose only others are considered deviations rather than variations. Encounter and proximity refuse the distance required for one to objectify and name another. And both encountering entities alter within their own nature and as a single new hybrid manifestation. By this can be cured the most monstrous but repressed of animal functions that man operates in his oppressive regimes:

> History hides the fact that man is the universal parasite, that everything and everyone around him is hospitable space. Plants and animals are always his hosts; man is necessarily their guest. Always taking, never giving. He bends the logic of exchange and of giving in his favour when he is dealing with nature as a whole. When he is dealing with his kind he continues to do so: He wants to be the parasite of man as well.[21]

Michel Serres shows that it is not the monster who needs normal man to liberate it but man who needs the monster to affirm himself and his status.

The monster is always liberated enough, too much, limitless. The monster's becomings with other monsters, already us as we are already them, is quelled by man's being as parasite. This relation, to know and name the monster, is an act of violence:[22]

> Consequently the basic combat situation reappears in knowledge. There.
> Just as we noted previously, a collectivity united by an agreement finds itself
> facing the world in a relation, neither dominated nor managed, of uncon-
> scious violence: Mastery and possession . . . Science brings together fact and
> law: whence it is now decisive place. Scientific groups, in a position to control
> or do violence to the worldwide world, are preparing to take the helm of the
> worldly world.[23]

Serres pleads for a natural contract, what Guattari would call an ecosophy of alterity and relations over law.[24] That science is law shows the fictitious nature of both, and monstrosity requires a certain lawlessness that, as a concept, is itself seen to be monstrous. It is not, it is simply not top-down. Traversal is active and activating. From abnormal thing to anomalous movement operates. Guattari names this the politics of traversal. Monsters show that all subjectivity must be considered pure singularity. Traversing domains of singularities, creating monstrous territories, promotes

> innovatory practices, the expansion of alternative experiences centred around
> a respect for singularity and through the continuous production of an autono-
> mising subjectivity that can articulate itself appropriately in relation to the
> rest of society. . . . Individuals must become both more united and increasingly
> different.[25]

Teratology from taxonomy to traversal celebrates the singularity of each monster while showing that we are all monsters in our singularity. Collectivity comes from the unlike, to transform groups based on expressions of creativity through differ-ence, not of power through knowledge. It also addresses the lived reality of mon-sters and their/our unique experiences of suffering and jubilance.

Conclusion

Guattari writes:

> We can no longer sit idly by as others steal our mouths, our anuses, our geni-
> tals, our nerves, our guts, our arteries, in order to fashion parts and works in
> an ignoble mechanism of production which links capital, exploitation and the
> family. We can no longer allow others to turn our mucous membranes, our

skin, all our sensitive areas, into occupied territory—territory controlled and regimented by others, to which we are forbidden access. We can no longer permit our nervous system to serve as a communications network for the system of capitalist exploitation, for the patriarchal state; nor can we permit our brains to be used as instruments of torture programmed by the powers that surround us. We can no longer allow others to repress our fucking, control our shit, our saliva, our energies, all in conformity with the prescriptions of the law and its carefully defined little transgressions. We want to see frigid, imprisoned, mortified bodies exploded to bits, even if capitalism continues to demand they be kept in check at the expense of our living bodies.[26]

Guattari emphasizes that the most monstrous bodies are those already available to us, from neither past nor future, and that are all that we are. The most basic and quiet of corporeal acts, if not enclosed in regimentation and signification, can cause horror, while grand experiments in posthumanism can reiterate the oppression and repression of bodies, depending on what symbolic values and by what means these bodies emerge and are encountered. "Pathology is not a general state of being, a disease which afflicts the whole system, but a local and readable lesion, a mappable topography."[27] Monsters are lesion bodies that must be extricated from the body politic, the corpus. They must be read before they can be encountered and removed, yet we could say that the encounter, which causes horror through aberration as ambiguity, is the catalyst for signification, where marveling converts to meaning. Marveling opens up the witness; meaning closes off the monster. It is a question of a revolutionary or reifying decision, the way the other is mapped. A lesion to be ablated, or a suppurating opening, what Guattari shows is that the way beyond the categorization of the human is what we have already repressed that is inherently part of and all that we are. And one could argue that cyborgs do not sweat, shit nor spit, while animals, including the human animal do, but we perceive it in either a ritualized or naturally innocent fashion.

Kristeva writes that "experimental multiplicity is entirely different from the emptiness and destruction experienced in the loss of identity."[28] Monsters, multiple, hybridic and metamorphic, find their place—a no-place, an every-place—in postmodernity as proliferation. They offer a vitalistic foil to the sometimes cynical, even nihilistic risks that the postmodern loss of identity may entail. The very nature of monsters as sicknesses of a failure to be human makes their dividuated corporeal aberrancies mirror their place in society as flaws or deformities of the social corpus. But when postmodernity facilitates posthumanity, monsters show the body already remapped. We are faced with our bodies as monstrous because the sites of what would be considered failures or flaws upon a human map, and signified as such, close off thinking the body differently, become openings toward life without and beyond humanity, actual lived experience, being without having to be a specified subject.

Monstrous "deformities" and symptoms traditionally punctuate a normal body as text to be read. These punctuative points can be encountered as *despositifs* that escape signification rather than functioning as an affirmation of the claimed necessity of normality. Lyotard states of the aberrant body that "the body is undone and its pieces are projected across libidinal space, mingling with other pieces in an inextricable patchwork."[29] Patching together despotic aberrations of the flesh, the genetic code connects points that are incommensurable with the normal human but that are also commensurable with each other. Where they are single points—conceptually and physically—that sully the smooth, sealed terrain of the human, they become multiple relations between other nonhumans, and each seam of the patchwork (and each despotic aberration has many sides, and thus many seams and many relations with others) is a unique connective tissue of creative singularity. It demands thought because it has never been encountered before. All bodies, perceived as formerly normal or not, have to think what relations they can make with multiple *despositifs*. Each body must therefore have more than one plane, side, or aspect, and each specific connection exacerbates these multiplications. This operation involves

> opening the body to connections that presuppose an entire assemblage, circuits, conjunctions, levels and thresholds, passages and distributions of intensities and territories and deterritorialisations measured with the craft of a surveyor . . . how can we unhook ourselves from the points of subjectification that secure us, nail us down to a dominant reality?[30]

Teratological connectivity fulfills certain qualities of the posthuman—multiplicity in the one, singularity in the many, the death of reproduction for production of the unlike. This mode of teratological experimentation in thought and practice does not need an actual element of alterity that is not human—animal, machine—but reminds us all that humanity is made up of its own elements of otherness that are repressed, denied, or cataloged. Teratological connectivity affirms that the category of human has never existed properly, but instead of co-opting elements opposed to the human, it celebrates and exploits that we already have everything we need to become posthuman monsters, without the need for fetishization or assimilation of those who cannot choose to become part of nonhuman assemblages, such as animals, or for access to overarching systems of modernity beyond the reach of most people, such as cyborg research. Teratological resignification of all bodies should not involve a forgetting of the realities of the lived experiences of those named monsters by dominant epistemes. While connections involve opening futures as becomings to come, no single body comes from nowhere and the memories of suffering and oppression are part of the specificity of each *despositif* to which each connector will have its own relation, such as shared oppression and accountability. What matters most is that, by refusing regimes of signification, we all become accountable, while all acknowledging the urgency with which and the reasons why experiments in teratological connectivity are as political as they are interesting, artistic, liberating, and, hopefully, fun.

Notes

1. Critical key texts that introduce this concept in relation to technology, biology, and popular culture include the following: Ihab Hassan, "Prometheus as Performer: Toward a Postmodern Culture?," in *Performance in Postmodern Culture,* ed. Michel Benamou and Charles Caramello (Madison, Wis.: Coda Press, 1977); N. Katherine Hayles, *How We Became Posthuman: Virtual Bodies in Cybernetics, Literature, and Informatics* (Chicago: University of Chicago Press, 1999); Neil Badmington, *Posthumanism,* Readers in Cultural Criticism (Basingstoke, U.K.: Palgrave Macmillan, 2000); Cary Wolfe, *What Is Posthumanism?,* Posthumanities 8 (Minneapolis: University of Minnesota Press, 2010); Robert Pepperell, *The Posthuman Condition: Consciousness beyond the Brain* (Exeter, U.K.: Intellect, 1995); Judith Halberstam and Ira Livingston, eds., *Posthuman Bodies* (Bloomington: Indiana University Press, 1995); Donna Haraway, *Simians, Cyborgs and Women: The Reinvention of Nature* (New York: Routledge, 1991); and Francis Fukuyama, *Our Posthuman Future: Consequences of the Biotechnology Revolution* (New York: Farrar, Straus, and Giroux, 2002).

2. For an elaboration of modes and purposes of teratological ontologies and their paradigmatic shift in contemporary culture, see Jeffrey Jerome Cohen, "Monster Culture (Seven Theses)," in *Monster Theory: Reading Culture,* ed. Jeffrey Jerome Cohen, 3–25 (Minneapolis: University of Minnesota Press, 1996), and Patricia MacCormack, "Perversion: Transgressive Sexuality and Becoming-Monster," *Thirdspace* 3, no. 2 (2004), http://www.thirdspace.ca/articles/3_2_maccormack.htm.

3. W. Clark, *A Case of Human Monstrosity,* Folio (Cambridge: Cambridge University Press, 1831), 2.

4. Haraway, *Simians, Cyborgs and Women,* 209.

5. Rodney Cotterill, *Enchanted Looms* (Cambridge: Cambridge University Press, 1998), 434–36.

6. In relation to the copy as a natural phenomenon and culture's fascination with both studying and creating copies, see Hillel Schwarz, *The Culture of the Copy* (New York: Zone Books, 1998).

7. Benedict Spinoza, *Ethics,* trans. Edwin Curley (London: Penguin, 1994), 12.

8. Pepperell, *Posthuman Condition,* 26.

9. The authors do not give examples of what they refer to here. They word their comment ominously, however, and so it is difficult to glean whether they are invoking eugenic projects, ultimate Frankensteinian man-making goals, or an extension of the human genome project.

10. C. Ben Mitchell, Edmund D. Pellegrino, Jean Bethke Elshtain, John F. Kilner, and Scott B. Rae, *Biotechnology and the Human Good* (Washington, D.C.: Georgetown University Press, 2007), 11.

11. For their home pages, see http://www.stalkingcat.net/ and http://www.thelizardman.com/.

12. For more on the problems of exemplification in discussions of body modification and animal-becomings, see Patricia MacCormack, "The Great Ephemeral Tattooed Skin," *Body and Society* 12, no. 2 (2006): 57–82.

13. In reference to devolutionary alterity, I do not here invoke "modern primitives." In the context of a discussion of teratology, they do not represent the hybridity which the cyborg and human-animal illustrate.

14. This project can be understood as not only assimilative of animal behavior as it is distorted by humans, but it problematically involves the "domestication," tethering, and incarceration of birds of prey. From the perspective of a Spinozan consideration of the nonhuman, this project is unethical. Monika Oechsler, *The Eagle Project,* performance at the James Hockney Gallery, 2007, http://monikaoechsler.co.uk/pages/eagle.html.

15. Cary Wolfe, introduction to *Zoontologies,* ed. Cary Wolfe (Minneapolis: University of Minnesota Press, 2003), x.

16. Keith Thomas, *Man and the Natural World* (New York: Pantheon, 1983), 41.

17. Giorgio Agamben, *The Open: Man and Animal,* trans. Kevin Attell (Stanford, Calif.: Stanford University Press, 2004), 29–30.

18. Gilles Deleuze, *Foucault,* trans. Sean Hand (London: Athlone Press, 1988), 98.

19. Gilles Deleuze and Félix Guattari, *A Thousand Plateaus,* trans. Brian Massumi (Minneapolis: University of Minnesota Press, 1987), 244.

20. Michel Foucault, "The Subject and Power," in *Michel Foucault: Beyond Structuralism and Hermeneutics,* ed. H. L. Dreyfus and P. Rabinow (Brighton, U.K.: Harvester, 1982), 220. Emphasis is original.

21. Michel Serres, *The Parasite,* trans. Lawrence Schehr (Minneapolis: University of Minnesota Press, 2007), 24.

22. Derrida points out that "a monster is a species for which we do not have a name. . . . [However], as soon as one perceives a monster in a monster, one begins to domesticate it." In Jacques Derrida, *Points . . . : Interviews, 1974–1994,* trans. Peggy Kamuf (Stanford, Calif.: Stanford University Press, 1995), 386.

23. Michel Serres, *The Natural Contract,* trans. Elizabeth MacArthur and William Paulson (Ann Arbor: University of Michigan Press, 2001), 22.

24. Felix Guattari, *The Three Ecologies,* trans. Ian Pindar and Paul Sutton (London: Athlone Press, 2000).

25. Guattari, 59, 69.

26. Félix Guattari, *Soft Subversions,* trans. Jarred Becker (New York: Semiotext(e), 1996), 31.

27. Catherine Waldby, *Visible Human Project: Bodies and Posthuman Medicine* (London: Routledge, 2000), 24.

28. Julia Kristeva, *Revolt, She Said,* trans. Brian O'Keeffe (New York: Semiotext(e), 2002), 131.

29. Jean-François Lyotard, *Libidinal Economy,* trans. Iain Hamilton Grant (Bloomington: Indiana University Press, 1993), 60.

30. Deleuze and Guattari, *A Thousand Plateaus,* 160.

PREVIOUS PUBLICATIONS

Chapter 1 was first published as Jeffrey Jerome Cohen, "Monster Culture (Seven Theses)," in *Monster Theory: Reading Culture,* edited by Jeffrey Jerome Cohen, 3–25 (Minneapolis: University of Minnesota Press, 1996).

Chapter 2 was first published as Sigmund Freud, "The Uncanny," in *The Standard Edition of the Complete Psychological Works of Sigmund Freud, Vol. 17, 1917–1919,* trans. Alix Strachey, 217–56 (London: The Hogarth Press, 1955).

Chapter 3 was first published as Masahiro Mori, "The Uncanny Valley" [1970], trans. Karl F. MacDorman and Norri Kageki, *IEEE Robotics and Automation* 19, no. 2 (2012): 98–100.

Chapter 4 was first published as Julia Kristeva, "Approaching Abjection," in *The Powers of Horror,* trans. Leon S. Roudiez, 1–17 (New York: Columbia University Press, 1982). Copyright 1982 Columbia University Press. Reprinted with permission of the publisher.

Chapter 5 was first published as Robin Wood, "An Introduction to the American Horror Film," in *The American Nightmare: Essays on the Horror Film* by Andrew Britton, Richard Lippe, Tony Williams, and Robin Wood, 7–28 (Toronto: Festival of Festivals, 1979).

Chapter 6 was first published as Noël Carroll, "Fantastic Biologies and the Structures of Horrific Imagery," in *The Philosophy of Horror,* 42–52 (New York: Routledge, 1990).

Chapter 7 was first published as Judith Halberstam, "Parasites and Perverts: An Introduction to Gothic Monstrosity," in *Skin Shows: Gothic Horror and the Technology of Monsters,* 1–27 (Durham, N.C.: Duke University Press, 1995). All rights reserved. Reprinted by permission of the copyright holder. http://www.duke upress.edu/.

Chapter 8 was first published as Alexa Wright, "Monstrous Strangers at the Edge of the World: The Monstrous Races," in *Monstrosity: The Human Monster in Visual Culture*, 8–26 and 168–71 (London: I. B. Tauris, 2013). Copyright 2013 Alexa Wright. I. B. Tauris is an imprint of Bloomsbury Publishing Plc.

Chapter 9 was first published as Bettina Bildhauer, "Blood, Jews, and Monsters in Medieval Culture," in *The Monstrous Middle Ages*, edited by Bettina Bildhauer and Rovert Mills, 75–96 (Toronto: University of Toronto Press, 2003). Reprinted with permission of the publisher.

Chapter 10 was first published as Barbara Creed, "Horror and the Monstrous-Feminine: An Imaginary Abjection," in *Screen* 27, no. 1 (1986): 44–77.

Chapter 11 was first published as Harry M. Benshoff, "The Monster and the Homosexual," in *Queer Cinema: The Film Reader*, edited by Harry M. Benshoff and Sean Griffin, 63–74 (New York: Routledge, 2004). Copyright 2004. Reprinted by permission of Taylor & Francis Books UK.

Chapter 12 was first published as Annalee Newitz, "The Undead," in *Pretend We're Dead: Capitalist Monsters in American Pop Culture*, 89–122 and 191–94 (Durham, N.C.: Duke University Press, 2006). All rights reserved. Reprinted by permission of the copyright holder. http://www.dukeupress.edu/.

Chapter 13 was first published as Elizabeth Grosz, "Intolerable Ambiguity: Freak as/at the Limit," in *Freakery: Cultural Spectacles of the Extraordinary Body*, edited by Rosemarie Garland Thomson, 55–66 (New York: New York University Press, 1996).

Chapter 14 was first published as Stephen T. Asma, "Monsters and the Moral Imagination," *The Chronicle Review* of *The Chronicle of Higher Education*, October 25, 2009, http://chronicle.com/article/Monstersthe-Moral/48886/.

Chapter 15 was first published as Timothy Beal, Introduction to *Religion and Its Monsters*, 1–10 (New York: Routledge, 2002).

Chapter 16 was first published as Margrit Shildrick, "The Self's Clean and Proper Body," in *Embodying the Monster: Encounters with the Vulnerable Self*, 48–67 (Thousand Oaks, Calif.: Sage: 2002). Reprinted with permission of Margrit Shildrick. Permission conveyed through Copyright Clearance Center, Inc.

Chapter 17 was first published as Michael Dylan Foster, "Haunting Modernity: *Tanuki*, Trains, and Transformation in Japan," *Asian Ethnology* 71, no. 1 (2012): 3–29.

Chapter 18 was first published as Jeffrey Andrew Weinstock, "Invisible Monsters: Vision, Horror, and Contemporary Culture," in *The Ashgate Research Companion to Monsters and the Monstrous*, edited by Asa Simon Mittman with Peter J. Dendle, 275–89 (Surrey, U.K.: Ashgate, 2012). Copyright 2012. Reprinted by permission of Taylor & Francis Books UK.

Chapter 19 was first published as Jasbir K. Puar and Amit S. Rai, "Monster,

Chapter 20 was first published as Jon Stratton, "Zombie Trouble: Zombie Texts, Bare Life, and Displaced People," *European Journal of Cultural Studies* 14, no. 3 (2011): 265–81. Reprinted by permission of SAGE Publications, Ltd.

Chapter 21 was first published as Erin Suzuki, "Beasts from the Deep," *Journal of Asian American Studies* 20, no. 1 (2017): 11–28. Copyright 2017 Johns Hopkins University Press. Reprinted with permission of Johns Hopkins University Press.

Chapter 22 was first published as Anthony Lioi, "Of Swamp Dragons: Mud, Megalopolis, and a Future for Ecocriticism," in *Coming into Contact: Explorations in Ecocritical Theory and Practice,* 17–38 (Athens: University of Georgia Press, 2007). Copyright 2007 by the University of Georgia Press.

Chapter 23 was first published as Donna Haraway, "The Promises of Monsters: A Regenerative Politics for Inappropriate/d Others," *Cultural Studies,* edited by Lawrence Grossberg, Cary Nelson, and Paula Treichler, 395–437 (New York: Routledge, 1992). Reprinted with permission of Routledge. Permission conveyed through Copyright Clearance Center, Inc.

Chapter 24 was first published as Patricia MacCormack, "Posthuman Teratology," in *The Ashgate Companion to Monsters and the Monstrous,* edited by Asa Simon Mittman with Peter J. Dendle, 293–310 (Surrey, U.K.: Ashgate, 2012). Copyright 2012. Reprinted by permission of Taylor & Francis Books UK.

CONTRIBUTORS

STEPHEN T. ASMA is professor of philosophy at Columbia College Chicago. He is the author of ten books, including *On Monsters: An Unnatural History of Our Worst Fears, Why We Need Religion, The Evolution of Imagination,* and *The Emotional Mind.* He writes regularly for the *New York Times,* the *Chronicle of Higher Education,* and *Aeon.*

TIMOTHY BEAL is interim dean of the College of Arts and Sciences and Florence Harkness Professor of Religion at Case Western Reserve University. He has published fourteen books, including *Religion and Its Monsters* and, most recently, *The Book of Revelation: A Biography,* which won a Public Scholar Award from the National Endowment for the Humanities.

HARRY BENSHOFF is the author of *Monsters in the Closet: Homosexuality and the Horror, Dark Shadows,* and *Film and Television Analysis: An Introduction to Theories, Methods, and Approaches.* He recently edited *A Companion to the Horror Film.* With Sean Griffin, he coauthored *America on Film: Representing Race, Class, Gender, and Sexuality at the Movies* and *Queer Images: A History of Gay and Lesbian Film in America,* and he coedited *Queer Cinema: The Film Reader.* His essays and book chapters cover topics such as blaxploitation horror films, Hollywood LSD films, *The Talented Mr. Ripley* (1999), *Brokeback Mountain* (2005), *Milk* (2008), and *Twilight* (2008).

BETTINA BILDHAUER is professor of modern languages at the University of St. Andrews (United Kingdom). She became interested in monstrosity when studying blood in medieval culture, specifically how blood undermined physical integrity and expectations of normative bodies. She is coeditor, with Robert Mills, of *The Monstrous Middle Ages* and has also published *Medieval Blood* and *Filming the Middle Ages*, as well as the edited collections *Medieval Film* (with Anke Bernau) and *The Middle Ages in the Modern World* (with Chris Jones).

NOËL CARROLL is Distinguished Professor of Philosophy at the Graduate Center of CUNY. He is the author of more than fifteen books, including *The Philosophy of Horror* and *Humour: A Very Short Introduction*.

JEFFREY JEROME COHEN is dean of humanities at Arizona State University. His research examines strange and beautiful things that challenge the imagination, phenomena that seem alien and intimate at once. He is especially interested in what monsters reveal about the cultures that dream, fear, and desire them. His book *Stone: An Ecology of the Inhuman* (Minnesota, 2015) received the 2017 René Wellek Prize for best book in comparative literature from the American Comparative Literature Association. He is also the author of *Of Giants: Sex, Monsters, and the Middle Ages* and the editor of *Monster Theory: Reading Culture*, both published by the University of Minnesota Press.

BARBARA CREED is Redmond Barry Distinguished Professor at the University of Melbourne. She is the author of six books in feminist film theory, gender, and horror, including *The Monstrous-Feminine: Film, Feminism, Psychoanalysis* and *Phallic Panic: Film, Horror, and the Primal Uncanny*. Her recent research is in animal studies, ethics, and the inhuman; her most recent book is *Stray: Human–Animal Ethics in the Anthropocene*. She has been on the boards of Writers Week and the Melbourne Queer Film Festival and film critic for *The Age*, ABC radio, and *The Big Issue*.

MICHAEL DYLAN FOSTER is professor of East Asian languages and cultures at the University of California, Davis. He is the author of *The Book of Yōkai: Mysterious Creatures of Japanese Folklore*, *Pandemonium and Parade: Japanese Monsters and the Culture of Yōkai*, and many essays on Japanese folklore, literature, and media. He coedited *The Folkloresque: Reframing Folklore in a Popular Culture World* and *UNESCO on the Ground: Local Perspectives on Intangible Cultural Heritage*.

SIGMUND FREUD is the founder of psychoanalysis and one of the twentieth century's most influential thinkers.

ELIZABETH GROSZ is the Jean Fox O'Barr Chair in Feminist Theory at Duke University. She has written primarily on feminism and French philosophy. Her most recent book is *The Incorporeal: Ontology, Ethics, and the Limits of Materialism*.

JACK HALBERSTAM is visiting professor of gender studies and English at Columbia University. Halberstam is the author of five books: *Skin Shows: Gothic Horror and the Technology of Monsters, Female Masculinity, In a Queer Time and Place, The Queer Art of Failure,* and *Gaga Feminism: Sex, Gender, and the End of Normal.* Halberstam has coedited several anthologies, including *Posthuman Bodies* with Ira Livingston and a special issue of *Social Text* with José Munoz and David Eng, "What's Queer about Queer Studies Now?"

DONNA HARAWAY is Distinguished Professor Emerita in the History of Consciousness department at the University of California, Santa Cruz. Attending to the intersection of biology with culture and politics, her work explores the string figures composed by science fact, science fiction, speculative feminism, speculative fabulation, science and technology studies, and multispecies worlding. Her books include *Staying with the Trouble: Making Kin in the Chthulucene; Manifestly Haraway* (Minnesota, 2016); *When Species Meet* (Minnesota, 2008); *The Companion Species Manifesto; The Haraway Reader; Modest_Witness@Second_Millennium; Simians, Cyborgs, and Women; Primate Visions;* and *Crystals, Fabrics, and Fields.* With Adele Clarke, she coedited *Making Kin Not Population,* which addresses questions of human numbers, feminist antiracist reproductive and environmental justice, and multispecies flourishing.

JULIA KRISTEVA is a psychoanalyst, critic, and novelist best known for her writings in psychoanalysis, semiotics, and philosophical feminism. She has authored more than thirty books, including *Powers of Horror: An Essay on Abjection, Black Sun: Depression and Melancholia, Strangers to Ourselves,* and *Hatred and Forgiveness.*

ANTHONY LIOI is associate professor of English at the Juilliard School in New York City, where he teaches contemporary literature, composition, and the environmental humanities. His writing has been published in *ISLE, Feminist Studies, Image-TexT, MELUS, Acoma, Ecozon@,* and many critical anthologies. He is a past president of ASLE: Association for the Study of Literature and Environment and an editor of *Resilience: A Journal of the Environmental Humanities.* He recently published *Nerd Ecology,* the first ecocritical study of nerds and nerd culture, and is now writing on fan cultures as agents of ecotopia.

PATRICIA MacCORMACK is professor of Continental philosophy at Anglia Ruskin University. Her books include *Post-Human Ethics* and *Cinesexuality.* She is the editor of *The Animal Catalyst* and coeditor of *The Schizoanalysis of Cinema.*

MASAHIRO MORI is a roboticist known for his pioneering work in robotics, automation, and religion.

ANNALEE NEWITZ writes science fiction and nonfiction. She is the author of the novel *Autonomous*, nominated for the Nebula and Locus awards, and winner of the Lambda Literary Award. As a science journalist, she has written for the *Washington Post*, *Slate*, *Ars Technica*, the *New Yorker*, and the *Atlantic*. Her book *Scatter, Adapt, and Remember: How Humans Will Survive a Mass Extinction* was nominated for the LA Times Book Prize in science. She was the founder of *io9* and served as the editor-in-chief of *Gizmodo*. In a previous life, she earned a PhD in English and American studies and worked as a lecturer at UC Berkeley.

JASBIR K. PUAR is professor and graduate director of women's and gender studies at Rutgers University. She is the author of *The Right to Maim: Debility, Capacity, Disability* and *Terrorist Assemblages: Homonationalism in Queer Times*, and her edited volumes include a special issue of *GLQ* ("Queer Tourism: Geographies of Globalization") and coedited volumes of *Society and Space* ("Sexuality and Space"), *Social Text* ("Interspecies"), and *Women's Studies Quarterly* ("Viral"). She writes for the *Guardian*, *Huffington Post*, *Art India*, *Feminist Review*, *Bully Bloggers*, *Jadaliyya*, and *Oh! Industry*.

AMIT S. RAI is senior lecturer in new media and communication at Queen Mary, University of London. He is the program director for MA in Creative Industries and Arts Organization. He is the author of *Rule of Sympathy: Race, Sentiment, and Power, 1760–1860* and *Untimely Bollywood: Globalization and India's New Media Assemblage*. His writing has been published in *Cultural Studies*, *Social Text*, *Discourse*, *Third Text*, *Screen*, *Diaspora*, *South Asian Popular Culture*, *Camera Obscura*, *Women's Studies Journal*, and *Environment and Planning*. His latest book is *Jugaad Time: Ecologies of Everyday Hacking in India*.

MARGRIT SHILDRICK is guest professor of gender and knowledge production at Stockholm University and adjunct professor of critical disability studies at York University, Toronto. Her research covers postmodern feminist and cultural theory, bioethics, critical disability studies, and body theory. Her books include *Leaky Bodies and Boundaries: Feminism, (Bio)ethics, and Postmodernism*, *Embodying the Monster: Encounters with the Vulnerable Self*, and *Dangerous Discourses of Disability, Sexuality, and Subjectivity*. She has recently been addressing the sociopolitical and embodied conjunction of microchimerism, immunology, and corporeal anomaly.

JON STRATTON is adjunct professor of cultural studies in the School of Creative Industries at the University of South Australia. He has published widely in cultural studies, Jewish studies, popular music studies, and Australian studies and about race and multiculturalism. His most recent books are *When Music Migrates: Crossing*

British and European Racial Faultlines, 1945–2010 and, coedited with Nabeel Zuberi, *Black Popular Music in Britain since 1945.*

ERIN SUZUKI is assistant professor of literature at the University of California, San Diego. Her research focuses on oceanic environments as critical sites for the construction of Asian American and Pacific Islander subjectivities in the wake of the colonial conflicts that shaped the emergence of Pacific Rim/transpacific discourse in the late twentieth century.

JEFFREY ANDREW WEINSTOCK is professor of English at Central Michigan University and an associate editor for the *Journal of the Fantastic in the Arts.* He has published twenty-two books, including *The Cambridge Companion to the American Gothic, The Age of Lovecraft* (with Carl Sederholm; Minnesota, 2016), *Goth Music: From Sound to Subculture* (with Isabella van Elferen), *Return to Twin Peaks: New Approaches to Materiality, Theory, and Genre on Television* (with Catherine Spooner), *The Vampire Film: Undead Cinema,* and *The Rocky Horror Picture Show.* Visit him at JeffreyAndrewWeinstock.com.

ROBIN WOOD was an influential English film critic. Among his many books are *Hitchcock's Films, Howard Hawks, Ingmar Bergman, Hollywood from Vietnam to Reagan,* and *Sexual Politics and Narrative Film: Hollywood and Beyond.*

ALEXA WRIGHT is a visual artist whose practice spans a variety of media, including photography, video, sound, interactive installation, and book works. She has worked at the intersection of art and medical science since the mid-1990s, when she created award-winning photographs of people with phantom limbs, *After Image.* Her art addresses questions of human identity and otherness and aims to raise public awareness of issues that surround physical and mental difference. She teaches at the University of Westminster in London. http://www.alexa wright.com/.

INDEX